HARRIETTE WILSON'S
MEMOIRS

Harriette Wilson (1786–1846) was one of the most glamorous and intelligent women of her age. She allowed herself to be seduced by Lord Craven at the age of 15 and rapidly acquired a string of rich and powerful lovers, chief among whom was the Duke of Wellington. After retiring from the courtesan life at the age of 35 she wrote a number of novels as well as her scandalous *Memoirs*.

Lesley Blanch, the editor of the present volume, is renowned for her bestselling book *The Wilder Shores of Love*, which studies the attraction exercised by the East over mid-nineteenth-century European women and which has been translated into over a dozen languages. Her other works include *Round the World in Eighty Dishes*, *The Sabres of Paradise*, *Under a Lilac Bleeding Star*, *The Nine Tiger Man*, *Journey into the Mind's Eye*, *Pavilions of the Heart* and *Pierre Loti: Portrait of an Escapist*. Her essays and articles have appeared in many of Britain's leading periodicals. Lesley Blanch was born in London, England, and has travelled over most of the globe. She now lives in France.

HARRIETTE WILSON'S MEMOIRS

Selected and Edited with an Introduction by

Lesley Blanch

PHOENIX

A PHOENIX PRESS PAPERBACK

First published in Great Britain
by John Murray in 1957
This paperback edition published in 2003
by Phoenix Press,
a division of The Orion Publishing Group Ltd,
Orion House, 5 Upper St Martin's Lane,
London WC2H 9EA

Printed and bound in Great Britain by
Clays Ltd, St Ives plc

Contents

Acknowledgments

I wish to thank Sir John Murray for his kind permission to photograph one of the Harriette Wilson–Lord Byron letters now in his possession. Other letters quoted in the Appendix are from the same sources and were first published in book form in 1939 under the title To Lord Byron, *by Peter Quennell. The letters of Harriette Wilson to Bulwer-Lytton, also given in the Appendix, are taken from Mr. Michael Sadleir's book,* Bulwer: a Panorama.

LESLEY BLANCH

Illustrations

Harriette Wilson

A Letter from Harriette Wilson to Lord Byron

Amy, Sophia and Julia

The Marquis of Worcester: a Dighton sketch

The Duke of Argyll: a Dighton sketch

Lord Ponsonby.   Sketch by Henry Bone of a portrait by Lawrence
   (By courtesy of the National Portrait Gallery.)

High stakes at Crockford's

A domestic interlude.   From a contemporary illustration to the
   Memoirs

'First Come First Served.'   A contemporary caricature

'The Cyprians' Ball.'   From *The English Spy*'s caricature

The *ton* disport themselves at Almack's

Lord Alvanley

Lord Nugent

Cutting a dash in Hyde Park.   (From an engraving by George
   Cruikshank.)

THE GAME OF HEARTS

INTRODUCTION

THE NINETEENTH CENTURY was an age of great personalities, a last splendid flowering before twentieth-century anonymity and mass living engulfed them in its drab tide. England was always a stronghold of eccentrics and individualists. At this moment they had reached their apogee. But beside the Wellingtons, Beckfords, Byrons or Lady Hester Stanhopes of the age, a small, giddy shade is still remembered with delight, if not with honour.

Harriette Wilson's life was deplorable—but how readable! She emerges from her *Memoirs* and other contemporary sources as a most engaging creature—though that is, after all, what would be expected of the most celebrated courtesan of her day (and one, moreover, who really relished her calling). There is always an especial interest in memoirs and journals which give us an unselfconscious, eyewitness account of the daily life of other ages; the vivid picture of everyday, medieval family life that emerges from the Paston letters could not be made so real to us by any other medium. The court of Louis XIV, with all its majesty and brittle intrigue, is brought to life for us by the pen of St. Simon. Pepys's odd jumble of household accounts, Stuart excesses, foreign policies and his private pornographic jottings make ·Restoration England relive for us. Perhaps an added zest attaches to those memoirs which verge on the *chroniques scandaleuses*, especially where they concern the private life of the great. Casanova's memoirs cannot be called everyday life, but they are certainly good reading—a puppet show of eighteenth-century European gallantry in the raw. The value of the great diarists often lies less in their personality than in their background. Creevey, sly wag, Greville, Gronow, Thomas Raikes, Mrs. Arbuthnot—all of them have created for us scenes which we remember principally because of their background: Regency London.

But Harriette Wilson's *Memoirs* stand apart. By nature of her profession a courtesan's memoirs must deal primarily with herself and give a close-range portrait of the men she came to know. Harriette's own evocation of the Regency scene is not so much a panorama as an interior with figures. And if at times we seem to be looking through the keyhole, it serves to sharpen our interest.

It might be asked why the memoirs of a courtesan, deliberately written with an eye to blackmail, should be of particular interest to us; but even if Harriette did extort money for suppressing, or removing, some of her memories of the great and the rich, it does not lessen the intensely personal authenticity of the pictures she paints. She is mischievous rather than malicious, outrageous but not pornographic. As Sir Walter Scott wrote: 'H.W. beats [the memoirs of] Con Philips and Anne Bellamy and all former demi-reps out and out.' She gives us a microcosm of one particular stratum of London life where she ruled supreme. She is her own Boswell. How could such a chronicle fail to enthrall?

Then, too, by the time we have followed Harriette through so many vicissitudes we have grown to love her—however monstrous her behaviour. We see why Harriette—shabbily treated by the Duke of Beaufort, done out of her pension, her looks and youth gone, falling from fashion, penniless, victim of her own extravagances, fighting to keep a hold on Rochfort, her fancy man—began to cast about desperately for a means of raising money. What else had she to sell now but her memories? Thus, fighting for life, she wrote the *Memoirs*—for money, not out of a clinging nostalgia nor, as has been said, for spite. At what stage of her work she thought of offering certain victims the chance of buying themselves out we do not know, nor do we know whether this was her own idea or that of Stockdale, her enterprising publisher, or the malign influence of Rochfort. Nor do we know how many men bought themselves out. Harriette kept her word; those who paid escaped, and, after all, the price she asked was not exorbitant, especially since the men she approached were all wealthy and privileged. ('She attacks no poor man, no single man, they cannot pay, or do not fear her calumnies.') Still, by the time she struck, just as she had fallen, so they had, in the main, risen to positions of dignity and eminence and could ill afford to appear in such a context. Consequently many of them paid up, and the reader is the poorer.

Harriette Wilson lived among and was an integral part of a wealthy society where privilege, arrogance and leisure flourished. This is the courtesan's natural background; once these things disappear, particularly the wealth which leisure implies, the courtesan is doomed. She does not flourish in an industrial age. She may be said to have vanished with the nineteenth century, the first half of which, specifically, was the heyday of all those women whose personality and style, more than beauty alone, were such that they could command, besides large sums of money, independence and respect. The basic difference between the courtesan and the prostitute was not so much a question of class as of personality. The legendary courtesans provided more than sex alone. In England, Harriette Wilson was an outstanding example of her profession. She was followed, in France, by Marie Duplessis. Between them these two widely different women personified their respective country and period, and between them they brought to a close the first half of the century and with it the great age of the classic and romantic courtesan.

True, there was a brilliant and superficially more striking era near the end of the century when the *grandes cocottes* such as Liane de Pougy, and Emillienne d'Alençon succeeded the Cora Pearls and Anna Deslions of the '60s and '70s. But it was a St. Martin's summer, a last blaze where extravagance and flamboyance were the keynote, a calculated extravagance, however, which was already tainted by big business methods. Publicity was the new god of the industrial age and it changed the demimonde too. These fabulous *cocottes*, or '*créatures*,' as they were called in the Paris salons, were, first of all, showpieces. Carriages, toilettes, jewels, even their whims, were calculated for effect; advertising had arrived, together with big business. An outward life of show came to occupy as important a place in the game as any alcove. The foyer, the 'other woman's establishment,' was suddenly less desirable than the best table at Maxim's: or a yacht. Suddenly, travel became fashionable; the great migratory trek from casino to spa, from winter resort to summer watering place had begun: Deauville, Biarritz, Monte Carlo, Biskra, Vichy. The pace was as killing as the price, so that the actress, Mrs. Patrick Campbell, spoke for many men when she pronounced on "the deep peace of the double bed after the hurly-burly of the chaise-longue." The twentieth century cast a long shadow before it, ominous and forbidding, and *la vie galante*, high gallantry, and the courtesan were all doomed.

Today we see that economic pressure and mass living have been far more destructive to *la vie galante* than any morality drives. In fact, they have been the first and only force to oppose sexual freedom in the sense of which I speak, in the sense of destroying the courtesan and her world. Mass living implies mass thought. A society of leisure could afford to live individually, could afford to keep life in separate compartments. Men had homes, families, wives, mistresses, clubs, and two social lives, one shared with their wife, the other one independent of her. Today, everything is reduced to the minimum—call girl, massage parlour or back seat.

Then it must be remembered that the decline of the marriage of convenience is also, in part, responsible for the decline of the courtesan.

When such marriages were customary the husband generally went in search of other women and, when circumstances permitted, another foyer or hearth. (Although today the distractions of sex can be obtained by varying degrees of expenditure, the maintenance of a separate establishment denotes a very high standard of living and leisure. It is, in fact, a luxury to which few men can now subscribe.)

In European polite society in the late eighteenth and early nineteenth centuries the wife, too, was conceded great freedom. The attentions of both *cicisbeo* and *cavaliere servente* were ambiguous. A man expected his first-born to be his own—but once the inheritance was firmly established with two or more little pledges, the wife was generally able to seek her diversions elsewhere, as her husband had done from the first. "One exists with one's husband—one *lives* with one's lover," says the Marquise de Vandenesse in Balzac's *Une fille d'Eve*.

In such a society, then, the courtesan played a very important part. She was not 'received,' but she had her own world—that hieratic demi-monde with its own etiquette and protocol. She never seems to have revolted against her exclusions or limitations. Perhaps she knew how firmly her half-world was entrenched behind the larger *beau monde* from which she drew her protectors. The courtesan derived from a society which surrounded sex not only with all those graces women once commanded, but also with that style men could once afford to demand.

She was, in fact, a *dame de compagnie* in the largest sense.

The courtesan was expected to provide all the shades of companionship without the oppressive limitations and implications of marriage. She offered not only the bed but the sofa, the alcove and the hearth, the dinner-table and the salon—all save the nursery and the kitchen. Her conversation as well as her company was courted. Her personality as much as her person had a price. To be seen with her during a drive in the park, at a restaurant or in her box at the theatre was regarded as an achievement. In Harriette Wilson's day the young noblemen used to drive down from Oxford or Cambridge for the express purpose of obtaining an introduction to her as she held court in her opera box. This box was not only the courtesan's showcase or shop window, but, according to her degree of fame, the gauge of her current lover's wealth and taste. Thus we see a system designed to surround the basic traffic with elegance.

In a society of individualists such as that of Regency England, Harriette Wilson had to match her own personality against those of the distinguished men who were her world. She was no beauty, but she was herself, like no one else, and her immense vitality, her wit and lively interest in many things, combined with her independent, take-me-or-leave-me terms, brought her to the top of her profession and made her the fashion. A merely lovely, compliant creature could not have stayed the course for long; she would have been just one more of the ranks of prostitutes who at that time, we are told, swarmed about the city of London.

And here we might speculate on how much education—not perhaps in the academic sense, but in that of general culture—Harriette acquired from her lovers, from years of association with men who, however much they might choose to masquerade as being interested only in the turf, prize-fighting and cards, did, in fact, stem from a cultivated aristocracy. There are many ways of learning. Harriette, who left home at fifteen and spent more time in bed than most, spoke fluent French and seems to have been well read. Her memoirs show her to have been far more than an agreeable rattlepate. She was born witty; but I think she acquired a considerable culture, the art of conversation and letter writing, and a philosophic way of thought which she did not owe to her family background but rather to those men who were her protectors—men who, one might say, came to sleep but stayed to dine; men who, probably unconsciously, paid for their entertainment with more than a mere fee. After all they were among the best minds, the greatest wits of the age. She was on good terms with such men as Tom Sheridan, son of the playwright, Lord Alvanley, the famous wit, Luttrell, who was considered the most brilliant conversationalist of his day, Henry Brougham, the great advocate, the Duke of Wellington, and many more. Association with men of this calibre must have been an education in itself.

The finer shades of what might be described as pleasing are many. The prostitute, the courtesan, the *femme entretenue*, or kept woman, are all variations on the theme. Harriette Wilson falls into the category of courtesan chiefly because of her independent attitude, her selective approach. She changed her lovers as easily as her shoes, says Julia Johnstone, her rival. But while the prostitute is to be bought by anyone, the courtesan selects her patrons, and the *femme entretenue* is kept, in exclusivity, by one protector, to be entirely at his disposal. Although Harriette was, we imagine, kept in exclusivity, for certain stretches of time, by the Duke of Argyll, Lords Ponsonby and Worcester, and others besides, she was essentially a courtesan. Her exclusivity was relative; and except in the case of Lord Ponsonby, the love of her life, it is doubtful that she ever intended or wished to be the property of any one man. She liked variety, and had, on her own admission, *le diable au corps*—brisk appetites.

·   ·   ·   ·   ·

'There can be no great age without its magnificent Aspasian figure,' wrote Balzac in 1838. 'See how perfectly the Dubarry fits the eighteenth century and Ninon de Lenclos the seventeenth century. These women are the poetry of their age. Laïs and Rhodope *are* Greece and Egypt.'

The flavour and tempo of an age is reflected in many ways: in the curve of a corset, a taste in wines, the argot of the moment. Such trivialities conjure an epoch as sharply as historic headlines. The various glittering facets of *la vie galante*, too, are sharply evocative. Through the long mirrors that lined Joséphine de Beauharnais' rooms in the Rue Chantereine, we see not only the febrile post-revolutionary society, but Bonaparte as a lovesick First Consul. Intrigues behind the Franco-Prussian war were played out against the ormolu and plush salons of La Païva's establishment. Dumas and Gautier and Liszt and all Romantic Paris crowd into Marie Duplessis' box at the Funambules. Munich overboils into revolution on the steps of Lola Montez' house. Wellington returns from the Peninsular Campaign to court Harriette Wilson, and, since her affections are otherwise engaged, she locks him out in a downpour.

Each nation, like each age, has its different idiom. The Greek hetaerae were votaries, a sect of beautiful and cultivated women, set apart, designed to please, to charm, as others were to breed. Greek logic saw things clearly: there were no half shades, no straggling ranks of amateurs, either way, whether to dull their delights or threaten their domestic peace. The hetaerae were not only desirable as women (though one of the most celebrated was positively plain) but they were schooled to provide the highest intellectual companionship too. (The Latin word *hetaera* derives from the Greek *hetaira*—a companion.) They consorted with the greatest statesmen and intellectuals, and were never admitted to the ranks until they had considerable attainments.

Turning eastward, where education has always sought to develop rather than extinguish the senses, as Gèrard de Nerval remarks wistfully, we find the same approach, the same blend of intellect and *volupté* combined in the traditions of Chinese gallantry. In Japan there was the stylized formality, as rigid and brilliant as the costumes, where the institution of the Yoshiwara Yuwaku, or professional prostitution (both male and female), was the essence of Oriental formality, as are those accounts of tenth-century love affairs recounted by the Lady Murasaki in her *Tale of Genji*.

In Japan, too, there is that temple dedicated to some benign deity who favours prostitutes. The women make ceremonial pilgrimages to donate an animal figure; the temple swarms with these rather grotesque and Disney-like creatures, in every kind of substance. There are little whiskered snouts in gold, or jade, or coral, with ruby eyes or enamelled ears; giant beasts in bronze, life-sized ones in crystal, infinitesimally small ones in ivory or ebony. Their size and splendour vary according to the value of the affair for which the prostitute renders thanks.

Another, rather less formalized East is reflected in the person of Schéhérazade, the story-teller of Bagdad, the slave girl whose conversational prowess, it is evident, outshone all the rest of her charms. Here we see a world of abandon and cunning, of cruel and capricious caliphs, a world where, to survive, a woman had to be more than merely beautiful.

A curiously muted, almost stealthy voluptuousness breathes from Carpaccio's paintings of Venetian prostitutes, Renaissance beauties sunning themselves on flat rooftops overlooking the Grand Canal. They braid one another's bleached golden hair, sit in attitudes of melancholy and repose, brooding over their pet doves or perhaps their fading youth. They droop; they are clinging vines, as minor in key as the green ghostly waterways of Venice. For all that, they wielded considerable influence, socially and politically. They were considered as one of the city's ornaments, almost a matter of civic pride. People came from afar merely to witness the state appearances of these beauties of whom the Republic was so proud.

All the roaring bawdry of Shakespeare's Bankside life is embodied in Doll Tearsheet the strumpet, a match for anyone. All the gusto of Restoration England is in Moll Flanders, Daniel Defoe's whore. Captain Macheath's doxies step straight from a canvas by Hogarth, and early Georgian London lives around them, as it did when John Gay wrote *The Beggar's Opera*. Such women epitomize the more ephemeral aspects of pleasing; they could be had for a night or an hour. And to go forward in time, when Emma Crouch leaped from obscurity in London to become Cora Pearl, the most notorious of all the Parisian demi-mondaines, she always remained the trollop, the coarse, rampageous tart, regardless of her princely lovers and satin-hung boudoirs. However seductive, she was not a courtesan (as was Marie Duplessis or Harriette Wilson) but rather 'la putaine anglaise,' whose conduct outraged even the men and women of her immediate circle, which is saying a great deal.

In the Marquise de Pompadour we find the perfect expression of both her nation and age. She too is the crystallization of a whole way of life, a whole school of taste, loosely described as *dix-huitième*. She is the apotheosis of the kept woman, a being set apart, mistress of the king, his inseparable companion. She was a woman of intellect, charm and wit, who held her lover in spite of, rather than because of, her flesh. It is well known that she failed to respond to his ardour. It tired her; it bored her. But she remained supreme to the end simply by supplying those graces and distractions, that *companionship* which the monarch never found elsewhere. She wielded enormous influence; her subtle sway changed policies, launched fashions and established painters and poets. Her frown spelled failure; her smile, fortune. She intellectualized the passions, interpreting them with the same frivolous air of elegance and artificiality we see in the painting of Boucher or Fragonard. She kept everything, even love, regulated by that excellent French sense of order and proportion which reached its highest expression in the writings of Voltaire or the architecture of Versailles. She is often accused of having supplied the king with young girls at a little hunting box, the Parc aux Cerfs. Probably she did, rather in the manner of an intelligent *maîtresse de maison* employing extra help for the heavy work. It was a sensible solution, in an age at once practical and profligate but never romantic.

Barely a century later, however, the Romantic heyday was to impose other standards. In the eighteen-thirties courtesans, and prostitutes too, were surrounded by a peculiarly emotional climate—especially those who fell by the way, who died young, of love, of consumption, of no matter what, so long as a pale cheek could shed a glistening tear, so long as renunciations and frustrations ensured a tragic ending to every love story. The archetype of all these romanticized daughters of joy is Marie Duplessis, the model for Dumas' Marguerite Gautier, and Verdi's Violetta, in *La Traviata,* and who was in real life Alphonsine Plessis. When Dumas *fils* wrote the preface to the novel in which he immortalized her as *La Dame aux Camélias,* he spoke of her as ephemeral, the embodiment of a brief moment of emotion. 'La Dame aux Camélias was written fifteen years ago; it could not be written today. Not only would it not be true—but it would not even be possible. One searches vainly for a woman who could inspire such emotion, who could develop such a love; who could make such a repentance, and such a sacrifice credible.' She was barely twenty-three when she died, but she had become a legend. Dickens; in Paris at the time, went to the auction of her possessions, and remarked that, to see the sorrow her loss occasioned, one might have believed it concerned a national hero, a Joan of Arc. Public enthusiasm knew no bounds when Eugène Sue bid for her prayer-book. And Liszt, with all Europe at his feet, and the ladies of every capital palpitating if he so much as glanced in their direction, found her 'the most perfect incarnation of Woman that has ever existed.' "A child, fallen asleep in a courtesan's bed," said her contemporaries, in ecstasies of grief. "A virgin, that chance made a courtesan; a courtesan that could, by chance, as well be the purest virgin."

This worship of the courtesan is one of the most striking aspects of a general exaltation of love, physical, mystical and abstract, which reigned among the poets, painters and aristocracy during the period. When love was thus exalted as the greatest emotion man could experience, it follows that the courtesan, who was its high priestess, appeared as a sort of divinity. They saw in her the incarnation of all they desired—not only a woman, but an ideal; not only their mistress, but their Muse. They approached her with rapture and reverence, as an almost sacred being, dedicated to the fulfilment of passion. No true Romantic, poet or dandy, could remain insensitive to one who could dispense the emotions which were their life's blood. The plain fact that she was paid, that her dispensations were to be bought, was seldom mentioned, or else it was glossed over in a tangle of high-flown phrases.

It was the flowering of an idealistic approach to free love—to love above all. "She has completed her life" was the fashionable way of saying that a woman had taken a lover; and though this phrase was applied not to the courtesan but to the married woman, whether of the aristocracy or bourgeoisie, the same tone of complacency surrounded anything concerning the passions. Within the various economic limitations, each stratum of society had its own version of the amorous theme. Even the penniless poets and students of Murger's *Scènes de la Vie de Bohème* had their *lorettes* or *grisettes*, those little workgirls who scraped their sous together to provide inspiration in the shape of a bottle of wine, offered along with their love. And the despised bourgeoisie, too, were united with the artists and the aristocracy in their craving for emotion—love for love's sake. The actress Marie Dorval spoke for her age when she wrote, 'Is it the senses which lure us on, eternally? No, it is a thirst for something more. It is the frenzy, the cravings to find true love which lures us and evades us, eternally.'

The dividing line between the *grande courtisane* and *grande amoureuse* (or women who loved for love's sake alone) was often very slight. The history of Romantic Paris is a grand chain of emotional entanglements. Ménage overlapped ménage; men slept with one another's mistresses and wives; mothers and daughters were embroiled with the same lover; fathers supplanted their sons, who in turn poached on the paternal preserves; Victor Hugo snatches Alice Ozy from his son Charles, and Esther Guimont from his friend Emile de Girardin. In the name of love this *monstre sacré*, this pseudo-mystical adulterer rides roughshod over so many, demands supreme sacrifices from his wife—from his mistress too, the lovely actress Juliette Drouet. Taking her, he imposes a bitter '*rédemption amoureuse*' of retirement, petty economies and domestic lectures, to which she submits voluptuously for years before she too is left to pine. How they carried on, those French Romantics! The ferment of passions was always kept at boiling-point.

When George Sand was unable to sweep Alfred de Musset out of his mother's sphere of influence, she found it quite normal to approach that lady and win her consent to the proposed Venetian idyll: her eloquence was such that even maternal opposition ceded. Installed at Danieli's, the lovers were able to concentrate on further complications. Alfred soon contrived to inject a morbid note into their raptures. "You thought yourself my mistress, but you were my mother! We have committed incest!" (It was simpler in Regency England. It was 'Yes,' or 'No'; 'Tonight,' or 'Tomorrow night.') Presently, an unhappy termination to George and Alfred's love made everything seem well worthwhile. Besides, it provided both writers with a prodigious amount of copy. 'A Romantic's work is but an extension of his personality' wrote one romantic. George Sand and Alfred de Musset had lived every page of *Elle et Lui* and *La Confession d'un Enfant du Siècle*, their two versions of the liaison. In this spirit, it will be seen that unhappy endings, high tragedies of renunciation—or fulfilment—were not only *à la mode*, but good business too.

While both Regency London and Romantic Paris approached life hedonistically, and were preoccupied with the pleasures of the flesh, the Romantics spoke of body in terms of soul, especially a tormented one. Thus we see that both Harriette Wilson and Marie Duplessis were a perfect reflection of their moment, and were each an aspect of that Aspasian figure Balzac evoked. Both women shared, besides their calling, a certain generous simplicity which few of their rivals could claim. Neither was rapacious. Neither shared the insensate greed of Rachel, who, although the greatest actress of early nineteenth-century France, was never too romantic, too exalted, to keep a burning dark eye on the main chance. Her rapacity led her to sell her favours to the highest bidders; yet she knew how to put an over-bold admirer in his place. On receiving a note at the theatre during a performance, demanding her terms—'*ou, quand, combien?*' she sent back the following reply: '*Chez moi, ce soir, pour rien*', a riposte which, while showing she could not resist the *bon mot* any more than the desire to rebuke a man arrogant enough to bid for her in such a way, was not, we feel, to be taken too literally. Rachel never gave anything, least of all herself, for nothing.

The century which produced such women as Harriette and her rival demi-reps now seems as remote as any Neanderthal age. Yet there are still people alive who must recall a woman who might be described as her next-of-kin, Skittles, another very high-stepping charmer, her direct descendant, who may be said to have flourished till the day of her death. Which leads me to reflect on that strange thread of chance, of fortune, which will lead two outwardly similar lives, one to success, the other to failure. Why should Harriette Wilson have sunk to oblivion and hard times, her youth and looks gone, and Skittles have lived to a ripe old age surrounded by an adoring circle of the most distinguished men? Skittles was perhaps the last of the spectacular English courtesans; she was born about 1840. She had, no doubt, more real beauty than Harriette, but beauty fades. Both were impudently gay, good company, and captivated not only the *coureurs*—men who, whether from psychological or physiological causes, chase after women indefatigably—but also men of an altogether different kidney. Harriette's personality alone seems to have won her the friendship of no less a figure than Henry Brougham, later the Lord Chancellor, who, she says (and it was never contradicted), gave her much valuable legal advice on how to proceed in her case against the Duke of Beaufort. Her professional successor, Skittles, entertained Mr. Gladstone to tea. Yet, both starting equal, both having the gift of acquiring friends as well as lovers, for Skittles life ended well, for Harriette badly.

Skittles (Catherine Walters), too, had begun early, working in a skittle (or bowling) alley among the tough Lancashire crowds. Soon she was fair game for street rhymesters, hawking their scandal sheets from door to door:

> *In Liverpool, in days gone by,*
> *For ha'pence and her wittles*
> *A little girl by no means shy*
> *Was settin' up the skittles.*

Yet by the time she was established as a legend in London (having for some while been under the protection of the Duke of Devonshire) her personality was such that, in her pampered old age, being wheeled around the park where once she had driven her famous team of Orloff blacks, she was accompanied by the most distinguished statesmen and men of letters, who hung on her words. Her eyes were still enormous, violet, melting; she swore like a docker. She had enslaved so many different kinds of men—potmen, the Prince of Wales, the poet Wilfred Scawen

Blunt. And to the end Lord Kitchener of Khartoum had been proud to push her bath-chair along the East Carriage Drive in Hyde Park.

By the middle of the nineteenth century, France, which usually set the tone in these matters, had replaced romantic miasmas with the harsh glitter of Second Empire gas-lamps. Even Berlioz and Victor Hugo could no longer impose their impassioned vision on the hard base of French logic and materialism. Under the glare of the street-lamps, we see, wafted in patchouli, the big-bosomed, tiny-booted street walkers of Constantin Guys' drawings. They mince along, inviting sidelong glances darting from below their frizzed bangs; they sprawl, sullen and lascivious, on curiously prim looking sofas while their patrons eye them arrogantly, like so much cattle. Nothing romantic here. Guys is the supreme painter of the demi-monde. No one knew better than he how to convey breeding in a horse, lack of it in a woman. It was Offenbach's world, the world of Cora Pearl, too, where the manners of the Empress Eugénie's court verged on those of the demi-monde. And, speaking of this age, we should perhaps recall Miss Howard, the English courtesan, whose love for the exiled Prince Louis Napoleon was proved in most positive terms. She placed her hard-won fortune at his disposal for the Bonapartist cause and was, not unnaturally, disappointed when, after becoming Emperor, Napoleon III married a Spanish commoner, Mademoiselle de Montijo.

In England, things were not following suit. Regency clarity was becoming shrouded in flannel. The snortings of the industrial age were accompanied by sniffs of disapproval. If Constantin Guys epitomized his era in France, Augustus Eggs' paintings of wayward, repentant matrons spoke for England. The rise of Victorian gentilities, and moral hypocrisy left no room for Harriette Wilson's tearing pace, her frank methods of livelihood, or any romantic miasmas. All were overcome by tidal waves of whitewash. The courtesans retreated to a colony of discreet villas around St. John's Wood, where high-walled gardens and roofed-in carriageways were effective in stilling any conjectures as to their visitors. 'Tarts' were never mentioned in polite society. The sons of those men whom Harriette Wilson had once enslaved busied themselves destroying all the papers or proof of their parents' infatuation. The *Memoirs* were burned, or languished out of reach on the top shelves of libraries.

There were still the 'flash cribs' around the Haymarket, which were frequented by the more draggled street walkers. And there were a bevy of 'pretty horse breakers,' as they were called—girls who could ride well, who worked in with a livery stable, horse and girl being loosed on the Park along a ride then reserved exclusively for ladies of the profession, where both the rider and her mount were calculated to obtain an advantageous offer; and it was here that Miss Howard's paces were first admired.

But gradually the English came to look elsewhere, specifically to France, to the 'Gay Paree' of tourists' legend, for their pleasures. Edwardian society, which now embraced *parvenus* and a new aristocracy of wealth, could afford the most scorching French *voluptés*, of which there were many levels: there were the Rue Chabanais and the Bal Tabarin: there were the *grues*, those haggard and vicious creatures whom Toulouse-Lautrec loved to paint; but they had nothing to do with the world of *grandes courtisanes*. They haunted the *boîtes* and dance halls of Montmartre and were seldom of any fixed abode, unless it were some run-down brothel; but to all the world they had come to represent 'Gay Paree.' It was the company of which Yvette Guilbert sang with such incomparable art and understanding. The stratum of French life which Colette has transfixed forever in *Chéri* shows us a whole hierarchy of *grandes cocottes,* who, well within living memory, were to be glimpsed, distractingly, across the ostrich boas and aigrettes at Maxim's, their first-water diamonds flashing in the last afterglow of agreeable dissipation. They lingered on, wasp-waisted, businesslike and daring, well into the early years of the twentieth century. But already they were retiring to properties at Biarritz or Monte Carlo, and after the First World War, when the ranks of both international financiers and Russian Grand Dukes were so thinned, they were seen no more. They took with them not only a way of life but the cumulative traditions of many centuries.

After World War II all the French establishments, both luxurious and sordid, were suppressed in a mood of purity hard to sustain; and it is indicative of the paucity, the economic pressure of this age that whether the ladies now operate in the shade or in the open, all of them—*grues, filles, trotteuses, belles de nuit, cocottes*—have now come to be known simply as *poutes*. All the Gallic philosophy and tradition, all the nuances between an eighteenth-century Manon Lescaut, or a nineteenth-century Païva, all the inmates of a Maison Tellier or a house in the Rue Chabanais have now been reduced by twentieth-century economics to *une putaine*.

The levelling of society is reflected in this aspect of life, too. In the United States, which boasts less class distinction than elsewhere (income brackets apart), we now see an even greater simplification—that of the call-girl. And here we might remark on the way in which the facility of American divorce tends to place some much-married ladies in the category of unofficial (or amateur) courtesans: though always with the spectre of alimony at the feast. In the early pioneer days, when the West was first opening up, there were flourishing chains of establishments, varying between brash saloons and log cabins. In San Francisco, women were such a rarity that a new arrival occasioned a journalistic review, in the manner now accorded a new play or book, where the lady's good and bad points were discussed in detail and a critical rating, usually of an indulgent nature, was given. By the late eighties and nineties American sporting houses were world famous. Those of Chicago and New Orleans in particular developed a legendary quality and are immortalized in popular ballads. As the wealth of the young, vital nation accumulated, the demand for extravagant pleasures grew. (As George Sand wrote to her daughter, Solange, 'Men with money to spend want women who know how to earn it.') So, while the come-by-chance fortunes of America were often being enjoyed by Diamond Lil and her rivals, there were champagne breakfasts and gold spittoons for the best clients, with perfumed fountains, four-piece orchestras scraping away tirelessly and, for very special occasions, clouds of live butterflies hovering gaudily. Today, in America, the courtesan may be said to have been replaced by the psychoanalyst. In place of the alcove there is the analyst's office. But basically the functions of both courtesan and analyst have the same principle. Both offer escape, relaxation and individual attention; both are expensive. And the couch is still there. *Plus ça change*.

2

Harriette Wilson belongs to the Regency: she first appears on the scene about 1803 and disappears from it about 1825. During the Napoleonic wars England had turned inward upon itself, being even more isolated from Continental influences than before (although it is known that no international tension ever prevented the Empress Josephine from receiving regular packages of English rose-trees for her garden at Malmaison). And the fashionable set laced their talk with French phrases, a habit which Harriette's *Memoirs* reflect on every page. It was considered elegant to speak in a curious sort of half-and-half lingo.

It was an age of toughness, of brutal sports and crude practical jokes. Humour was coarse, wit steely. The noblemen, while retaining all the arrogance and privilege of their eighteenth-century forebears, acquired a variety of affectations which they cultivated along with the manners of the jockeys and prize-fighters with whom they consorted. The men about town, bucks, or Corinthians, rode like jockeys and boxed like professional pugilists. Lord Barrymore, a celebrated Corinthian, limped and was known as 'Cripplegate'; his two brothers, a disreputable pair, were 'Hellgate' and 'Newgate' (after the prison), while their sister was known as 'Billingsgate,' in reference to her language. One sporting dandy had his front teeth filed to points the better to whistle through them in the manner of the stage-coach drivers among whom he spent his days.

The diarist, Captain Gronow, writing in the 1860's, remembered the Regency dandies thus: 'How unspeakably odious—with a few brilliant exceptions such as Alvanley and others—were the dandies. They hated everybody and abused everybody, and would sit together in White's bay window, or the pit boxes at the Opera, weaving tremendous crammers [tall stories]. They swore a good deal, never laughed, had their own particular slang, looked hazy after dinner, and had most of them been patronized at one time or another by Brummell and the Prince Regent.' Hunting, racing, horse breeding, cock-fighting, gambling for enormously high stakes, drinking themselves under the table, keeping a mistress such as Harriette, or Emma Hart—these were the diversions of Regency men of wealth and fashion.

They had little time, or inclination, to spare for women of breeding. They married them, begat heirs and occasionally escorted them to a Court Ball, or one of those evenings at Almack's, where to become a member was almost equal to presentation at Court. Encouraged by the example of the Prince Regent, the First Gentleman of Europe, that glowing Prince Florizel who had, with time, become an obese, debauched figure, the butt of Rowlandson's most savage caricatures, Regency men considered it amusing to cuckold a friend or acquaintance. But in the main the women of their own station were neglected for a less exigent circle, such as that of Harriette Wilson and her sisters, 'the Fashionable Impures,' or Cyprians, as they were called. Among such women they could forget current affectations and, for a while, be themselves. Although these men were lavish in their way of life—and their credit seemed inexhaustible—it was not so much on their women as on gambling and their stables that the largest sums of money were spent. Play ran very high at all the clubs along St. James's. Faro and macao were the favourite card games. At Crockford's the players wore a curious sort of wide-brimmed straw hat to shadow their faces, thus concealing any tell-tale emotions from the other players.

Bloodstock and extravagant equipages were another passion. Curricles, britzkas, tilburys and phaetons as high as a second-floor window skimmed about the streets like so many glittering, brilliant-coloured insects. Their line, carriage work and upholstery were triumphs of the carriage-maker's art. Generally the owner liked to drive himself; the bucks were famous for 'tooling the ribbons' or, to continue their language, 'coming coachy in prime style.' They enjoyed dashing along the Bath or Brighton Road, driving a four- or six-in-hand, horse-whipping the turnpike men out of their way, overturning market carts and generally calling attention to their insufferable manners. They dressed themselves and their little tigers, or grooms, to harmonize with the general turnout. Lord Petersham drove brown horses, had a brown carriage, wore a brown greatcoat and beaver hat, this serving, it was said, as a reminder of his unrequited passion for a beautiful widow of that name. Tommy Onslow, another celebrated buck, chose an all-black turnout and was criticized for looking like a hearse. But all of them paled beside a Mr. Cope, who was known as 'the Green Man.' His clothes, equipage and harness were all bright green; he powdered his hair green, was never seen to eat anything but spinach and was always accompanied by a poodle of greenish tinge.

In that age of individualists men were able not only to dress as they pleased but to live and love as they chose, besides ranging a whole field of amorous encounter, selecting a mistress of angelic or diabolic qualities and enjoying her for a night or a season in circumstances of anonymity or in the full glare of publicity. They were as personal, as exigent, in their choice of food. Lord Sefton, a great gourmet, employed Ude, the celebrated chef, at a considerable salary and undertook to leave him the same amount in an annual legacy, provided he retained his services to the end. But in such an age of individualism chefs too adopted a selective attitude. They were treated *en prince*; in some great houses the chef's name would be printed on the menu after the dish he had created, in the manner of a star performer. Carême, sure of his genius, declined to stay with no less a *bon viveur* than the Prince Regent. "His Royal Highness' cuisine is too bourgeois," he stated, and was joined by another chef who refused to follow his ducal master to Dublin since there was no opera there. Small wonder, then, that Harriette, conquering this world as she did, was a very remarkable creature.

London, as Harriette Wilson and her world knew it, comprised the small area of Mayfair, bounded on the north by Grosvenor Square, on the south by St. James's Park, on the east by Bond Street and on the west by Park Lane. Beyond the turnpike at Hyde Park Corner lay fields dotted with the villages of Chelsea, Brompton and Kensington. From Oxford Street, then known as the Oxford Road, there were uninterrupted vistas of Hampstead.

St. Paul's and the city lay outside the fashionable perimeter; they were for merchants and lawyers, just as the rookeries of St. Giles, Seven Dials and Drury Lane were for the cut-throats and drabs. The *ton*, among whom Harriette moved, were all congregated in or around Mayfair. Some of the streets she knew and the houses where she lived still stand much as they did in her day. The little plum-red brick alleys of Shepherd Market, the sober elegance of Curzon Street, Chesterfield Street or Hertford Street are not greatly changed outwardly. In Charles Street, at No. 16, once the town house of the Earl of Craven, later the Guards Club, its splendid portals flanked by stone obelisks, Harriette's life of adventure might be said to have begun, if we are to believe the incomparable opening to her *Memoirs*. Here she is, recounting her fall:

I shall not say why, or how, I became, at the age of fifteen, the mistress of the Earl of Craven. Whether it was love, or the severity of my father, the depravity of my own heart, or the winning arts of the noble Lord, which induced me to leave my paternal roof and place myself under his protection, does not now much signify: or if it does, I am not in the humour to gratify curiosity in this matter.

Before that she had lived at her father's house, No. 23 Queen Street, a few doors away from No. 16 Charles Street. She and her sisters used to sit in the window of the family parlour, eyeing the mansion down the street, eyeing, too, the fine gentlemen who used to issue from its doorway and lounge down Queen Street with such a marked rallentando opposite No. 23. Presently Harriette kicked over the traces, dashed up the street to Lord Craven's arms and was never to return to her family again. But I anticipate.

In the London of that moment: oil-lamps were only beginning to give place to gas-lamps in 1816. In the obscurity crime flourished. Cut-throats, garroters, pickpockets and street walkers abounded. There was no organized police force until 1820. The press gang struck terror wherever it went, seizing men for forced service in the navy. Malefactors were transported and sent to the dreaded hulks, or prison galleys; others were hanged at Tyburn or outside Newgate gaol, where huge crowds, which had paid high prices to get a place beside the scaffold, turned the matter into a sort of public holiday. Debtors were lodged at the Fleet or the Marshalsea Prison, where those who could afford to pay could still live in comfort, sending out for foods and wines and receiving their visitors alongside the more wretched, forgotten inmates. Lunatics were chained, existing in ghastly conditions at the Royal Bethlehem Hospital, where the public often repaired to observe their curious behaviour. Other diversions were Punch-and-Judy shows, raree-shows of performing fleas, or travelling fairs, with their mountebanks, wirewalkers and bearded women.

There were, besides, the circus, the theatre and the pleasure gardens at Vauxhall. The Argyle Rooms were celebrated for being the scene of an annual event, the Cyprians' Ball, given by the 'Fashionable Impures,' the demi-reps, who played hostess *en masse* to their admirers and protectors. In Cruikshank's drawing we see the sort of evening it was. Joy is obviously unrestrained; the ladies are waltzing giddily, offering their charms to whiskered oglers. Harriette, seen at the right, splendidly plumed, is on the arm of the publisher, Stockdale; her sister Amy, sitting below the cellist, displays a great deal too much leg. Bosoms, shoulders, all are for show or for sale. In a contemporary account of the revels we are told that 'while the snowy orbs of nature undisguised heaved like the ocean with circling swell, the amorous lover palmed the melting fair and led her to where shame-faced Aurora . . . might hope in vain to draw aside the curtain and penetrate the mysteries of Cytherea.'

The writer goes on to say that in this territory of the Paphian Goddess, female invitations to the ball were confined to the stars and planets of the demi-monde. Distinguished personages of the other sex abounded, all the leading roués of the day being present. Listing 'the fair Dulcineas,' he speaks of The Venus Mendicant, The Mocking Bird, and Brazen Bellona, who, her father being a market gardener near Eton, had been launched on her career by the Etonians. Another, The White Doe, 'now reclines upon the velvet cushion of Independence,' while Laura, 'has money in the Funds.' In short, the assembled ladies represented the flower of their profession.

For the well-to-do, rather than the musical, there was the opera. This was regarded more as a fashionable promenade, or rendezvous, than as a musical entertainment, and for the men Court dress, knee breeches and *chapeaux bras* were *de rigueur*. Women of both the aristocracy and the demi-monde held court in their boxes each night; they eyed, and were eyed by, the whole house. To the demi-reps, to Harriette and her rivals, an opera box was a necessity—their showcase. Prices were high. For a box in the first tier, Harriette tells us, she paid 200 guineas a season, a considerable sum then and one which would today represent about £800.

Apart from the extreme luxury and sophistication of a small circle, London still retained much that was primitive in its tenor of life. Refuse accumulated and rotted in the gutters. Slops were flung from windows. The lack of any kind of hygiene was responsible for a high rate of infant mortality. It was not thought worth while to notify half the deaths; many were merely listed as being caused by 'convulsions.' In a city report about this time we read that of the 21,780 deaths notified during the year, 4,809 were from consumption, largely due, no doubt, to the conditions of living half starved in overcrowded slums. There were 172 deaths in childbed, 11 from excessive drinking (excessive eating was not mentioned, unless we count the 223 deaths from apoplexy). Cancer claimed only 42. The French pox, or syphilis, carried off 65, leprosy 2. The Thames being then used as a highway, 138 were drowned. There were 5 murders, 34 suicides, 8 who were overlaid mysteriously, 3 who died of grief, as well as some deaths attributed to St. Anthony's Fire and 'the rising of the lights,' which latter we must presume to have been a digestive complaint.

The apothecary dealt with minor ailments; teeth were still drawn at the street corner by itinerant quacks. The chiropodist, too, did a brisk, passing trade, taking up his pitch at a busy thoroughfare, brandishing his knife and scissors, crying "Corns to pick!" Most confinements were attended by the male midwife, reminiscent of Sterne's Dr. Slop. Harriette gives us a lively description of her sister Amy's accouchement, presided over by Dr. Sam Merriman, in circumstances of great luxury provided by Amy's current protector and Harriette's former lover, the Duke of Argyll, who although in such a taking (being then anxious to end the liaison and marry Lady Anglesey) performed all the rituals of an expectant father and ordered straw to be laid down before the house and the door knocker to be muffled at least three weeks before the birth. It was customary to speak of ladies in a delicate condition as being 'in the straw.'

There was little or no drainage system in the city; even the most commodious houses were only beginning to install water closets. Although these had been first introduced from Italy in the reign of Queen Elizabeth, they had not become popular, a chamber pot serving quite well enough for the next two centuries until water closets were at last reintroduced by Dr. Darwin, the biologist's grandfather. Beau Brummell was regarded as unbalanced in his passion for daily ablutions. His ritualistic morning toilet took upwards of five hours, one hour spent inching himself into his skin-tight buckskin breeches, an hour with the hairdresser and another two hours tying and 'creasing down' a series of starched cravats until perfection was achieved. But first of all two hours were spent scrubbing himself with fetish zeal from head to toe in milk, water and eau-de-Cologne. He was a close friend of Harriette's, though she tells us little of his idiosyncrasies. Beau Brummell said he used only the froth of champagne to polish his Hessian boots. He had 365 snuff boxes, those suitable for summer wear being quite unthinkable in winter, and the fit of his gloves was achieved by entrusting their cut to two firms— one for the fingers, the other for the thumbs. Sometimes, however, the tyranny of elegance became altogether insupportable. A Mr. Boothby committed suicide and left a note saying he could no longer endure the ennui of buttoning and unbuttoning.

The niceties of masculine fashion seem to have taken precedence over female fashion at this time. No doubt there were elegant women and dowdy ones, but man was the *arbiter elegantiarum* of the age. Military uniforms reached a degree of brilliance that belied their wearers' martial spirit. The officers of the Guards were wont to shelter their splendours under umbrellas, even on the field of battle, unless engaged in particularly active combat. But this practice was finally proscribed by the Duke of Wellington in his Peninsular campaign, during a season of torrential rains.

Both Wellington and Napoleon were eminently practical men. They knew there was a time for dressing-up and a time for undressing too. I am reminded of the anecdote told by Wellington to his confidante, Mrs. Arbuthnot, on the methods Napoleon wished to employ in order to distract the Parisian public's attention from the appalling losses in the Russian campaign then in progress. He ordered that the ballet dancers at the opera were to appear *sans culotte*. The order was given, but the dancers flatly refused to comply. 'Wellington added,' says Mrs. Arbuthnot in her journal, 'that if the women had consented he did not doubt but that it would have obliterated all recollection of the Russian losses. Wellington was categoric. "This anecdote," he said, "he knew for a fact." ' The Iron Duke had a sound understanding of human nature: and he was being realistic, rather than cynical, when, during the Peninsular campaigns he set a limit of forty-eight hours for his officers' leaves in Lisbon, or behind the lines. This, he said, was as long as any reasonable man could wish to spend in bed with any woman.

While the Prince Regent and Beau Brummell led masculine fashion, the ladies of the royal family—the Prince's retiring mother, Queen Charlotte, and her stodgy daughters—lived withdrawn. The wives and mistresses of his brothers, too, did not set up to be *élégantes*. In his choice of mistresses, such as Lady Hertford or Lady Conyingham, the Prince always showed an irresistible attraction for maturity bordering on the elderly. When Lady Conyingham was first installed as the favourite, the diarist Greville notes that Lord Beauchamp, a cynical young peer, encountered her riding in the park with her royal lover, which caused him to say, "By God, our grandmother will have to learn to ride or it will be all up with us."

There were some women's magazines, such as *La Belle Assemblée*, which printed coloured fashion plates inspired by Paris, where mantuamakers, milliners, perfumiers, glove and shoemakers advertised their wares. Advertisements dwelled on the merits of 'long stays which compass into form the chaos of the flesh.' We read of all kinds of cushions, plumpers and padded rolls to hide defects, though of these Harriette could have had no need. There are frequent references to her lovely figure, her small waist and voluptuous bosom. Paint was lavishly used: red, black and white, a primitive palette. There were fearful concoctions of white lead and vegetable rouge, and, only a generation back, one of the lovely Gunning sisters had died of lead poisoning induced by the excessive use of cosmetics.

Dental skill being in its infancy, teeth were either good or bad. False teeth were an expensive luxury, and we are told that Mrs. Fitzherbert's charms were much impaired by an ill-fitting set. Different ages have different standards of conduct, and beauty too. Small hands and feet were one of the first essentials of beauty to nineteenth-century Europe. From the Thames to the Neva, poets were intoxicated by glimpses of their mistresses' tiny feet. Oddly, this standard seems to have been applied to men too. There are frequent references in Harriette's *Memoirs* to the 'small, white, soft' hands of the men upon whom she dotes; Lord Byron and Lord Ponsonby are both described as having 'little hands.'

Judging by the portraits of the period—particularly the Dighton series of celebrated London personalities, many of them Harriette's protectors or friends—we see that even the young were of a portly inclination. Lord Alvanley, choked into a high, starched stock, a beaver hat crammed down on his wine-flushed face, is the perfect image of a Regency buck, but he wears his weight well. And his wit was airy. Creevey called him a natural wag. Greville found him the delight and ornament of society, but

O'Connell, with whom he fought a duel, called him a bloated buffoon. He lived high, and once ordered a dish which cost him £108. He was partial to cold apricot tart, which he insisted on having on his side table every day, all the year round. Continuing the fashionable cult of individualism, he liked to read in bed but not to blow out the candle. Therefore, he would hurl the candle on to the floor; if it still burned he would fling a pillow at it. This reckless arrogance recalls Lord Cardigan (of the Light Brigade), who, when picknicking in his carriage, always flung the tray, with all its luxurious silver, glasses and porcelain, out of the carriage window, saying it was the only way to picnic without a mess. Arrogance was inbred in these men. They were patricians and intended to avail themselves of every privilege which their birth accorded them and their wealth obtained.

Even the great Wellington, always far removed from the more spectacular follies of his age, reveals an unconscious hauteur and a contempt for both progress and the masses when he dismisses the new steam railway as 'a project which would encourage the lower classes to move about needlessly.' This same mixture of imperiousness and common sense, this sureness of themselves which was ever a fundamental characteristic of the British aristocracy, is found again, years later, when the Duke, an old man, admonishes the young heiress, Angela Burdett-Coutts, twenty-five and deeply in love with him. Casting discretion to the winds, she visited him unaccompanied and wished to plunge into an entanglement. 'My dearest,' writes the Duke, 'I tell you very firmly I will not allow it. I did not think you would be guilty of such folly.' He goes on to remind her that she will be still young when he is a wreck. What supreme confidence is shown here by the old general, still so shrewd, so vital, so sure of himself as a man! 'I entreat you again, in this way, not to throw yourself away upon a Man old enough to be your Grandfather, who, however Strong, Hearty and Healthy at present, must and will certainly *in time*' (the italics are mine) 'feel the consequences and infirmities of Age.' Even at seventy the Duke spoke of infirmity and age as a melancholy prospect rather than an existing fact.

Harriette's *Memoirs* are very personal; they do not reflect the larger aspects of her age as do those of the classic diarists, Creevey, Greville or Gronow. There is some mention of the Napoleonic wars, since many of her beaux saw action in the various campaigns, and Wellington himself was one of them. But of outstanding events, whether Nelson's death in 1805, the first performance of a Mozart opera in England, at His Majesty's

Theatre in 1806, Pitt's Abolition of Slavery, or the Congress of Vienna, we hear nothing. Bonaparte is mentioned only once.

London has always consisted of a series of overlapping but completely separate quarters. The *ton*, living in Mayfair, found it impossible to envisage anything farther east than the Haymarket. Beau Brummell spoke for all of them when, in reply to an invitation to dine in Bloomsbury, he accepted, 'providing my coachman can find his way there.' Literary London—that is, the successful and fashionable authors—all congregated at 50 Albemarle Street, then, as now, the beautiful premises of the publishing firm of John Murray. "My Murray," says Byron, who treated the place as his club, bank, home and refuge from the more importunate ladies, such as Caroline Lamb. Here, in the red drawing-room, he used to meet with all the men of letters of the day, and when Harriette Wilson tried to crash these gates and set up in authorship, she could never forgive Mr. Murray's unenthusiastic behaviour. One of Harriette's rivals, Julia Johnstone, insisted that Harriette's culture was mere affectation, since she and her sisters were nourished on Monk Lewis and Mrs. Radcliffe's horrific novels . . . 'I have often written out quotations from Shakespeare and Milton and others for Harriette to use in conversation.' And from the same source we learn that Harriette's literary aspirations led her, not only to quote Shakespeare, but to write a farce which she herself took very seriously, and submitted to John Kemble. But it seems this manuscript met with no better success than the one she offered to Mr. Murray.

A less successful literary group was found at Euston, where, in an atmosphere vibrant with passions and higher thought, Mary Wollstonecraft, author of *Vindication of the Rights of Women*, had lived with her husband, Godwin, and where their daughter grew into the gentle, unhappy idealist who was to marry Shelley and write *Frankenstein*. The pompous city merchants were centred around Bloomsbury. Somers Town was a favourite neighbourhood for the Cyprians of second rank, who were installed there, in comfort if not in style, by their lovers. It was conveniently removed from Mayfair, yet easy of access. Harriette Wilson lived there for a short while in her early days when under the protection of Fred Lamb, and prior to engaging the affections of the Duke of Argyll, then Marquis of Lorne, who soon removed her to Argyll House, Mayfair and fame.

All these changes of house or lover are recorded with candour, though perhaps not always with accuracy. Harriette has a fine disregard for exactitude, either in names, places or dates. Incidents which most likely occurred, are set wildly, some years out of date. Wellington is referred to as the Duke some years before he obtained that title. The Duke of Argyll, who during their liaison was Marquis of Lorne, is called both Lorne and 'Argyle'. The Marquis of Hertford is sometimes Lord Yarmouth. Harriette and Byron discuss Lady Caroline Lamb's *roman à clef, Glenarvon,* seven years before it is published—that is, if they discussed it at Wattier's Masquerade, as she says. But does it signify? Dates make ladies nervous and stories dry, says Harriette—no lady and never dry.

The *Memoirs* may be said to derive directly from the sixth Duke of Beaufort. We must always be grateful. Without his stinginess, without the backsliding of his son and heir, the Marquis of Worcester, we might never have had them. When, some years earlier, Worcester was at the height of his passion for Harriette, to whom he was in the habit of writing the most imprudent promises of marriage, addressed to his adored 'wife,' his 'angelick' Harriette, he was kept from the altar only by the fact that he had not reached his majority and, Harriette assures us, by her refusal, her positive refusal, to become a Marchioness. Be that as it may, the Duke and Duchess of Beaufort began to grow very uneasy after two years of their son's spectacular constancy. Every effort was made to separate the lovers without success. Presently the Duke's lawyers approached Harriette, offering her a sum of money for the return of Lord Worcester's letters. Harriette's own lawyer advised her they were worth about £20,000, but Harriette, incurably sentimental, wished to get on good terms with her lover's family. She returned most of the letters (though retaining enough worldly sense to hold some back) and wrote an affecting letter saying her only wish was to be considered more kindly by the Beauforts. Naturally this remained unanswered.

The Duke now succeeded in having his son ordered off to the wars. He was to join Wellington's staff in the Peninsula. Lord Worcester spoke of suicide. Tears streamed down his cheeks; Harriette began to feel she had perhaps set too little value on the young man's passion. Grief ruled the day; the lovers could hardly be parted for an hour during the last weeks together. Indeed, Lord Worcester's uncle was dispatched to drag him from Harriette's arms and see him aboard the ship for Spain. Meantime Harriette undertook to remain true to her love (on a modest allowance provided by the family lawyers). Lord Worcester was a splendid catch. Young, ardent, romantic, his beaky parrot nose spoke of his Plantaganet and FitzRoy ancestry, while his quarterings displayed the *fleur-de-lis* of France and the lion of England. His father was the sixth Duke of Beaufort. The family had always been closely associated with the Crown.

Their name recurs nobly throughout English history and their historic home, Badminton, was only one of several splendid estates. After all, Harriette might have argued, was she really aiming too high? There was the case of Mary Anne Clarke, who, with no more pretensions to beauty or breeding than Harriette, had been set up by H.R.H. the Duke of York, brother of the Prince of Wales, the Duke having agreed to pay Mrs. Clarke £1,000 a month. On this understanding the lady had filled her stables with bloodstock, kept twenty servants, including three chefs, and never ate off anything but gold or silver plate. 'Gay goings-on in Gloucester Place,' says a contemporary before Mary Anne Clarke found that, due to her allowance being paid to her so very irregularly, she was obliged to traffic in military appointments and preferments, this course being made easy for her as the Duke of York was Commander-in-Chief of the British Army. This eventually led to her public examination in the House of Commons on a charge of corruption. She was by then a fallen favourite. But this did not happen till 1809. When Harriette was discomforting the Beaufort family Mary Anne Clarke was still supreme, an object lesson in triumphant depravity. So Harriette held out for her marquis and the Beauforts placed their faith in time and distance.

The better to avoid those snares of fashionable society of which Lord Worcester was so apprehensive, Harriette promised to bury herself in a village in Devon. She was to spend a year there, awaiting her lover's majority. Upon which, it was agreed between them that she should join him in Spain and nothing on earth should prevent the marriage. But reading between the lines, we see that life in the country, for Harriette, was no life at all. 'She had no idea of ruralizing, she was a real city madam,' says Julia, who, according to her *Confessions*, shared Harriette's exile, and even endeavoured to restrain her friend's exuberance. 'Once,' she says, 'Harriette nearly betrayed her calling as we were going to church, by holding up her leg on a passing stile and desiring the clergyman to fasten her bootlace. He had once been a dasher on the London streets and very gallantly complied with her request, saying with a smile, "Don't your garters want tightening, my love?" I could have brained her with my fan,' adds the refined Julia.

Even with such diversions, Harriette chafed: and since the Beaufort lawyers were always in arrears with her allowance, she decided to have done with dullness and Devon. She wrote to Worcester and agreed to join him without further delay. Alas, she had gone no farther than Falmouth, where she was awaiting the packet-boat, when news reached her of Lord

C

Worcester's infatuation with a paymaster's wife. It was not to be borne. She returned to London and her former ways.

High dramas ensued, which the *Memoirs* relate in full. When threatened with a breach of promise case the Beaufort family were prompt with their payments; but when they tried to wriggle out of their undertakings by offering a cash settlement of £1,200 down, Harriette's ire was roused. On the advice of no less an advocate than Lord Brougham, she says, she took the Duke to court and would have won her case had not Lord Worcester stepped in and revealed that by certain letters she had written him from Devonshire she had broken her side of the agreement. Thus, on her late lover's evidence, Harriette lost her case. Gradually she fell from fashion, her looks faded and she had to accept second-rate men and second-rate terms. She moved to Paris around 1815 and for the first time a note of lasting melancholy creeps into the *Memoirs*. She learned, now, to be content with tawdry triumphs. Most of her old friends were marrying, or forgetting her determinedly. She was not of much consequence in Paris, and we sense with what eagerness she welcomes the few Englishmen whom she encounters. But, as she says, 'it won't do to play the game of hearts in Paris.'

There is a silence of some years before we hear of her, now really hard pressed for money, and under the influence of the disreputable Colonel Rochfort, welcoming the publisher Stockdale's scheme for producing her *Memoirs* in a manner most calculated to bring the biggest returns. As has been remarked, Harriette was not by nature spiteful; she seldom bore malice. But here, we feel, she fell in with Stockdale with a special gusto. It must have been a great pleasure to discomfort the Beaufort family once more; they had treated her very shabbily. And Lord Worcester, now suitably married, presented a perfect target. I think it likely that the *Memoirs* would never have been written had she been able to settle down into a snug middle age on a Beaufort pension.

Harriette now circularized all her former friends and lovers, advising them of her intentions. Two hundred pounds down by return of post was her price of omission from the *Memoirs*, and she kept her word. We imagine with what alarm such letters were received, an alarm tinged with exasperation, since Harriette was in the habit of sealing her letters with her own seal or device. One bore the message *Andante Felice*—go in happiness; another, with the image of a cupid, bore one word—'Hush'! Their irritant qualities, in the present circumstances, were not lost on Harriette, we feel. It must have added to the fun. Many apprehensive gentlemen paid up by return, and felt it well worth while. Some braved it out and writhed as each new instalment appeared, published with a great flourish by Joseph Stockdale, a 'Caliban figure' lurking in the shady purlieu of the Opera Colonnade, off the Haymarket, where a besieging mob had to be held back by barricades, so overwhelming was the demand for the first instalment. St. James's was in a ferment. Boodles, Crockford's, White's—the sober façade of each club concealed an uproar. The noble members, now come into their honours and titles, ministers of the Crown, married, fathers of families, setting into a triumphant maturity, found themselves pilloried, their callow follies, their passions and weaknesses displayed with a ruthless objectivity. Once again, we feel that Harriette was enjoying her work.

It would seem that she chose her moment well. Just as she had led the unfettered, hedonistic life of her inclination during the Regency, so now, at its close, she found, with her decline, the perfect moment to extract a price for her silence. Times had changed. Yet even twenty years earlier that England which had countenanced so many follies and excesses, and had accepted the lovely dissolute Emma Hart becoming not only Lady Hamilton but British Ambassadress at the Court of Naples, could not countenance her being bequeathed to the nation by the nation's hero, Nelson. Lady Hamilton and Horatia, her child by Lord Nelson, were left to perish. Even in 1805 a line was drawn between private life and public gestures.

From Creevey we learn that Mrs. Fitzherbert, who was the Prince Regent's mistress and probably his wife, was also opposed to Lady Hamilton's influence. The Prince was greatly affected by the news of Lord Nelson's death, 'but Mrs. Fitzherbert at once entered into an account of the domestic failings of Lord Nelson, in a way infinitely creditable to her. . . .' We visualize the scene: the portly Prince, fidgety but respectful while Mrs. Fitzherbert pronounced, his bulging eyes straying sometimes beyond the green lawns of the Pavilion to the Steyne gardens, where fair passers-by were glimpsed beyond the flower-beds that bordered the royal residence. Mrs. Fitzherbert was entirely for Lady Nelson, we learn. Lady Hamilton, she said, '*overpowered* Lord Nelson, hero though he was, and took possession of him quite by force. . . .' But in 1806 the Prince fell desperately in love with Lady Hertford and Mrs. Fitzherbert's censure was of no more consequence.

There followed a few more years of latitude before respectability took over with growing momentum. By the time Harriette struck, twenty years later, the effect was cataclysmic. London society spoke of nothing else; pirated editions appeared rapidly, and broadsheets, crudely illustrated, were sold in the thousands. There were the most entertaining pictures of the Marquis of Worcester lacing Harriette Wilson's stays with one hand and toasting her breakfast bread with the other. There were pictures of Harriette pursuing Lord Ponsonby, and of Lord Deerhurst accosting her sister Sophia. No one was immune. Sir Walter Scott wrote in his journal, 'The gay world has been kept in hot water lately by the impudent publication of the celebrated Harriot Wilson, who lived with half the gay world at hack and manger, and now obliges such as will not pay hush money with a history of whatever she knows or invents about them.' Scott conceded 'she has some good retailing of conversations, in which the style of the speaker, so far as known to me, is exactly imitated'. It was this very quality which made the *Memoirs* so unpalatable, so unforgivable, to many of her former friends.

The manner in which Stockdale announced each successive instalment was calculated to obtain the maximum attention. Encouraged by the success of the opening numbers, he announced the next in these terms:

> *Part VII will be ready on Monday, 4th April, at 2 o'clock precisely, and Part VIII on Monday, 18th April, at the same hour.*

Preceding this there had been a statement intended to arouse alarm and the most lively curiosity. The noble persons mentioned in the *Memoirs* had been listed like an inventory. Under the heading *Exhibits in Parts IV, V and VI* he had announced:

> *Dukes.* Argyll, Beaufort (and Duchess), de Guiche, Leinster, Wellington.
> *Marquesses.* Anglesea, Bath, Headfort, Sligo, Worcester . . .

and so on down, through Earls, Barons, Honourables, to Colonels, Captains and even the modest Esquire. An equal treat was promised in the forthcoming instalments.

For some while Harriette had been sending each successive instalment through the bag—the Foreign Office official valise. When the new Ambassador to France turned out to be none other than that pompous Lord Granville whom Harriette had tried out and found wanting on the hot, long walk to Hampstead and back so many years ago, he quickly put a stop to the practice. But he had not reckoned with Harriette, who wrote telling him that she had been looking about for a fool to fill up her *Memoirs* and that he had presented himself just in time.

The whole affair engendered a great deal of unpleasantness and more and more gentlemen now took almost permanent refuge in their clubs, where, among themselves, Harriette's victims discussed how best to defend themselves against her onslaughts. The Hon. Edward 'Bear' Ellice, M.P. for Invergarry, Secretary to the Treasury, a wealthy man owning vast estates in Canada, was one of those who had no intention of paying Harriette's price. On receiving a letter from her, he published it in an effort to unite action against her. Here is Harriette, impertinent and impenitent:

> *Paris. 111 Rue du Faubourg*
> *St. Honoré,*
> *March 8, 1825.*

Sir—

> *People are buying themselves so fast out of my book, 'Memoirs of Harriette Wilson,' that I have no time to attend to them. Sh'd be sorry not to give each a chance if they chuse to be out. You are quizzed most unmercifully. Two Noble Dukes have taken my word and I have never named them. I am sure————wd say you might trust me not to publish or cause to be published aught about you if you like to forward £200 directly to me, else it will be too late as the last volume in which you shine will be the property of the Editor, and in his hands. Lord————[name removed by Ellice] says he will answer for aught I agree to, and so will my husband. Do just as you like. Consult only yourself. I get as much for a small book as you will give me for taking you out, or more. I attack no poor men because they cannot help themselves. Adieu!—Mind, I have no time to write again, as what with writing books and then altering them for those who buy out, I am done up—frappé en mort. What do you think of my French?*

> Yours, H. ROCHFORT. late Wilson

P.S. Don't trust the bag with your answer.

It is sometimes said that Lord Ponsonby (Harriette's great love) owed the start of his diplomatic career to the fact that he had given Harriette some of his old love letters, notably those of Lady Conyingham, once his mistress and now George IV's favourite. Harriette threatened to publish these letters, it is alleged. But Prime Minister Canning settled things by nominating Ponsonby Ambassador to a new capital, Buenos Aires, thus removing him from Harriette's reach and from Lady Conyingham's too, which greatly relieved the King, jealous to distraction over his inamorata. In any case, nothing more was ever heard of the letters, and Lord Ponsonby's diplomatic career kept him out of England for many years.

The Duke of Wellington was one of those who refused to be exploited. With the same vigour and dispatch with which he once sought Harriette's embraces he is said to have sent back her demands with the famous phrase 'Publish and be damned' scrawled across it in red ink. In his daily walks and talks with his confidante, Mrs. Arbuthnot, he had to explain that it had all been a very long time ago, that he doubted that he would even recognize Harriette if he saw her now. Mrs. Arbuthnot noted it all down in her journal and seemed quite satisfied.

Not so Harriette. It would never do if men began to brave it out. It is not surprising, therefore, that the Duke cuts a rather poor figure in the *Memoirs*. This was Harriette's method of revenging herself on those who did not co-operate. 'Men are more hurt at being painted weak silly creatures than gross blackguards,' she wrote apropos of her methods of extortion, and we see the Iron Duke, Marquis of Douro, Field Marshal of Great Britain, Duke of Ciudad Rodrigo, Prince of Waterloo in the Netherlands, and so many more titles besides, as a faintly comic character, 'looking,' she said, 'rather like a rat-catcher.' Even so, something of his essential largeness—his generosity and chivalresque attributes—emerges from the pages. However Harriette chooses to present her subjects, it must be agreed she has an acute, Dickensian sense of character. No doubt it was convenient for her subjects to denounce the *Memoirs* as a tissue of lies. Yet, inaccurate or no, a ring of most unmistakable truth pervades the whole, and where I have ventured to cut the enormous original, it is only to avoid the more repetitious or padded passages.

Harriette Dubochet—for Wilson she chose as her professional name (it never seems to have been associated with any of her protectors)—was born in London, in Mayfair, on February 2, 1786, 'at ten minutes before 8 o/c.' This date is almost the only one in all her life of which we are sure. She was christened in the parish church of St. George's, Hanover Square, as the daughter of John Dubochet and Amelia Cook, his wife. They lived in a little house, No. 2 Carrington Street, Shepherd Market, now vanished.

There were fifteen children; of the nine who survived, only three of the girls followed the path of virtue. Mary, and Diana, whom Harriette speaks of as Paragon, and the youngest, Charlotte, appear seldom in the *Memoirs*; they lived in retired or domestic circumstances far removed from the raffish society frequented by Harriette. (Creevey makes one mysterious reference: 'Lord Lascelles' son has married Harriette Wilson's sister,' he writes in 1819. Which sister? Nothing in the Lascelles family bears out Creevey's statement.)

Amy, the eldest, a dark-eyed virago, Fanny, a golden creature for whom no one ever had a harsh word, Harriette, and their younger sister, Sophia, who set out to copy her sisters' way of life and bagged Lord Deerhurst at thirteen—all were stylish courtesans. But with this difference: while the legendary charmers of history, the hetaerae, the geishas and most of the more celebrated courtesans of other ages lived in an atmosphere of mystery, as high priestesses of seduction, the Dubochet sisters retained a cosy and most down-to-earth simplicity. Their amours were set less, it seems, in the voluptuous décor of the alcove, such as French eighteenth-century engravings have immortalized (those inviting little supper-tables set beside a canopied bed, tumbled with curtains, laces and discarded chemises), than in a setting at once more brisk and matter-of-fact—at a coaching inn on the Bath Road maybe, or in one of those snug little dun-brick London houses which still abound between Bond Street and the Park.

We read of a very pressing suitor shown into Harriette's parlour just as the cloth was being laid for supper; of Lord Berwick hurling a leg of mutton at the footman's head. Amy entertains the dandies, the beau monde, the émigré French princes of the Blood and all the diplomatic corps at her little love nest in York Place, the tiny, narrow hallway and stairs crammed with fine gentlemen, the upstairs drawingroom wedged with half Burke's Peerage. She feeds them cold chicken, washed down by claret and champagne; but it goes against the grain. Amy is mean; she herself is nourished on black pudding, a rather unromantic dish which she endeavours to conceal from her elegant patrons. Sophia, a glum girl, 'dumb' in modern parlance, is dispatched by Amy to fetch home this plebeian sausage and suffers agonies of mortification when, seeing Lord Deerhurst approaching, she vainly tries to dispose of the black pudding in the gutter and it is returned to her by a passer-by. These are homely incidents, and it was perhaps these very natural qualities which made the Dubochet sisters so irresistible to the men of fashion, who had to spend so much time maintaining standards of excessive artificiality if they wished to follow the tone set by Beau Brummell.

Above all, the Dubochet sisters must have been good company. We long to have known them. Across the century and a half that separates us we catch echoes of the chatter, the murmurs of admiration, the gaiety and the bursts of laughter which accompanied them wherever they went. These lusty young creatures, so full of life, so amoral, so frankly enjoying themselves, must have been delicious to know. Impossible to imagine a dull moment in their society. If not beautiful, they were alluring, with that special allure of the woman who knows she is desired by many. They were elegant, had cultivated graces; they were good linguists and musicians; they could discuss politics and current literature as well as the newest scandal. They were witty, improvident, imprudent—and to be had. The mixture must have been irresistible.

Alas, they missed being photographed by a mere thirty-five years. If only we could see them, fixed forever, smiling out at us from the opaque shadows of a daguerreotype! The earliest tintypes give us a sense of verity no portrait can. The turn of a nèck, the curve of a hand, an expression in the eyes—these things are irrefutable in a photograph, however faded and stiff. By 1840 Fox-Talbot was posing those quiet family groups on the lawns of Laycock Abbey. Only thirty-five years separate us from the possibility of gazing today at a laughing group of girls—Amy, Fanny, Harriette, Julia and Sophia.

Harriette was the most successful of all the sisters, unless we allow that Sophia, by marrying Lord Berwick and withdrawing to propriety and Leamington Spa, succeeded better. Harriette was the rage; all fashionable London aspired to be her lover for a night or two, or her protector for longer, or, at least, to be one of the crowd who jammed themselves into the opera box where she held court, levelling her glasses across the house, fancying this man or that, quizzing the pit and the parterre. "Pray send your patting men to me," says Mrs. Julia Johnstone, her rival, to Amy, who always professes innocence yet claims to have been able to obtain £100 at will, merely by allowing a Mr. Hart Davis to pat her arm. Not that Harriette would have been contented with pats. It must be admitted that she took a most unprofessional delight in her calling. Although the *Memoirs* are neither pornographic nor even erotic in the sense of the writings of Casanova or Paul de Kock, yet sandwiched between her pawky accounts of daily life (her daily life making, it must be remembered, very racy reading) are passages which disclose besides her roaring appetites ('not that I love a saint, but something which is most luxuriously sly and quiet . . .') her passionate love for Lord Ponsonby.

This affair was to shadow all the rest of her life. It was to her something which transcended mere mortal bliss. Writing to Lord Byron fifteen years after it was all over, she says, 'Don't despise me, nothing Lord Ponsonby has dearly loved can be vile or destitute of merit.' Ponsonby was, to her, a man apart, a god. She speaks of her sufferings when he terminated the relationship as mortal agony. She who loved life, men, and love, and had so much of all three, did, I believe, centre the whole force of her emotion on Ponsonby. After he had gone there was shadow and sunlight, money to be earned, appetites to be gratified, bills to be paid, a losing battle to be fought courageously against ill-health and age—but never again the bright chimera of love as she had known it centred in him. Still, she had dwelled with the rose.

In the beginning, about 1799, when she and her sisters used to sit in the window of the Dubochet home in Queen Street, times were hard and the girls passed as stocking menders. Their mother, whom Harriette adored, seems to have been a gentle and loving parent. Her business of Stocking Repairs flourished at that moment, for knee breeches were still generally worn and went out of fashion only around 1820. Unkind tongues hinted that Mrs. Dubochet had also followed the profession her daughters later embraced; but she is also said to have been the illegitimate child of a country squire, adopted and brought up in loving kindness by a Mr. and Mrs. Cook, stocking menders by trade, from whom the little Amelia obtained her surname and her skill at darning. When she married Dubochet, the Swiss watchmaker, twenty years her senior, he made some pretence of earning, being employed in the office of a coal wharf, but for the most part he was absorbed in mathematical calculations and accepted his wife's earnings unquestioningly. He appears to have been a detestable character, a domestic tyrant, violent-tempered, and one in whom his family, not unnaturally, did not confide. The only occasion when he sounds human is when his youngest daughter, Sophia, marries Lord Berwick and he is able to preen it over a patronizing neighbour. He came from the canton of Berne and was said, though not by Harriette, to be the child of that Elizabeth Dubochet who had been seduced by Lord Chesterfield and who was the mother of his son, Philip, to whom he addressed his celebrated *Letters*.

There is one highly coloured account of his ancestry which describes how a Mlle. Debouchette, a lovely young creature, a *limonadière* at the Hague, attracted the attention of a party of profligate English noblemen— the Earl of Chesterfield among them. She resisted all his advances until, at last, determined to win a bet on the subject, he adopted a course of action suggested by his Italian valet, no doubt an expert in such matters. A carriage was stationed near by while the Earl and his valet held a lighted sheet, saturated with spirits, at her window, crying fire. When she rushed out they seized her and made off with her to the coach. Her brother challenged Lord Chesterfield since he refused to marry his victim. But, having settled a considerable sum of money on her, he was at last permitted to take her to England. There she lived under Chesterfield's protection, in discreet retirement at Chelsea, where Harriette Wilson's father was born. With such animated parental backgrounds on both sides it is not surprising that, one by one, the lovely Dubochet sisters left home to set up for themselves.

Amy went first, and, having decided to walk about London till she met her destiny, she accepted a Mr. Trench for no other reason than that it seemed difficult to refuse him longer than two days. He was succeeded by General Madden, and then Mr. Sydenham, by whose name she was generally known. But there were many other interludes—with the *Corps Diplomatique* in particular, Counts Benckendorff, the Duke of Palmella, and others. In her forties Amy married an Italian harpist, Signor Bochsa, who behaved very badly to her and was a most unsatisfactory husband.

Fanny was the next to go; she had many adorers but seems to have been steadily under the protection of the Marquis of Hertford, Lord Yarmouth or 'Red Herrings' in his younger days. Colonel Parker was her undoing. They set up an establishment together, and Fanny, gentle, pretty, kindly Fanny, believed she had found peace. The Colonel wished her to be known as Mrs. Parker; she was treated with great respect by all his fellow officers, and he seems to have accepted unquestioningly the presence of George, her son by an earlier liaison. But after a few years of this quasi-domestic bliss, Colonel Parker coolly announced he was about to be married. Fanny never recovered from the blow. Complaining of a pain in her heart, she withdrew from the world, pined and faded. Her last hours were made easier by the kindness of Lord Hertford, whom Thackeray has painted as the profligate Marquis of Steyne in *Vanity Fair*. He had her moved to the then rustic freshness of Brompton Road and himself rushed to Piccadilly and back at the gallop to fetch her eau-de-Cologne. But no one could bring back Colonel Parker. Fanny sank and died, one summer evening, in Harriette's arms.

However, before that melancholy end, there were a number of years, from about the beginning of the century to 1815, when the three sisters swam in an aura of gaiety and adventure. Harriette soon followed her two elder sisters, starting out, according to the *Memoirs*, at fifteen as Lord Craven's mistress. Later she was followed by Sophia, an early starter at thirteen. Although they all remained on close terms, the atmosphere was often charged with vituperation; they confided in one another, borrowed one another's clothes and poached on one another's preserves. Amy, or Mrs. Sydenham, was always a little removed; less successful, she was jealous and unscrupulous. She was constantly trying to acquire her sisters' more spectacular conquests and sometimes succeeded.

Fanny, Harriette and their friend and rival, Julia Johnstone, were known as the Three Graces, while Amy was unkindly known as one of the Furies. All of them took a sisterly interest in Sophia and gave her much advice which, however, she does not seem to have needed, for she very soon persuaded Lord Berwick to marriage and from her rarefied position as a peeress snubbed, patronized and finally ignored her family. Sir Walter Scott relates that at the opera Harriette's box was directly above that of Lady Berwick, and Harriette used occasionally to remind her reformed sister of her presence by spitting on her head.

Julia Johnstone occupies a special place in these pages, for not only was she a professional friend and rival of Harriette's but she has left her *Confessions* in which she has sought to vilify Harriette and to give us other accounts of the events which Harriette records. Her version of Harriette's beginnings is very different from that cited in the *Memoirs*. Julia Johnstone writes spitefully; she is of no weight, and is far more inaccurate than Harriette. For example, she flatly states that Harriette was never *regularly* under Lord Worcester's protection but that she was sometimes favoured with his attentions. This was patently said to denigrate Harriette's charms, or the rank of her lovers. Yet in the correspondence between Lady Bessborough and Lord Granville Leveson-Gower, dated September 24, 1813, we read: 'Harriette Wilson is living at Ryde in great retirement, she passes for the most Virtuous Woman in the Island; she is waiting for Lord W.'s coming of age when he is to return and marry her. She shew'd some of his letters, all ending with yr affecn Husband . . .' As Lord Granville was the Duchess of Beaufort's brother, Lady Bessborough was no doubt only reporting a situation which was already causing lively anxiety in the Beaufort family.

Still, I quote Julia's *Confessions* at some length, since they form a sort of counterpoint by which the reader sees two opposing views or accounts of events and people.

Mrs. Johnstone was a charmer whose languid, high-bred manners concealed a most sensuous nature. Twelve children were the fruits of her passions, and when she loved it was with overwhelming solemnity. She was ahead of her time; already in Julia we sense that Victorian cant so far from the roaring Regency mood. For a while she and Harriette were inseparables. Although Harriette's *Memoirs* seldom miss a chance to diminish Julia's charms, it is with an offhanded, good-natured patronage rather than with the cold fury Julia reserves for Harriette. When the *Memoirs* were first published Julia reappeared from the shadows. Harriette had categorically stated that Julia was dead and that she, Harriette, had visited her on her deathbed. But a most lively shade returned: languor had given place to rage. Within two months of the *Memoirs'* publication Julia rushed into print with *The True Confessions of Julia Johnstone, written by herself, in contradiction to the Fables of Harriette Wilson*. They fell very flat. Even then it was seen that she was activated by purely personal motives; she wished to whitewash herself and pour venom and scorn, however late, on her one-time rival. Her description of Fanny's death is savage. She attributes it to drink. 'She screamed to live and had no hope of a blessed hereafter; I fear it may prove a family deathbed,' she says, at once unctuous and cruel.

Her description of Harriette at forty is as cruel but probably more exact. 'Imagine to yourself a little woman in a black beaver hat and long grey cloak. No tightening at the waist to show the figure of the wearer, nor any ornament to be seen whatever. Her figure, at a short distance, might not ineptly be compared to a mile-stone with a carter's hat resting on its summit. Her once little feet are now covered with list shoes to defend them from attacks of a desultory gout which she has suffered long in both extremities. Her face, at the time I'allude to, was swollen with this disorder to distortion. She has no colour, *le couleur de rose a disparu* [sic] and in its place appears a kind of dingy lilac which spreads all over her once light countenance and appears burnt into her lips. The crows feet are wide-spreading beneath her eyes, which, though sunken, still gleam with faded lustre through her long dark eyelashes. She bears the remains of what was once superlatively lovely—the wreck of the angel's visage is yet to be seen; it looks interesting in decay—not the decay brought by age and infirmity [such as even she, Julia Johnstone must suffer, she implies] but beauty hurried away prematurely, from the practices of a licentious and dissolute life; such is the once celebrated Miss Dubochet, alias Wilson.' Julia states that she repudiates, at the urgent request of her friends, 'the vile aspersions cast on me by one who was indebted to me not only for pecuniary services, but introducing her to fashionable life. . . .'

She is plainly mortified at the financial success of Harriette's *Memoirs*, and hopes to do as well herself. Julia, in her own words, had 'no editor like Stockdale, to wrap up in equivocal language the most sensual tales and clothe *vice* in the raiment of *virtue*. . . .' After a torrent of scandalous tattle she ends on a high-flown note. Her whole effort has been to repair the injury done to others by Harriette's *Memoirs*. 'Reader, I say with St. Paul, I have fought the good fight. I have finished my course, and now I care not what men can say against me.' Alas, no one bothered to say anything, for or against. The *Confessions* were a failure. She had, we suspect, been a bore in her youth and she did not change with age.

Although the manner in which Julia is described by Harriette is sometimes irritating, it is not wantonly vicious, as are all Julia's disclosures on
Harriette. In the index to one edition of the *Memoirs* Julia is listed as
Julia Storer, a girl at Hampton Court, ruined on the staircase of. A bald
statement, but it appears to have been true. She was brought up in genteel
poverty, her mother being, she says, a maid of honour to Queen Charlotte.
The pay was trifling and Julia often wore royal cast-offs. When the court
moved to Hampton Court Palace, Julia, at fourteen, found the etiquette of
the elderly Queen's court oppressive. 'One day I was handed out of the
carriage by a military officer. The sight inspired me with unusual pleasure: a hussar's cap and feather gives such a fillip to the spirits of a young
miss in her teens, you don't know.' She was now thrown into the society
of Colonel Cotton, dashing husband of an austere lady to whose children
Julia acted in the capacity of governess–companion. Soon there followed
the seduction on the staircase. Inflamed with passion, the lovers threw
discretion to the winds. 'When I discovered myself to be in a peculiar
situation,' says Julia, 'the Colonel removed me to a cottage near Primrose
Hill, where I had all the conveniences and comforts of life. . . .' (And
five children, says Harriette.)

It was in this modest abode about the year 1802 that Harriette first encountered Julia, who now passed as Mrs. Johnstone, the Colonel being
known as Mr. Johnstone. Harriette, then a beginner at the game, had only
recently exchanged Lord Craven, 'a dead bore,' for the Honourable Fred
Lamb, not much better, who had installed her in Somers Town, an easy
walk from Primrose Hill. The ladies fell into conversation and, while each
knew nothing of the other's circumstances, like calls to like, and a friendship was struck. 'When Lamb left Harriette alone, which was four out of
six nights,' says Julia, 'she came to me, danced or romped with the children; she was all animal spirits. I believe nothing could have made her
grieve for an hour but the loss of her beauty.' One Sunday the two ladies
were alone. 'Fred Lamb always dined at home that day, like a good boy.'
'Mr. Johnstone' was also absent. The ladies were soon exchanging confidences. 'We had no music and were rather dull.' But not for long.

"Come, Julia," said Harriette, "I will dispel this ennui by telling you
my history." She started counting up her lovers, which, according to
Julia, was a most shocking admission. Julia's retrospectively sancti-
monious tone does not ring true. She goes on to say that Harriette's
family lived in a nook at Hammersmith, burrowed together like rabbits.
(No mention here of the Dubochets' house, which, however modest, was
still in Mayfair.) Harriette's first love was, according to Julia, not Lord

Craven but the son of a washerwoman who kept a wherry-boat on the Thames below Hammersmith, where he plied for hire. 'A lusty, carroty lad, with the finest set of . . . teeth I ever saw': thus Harriette, according to Julia, who goes on to say that Harriette and Amy often took trips to Isleworth and back to visit another humble lover, this time Amy's, a miller, locally celebrated for his amorous prowess. For all one summer the river idyll continued, the sisters drifting up the pale, misty reaches of the Thames, past Chiswick Mall and Strand-on-the-Green (much as it remains today), on, past the willow-fringed islands and the little Dutch palace at Kew, to the silent reaches of Sion, where the herons fly at evening and the bells of Isleworth church sound faintly across the water meadows. So they drifted, Harriette clasped to her wherry-boy, Amy in the arms of her miller. Such was the modest beginning of two such high-steppers. If we are to believe Julia, this was their true embarkation for Cytherea.

Julia says she was greatly astonished at Harriette's disclosures. '"Can this be true?" interrupted I. "True as eggs is eggs," cried Harriette, and continued, "Then I fell sick for a recruiting sergeant who beat such a tattoo on my heart he fairly turned it topsy-turvy."' The young Harriette eloped with him, we learn, but he made off with her best clothes and her watch. 'This cooled her for low life, and she resolved to look higher,' says Julia, obviously satisfied to have denied the more stylish version with which Harriette opens her own tale. Since Julia Johnstone's *Confessions* are little known, and hard to come by, these extracts are of particular interest in our reconstruction of Harriette herself. And they give us a delicious picture of Miss Wilson preparing for bed. 'Harriette was a perfect nightmare in the same room with you, taking as much pains in doing up her fine hair and folding her laced night-gown and cap as though she were preparing for a ballroom. I remonstrated with her, once, on the folly of spending two hours thus, and then waking me out of my sleep to give my opinion on how her night-clothes became her, whether she looked most like Cleopatra waiting for Anthony, or the wife of Potiphar trying to seduce Joseph. Harriette said she would not for the world go to bed otherwise than elegant, for fear of dying in the night and not making an elegant corpse.'

However much they may have bickered in private, the Three Graces presented a united front to the world. Besides sharing one another's boxes at the opera, they moved in and out of one another's houses, exchanged hats, lovers, good advice and confidences, and put their heads together to invent all manner of elaborate ruses to catch this man or that, Harriette taking a specially sympathetic interest in 'poor Julia's' inability to retain the affections of Sir Harry Mildmay, 'the violet-breathing baronet,' as Julia described him.

All Three Graces were concerned over Sophia's precocious entry into the world of gallantry. '"*She is off!* Sophia is off! run away, nobody knows where," was the cry of all my sisters one fine morning,' says Harriette, and goes on to recount a curious instance of the law at that time. Sophia was thirteen and had gone to Lord Deerhurst, who seduced her and then, alarmed at the protestations made by Harriette, returned Miss Sophia to her family. When they threatened to sue him, claiming he must provide for her, it was found that 'the only legal grounds for obtaining provision for a girl thus unfortunately situated is that of the parents having lost her domestic services.' Deerhurst being at last prevailed upon to provide for Sophia, his parsimony was made apparent by his choice of 'two small dark parlours near Grosvenor Place,' but, to make amends, he sent her six bottles of red-currant wine, declaring it to be far more conducive to health than any 'foreign vintage.' He further provided her with the most trumpery bits of brass and glass jewellery, which he cunningly presented in boxes bearing the label of the best jeweller's in town. Sophia's elder sisters were particularly incensed at this cruel deception, and all of them were delighted to plead Lord Berwick's cause when he wished to remove Sophia from such a stingy lover and make her his own.

Julia, however, is warm in her defence of Lord Deerhurst. 'His lordship took lodging for her near Hyde Park Corner, but it was so far from being the mean one Harriette describes that it was a first floor *in every way* becoming to the mistress of a Peer.' Sophia, she sums up as 'a pert and forward child. Harriette foolishly, if not wickedly, cockered-up her ideas with hopes of making conquests—of bringing this lord or that knight to her feet. . . . In a very short time the little creature talked of nothing else but *levelling* a peer, *winging* a duke, *dropping* a baronet; even *hamstringing* an alderman—a vocabulary culled from the sporting peers who were Harriette's admirers.'

Sophia appears to have been so determined on her fall that we conclude she was influenced in early life by the example of a young lady called Rachel Lee, the story of whose rape by two gentlemen (one of them in holy orders) occupied a great deal of space in the press during the year 1804. Cross-examined during the trial of these men, Rachel Lee had admitted that, when forced into the post-chaise, she found further resistance useless and, tearing from her breast a camphor bag (evidently powerless against assault, whatever it might promise against moths), she flung it from the window and exclaimed, "The charm that has hitherto preserved my virtue is dissolved! Now welcome pleasure!" This admission proved fatal to the prosecution, and the accused gentlemen were given their liberty amid loud cheers from the assembled public. *Now welcome pleasure!* How often the Dubochet sisters echoed this! It was, indeed, their lifelong maxim, their guiding principle.

The Three Graces always drove together in the park on fine afternoons. It was a ritualistic outing, as much a part of their professional life as their nightly appearance at the opera. Here the fair Cyprians, in their splendid equipage, circled under the trees, escorted by a cavalcade of trotting beaux. Their carriages were usually upholstered in a colour calculated to cast the most becoming glow upon the occupant. Sky-blue satin was said to set off a milky complexion best; ruby velvet was a glowing foil for a brunette. Fine horses, footmen and coachmen were *de rigueur*. 'The servants' hats are spiked with a cockade to imply their mistresses have seen service,' says a contemporary observer, the English Spy who gives us much information on the Fashionable Impures. He tells us he was walking in the park towards Cumberland Gate, with his friends, Eglantine, Blackmantle and Crony, when they were passed by several fine equipages containing the demi-reps, out for an airing. 'In London,' he observes, 'these daughters of pleasure are like physicians, travelling about to destroy in all sorts of ways.' He goes on to say that the demi-reps had the discretion to leave heraldic emblazonment alone (though one flaunted a crest; it was a serpent coiled and prepared to strike). Coronets and escutcheons were the wages of virtue, and poor company many of the neglected wives found them. The Duchess of Wellington, loaded with the honours of her husband's glory, was often to be seen driving alone, buried in a book; she was so shortsighted she could not recognize a face, and so shy she could never greet anyone.

A constant thread of financial worry runs through Harriette's *Memoirs,* and from time to time (as when Julia's furniture was seized by the bailiffs) there are acute crises. Still, the ladies seem to have lived in considerable style. It was every courtesan's dream to have 'money in the Funds,' the mere phrase conjuring up the most relaxing vistas of security. The Count, later Duke, of Palmella, then Portuguese Ambassador to the Court of St. James's, was so struck by Amy's swarthy charms that he won her away from a visiting Russian, Count Benckendorff, and set her up handsomely in Curzon Street, with '£200 a month paid in advance and the use of his carriage.' Such were the terms. We wonder how the Countess viewed this last concession. According to Julia, Harriette squandered her money on gewgaws, and sometimes settled the jeweller's bill by payment in kind. She tells of an occasion when she accompanied Harriette to plead with old Courtois, the hairdresser and débauché, who threatened to sue for the £300 he had lent her. He had, besides, provided her with £800 worth of jewels, says Julia (although Harriette always says she disdained jewels, save earrings, preferring to have the distinction of a simple, elegant toilette unadorned by ornament). Harriette and Courtois retired to an inner room, says Julia, who waited in the antechamber. After half an hour the old miser returned, all smiles; he kissed Harriette's hand, calling her very kind—very pretty, very kind. And no more was heard of the debt.

Harriette's extravagances, says Julia, were a drain even on Mr. Meyler, the wealthy sugar baker. 'He long afterwards felt the effects of his profusion. Her establishment in Lisson Grove was kept up in great style . . . servants, equipages . . . as well as his own house in Grosvenor Square.' But this was towards the end of Harriette's career. At first she seems to have been able to obtain money all around, even from those who were not technically her lovers. Prince Esterhazy, who had economical notions about love and sought diversions among the cut-rate girls of Cranborne Alley, had the effrontery to offer Harriette a ten-pound note on suggesting she should play pander for him. "There are many girls who are determined on their own fall," he said. "All I want is that when you should see them going downhill you should give them a gentle push." Harriette was outraged, refused to oblige the Prince and read him a stiff lecture on the spot. But she pocketed the note all the same.

Gewgaws apart, she seems to have lived expensively. There are constant references to her footman (the lugubrious Will Halliday), her cook, the *femme-de-chambre*, the housekeeper, coachman and her *dame-de-compagnie*, whose exact function is not clear. She does not seem to have entertained as much as Amy and Fanny, though no doubt, since she was such excellent company, she was in great demand, and she very often refers to supper-parties at Lord Hertford's and elsewhere. Such women were always expected to live stylishly, to have, besides a good address, an elegantly furnished house, first-rate food and a well-stocked cellar.

Then there were the lesser but necessary expenses on which so much depended—the art of the staymaker, the coiffeur and the shoemaker. Small, beautifully shaped feet were Harriette's special pride, and she spent considerable sums on her shoes. Then, too, although when under steady protection mantuamakers' and milliners' bills were generally met by the current protector, when the Cyprians lived more freely there were stretches of time when they had no one to rely on for any steady income. Harriette was always very selective. She never suffered middle-class men willingly; it had to be aristocrats or 'the lower orders.'

When the Prince Regent moved to Brighton and established himself in his fabulous Hindu-Gothic Pavilion, the Court followed, the crack regiments were quartered there, the beau monde flocked and it suddenly became imperative for Harriette and her kind to be there too. Some set off in a spirit of adventure, of chase; others, such as Sophia, more fortunate, were invited there on very special terms. She had at last been persuaded to inhabit the same house as the besotted Lord Berwick, but she had not yet decided whether she could tolerate him on closer terms. This hypocritical young creature determined, even now, not to appear compromised. She insisted that her protector go ahead in a coach-and-four, followed by his servants, a *batterie de cuisine* and the silver. Miss Sophia came last, in a neat little chariot, accompanied by Julia, because, says Harriette, 'Mademoiselle Sophie wished to parade the remains of her rather shaky virtue.'

Sometime during the year 1811 Harriette was installed at Brighton under Lord Worcester's protection. The young lover was in a fever; he had taken a house, engaged servants, ordered meals, and, fiercely impatient, galloped fifteen miles along the Brighton Road to meet his mistress. Harriette was overwhelmed with his passions and attentions. When he presented her with a richly embroidered side-saddle, which he insisted should be kept in his dressing-room, unsullied by any groom's hand, Harriette was especially touched. The accounts of their ménage at Rockcliffe Gardens are among her most entertaining pages.

According to Julia, a *rational* tone prevailed in the Worcester-Wilson ménage.... 'Domestic calmness shed its blessings ... at one time I thought Harriette stood a good chance, so firmly had she drawn the leading-strings around Worcester. He was, of all the men I ever knew, the most partial to fireside comforts and rational society.'

At that moment Brighton presented a curious spectacle. The small fishing village had been transformed overnight into the setting for every extravagance of fashionable life, from the fabulous onion domes, pagodas and turrets of the Royal Pavilion to the eccentricities of costume and behaviour adopted by the *ton*. The Court, the beau monde, the officers and their fancy ladies were all lodged in the little black-pebble or bow-fronted houses along the various Marine Parades, Terraces and Gardens that faced the sparkling, pale-blue expanse of the sea. The narrow lanes and winding streets were hugger-mugger with the splendour of newly imposed classic porticoes and those houses built around the Pavilion for the Prince Regent's immediate entourage. Mrs. Fitzherbert, who never inhabited the Pavilion, was ensconced in a commodious, balconied villa adjacent to and allegedly connected with it by an underground passage. Later this house was taken over by the Young Men's Christian Association.

The tracing of living links with other ages, with what appears the remote past, is a peculiarly fascinating study. In some cases the Restoration, and even the Tudor age, has been reached by three or four lives. The present writer remembers an old resident of Brighton who had known Mrs. Fitzherbert. Creevey mentions a certain 'young giant Spencer,' a child of the Bessborough circle, and this boy, as Sir Spencer Ponsonby Fane, was living, perfectly sound in memory, until 1915. Harriette's sister Sophia died only in 1875. That Lord Ebrington who had been so assiduous in his attentions to Harriette in Paris was survived by his widow till 1896, within four years of the last century, while Fred Lamb's widow lived till 1894. Perhaps the two old ladies were friends and sat together over the teacups, their veined, bony, heavily ringed hands rattling among the silver as, their footmen and companions withdrawn to a discreet distance, they spoke of the past, the trouble with husbands and the particular troubles brought about by the *Memoirs* of that forgotten temptress who had been so disgracefully outspoken about poor dear Fred and Hugh.

At Regency Brighton the sportsmen, led by Jockey Norfolk—The Duke—bet heavily on the races and spent their days between the Downs and the stables. From the banqueting rooms of the Pavilion (where gilded dragons twined, and every Oriental conceit was incorporated in the decoration) came exotic wafts of high living, pâtés and curries, soufflés and such, mingling with the scent of the fresh currant buns baked by the pastrycooks of East Street. It was at once innocent and raffish, and the Three Graces installed there, continued the sophisticated tenor of their London life, lovers and tattle, high passions and intrigue, besides buneating and donkey-rides along the sands.

Harriette was no stranger to Brighton. She had lived in a house on the Steyne with Lord Craven (the dead bore) in her earliest days. It was at Brighton, too, that she had made her overtures to the Prince of Wales. The manner in which she was established there by Lord Worcester shows us how these ladies were accepted by the men of *ton*, by the regimental commanders too. Harriette rides with the officers, her riding habit being an exact copy of the 10th Hussars uniform. She dines in their mess (the only woman present) and dinner is kept back an hour to suit her. She promises the Colonel personally to be responsible for Lord Worcester being on parade at 8 a.m., just as she had no doubt been responsible for his failing to be there on time so many other mornings. Harriette, more than the rest of the Cyprians, seems to have queened it over the army. It will be recalled she always had a weakness for the military of all ranks. Indeed, Julia tells us she was once ordered off the parade ground by General Hill, 'since her flirting was so insufferably indelicate that she occupied the attention of the entire regiment.'

Edmond de Goncourt observes that there is a natural partnership between the soldier and the prostitute. 'Woman's love of force, her attraction towards brutality are even more marked among such women. The soldier may be coarse, but he is neither sarcastic nor vicious, as are so many *petits bourgeois*. The prostitute feels herself the soldier's equal—his mistress—while with the other men she is simply an instrument of pleasure. But the soldier, with his hard life of discipline and danger, remains more simple. His passions are more direct. He spends his money on her generously and parades her proudly. There is no condescension.'

Perhaps this reasoning affected Harriette subconsciously. In any case she, her sisters and friends always showed a marked liking for military men—Julia for Colonel Cotton, Fanny for Colonel Parker, Amy for General Madden—and Harriette, while snubbing Wellington, seemed more partial to the Marquis of Worcester once he had donned his regimentals.

While the likenesses of many of the men who formed Harriette's immediate circle are left to us in family portraits or caricatures such as the well-known series by Dighton, some of which are reproduced here, Harriette and her sisters are less well served. Of beautiful Fanny, with her laughing dark-blue eyes, I can find no trace. Lord Hertford, connoisseur of both art and women, wished to have her painted by Sir Thomas Lawrence, but this was never done. In the crude engravings of the period Sophia, Amy, Harriette and Julia all appear plain. Sophia is downright hideous. Harriette's looks must have depended largely on her vivacity. 'She possessed a considerable portion of humour,' we learn, 'and could perform "High life below stairs" *au merveille*.' Sir Walter Scott found her ugly—men sought her more for her wit, he said. Although even Julia speaks of her once superlative loveliness, I fancy she was never, in the strict sense, a beauty. We know that she had a lovely figure, bright hazel eyes fringed with dark lashes; that she wore her brown hair dressed in loose curls; that her feet and ankles were particularly well formed;

that she seldom wore colours, preferring to appear in the evening in 'a rich white figured French gauze'; that her only ornaments were long earrings, ruby, turquoise or pearl. She seems to have dressed with a restrained elegance, at once *à la mode* and in her own style.

She had her own, highly personal manner of speaking, too. In a letter to Byron she speaks of herself as 'never being one to think of forms much.' Her turn of phrase, her slang, are lively. She is 'struck all of a heap' when the Beauforts withhold her allowance. According to Julia Johnstone, her oaths were startling. Sir Jospeh Nourse, said Julia, held that 'Harriette would have made an excellent sailor's wife, she swore such good round oaths. . . . She thought it gave zest to her conversation as olives do to wine. . . .' Thus Julia, all prunes and prisms, and we catch a sudden flash of another Harriette, the *gamine*, who to some of her lovers was 'Harry' and to others 'little fellow'—a saucy boy rather than a passionate woman. 'No one likes me a *little*, or forgets me, when they have once liked,' she writes to Edward Bulwer-Lytton, the young novelist, in a revealing letter, which is quoted in full in the Appendix.

Although she often speaks of fevers, coughs and ill-health, she was in fact remarkably wiry. Not for her the swooning style of *La Dame aux Camélias*. She lived hard, rode hard and walked hard too. She was, in modern parlance, athletic. She loved to walk and, before making a rendezvous with a new lover, thought nothing of trying out his paces from Hyde Park up to Primrose Hill and down again, a walk of some eight miles or more and one which she accomplished without turning a hair (this after nights which left little time for repose) but which on one occasion left the gentleman in question, Lord Granville Leveson-Gower, in a sweat of exhaustion. While he mopped his brow on Harriette's doorstep in Grosvenor Street and begged to be allowed to enter to recover himself, she decided he would not suit and packed him off. Found wanting on the walk, he was given no chance to justify himself otherwise.

Harriette was ever high-handed. Prospective clients who called without being correctly introduced were given short shrift. Occasionally she unbent sufficiently to say a fifty-pound note would do as well as a regular introduction—fifty pounds being, at that time, a very large sum. Once a peer of the realm made so bold as to send his footman with a note soliciting the honour of a rendezvous that night. This businesslike request flung Harriette into a rage. She pealed her bell (one of her favourite gestures) and ordered the footman out, but not before she had returned his master's letter to him—unsealed, unfolded, for all the world to read—saying, 'This letter could not be meant for me, to whom his Lordship was only presented yesterday. Take it back, young man, and say from me that I request he will be careful how he misdirects them in future—an accident which was no doubt caused by his writing them after dinner.' We imagine with what pleasure the footman must have loitered on the way back, recounting it all among the shopkeepers, stable-boys and publicans of Mayfair.

On the other hand, Harriette herself often made overtures to gentlemen she fancied, or whose money she coveted, and she was always very much put out if they did not respond favourably; but on the whole she had few rebuffs and seems not only to have enjoyed the exercise of her calling but to have been able to pick and choose among the quality. We have it on her own authority that she sometimes suffered from *le diable au corps* and allowed herself to be carried away by an enthusiasm fatal to her profession. She found Mr. Meyler, 'the damned sugar baker,' as Lord Alvanley called him, perfectly irresistible. 'There was in fact an expression in Meyler's countenance of such voluptuous beauty that it was impossible for any woman to converse with him, after he had dined, in cold blood.' Harriette, decidedly warm-blooded, led him a dance equalled only by that which he led her. She took an understandable pleasure, too, in taking him away from the Duchess of Beaufort, Lord Worcester's mother, who had been so unsympathetic to Harriette's affair with her son.

Although Harriette had such a weakness for the military, she shows also a particular liking for gentlemen of a more intellectual kind. Lord Ponsonby was not a Corinthian; he was considerably older than she and of a more studious cast than most of his contemporaries. In fact, to be worthy of his love, Harriette shut herself up and read Seneca. 'The Greeks employed me for two whole days,' she says, 'and the Romans six more.... I then read Rousseau's *Confessions*, then Racine's Tragedies, and, afterwards, Boswell's *Life of Johnson*. I allowed myself only ten minutes for my dinner,' adds this ardent creature who never did anything by halves.

Julia speaks of Harriette having literary aspirations, and it is certain that she revered Byron the poet beyond the fashionable cult of Lord Byron as the rage and scandal of the town. ('I always should have been more proud of the slightest acquaintance with you than being loved dearly as I was by Wellington and other great men in my time,' she writes.) In her attitude towards him she shows an almost maternal solicitude. It is, perhaps, only in her letters to Lord Byron that we can gauge Harriette's nature fully. In these letters we see something more than the 'smart, saucy girl' Sir Walter Scott remembered. In the *Memoirs* she quotes some remarkably dull letters which she says are among those she sent to Byron. Evidently she did not keep copies and had forgotten all but their purport. A century later a small packet of her letters to the poet was discovered among the Byron papers in the possession of Sir John Murray, whose great-grandfather had been the poet's publisher and confidant.

These letters give us the living, warm, witty Harriette as she was when no considerations of her calling came between her and the object of her affection.* Harriette emerges from the spidery scrawl as a woman full of common sense, humour, tenderness too, which her conduct regarding the *Memoirs* might lead us to suppose she had long lost. Besides the letters to Lord Byron there are three which she addressed ten years or so later, probably in 1829, to the novelist Edward Bulwer-Lytton. Here we see, once again, the forgotten demi-rep at forty-three, still longing, if not for conquests, for some link with that world of gaiety, literature and politics in which she had once lived. These letters are less emotional than those to Lord Byron, but they give as Harriette's lively self and show conclusively her own style—the style of the *Memoirs*, thus proving that these were not, as is sometimes said, the work of either Stockdale or some unknown hack.

Here is Harriette writing to Byron. The letter is undated but probably can be set around 1818. 'I love you honestly and dearly. . . . *Your* love I never desired. . . . Pray, dear Lord Byron, think of me a little, now and then (I don't mean as a woman for I shall never be a *woman* to you) . . . forget me when you are happy; but in gloomy moments, chilly, miserable weather, bad razors and cold water, perhaps you'll recollect and write to me. . . .' 'Miserable weather, bad razors and cold water.' How succinctly she sums up those moments of *cafard*, moments when love means little and friendship alone can cheer. There are a number of such solicitous letters. True, she importuned for money (which Byron sometimes sent), but always, to him, she offered warmth and tenderness. 'I wish I could learn something of your *health*, dear Lord Byron.' In another, chiding him for some splenetic outburst, some passage she considers unworthy of his genius, occasioned, she suspects, by liver: 'Throw away your pen, my love, and take a little calomel,' she urges. And if he replied, the letters have vanished, along with other traces of Harriette Wilson's life, her possessions or souvenirs.

There is a legend, which I am unable to trace, that somewhere in the green, quiet landscape of northern England a house still stands richly furnished but unoccupied since Harriette refused it. One of her more

---

*Two of those letters are printed in full on pp. 422 and 423.

49

generous admirers had hoped to lure her to the country and his embraces by preparing this gilded cage. But Harriette, 'never one for ruralizing,' would have none of it. The house has stood empty ever since; by the terms of the owner's will it may not be sold, let or in any way changed.

Of Harriette's taste in houses and furniture we know nothing. Egyptian and Gothic extravaganzas were now the rage in many of the stateliest homes. Remodelled dining-rooms became echoing vaults; there were monastic corridors and vast cathedral bedrooms with pinnacled, fretted, tomblike beds and dressing-tables resembling high altars. It is in such a setting that we imagine the sinister witch-women that Fuseli's drawings represent, all evil in their beckoning glance. They are the fitting denizens of such a horrific setting. Impudent and robust Harriette has no place here. Creevey writing of Knowsley, when the new Gothic dining-room was opened, and describing it as being fifty-three by thirty-seven feet and 'such a height that it destroys the effect of all the other apartments. . . . You enter it from a passage, by two great Gothic church-like doors the whole height of the room.' (It will be recalled that when Beckford built Fonthill Abbey—where the arches of the great hall were one-third higher than the loftiest arches of the nave in Westminster Abbey—he stationed a dwarf at the doors to emphasize their height.) Creevey goes on, 'General Grosvenor was heard to remark, "Pray are those great doors to be opened for every pat of butter that comes into the room?"' In spite of two fireplaces, thirty-six wax candles and ten great pedestal lamps, the cold was still quite petrifying and Creevey says they were soon obliged to abandon the room entirely.

And now the mood changes, the skies cloud over and the villain appears. Harriette had known high comedy, drama, and a certain pathos too; but not until she encountered the sinister figure of William Henry Rochfort did her way lead irrevocably into the shadows. The swaggering creature who now appears was to become the baleful influence of her life. Up to this time Harriette's path, however thorny, had been lighted by the brightness of youth and health and hope, a morning glow, where adventures, loves and griefs, however desperate, were all part of the pattern of a demi-rep's life, unshadowed by what was to follow. Even the spectre of age, advancing so implacably, had been foreseen and accepted as something inevitable, as she herself said in a letter to Byron:

'*I will hope that we shall one day, some twenty years hence, take a pinch of snuff together before we die—and as you watch me in my little pointed cap, spectacles, bony ankles and thread stockings, stirring up and tasting my pot-au-feu, you'll imagine Ponsonby's, Worcester's and Argyle's Angelick Harriette.'*

With this melancholy but classic end in view, Harriette had withdrawn to Paris, where she was declining by stages, from a *réchauffée* of rather indifferent ex-lovers and second-rate, come-by-chance protectors to boys such as the very young Secretary of Embassy, whom, in another letter to Byron, she tells us she set to searching out her grey hairs.

Old ways die hard. The habits of coquetry and badinage, the thirst for admiration and power over men, the craving for the stimulus of adventure were ingrained, and, like her lusty appetites, her passions and frailties had been fostered by the example of her giddy elder sisters. Those habits, begun so young, had become the inclinations and necessities, the very mainspring, of a lifetime. How could she change her whole nature? As long as there were men to fool, to flirt with and, who knows, perhaps still to love, the game of hearts must continue.

But boys, even those enamoured young scions of nobility, who had been reared on whispered legends of Harriette's glory, could be no more than puppet partners in a twilight epilogue. Decidedly it did not do to play the game of hearts in Paris.

Sometimes between the years 1815–1820 she returned to London, drawn there perhaps by a nostalgia for the scenes of her former triumphs, by loneliness, by family ties and the fading hopes of encountering some long-lost love—of catching a glimpse of Ponsonby, even. Who knows what secret longings, what romantic hopes she cherished beneath what was becoming a rather battered but still brave exterior? That Harriette was capable of loving deeply, of suffering, there is no doubt. Anguish sounds occasionally through her flippancies. In yet another letter to Lord Byron, written, it would seem, about this time, we see the real woman, all barriers down. It is a tragic cry, wrung from the heart:

'Lord, if only you could suffer for a single day the agony of mind I endured for more than two years after Ponsonby left me, because Mrs. Fanny [Lord Ponsonby's wife] would have it so, you would bless your stars and your good fortune, blind, deaf and lame at eighty-two, so that you could sleep an hour in forgetfulness, eat a little bit of batter pudding. Heavens! how I have prayed for death, nights, days and months together, merely as a rest from suffering . . .'

Unhappily there was never any rest for Harriette; she was a constant prey to both her emotions and her appetites. Now, once more, her heart was to be wrung, this time for a far less worthy subject than Lord Ponsonby. The scene is London; the occasion one of her rare visits, when we imagine her wandering forlornly through the settings of her heyday, wandering like a revenant down St. James's where 'the rattle and dash of the dice-box' still sounded, or, turning northward, catching faint echoes of the laughter, the sound of corks being drawn, the gaiety and chatter as it drifted out on the night air from the little house in York Place where she and Amy and Fanny and Julia had once held court, catching, perhaps, the echo of a door slamming shut—Lord Ponsonby's door in Upper Brook Street, shutting her out forever from his life.

On one of these sad evenings, as she walked home to her lodgings in Lisson Grove, near to that establishment she had once shared with the voluptuous Mr. Meyler, a dark shadow fell across her path and she met her destiny in the person of Rochfort. It was a pick-up, a street acquaintanceship, struck as the flash bully and the fading charmer came face to face under the flickering gas-lamps of Marylebone. For Harriette it was a lightning dart of passion; a violent, pent-up force of emotion was now loosed, sweeping her along. Rochfort was a prince among men! Apollo, Mars, the King of Hearts! We imagine this swarthy, swaggering individual who worked such havoc, whose insolent glance was so seducing, and the haggard, eager woman Harriette had become, levelling the full battery of her practised arts only to be met with a contemptuous offhand acquiescence. We do not know what Rochfort thought of Harriette; certainly he did not return her affections wholeheartedly. To him she was probably just one more of a string of easy conquests—one who was to show great devotion, however, and whose energy and dispatch in attending to his welfare made her worth cultivating. Also one who, as he came to know her better, offered all kinds of interesting possibilities of financial returns which he was, in due course, to exploit to the full.

William Henry Rochfort is a mysterious character. He appears suddenly on the scene and, having played out his part, disappears as abruptly. He claimed to be the rightful heir to an Irish earldom which had become extinct in 1814. When pressed for details, however, he always became very vague. His claims centred around the probable indiscretion of the wife of the first Earl of Rochfort. William Henry held that he was the child of a son of Lady Rochfort's by an unknown lover. Lord Rochfort refused to acknowledge this son. On the death, without issue, of the rightful heir, William Henry Rochfort claimed that the titles and estates in Ireland were his by rights. In any case, however plausible women—and

Harriette in particular—found him, the law was less sympathetic, and he never succeeded in establishing his claims. In fact, on one occasion he ran foul of the law and was indicted on a charge of larceny. Julia Johnstone tells us that he had been 'for a very short time a Colonel in some unknown corps of South American Independents, and a full Cornet in Lincoln Stanhope's regiment, the 17th Dragoons, and has never clipped his moustachioes since'—a heavy sarcasm this, for the rank of cornet was very small fry, lowliest of all the officers, corresponding to a junior second lieutenant. There are few contemporary sources, reliable or otherwise, from which anything can be gleaned about the Colonel; even his place in Lincoln Stanhope's Central American Independents remains obscure.

At this time Central and South America exercised a powerful spell over the imaginations of Europeans. This part of the world had only lately appeared on their horizons, a remote, exotic panorama. It is probable that Rochfort took full advantage of a background at once so rare and so much in vogue. No doubt he realized that such a setting added great lustre to any adventures which he recounted to Harriette, or any of the other impressionable ladies to whom he was addicted. No doubt they saw him striding fearlessly across cactus-studded deserts, swimming crocodile-infested yellow rivers which wound through tropical jungles where swarms of butterflies darkened the blazing noonday sun. They saw him, Simón Bolívar's peer, riding a plunging mustang towards liberation, his sword flourished aloft.

Did they perhaps see him as one of the few survivors, one of the guard which had accompanied that band of gullible fools, two hundred or more, victims of 'The Poyais Hoax', who, about this time, had been persuaded to pay fancy prices to the 'agents' of some promised faraway land in Central America where they were to take up the high offices and positions they had bought so trustingly in London? The celebrated hoax had appeared so convincing that, led on by accounts of streets paved with silver and hills veined with gold, of pomegranates and plenty, the two hundred citizens had embarked trustingly, accompanied by their families, servants and a troop of mercenaries.

Their true situation was revealed to them only when the ships put in to a barren stretch of coast where nothing stirred, where no sign of life was to be seen. They had been duped, they realized, and now they were to be dumped, left to perish. Hostile natives and fever decimated their ranks; soon almost all of them were dead. Only a handful of survivors managed to return to tell the tale. It would be a dramatic episode in Rochfort's life, a properly flamboyant background for his villainy, but unfortunately there is absolutely no evidence that supports the supposition, beyond the fact that he had seen service with some Central American Independents. In London, he soon so worked on Harriette's feelings that she was in a pining state. She learned that he was a prisoner within the Rules—the confines set for the inmates of the Debtors' Prison, confines which still left considerable freedom to move about. Before long she had paid his debts and liberated him, perhaps on the understanding that they should go through a form of marriage, and they left England together to take up their residence in Paris, Harriette now passing as Mrs. Rochfort. We imagine with what naïve delight she saw herself setting out on a last, shining, eternal love—a love that was to be her all, the redemption of her former ways. She would love the Colonel as she had never loved before, his every wish her law. Now that his debts were paid, now that she had detached him from the various ladies who had surrounded him so jealously in London, Harriette must have felt he was indeed all hers to cosset.

It is sentimental and probably misguided to see Harriette as a pathetic figure. But while never approaching tragic stature and being far too gallant, too much of a fighter, too little of a sniveller to be 'in the pathetics' (her own phrase) for long, she is often touched with melancholy. When we observe her more closely, weighing up her outrageous conduct and the circumstances of her life, giving her the sober consideration she is seldom accorded, she emerges as something far less two-dimensional than a first estimate presupposes. Compare her to another, even higher flying courtesan who cloaked her activities under political intrigues, a *mari complaisant* and an Imperial lover—the Contessa Castiglione. She was the pawn of Cavour, the Italian statesman, the greatest beauty and a scheming, arrogant, humourless egocentric. When her beauty faded nothing was left but darkness, moanings, shrouded mirrors and shuttered windows. She became a shapeless bag of self-pity, living in the past, creeping out at night to rummage in the garbage bins. No backbone, no personality emerged when the façade crumbled.

Harriette, on the contrary, while often appalling us by her conduct, steadily gains our affections and interest. We follow patiently, with sympathy, her sentimental vacillations between the Duke of Leinster and Lord Worcester, or, history repeating itself, between Lord Ebrington and Mr. Meyler. We positively respect her delicacy in disliking to be on with the new love while the old love still breathes the same air—though it must be said that such delicacy, in her profession, amounts to a disadvantage. It is not businesslike, and Harriette is always the one to suffer. If only we could talk a little common sense into the girl! All those longings and regrets over Lord Ponsonby are sad reading, no part of a demi-rep's make-up. As for her impetuous decision to write to Lord Worcester after undertaking (the price of her pension) to remain aloof, it shows a most foolish fondness. But she will never learn. Her passion for Colonel Rochfort fills us with misgivings. He is a cad. But, as Shakespeare says, ''tis the strumpet's plague to beguile many, but be beguiled by one. . . .' Harriette cannot rest till she has obtained the doubtful satisfaction of a Fleet marriage to her Colonel, 'Moustachio,' as she calls him. We could wish it otherwise. In short, she has become a matter of concern to us. She has come alive, and, with all her failings, we love her to the end.

There is a silence of some years before Harriette again emerges from the shadows. These years must have been sadly disillusioning. Harriette's looks have vanished; Rochfort leads her a terrible dance and drink is the only panacea. Life is hard now and getting harder with each passing day. The Colonel must be kept in those luxuries without which he becomes sulky and restive. What course is left open to the ruined, forgotten demi-rep Harriette has become? She is shrewd enough to know she can hold him just as long as she can provide for him well. Drink, snug quarters, money for gambling and for other women—those are the Colonel's requirements. Harriette casts about desperately for a means of raising money. Once she had been in the habit of plaguing her old friends for donations, but gradually they had proved less and less responsive. Harriette tells us that she cared little about money for herself; but Rochfort's spell changed everything. It has been said that Rochfort bore a certain resemblance to Harriette's great love, Lord Ponsonby, and in her now rather clouded mind it is likely that Rochfort came to represent all love, that he seemed the embodiment of Romance, as once Lord Ponsonby had been. The lodestar of her life had changed its outward semblance perhaps, but its essence may have remained the same, an unattainable, tormenting mirage.

Although there is no portrait of Rochfort to support the theory that he resembled Lord Ponsonby, it is very possibly true, for again and again we see men and women seeking to find once more in a new love some resemblance to the features, voice, eyes or mannerisms of the first person deeply loved. And it often happens that in so doing they blind themselves to failings of character or differences of birth and education in a touching effort to catch echoes of what had once meant so much to them. Women in particular have been known to follow men of dissolute or even criminal character, drunkards, bullies and murderers only because of a way of smiling, a look in the eyes, that gave them once again the illusion of some lost love.

This may have been Harriette's case. To the objective reader it would explain Rochfort's hold on her; how otherwise accept that such a man, so low a type, could have such complete power over a woman like Harriette, who had known, and been loved by, men of a very different order? Was she following the usual course of a prostitute's life by ending with a hard-drinking bully for her mate? Did Rochfort, with his bogus rank and his pretensions to breeding, represent someone whom she could present to the world as her husband but who in fact took the place of those lusty common soldiers whom, by all accounts, Harriette had found irresistible in the past? Or did Rochfort, in one person, combine both her love for Ponsonby and her taste for low life? Did he represent to her both sacred and profane love?

While Harriette is still fixed on the tormenting mirage of perfect love, the Colonel has other ideas. His is a wolfish temper. The frustrated child of a bastard son, he feels himself slighted, denied; he longs for vengeance on that class which had ignored him and to which he feels he rightfully belongs. And so, by stages, he comes to the idea of working off his own old scores on the aristocracy as a whole through the medium of Harriette, while at the same time putting a handsome sum of money into both their pockets. Harriette can be a unique instrument of vengeance, for she knows all their secrets. She can easily enough be persuaded to fall in with any plan he presents; the Colonel knows his hold on her, knows how to crack the whip. 'I am not my own mistress,' she writes to Bulwer-Lytton some years later. No doubt where the Colonel was concerned Harriette remained obedient. Again she harps on her changed ways: 'In fact, I am a true faithful wife leading about as innocent a life as a hermit can well do.'

Did Rochfort approach Stockdale and suggest the publication of the *Memoirs*? It is perhaps not too much to imagine this may have been the case. At any rate, once Stockdale had sounded Harriette, the die was cast. Harriette saw it in its simplest light, a way—her only remaining way—to earn the money she needed to keep Rochfort by her side. The *Memoirs* were begun and, no doubt spurred on by a suddenly transformed, affectionate Rochfort, Harriette's pen raced along the page, recalling this audacity or that. Stockdale, delighted by the first instalment, assured her of a huge sale. The Colonel hung over her tenderly; and together, in a most unwonted harmony, they discussed the future instalments.

We imagine them in some grey, panelled salon, a little room in one of those shuttered houses along the Faubourg St. Honoré, where, built around an inner courtyard, the ground-floor rooms, however brightly lighted by chandeliers and candles, are forever gloomy and overcast. Harriette wears an elegant if rather shabby, satin dress; her greying hair still in those careless curls which were Lord Worcester's undoing that evening at the opera when he was coquettishly invited to tumble them. She is seated at a desk overflowing with papers, journals, old household accounts, dunning letters, *billets doux* and bundles of Lord Worcester's effusions carefully tied up with pink tape, last traces of the lawyers who had conducted her case against the Duke of Beaufort. The lamplight falls on her haggard face. She glances apprehensively up at Rochfort, who stands over her. Harriette is as clay. She begins to scribble obediently, and as she writes a gleam of the old fun flashes from beneath the long dark lashes that even Julia Johnstone could not deny her. To Julia all the villainy was centred in Harriette. Rochfort was her fancy man, a mere accessory. But then Julia, 'seldom in the melting mood,' especially when writing her *Confessions,* never saw Harriette other than as a monster of depravity. Her malice seems only to produce a caricature, the devil in petticoats. If Julia had really believed Harriette to be so evil, why had she been such a close friend of hers for so many years when they were both young? No, we remain unconvinced and cast about for more logical, or psychological, explanations of Harriette's action. To the present writer the key is Rochfort and the spell he cast over his inamorata.

With the publication of the *Memoirs* Harriette's financial worries were over—for a while, at any rate. Julia states that between them Harriette and Stockdale 'fingered £10,000 of the public's money.' But while they had shared these rich profits, Stockdale, as publisher, was presently involved in a series of law suits for libel and damages which, however, did not involve Harriette. The wretched man emerged from one suit only to be engulfed by another. Prison followed, on technicalities regarding other, more positively pornographic or obscene publications, until at last he was ruined. Harriette seems to have had no remorse. Indeed it is difficult to be sympathetic towards Stockdale. He was an unctuous, creeping character, hypocritical, mean, sly, parasitic and unscrupulous, whose persecutions, as he called them, were the fruits of many years of villainy and culminated only in the business of the *Memoirs.*

And so Harriette now found herself snugly placed with the proceeds of the *Memoirs* in her bank, the Colonel at her side. She had become a best-selling author. Thirty-one editions were sold in the first year, and pirated editions appeared all over Europe. Harriette next tried her hand at a novel, the story of English people on a visit to Paris. This indifferent piece of work, *Paris Lions and London Tigers,* is a *roman à clef* which, once the characters are established—Sir Violet Sigh-away for Sir Harry Mildmay and such—has no further interest and is best forgotten, although one brief autobiographical flash can be detected. Harriette writes of a Mr. Bellfield, a paragon, evidently modelled on her image of the Colonel, and we hear Harriette, with all her longings, doubts and regrets, sounding through the paeans. "'Mr. Bellfield is a *fine* man," sighed the heroine, for with all her vanity, long experience had put it beyond a doubt that such first-rate beauties as Bellfield were past praying for.' And it is in the preface to this book that the following characteristic passage occurs: "'Here's a piece of pork and greens," as exclaimed a good-humoured countryman who got into some dilemma with his carthorse one day. "Here's a piece of pork and greens!"'

And a piece of pork and greens it was, every time Harriette reappeared on the English scene or was reported to be brewing some further mischief. She had no sooner landed at Dover than she was set on by an outraged lady (perhaps one whose husband figured in the *Memoirs*) who knocked her down and dragged out her hair in fistfuls. The *Memoirs* had succeeded in destroying the piece of mind of married women of all ranks. Although the book was, naturally, kept away from young ladies, those who were fortunate enough to lay hands on a copy found their confidence in the married state sadly shaken. On the other hand, hitherto undreamed-vistas were now revealed to them of an alluring, independent life passed in the company of half the most desirable gentlemen in England. Harriette had much to answer for, and it is surprising she contrived to end her days in England, although as to how and where she died we remain in the dark.

Her last public appearance was in 1829, when she had returned from Paris and was living in Trevor Square, still with the Colonel, her brother, and a French maid, whom Harriette accused of improper relations with her brother. The maid retaliated by taking Harriette to court on a charge of assault. Harriette's reappearance in the limelight was a brief, inglorious flash. On February 15 she was hailed before the magistrate at Marlborough Street. Harriette and the Colonel found themselves very unsympathetically treated by the newspapers, which gloated over her vanished looks, the Colonel's inability to establish his ancestry, and their joint inability to raise bail. There were many persons of quality, said Harriette, who would vouch for her but whom she hardly liked to trouble on so trivial a matter. After a lot of unpleasantness, she and the Colonel were allowed to depart.

It was from Trevor Square in 1830 that Harriette, anonymously, published another *roman à clef*, called *Clara Gazul*, in which she refers to herself as 'Harriette Memoirs' and gives us, besides some account of her beginnings, further impudent anecdotes of the world in which she no longer figured. There is no explanation as to why she selected the name Prosper Merimée had chosen, in 1825, for his *Théâtre de Clara Gazul*. The book aroused considerable anxiety all around, and it is probable that she was persuaded to suppress most of the copies and disappear, conveniently, on receipt of a lump sum. In any case, examples of the book are very rare and it does not seem to have circulated widely.

She gave up the house in Trevor Square in 1830. After 1832 she vanishes from sight. The rest is rumour and conjecture. The little house, No. 16, at the south-east corner looks much as it did during her occupancy. The prim brick-and-plaster façade overlooks the gardens of the square where lilac, laurel and acacia tangle behind the iron railings. These quiet, elegant little streets and squares around Knightsbridge and the Park, are especially evocative of Regency life and loves. Trevor Square, Montpelier Terrace, and Hill Street (now called Trevor Place) were all favourites of the demi-reps.

Sometimes, walking at night along these deserted pavements, where only a few gas lamps light the way, where, behind the ornate balconies, muslin curtains filter an apricot glow of warmth and firelight plays across the ceiling of an upstairs room, I fancy I catch a burst of laughter, a snatch of song and the chink of glasses as the Cyprians entertain their friends. Far away, wafted across the chimneys and tiled rooftops, comes the faint sound of a street organ, grinding out some forgotten tune. Harriette's house stands mute, telling nothing of that life it once framed. In 1975 the owners, who were unaware of its history, told me they thought it was haunted. The ghost is a quiet one; it walks upstairs and goes into the bedroom—which is, after all, what might be expected of Harriette Wilson's shade.

Lesley Blanch, 1957, 2002

THE LADY AND THE GAME

Harriette Wilson's Memoirs
of Herself and Others

CHAPTER 1

I SHALL NOT say why and how I became, at the age of fifteen, the mistress of the Earl of Craven. Whether it was love, or the severity of my father, the depravity of my own heart, or the winning arts of the noble Lord, which induced me to leave my paternal roof and place myself under his protection, does not now much signify: or if it does, I am not in the humour to gratify curiosity in this matter.

I resided on the Marine Parade, at Brighton; and I remember that Lord Craven used to draw cocoa trees, and his fellows, as he called them, on the best vellum paper, for my amusement. Here stood the enemy, he would say; and here, my love, are my fellows: there the cocoa trees, etc. It was, in fact, a dead bore. All these cocoa trees and fellows, at past eleven o'clock at night, could have no peculiar interest for a child like myself, so lately in the habit of retiring early to rest. One night, I recollect, I fell asleep; and, as I often dream, I said, yawning, and half awake, "Oh, Lord! oh, Lord! Craven has got me into the West Indies again." In short, I soon found that I had made a bad speculation by going from my father to Lord Craven. I was even more afraid of the latter than I had been of the former; not that there was any particular harm in the man, beyond his cocoa trees; but we never suited nor understood each other.

I was not depraved enough to determine immediately on a new choice, and yet I often thought about it. How, indeed, could I do otherwise, when the Honourable Frederick Lamb was my constant visitor, and talked to me of nothing else? However, in justice to myself, I must declare that the idea of the possibility of deceiving Lord Craven, while I was under his roof, never once entered into my head. Frederick was then very handsome; and certainly tried, with all his soul and with all his strength, to convince me that constancy to Lord Craven was the greatest nonsense in the world. I firmly believe that Frederick Lamb sincerely loved me, and deeply regretted that he had no fortune to invite me to share with him.

Lord Melbourne, his father, was a good man. Not one of your stiff-laced moralizing fathers, who preach chastity and forbearance to their children. Quite the contrary; he congratulated his son on the lucky circumstance of his friend Craven having such a fine girl with him. "No such thing," answered Frederick Lamb; "I am unsuccessful there. Harriette will have nothing to do with me."—"Nonsense!" rejoined Melbourne, in great surprise; "I never heard anything half so ridiculous in all my life. The girl must be mad! She looks mad: I thought so the other day, when I met her galloping about, with her feathers blowing and her thick dark hair about her ears."

"I'll speak to Harriette for you," added His Lordship, after a long pause; and then continued repeating to himself, in an undertone, "Not have my son, indeed! six feet high! a fine, straight, handsome, noble young fellow! I wonder what she would have!"

In truth, I scarcely knew myself; but something I determined on: so miserably tired was I of Craven, and his cocoa trees, and his sailing boats, and his ugly cotton nightcap. Surely, I would say, all men do not wear those shocking cotton nightcaps; else all women's illusions had been destroyed on the first night of their marriage!

I wonder, thought I, what sort of a nightcap the Prince of Wales wears? Then I went on to wonder whether the Prince of Wales would think me so beautiful as Frederick Lamb did? Next I reflected that Frederick Lamb was younger than the Prince; but then, again, a Prince of Wales! ! !

I was undecided: my heart began to soften. I thought of my dear mother, and wished I had never left her. It was too late, however, now. My father would not suffer me to return; and as to passing my life, or any more of it, with Craven, cotton nightcap and all, it was death! He never once made me laugh, nor said nor did anything to please me.

Thus musing, I listlessly turned over my writing-book, half in the humour to address the Prince of Wales. A sheet of paper, covered with Lord Craven's cocoa trees, decided me; and I wrote the following letter, which I addressed to the Prince.

BRIGHTON.

I am told that I am very beautiful, so, perhaps, you would like to see me; and I wish that, since so many are disposed to love me, one, for in the humility of my heart I should be quite satisfied with one, would be at the pains to make me love him. In the mean time, this is all very dull work, Sir, and worse even than being at home with my father: so, if you pity me, and believe you could make me in love with you, write to me, and direct to the post-office here.

By return of post, I received an answer nearly to this effect: I believe, from Colonel Thomas.

Miss Wilson's letter has been received by the noble individual to whom it was addressed. If Miss Wilson will come to town, she may have an interview, by directing her letter as before.

I answered this note directly, addressing my letter to the Prince of Wales.

SIR,

To travel fifty-two miles, this bad weather, merely to see a man, with only the given number of legs, arms, fingers, etc., would, you must admit, be madness, in a girl like myself, surrounded by humble admirers, who are ever ready to travel any distance for the honour of kissing the tip of her little finger; but if you can prove to me that you are one bit better than any man who may be ready to attend my bidding, I'll e'en start for London directly. So, if you can do anything better, in the way of pleasing a lady, than ordinary men, write directly: if not, adieu, Monsieur le Prince.

I won't say Yours,
By day or night, or any kind of light;
Because you are too impudent.

It was necessary to put this letter into the post-office myself, as Lord Craven's black footman would have been somewhat surprised at its address. Crossing the Steyne, I met Lord Melbourne, who joined me immediately.

"Where is Craven?" said His Lordship, shaking hands with me.

"Attending to his military duties at Lewes, my Lord."

"And where's my son Fred?" asked His Lordship.

"I am not your son's keeper, my Lord," said I.

"No! By the by," inquired His Lordship, "how is this? I wanted to call upon you about it. I never heard of such a thing, in the whole course of my life! What the Devil can you possibly have to say against my son Fred?"

"Good heavens! my Lord, you frighten me! I never recollect to have said a single word against your son, as long as I have lived. Why should I?"

"Why, indeed!" said Lord Melbourne. "And since there is nothing to be said against him, what excuse can you make for using him so ill?"

"I don't understand you one bit, my Lord." (The very idea of a father put me in a tremble.)

"Why," said Lord Melbourne, "did you not turn the poor boy out of your house, as soon as it was dark; although Craven was in town, and there was not the shadow of an excuse for such treatment?"

At this moment, and before I could recover from my surprise at the tenderness of some parents, Frederick Lamb, who was almost my shadow, joined us.

"Fred, my boy," said Lord Melbourne, "I'll leave you two together; and I fancy you'll find Miss Wilson more reasonable." He touched his hat to me, as he entered the little gate of the Pavilion, where we had remained stationary from the moment His Lordship had accosted me.

Frederick Lamb laughed long, loud, and heartily at his father's interference. So did I, the moment he was safely out of sight; and then I told him of my answer to the Prince's letter, at which he laughed still more. He was charmed with me for refusing His Royal Highness. "Not," said Frederick, "that he is not as handsome and graceful a man as any in England; but I hate the weakness of a woman who knows not how to refuse a prince, merely because he is a prince."

Frederick Lamb now began to plead his own cause. "I must soon join my regiment in Yorkshire," said he (he was, at that time, aide-de-camp to General Mackenzie); "God knows when we may meet again! I am sure you will not long continue with Lord Craven. I foresee what will happen, and yet, when it does, I think I shall go mad!"

For my part, I left flattered and obliged by the affection Frederick Lamb evinced towards me; but I was still not in love with him.

At length the time arrived when poor Frederick Lamb could delay his departure from Brighton no longer. On the eve of it, he begged to be allowed to introduce his brother William to me.

"What for?" said I.

"That he may let me know how you behave," answered Frederick Lamb.

"And if I fall in love with him?" I inquired.

"I am sure you won't," replied Fred. "Not because my brother William is not likeable; on the contrary, William is much handsomer than I am; but he will not love you as I have done, and do still; and you are too good to forget me entirely."

Our parting scene was rather tender. For the last ten days, Lord Craven being absent, we had scarcely been separated an hour during the whole day. I had begun to feel the force of habit; and Frederick Lamb really respected me, for the perseverance with which I had resisted his urgent wishes, when he would have had me deceive Lord Craven. He had ceased to torment me with such wild fits of passion as had, at first, frightened me; and by these means he had obtained much more of my confidence.

Two days after his departure for Hull, in Yorkshire, Lord Craven returned to Brighton, where he was immediately informed, by some spiteful enemy of mine, that I had been, during the whole of his absence, openly intriguing with Frederick Lamb. In consequence of this information, one evening, when I expected his return, his servant brought me the following letter, dated Lewes:

A friend of mine has informed me of what has been going on at Brighton. This information, added to what I have seen with my own eyes, of your intimacy with Frederick Lamb, obliges me to declare that we must separate. Let me add, Harriette, that you might have done anything with me, with only a little more conduct. As it is, allow me to wish you happy; and further, pray inform me, if, in any way, à la distance, I can promote your welfare.

CRAVEN.

This letter completed my dislike of Lord Craven. I answered it immediately, as follows:

MY LORD,

Had I ever wished to deceive you, I have the wit to have done it successfully; but you are old enough to be a better judge of human nature than to have suspected me of guile or deception. In the plenitude of your condescension, you are pleased to add, that I 'might have done anything with you, with only a little more conduct,' now I say, and from my heart, the Lord defend me from ever doing any thing with you again! Adieu.

HARRIETTE.

My present situation was rather melancholy and embarrassing, and yet I felt my heart the lighter for my release from the cocoa trees, with its being my own act and deed. It is my fate! thought I; for I never wronged this man. I hate his fine carriage, and his money, and everything belonging to, or connected with him. I shall hate cocoa as long as I live; and, I am sure, I will never enter a boat again, if I can help it. This is what one gets by acting with principle.

The next morning, while I was considering what was to become of me, I received a very affectionate letter from Frederick Lamb, dated Hull. He dared not, he said, be selfish enough to ask me to share his poverty, and yet he had a kind of presentiment, that he should not lose me.

My case was desperate; for I had taken a vow not to remain another night under Lord Craven's roof. John, therefore, the black, whom Craven had, I suppose, imported, with his cocoa trees from the West Indies, was desired to secure me a place in the mail for Hull.

It is impossible to do justice to the joy and rapture which brightened Frederick's countenance, when he flew to receive me, and conducted me to his house, where I was shortly visited by his worthy general, Mackenzie, who assured me of his earnest desire to make my stay in Hull as comfortable as possible.

We continued here for about three months, and then came to London. Fred Lamb's passion increased daily; but I discovered, on our arrival in London, that he was a voluptuary, somewhat worldly and selfish. My comforts were not considered. I lived in extreme poverty, while he contrived to enjoy all the luxuries of life; and suffered me to pass my dreary evenings alone, while he frequented balls, masquerades, etc. Secure of my constancy, he was satisfied—so was not I! I felt that I deserved better from him.

I asked Frederick, one day, if the Marquis of Lorne was as handsome as he had been represented to me. "The finest fellow on earth," said Frederick Lamb, "all the women adore him"; and then he went on to relate various anecdotes of His Lordship, which strongly excited my curiosity.

Soon after this, he quitted town for a few weeks, and I was left alone in London, without money, or, at any rate, with very little; and Frederick Lamb, who had intruded himself on me at Brighton, and thus become the cause of my separation from Lord Craven, made himself happy; because he believed me faithful, and cared not for my distresses.

This idea disgusted me; and, in a fit of anger, I wrote to the Marquis of Lorne, merely to say that, if he would walk up to Duke's Row, Somerstown, he would meet a most lovely girl.

This was his answer:

If you are but half as lovely as you think yourself, you must be well worth knowing; but how is that to be managed? not in the street! But come to No. 39, Portland Street, and ask for me.

L.

My reply was this:

No! our first meeting must be on the high road, in order that I may have room to run away, in case I don't like you.

HARRIETTE.

68

The Marquis rejoined:

Well, then, fair lady, tomorrow, at four, near the turnpike, look for me on horseback; and then, you know, I can gallop away.

L.

We met. The Duke (he has since succeeded to the title) did not gallop away; and, for my part, I had never seen a countenance I had thought half so beautifully expressive. I was afraid to look at it, lest a closer examination might destroy all the new and delightful sensation his first glance had inspired in my breast. His manner was most gracefully soft and polished. We walked together for about two hours.

"I never saw such a sunny, happy countenance as yours in my whole life," said Argyle to me.

"Oh, but I am happier than usual today," answered I, very naturally.

Before we parted, the Duke knew as much of me and my adventures as I knew myself. He was very anxious to be allowed to call on me.

"And how will your particular friend, Frederick Lamb, like that?" inquired I.

The Duke laughed.

"Well, then," said His Grace, "do me the honour, some day, to come and dine or sup with me at Argyle House."

"I shall not be able to run away, if I go there," I answered, laughingly, in allusion to my last note.

"Shall you want to run away from me?" said Argyle; and there was something unusually beautiful and eloquent in his countenance, which brought a deep blush into my cheek.

"When we know each other better?" added Argyle, beseechingly, "*En attendant*, will you walk again with me tomorrow?" I assented, and we parted.

I returned to my home in unusual spirits; they were a little damped, however, by the reflection that I had been doing wrong. I cannot, I reasoned with myself, I cannot, I fear, become what the world calls a steady, prudent, virtuous woman. That time is past, even if I was ever fit for it. Still I must distinguish myself from those in the like unfortunate situations, by strict probity and love of truth. I will never become vile. I will always adhere to good faith, as long as anything like kindness or honourable principle is shown towards me; and, when I am ill-used, I will leave my lover rather than deceive him. Frederick Lamb relies in perfect confidence on my honour. True, that confidence is the effect of vanity. He believes that a woman who could resist him, as I did at Brighton, is the safest woman on earth! He leaves me alone, and without sufficient money for common necessaries. No matter, I must tell him tonight, as soon as he arrives from the country, that I have written to, and walked with Lorne. My dear mother would never forgive me, if I became artful.

So mused, and thus reasoned I, till I was interrupted by Frederick Lamb's loud knock at my door. He will be in a fine passion, said I to myself, in excessive trepidation; and I was in such a hurry to have it over, that I related all immediately. To my equal joy and astonishment, Frederick Lamb was not a bit angry. From his manner, I could not help guessing that his friend Lorne had often been found a very powerful rival.

I could see through the delight he experienced, at the idea of possessing a woman whom, his vanity persuaded him, Argyle would sigh for in vain; and attacking me on my weak point, he kissed me, and said, "I have the most perfect esteem for my dearest little wife, whom I can, I know, as safely trust with Argyle as Craven trusted her with me."

"Are you quite sure?" asked I, merely to ease my conscience. "Were it not wiser to advise me not to walk about with him?"

"No, no," said Frederick Lamb; "it is such good fun! bring him up every day to Somerstown and the Jew's Harp House, there to swallow cyder and sentiment. Make him walk up here as many times as you can, dear little Harry, for the honour of your sex, and to punish him for declaring, as he always does, that no woman who will not love him at once is worth his pursuit."

"I am sorry he is such a coxcomb," said I.

"What is that to you, you little fool?"

"True," I replied. And, at that moment, I made a sort of determination not to let the beautiful and voluptuous expression of Argyle's dark blue eyes take possession of my fancy.

"You are a neater figure than the Marquis of Lorne," said I to Frederick, wishing to think so.

"Lorne is growing fat," answered Frederick Lamb; "but he is the most active creature possible, and appears lighter than any man of his weight I ever saw; and then he is, without any exception, the highest-bred man in England."

"And you desire and permit me to walk about the country with him?"

"Yes; do trot him up here. I want to have a laugh against Lorne."

"And you are not jealous?"

"Not at all," said Frederick Lamb, "for I am secure of your affections."

I must not deceive this man, thought I, and the idea began to make me a little melancholy. My only chance, or rather my only excuse, will be his leaving me without the means of existence. This appeared likely; for I was too shy and too proud to ask for money; and Frederick Lamb encouraged me in this amiable forbearance!

The next morning, with my heart beating very unusually high, I attended my appointment with Argyle. I hoped, nay, almost expected, to find him there before me. I paraded near the turnpike five minutes, then grew angry; in five more, I became wretched; in five more, downright indignant; and, in five more, wretched again—and so I returned home.

This, thought I, shall be a lesson to me hereafter, never to meet a man: it is unnatural; and yet I had felt it perfectly natural to return to the person whose society had made me so happy! No matter, reasoned I, we females must not suffer love or pleasure to glow in our eyes until we are quite sure of a return. We must be dignified! Alas! I can only be and seem what I am. No doubt my sunny face of joy and happiness, which he talked to me about, was understood, and it has disgusted him. He thought me bold, and yet I am sure I never blushed so much in any man's society before.

I now began to consider myself with feelings of the most painful humility. Suddenly I flew to my writing-desk: he shall not have the cut all on his side neither, thought I, with the pride of a child. I will soon convince him I am not accustomed to be slighted; and then I wrote to His Grace, as follows:

It was very wrong and very bold of me, to have sought your acquaintance, in the way I did, my Lord; and I entreat you to forgive and forget my childish folly, as completely as I have forgotten the occasion of it.

So far, so good, thought I, pausing; but then suppose he should, from this dry note, really believe me so cold and stupid as not to have felt his pleasing qualities? Suppose now it were possible that he liked me after all? Then, hastily, and half ashamed of myself, I added these few lines:

I have not quite deserved this contempt from you, and, in that consolatory reflection, I take my leave—not in anger, my Lord, but only with the steady

*determination so to profit by the humiliating lesson you have given me, as
never to expose myself to the like contempt again.*

Your most obedient servant,

HARRIETTE WILSON.

Having put my letter into the post, I passed a restless night; and, the
next morning, heard the knock of the twopenny postman, in extreme
agitation. He brought me, as I suspected, an answer from Argyle, which
is subjoined.

*You are not half vain enough, dear Harriette. You ought to have been quite
certain that any man who had once met you, could fail in a second appointment,
but from unavoidable accident—and, if you were only half as pleased with
Thursday morning as I was, you will meet me tomorrow, in the same place, at
four. Pray, pray, come.*

LORNE.

I kissed the letter, and put it into my bosom, grateful for the weight it
had taken off my heart. Not that I was so far gone in love, as my readers
may imagine, but I had suffered severely from wounded pride, and, in
fact, I was very much *tête montée*.

The sensations which Argyle had inspired me with, were the warmest,
nay, the first of the same nature I had ever experienced. Nevertheless,
I could not forgive him quite so easily as this, neither. I recollected
what Frederick Lamb had said about his vanity. No doubt, thought I,
he thinks it was nothing to have paraded me up and down that stupid
turnpike road, in the vain hope of seeing him. It shall now be his turn:
and I gloried in the idea of revenge.

The hour of Argyle's appointment drew nigh, arrived, and passed
away, without my leaving my house. To Frederick Lamb I related everything—presented him with Argyle's letter, and acquainted him with my
determination not to meet His Grace.

"How good!" said Frederick Lamb, quite delighted. "We dine
together today, at Lady Holland's; and I mean to ask him, before
everybody at table, what he thinks of the air about the turnpike in
Somerstown."

The next day I was surprised by a letter, not, as I anticipated, from
Argyle, but from the late Tom Sheridan, only son of Richard Brinsley
Sheridan. I had, by mere accident, become acquainted with that very
interesting young man, when quite a child, from the circumstances of his
having paid great attention to one of my elder sisters.

He requested me to allow him to speak a few words to me, wherever I pleased. Frederick Lamb having gone to Brocket Hall, in Hertfordshire, I desired him to call on me.

"I am come from my friend Lorne," said Tom Sheridan. "I would not have intruded on you, but that poor fellow, he is really annoyed: and he has commissioned me to acquaint you with the accident which obliged him to break his appointment, because I can best vouch for the truth of it, having, upon my honour, heard the Prince of Wales invite Lord Lorne to Carlton House, with my own ears, at the very moment when he was about to meet you in Somerstown. Lorne," continued Tom Sheridan, "desires me to say, that he is not coxcomb enough to imagine you cared for him; but, in justice, he wants to stand exactly where he did in your opinion, before he broke his appointment: he was so perfectly innocent on that subject. 'I would write to her,' said he, again and again; 'but that, in all probability, my letters would be shown to Frederick Lamb, and be laughed at by them both. I would call on her, in spite of the devil, but that I know not where she lives.'"

"I asked Argyle," Tom Sheridan proceeded, "how he had addressed his last letters to you? To the post-office, in Somerstown, was his answer, and thence they were forwarded to Harriette. He had tried to bribe the old woman there, to obtain my address, but she abused him, and turned him out of her shop. It is very hard," continued Tom, repeating the words of his noble friend, "to lose the goodwill of one of the nicest, cleverest girls I ever met with in my life, who was, I am certain, civilly, if not kindly disposed towards me, by such a mere accident. Therefore," continued Tom Sheridan, smiling, "you'll make it up with Lorne, won't you?"

"There is nothing to forgive," said I, "if no slight was meant. In short, you are making too much of me, and spoiling me, by all this explanation; for, indeed, I had, at first, been less indignant; but that I fancied His Grace neglected me, because——" and I hesitated, while I could feel myself blush deeply.

"Because what?" asked Tom Sheridan.

"Nothing," I replied, looking at my shoes.

"What a pretty girl you are," observed Sheridan, "particularly when you blush."

"Fiddlestick!" said I, laughing; "you know you always preferred my sister Fanny."

"Well," replied Tom, "there I plead guilty. Fanny is the sweetest creature on earth; but you are all a race of finished coquettes, who delight in making fools of people. Now can anything come up to your vanity in writing to Lorne, that you are the most beautiful creature on earth?"

"Never mind," said I, "you set all that to rights. I was never vain in your society, in my life."

"I would give the world for a kiss at this moment," said Tom; "because you look so humble, and so amiable; but"—recollecting himself—"this is not exactly the embassy I came upon. Have you a mind to give Lorne an agreeable surprise?"

"I don't know."

"Upon my honour I believe he is downright in love with you."

"Well?"

"Come into a hackney-coach with me, and we will drive down to the Tennis Court, in the Haymarket."

"Is the Duke there?"

"Yes."

"But—at all events, I will not trust myself in a hackney-coach with you."

"There was a time," said poor Tom Sheridan, with much drollery of expression, "there was a time when the very motion of a carriage would —but now!"—and he shook his handsome head with comic gravity—"but now! you may drive with me, from here to St. Paul's, in the most perfect safety. I will tell you a secret," added he, and he fixed his fine dark eyes on my face while he spoke, in a tone, half merry, half desponding, "I am dying; but nobody knows it yet!"

I was very much affected by his manner of saying this.

"My dear Mr. Sheridan," said I, with earnest warmth, "you have accused me of being vain of the little beauty God has given me. Now I would give it all, or, upon my word, I think I would, to obtain the certainty that you would, from this hour, refrain from such excesses as are destroying you."

"Did you see me play the methodist parson, in a tub, at Mrs. Beaumont's masquerade, last Thursday?" said Tom, with affected levity.

"You may laugh as you please," said I, "at a little fool like me pretending to preach to you; yet I am sensible enough to admire you, and quite feeling enough to regret your time so misspent, your brilliant talents so misapplied."

"Bravo! Bravo!" Tom reiterated, "what a funny little girl you are! Pray, Miss, how is your time spent?"

"Not in drinking brandy," I replied.

"And how might your talent be applied, Ma'am?"

"Have not I just given you a specimen, in the shape of a handsome quotation?"

"My good little girl—it is in the blood, and I can't help it—and, if I could, it is too late now. I'm dying, I tell you. I know not if my poor father's physician was as eloquent as you are; but he did his best to turn him from drinking. Among other things, he declared to him one day, that the brandy, Arquebusade, and eau-de-Cologne he swallowed, would burn off the coat of his stomach. Then, said my father, my stomach must digest in its waistcoat; for I cannot help it."

"Indeed, I am very sorry for you," I replied; and I hope he believed me; for he pressed my hand hastily, and I think I saw a tear glisten in his bright, dark eye.

"Shall I tell Lorne," said poor Tom, with an effort to recover his usual gaiety, "that you will write to him, or will you come to the Tennis Court?"

"Neither," answered I; "but you may tell His Lordship that, of course, I am not angry, since I am led to believe he had no intention to humble nor make a fool of me."

"Nothing more?" inquired Tom.

"Nothing," I replied, "for His Lordship."

"And what for me?" said Tom.

"You! what do you want?"

"A kiss!" he said.

"Not I, indeed!"

"Be it so, then; and yet you and I may never meet again on this earth, and just now I thought you felt some interest about me"; and he was going away.

"So I do, dear Tom Sheridan!" said I, detaining him; for I saw death had fixed his stamp on poor Sheridan's handsome face. "You know I have a very warm and feeling heart, and taste enough to admire and like you; but why is this to be our last meeting?"

"I must go to the Mediterranean," poor Sheridan continued, putting his hand to his chest, and coughing.

To die! thought I, as I looked on his sunk, but still very expressive dark eyes.

"Then God bless you!" said I, first kissing his hand, and then, though somewhat timidly, leaning my face towards him. He parted my hair, and kissed my forehead, my eyes, and my lips.

"If I do come back," said he, forcing a languid smile, "mind let me

F

find you married, and rich enough to lend me an occasional hundred pounds or two." He then kissed my hand gracefully, and was out of sight in an instant.

I never saw him again.

The next morning my maid brought me a little note from Argyle, to say that he had been waiting about my door an hour, having learned my address from poor Sheridan; and that, seeing the servant in the street, he could not help making an attempt to induce me to go out and walk with him. I looked out of the window, saw Argyle, ran for my hat and cloak, and joined him in an instant.

"Am I forgiven?" said Argyle, with gentle eagerness.

"Oh yes," returned I, "long ago; but that will do you no good, for I really am treating Frederick Lamb very ill, and therefore must not walk with you again."

"Why not?" Argyle inquired. "*Apropos*," he added, "you told Frederick that I walked about the turnpike looking for you, and that, no doubt, to make him laugh at me?"

"No, not for that; but I never could deceive any man. I have told him the whole story of our becoming acquainted, and he allows me to walk with you. It is I who think it wrong, not Frederick."

"That is to say, you think me a bore," said Argyle, reddening with pique and disappointment.

"And suppose I loved you?" I asked, "still I am engaged to Frederick Lamb, who trusts me, and——"

"If," interrupted Argyle, "it were possible you did love me, Frederick Lamb would be forgotten: but, though you did not love me, you must promise to try and do so, some day or other. You don't know how much I have fixed my heart on it."

These sentimental walks continued more than a month. One evening we walked rather later than usual. It grew dark. In a moment of ungovernable passion, Argyle's ardour frightened me. Not that I was insensible to it: so much the contrary, that I felt certain another meeting must decide my fate. Still, I was offended at what, I conceived, showed such a want of respect. The Duke became humble. There is a charm in the humility of a lover who has offended. The charm is so great that we like to prolong it. In spite of all he could say, I left him in anger. The next morning I received the following note:

If you see me waiting about your door, tomorrow morning, do you not fancy I am looking for you; but for your pretty housemaid.

76

I did see him from a sly corner of my window; but I resisted all my desires, and remained concealed. I dare not see him again, thought I, for I cannot be so very profligate, knowing and feeling, as I do, how impossible it will be to refuse him anything, if we meet again. I cannot treat Fred Lamb in that manner! besides, I should be afraid to tell him of it: he would, perhaps, kill me.

But then, poor dear Lorne! to return his kisses, as I did last night, and afterwards be so very severe on him, for a passion which it seemed so out of his power to control!

Nevertheless we must part, now or never; so I'll write and take my leave of him kindly. This was my letter:

At the first, I was afraid I should love you, and, but for Fred Lamb having requested me to get you up to Somerstown, after I had declined meeting you, I had been happy: now the idea makes me miserable. Still it must be so. I am naturally affectionate. Habit attaches me to Fred Lamb. I cannot deceive him or acquaint him with what will cause him to cut me, in anger and for ever. We may not then meet again, Lorne, as hitherto: for now we could not be merely friends: lovers we must be, hereafter, or nothing. I have never loved any man in my life before, and yet, dear Lorne, you see we must part. I venture to send you the inclosed thick lock of my hair; because you have been good enough to admire it. I do not care how I have disfigured my head, since you are not to see it again.

God bless you, Lorne. Do not quite forget last night directly, and believe me, as in truth I am,

> *Most devotedly yours,*
> HARRIETTE.

This was his answer, written, I suppose, in some pique.

True, you have given me many sweet kisses, and a lock of your beautiful hair. All this does not convince me you are one bit in love with me. I am the last man on earth to desire you to do violence to your feelings, by leaving a man as dear to you as Frederick Lamb is; so farewell, Harriette. I shall not intrude to offend you again.

> LORNE.

Poor Lorne is unhappy; and, what is worse, thought I, he will soon hate me. The idea made me wretched. However, I will do myself the justice to say, that I have seldom, in the whole course of my life, been tempted by my passions or my fancies, to what my heart and conscience told me was wrong. I am afraid my conscience has been a very easy one; but, certainly, I have followed its dictates. There was a want of heart and delicacy, I always thought, in leaving any man, without full and very sufficient reasons for it. At the same time, my dear mother's marriage had proved to me so forcibly, the miseries of two people of contrary opinions and character, torturing each other to the end of their natural lives, that, before I was ten years old, I decided, in my own mind, to live free as air from any restraint but that of my conscience.

Frederick Lamb's love was now increasing, as all men's do, from gratified vanity. He sometimes passed an hour in reading to me. Till then, I had no idea of the gratification to be derived from books. In my convent in France, I had read only sacred dramas; at home, my father's mathematical books, *Buchan's Medicine, Gil Blas,* and the *Vicar of Wakefield,* formed our whole library. The two latter I had long known by heart, and could repeat at this moment.

My sisters used to subscribe to little circulating libraries, in the neighbourhood, for the common novels of the day; but I always hated these. Fred Lamb's choice was happy—Milton, Shakespeare, Byron, the Rambler, Virgil, etc. I must know all about these Greeks and Romans, said I to myself. Some day I will go into the country quite alone, and study like mad. I am too young now.

In the meantime, I was absolutely charmed with Shakespeare. Music, I always had a natural talent for. I played well on the pianoforte; that is, with taste and execution, though almost without study.

There was a very elegant-looking woman, residing in my neighbourhood, in a beautiful little cottage, who had long excited my curiosity. She appeared to be the mother of five extremely beautiful children. These were always to be seen with their nurse, walking out, most fancifully dressed. Everyone used to stop to admire them. Their mother seemed to live in most complete retirement. I never saw her with anybody besides her children.

One day our eyes met: she smiled, and I half bowed. The next day we met again, and the lady wished me a good morning. We soon got into conversation. I asked her, if she did not lead a very solitary life? "You are the first female I have spoken to for four years," said the lady, "with the exception of my own servants; but," added she, "some day we may know each other better. In the meantime will you trust yourself to come and dine with me today?"—"With great pleasure," I replied, "if you think me worthy of that honour." We then separated to dress for dinner.

When I entered her drawing-room, at the hour she had appointed, I was struck with the elegant taste, more than with the richness of the furniture. A beautiful harp, drawings of a somewhat voluptuous cast, elegant needlework, Moore's poems, and a fine pianoforte, formed a part of it. She is not a bad woman—and she is not a good woman, said I to myself. What can she be?

The lady now entered the room, and welcomed me with an appearance of real pleasure. "I am not quite sure," said she, "whether I can have the pleasure of introducing you to Mr. Johnstone today, or not. We will not wait dinner for him, if he does not arrive in time." This was the first word I had heard about a Mr. Johnstone, although I knew the lady was called by that name.

Just as we were sitting down to dinner, Mr. Johnstone arrived, and was introduced to me. He was a particularly elegant handsome man, about forty years of age. His manner of addressing Mrs. Johnstone was more that of an humble romantic lover than of a husband; yet Julia, for so he called her, could be no common woman. I could not endure all this mystery, and, when he left us in the evening, I frankly asked Julia, for so we will call her in future, why she invited a strange madcap girl like me to dinner with her?

"Consider the melancholy life I lead," said Julia.

"Thank you for the compliment," answered I.

"But do you believe," interrupted Julia, "that I should have asked you to dine with me, if I had not been particularly struck and pleased with you? I had, as I passed your window, heard you touch the pianoforte with a very masterly hand, and therefore I conceived that you were not uneducated, and I knew that you led almost as retired a life as myself. *Au reste*," continued Julia, "some day, perhaps soon, you shall know all about me."

I did not press the matter further at that moment, believing it would be indelicate.

"Shall we go to the nursery?" asked Julia.

I was delighted; and, romping with her lovely children, dressing their dolls, and teaching them to skip, I forgot my love for Argyle, as much as if that excellent man had never been born.

Indeed I am not quite sure that it would have occurred to me even when I went home, but that Fred Lamb, who was just at this period showing Argyle up all over the town as my amorous shepherd, had a new story to relate of His Grace.

Horace Beckford and two other fashionable men, who had heard from

Frederick of my cruelty, as he termed it, and the Duke's daily romantic walks to the Jew's Harp House, had come upon him, by accident, in a body, as they were galloping through Somerstown. Lorne was sitting, in a very pastoral fashion, on a gate near my door, whistling. They saluted him with a loud laugh. No man could, generally speaking, parry a joke better than Argyle: for few knew the world better: but this was no joke. He had been severely wounded and annoyed by my cutting his acquaintance altogether, at the very moment when he had reason to believe that the passion he really felt for me was returned. It was almost the first instance of the kind he had ever met with. He was bored and vexed with himself, for the time he had lost, and yet he found himself continually in my neighbourhood, almost before he was aware of it. He wanted, as he has told me since, to meet me once more by accident, and then he declared he would give me up.

The next day Julia returned my visit; and, before we parted, she had learned, from my usual frankness, every particular of my life, without leaving me one atom the wiser as to what related to herself. I disliked mystery so much that, but that I saw Julia's proceeded from the natural extreme shyness of her disposition, I had, by this time, declined continuing her acquaintance. I decided, however, to try her another month, in order to give her time to become acquainted with me. She was certainly one of the best-mannered women in England, not excepting even those of the very highest rank. Her handwriting, and her style, were both beautiful. She had the most delicately fair skin, and the prettiest arms, hands, and feet, and the most graceful form, which could well be imagined; but her features were not regular, nor their expression particularly good. She struck me as a woman of very violent passions, combined with an extremely shy and reserved disposition.

Mr. Johnstone seldom made his appearance oftener than twice a week. He came across a retired field to her house, though he might have got there more conveniently by the roadway. I sometimes accompanied her, and we sat on a gate to watch his approach to this field. Their meetings were full of rapturous and romantic delight. In his absence, she never received a single visitor, male or female, except myself; yet she always, when quite alone, dressed in the most studied and fashionable style.

There was something dramatic about Julia. I often surprised her, hanging over her harp so very gracefully, the room so perfumed, the rays of her lamp so soft, that I could scarcely believe this *tout ensemble* to be the effect of chance or habit. It appeared arranged for the purpose, like a scene in a play. Yet who was it to affect? Julia never either received or expected company!

Everything went on as usual for another month or two: during which time Julia and I met every day, and she promised shortly to make me acquainted with her whole history. My finances were now sinking very low. Everything Lord Craven had given me, whether in money or valuables, I had freely parted with for my support. Fred Lamb, I thought, must know that these resources cannot last for ever; therefore I am determined not to speak to him on the subject.

I was lodging with a comical old widow, who had formerly been my sister Fanny's nurse when she was quite a child. This good lady, I believe, really did like me, and had already given me all the credit for board and lodging she could possibly afford. She now entered my room, and acquainted me that she actually had not another shilling, either to provide my dinner or her own.

Necessity hath no law, thought I, my eyes brightening, and my determination being fixed in an instant. In ten minutes more, the following letter was in the post-office, directed to the Marquis of Lorne.

If you still desire my society, I will sup with you tomorrow evening in your own house.

Yours, ever affectionately,

HARRIETTE.

I knew perfectly well that on the evening I mentioned to His Grace, Fred Lamb would be at his father's country house, Brocket Hall.

The Duke's answer was brought to me by his groom, as soon as he had received my letter; it ran thus:

Are you really serious? I dare not believe it. Say, by my servant, that you will see me, at the turnpike, directly, for five minutes, only to put me out of suspense. I will not believe anything you write on this subject. I want to look at your eyes, while I hear you say yes.

Yours, most devotedly and impatiently,

LORNE.

I went to our old place of rendezvous to meet the Duke. How different, and how much more amiable, was his reception than that of Fred Lamb in Hull! The latter, all wild passion; the former, gentle, voluptuous, fearful of shocking or offending me, or frightening away my growing passion. In short, while the Duke's manner was almost as timid as my own, the expression of his eyes and the very soft tone of his voice, troubled my imagination, and made me fancy something of bliss beyond all reality.

We agreed that he should bring a carriage to the old turnpike, and thence conduct me to his house. "If you should change your mind!" said the Duke, returning a few steps after we had taken leave: "*mais tu viendras, mon ange? Tu ne seras pas si cruelle?*" Argyle is the best Frenchman I ever met with in England, and poor Tom Sheridan was the second best.

"And you," said I to Argyle, "suppose you were to break your appointment tonight?"

"Would you regret it?" Argyle inquired. "I won't have your answer while you are looking at those pretty little feet," he continued. "Tell me, dear Harriette, should you be sorry?"

"Yes," said I, softly, and our eyes met, only for an instant. Lorne's gratitude was expressed merely by pressing my hand.

"*À ce soir, donc,*" said he, mounting his horse; and, waving his hand to me, he was soon out of sight.

CHAPTER 2

I WILL NOT say in what particular year of his life the Duke of Argyle succeeded with me. Ladies scorn dates! Dates make ladies nervous and stories dry. Be it only known then, that it was just at the end of his Lorne shifts, and his lawn shirts. It was at that critical period of his life, when his whole and sole possessions appeared to consist in three dozen of ragged lawn shirts, with embroidered collars, well fringed in his service; a threadbare suit of snuff colour, a little old hat with very little binding left, an old horse, an old groom, an old carriage, and an old château. It was to console himself for all this antiquity, I suppose, that he fixed upon so very young a mistress as myself. Thus, after having gone through all the routine of sighs, vows, and rural walks, he, at last, saw me blooming and safe in his dismal château in Argyle Street.

Joy produced a palpitation which had, well nigh, been fatal to . . . No matter, to be brief . . .

A late hour in the morning blushed to find us in the arms of each other, as Monk Lewis, or somebody else says; but the morning was pale when compared to the red on my cheek—aye, ladies, pure red, when I, the very next day, acquainted Fred Lamb with my pretty, innocent, volatile adventure!

Fred was absolutely dumb from astonishment, and half choked with rage and pride. I would not plead my poverty; for I conceived that common sense and common humanity ought to have made this a subject of attention and inquiry to him.

"You told me he was, when he pleased, irresistible," said I.

"Yes, yes, yes," muttered Fred Lamb, between his closed teeth; "but a woman who loves a man is blind to the perfections of every other. No matter, no matter, I am glad it has happened. I wish you joy. I——"

"Did I ever tell you I was in love with you?" said I, interrupting him. "Indeed, it was your vanity deceived you, not I. You caused me to lose Lord Craven's protection, and, therefore, loving no man at the time, having never loved any, to you I went. I should have felt the affection of a sister for you, but that you made no sacrifices, no single attempt to contribute to my comfort or happiness. I will be the mere instrument of pleasure to no man. He must make a friend and companion of me, or he will lose me."

Fred Lamb left me in madness and fury; but I knew him selfish, and that he could dine on every imagined luxury, and drink his champagne, without a thought or care whether I had bread and cheese to satisfy hunger. Then who, with love, first love! beating in their hearts, could think of Frederick Lamb?

I immediately changed my lodgings for a furnished house at the west end of the town, better calculated to receive my new lover, whose passion knew no bounds. He often told me how much more beautiful I was than he had ever expected to find me.

I cannot, he wrote to me, during a short absence from town, I cannot, for circumstances prevent my being entirely yours. I fancied he alluded to his old flame, Lady W——, with whom the world said he had been intriguing nineteen years, but nothing can, nor shall, prevent my being, for ever, your friend, etc. etc.

If, thought I, this man is not to be entirely mine, perhaps I shall not be entirely his. I could have been—but this nasty Lady W—— destroys half my illusion. He used to sit with her, in her box at the opera, and wear a chain which I believed to be hers. He often came to me from the opera, with just such a rose in his bosom, as I had seen in hers. All this was a dead bore. One night I plucked the rose from his breast, another time I hid the chain, and all this, to him, seemed the effect of pure accident: for who, with pride, and youth, and beauty, would admit they were jealous?

One night (I am sure he will recollect that night, when he thought me mad), one night, I say, I could not endure the idea of Lady W——. That night we slept in Argyle House, and he really seemed most passionately fond of me. The idea suddenly crossed my mind, that all the tenderness and passion he seemed to feel for me, was shared between myself and Lady W——.

I could not bear it.

"I shall go home," said I, suddenly jumping out of bed, and beginning to dress myself, at three o'clock on a cold morning in December.

"Going home!" said the Duke. "Why, my dear little Harriette, you are walking in your sleep"; and he threw on his dressing-gown, and took hold of my hand.

"I am not asleep," said I; "but I will not stay in your room, nor go into your bed again; I cannot. I would rather die"; and I burst into tears.

"My dear, dear Harriette," continued Argyle in great alarm; "for God's sake, tell me what on earth I have done to offend you?"

"Nothing—nothing," said I, drying my tears. "I have but one favour to ask: let me alone, instead of persecuting me with all this show of tenderness"; and I continued putting on my clothes.

"Gracious God!" said Argyle, "how you torment me! If," he proceeded, after pausing, "if you have ceased to love me—if—if you are disgusted——"

I was silent.

"Do speak! pray, pray!" said he.

His agitation astonished me. It almost stopped his breathing. This man, thought I, is either very nervous, or he loves me just as I want to be loved. I had my hand on the door, to leave him. He took hold of me, and threw me from it, with some violence; locked it and snatched the key out; took me in his arms, and pressed me with almost savage violence against his breast.

"By heavens!" said he, "you shall not torture me so, another moment."

This wildness frightened me. He is going to kill me, thought I. I fixed my eyes on his face, to try and read my doom. Our eyes met, he pushed me gently from him, and burst into tears.

My jealousy was at an end, *au moins pour le moment*.

"I am not tired of you, dear Lorne," said I, kissing him eagerly. "How is it possible to be so? Dear Lorne, forgive me!"

Nothing was so bright nor so brilliant as Lorne's smile through a tear. In short, Lorne's expression of countenance, I say it now, when I neither esteem, nor love, nor like him—his expression, I say, is one of the finest things in nature.

Our reconciliation was completed, in the usual way, and on the spot.

The next morning, I was greatly surprised by a visit from my dear, lively sister Fanny, on her arrival from the country. Fanny was the most popular woman I ever met with. The most ill-natured and spiteful of her sex, could never find it in their hearts to abuse one who, in their absence, warmly fought all their battles, whenever anybody complained of them, where she was.

I often asked her why she defended, in society, certain unamiable persons? "Merely because they are not here to defend themselves, and therefore it is two to one against them," said Fanny.

Fanny, as the Marquis of Hertford uniformly insisted, was the most beautiful of all our family. He was very desirous of having her portrait painted by Lawrence, to place it in his own apartment. "That laughing dark blue eye of hers," he would say, "is unusually beautiful." His Lordship, by-the-by, whatever people may say of the coldness of his heart, entertained a real friendship for poor Fanny; and proved it, by every kind attention to her during her last illness. He was the only man she admitted into her room, to take leave of her before she died, although hundreds, and those of the first rank and character, were sincerely desirous of doing so. I remember Lord Yarmouth's last visit to Brompton, where my poor sister died, after an illness of three weeks. "Can I, or my cook, do anything in the world to be useful to her?" said he. I repeated that it was all too late—that she would never desire anything more, and all I wanted for her was plenty of eau-de-Cologne, to wash her temples with; that being all she asked for. He did not send his groom for it, but galloped to town himself, and was back immediately.

This was something for Lord Yarmouth; but to proceed, Fanny was certainly very beautiful; she had led a most retired steady life for seven years, and was the mother of three children at the death of their father, Mr. Woodcock, to whom Fanny would have been married, could he have obtained a divorce from his wife. Everybody was mad for Fanny, and so they had been during Mr. Woodcock's life; but it was all in vain. Now there was a better chance for them, perhaps.

Fanny and our new acquaintance, Julia, soon became sworn friends. Most people believed that we were three sisters. Many called us the Three Graces. It was a pity that there were only three Graces!—and that is the reason, I suppose, why my eldest sister, Amy, was cut out of this ring, and often surnamed—one of the Furies. She was a fine dark woman too. Why she hated me all her life, I cannot conceive; nor why she invariably tried to injure me in the opinion of all those who liked me, I know not: but I can easily divine why she made love to my favourites; for they were the handsomest she could find. It was Amy, my eldest sister, who had been the first to set us a bad example. We were all virtuous girls, when Amy, one fine afternoon, left her father's house and sallied forth, like Don Quixote, in quest of adventures. The first person who addressed her was one Mr. Trench, a certain short-sighted pedantic man, whom most people know about town. I believe she told him that she was running away from her father. All I know for certain is, that when Fanny and I discovered her abode, we went to visit her, and when we asked her what on earth had induced her to throw herself away on an entire stranger whom she had never seen before, her answer was, "I

86

refused him the whole of the first day; had I done so the second, he would have been in a fever."

Amy was really very funny, however spitefully disposed towards me. To be brief with her history: Trench put her to school again, from motives of virtue and economy. From that school she eloped with General Maddan.

Amy's virtue was something like the nine lives of a cat.

With General Maddan she, for several years, professed constancy; indeed, I am not quite certain that she was otherwise. I never, in my occasional visits, saw anything suspicious, except, once, a pair of breeches!!

It was one day when I went to call on her with my brother. General Maddan was not in town. She wanted to go to the opera. The fit had only just seized her, at past nine o'clock. She begged me to make her brother's excuse at home, as, she said, he must accompany her. "What, in those dirty boots?" I asked—"I have got both dress-stockings and breeches upstairs, of Maddan's," replied Amy; and I assisted at the boy's toilette. In handing him the black pair of breeches, which Amy had presented me with, I saw marked, in India ink, what, being in the inside, had probably escaped her attention. It was simply the name of Proby.

"How came Lord Proby's black small-clothes here?" said I.

Amy snatched them out of my hand in a fury, and desired me to go out of the house. *Au reste*, she had often, at that time, three hundred pounds in her pocket at once, and poor Maddan had not a shilling. All this happened before I had left my home.

At the period I now write about, I believe that Maddan was abroad, and Amy lived in York Place, where she used to give gay evening parties to half the fashionable men in town, after the opera. She never came to me but from interested motives. Sometimes she forced herself into my private box, or teased me to make her known to the Duke of Argyle.

This year, we three Graces, as we were called, hired an opera box for the season together. Amy had another near us, for herself and her host of beaux. Her suppers on Saturday nights were very gay. Julia and Fanny were always invited, but she was puzzled what to do with me. If I was present, at least half the men were on my side of the room: if I stayed away, so did all those who went only on my account.

This difficulty became a real privation to such men as delighted in us both together. Among these was Luttrell; everybody knows Luttrell, or if they do not, I will tell them more about him by and by. Luttrell, I say, undertook to draw up a little agreement, stating, that since public parties ought not to suffer from private differences, we were thereby requested to engage ourselves to bow to each other in all societies, going through the forms of good breeding, even with more ceremony than if we had liked each other, on pain of being voted public nuisances and private enemies to all wit and humour.

Signed with our hands and seals. . . .

"Now," said Fanny one day to Julia, soon after our first opera season had begun, "Harriette and I propose cutting you, Mrs. Julia, altogether, if you do not, this very evening, give us a full and true account of yourself, from the day you were born, and the date thereof, up to this hour."

"No dates! no dates! I pray!" said Julia.

"Well, waive dates," added I, "and begin."

Julia then related, in her shy, quiet way, what I will communicate as briefly as possible.

Julia's real name was Storer. She was the daughter of the Honourable Mrs. Storer, who was one of the maids of honour to our present king's royal mother, and the sister of Lord Carysfort.

Julia received part of her education in France, and finished it at the palace of Hampton Court, where her mother sent her on a visit to the wife of Colonel Cotton, who was an officer in the 10th Dragoons.

Mrs. Cotton had a family of nine children, and very little fortune to support them. Julia had been, from the earliest youth, encouraging the most romantic passions which ever fired a youthful breast. With all this, her heart, unlike mine, was as cold as her imagination was warm. What were parents, what were friends to her? What was anything on earth, to love?

The first night Colonel Cotton danced with her, she was mad! In four months more, she was pregnant. In nine months more, having concealed her situation, she was seized with the pangs of labour, while in the act of paying her respects to her Majesty! and all was consternation in the *beau château de Hampton!*

Mrs. Cotton, instead of sending for the *accoucheur*, with extreme propriety, though somewhat *mal-apropos*, loaded poor Julia with abuse! "Have yet a little mercy," said Julia, "and send for assistance."—"Never never, you monster! you wretch! will I so disgrace your family," exclaimed Mrs. Cotton. Poor Julia's sufferings were short; but dreadfully severe. In about five hours, unassisted, she became the mother of a fine boy.

Julia could not attempt to describe the rage and fury either of her mother or brother. It was harsh, it was shocking, even as applied to the most hardened sinner, in such a state of mental and bodily suffering. Julia was, with her infant, by her noble relatives, hurried into the country, almost at the risk of her life, and Colonel Cotton was called out by young Storer, Julia's brother, and, I believe, wounded.

From her retirement, Julia had contrived to write to Colonel Cotton, by means of Colonel Thomas, to declare to him, that, if they were to meet no more, she would immediately destroy herself. In short, Cotton was raving mad for Julia, and Julia was wild for Cotton—*le moyen de les séparer?*

A very retired cottage near town was hired by Cotton for Julia, who inherited a small fortune over which her parents had no control; and on that she had supported herself, in the closest retirement, for more than eight years, when I, accidentally, became acquainted with her. Cotton was dismissed from his regiment, by his royal commander.

I never saw such romantic people, after nine years and five children! Julia! adored Julia! so he would write to her, if you love but as I do, we shall, tomorrow, at eight in the evening, enjoy another hour of perfect bliss! Julia! angel Julia! my certain death would be the consequence of your inconstancy, etc.

Julia used to show me these rhapsodies from Cotton, at which I always laughed heartily, and thus I used to put her in a passion continually.

At the opera I learned to be a complete flirt; for there I saw Argyle, incessantly, with Lady W——, and there it became incumbent on me either to laugh or cry. I let him see me flirt and look tender on Lord Burghersh, one night, on purpose, and the next day, when we Three Graces met him in the park, I placed in his hand a letter, which he was hastily concealing in his pocket, with a look of gratified vanity, believing, no doubt, that it was one of my soft effusions on the beauty of his eyes. "For the post," said I, nodding, as we were turning to leave him, and we all three burst into a loud laugh together. The letter was addressed to Lord Burghersh, merely to tell him to join us at Amy's after the next opera.

The next opera was unusually brilliant. Amy's box was close to ours, and, almost as soon as we were seated, she entered, dressed in the foreign style, which best became her, accompanied by Counts Woronzow, Beckendorff, and Orloff. Beckendorff was half mad for her, and wanted to marry her with his left hand.

"Why not with the right?" said Amy.

"I dare not," answered Beckendorff, "without the consent of the Emperor of Russia."

Amy had desired him to go to Russia, and obtain this consent from the Emperor, more than a month before; but still he lingered.

Our box was soon so crowded, that I was obliged to turn one out as fast as a new face appeared. Julia and Fanny left me to pay a visit to the enemy, as Luttrell used to call Amy. Observing me, for an instant, the Duke of Devonshire came into my box, believing that he did me honour.

"Duke," said I, "you cut me in Piccadilly today."

"Don't you know," said thick-head, "don't you know, *belle Harriette*, that I am blind as well as deaf, and a little absent too?"

"My good young man," said I, out of all patience, "*allez donc à l'hôpital des invalides*: for really, if God has made you blind and deaf, you must be absolutely insufferable when you presume to be absent too. The least you can do as a blind, deaf man, is surely to pay attention to those who address you."

"I never heard anything half so severe as *la belle Harriette*," drawled out the Duke.

Luttrell now peeped his nose into my box, and said, dragging in his better half, half-brother I mean, fat Nugent, "A vacancy for two! How happens this? you'll lose your character, Harriette."

"I'm growing stupid, from sympathy, I suppose," I observed, glancing at His Grace, who, being as deaf as a post, poor fellow, bowed to me for the supposed compliment.

"You sup with Amy, I hope?" said I to Luttrell. "And you?" turning to Nugent.

"There's a princess in the way," replied Nugent, alluding to the late Queen.

"Nonsense," said Luttrell, "Her Royal Highness has allowed me to be off."

"You can take liberties with her," Nugent remarked. "You great wits can do what you please. She would take it very ill of me; besides, I wish Amy would send some of those dirty Russians away. Count Orloff is the greatest beast in nature."

Lord Alvanley now entered my box.

"*Place pour un*," said I, taking hold of the back of the Duke of Devonshire's chair.

"I am going," said His Grace; "but, seriously, Harriette, I want to accomplish dining alone some evening, on purpose to pay you a visit."

"There will be no harm in that," said I.

"None! None!" answered Luttrell, who took my allusion.

Alvanley brought me a tall, well-dressed foreigner, whom he was waiting to present to me, as his friend.

"That won't do, Lord Alvanley," said I; "really, that is no introduction, and less recommendation. Name your friend, or away with him."

"*Ma foi, madame,*" said the foreigner, "*un nom ne fait rien du tout. Vous me voyez là, madame, honnête homme, de cinq pieds et neuf pouces.*"

"*Madame est persuadée de vos cinq pieds, mais elle n'est pas si sûre de vos neuf pouces,*" Alvanley observed.

"*Adieu, ma belle Harriette,*" said the Duke, at last, taking my hint; and rising to depart.

Julia and Fanny now returned; the latter, as usual, was delighted to meet Alvanley.

"Do you come from the enemy?" Luttrell inquired of them.

"Yes," replied Fanny, laughing.

"My dear Fanny," said Luttrell, in his comical, earnest, methodistical manner, "my dear Fanny, this will never do!"

"What won't do?" inquired Fanny.

"These Russians, my dear."

"She has got a little Portuguese, besides the Russians, coming to her tonight," said I. "The Count Palmella."

"The ambassador?" Nugent asked.

"God bless my soul!!" said Luttrell, looking up to the ceiling with such a face! Tom Sheridan would have liked to have copied it, when he played the methodist, in a tub, at Mrs. Beaumont's masquerade.

"They are only all brought up upon trial," I observed; "she will cut the rest, as soon as she has fixed on one of them."

"Yes; but you see, coming after these cossacks is the devil!" lisped Alvanley, with his usual comical expression. "God bless your soul, we have no chance after these fellows."

"There is Argyle looking at you, from Lady W——'s box," Nugent said.

The remark put me out of humour, although I did observe that, though he sat in her ladyship's box, he was thinking most of me. Nevertheless, it was abominably provoking.

Lord Frederick Bentinck next paid me his usual visit.

"Everybody is talking about you," said His Lordship. "Two men, downstairs, have been laying a bet that you are Lady Tavistock. Mrs. Orby Hunter says you are the handsomest woman in the house."

Poor Julia, all this time, did not receive the slightest compliment or attention from anybody. At last she kissed her hand to someone in a neighbouring box.

"Who are you bowing to?" I inquired.

"An old flame of mine, who was violently in love with me, when I was a girl, at Hampton Court," whispered Julia. "I have never seen him since I knew Cotton."

"What is his name?" I asked.

"George Brummell," answered Julia.

I had never, at that time, heard of George Brummell.

"Do you know a Mr. George Brummell?" said I to Lord Alvanley.

Before His Lordship could answer my question, Brummell entered the box; and, addressing himself to Julia, expressed his surprise, joy, and astonishment, at meeting with her.

Julia was now all smiles, and sweetness. Just before Brummell's arrival she was growing a little sulky. Indeed she had reason, for in vain did we cry her up, and puff her off, as Lord Carysfort's niece, or as an accomplished, elegant, charming creature, daughter of a maid of honour: she did not take. The men were so rude as often to suffer her to follow us, by herself, without offering their arms to conduct her to the carriage. She was, in fact, so reserved, so shy, and so short-sighted, that, not being very young, nobody would be at the trouble of finding out what she was.

In the round room we held separate levees. Amy always fixed herself near enough to me to see what I was about, and try to charm away some of my admirers. Heaven knows! Fanny and I had plenty to spare her; for they did so flock about us, they scarcely left us breathing room. Argyle looked as if he wanted to join us, but was afraid of Lady W——.

"Are you not going home, pretty?" he would say to me, between his teeth, passing close to my ear.

"Do speak louder, Marquis," I answered, provoked that he should be afraid of any woman but myself. "I am not going home these three hours. I am going first to Amy's party."

Lorne looked, not sulky, nor cross, as Fred Lamb would have done; but smiled beautifully, and said: "At three, then, may I go to you?"

"Yes," answered I, putting my hand into his, and again I contrived to forget Lady W——.

There was all the world at Amy's, and not half room enough for them. Some were in the passage, and some in the parlour, and in the drawing-room one could scarcely breathe. At the top of it, Amy sat coquetting with her tall Russians. The poor Count Palmella stood gazing on her, at a humble distance.

The little delicate weak gentlemanlike Portuguese was no match for the three cossacks. I do not believe he got in a single word the whole evening, but once; when Amy remarked, that she should go the next evening to see the tragedy of Omeo.

"What tragedy is that, pray?" drawled out the Honourable John William Ward, starting from a fit of the dismals, just as if someone had gone behind him and, with a flapper, reminded him that he was at a party, and ought to *faire l'aimable aux dames.*

"You may laugh at me as much as you please," answered Amy, "and I must have patience and bear it, ight or ong; for I cannot pronounce the letter *r.*"

"How very odd!" I remarked. "Why, you could pronouce it well enough at home!" I really did not mean this to tease her: for I thought, perhaps, lisping might grow upon us, as we got older, but I soon guessed it was all sham, by the gathering storm on Amy's countenance. The struggle between the wish to show off effeminate softness to her lovers, and her ardent desire to knock me down, I could see by an arch glance at me, from Fanny's laughing eye, and a shrug of her shoulder was understood by that sister, as well as by myself. Fanny's glance was the slyest thing in nature, and was given in perfect fear and trembling.

"Harriette's correctness may be, I am sorry to say——" and she paused to endeavour to twist her upper lip, trembling with fury, into the shape and form of what might be most pure and innocent in virtuous indignation!

Count Beckendorff eyed me with a look of pity and noble contempt, and then fixed his eyes, with rapture, on his angel's face!

Joking apart, he was a monstrous fool, that same Count Beckendorff, in the shape of a very handsome young cossack.

"Where's the treaty of peace?" said Nugent, dreading a rupture, which would deaden half the spirit of the little pleasant suppers he wished to give us, at his own rooms in the Albany. "No infringement, we beg, ladies. We have the treaty, under your pretty hands and seals."

"Peace be to France, if France, in peace, permit it!" said I, holding out my hand to Amy, in burlesque majesty.

Amy could not, for the life of her, laugh with the rest; because she saw that they thought me pleasant. She, however, put out her hand hastily, to have done with what was bringing me into notice; and, that the subject might be entirely changed, and I as much forgotten, she must waltz, that instant, with Beckendorff.

"Sydenham!" said Amy, to one of her new admirers, who, being flute-mad, and a beautiful flute-player, was always ready.

"The flute does not mark the time enough for waltzing," said he, taking it out of a drawer; "but I shall be happy to accompany Harriette's waltz on the pianoforte, because she always plays in good time."

"Do not play, Harriette," said Amy, for fear it should strike anyone that I played well; "if I had wished her to be troubled, I should have asked her myself. The flute is quite enough"; and she began twirling her tall cossack round the room. He appeared charmed to obey her commands, and sport his really graceful waltzing.

"I do not think it a trouble, in the least," I observed, opening the instrument, without malice or vanity. I was never vain of music; and, at that early age, so much envy never entered my head. I hated playing too; but fancied that I was civil in catching up the air, and accompanying Colonel Sydenham.

"Harriette puts me out," said Amy, stopping, and she refused to stand up again, in spite of all Sydenham could say about my very excellent ear for music.

"*Madame a donc le projet d'aller à Drury Lane, demain?*" said the Count Palmella at last, having been waiting, with his mouth open, ever since Amy mentioned Omeo, for an opportunity of following up the subject.

Amy darted her bright black eyes upon him, as though she had said, *Ah! te voilà! d'où viens tu?* but without answering him, or, perhaps, understanding what he said.

"*Si madame me permettera,*" continued the Count, "*j'aurai l'honneur de lui engager une loge.*"

"*Oui, s'il vous plaît, je vous en serai obligée,*" said Amy, though in somewhat worse French.

The celebrated beau, George Brummell, who had been presented to Amy by Julia, in the round room at the opera, now entered, and put poor Julia in high spirits. Brummell, as Julia always declared, was, when in the 10th Dragoons, a very handsome young man. However that might have been, nobody could have mistaken him for anything like handsome, at the moment she presented him to us. Julia assured me that he had, by some accident, broken the bridge of his nose, and which said broken bridge had lost him a lady, and her fortune of twenty thousand pounds. This, from the extreme flatness of it, of his nose, I mean, not the fortune, appeared probable.

He was extremely fair, and the expression of his countenance far from disagreeable. His person, too, was rather good; nor could anybody find fault with the taste of all those who, for years, had made it a rule to copy the cut of Brummell's coat, the shape of his hat, or the tie of his neck-cloth: for all this was in the very best possible style.

"No perfumes," Brummell used to say, "but very fine linen, plenty of it, and country-washing."

"If John Bull turns round to look after you, you are not well dressed; but either too stiff, too tight, or too fashionable."

"Do not ride in ladies' gloves, particularly with leather breeches."

In short, his maxims on dress were excellent. Besides this, he was neither uneducated nor deficient. He possessed, also, a sort of quaint dry humour, not amounting to anything like wit; indeed, he said nothing which would bear repetition; but his affected manners and little ab-surdities amused for the moment. Then it became the fashion to court Brummell's society, which was enough to make many seek it who cared not for it; and many more wished to be well with him, through fear, for all knew him to be cold, heartless, and satirical.

It appeared plain and evident to me, that his attention to Julia was no longer the effect of love. Piqued at the idea of having been refused marriage by a woman with whom Cotton had so easily succeeded, *sans cérémonie*, he determined in his own mind soon to be even with his late brother officer.

And pray, madam, the reader may ask, how came you to be thus early acquainted with George Brummell's inmost soul?

A mere guess. I will tell you why.

Brummell talked to Julia, while he looked at me; and, as soon as he could manage it with decency, he contrived to place himself by my side.

"What do you think of Colonel Cotton?" said he, when I mentioned Julia.

"A very fine dark man," I answered, "though not at all to my taste, for I never admire dark men."

"No man in England sticks like Cotton," said Brummell.

Ah! ah! thought I, *me voilà au fait!*

"A little eau-de-Portugal would do no harm in that quarter, at all events," I remarked, laughing, while alluding to his dislike of perfumery.

Amy gave us merely a tray-supper in one corner of the drawing-room, with plenty of champagne and claret. Brummell, in his zeal for cold chicken, soon appeared to forget everybody in the room. A loud dis-cordant laugh from the Honourable John Ward, who was addressing something to Luttrell at the other end of the table, led me to understand that he had just, in his own opinion, said a very good thing; yet I saw his corner of the room full of serious faces.

"Do you keep a valet, Sir?" said I.

"I believe I have a rascal of that kind at home," said the learned ugly scion of nobility with disgusting affectation.

"Then," I retorted, "do, in God's name, bring him next Saturday to stand behind your chair."

"For what, I pray?"

"Merely to laugh at your jokes," I rejoined. "It is such hard work for you, Sir, who have both to cut the jokes and to laugh at them too!"

"Do pray show him up, there's a dear creature, whenever you have an opportunity," whispered Brummell in my ear, with his mouth full of chicken. "Is he not an odious little monster of ill-nature, take him altogether?" I asked.

"And look at that tie!" said Brummell, shrugging up his shoulders, and fixing his eyes on Ward's neckcloth.

Ward was so frightened at this commencement of hostilities from me, that he immediately began to pay his court to me, and engaged me to take a drive with him the next morning, in his curricle.

"Go with him," whispered Brummell in my ear. "Keep on terms with him, on purpose to laugh at him." And then he turned round to Fanny, to ask her who her man of that morning was.

"You allude to the gentleman I was riding with in the Park?" answered Fanny.

"I know who he is," said Alvanley. "Fanny is a very nice girl, and I wish she would not encourage such people. Upon my word it is quite shocking."

"Who did you ride with today, Fanny?" I inquired.

"A d——d sugar-baker," said Alvanley.

"I rode out today," replied Fanny, reddening, "with a very respectable man, of large fortune."

"Oh yes!" said Alvanley, "there is a good deal of money to be got in the sugar line."

"Why do not you article yourself then to a baker of it," I observed, "and so pay some of your debts?" This was followed by a laugh, which Alvanley joined in with great good humour.

"What is his name?" inquired Luttrell.

"Mr. John Mitchel," answered Fanny. "He received his education at a public school, with Lord Alvanley."

"I do not recollect Mitchel," retorted Alvanley; "but I believe there were a good many grocers admitted at that time."

Fanny liked Lord Alvanley of all things, and knew very little of Mr. Mitchel, except that he professed to be her very ardent admirer; yet her defence of the absent was ever made with all the warmth and energy her shyness would permit. "Now, gentlemen," said Fanny, "have the goodness to listen to the facts as they really are." Everybody was silent, for everybody delighted to hear Fanny talk.

"That little fat gentleman there"—looking at Lord Alvanley—"whom you all suppose a mere idle, lazy man of genius, I am told, studies *bons mots* all night in his bed. (A laugh.) Further, I have been led to understand, that, being much lower down in the class than Mitchel, though of the same age, His Lordship, in the year eighteen hundred and something or other, was chosen, raised, and selected, for his civil behaviour, to the situation of prime and first fag to Mr. Mitchel, in which said department, His Lordship distinguished himself much, by the very high polish he put upon Mr. J. Mitchel's boots and shoes."

There was not a word of truth in this story, the mere creation of Fanny's brain; yet still there was a probability about it, as they had been at school together, and which, added to Fanny's very pleasing, odd mode of expression, set the whole room in a roar of laughter. Alvanley was just as much amused as the rest; for Fanny's humour had no real severity in it at any time.

"But, Fanny, you will make a point of cutting this grocer, I hope?" observed Brummell, as soon as the laugh had a little subsided.—"Do pray, Fanny," said I, "cut your Mitchels. I vote for cutting all the grocers and valets who intrude themselves into good society."

"My father was a very superior valet," Brummell quickly observed, "and kept his place all his life, and that is more than Palmerston will do," he continued, observing Lord Palmerston, who was in the act of making his bow to Amy, having just looked in on her, from Lady Castlereagh's.

"I don't want any of Lady Castlereagh's men," said Amy. "Let all those who prefer her Saturday night to mine, stay with her."

"Who on earth," said Luttrell, with his usual earnestness, "who on earth would think of Lady Castlereagh, when they might be here?"

"Why, Brummell went there for an hour, before he came here," said Alvanley.

"Mr. Brummell had better go and pass a second hour with Her Ladyship," retorted Amy, "for we are really too full here."

"I am going for one," I said, putting on my shawl; for I began to think it would not do to neglect Argyle altogether. I made use of one of the Russian's carriages, to which Brummell handed me.

"To Argyle House, I suppose?" said Brummell, and then whispered in my ear, "You will be Duchess of Argyle, Harriette."

I found Argyle at his door, with his key, a little impatient. I asked him why he did not go to Amy's?

"I don't know your sister," answered His Grace, "and I dislike what I have seen of her. She makes so many advances to me!" I defended my sister, as warmly as though she had really treated me with kindness, and felt, at that time, seriously angry with the Duke for abusing her.

The next morning, from my window, I saw Amy drive up to my door, in the Count Palmella's barouche. She wants me to write a copy of a letter, for some of her men, thought I, well knowing that affection never brought Amy to visit me.

"Are you alone?" asked Amy, bouncing into the room.

"Yes," said I.

"Then tell that count, downstairs, he may go home," addressing my servant.

"Poor little man!" I remarked, "how terribly rude! I could not be rude to such a very timid gentlemanly man as that!"

"Oh, he makes me sick," said Amy, "and I am come to consult you as to what I had better do. I like liberty best. If I put myself under the protection of anybody, I shall not be allowed to give parties, and sit up all night; but then I have my desk full of long bills, without receipts!"

"I thought you were to marry Beckendorff, and go to Russia," I observed.

"Oh, true, I have come to tell you about Beckendorff," said Amy. "He is off for Russia this morning, to try to obtain the consent of the Emperor and that of his own family. There was no harm in sending him there, you know! for I can easily change my mind when he comes back, if anything which I like better occurs. He wished George to be his aide-de-camp; but George would not go. Well, never mind Beckendorff," Amy went on impatiently. "I want two hundred pounds directly. It spoils all one's independence, and one's consequence, to ask Englishmen for money. Palmella wishes to have me altogether under his protection. He is rich; but—but I like Colonel Sydenham best."

"Sydenham has no money," said I. "Palmella seems disposed to do a great deal for you, and he is very gentlemanlike: therefore, if a man you must have, my voice is for Palmella!"

"Well," said Amy, "I cannot stop! I do not much care. Palmella makes me sick too. It cannot be helped. You write me a copy, directly, to say I consent to enter into the arrangement, as he calls it, which he proposed: namely, two hundred pounds a month, paid in advance, and the use of his horses and carriage." This letter was soon dispatched to His Excellency Palmella; and Amy, shortly afterwards, took her leave.

The next day, as I was returning home from my solitary walk, reflections the most despondingly melancholy crowded on my mind. I thought of the youth I was passing away, in passions wild and ungovernable; and though ever ready to sacrifice more than life for those I have loved, with real genuine warmth and tenderness of heart, yet I had, perhaps, deserved that none should, hereafter, remember me with affection; for my actions had been regulated by the impulses and feelings of that heart alone, void of any other principle than what it had dictated. I was roused by a sudden tap on the shoulder, from the coarse, red, ungloved hand of my old friend, Lord Frederick Bentinck.

"My lord, I was just going to drown myself, therefore pray do not leave me here alone."

"I must," said His Lordship, panting, "for I have a great deal to do. I ought to be at the Horse Guards at this moment."

"Nonsense! But if you really can do anything, I wish to heaven you would put on a pair of gloves."

"I only wish," answered His Lordship, speaking loud, in a good-natured passion, "I only wish that you were compelled to listen to the sort of things I am obliged to attend to daily. Everybody wants promotion. No man will be satisfied with an answer. For my part, I have got into a way of writing my letters, as soon as I have stated all that is to be said. I hate talking, many people expose themselves in that way, so *adio*." It occurred to me, as soon as His Lordship had left me, how unfortunate for his taciturn disposition was the meeting of Sir Murray Maxwell's friends, which took place some time ago, to commemorate that highly-respected gentleman's broken pate. The noble lord was chosen steward of the feast, and, whatever might be the exposure, either in the way or lack of intellect, Lord Frederick must inevitably come forward with a maiden speech. The said discourse, however, would no doubt have redounded to the credit and glory of His Lordship's able attorney, in spite of the many restrictions he had received, not to put in any break-teeth long words; but, alas! His Lordship was not aware of the defect of a memory, which had never been so exerted, and, at the very critical moment, after he had risen to address the attentive assembly, he discovered, with dismay, that he had forgotten every word of his speech. What was to be done? He resolved to address them in detached sentences, delivered in a voice of thunder; such as, My principles, gentlemen—likewise,—observe—my friends,—but I therefore—being, as I say, —a man of few words, gentlemen. The intervals being filled up with much gesticulation, everybody advanced their heads and redoubled their attention, to try to hear what could not be heard. Those who were at a distance said, "We are too far off," and those immediately next to him, thought themselves too near, or suspected the wine had taken an unusual effect, owing to the heated atmosphere of the crowded apartment. All resolved to secure better situations on the next meeting, that they might profit by so fine and affecting a discourse.

The season for Argyle's departure from London, for the north, was now drawing very near. He often spoke of it with regret, and sometimes he talked about my accompanying him.

"Not I, indeed!" was my answer: for I was an unsettled sort of being; and nothing but the whole heart of the man I loved could settle me.

Lorne had fascinated me, and was the first man for whom I had felt the least passion; but his age made him fitter to be my father than my friend and companion: and then this Lady W——! How could I fix my affections on a man whom I knew to be attached still to another woman! Indeed, even his inconstancy to Lady W—— often disgusted me.

"You will not accompany me to Scotland then?" said the Duke.

"No!"

"*Cella, donc, est décidé.*"

"*Oui.*"

CHAPTER 3

I WAS GETTING into debt, as well as my sister Amy, when it so came to pass, as I have since heard say, that the—immortal!!! No; that's common; a very outlandish distinction, fitter for a lady in a balloon. The terrific!!! that will do better. I have seen His Grace in his cotton nightcap. Well, then, the terrific Duke of Wellington!! the wonder of the world!! Having six feet from the tail to the head, and—but there is a certain technicality in the expressions of the gentleman at Exeter 'Change, when he has occasion to show off a wild beast, which it would be vanity in me to presume to imitate; so leaving out his dimensions, etc. etc., it was even the Duke of Wellington, whose laurels, like those of the giant in the *Vicar of Wakefield*, had been hardly earned by the sweat of his little dwarfs' brows, and the loss of their little legs, arms, and eyes; who, feeling himself amorously given—it was in summer—one sultry evening, ordered his coachman to set him down at the White Horse Cellar, in Piccadilly, whence he sallied forth, on foot, to No. 2 or 3, in Berkeley Street, and rapped hastily at the door, which was immediately opened by the tawdry, well-rouged housekeeper of Mrs. Porter, who, with a significant nod of recognition, led him into her mistress's boudoir, and then hurried away, simpering, to acquaint the good Mrs. Porter with the arrival of one of her oldest customers.

Mrs. Porter, on entering her boudoir, bowed low; but she had bowed lower still to His Grace, who had paid but shabbily for the last *bonne fortune* she had contrived to procure him.

"Is it not charming weather?" said Mrs. Porter, by way of managing business with something like decency.

"There is a beautiful girl just come out," said His Grace, without answering her question; "a very fine creature; they call her Harriette, and——"

"My Lord," exclaimed Mrs. Porter, interrupting him, "I have had three applications this very month for the girl they call Harriette, and I have already introduced myself to her."

This was a fact, which happened while I was in Somerstown, and which I have forgotten to relate.

"It was," continued Mrs. Porter, "at the very earnest request of General Walpole. She is the wildest creature I ever saw. She did not affect modesty, nor appear in the least offended at my intrusion. Her first question was, is your man handsome? I answered frankly, that the General was more than sixty years of age; and at which account she laughed heartily; and then, seeming to recollect herself, she said, she really was over head and ears in debt, and therefore must muster up courage to receive one visit from her antiquated admirer, at my house."

"Well?" interrupted Wellington, half jealous, half disgusted.

"Well, my Lord," continued Mrs. Porter, "the appointment was made for eight o'clock on the following evening, at which hour the old General was punctual, and fidgeted about the room over this, my Lord, for more than three-quarters of an hour. At last, he rang the bell violently: I answered it; and he told me, in a fury, he would not thus be trifled with. I was beginning very earnest protestations, when we heard a loud rap at the street door, and, immediately afterwards, my housekeeper entered, to inform me that a lady, whose face was covered with a thick black veil, had just arrived in a hackney-coach, and she had shown her into the best room."

"She came then?" inquired Wellington impatiently, and blowing his nose.

"You shall hear, my Lord," continued Mrs. Porter. "The old General, in a state of perfect ecstasy, took me by the hand, and begged me to pardon his testy humour, assuring me, that he had been for more than a year following Harriette, and therefore, that this disappointment had been too much for his stock of patience.

"I led the way to the room, where we expected to find Harriette. The black veil did not surprise us. She was too young to be expected to enter my house, void of shame. Judge our astonishment, my Lord, when the incognita, throwing back her veil with much affectation, discovered a wrinkled face, which had weathered at least sixty summers, aye, and winters too! 'The Lord defend me!' said I. 'Who the devil are you?' said the General. 'A charming creature,' replied the hag, 'if you did but know me. A widow, too, dear General, very much at your disposal; for my dear good man has been dead these sixty years.' 'You are a set of——' The General was interrupted by his fair incognita, with—'Here is gallantry! here is treatment of the soft sex! No, Mr. General, not the worst of your insinuations shall ever make me think the less of myself!'

"The General, at this moment, beginning to feel a little ashamed, and completely furious, contrived to gain the street, declaring that he would never enter my house again. His fair one insisted on following him; and all I could say or do would not prevent her. I know not what became of them both."

"My good woman," said Wellington, without making any remarks on her story, "my time is precious. One hundred guineas are yours, and as much Harriette's, if you can induce her to give me the meeting."

"My dear Lord," said Mrs. Porter, quite subdued, "what would I not do to serve you? I will pay Harriette a visit early tomorrow morning; although, my Lord, to tell you the truth, I was never half so afraid of any woman in my life. She is so wild, and appears so perfectly independent and careless of her own interests and welfare, that I really do not know what is likely to move her."

"Nonsense!" said Wellington, "it is very well known that the Marquis of Lorne is her lover."

"Lord Lorne may have gained Harriette's heart," said Mrs. Porter, just as if she understood the game of hearts! "However," added she, "I will not give up the business till I have had an interview with Harriette."

"And make haste about it," said Wellington, taking up his hat; "I shall call for your answer in two days. In the meantime, if you have anything like good news to communicate, address a line to Thomas's Hotel, Berkeley Square."

These two respectable friends now took leave of each other, as we will of the subject, *pour le moment au moins.*

I rather think it must have been on the very day the above scene took place, that Fanny, Julia, and myself dined together at my house; and Amy, unasked, joined us after dinner, because she had nothing better to do.

"You are welcome," said I to Amy, "so that you bring me no men; but men I will not admit."

"Why not?" Amy inquired.

"Why? because I am not a coquette, like you; and it fatigues me to death to be eternally making the agreeable to a set of men who might be all buried, and nobody would miss them. Besides, I have seen such a man!!!"

"What manner of man have you seen?" asked Fanny.

"A very god!" retorted I.

"Who is he?" inquired Amy.

"I do not know," was my answer.

"What is his name?"

"I cannot tell."

"Where did you see him?"

"In Sloane Street, riding on horseback, and followed by a large dog."

"What a simpleton you are," observed Amy.

"I never made myself so ridiculous about any man yet," I observed, "as you have done about that frightful, pale William Ponsonby."

"Oh, he is, indeed, a most adorable heavenly creature," rejoined Amy, turning up her eyes in a fit of heroics.

"Good gracious! how can people be so blind?" exclaimed I. "Why, he has not a single point of beauty about him, and besides, he treats you like a dog."

"So he does," acknowledged Amy, waxing indignant.

"How do you think he treated me last night?"

"God knows!" interposed Julia.

"He got into my bed!" continued Amy.

"Mercy on us!!" exclaimed Julia.

"Why, that is the very thing you have been wanting him to do for the last six months," returned I. "My fingers ache with all the pressing invitations you have made me write to William Ponsonby. And——"

"Which you know he always refused," continued Amy. "Last night I went home late," she proceeded, "and therefore hurried up to bed, and began undressing myself, making use of every convenience in my bedroom, without delicacy or ceremony. Only imagine my dismay, just as I was stepping into bed, to hear a loud laugh, and see William Ponsonby's face peeping between the curtains."

"What a brute William Ponsonby must be," said I.

"Pray how came he there?" inquired Julia.

He had called in Amy's absence, and the servants having strict orders to admit William Ponsonby at any time, he was shown into the drawing-room, from which, being very drunk, he had marched into her bedroom, where he had slept himself sober, in his clothes. The servants, concluding that no man would have done this, without particular permission from their mistress, did not mention the circumstance to Amy. Ponsonby's apology to Amy was drunkenness. He hastened out of the room, rudely observing that he came there to seek repose, not a companion.

"And you still like this brute?" observed I.

"Brute!" retorted Amy, "he is a god!" and this wretched fellow went by the name of Amy's god ever afterwards. I allude to William Ponsonby of the Besborough family.

"Amy's story," said Julia, "reminds me of something very ridiculous which happened to me at Hampton Court, while I was staying with Mrs. Cotton."

We pressed her to tell us all about it.

"Did I ever tell you where and how Cotton first succeeded with me?" inquired Julia.

"It was at Hampton Court," I answered.

"On a stone staircase," added Julia. "But to proceed with my story: I can scarcely describe to you the difficulty which existed in the palace, of securing a *tête-à-tête*: with all joint inventions on the stretch, and all our hopes of happiness depending on it, we did not accomplish more than three private interviews in a month.

"My bedroom," continued Julia, "was next to mamma's. My sister always shared her mother's bed; but used my room as her dressing-room, wherein was deposited the whole of her wardrobe.

"'Suppose,' said Cotton one day to me, 'suppose I were to conceal myself under your bed?'

"'But then my mamma always comes into my room before she sleeps, to kiss me, and wish me good night.'"

"'I will wait patiently till all are retired to rest.'

"'How will you endure to be under a bed for three or four hours?'

"'What would I not endure?'

"'But then this is my sister's dressing-room, and here she always undresses.'

"'I will be silent as the grave,' said Cotton."

In short, they had no better remedy.

"Fancy him then," Julia went on, "safely concealed under my bed. Fancy myself and sister about to undress together. Fancy the contrast! while I was studying my attitudes, as I folded my hair gracefully round my head, and bathed my hands and face with rose-water, just as might be expected by any woman who believed herself watched by an adoring romantic lover; my sister was carelessly washing, splashing, and rattling, and talking to me of her sensations, her pimples, her warts, and her wishes, etc. I really thought I should have fainted with terror and dismay."

"Now," said I to Amy, "since it seems we are in the humour to relate some of our adventures, suppose you confess."

"I confess! what?"

"Confess," added I, "how you came by all those nice-looking hundred-pound notes, which I used to see you with, when you were with poor Maddan, and I was a good little girl at home."

"It is all a story of Harriette's making," said Amy.

"Come, come," Fanny observed, "what is the use of being sly as to what happened so long ago? Give us the whole history of these self-same bank notes."

"Why, you must know, Hart Davis——"

"Good heavens!" exclaimed I, "did you have that frightful creature, Hart Davis?"

"Never," said Amy. "The whole of all that money came out of his pocket, notwithstanding."

"And all in the way of honesty?" inquired Julia.

"Not quite," proceeded Amy; "he used to pat me."

"How, pat you!" we eagerly and inquisitively cried out with one consent.

"So," said Amy, showing me with her hand on my arm.

"Was that all?" asked I.

"Do pray send your patting men to me," remarked Julia.

"That was all," said Amy, "I assure you. 'Aamy! Aamy!' he used to say, drawing down his bushy eyebrows, and patting me thus—'Aamy! Aamy! does that feel nice?'—'No! to be sure not,' I used to answer, very fiercely; but, at last, one day when he called, I wanted a hundred pounds, of all things, to hire an opera box. So when he began with his usual 'Aamy, Aamy, does that feel nice?' I made a face so...."

"How?" said Julia, and I, and Fanny, all at once.

"So...." repeated Amy.

The face was too ridiculous, and yet we laughed immoderately.

"Pray," said I, at length, "did that face take, with your friend Hart Davis?"

"Yes," said Amy, "I made this sort of face, and said, 'Ye-s, thank you—I think it does feel ra-ther nice.'

"This confession was always enough to secure me a hundred pounds from Hart Davis, whenever I could find it in my heart to make it, which you may conceive, was only on great occasions!"

"And what," asked I, "have you done with Palmella?"

"Oh!" replied Amy, in some little confusion, "I have never seen him since."

"Did you send the letter I wrote for you?"

"Yes," answered Amy.

"And did he send you the two hundred pounds?"

"Directly," rejoined Amy, "with a letter full of professions of the deepest gratitude."

"And where is that poor dear little man now?" inquired I.

"God knows!" replied Amy. "I have been denied to him ever since. Sydenham has been telling me that I am too beautiful, and it would really be too great a sacrifice, for me to throw myself away on Palmella."

"Did Sydenham say your returning the two hundred pounds would be too great a sacrifice also?"

"No! but I have spent it."

It was now growing late, and we separated.

The next morning, my servant informed me that a lady desired to speak a word to me. Her name was Porter.

"You are come to scold me for sending my old nurse to console the General?" said I, when I entered the room where she was waiting.

"Not at all, my dear, wild young lady," answered Mrs. Porter; "but I am now come to inform you, that you have made the conquest of a very fine, noble, most unexceptionable man."

"Delightful!" said I. "Who is he?"

"I dare not tell you his name," interrupted Mrs. Porter; "but you may rest assured that he is a man of fashion and rank."

"It will not do," reiterated I, striking my head. "Tell your friend that I have no money, that I do not know how to take care of myself, and Argyle takes no care of me. Tell him that nobody wants a real steady friend more than I do; but I cannot meet a stranger as a lover. Tell him all this, if he is really handsome, that is to say (for the stranger I had twice met, riding down Sloane Street, accompanied by his large dog, had lately run often in my head) and let me know what he says, to-morrow."

Mrs. Porter acquiesced, and, hearing a loud rap at my door, she hastily took her leave.

This was Fanny. At his own earnest request, she had brought me the son of the rich Freeling, secretary to the General Post Office; saying: "Mr. Freeling will allow me no rest till I have made him known to you."

The young man was civil and humble, and kept a proper distance; and was rather a bore. In point of fact, at least in my humble opinion, there is no endurable medium between men of the very highest fashion, and honest tradesmen, to those who have once acquired a taste and habit of living with high-bred people. Young Freeling was, however, as well as could be expected, as they say of ladies in the straw. He was a gentleman as far as grammar, and eating with his fork, went; and Fanny proposed our going to Covent Garden together that evening. She wanted to

H

show little Fanny (for by that appellation we distinguished her eldest daughter) the Harlequin farce, before she returned to school.

"What is the play?" said I.

"*Julius Caesar*," answered Freeling.

I was pleased beyond measure at the idea of seeing this play.

I had been at but three plays in my life, all comedies. I shall never forget the delight I experienced in witnessing that fine scene between Brutus and Cassius where they quarrel, performed by John Kemble and Charles Young! Were I to live to the age of a hundred, I should not forget John Kemble's energetic delivery of those beautiful lines, so finely expressive of virtuous indignation, so rich in eloquence, in force, and in nerve. In short, I, like Mark Antony, being no scholar, can only speak right on, and know not how to praise the poet as he merits. Yet few, perhaps, among the most learned, have in their hearts done more honour to some of the natural beauties of Shakespeare than I have.

I am not sitting down here to write a book of quotations; but I could not help offering my mite of praise to the memory of that great actor, whose likeness I shall never behold again on earth; and such was the impression Kemble made on me, that methinks I hear his accent in my ear, and the very tone of that voice which made my heart thrill so long ago, while he was thus taking leave of Cassius:

> And whether we shall meet again, I know not;
> Therefore our everlasting farewell take.
> For ever, and for ever, farewell Cassius!
> If we do meet again, why we shall smile;
> If not, why then this parting was well made.

I begged to be excused remaining to see the Harlequin farce, as it would have been impossible for me to have witnessed such an exhibition after *Julius Caesar,* and I was allowed to drive home alone, for I insisted on not robbing Fanny of the protection of our worthy general postman.

The next morning I received another visit from Mrs. Porter, who informed me that she had just had an interview with my new lover, and had reported to him all I had desired her to say.

"Since you object to meet a stranger," continued Mrs. Porter, "His Grace desires me to say, he hopes you can keep a secret, and to inform you, that it is the Duke of Wellington who so anxiously desires to make your acquaintance."

"I have heard of His Grace often," said I, in a tone of deep disappointment: for I had been indulging a kind of hope about the stranger with the great Newfoundland dog, with whose appearance I had been so unusually struck as to have sought for him every day, and I thought of him every hour.

"His Grace," Mrs. Porter proceeded, "only entreats to be allowed to make your acquaintance. His situation, you know, prevents the possibility of his getting regularly introduced to you."

"It will never do," said I, shaking my head.

"Be assured," said Mrs. Porter, "he is a remarkably fine-looking man, and, if you are afraid of my house, promise to receive him in your own, at any hour when he may be certain to find you alone."

Well, thought I, with a sigh; I suppose he must come. I do not understand economy, and am frightened to death at debts. Argyle is going to Scotland; and I shall want a steady sort of friend, of some kind, in case a bailiff should get hold of me.

"What shall I say to His Grace?" Mrs. Porter inquired, growing impatient.

"Well then," said I, "since it must be so, tell His Grace that I will receive him tomorrow at three; but mind, only as a common acquaintance!"

Away winged Wellington's Mercury, as an old woman wings it at sixty; and most punctual to my appointment, at three on the following day, Wellington made his appearance. He bowed first, then said—

"How do you do?" then thanked me for having given him permission to call on me; and then wanted to take hold of my hand.

"Really," said I, withdrawing my hand, "for such a renowned hero you have very little to say for yourself."

"Beautiful creature!" uttered Wellington, "where is Lorne?"

"Good gracious," said I, out of all patience at his stupidity—"what come you here for, Duke?"

"Beautiful eyes, yours!" reiterated Wellington.

"Aye, man! they are greater conquerors than ever Wellington shall be; but, to be serious, I understood you came here to try to make yourself agreeable?"

"What, child! do you think that I have nothing better to do than to make speeches to please ladies?" said Wellington.

"*Après avoir dépeuplé la terre, vous devez faire tout pour la repeupler,*" I replied.

"You should see me where I shine," Wellington observed, laughing.

"Where's that, in God's name?"

"In a field of battle," answered the hero.

"*Battez-vous, donc, et qu'un autre me fasse la cour!*" said I.

But love scenes, or even love quarrels, seldom tend to amuse the reader, so, to be brief, what was a mere man, even though it were the handsome Duke of Argyle, to a Wellington!!!!

Argyle grew jealous of Wellington's frequent visits, and, hiding himself in his native woods, wrote me the following very pathetic letter:

I am not quite sure whether I do or do not love you—I am afraid I did too much;—but, as long as you find pleasure in the society of another, and a hero too, I am well contented to be a mere common mortal, a monkey, or what you will. I too have my heroines waiting for me, in all the woods about here. Here is the woodcutter's daughter, and the gardener's maid always waiting for my gracious presence, and to which of them I shall throw the handkerchief I know not. How then can I remain constant to your inconstant charms? I could have been a little romantic about you, it is true; but I always take people as I find them, "et j'ai ici beau jeu." Adieu.

I am very fond of you still, for all this.

ARGYLE.

This was my answer:

Indeed you are, as yet, the only man who has ever had the least influence over me, therefore, I entreat you, do not forget me! I wish I were the woodcutter's daughter, awaiting your gracious presence in the woods for days! weeks! months! so that, at last, you would reward me with the benevolent smile of peace and forgiveness; or that illumined, beautiful expression of more ardent feeling, such as I have often inspired and shall remember for ever, come what may, and whether your fancy changes, or mine. You say you take people as you find them; therefore, you must and you shall love me still, with all my imperfections on my foolish head, and that dearly.

HARRIETTE.

Wellington was now my constant visitor—a most unentertaining one, Heaven knows! and, in the evenings, when he wore his broad red ribbon, he looked very like a rat-catcher.

"Do you know," said I to him one day, "do you know the world talks about hanging you?"

"Eh?" said Wellington.

"They say you will be hanged, in spite of all your brother Wellesley can say in your defence."

"Ha!!" said Wellington, very seriously, "what paper do you read?"

"It is the common talk of the day," I replied.

"They must not work me in such another campaign," Wellington said, smiling, "or my weight will never hang me."

"Why, you look a little like the apothecary in Romeo already," I said.

In my walks Brummell often joined me, and I now walked oftener than usual—indeed, whenever I could make anybody walk with me; because I wanted to meet the man with his Newfoundland dog, who was not the sort of man, either, that generally strikes the fancy of a very young female—for he was neither young nor at all gaily dressed. No doubt he was very handsome; but it was that pale expressive beauty, which oftener steals upon us, by degrees, after having become acquainted, than strikes at first sight.

I had, of late, frequently met him, and he always turned his head back, after he had passed me; but whether he admired, or had, indeed, observed me, or whether he only looked back after his large dog, was what puzzled and tormented me. Better to have been merely observed by that fine noble-looking being, than adored by all the men on earth besides, thought I, being now at the very tip-top of my heroics.

Dean Swift mentions having seen, in the grand academy of Lagado, an ingenious architect, who had contrived a new method of building houses, by beginning at the roof, and working downwards to the foundation; and which he justified by the like practice of those two prudent insects, the bee and the spider. The operation of my love, then, was after the model of this architect. The airy foundation on which I built my castles, caused them ever to descend. Once in my life, when I raised my air-built fabric unusually high, it fell with such a dead weight on my heart, that the very vital spark of existence was nearly destroyed. I have never enjoyed one hour's health since. Now, however, I look on all my past bitter suffering, caused by this same love, which many treat as a plaything and a child, and which I believe to be one of the most arbitrary, ungovernable passions in nature, as a wild dream, remembered by me merely as I recollect three days of delirium, by which I was afflicted after the scarlet fever, with the idea of rats and mice running over my head, and which thus kept me in a frenzy, from the mere working of a disordered brain.

Characters and feelings, unnaturally stretched on the sentimental bed of torture, must return with violence to their natural tone and dimensions, says a celebrated French writer. The idol of romantic passion, in some unlucky moment of common sense, or common life, is discovered to be the last thing their worshippers would wish the idol to be found—a mere human being! with passions, and infirmities, and wants, utterly unprovided for by the statutes of romance. Soon we find, too, a certain falling off in our own powers of human life, a subjection to common accidents, ill-health and indigence, which sicklies o'er the rich colouring of passion with the pale cast of humanity.

But to proceed—if, in my frequent walks about Sloane Street and Hyde Park, I failed to meet the stranger whose whole appearance had so affected my imagination, I was sure to see George Brummell, whose foolish professions of love I could not repeat, for I scarcely heard them.

One day, just as I was going to sit down to dinner, with Fanny, and Amy, who was passing the evening with her, I felt a kind of presentiment come over me, that, if I went into Hyde Park at that moment, I should meet this stranger. It was past six o'clock. I had never seen him but at that hour. They both declared that I was mad, and Lord Alvanley calling on Fanny at that moment, they retailed my folly to His Lordship.

"I dare say he is some dog-fancier or whipper-in, or something of the sort," said Alvanley. "God bless my soul! I thought you had more sense. What does Argyle say to all this?"

Lord Lowther now entered the room.

"How very rude you all are," said Fanny. "I have told you frequently, that this is my dinner hour, and you never attend to it!"

"It is those d——mn grocers, the Mitchels," said Alvanley, "who have taught you to dine at these hours! Who the d——l dines at six? Why, I am just out of bed!"

Lord Lowther made many civil apologies. He wanted to have the pleasure of engaging us three to dine with him on the following day, to meet the Marquis of Hertford, then Lord Yarmouth; a Mr. Graham, the son of Sir James Graham, Bart.; Street, the editor of the *Courier* newspaper; and J. W. Croker, M.P., of the Admiralty.

We accepted the invitation, and Lord Lowther, after begging us not to be later than half past seven, took his leave. Alvanley accompanied me as far as Hyde Park, laughing at me and my man and his dog all the way. The Park was now entirely empty—nothing like a hero, nor even a dog, to be seen.

"I must now wish you good morning," said Alvanley. "I am not going to be groom," he added in my ear.

I shook hands with him, without at all understanding what he meant, and walked down towards that side of the river where I had once or twice seen the stranger coaxing his dog to swim, by throwing stones into the water.

If I could but once see him walking with any man I had ever met before, then, at least, I should have a chance of learning his name. I continued to wander up and down the river, for nearly an hour. As I was returning home disappointed, as usual, I met an elderly gentleman, whose name I forget, though we had often seen each other in society. He stopped to converse with me, on common subjects for a few minutes, and just as he had taken his leave, and was slowly walking his horse away, a very clean, aged woman came up to me and begged assistance. Her manners were unlike those of a common beggar. She smiled on me, and looked as if she would have been nearly as much pleased by a few kind words, as with money.

I always liked very old people, when they were clean and appeared respectable, and I was unusually interested by this woman's demeanour. I eagerly searched my reticule. Alas! it was empty. I turned a wishful eye towards the old gentleman who had left me. His prim seat, on horseback, struck me, altogether, as too formidable. If I knew him a little better, thought I, hesitating, as I saw him stop to speak to his groom. He turned his harsh-looking countenance, at that moment, towards me. It will never do, thought I, and then I expressed my sincere regret to the poor old woman, that I had nothing to give her.

"Never mind," replied the good old creature, smiling very kindly on me, "never mind, my dear young lady. Many, I bless God, are more in want than I am."

"Wait here a minute," said I.

My desire to assist her now overcoming my repugnance, I ran as fast as I possibly could after the old gentleman, who was disappearing, and, quite out of breath, and in the deepest confusion, told him I had forgotten my purse, and had occasion for half a crown, which I hoped he would lend me.

"Certainly, with pleasure," said the old gentleman, drawing out his purse and presenting me with what I had asked for.

I made him many confused apologies; and turning hastily towards some trees, which led, by rather a shorter road, to where I had left the old woman, I came immediately in close contact with the stranger, whose person had been concealed by two large elms, and who might have been observing me for some time. I scarcely dared encourage the flattering idea. It made me wild; and yet, why should such a noble, fashionable-looking man have pulled up his horse between two trees, where there was nothing else to be seen?

After all, I was only encouraging the most absurd vanity, contrary to common sense. Might he not be watching his dog? Did he ever look at me? I know not! After passing days and days in looking for him, his sudden appearance caused such a tremulousness to come over me, that I wanted courage once to raise my eyes to his face; so that I rather felt than knew I was near him, whom now I passed as quickly as my extreme agitation would permit, and soon came up with the old woman, and presenting the half-crown, and my card, desired her to call and see me.

The poor old nervous creature shed tears of gratitude, called me a dear, sweet, young lady, assured me that she had kept a respectable inn, for thirty years, at Glasgow, which, from her language, I was inclined to believe, and then took her leave.

I now ventured to turn my head back, believing myself at a safe distance from the stranger. He had quitted his hiding-place, and was slowly walking his very fine horse towards me. There he is, thought I. No one is near us, and yet, in another minute or two, he will have passed me, and be, perhaps, lost to me for ever. I began to muster all the energies of my character, generally fertile in resources, to consider of a remedy for this coming evil. If any man could be bribed to follow him slyly! thought I, hastily looking about me. The stranger drew nearer. Alas! he will have passed me for ever, perhaps, in another instant. Surely I might have said, with King Richard, "A horse, a horse! my kingdom for a horse!" since, without one, who could follow the stranger? I heard the sound of his horse's feet close behind me. I will fix my eyes upon his face, this time, to ascertain if he looks at me, said I to myself with a sudden effort of desperate resolution; which I put in practice the next moment. I thought our eyes met, and that the stranger blushed; but his were so immediately withdrawn from my face, that I went home, still in doubt whether he had, or had not, taken sufficient notice of me even to know me again by sight.

I related this adventure to Fanny, on my return. She gave me some dinner, and advised me, with friendly seriousness, not to make such a fool of myself, about a man I had never spoken to, and who, after all, might turn out to be vulgar, or ill-mannered, or of bad character.

"True," answered I, "and I shall be glad to learn that this man is either of those, for vulgarity will make me heart-whole again in an instant. In short, at any rate, I look for my cure in a future knowledge of this man's character. Nothing is perfect under the sun; and rank, talents, wit, beauty, character, manners, all must combine, in that human being who shall make me die of a broken heart. Therefore I am safe."

"I had not an idea that you were such a simpleton, or half so sentimental," retorted Fanny. "I wonder if I should admire the man !"

"We will try and meet him together," I replied; "but enough of a subject, which begins to make me melancholy, as though he were my fate ! How many fine, elegant-looking young men have I not met about the streets, and at the opera, without their making the slightest impression on me. And what do I know of this man, beyond mere beauty of countenance ? yet I think if I could but touch, with my hand, the horse he rode, or the dog he seems so fond of, I should be half wild with joy."

"What incredible nonsense, my dear Harriette," said Fanny.

"But true, upon my word," I replied, "and I cannot help myself."

Fanny shook her head at me, and I left her, to dream of the stranger.

By a little before eight on the following evening, the party, I have before mentioned, all sat down to dinner, at Lord Lowther's in Pall Mall. Lord Yarmouth was at the bottom of the table, opposite to Lord Lowther; Amy, on Lowther's right hand, Fanny at his left: Street, the editor, was her neighbour; and I sat next to Croker. Poor Julia had not been invited. Lord Hertford, who, at his own table, is always particularly entertaining, was a little out of sorts here, which generally happened to him when he dined with Lowther, who gave a very bad dinner.

Lord Hertford very candidly owns that he dislikes a bad dinner; and I had heard him own it so often to Lord Lowther, that I was surprised His Lordship invited him at all, unless he had thought proper to have provided a good one.

The claret, Lowther said, he wanted Lord Hertford's opinion about, having just provided himself with a large quantity of it, in consequence of its quality having been strongly recommended to him.

Our first glass had scarcely gone round, when Lord Hertford said, in his usual loud, odd voice, addressing Lowther, "You asked me for my opinion, and I will give it you; your claret is not worth a d——n."

Poor Lowther looked a little annoyed.

Croker fought on his side. "I must differ in opinion with you, Lord Hertford," said he in his starched pragmatical manner; "I think the claret excellent."

"With all my heart," said Hertford, in a tone and manner of the most perfect indifference.

Mr. Graham sat on my left hand, and was as attentive to me as possible. Graham was a beauty; a very Apollo in form, with handsome features, particularly his teeth and eyes; sensible, too, and well educated.

"I brought you two together, because I knew you would fall in love with each other," said Lowther.

How impossible, thought I, as the stranger in Hyde Park, as I last saw him, or fancied I saw him blush, crossed my mind. I was not disposed to admire anything else, indeed; but I rather think Graham was pedantic.

He spoke to me, a good deal, of Fred Lamb, with whom he had been travelling on the Continent.

"Fred Lamb has often been jealous of me," said Graham; "but he would be jealous of any man; yet I have always liked Fred, much better than ever he liked me."

"His passion for women is so very violent," I observed, "that somehow or other it disgusted me."

"All ladies are not so refined," replied Graham, laughing.

"Perhaps not," answered I; "perhaps I may not be so refined, when I like my man better."

Street was, all this time, making hard love to Fanny. Poor Street, though a very pleasant man, is, as he knows, a very ugly one. Fanny's extreme good nature was always a Refuge for the Destitute. If ever there was a lame, a deaf, a blind, or an ugly man in our society, Fanny invariably made up to that man immediately, to put him in countenance. Nay, she would, I believe, have made up to the Duke of Devonshire, blind, deaf, absent and all, had he fallen in her way.

I now grew tired of waiting for Amy to make a first move, and began to think she was ill disposed, in the humility of her heart, to take upon her the privilege of eldest sister; so I made it for her, and we retired to Lowther's drawing-room, from which we took a peep into his dressing-room, where we found a set of vile, dirty combs, brushes, towels and dressing-gowns. Lowther, who always has a pain in his liver, and knows not how to take kindly to his bottle, entered his apartment, just as we were loudest in our exclamations of horror and dismay, as these said dirty objects offered themselves to our view.

"For heaven's sake," said Amy, with whom Lowther was certainly in love, "do turn away your valet, and burn these nasty dirty brushes and things."

"It will be no use, I believe," replied Lowther; "for every valet will copy his master."

"What! then," exclaimed Amy, "you admit the master is dirty?"

Lowther feared he must plead guilty.

"I am glad I ran away from you," retorted Amy, who had gone with him into the country, and afterwards cut him because he did not ask for a separate dressing-room at the inns on the road.

The other gentlemen soon joined us in the drawing-room, drank their coffee, and then we were all off to the opera.

I had the honour of taking Mr. Graham there in my carriage, with Fanny. Amy went with Lord Lowther.

We found Julia in our private box, alone, and half asleep, dressed very elegantly; and, in my opinion, looking very interesting and well.

"What, alone?" said I. "Why do not you make the men more civil?" and I introduced her to that most fresh and juicy-looking large beauty, young Graham.

Julia had lately got nearly to the bottom of her heroics with Cotton. She was ashamed to admit the idea, even to herself; she never would own it to me: but the fact was, she was tired of Cotton, and dying, and sighing, and longing secretly for something new. Young and beautiful, her passions, like those of a man, were violent and changeable; in addition to which, she had lately suffered every possible indignity and inconvenience which debts and duns could inflict; besides, Fanny and I, who knew that Mr. Cotton had a wife and large family at home, had laboured with all our hearts to disgust Julia with Cotton, believing that it would be for the good of both that they separated for ever. Cotton had not a shilling to spare for the support of Julia's children; and Julia's *accouchements* took place regularly once in eleven months. She had often vainly applied to her parents, as well as to her uncle, Lord Carysfort, who only wrote to load her with reproaches.

As soon as Graham had left us, Julia expressed her admiration of him in very warm terms.

"He has no money," said Fanny; "besides, I can see that he is making up to Harriette. Do, my dear Julia, consider all your beautiful children; and, if you can leave Cotton to his poor wife, and must form another connection, let it be with someone who can contribute to the support of your young family."

Julia assured us she was, at that moment, actually in expectation of being arrested; and she entreated that Fanny or I would make an application to some of her noble relations, which she promised to do.

This point being decided, she again talked of Graham's beauty, wondered where he was, and anxiously inquired whether I was sure that he had taken a fancy for me?

"Not a bit sure," I replied. "I know nothing at all of the matter, neither do I care."

Fanny then related all about my last meeting with my stranger and his dog, to Julia, who seemed to understand my sensations much better than Fanny did.

"Oh, *mon Dieu!*" interrupted I, "there is, in that box next to Lady Foley's, a man—no, it is still handsomer than my stranger! and yet—(the stranger turned his head towards our side of the house)—Oh!" continued I, taking hold of Fanny's hand in a fit of rapture, "it is he! only his hat, till now, concealed that beautiful head of hair."

"Where? Where?" cried out they both at once.

"Oh! that someone would come into our box, now, and tell us who he is!" I exclaimed.

"How provoking you are," said Julia. "Why do not you point out the man to us?"

"It is that man who is laughing. Oh! I had no idea that his teeth were so very beautiful!"

"Dear me, how tiresome," observed Fanny, quietly. "If you will not tell us which is your man, let us talk of something else."

"He is there," replied I, "next to Lady Foley's box, leaning on his arm."

Julia put her glass to her eye, as usual; being remarkably shortsighted, she could distinguish nothing without it.

"I know him," said Julia, after gazing on him for some time.

"Not much?" I observed, almost breathless. "Did you ever speak to him?"

"I have met him in society, when I was a girl," continued Julia; "but I was intimate with a girl to whom, when young, he proposed. Her wedding clothes were made; she used to sleep in my room, with his picture round her neck. She adored him beyond all that could be imagined of love and devotion, and, within a few days of their proposed marriage, he declared off. His excuse was that his father refused his consent.

"For many years," continued Julia, "my friend's sufferings were severe; her parents trembled for her reason. No one was permitted to name her former lover in her presence. She is now Lady Conyngham."

"And his name?" said I.

"Lord Ponsonby, who is supposed to be the handsomest man in England: but he must now be forty, if not more," replied Julia.

"I wish he were sixty," I answered. "As it is, I have no chance: but, indeed, I never thought I had. He is a sort of man I think I could be wicked enough to say my prayers to. I could live in his happiness only, without his knowing me. I could wait for hours near his house, for the chance of seeing him pass, or hearing his voice."

Fanny laughed outright.

Julia only exclaimed, "Well done, Harriette! You are more romantic than ever I was at your age, and I thought that was impossible."

"You did not love Lord Ponsonby," retorted I.

"True," said Julia; "badinage apart, Ponsonby is, as I have always been told, very near perfection. But what chance can you have? He is married to the loveliest creature on earth—the youngest daughter of Lord Jersey."

"I knew very well," sighed I, despondingly, "before I heard of his marriage, that I should never be anything to him."

"I will tell you where he lives," said Julia. "It is in Curzon Street, Mayfair."

"Well then," thought I, "at least when he passes me I shall not, as yesterday, fancy I am looking at him for the last time."

Upon the whole, my spirits were violently elated this evening. Lord Ponsonby, I believe, did not perceive me. I was most anxious, yet afraid to see his wife.

"I cannot find her box," observed Julia, "else I should know her immediately."

We now lost sight of His Lordship for some time, he having left the box I first saw him in. I perceived him, for an instant, afterwards, but missed him altogether before the opera was over.

"I am glad I have not seen his wife," said I, after we were seated in the carriage. "I hope I shall never see her as long as I live."

I resolved, now, to make no kind of advances to become acquainted with Lord Ponsonby; but, on the very next evening, I indulged myself in passing his house at least fifty times. I saw and examined the countenances of his footmen, and the colour of his window-curtains: even the knocker of his door escaped not my veneration, since Lord Ponsonby must have touched it so often. My very nature seemed now to have undergone a change. I began to dislike society, and considered the unfortunate situation I had fallen into, with horror, because I fancied Lord Ponsonby would despise me. I often reflected whether there might yet be some mighty virtue in my power, some sacrifice of self, some exertion of energy, by which I might, one day, deserve to be respected, or to have my memory respected by Lord Ponsonby after I was dead.

The fact is, I really now lived but in his sight, and I only met him once or twice in a week, to see him pass me without notice. At last I began to believe he really did see me in the park, with pleasure, when, by any accident, late in the evening, I happened to be alone, and the park empty. Once he rode behind me, to my very door, and passed it, without seeming to look at me: the dread of being by him accused of boldness, ever prevented my observation.

This day, on entering my house, I mounted hastily up into my garret, and got out upon the leads, there to watch if Lord Ponsonby turned back, or whether he had merely followed me by accident, on his way somewhere else. He rode on, almost as far as I could see, and then turned back again, and galloped hastily by my door, as though afraid of being observed by me.

Suppose he were to love me! thought I, and the idea caused my heart to beat wildly. I would not dwell upon it. It was ridiculous. It would only expose me to after-disappointment. What was I, that Lord Ponsonby should think about me? What could I ever be to him? Still there was no reason, which I could discover, why I might not love Lord Ponsonby. I was made for love, and looked for no return. I should have liked him to have been assured that for the rest of his life mine was devoted to him. In short, though I scarcely ventured to admit it, hope did begin to predominate. I was young, and my wishes had, hitherto, rarely been suppressed by disappointment.

My reflections were interrupted by my servant, who brought me a letter from George Brummell, full of nonsensical vows and professions. "When," he wrote, "beautiful Harriette, will you admit me into your house? Why so obstinately refuse my visits? Tell me, I do entreat you when I may but throw myself at your feet, without fear of derision from a public homage on the pavement, or dislocation from the passing hackney-coaches!" The rest I have forgotten.

Wellington called on me the next morning before I had finished my breakfast. I tried him on every subject I could muster. On all, he was most impenetrably taciturn. At last he started an original idea of his own; actual copyright, as Stockdale would call it.

"I wonder you do not get married, Harriette!"

(By the by, ignorant people are always wondering.)

"Why so?"

Wellington, however, gives no reason for anything unconnected with fighting, at least since the convention of Cintra; and he, therefore, again became silent. Another burst of attic sentiment blazed forth.

"I was thinking of you last night, after I got into bed," resumed Wellington.

"How very polite to the Duchess," I observed. "*Apropos* to marriage, Duke, how do you like it?"

Wellington, who seems to make a point of never answering one, continued, "I was thinking—I was thinking that you will get into some scrape, when I go to Spain."

"Nothing so serious as marriage neither, I hope!"

"I must come again tomorrow, to give you a little advice," continued Wellington.

"Oh, let us have it all out now, and have done with it."

"I cannot," said Wellington, putting on his gloves and taking a hasty leave of me.

I am glad he is off, thought I, for this is indeed very uphill work. This is worse than Lord Craven.

As soon as he was gone, I hastened to Curzon Street. The window-shutters of Lord Ponsonby's house were all closed. How disappointed and low-spirited I felt at the idea that His Lordship had left town! Suspense was insufferable; so I ventured to send my servant to inquire when the family were expected in London.

In about a month, was the answer. I must forget this man, thought I, it is far too great a bore; and yet I felt that to forget him was impossible.

Things went on in the same way, for a week or two. Amy had closed with Mr. Sydenham's proposal, and changed her name to that of Mrs. Sydenham. She called on Fanny, one morning, when her drawing-room was half full of beaux.

"Beautiful Amy, how do you do?" said Nugent, with that eternal smile of his! It is so vulgar to be always looking joyful and full of glee, I cannot think what he can mean by it.

"Oh," said Amy, withdrawing her hand, "I must never flirt, nor have any beaux again."

"A-a-my! A-a-my! will that feel nice?" said I, in humble imitation of Mr. Hart Davis, M.P.

"I must now lead a pure, virtuous, chaste, and proper life," proceeded Amy.

"Who has laid such an appalling embargo on you?" I asked.

"Why, do not you know that Sydenham and I are become man and wife and that I have changed my name and my home for his?"

"Alas, poor Beckendorff!" I ejaculated.

After wishing Mrs. Sydenham joy, I took my leave. On reaching home, I found young Freeling in my drawing-room, waiting to pay his respects to me.

I began to think I had scarcely done this young man justice, he appeared so very humble, quiet, and amiable. He blushed exceedingly when I addressed him, but—never mind the vanity—it proceeded more from a sort of respectful growing passion towards me, than as I had at first imagined, from *mauvaise honte*.

Freeling was not fashionable, as I have said before; but I must add, that I believe even his enemy could say nothing worse of him.

"I will not deceive you," said I to him one day, seeing he was inclined to follow the thing up steadily, under the impression, perhaps, that faint heart never won fair lady. "Some women would make use of your attentions, your money, and your private boxes, as long as possible. I shall receive you with pleasure, as a friend, at any time; but if you were to sit down and sigh for a twelvemonth, you would never get any further. No speeches now! You are an interesting young man, whom thousands of amiable women would like, and life is short. *L'amour ne se commande pas*, perhaps you are going to tell me; and my answer is, that I am sure it cannot long survive hope, and for you, indeed, there is none."

Freeling blushed and looked melancholy and undecided.

"Shake hands and forgive me," said I.

"There now, I see it is over already," I continued, and changed the subject, which Freeling had the good sense and good taste never to renew; and what is more, the good heart to take an opportunity of doing me a very essential service, some months afterwards, when I believed he had forgotten me altogether.

Some short time after this the Duke of Wellington, who, I presume, had discovered the tough qualities of his heart, which contributed to obtain him such renown in the field of battle, possessed no more merit for home service, or ladies' uses, than did his good digestion, betook himself again to the wars. He called to take a hasty leave of me, a few hours before his departure.

"I am off for Spain directly," said Wellington.

I know not how it was, but I grew melancholy. Wellington had relieved me from many duns, which else had given me vast uneasiness. I saw him there, perhaps for the last time in my life. Ponsonby was nothing to me, and out of town; in fact, I had been in bad spirits all the morning, and strange, but very true, and he remembers it still, when I was about to say, God bless you, Wellington! I burst into tears. They appeared to afford rather an unusual unction to his soul, and his astonishment seemed to me not quite unmixed with gratitude.

"If you change your home," said Wellington, kissing my cheek, "let me find your address at Thomas's Hotel, as soon as I come to England; and, if you want anything in the meantime, write to Spain; and do not cry; and take care of yourself; and do not cut me when I come back.

"Do you hear?" said Wellington, first wiping away some of my tears with my handkerchief; and then, kissing my eyes, he said, "God bless you!" and hurried away.

Argyle continued to correspond with me; but, if one might judge from the altered style of his letters, Wellington had made a breach in His Grace's late romantic sentiments in my favour. Breach-making was Wellington's trade, you know: and little as men of Argyle's nation might be expected to care about breaches, yet, the idea of Wellington often made me sigh; and sometimes he whistled; which, with Argyle, was just the same thing.

I forgot to mention that, on the day after I met a certain great man, at Julia's house, my servant informed me a gentleman in the parlour desired to speak to me.

"Why do not you bring his name?" said I.

"The gentleman says, it does not signify," was my footman's answer.

"Go and tell him that I think it does signify; and that I will not receive people who are ashamed either of me, or themselves."

The man hesitated.

"Stay," said I, "I will put it down for you," and I wrote what I had said on a bit of paper.

My servant brought me back the paper, on the blank side of which was written, with a pencil, one word.

I sent it down again, with these words written underneath the word, on purpose to put him in a passion: *Don't know anybody in that shire.*

The servant returned once more, with one of His Lordship's printed cards, assuring me the gentleman in the parlour was walking about in a great passion.

I desired him to be showed upstairs, and, when he entered, I stood up, as though waiting to hear why he intruded on me.

"I believe, Madam," said His Lordship, "some apology is due to you, from me."

"Are you going to tell me that you were tipsy, when you last did me the favour to mistake my house for an inn, or something worse?"

"No! certainly not," answered the peer.

I

"Were you quite sober?"

"Perfectly."

"Then your late conduct admits of no apology, and you could offer none which would not humble and greatly wound my pride, to avoid which, I must take the liberty of wishing you a good morning."

I then rang my bell and left him.

CHAPTER 4

MORE THAN A month had now elapsed since Lord Ponsonby left London, and I perceived no signs of his return. Yet I never forgot him, although half the fine young men in town were trying to please me.

Amy continued to give her parties; but soberly: that is to say, Sydenham insisted on having his house quiet before three in the morning. One evening, when Fanny and Julia dined with me, I got up from my table to open my window, and I saw Lord Ponsonby, who was slowly riding by my house, with his face turned towards my window. This time there could be no doubt as to his blushing. My happiness was now of a nature too pure to be trifled with, and I knew I could not endure to have it intruded on by any commonplace remarks. I kept his appearance, therefore, a profound secret; although I found it the most difficult thing possible, to talk on any other subject. I thought these women never would have left me. They took their leave, however, at last; but not till near twelve o'clock.

I could not sleep a wink all night! At nine the next morning I rang my bell, being quite worn out with attempting it. My maid entered my room, with a letter which had just arrived by the twopenny-post. It was as follows:

I have long been very desirous to make your acquaintance: will you let me? A friend of mine has told me something about you; but I am afraid you were then only laughing at me; "et il se peut, qu'un homme passe, ne sait bon que pour cela!" I hope, at all events, that you will write me one line, to say you forgive me, and direct it to my house in town.

P.

I will not attempt to describe all I felt, on the receipt of this first epistle from Lord Ponsonby. I am now astonished at that infatuation, which could render a girl, like me, possessed, certainly, of a very feeling, affectionate heart, thus thoughtless, and careless of the fate of another: and that other a young, innocent and lovely wife! Had anybody reminded me that I was now about to inflict, perhaps, the deepest wound in the breast of an innocent wife, I hope and believe I should have stopped there; and then what pain and bitter anguish I had been spared: but I declare to my reader, that Lady Fanny Ponsonby never once entered my head.

I had seen little or nothing of the world, I never possessed a really wise friend, to set me right, advise or admonish me. My mother had ever seemed happiest in my father's absence, nor did she vex or trouble herself to watch his steps; and I did not know, or at all events, I did not think, my making Lord Ponsonby's acquaintance would be likely to injure any one of my fellow-creatures; or I am sure such a reflection must have embittered that pure state of happiness I now enjoyed.

This was my answer to Lord Ponsonby's letter:

For the last five months, I have scarcely lived but in your sight, and everything I have done or wished, or hoped, or thought about, has had a reference to you and your happiness. Now tell me what you wish.

HARRIETTE.

Reply:
I fancy, though we never met, that you and I are, in fact, acquainted, and understand each other perfectly. If I do not affect to disbelieve you, you will not say I am vain; and, when I tell you that we cannot meet immediately, owing to a very severe domestic calamity, you will not say I am cold. In the meantime will you write to me? The little watch I have got for you, I am not quite satisfied with. I have seen one in better taste, and flatter. But my poor father is dying, and counts the minutes of my absence, or I could have found one to please you. However, you will keep this for my sake. I will leave it myself at your house this evening. I can scarcely describe to you how exhausted I am; for I have passed the whole of the three last nights, by the bedside of my sick father, without rest. I know he will have your prayers. At midnight, let us pray for him together. He has been suffering more than five months. Adieu, dear Harriette.

Lord Ponsonby's solitary rides, with his dog, his paleness, and that melancholy expression of countenance, which at once interested me so deeply, were now accounted for. During three weeks more, we corresponded daily. His father continued to exist, and that was all. I learned from His Lordship's letters, that, on the night we saw him for a few moments at the opera, his father was pronounced out of danger, and country air was recommended to him, which, having produced no favourable change, nothing now could save him. My happiness, while that correspondence went on, was the purest, the most exalted, and the least allied to sensuality, of any I ever experienced in my life. Ponsonby, I conceived, was now mine, by right; mine by that firm courage which made me feel ready to endure any imaginable evil for his sake. I was morally certain that nothing in existence could love Lord Ponsonby, or could feel the might and majesty of his peculiarly intellectual beauty, as I did.

My beloved, so he wrote to me at last, *my spirits and health fail me; they are worn out and exhausted with this close confinement. My poor father no longer suffers, or is scarcely sensible. My brother George will take my place by his bedside. Let us meet this evening, and you will console me. I shall go to you at nine.*

Lord Ponsonby was then coming to me at last! I began to fear the expression of his eyes, so penetrating, so very bright, I began to think myself under the influence of a dream, and that he was not coming; then I feared sudden death would deprive me of him. I heard the knock, and his footsteps, on the stairs; and then that most godlike head uncovered, that countenance so pale, so still, and so expressive, the mouth of such perfect loveliness; the fine clear, transparent, dark skin. I looked earnestly in his face, I watched for that characteristic blush which made me fancy his body thought, to be certain of my own happiness! and then my overflowing heart was relieved by a flood of tears.

"My dear, dear little Harriette," said Ponsonby, drawing me towards him, and passing his arm softly round my waist, "let us be happy now we are met." My smile must have been expressive of the most heartfelt felicity; yet our happiness was of that tranquil nature, which is nearer allied to melancholy than to mirth. We conversed together all night, with my head resting on his breast. An age could not have made us better acquainted! Ponsonby's health and spirits were, evidently, quite exhausted by anxiety and want of rest. Neither of us desired anything, while thus calmly engaged in conversation. Yes, perhaps I did, as my eyes were fixed, for hours, on his beautiful and magnificent countenance, feel my own lips almost tremble, as I thought they would be pressed to his, and Ponsonby seemed to understand and feel my wishes, for he said, in answer to nothing but the expression of my eyes:

"No, not tonight! I could not bear your kiss tonight. We will dream about it till tomorrow."

Ponsonby assured me, in the course of our *tête-à-tête*, that the first time he had seen me, was one day when I lived at Somerstown, two years before. For three or four days after that, he could think of nothing else. He met me with Argyle again, and wished to forget me; "but," added he, "I, being the shyest poor wretch in the world, have ever held anything like notoriety in the greatest dread. I abhor it! therefore, when you came out at the opera, and I heard all the fine young men talking about you, it was not so difficult to forget you; and yet, though you did not see me, I was always looking at you, and trying to hear someone talk about you. When we met, latterly, in the park, there was something so natural and unaffected, and wild, about your manner, that I began to forget your notoriety."

Ponsonby then told me all about the poor old woman to whom I had given half a crown in the park; but what he said on that head was far too flattering for me to repeat. It was past five in the morning when we separated.

"You are so ill and fatigued," said I, "dear Ponsonby, that I will not let you come to me tomorrow night."

"Oh, but I must!" answered Ponsonby.

"Indeed you must rest."

"Impossible!" he replied.

We made no professions of love to each other—not one; for we were as certain, as of our existence, that we were mutually adored; and yet we passed the night together, and parted, without a kiss, to meet early the following evening.

Heavy work, ma'am, all this love and stuff, says my fair reader of sixty, taking off her spectacles—for we are always fair—and my young reader does not like playing second fiddle, which is my own reason for hating novels.

Examinez votre propre cœur, et vous pouvez, en quelque sorte, connâitre les hommes, says Voltaire, or La Bruyère, or somebody else.

Well, ladies, I wanted to leave out this love of mine, altogether, and had done so, but that my editor insisted on the love, above all things. Nevertheless I will make shorter of our second night.

I have one advantage over other bad female writers and prosing ladies, which is, that I do not think myself agreeable. Now there are many ladies, virtuous ladies too, to whom it is my duty and my wish to look up, who really are enough to kill one, in that way; and, though out of the high veneration in which I hold virtue, *à la distance*, I have never in my whole life presumed to intrude my unworthy society on any one immaculate female, yet it is astonishing what a knack they have always had, of intruding themselves upon me. I remember I had the whole family of the Pitchers on my back at once, whether I would or not, some time ago, when I went down to study Voltaire, and Roman history, by myself, for a week or two at Salt Hill; nor could I, in any way, get rid of their pressing invitations to visit them in town, without the humiliating confession of all my sins! It surely was disagreeable, and hardly fair, that such errors should be extorted from a person like me, who has ever had plenty of people to abuse her, without abusing herself.

I hit upon a new plan for getting rid of Mrs. Nesbit, a certain widow lady, now living with her family at Versailles, a relation, I believe, of Lord Bathurst. I will tell you all about it. My being thrown into her honourable society was a mere accident, and I was well disposed to keep my distance, and talk only to the male part of our company. Mrs. Nesbit not only put herself forward, and took an active part in our conversation, but she called me, My dear, took me aside, and declared that she had taken a great fancy to me; hoped we should meet in town; detailed to me all the beauties of her young family; and further, to prove her unreserved friendship, took me out of the society of some very pleasant young men, into a cold, dirty bedroom, where she acquainted me with an affliction which had befallen that part of her person, which made it impossible for her to sit down without torture. I was very sorry, and duly condoled with her, of course; but I never saw the lady in my life before, and, if I had, how could I help her tremendous boils, or their very critical situation! I expressed my unfeigned surprise at her temerity in having ventured out in her present misery, instead of reclining on her sofa at home, and concluded with strongly recommending her recurrence to the horizontal position.

"Oh, my dear," said Mrs. Nesbit, "it is absolutely shocking! I have brought you up here on purpose to show it you."

I began to declare off altogether, earnestly remarking that, really, since my examining the part affected could do it no manner of good, I saw no necessity for so ungainly an exhibition.

"Oh, my love, I have taken a great liking to you," rejoined Mrs. Nesbit, "and therefore, I particularly wish you to see it"—suiting the action to the word.

It was just before our dinner, and I lost not a moment to declare myself satisfied with the unctuous and glowing spectacle.

"It is very bad, indeed, Madam; had you not better cover it up?"

But she insisted on my luxuriating in the fullest view!

I am not modest, as this woman is, thought I, according to the world's acceptation of that word, and yet I could not, I am sure, do this, even with my own sister!

We soon returned to the dining-room, where I set my wits to work, how best and soonest to destroy Mrs. Nesbit's so rapidly-matured friendship for me.

At dinner she talked politics: I suppose because she was past forty, and virtuous, and related to a noble politician.

What shall I do to disgust her? thought I; for we were a large party, travelling on the Continent together; and I saw myself, what is vulgarly called, in for it.

I listened to her conversation, eagerly attending to her antipathies, in order that I might practise some of them upon her directly, as if by mere accident. At last I got her from politics, to lecture on decorum. She mentioned her friend, Lady Emily Stuart, the English ambassador's wife at Paris. She had been under the necessity of refusing that lady's invitation to see masks at the carnival; because Lady Aldborough was invited.

"I told my Lady Emily, frankly," continued Mrs. Nesbit, "that as a mother, and one who, I thanked God, had hitherto contrived to escape censure—(Mrs. Nesbit must have been, even in her youth, extremely plain)—by the strictest adherence to propriety, even in its slightest forms."

This was a temptation too great for me to contend with.

"What could it signify," observed I, carelessly, delighted at the prospect of getting off so much easier than with the warm-hearted, friendly Pitchers.

"Signify!" reiterated Mrs. Nesbit, with astonishment.

"Aye," said I, yawning; "point me out anyone, man or woman, to whom all this could possibly signify a straw!"

"I do not understand you, Madam!" said Mrs. Nesbit.

"Why, who cared?" said I, impatiently.

"Who cared!!!" echoed she.

"Yes, who cared," repeated I. "Can you bring forward one person, in the whole wide world, who did care, does care, or will ever care hereafter, how many forms you missed, and how many you observed? For my part," I added, seeing Mrs. Nesbit's eyes distended, and mouth wide open, in astonishment, and, resolving to make short work of it, to avoid the favour of a second exhibition, which I could ill have endured immediately after my dinner—so taking my little fur travelling-cap off my head, and twisting it into the form and appearance of a hare, in presence of all the party, for which, I dare say, my reader will think that I ought to have been excommunicated, and in which act I did blush, but only consider the emergency!—"For my part, I hate forms of all sorts, and most particularly the form of this cap." Then, putting it on a clean plate, after I had really made it look like a hare, I asked the waiter, in French, if he had any currant jelly?

"I must leave the table," cried Mrs. Nesbit, reddening. "For shame!!" and, seizing my poor cap, she threw it wrathfully to the other end of a dirty, sandy French room.

I was now in an unfeigned passion myself. Since it was a public table, I thought the virtuous Mrs. Nesbit had no excuse for throwing my new cap into the sand. The handsome young man on the other side, whom she had been lecturing into a fever, jumped up, and, after wiping off the sand, presented me my cap, laughing, but respectfully saying he hoped it was not dirtied.

I am not the meekest creature on earth, nor quite as easily lead, as my sister, Lady Berwick, so I carefully again made a hare of my cap, which I once more replaced in the plate, while everybody was laughing, saying: "Take care of your Indian shawl, Mrs. Nesbit, the next time you meddle with my new cap, unless you are fond of French expectorations and French sand."

"I must leave the table then!" said Mrs. Nesbit, with a countenance of dreadfully gathering rage.

"I have just been recommending a more horizontal position to you, Madam, *et pour cause, vous savez*," and then added, in her ear, although there was not a person at table who understood a word of English (it was at Amiens), "I am puzzled to guess, with such a nice sense of propriety and love of decorum, how you came to show me, an utter stranger, your bum-fiddle!"

"This," said Mrs. Nesbit, rising to leave the room, with as dignified and reserved an air as if she had done no such thing, "this shall be a lesson to me against forming hasty friendships."

"Or showing your bum-fiddle," I added, laughing, which remark did not in the least alter, or affect her majestic, and truly dramatic, manner of making her exit from the room.

SECOND NIGHT'S ENTERTAINMENT:

Not Arabian, but Irish, and that is better. At nine o'clock on the following evening, Ponsonby entered the room, an altered man. He was one of the very few persons I have met with in my life, who, from the natural, extreme reserve and shyness of their disposition, absolutely required to be a very little tipsy, before they can give their brilliant imaginations fair play. Ponsonby had slept, drank a little more claret, and what, lately had been unusual to him, owing to his father's lingering illness, had put on an evening dress. He appeared now so much more beautiful than I had ever imagined any mortal mixture of earth's clay, that I began to lose my confidence in myself, and tremble. There was, too, a look of success about him, for indeed the humblest man on earth must have borrowed courage from the reflection of Ponsonby's looking glass on that evening: and there he sat, for half an hour, laughing, and showing his brilliant teeth, while he related to me many witty things, which had been said by his uncle whom he had just left—the George Ponsonby, now no more, who spoke so well on the opposition side.

Can one endure this any longer, thought I. I was getting into a fever. Perhaps he does not love me.

"You are so proud of being dressed tonight!" I remarked with some drollery, and I thought he never would have ceased laughing at me.

It was very tiresome.

"The fact is," said Ponsonby, in his sweet voice, the beauteous tones of which nobody ever did or will dispute, "the fact is, I really am proud of it; for I have not worn shoes before, for these last three months; but," added he, "do you know what I am most proud of in the world, and which, poor as I am, upon my honour, I would not exchange at this moment, for a hundred thousand dollars?"

"No!——"

"I will tell you—my place in your heart, and your arms, this evening." He put his arms round my waist, and my lips were nearly touching his. Ponsonby's cheek was now tinged with the glowing blush of passion; yet he turned from my kiss, like a spoiled child.

"No!" said Ponsonby, shaking his head, "I have a thousand things to tell you."

"I cannot listen to one of them," said I, faintly, and our lips met in one long, long delicious kiss! so sweet, so ardent! that it seemed to draw the life's warm current from my youthful heart, to reanimate his with all its wildest passion.

And then!—yes, and then, as Sterne says—

And then—and then—and then—and then—and then we parted.

The next day, at past three o'clock, Fanny found me in bed.

"How abominably idle!" said Fanny.

I answered that I was not well.

"You do not look very bad," Fanny replied; "on the contrary, I have not seen you look so well, nor your eyes so bright, for some time."

"Well," said I, "if you really think me out of danger, I will get up."

"Come!" answered Fanny, "shall I ring for your maid? I want you to take me to Julia's."

While I was dressing, Fanny informed me that she had given up her own house, to go and live with Julia.

"I rather prefer living alone," she continued, "but Julia is so very dull, and my paying half her rent will also be of service to her."

"And some of your beaux may, perhaps, be brought to flirt with her, poor thing!" added I, "for really their neglect is very hard upon her." Much more beauty, it should seem, is required to please without virtue than with it, since it is said that Julia, at her mamma's, made conquests everywhere and every hour. Even the Regent himself once said he would travel a hundred miles to have the pleasure of seeing her dance.

Her dancing, we both agreed, was perfection: speaking of what was most truly graceful, effeminate and lady-like.

"Brummell has been with her, making strong love lately," said Fanny.

"Oh, the shocking deceiver! Tell Julia not to believe one word he says."

I inquired how Amy and Sydenham went on.

"Pretty well," answered Fanny. "Sydenham is not only a very good-natured, but a remarkably clever and well-bred man. Amy tries his patience too, a little, with his passion for books; she is always taking them out of his hand, and making him look at her attitudes before the glass, or her attempts at the shawl-dance."

"What does Sydenham do for the Marquis of Wellesley?" I asked.

"Everything, I believe," Fanny replied. "He appears to write all his letters and papers, in the shape of business; and so, I believe, he did in India; but I know that Wellesley does nothing except by his advice."

"Pray does Lord Wellesley make his love too, as well as his reputation, by proxy?"

"I do not know," answered Fanny, laughing, "although I believe he passed a good deal of his time, formerly, with the lady they call Mrs. Moll Raffles" (as Fanny designated her, in her zeal to be civil).

"I never saw anybody in such spirits as you today," Fanny remarked to me, when we got into the carriage. "I am afraid there is some mischief in the wind. What has become of Lord Ponsonby?"

I was too happy to talk about it, so I contrived to change the subject. "Where shall I take you to?" I inquired.

"To Julia's, where I am now settled. I went there yesterday," was Fanny's answer.

"This world is really made to be laughed at," said Fanny, suddenly leaning her head out of the carriage window.

"What is the matter?" I asked.

"That man," said Fanny, "with his grave face, and his large board hoisted up, standing there challenging the world, as if he were Don Quixote come to life again."

"What for?" said I.

"Bayley's Blacking. Can one conceive anything so absurd?"

I set her down, as desired, and begged her to make my excuse to Julia, who was at her window with Horace Beckford, the handsome nephew of Lord Rivers. He appeared inclined to pay her attention, if one might judge by the soft smile which was playing about his features: but then he was eternally smiling.

I found my very constant and steady admirer, Lord Frederick Bentinck, waiting for me, prepared, as usual, to give me a world of advice. He told me that I was going on in a very bad way, and asked me whither I expected to go.

"Where are you going to?" said I, as he walked into my dressing-room, and seemed to admire himself in my large glass.

"I am going to see the Duchess of York," said Fred Bentinck.

"What of that?" I returned. "Where are your gloves?"

"I never wear them, unless at court; but I have got on a new pair of leather breeches, today, and I want to see how they fit, by your glass."

Brummell at this moment was announced.

"How very *apropos* you are arrived," I remarked. "Lord Frederick wants your opinion of his new leather breeches."

"Come here, Fred Bentinck!" said Brummell. "But there is only one man on earth who can make leather breeches!"

"Mine were made by a man in the Haymarket," Bentinck observed, looking down at them with much pride; for he very seldom sported anything new.

"My dear fellow, take them off directly!" said Brummell.

"I beg I may hear of no such thing," said I, hastily—"else where would he go to, I wonder, without his small-clothes?"

"You will drive me out of the house, Harriette," said Fred Bentinck; and then putting himself into attitudes, looking anxiously and very

134

innocently from George Brummell to his leather breeches, and from his leather breeches to the looking-glass.

"They only came home this morning," proceeded Fred, "and I thought they were rather neat."

"Bad knees, my good fellow! bad knees!" said Brummell, shrugging up his shoulders.

"They will do very well," I remarked. "Fred Bentinck, do start a new subject, for first with my latter end, and then with your own, this is quite worn out."

Lord Ponsonby and myself met every evening, for more than a week. We were never tired of conversing with each other. His humour exactly suited mine. In short, though I have been called agreeable all my life, I am convinced that I was never half so pleasant or so witty as in Ponsonby's society. We seldom contrived to separate before five or six o'clock in the morning, and Ponsonby generally came to me as soon as it was dark. Nor did we always wait for the evening to see each other, though respect for Lady Ponsonby made us ever, by mutual consent, avoid all risk of wounding her feelings; therefore, almost every day after dinner, we met in the park, by appointment, not to speak, but only to look at each other.

One morning, being greatly struck with the beauty of a young lady who drove by me in a very elegant little carriage, while I was expecting to see Lord Ponsonby, I inquired of the gentleman who was walking with me, if he knew who she was? It was the man, well known in the fashionable world by the appellation of Poodle-Bing; the title of Poodle having been bestowed on him, owing to his very curly, white locks, in defence of which, he always declared that his head was the original from which all the young men and their barbers took base copies.

"It is," answered Poodle, "that most lovely creature, Lady Fanny Ponsonby, whom we are all sighing and dying for."

She was indeed very lovely, and did not appear to be more than eighteen. I considered her with respect and admiration, unmixed with jealousy. This was not the rose; but she had dwelled with it. I thought that she resembled Lord Ponsonby, and I felt that I could have loved her dearly. Thank heaven, thought I, this beautiful girl appears quite calm and happy; therefore I have done her no harm.

In the evening I was eager to praise her to her husband. "She possesses all the beauty of all the Jerseys," said I to him; "and what a pretty little foot!" This I had observed as she got out of her carriage in Curzon Street.

"How very odd!" Ponsonby remarked.

"What is odd?"

"Why, I do believe you like Fanny!"

"Be sure of it then," I answered. "I like her as much as I should dislike any woman who did not love you dearly. Listen to me, Ponsonby," I continued, taking his hand, and speaking with steady firmness. "All my religion is from my heart, and not from books. If ever our intimacy is discovered, so as not to disturb her peace of mind, on that day we must separate for ever. I can but die, and God, I hope, will have mercy on me, very soon after our separation, if ever it should be found necessary: but we are not monsters! therefore, we will never indulge in selfish enjoyments at the expense of misery to any one of our fellow-creatures, much less one who depends on you for all her happiness."

"And she is very happy, thank God," said Ponsonby, "and I would rather forfeit my life than destroy her peace."

"Be firm in that, I entreat you," I replied, "for there can be no rest, here nor hereafter, without the acquittal of our hearts. Mine was devoted to you with that sincere ardour and deep character of feeling which is so natural to me, before I knew that you were married. I know it now, too late to endure life when you shall have left me; but I can die when her happiness shall require it. Alas! I knew not half the anguish and suffering the human frame can endure, and yet survive!"

One night, about a week from the day Ponsonby first visited me, when I did not expect him till midnight, I retired to bed and fell fast asleep, which said long nap neither Ponsonby nor anyone else had disturbed. When I awoke, the sun was shining through my curtains. My first waking thoughts were always on Ponsonby, and I recollected, with a deep feeling of disappointment, that he had promised, the night before, to come to me by midnight, and I had desired my maid to send him up into my room as soon as he arrived. I felt for his little watch, which I always placed under my pillow; judge my astonishment, to find, attached to it, a magnificent gold chain of exquisite workmanship. I began to think myself in the land of fairies! and still more so, when I observed a very beautiful pearl ring on one of my fingers. I rubbed my eyes, and opened them wide, to ascertain, beyond a doubt, that I was broad awake. A very small strip of writing paper, which I had drawn from under my pillow, with my watch now caught my attention, and I read, written with a pencil, in Ponsonby's small, beautiful characters: *Dors, cher enfant, je t'aime trop tendrement pour t'éveiller.*

It was very sentimental and affectionate, for Ponsonby knew how much I required rest. I was very grateful, and yet I thought it altogether exceedingly provoking! How could I be so stupid as not to awake, even when he had his hand under my pillow, in search of my watch! I rang my bell, and inquired of my maid how long she thought Lord Ponsonby had stayed with me the night before?

More than an hour, was the reply.

"Dear Ponsonby," said I, as soon as she had quitted the room, while I bestowed a thousand eager kisses on the beautiful watch and chain, "you are the first man on earth, who ever sacrificed his own pleasure and passions to secure my repose!"

Lord Ponsonby's father still continued another fortnight, in the same hopeless state. His favourite son deeply lamented his illness, and had been indefatigable in his attentions, refusing to visit me, or anybody, as long as there was hope, or while his father could derive comfort from his son's affections; but when nothing more could be done, he had sought comfort in the society of the person who loved him best. I should do Lord Ponsonby great injustice, were I to say that he ever forgot or neglected his father.

I asked a friend of Lord Ponsonby's one day, why he did not adore his beautiful wife? He had no idea that I was acquainted with His Lordship.

"Lord Ponsonby is always very kind and affectionate to her," was the reply.

"True," I continued; "but I have heard that he does not fly to her for consolation when he is melancholy, nor consult her, nor make a friend of her."

"Lady Fanny is a sweet-tempered child," said he, "but not at all clever: and then, poor thing! she is very deaf, which affliction came on after a violent attack of scarlet fever."

"What a beautiful, sweet, and calm expression of countenance she possesses," I remarked, "so pale, that her features, at first sight, appear only pretty; but, on examination, they are found perfect; and her dark, clear, brown eyes——"

"So like your own," said the gentleman, interrupting me.

"I have heard that remark made before," I replied, blushing deeply; "but I am not vain enough to credit it."

"With all their beauty," remarked Ponsonby's friend, "men soon grow tired of those Jerseys, with the exception only of Lady——, with whom the wicked world say the Duke of Argyle has been in love more than twenty years."

"Is not the boy they call Frank supposed to be a son of the Duke?" I asked.

"I have heard so; but let us hope it is all vile scandal."

"With all my heart; but how does Lady Fanny Ponsonby pass her time?"

"She draws prettily"—he observed; "and she has now got a little companion she is very fond of."

"Who is that?" said I.

"A mouse! which having, one night, showed its little face to Her Ladyship, in her drawing-room, she so coaxed him with her dainties, for three weeks together, that she contrived to tame him; and now he will eat them out of her lovely hands."

"But then after the mouse is gone to bed," said I, "how does Her Ladyship amuse herself?"

"With her youngest sister, or in writing, or drawing. Lady Fanny does not much care for society."

"She is not a flirt, I believe?"

"What man can she think it worth while to flirt with," answered he, "being married to such a one as Ponsonby?"

I was charmed to hear my own sentiments from the lips of another, and one of his own sex too.

"You admire Lord Ponsonby then?" said I.

"Admire! depend upon it there is nothing like him in all Europe. I speak of him altogether, as to his beauty, his manners, and his talents; but Lord Ponsonby," he continued, "owing to his extreme reserve and his excessive shyness, is very little known. He never desires to be known or appreciated but by his own particular friends; yet I know few so capable of distinguishing themselves anywhere, particularly in the senate, as His Lordship: his remarkably fine voice, and his language, always so persuasive and eloquent; besides, he is such an excellent politican. He will now shortly, by the expected death of his father," continued the gentleman, whose name, if I recollect well, was Matthew Lee, "become one of the peers of the United Kingdom. I was telling him, the other day, how much we should be disappointed if he did not take a very active part in the debates.—'God forbid!' said Ponsonby. 'It is all I can do to find nerve for yes or no, when there is a question in the House, and that in a whisper.'"

"How came he to be so shy?" I asked.

"And how came it to become him so well?" returned his friend, "for it would make any other man awkward, and Ponsonby is most graceful when he is most embarrassed. I have known him from a boy. We were at school together. The ladies were all running mad for him before he was fifteen, and I really believe that, at eighteen, Ponsonby, with the true genuine Irish character, and warmest passions, had not looked any woman full in the face; and to this day, his friends are obliged to make him half tipsy in order to enjoy his society. Yet, with all this timidity," he went on (observing that I was never tired of the subject, and could pay attention to no other), "Ponsonby has a remarkably fine, high spirit. One night, very late, near Dublin, he met two of his brothers, just as they had got into a violent row, with three raw-boned, half-naked Irish pats.

"Seeing that his brothers were drunk, Ponsonby began to remonstrate with them, and strove to persuade them to come home quietly, when one of those ruffians struck his youngest brother a very unfair blow, with a stick.

"'Now, d——n your hearts and b——ds!' said Lord Ponsonby, stripping, and setting to with the strength and spirit of a prize-fighter.

"His own mother, at this moment, could not have known her son: the metamorphosis was nearly as laughable as it was astonishing."

I asked how long he had been married.

"Not five years."

"And Lady Fanny's age?"

"Twenty."

I then asked if he married her for love or money?

"Money!!" said Lee, indignantly. "It is now clear to me that you do not know Lord Ponsonby. I was just beginning to suspect, from the multiplicity of your questions, that you did."

"He was very much in love with her then?" I inquired, without attending to this observation.

"She was not fourteen," answered Lee, "when Ponsonby first met her, at her mother's, Lady Jersey's. He was, of course, like everybody else, speedily struck with her beauty. She was not deaf then, but, shortly afterwards, she had a violent attack of the scarlet fever, during which her life was despaired of for several weeks: indeed, there was scarcely a hope of her recovery. I remember Ponsonby said to me, one night, as we passed by Lady Jersey's house together—'The loveliest young creature I ever beheld on earth lies in that room, dying.' The first time Lady Fanny appeared in her mother's drawing-room, she resembled a spirit; so fair, so calm, so transparent. All her magnificent hair, which had before reached, and now again descends much below her waist, had been shorn from her beautiful little head. She often took her lace cap off, and exhibited herself thus to anybody, to raise a laugh; or perhaps she knew that she was, even without hair, as lovely as ever.

"Lord Ponsonby, as he had told me since, was present when Her Ladyship first left her room, and soon discovered that she was now afflicted with deafness. He felt the deepest interest, admiration and pity for her. He considered, with horror, the bare possibility of this sweet, fragile, little being, becoming the wife of some man who might, hereafter, treat her harshly. Added to this, I fancy," continued Lee, "Ponsonby had discovered that he was not indifferent to Her Little Ladyship; so, to secure her from any of these evils, he resolved to propose for her himself. I need not add, that he was joyfully accepted, by both mother and daughter. He might have done better," added Lee; "and, I fancy Ponsonby sometimes wishes that his wife could be his friend and companion; but that is quite out of the question. Her Ladyship is good, and will do as she is bid; but besides her deafness, her understanding is neither bright nor lively. Lord Ponsonby shows her the sort of indulgence and tenderness which a child requires; but he must seek for a companion elsewhere."

Mr. Lee then took leave of me; and a very few days after this conversation had taken place, Lord Ponsonby's father breathed his last, in the arms of his son, who immediately left town without seeing me; but he wrote to me most affectionately.

A few days after his departure, I was surprised by a visit from Sir William Abdy, with whom I was but very slightly acquainted. I thought it strange his paying any visits so immediately after the elopement of his wife, who was the natural daughter of the Marquis Wellesley, by a French woman who, as I am told, once used to walk in the Palais Royal, at Paris, but afterwards became Marchioness of Wellesley!

"I have called upon you, Miss Harriette," said Sir William, almost in tears; "in the first place, because you are considered exactly like my wife (my likeness to Lady Abdy had often been thought very striking), and in the second, because I know you are a woman of feeling! !"

I opened my eyes in astonishment.

"Women," he continued, "have feeling, and that's more than men have."

I could not conceive what he would be at.

"You know, Miss Harriette, all about what has happened, and my crim. con. business, don't you, Miss?"

"Yes."

"Could you have thought it?"

"Oh yes!"

"And yet, I am sure, Charles Bentinck is worse than I am."

"In what way, pray?"

"Why, a worse head," said Sir William, touching his forehead, "and I don't pretend to be clever myself."

"Is that all? But I would not be so very demonstrative as to touch my forehead, if I were you."

"That Charles Bentinck," said he, half angry, "is the greatest fool in the world; and in Paris we always used to laugh at him."

"But," said I, "why did you suffer His Lordship to be eternally at your house?"

"Why, dear me!" answered Abdy, peevishly, "I told him in a letter, I did not like it, and I thought it wrong; and he told me it was no such thing."

"And therefore," I remarked, "you suffered him to continue his visits as usual?"

"Why, good gracious, what could I do! Charles Bentinck told me, upon his honour, he meant nothing wrong."

This man is really too good! thought I, and then I affected the deepest commiseration of his mishap.

"Why did she run away from you?" said I. "Why not, at least, have carried on the thing quietly?"

"That's what I say," said Abdy.

"Because," I continued, "had she remained with you, Sir, you would have always looked forward with hope to that period when age and ugliness should destroy all her powers of making conquests."

"Oh," said Abdy, clasping his hands, "if any real friend, like you, had heartened me up in this way, at the time, I could have induced her to have returned to me! But then, Miss Wilson, they all said I should be laughed at, and frightened me to death. It was very silly to be sure, of me to mind them; for it is much better to be laughed at, than to be so dull and miserable, as I am now."

"Shall I make you a cup of tea, Sir William?"

"Oh! Miss, you are so good! tea is very refreshing, when one is in trouble."

I hastened to my bell, to conceal the strong inclination I felt to laugh in his face, and ordered tea.

"Green tea is best, is it not, Miss?" said Sir William.

"Oh, yes," answered I, "as green as a willow leaf: and, in extreme cases, like yours, I am apt to recommend a little gunpowder."

"Just as you please, Miss."

I asked him, after he had swallowed three cups of tea, whether he did not feel himself a little revived.

"Yes, Miss, I should soon get better here; but you know my house is such a very dull house, and in such a very dull street too! Hill Street is, I think, the dullest street in all London, do you know, Miss Wilson."

"True, Sir William! would not you like to go to Margate?"

"Why, I was thinking of travelling, for you know, in Hill Street, there is her sofa, just as she left."

"Very nervous indeed," said I, interrupting him. "I would burn the sofa, at all events."

"And then there is her pianoforte."

"Lady Abdy was musical then?"

"Oh, very. She was always at it! I used to be tired to death of her music, and often wished she would leave off: but now she is gone, Miss Wilson, I would give the world to hear her play Foote's minuet!"

"Or, *Off She Goes*," added I.

"What is that, pray, Miss?"

"A very lively dance," I answered.

"True, Miss, I recollect my wife used to play it."

"Dear me, Sir William, how could she be so foolish as to run away? I dare say you never interfered with her, or entered her room without knocking."

"Never, upon my honour."

"Well, I always heard you were a very kind, obliging, good-natured husband."

"Yes, and sometimes, when I used to knock latterly, Lady Abdy would not open the door!"

"That was wrong," said I, shaking my head, "very wrong."

"And how could that nasty, stupid fellow seduce her, I cannot think!"

"There was good blood in her veins, you know, by the mother's side. Besides, to tell you the truth, I don't think Charles Bentinck did seduce Lady Abdy from you."

"Oh! dear, Miss Wilson, what do you mean?"

"Shall I speak frankly?"

"Oh, Lord a mercy! pray do! I am quite in a fright!"

"I think Fred Lamb was one of her seducers; but how many more may have had a finger in the pie, I really cannot take upon myself to say."

"Oh, Lord! oh, Lord! Miss Wilson!" said Sir William, grasping my arm with both his hands, "you do not say so? What makes you think so?"

"I have seen Fred Lamb daily, and constantly, riding past her door. I know him to be a young man of strong passions, much fonder of enjoyment than pursuit; and further, my sister Fanny, one of the most charitable of all human beings, told me she had seen Fred Lamb in a private box at Drury Lane with your wife, and her hand was clasped in his, which he held on his knee."

"Oh, la, Miss! !"

"Come, do not take on so," said I, in imitation of Brummell's nonsense, and striving to conceal a laugh, "leave your dull house in Hill Street, and set off tomorrow morning on some pleasant excursion. Be assured that you will find fifty pretty girls, who will be so delighted with you, as soon to make you forget Lady Abdy."

"But then," said Sir William, "I cannot think how she came to be in the family-way: for I am sure, Miss Wilson, that during all the years we have lived together, I always——"

"Never mind," interrupted I, "go home now, and prepare for your journey, and be sure to write to me, and tell me if your mind is easier."

"Thank you, Miss Wilson! you are all goodness. I'll be sure to write, and I mean to set off tomorrow morning, and I'll never come back to that nasty, dull, large house of mine again."

"Get the sofa removed," said I, "at all events."

"Yes, Miss, I will, thank you; and the pianoforte. So good-bye, Miss "; and then returning, quite in a whisper, he said, "perhaps, Miss Wilson, when you and I become better acquainted, you'll give me a kiss!"

I only laughed, and, bade him take care of himself, and so we parted.

All this nonsense was, however, very poor amusement to me, now that I had lost Lord Ponsonby. I considered that although I was, by my hard fate, denied the pleasure of consoling his affliction, I might yet go into the country, and lead the same retired sort of life which he did; and there endeavour, by study, to make myself rather more worthy of him. I am a very ignorant little fool, thought I, but it does not therefore follow that I should remain a fool all my life, like Sir William Abdy. My plan was settled and arranged in less than an hour, and my small trunk packed, my carriage filled with books, and I and my *femme de chambre* on our road to Salt Hill.

I told the landlady of the Castle Inn, that I was come to take up my residence with her for a fortnight, and that I should require a quiet comfortable room to study in. The word study sounded very well, I thought, as I pronounced it; and, after arranging my books in due order, in the pretty rural room allotted to me by my civil landlady, I sat down to consider which of them I should begin with, in order to become clever and learned at the shortest notice, as that good lady provided people with hot dinners.

Ponsonby being forty already, thought I, will be downright old, while I continue to bloom; therefore, when this idea makes him more timid and humble, I should like to improve my powers of consoling him and charming away all his cares. Let me see! What knowledge will be likely to make me most agreeable to him? Oh, politics. What a pity that he does not like something less dry, and more lively! But no matter! and I turned over the leave of my History of England, for George the Second and George the Third, and I began reading the Debates in Parliament. Let me consider! continued I, pausing. I am determined to stick firm to the opposition side, all my life; because Ponsonby must know best; and yet it goes against the grain of all my late aristocratical prejudices, which by-the-bye, only furnish a proof how wrong-headed young girls often are.

I began to read a long speech of Lord Ponsonby's late intimate friend, Charles James Fox. This man, thought I, when I had finished his speech, appears to have much reason on his side; but then all great orators seem right, till they are contradicted by better reasoners; so if I read Pitt's answer to this speech, I shall become as aristocratical as ever. I must begin with Pitt, and finish with Fox's answer and objections to Pitt's plan. I tried this method of making a little Whig of myself, *pour les beaux yeux de mi* Lord Ponsonby. After all, said I, pausing, it will be no use and very mean of me to think one way, and profess to think another; and it still strikes me the better reason and the sounder judgment is with Pitt, who seems to go farther, and embrace a vaster and more solid plan, than Fox. The latter finding all that wit and brilliant exercise of humour necessary, makes his appear to me the worse course; then there is too much method in these Whigs, and their abuse of administration becomes pointless; because it seems as though perpetually ready cut and dried; and so vulgar! and opposition is such a losing game!! and then I have a sneaking kindness for my king.

Quelle dommage! I cannot be a Whig for the life of me! said I, throwing away the book, and quietly reclining my head on my hand, in deep thought as to what next I should study, having determined at once, out of respect to Lord Ponsonby, to stand neuter in regard to politics, since I could not make a Whig of myself.

My landlady came in to know what I would have for dinner.

"Oh, ma'am," I exclaimed, pushing aside my book, and walking towards the window, "it is impossible for persons to study, if they are to be interrupted by such absurd questions."

The woman begged my pardon.

"Listen to me, madam," said I, with the utmost concentration of dignity; "I have come into this retirement for the purpose of hard reading; therefore, instead of asking me what I want for dinner every day, or disturbing my books or papers, I shall thank you to bring up a tray with a fowl, or anything you like, exactly at five; and, placing it upon that little table, you must, if you please, go out of the room again, without saying a single word; and when I am hungry, I will eat."

Being once more left to myself, I snatched up a volume of Shakespeare, *pour me désennuier un moment*, and opened it at this passage, in the tragedy of Antony and Cleopatra:

> The barge she sat in, like a burnish'd throne,
> Burn'd on the water; the poop was beaten gold,
> Purple the sails, and so perfumed, that
> The winds were love-sick with them;

How beautiful! said I, throwing down the book. However, I came here to study—and Shakespeare is too amusing to be considered study. Therefore I'll study history; one must know something of that. I'll begin with ancient Greece, never mind English history, we can all get credit for that.

The Greeks employed me for two whole days, and the Romans six more: I took down notes of what I thought most striking. I then read *Charles the Twelfth*, by Voltaire, and liked it less than most people do; and then, Rousseau's *Confessions*, then, Racine's *Tragedies*, and afterwards, Boswell's *Life of Johnson*. I allowed myself only ten minutes for my dinner.

In short, what might I not have read, had not I been barbarously interrupted by the whole family of the Pitchers? who having once taken a fancy to my society, I had no chance but returning to town, as fast as possible, after a three weeks' residence at Salt Hill, during which time I had constantly heard from Lord Ponsonby, who was in Ireland; but hoped, shortly, to join me in town.

I was soon visited by my dear mother. She wished to consult me about what was best to be done to put my young sister out of the way of that most profligate nobleman, Lord Deerhurst, who was, she said, continually watching her in the Park, and streets, whenever she went out. I could hardly believe that anything wrong could be meant, towards a child scarcely thirteen years of age; but my mother assured me that he had been clandestinely writing to her, and sending her little paltry presents of gilt chains, such as are sold by Jews in the streets; these said trumpery articles being presented to my sister Sophia, in old jewel boxes of Love and Wirgman, in order to make it appear to the poor child that they were valuable.

"I see no remedy," said my dear mother, "but sending Sophia to some school, at a distance; and I hope to obtain her father's consent for that purpose, as soon as possible. No time is to be lost, Sophia being so sly about receiving these things, that I only found it out by the greatest accident. The last were delivered to her by a young friend of hers, quite a child, to whom Lord Deerhurst addressed himself, not having been able to meet with Sophia lately."

I was very much disgusted with this account, and quite agreed with my mother, that it would be the safest plan to send the child away.

Before she took her leave she assured me that, if possible, Sophia should depart immediately.

The next day I went to visit Fanny. Colonel Armstrong was with her. I allude to the Duke of York's aide-de-camp. The Earl of Bective was also there.

I inquired how Amy went on.

Sydenham was beginning to consider her evening parties rather a bore, since William Ponsonby had condescended to attend them. Julia, they said, was growing more gracious towards George Brummell than Colonel Cotton liked.

Armstrong, happening to be disengaged, which was seldom the case, proposed our taking Amy, who was a great favourite of his, by surprise, in the absence of Sydenham, who was at Brighton assisting Lord Wellesley to take care of Moll Raffles.

"Do you propose dining with her?" said I.

"Why not?" inquired Colonel Armstrong.

"I hope she will treat you better than she does her own sisters, when we try her pot-luck."

"I am not at all particular," said Armstrong.

"I never saw but one man," retorted I, "among all Amy's train of admirers, whom she did not contrive to cure of their temerity in intruding themselves to dinner.

"The baron Tuille's ardent love was, for six months, proof against Amy's bill of fare. Amy used to sit and sit, till hunger would not permit her to fast any longer, and, at last, she would say, 'Baron! I am going down to dinner; but I have nothing to offer you but a black pudding!'"

"'Note!!' the Dutchman always answered, 'Note! noting I like so vel!'"

"What," said Armstrong, "does she never have anything but black pudding?"

"Oh! yes," I replied, "sometimes toad-in-a-hole, or, hard dumplings; but black puddings take the lead."

Fanny, with all her good nature, began to laugh as she related the following little anecdote, which had occurred while I was at Salt Hill, *apropos* to Amy's penchant for a black pudding. My little sister Sophia had been permitted to go and dine with Amy one day, having been particularly invited a week before. Nevertheless, when she arrived, Amy appeared to start, as though surprised, and said, "Oh! by-the-bye, I forgot to order my dinner, and my maid and man are both out with letters and cards of invitation. However, I can soon manage to get a black pudding broiled. You will not mind running to South Audley Street for a pound of black pudding? Shall you, my dear?"

"Oh, no!" replied Sophia, reddening up to the eyes at the vile proposal, having lately become a coquette, from being told that she was an angel, and being really a very ladylike girl at all times; and just now she wore her smartest dress. However, she always said yes, to whatever people asked her, wanting courage or character to beg leave to differ from anybody's opinion.

The said black pudding, then, was put into her hand by the vulgar, unfeeling pork-butcher, enveloped only by a small bit of the dirty *Times* newspaper, just sufficiently large for her to take hold of it by, in the middle.

Sophia, being a remarkably shy, proud girl, felt herself ready to sink as she walked down South Audley Street, at that very fashionable hour of the day, with such a substitute for a reticule, flourishing, quite bare in her hand, as a greasy black pudding! She tried hanging down her arm: but rose it again in alarm, lest she should spoil her gay new frock. Then a ray of good sense which shot across her brain, her head I mean, induced her, with an effort of desperation, to hold the thing naturally, without attempting to conceal it; but, oh luckless fate! at the very moment poor Sophia had obtained this victory over her feelings, who should she bolt against, all on a sudden, in turning down South Street, but the first flatterer and ardent admirer of her young grace's, Viscount Deerhurst! ! !

The black pudding was now huddled up into the folds of her new frock: then she rued the day when pocket-holes went out of fashion. Deerhurst now holding out his hand to her, her last desperate resource was to throw down the vile black pudding, as softly as possible, behind her, and she then shook hands with His Lordship.

"Miss! Miss!" bawled out at this instant, a comical-looking, middle-aged, Irish labourer, who happened to be close behind her, and had picked up the delicate morsel, at the instant of its fall.

Thrusting forward the spectral lump, "Miss! Miss! how come you then, dear, to let go o' this and never miss it? Be to laying hold of it at this end, honey? It's quite clean, dear, and sure and you need not be afeard to handle it at the same end," added Pat, giving it a wipe with the sleeve of his dirty ragged jacket.

Deerhurst, who, it must be allowed, possesses a great deal of natural humour, could stand this scene between Pat and Sophia no longer, and burst into an immoderate fit of laughter, while poor Sophia, almost black in the face with shame and rage, assured the man she had dropped nothing of the sort, and did not know what he meant—and then she ran away so fast, that Deerhurst could not overtake her, and she got safe home to her mother's, leaving Amy to watch, at her window, the arrival of her favourite black pudding.

Colonel Armstrong was absolutely delighted with this account; but said he should decline her pot-luck, as it is vulgarly called. He nevertheless wished us, of all things, to accompany him to her house, and which we agreed to.

We found Amy in the act of turning over the leaves of Mr. Nugent's music book, and Mr. Nugent singing an Italian air, to his own accompaniment, ogling Amy to triple time.

The man commonly called King Allen, now Lord Allen, appeared to be only waiting for a pause of harmony, in order to take his leave.

"Ha! how do you do?" said Amy, and Nugent arose to welcome us with his everlasting laugh.

"Well, Harriette," said Amy, "you are come back, are you? I have heard that you went into the country with your whole library in your carriage, like Dominie Sampson; and let me see, who was it told me you were gone mad?"

"Your new and interesting admirer, His Grace of Grafton, perhaps, for I have heard that he is matter-of-fact enough for anything."

"It is a pity, my dear Harriette, that you continue to have such coarse ideas!" retorted Amy, *en faisant la petite bouche* with her usual look of purity, just as if she had not been lately receiving the sly hackney-coach visits of the old beau.

"A-a-my! A-a-my! was Grafton nice?" I asked.

Armstrong, seeing her rising fury, changed the conversation, by telling her that he had some idea of intruding upon her to dinner the next day.

"Oh, I really shall give you a very bad dinner, I am afraid," said Amy, having recovered from her growing anger towards me, in real alarm.

"My dear Mrs. Sydenham," replied Colonel Armstrong, earnestly, "I hate apologies, and indeed, am a little suprised that you should pay yourself so poor a compliment as to imagine, for a moment, any man cared for dinner, for vile, odious, vulgar dinner, in your society. Now, for my part, I request that I may find nothing on your table tomorrow, but fish, flesh, fowl, vegetables, pastry, fruit, and good wine. If you get anything more, I will never forgive you."

Amy's large round eyes opened wider and wider, and so did her mouth, as Armstrong proceeded; and before he had got to the wine, she became absolutely speechless with dismay. Armstrong, however, appeared quite satisfied, remarking carelessly that he knew her hour, and would not keep her waiting.

"Is anybody here, who can lend me two shillings to pay my hackney-coach?" said Allen.

"No change," was the general answer; for everybody knew King Allen!

The beaux having left us, Amy opened her heart, and said we might partake of her toad-in-the-hole, if we liked; but that she must leave us the instant after dinner.

"What for?" Fanny inquired.

"Nothing wrong," answered Amy, of course.

"Very little good, I presume," said I, and I took my leave.

CHAPTER 5

THE NEXT MORNING, I received a letter from Lord Ponsonby, to acquaint me that I might expect him in town by eight o'clock on the following evening. It is not, however, my intention to enter into many more minute details relative to my former unfortunate passion for Lord Ponsonby. This is not a complete confession, like Jean Jacques Rousseau's, but merely a few anecdotes of my life, and some light sketches of the characters of others, with little regard to dates or regularity, written at odd times, in very ill health. The only thing I have particularly attended to in this little work, has been, not to put down one single line at all calculated to prejudice any individual in the opinion of the world, which is not strictly correct; and, though I have, in writing of people as I have found them, only done as I would be done by, and as I request my friends will do by me, who never wished, yet, to pass for better than what I really am; yet my gratitude has not permitted me to publish even the most trifling faults of the few who have acted kindly towards me.

With regard to my sisters, I never had but one, and she has ceased to exist, who evinced the least regard for me. I am naturally affectionate, and my heart was disposed to love them all, till years of total neglect have at last compelled me to consider them as strangers. Some of them are my enemies. My sister Amy made it her particular study to wound my feelings, and do me all the injury in her power; and having occasion, in a moment of the deepest distress, to apply to Lady Berwick for a little assistance, she refused me a single guinea, notwithstanding in promoting her marriage with Lord Berwick, and on various other occasions, I certainly did my best, and had done many acts of friendship towards her previous to that period. Neither does this want of feeling for me, proceed from any ill opinion they have formed of my heart or character; for during our dear mother's last illness, Lady Berwick remained at her country house, in spite of all I could say to her, in my daily communications, as to the immediate danger of that dear parent; and her excuse, which she has often expressed for this heartless conduct, was that, since Harriette remained with her mother, she felt sure that no care or attention would be wanting that anybody could afford her. However, it is necessary for the sake of justice to relate the good with the bad : thus, then, be it known that if Lady Berwick would not come up to town, to attend the dreary couch of a most tender parent, she wrote to me every day, notes of inquiry, nay, more, she sent fine apples, and baskets of grapes, from her garden, up to the hour of my lamented mother's death.

These sketches, or memoirs, or whatever my publisher and editor may think proper to designate them (for my own part I think it quite tiresome enough to write a book, as fast as I can scribble it, without composing either a preface or a new name for it), were begun several years ago, merely to amuse myself. I am now only alluding to a few pages of it, for I soon grew tired of my occupation. However, the little I had done pleased my own acquaintances so much, that they all advised me to continue.

The Hon. George Lamb having been good enough to read a comedy which I attempted, was so polite as to say (and I have his letter now before me), that although it was too long, and deficient in stage-tact, there was no lack of wit and native humour about it; and further, he thought my talents well calculated for writing a light work, in the form of either novel or sketch-book. He also advised me to put the name of Harriette Wilson to the work, which he doubted not would the better ensure its sale.

Thus, being almost flattered into something like a good opinion of myself, I ventured one morning to wrap myself up in my large cloak, and put my little unfinished manuscript into my reticule, for I determined not to write another page till I had ascertained whether it was worth publishing. Thus equipped, I ventured in much fear and trembling, to wait upon the great Mr. Murray, as Lord Byron always satirically called him. He, thought I, being the friend and publisher of Lord Byron (as Dr. Johnson has it, who slays fat oxen, must himself be fat), should be wiser than George Lamb or anybody else, except Lord Byron alone; therefore I will stand by his decree.

I told Murray that I had so little confidence in myself, that I really could not be induced to go on with my work, till I had obtained his verdict on the few pages I ventured to offer for his inspection.

Murray looked on me with as much contempt as though Ass had been written in my countenance. Now I know this is not the case. He said, with much rudeness, that I might put the manuscript on his table, and he would look at it, certainly, if I desired it.

I asked when I should send for it.

Whenever you please, was his answer; as though he had already recorded his decision against me, and made his mind up not to look at it.

I promised to send for it the next evening. I did so, and the manuscript was returned without an observation. No doubt, thought I, it is all nonsense. I only wish I was quite sure that he had read it! because else it were really cruel thus to damp a beginner—who might have done something perhaps, with due encouragement. I am almost certain that it is trash; but I will be still more assured, lest the mania of scribbling should, in some moment of poverty, attack me again. However, beginning now to feel as much contempt for my manuscript as the Vicar of Wakefield did for his horse, or as I have since felt for the famed Bibliopolist of Albemarle Street, notwithstanding his carriage was numbered with those which followed in the funeral procession of the lamented Byron! I could not present my lucubrations to another publisher, as my own: my nerves would not permit it, and I therefore offered it to Messrs. Allman, of Princes Street, Hanover Square, as the first attempt of a young friend of mine. I was received by one of those gentlemen, with much politeness, and was requested to allow them four days to send their answer. They fixed their time, and I promised to send for my little manuscript on the day they appointed. It was sealed up and directed, ready for my servant, when he called for it. The envelope inclosed a few lines from Messrs. Allman, stating their readiness to publish the work, which they did not consider libellous—sharing the expenses and the profits with me. On the receipt of this note, which I have now in my possession, I got into a rage with old purblind Murray. I wish, I thought, I wish I could make rhymes! I would send him a copy of verses to thank him for being so rude to me.

To proceed with my story, I perhaps ought to relate, at large, all the raptures of my meeting with Lord Ponsonby, when he returned from Ireland; how struck I was with the pale cast of thought which enfeebled the brightness of that sweet countenance, only to increase the interest he previously inspired; how infinitely his deep mourning became him; how he had loved me, for the very thing cross Amy had laughed at me, and called me Dominie Sampson for; how he sent me Voltaire's tragedy of Zaîre, and how delighted he was to find that I felt and understood all its beauties; how he, one day, one night I mean, called me his angelic Harriette! and further declared that, had he known me sooner, he would never have married any other woman? How I used to fancy I could feel his entrance into his wife's private box, at the opera, without seeing him, as though the air suddenly should become purer; how I have astonished Fanny, by guessing the very instant of his approach, without looking towards his side of the house; how he would watch and follow me, in my walks; how he declared that he had never, in his whole life, felt such tenderness of affection for any woman on earth, combining all a father ought to feel, with the wildest passion his first youth had been capable of, with many other matters which it would be tedious to write now; but all this love is gone by, and, for the crime of attaching myself to a married man, I have deeply suffered: and all my affections are now fixed on another, to whom I am bound for life; and being just about to keep a pig and a few chickens, I really cannot mount up the ladder again; and why should I dwell too long on the wild romantic follies of my very youthful days?

During the three short years our intercourse lasted, our passion continued undiminished—increase, it could not. I do, in truth, believe, though it was a wicked thing, no two people on earth ever loved each other better, and the restraint and difficulties we laboured under, kept our passion alive, as it began. Often, after passing the early part of the evening together, finding it so difficult to separate, we drove down in a hackney-coach to the House of Lords, and in that coach have I waited half the night, merely for one more kiss, and the pleasure of driving with Ponsonby to his own door.

These three happy years of my life produced very few anecdotes which I can recollect worth relating; for I had neither eyes, nor ears, nor thoughts, but for Ponsonby. The old Scotch beggar woman in the Park, who had been the cause of my appearing advantageously to His Lordship, was my constant visitor, and I contributed to her comforts, as far as I could. She had once been in very easy circumstances, and was then in the habit of receiving every possible attention from her kind countrywoman, Lady Cottrell.

The old woman used to come to dine with me in a rich brocade silk gown, which stood absolutely alone, and once caused my equally stiff, old, powdered footman to laugh! but as it was I believe for the first time in his life, I forgave him.

Apropos of that same Mr. Will Halliday, who, though always in print, never expected the honour of being published, everybody wished to know why I kept such a clockwork, stiff, powdered, methodistical-looking servant, with a pig-tail? whom one might have taken for Wilberforce himself, instead of Will Halliday; and yet that piece of mechanism, with his eyes turned towards the ceiling, and his hair to match, used to steal my wine, as though he had forgotten all about his commandments; and when I reproached him with it, he declared that it was impossible,

"because," to use his own words, "I am the most particlerst man as is";
and, because I preferred losing my wine to being talked to, I submitted.

"Mr. Will," I used to say, "yes and no are all I want to hear from any
footman; if they will say more to me than this, I shall wait upon myself."

Will would console himself, on these occasions, with a young companion of mine, while she remained with me, whenever he could find her
disengaged, or she had the misfortune to be in the parlour while he was
laying the cloth.

"Miss Hawkes," he would begin, to her great annoyance, "Miss
Hawkes, now you see my missis don't like a sarvant to say nothing but yes
and no. Now sometimes, as I says, Miss Hawkes, yes or no won't do for
everything. Missis was very angry about my speaking yesterday; but if I
haddunt a told her I was the most particlerst man as is, she might a thort I
drinkt her wine, because I keeps the key of the cellar; and then again,
Miss Hawkes, respecting o' my great coat; I wants to tell Missis, as how
it's a mile too wide in the back: for you see, Miss, Missis don't observe
them ere things. Will you be so good, Miss, as to mention that I wants to
show he how my great coat sets behind?"

"I will go and tell her directly," said Miss Hawkes, delighted with an
excuse to get away.

"Well then," said I, in answer to what Miss Hawkes told me, "I will
look at the man's coat after dinner, only I am sure I shall laugh if he is to
walk about the room sporting his beautiful shape."

Having thus for once give Will liberty to speak, I was in dread of its
consequences all dinner-time. As soon as he had withdrawn the cloth,
and placed the dessert upon the table, he began to cough, and place himself in an attitude of preparation. Now it is coming! thought I, and I saw
Miss Hawkes striving to restrain her inclination to laugh out loud, with all
her might.

Will began sheepishly, with his eyes and his fingers fidgeting on the
back of a chair; but he grew in height, and in consequence, as he went on.
"I was a saying to Miss Hawkes, madam, that respecting o' your commands, that yes and no won't do for everything. Now, ma'am, respecting
o' my great coat——"

"You had better put it on, William," said I, holding down my head,
that I might not look at Miss Hawkes.

"Yes, ma'am; sartanly, ma'am," said Will, bustling out of the room,
and returning in an instant, equipped in a drab great coat, so very large
behind, that it made him look deformed; but did not, in the least, alter his
usual way of strutting about the room, like a player.

"Take it off, William," said I, faintly, and without venturing to raise my head, feeling that another glance at Will, eyeing his person all over, with his sharp little ferret-eyes, would have finished me. "Take it off, and carry it to the tailor's."

But Will, having once received a *carte blanche* for more than his usual yes and no, was not so easily quieted.

"Thank you, ma'am, you are very good, ma'am. I'll step down to-night with it; for the other evening, ma'am, when you sent me to carry back that there pheasant, my Lord Lowther's servant brought you, I says, says I, to Sally, 'as it is such a wet night, Sally, I won't put on my laced hat, so I claps on an old plain one; and, when I comed to St. James's Street, there was a bit of a row with some of they there nasty women at the corner, and you see, ma'am, this ere coat sticking out, in this ere kind of a way behind, and with that large cane of mine, there was a man says, says he to me, here, watchman! why don't you do your duty?'"

It was now all over with our dignities. Will, in finishing his pathetic speech, appeared almost on the point of shedding tears. We both, in the same instant, burst into an immoderate fit of loud laughter, when Will had the good sense to leave us.

The next day, Fanny, Miss Hawkes, and myself, drove into Hyde Park. We there met Sophia, with her eldest sister, looking very pretty and, above all, very modest. My carriage was soon surrounded by trotting beaux, whom I could not listen to, because that adored, sly, beautiful face of Ponsonby's was fixed on me *à la distance*. With all my rudeness and in-attention, I could not get rid of Lord Frederick Beauclerc. The rest went round to Fanny's side. This was better than going over to the enemy.

Ponsonby knew me and himself too well to be jealous; but, not daring to speak to me, or hear what I said, he looked unhappy, as I guessed, at his friend Fred Beauclerc's persevering attention; so I proposed to Fanny that we should take a drive down Pall Mall.

"Is that Mr. Frederick Lamb's ghost?" said Fanny.

"Where do you mean?" I inquired, and turning my head round, indeed saw Fred Lamb, who had, I believe, just returned from abroad. He blushed a little, and ordering my coachman to stop, told me that I looked remarkably well, and that he knew all about me.

"So you have cut poor Argyle, and are in love again, with a man of my acquaintance?" he continued.

"You are mistaken," said I, reddening.

"It may be so," rejoined Fred, "but I rather think I am right."

I shook hands with him and hoped we were parting good friends.

About ten o'clock in the evening, when Miss Hawkes had retired to rest, and I was sitting alone with my book, Fred Lamb was announced to me. I desired William to say that it was rather too late, and that I was shortly going to bed.

He returned to inform me that Mr. Lamb knew I never went to bed before midnight, and therefore begged I would permit him to chat with me for half an hour: so, feeling puzzled how to excuse myself, he was desired to walk upstairs.

He talked to me for more than an hour, of Argyle, Lord Ponsonby, and his own former affection for me. He then became a little more practical than I liked; first taking hold of my hand, and next kissing me by force. I resisted all his attempts with mild firmness. At last he grew desperate, and proceeded to very rough, I may say brutal, violence, to gratify his desires against my fixed determination. I was never very strong; but love gave me almost supernatural powers to repel this very tiger; and I contrived to pull his hair with such violence that some of it was really dragged out by the roots.

Fred Lamb was not of a mild, or patient, temper. In a moment of disappointment and fury, at the pain I must have inflicted on him, though it was certainly done only in self defence, he placed his hand on my throat, saying, while he nearly stopped my breath and occasioned me almost the pangs of suffocation, that I should not hurt him another instant. He spoke this in a smothered voice, and I did in truth, believe that my last moments had arrived. Another instant would have decided the business; but he, thank God, relinquished his grasp at my throat. He is, however, mistaken if he believes I have ever forgotten the agony of that moment. We arose from the sofa; his rage, I fancy, being converted into shame, and fear of what I might tell the world, or perhaps he was really shocked at the violence which he had been guilty of. It may easily be imagined that once free from so frightful a grasper of throats, I was not long in obtaining my room upstairs and double-locking my door. Fred Lamb did not attempt to speak to, much less detain me, and in a very few minutes afterwards, I heard him leave the house.

Thank God! I ejaculated, from the very bottom of my heart; and I began to breathe more freely, although it was some time before I recovered my fright.

Fred Lamb was a man of the world; and the next day, he no doubt said to himself, this is a bad story both for my vanity and my character: for I have been very brutal. The best way, now, will be for me to tell it first, to all her friends; and he accordingly went about making light of the story, as though he had not any reason to be ashamed.

"Do you know," said he to several of my acquaintances, who afterwards repeated it, "do you know that Harriette is so in love with John Ponsonby, that she was cruel even to me last night! I tried force too; but she resisted me like a little tiger, and pulled my hair!"

Be it so, thought I, and I never told the story till now. In fact, I was a good deal afraid of Fred Lamb at that time, and could not but feel provoked at the idea of a young man going about the world, always laughing, and showing off the characteer of a fine, good-tempered, open-hearted, easy, generous, sailor-like fellow, and who, yet, could take me from a rich man, to leave me starving at Somerstown, as he had done, without once making me the offer of a single shilling, and then return to me, as though all this selfishness had secured him a right over my person, to persecute me with brutal force, and lay hold of my throat, so as to put me in fear of my life, because I was not his humble slave, any day in any week, when he happened to return from the Continent; and I am sure Mr. Frederick Lamb cannot assert that, on the day I believed he meant to have been my last, he had ever given me one single guinea, or the value of a guinea.

He is now an ambassador, and just as well off as ambassadors usually are; yet, in my present poverty, I have vainly attempted to get an hundred pounds out of him. He has occasionally, indeed, sent me ten or five pounds; but not without much pressing; and he has not yet paid my expenses to Hull and back.

So much for the high-spirited Fred Lamb! With his brother George, I have only a very slight acquaintance; but am much indebted for the very polite, friendly, and condescending interest that gentleman has been pleased to take in my welfare.

Lord Ponsonby often rated me about Lord F. Beauclerc, his relation, whom he always called Fred Diamond Eye; and Fred Beauclerc was continually teasing me about Ponsonby. I assured him that it was all nonsense.

"I know better," F. Beauclerc would answer, "and yet I am fool enough to love a woman who is going mad for another man. However, if I get well over this folly, I will, for the rest of my life, reign lord paramount or nothing."

His Lordship really loved me, and, above all, he loved my foot. I was never, in his opinion, *assez bien chaussée*, therefore, he used to go about town with one of my shoes in his pocket, as a pattern to guide him in his constant search after pretty shoes for me.

Fred Beauclerc is a sly, odd man, not very communicative, unless one talks about cricket. I remember when the Marquis of Wellesley did me the honour to call on me and tell me what a great man he was, and how much he had been talked of in the world—how often carried on men's shoulders without nags, with other reminiscences of equal interest, Fred Beauclerc the Diamond Eye, cut me for Moll Raffles. I accused him of it, laughing, and he, laughingly, acknowledged the intrigue.

"I could not endure the idea of your receiving that vain old fool, Lord Wellesley," said Beauclerc.

"No harm, believe me!" I replied. "Mere curiosity induced me to have the man up, to see if he was like his brother; but you are very welcome to Mrs. Raffles; she'll make an excellent wife to a divine. Not that I know or care anything about the lady!"

"And what think you of Wellesley?" said the little parson.

"Why, I suppose I must either say he is clever and brilliant, or be called a fool myself; so instead of answering your question, I'll tell you what he says to me tomorrow, after I shall have acquainted him with your intrigue with his *belle amie* Raffles."

"You are not serious?" said the good clergyman in a great fright.

"Yes, I am quite serious, I assure you."

"What! You spoil sport! You make mischief! I would not have believed this of you."

"You only do me justice—but I will tell, notwithstanding; and if I either spoil your intrigue, or do mischief to anybody except the noble Marquis, never forgive me."

"I never will," said Beauclerc, seriously, and so we parted.

In the evening a remarkably fine-looking man requested to speak to me, from the Marquis of Wellesley. He wore a large brilliant on the third finger of his very white hand, and was peculiarly elegant in his dress. I offered him a chair with much politeness, feeling really something like respect for Lord Wellesley's good taste in sending me such an amiable substitute for a little, grey-headed, foolish old man. The gentleman bowed low, and refused to sit. He told me that he came from the Marquis of Wellesley, merely to say that if I were disengaged, he would have the pleasure of calling on me in less than an hour.

C'est son valet, sans doute, thought I; and sent my compliments to Lord Wellesley.

Wellesley's carriage drove up to my door, in less than an hour after his gentleman had left me. His Lordship appeared the very essence of every-thing most *recherché*, in superfine elegance. He was, in fact, all essence! Such cambric, white as driven snow! Such embroidery! Such diamonds! Such a brilliant snuff-box! Such seals and chain! And then, the pretty contrast between the broad new blue ribbon across his breast, and his delicate white waistcoat!

It was too much, too overpowering for a poor, honest, unaffected Suissess like me: for never before stood I in such presence, nor breathed I in such essence! What a pretty little thing too, it would be, methought, if it were but once deposited, unhurt, in one's bonnet-box, and one could shut him down whenever the essence became too strong for one's nerves. It was a graceful thing too, in miniature, and its countenance was good, and its speech was all honey, until I, very quietly, and very unceremoni-ously, mentioned the worthy clergyman having passed the whole of the night preceding with Moll Raffles, consoling her, *en prêtre*, for His Lord-ship's absence.

His Lordship now asked me, in a voice trembling more with agitation than age, or rage, what I meant.

"Simply what I have stated."

"Merciful powers! what do you say? what do you mean? what do you hint at? what do you think? what are you doing?" If His Lordship's want of breath had not given a momentary check to his volubility, and proved a kind of turnpike in his rapid course, and if I had not caught the critical opportunity to say—

"Nothing—your fair friend must do for us both"—I have little doubt that the little Marquis must and would have fallen a victim to exhaus-tion: but thus, having happily had a moment to recover himself, he proceeded.

"Nay, nay, nay," and laying his white hand, rings and all, on my shoulder, in much tribulation and hurry of speech and manner, "Nay—think of what you are saying—think how you may be in-juring that lovely sweet being—that sweetest unsophisticated! lovely! sweet!!"

"Oh, what a bed of sweets yours must be!" interrupted I.

"I know well enough," continued Wellesley, pacing up and down the room with a feverish rapidity, "I know she went to Vauxhall with Beauclerc—but then she told me there was nothing in all this."

"Poor Beauclerc!" ejaculated I—"and what can His Lordship do better, than attend so sweet a creature? Come, come," I continued, "my Lord! Don't be such an ape! Mrs. Raffles is rich, and can do without you, kindly assisted as she is by the little parson!—Don't fret for her, nor for yourself; but if you still love her, receive her from the hands of the good clergyman."

"Impossible!" Wellesley exclaimed. "I must reproach her with her faults and then—she will throw the plates and dishes in my face!"

"No! would she be so vulgar?"

"It is not vulgarity in her," said Wellesley.

"What then?"

"Nature," was his reply.

"Well then, since it is natural to break your head, which fact I do not in the least dispute, may it not be as natural to adorn it occasionally? and may it not be her nature to intrigue with Fred Beauclerc? Do not think about it, my Lord. Make yourself happy and comfortable, and——"

Wellesley took up his hat, and ran downstairs. I followed him, laughing loudly, till he got into his carriage.

Beauclerc was in due time tired of his *bonne fortune*, and this gave Wellesley the delicious opportunity of pressing his charmer to his faithful and doating heart with renovated rapture.

La Belle Nature!!

About this time, or else some other time, a Mr. Somethingdoff was presented to me, hot from Russia. I forget the beginning of his name. I recollect that he brought, at the ends of his fingers, a very odd waltz, which seemed to have been composed on purpose to warm them. I asked him, since he was on the Emperor's staff, if he had met with the General Beckendorff.

"Oh, yes!" answered he, laughing, "Beckendorff is my particular friend. He wanted to come to England with me; but, he assured me, he had made such a fool of himself about a woman here, Amy, I think he called her, that he was ashamed to show his face within a thousand miles of herself or her friends."

Now, gentle readers, you shall hear of the shocking seduction of the present Viscountess Berwick, by Viscount Deerhurst!

"She is off! Sophia is off! run away, nobody knows where," was the cry of all my sisters, one fine morning.

"When, how, where?" said I.

"Last night," answered Fanny, "she was missing. Her father has been to call on Lord Deerhurst: answer, nobody in town. So mother is coming to consult with you."

I waited for no more; but sat down to address Lord Deerhurst, begging him to consider the risk he ran in detaining such a child. I asserted the determination of my father to put in force the utmost rigour of the law; and I implored him, if he was not really dead to shame, and all the best feelings of a man, to repair his fault by bringing Sophia back to me immediately.

That prince of hypocrites, having forcibly obtained all he wished, and, in hopes that this would be the cheapest way of getting rid of the business, made a great merit of bringing her back to my house, being, as he said, touched, even to tears, by my letter, and the monster began to blubber, and declared that nothing wrong had occurred, he having passed the night with Sophia in mere conversation.

The poor child looked dreadfully frightened. It is indeed my firm belief that she went away with Lord Deerhurst, being innocent as an infant as to the nature of seduction, and its consequence. All she was blameable for, was her obstinate boldness in persisting, while so very young, and with that innocent face of hers, in keeping up a sly intercourse with a man like Lord Deerhurst, and throwing herself under his protection, at an age when girls less shy-looking had been afraid to have listened or spoken to any man, unsanctioned by the presence of their mother or sister.

Sophia was a child, and not a very clever one; but she went away willingly, and immediately after both her mother and myself had represented the striking profligacy and disgusting meanness of Lord Deerhurst, in passing off trumpery chains and rings for valuable jewellery. The child who could forsake her parents for such a man as Deerhurst, in spite of every caution, must have been either very vicious, or the greatest simpleton on earth.

The poor foolish girl was now kept out of everyone's sight, and applications were made to Deerhurst, for a provision for her, with a threat of law-proceedings in case of refusal.

It seems that the only legal plea for obtaining a provision for a girl thus unfortunately situated, is that of the parents having lost her domestic services. Deerhurst, after some months, at last said that, if Sophia remained with him, he would settle three hundred pounds a year on her, as long as no proof of inconstancy to him should be established against her; but, on such an event taking place, the annuity was to be reduced to an allowance of one hundred a year.

I saw that Sophia was growing idle, and much more likely to get into worse scrapes than to reform; therefore, having tried the generosity and honour of men myself, I advised her to secure the annuity, at any rate.

Deerhurst employed a —— of a lawyer to draw up a settlement according to the above plan, and, in about ten months after His Lordship first seduced Sophia, he hired a very miserable lodging for her, consisting of two small dark parlours, near Grosvenor Place; but then, to make her amends, he sent her in six bottles of red currant-wine, declaring to her that such wine was much more conducive to health than any foreign wine could possibly be. Here we must leave Sophia for a short time, while I return to my own house, to learn, of Will Halliday, who had called in my absence. These were, a gentleman who would not leave his name, and a tradesman of the name of Smith—both were to return in the evening.

"Very well," I said, "let Smith come upstairs; but be sure to send away the man who is ashamed of his name."

After dinner, Will told me that the strange gentleman begged to be allowed to speak to my *femme de chambre*, Mrs. Kennedy.

I desired Kennedy to attend me.

She returned to say that the gentleman sent me word, in confidence, that he was Lord Scarborough, who had been so long, and so very desirous to make my acquaintance—and regretted the impossibility of getting presented, since he was not a single man.

"Go and tell him," I answered, "that the thing is quite impossible, more men being regularly introduced to me by others, and of the first repectability, than I liked."

He entreated Kennedy to come up to me again. She declared that she could not take such a liberty with me. Lord Scarborough having, as she afterwards confessed, softened her heart by a five-pound note, induced her to carry me up his watch, with his arms on the seal, that I might be certain who he was.

I was in a great passion with Kennedy, and down she went, declaring she had lost her place.

I rang the bell, it having just struck me that the man ought to pay for putting me in a passion and giving us all this trouble; therefore, "Tell him," I said, when Kennedy returned, "that a fifty-pound note will do as well as a regular introduction, and, if he leaves it tonight, I will receive him tomorrow at ten."

He hesitated—wished he could only just speak to me, and give me the draft himself.

"Do as you like," Kennedy replied. "Miss Wilson is not at all anxious for you or your fifty pounds; but she has company, and will not be disturbed tonight."

"Well," said my Lord, "I think you look like an honest, good sort of woman, who will not deceive me."

"Never," said Kennedy with earnestness; and he wrote a draft for me, for fifty pounds, begging she would herself be at hand, to let him in when he should arrive the next night. "I will be very punctual," continued His Lordship.

"So will I too," repeated Kennedy; "I will wait for you in the passage"; and with this they took leave, and I immediately rang my bell for Will Halliday.

"William," said I, "that gentleman will be here at ten tomorrow, and he will, probably, again ask for Kennedy. Can you look quite serious, and declare to him you never heard of such a person?"

"As grave as I do now, ma'am."

"Very well, that is quite enough; but he will, no doubt, proceed to ask for me, by my name. Can you still be serious, while declaring that you have no mistress, and that your master is, you know, well acquainted both with His Lordship and his lady wife?"

"Most certainly, ma'am," said Will, as seriously as though he had been at vespers; "I will just clap your directions down in my pocket-book; so you need not be afraid of me, ma'am; because you see, as I told you before, I'm the most particlerst man as is."

"But suppose he insists, William?"

"Oh, ma'am! I'll tell him I've got my knives to clean, and shut the door, very gently, in his face."

"Thank you, William, I shall feel obliged to you."

Smith, the haberdasher of Oxford Street, was the next person announced to me; and he followed William into the drawing-room. He is a short, thick-built man, with little twinkling eyes, expressive of eager curiosity, and a bald head. This man had known me when I was quite an infant, having served my mother, I believe, before I was born, and often talked and played with us all while children. As I grew up, his extreme vulgarity, and the amorous twinkle of his little eyes, furnished me with so much real sport and amusement, that, in gratitude for his being so very ridiculous, I had, by degrees, lost sight of all my usual reserve towards these sort of people; and once, when I was about eleven years of age, this man caught me in the very act of mimicking his amorous leers at our maidservant. I was close behind him, and he saw me in the looking-glass.

"Oh, you rogue!" said Smith; and from that day, good-bye all serious reserve between Smith and me. I would have cut him, only nobody sold such good gloves and ribbons. I often took people to his shop to amuse them, while I encouraged Smith to be as ridiculous as possible, by affecting to be rather flattered by his beautiful leering and his soft speeches.

Smith was as deaf as a post, and never spoke without popping his ear against one's mouth, to catch the answer, and saying, hay! hay! long before one's lips could move to address him.

I guessed at the motive for his visiting me on this occasion; for I knew that two of my promissory notes of hand, for fifty pounds each, had been returned to him on that morning, as they had also been three months before, when I made him renew them. Not that I was in any sort of difficulty during the whole period I remained with Lord Ponsonby, who always took care of me, and for me; but Smith's scolding furnished me with so much entertainment, that I purposely neglected his bills, knowing his high charges, and how well he could afford to give long credit. He came into the room with a firmer step than usual, and his bow was more stately.

"Your sarvant, Miss."

"Smith," said I, "those bills were paid today, I hope?"

Smith shook his head. "Too bad, too bad, Miss, upon my word!"

I laughed.

"You are a pretty creature!" said Smith, drawing in his breath, his amorous feelings, for an instant, driving the bills out of his head, and then added hastily, with an altered expression of countenance, "But you really must pay your bills!"

"You don't say so?"

"If," continued Smith earnestly; "if you had but ha' let me ha knode, you see; but, in this way, you hurt my credit in the city."

"What signifies having credit, in such a vulgar place as that?"

"You talk like a child," exclaimed Smith, impatiently.

"Come," said I, "Smith, hand out your stamps."

"And, Miss, do you expect me to find you in stamps too?"

I laughed.

"But," continued Smith, growing enthusiastic all at once, "you look so beautiful and charming, in your little blue satin dress. You bought that satin of me, I think? Ah, yes, I remember—you do look so pretty, and so tempting, and so, so—oh Lord."

"Mr. Smith, I really will speak to Mrs. Smith, if you will go into these sort of raptures."

"Beg your pardon! beg your pardon! Have got a curious little article here to show you (pulling something from his breeches pocket, which proved to be some embroidered, covered buttons). Beg your pardon, but bless you! ! You are so well made, you see about here (touching his own breast). There is never a one of your sisters like you about here. I always said it. Hay? hay? I was a saying so, you see, to my young man, yesterday, when you came into the shop. Now, there's Miss Sophy, pretty creature too! very, but oh, Lord! you beat them all, just about here."

"Mr. Smith, I really must send a note to your wife tomorrow."

"Oh, no! I am sure you won't. You would not be so hard-hearted," He then proceeded, in a whisper, "The fact is, there's never a man in England as don't have a bit of frolic; only they doesn't know it you see. Pretty hair! !——"

"Mr. Smith, if you meddle with my hair, I shall seriously be angry, and ring for my servant."

"Beg pardon—thousands of pardons—it's the worst of me, I'm so imperdent, you see!—can't help it—been so from a child—never could keep my hands off a fine woman! and Mrs. Smith is confined, you see: that's one thing! hay? hay? but it shan't happen again. Now, about these here bills? If I draw you up two more, now, will you really give me your word they shall be paid?"

"No," answered I.

"You won't?"

"No!"

"Then I'll tell you what, Miss! I can't say as you treat me exactly like a lady, and—now don't laugh—oh, you sly, pretty rogue!—hay? hay? beg pardon—it's my only fault, you see. So very imperdent! Come, I'll draw up these here bills."

He began writing, and I laughed at him again. He shook his head at me. "Sad doings, Miss, these here bills being returned."

"It's the worst of me," said I, mimicking his manner. "It's the worst of me, that I never do pay my bills. Have been so from a child!"

Lord Ponsonby's well-known rap at the door occasioned Smith to be bundled into the street, bills and all, without the slightest ceremony.

I have, I believe, already said that I would not dwell much on that period of my life which I passed so happily with Lord Ponsonby, and which lasted, I think, three years. Lord Rivers used to say to me, "Your little, light feet seem scarcely to touch the earth, as though you could almost fly!"

Happiness is a stupid subject to write upon; therefore, I will revert to that of the present Lady Berwick, whom I often visited after she took possession of the poor, humble lodging which Deerhurst's parsimony had provided for her. First, however, the respect I feel for the memory of a most tender parent, makes me anxious that she should be acquitted from every shadow of blame, which might, by some, perhaps, be imputed to her, in consequence of her daughters' errors, and the life they fell into.

My mother was a natural daughter of a country gentleman, of great respectability, and good estate, Mr. Cheney. His only son, General Cheney, was an old guardsman, and died some few years ago. The late Lady Frederick Campbell, aunt of His Grace the Duke of Argyle, was so struck with the beauty of my mother, as to adopt her, and bring her up as her own child. After her marriage, Her Ladyship still continued her friendship, and, indeed, almost up to the time of the very lamented death of that amiable lady.

I remember the ceremony of our being all dressed up in our best frocks, to go out of town, and pass the day with Her Ladyship, who was kind enough to stand godmother to my eldest sister. My mother was the most beautiful woman, and possessed the finest and most benevolent countenance, I have ever seen in my whole life. Her education had been carefully attended to by Lady Frederick, and she possessed a most excellent understanding; but marrying, so very young, a man more than twenty years her senior, and being remarkably meek and gentle, she acquired such a habit of blind submission to his will that, at home, she was more like our sister than our parent. She was powerless to contribute either to our good or our comfort, in any one thing which did not suit my father's humour. Having no fortune to bestow on us, she gave us the best education in her power; and, what ought to have done us still more good, she ever set us the very best example; for she was not only virtuous, but patient, industrious, and invariably amiable in her temper. She was the mother of fifteen children when she died, lamented and respected by everyone who knew her.

Our home was truly uncomfortable; but my dearest mother ever made it the study of her life, to contribute to the ease and welfare of her family.

This, as I have said before, is not a complete confession; but nothing is stated of consequence to any individual, which is not strictly true.

When I called on Sophia, I generally found two or three beaux talking nonsense to her. Among them, Henry De Roos was the most favoured. Sophia appeared to dislike Lord Deerhurst of all things, and complained that he was usually sparing of soap and water, at his toilette.,

"He dresses completely," said Sophia, "before he touches water; and, being equipped, he wets a very dirty hair-brush, and draws it over his head; and this is what he calls washing it—and then, having thus washed his hands and face, he says that he feels fresh and comfortable."

One day Deerhurst insisted on my accompanying him and Sophia, in his curricle, to go out of town, somewhere, to dinner.

"Three in a curricle?" said Sophia.

"Oh, it is no matter, at this time of the year," Deerhurst replied.

I inquired where we should dine.

Deerhurst named some small place, about eight miles from town, but I have forgotten what he called it. He took us to a common village pot-house, where nothing could be put on the table besides fried eggs and bacon.

"Most excellent!" exclaimed Deerhurst; "an exquisite dish—and so very rural!"

Our rural dinner was soon dispatched; and, as I could not endure the strong smell of tobacco, which issued in copious fumes from the tap-room, I proposed returning to town as fast as possible.

Sophia, who always agreed with everybody, was asked first by Deerhurst, if eggs and bacon were not a delightful dish.

She answered, "Very much so indeed."

I then asked her, if it were not enough to make us sick, on such a hot day.

To which her reply was, "I am quite sick already."

In coming home, Deerhurst put his horses all at once into a full gallop, as we drew near the turnpike, bent on the noble triumph of cheating— I will not use the technical word—the man, of twopence!! the lord of the gate, in a fury, ran after Deerhurst, and with some difficulty, contrived to catch hold of his whip.

"Let go my whip!" vociferated Deerhurst.

"You sneaking b——kg——d!" said the man, still holding fast by one end of the whip; "this is not the first time you have attempted to cheat me."

"Let go my whip, and be d——d to you!" bawled Deerhurst.

The man, however, refused, and, in the struggle it was broken.

"Now, d——n your soul," said Deerhurst, darting from the curricle, without the least regard to our fears, and leaving us to manage two spirited horses how we could. In an instant he had stripped off his coat, and was hard at it with the fat, dirty turnpike-man.

"Oh!" ejaculated I, in despair, "that ever I should have ventured out in such disgusting society!"

"Very disgusting indeed," echoed Sophia.

Once Deerhurst was down; but we soon discovered that the fat turnpike man was undermost, and "Go it, my Lord! you a lord? a rum lord!" burst from a Babel-like confused world of voices.

The Honourable Arthur Upton happened to be passing at this moment. I called out to him by his name, and he came up to the curricle. I told him that we were frightened, almost to death at the scene which presented itself; and our peculiar situation, having no proper dresses, nor shoes, for walking, and requested that he would make somebody stand at the heads of the horses.

He did so, and afterwards obligingly made his way to Lord Deerhurst. He begged His Lordship would excuse the liberty he took, adding, "We know each other personally, Lord Deerhurst, and I cannot help feeling hurt and grieved to see you so engaged, particularly with two young ladies under your immediate protection. I feel myself bound, seeing so many blackguards against you, to stand by you, as long as you choose to keep me in this very disgraceful situation."

"What," cried out the many-mouthed-mob, "you are another lord, I suppose? Here's rum lords for you! cheating a poor man out of twopence, and then stopping to fight in the road. My sarvices to you, my lord! Who would not be a lord?"

"Out of respect for you, Mr. Upton," said Deerhurst, "I will pay this fellow"; and thus, after knocking the poor man about till he was black and blue, His Lordship being possessed of all such skill as his friends Crib and Jackson had taught him, he paid him the twopence which was originally his due, and was hissed and hooted till he drove out of sight.

When he rejoined us, his nose and fingers were covered with blood.

"Did you ever see such an impudent rascal, my dear Sophia," said Deerhurst to her.

"Never in my life," prettily repeated Sophia, in her cuckoo-strain.

Some days after this interesting rural party, I called, with Fanny to see, Amy, and found the door of her drawing-room locked.

"Good gracious," said Amy, as she opened it, after keeping us some time, "why does not John send the locksmith to this vile door, as I have so constantly desired him! It's quite a nuisance, being obliged to lock it in order to keep the wind out."

I shall not easily forget the figure Arthur Upton cut. When we entered, his powder and pomatum was rolling down his face, in large drops! I can't conceive what it could all mean!!

But beg security to bolt the door,

as Lord Byron somewhere has it.

"Amy," said I, "I have news for you of your sighing, waltzing Beckendorff."

"Oh, lord!" answered Amy, "I am sorry the poor fool is returned; for I really cannot marry him now."

"I do not think you can," answered I, and then related what I had heard.

"He is the fox, and I am the grapes," said Amy; "for, no doubt, he has heard I am Mrs. Sydenham."

"Alias Upton," continued I.

"Harriette judges of other people by herself," retorted Amy; "but, being innocent, these things never wound my feelings."

CHAPTER 6

To such of the kind public as may have a perverted taste for the serious, I beg leave to state that I am now making my debut in a tragic part; but venture, humbly, to express the hope that my tragical adventures will furnish more interest to my readers, than they supplied amusement to me.

I have twice before stated, that Lord Ponsonby's attachment to me continued, or appeared to continue, unabated, for the space of nearly three years: *et savez-vous, mes belles dames, que cela est beaucoup?* Towards the end of that period, he one evening appeared to me unusually melancholy. I had frequently reproached him with making a mystery to me of something which must have happened to him; but he not only assured me that I was mistaken, but began to affect more than his accustomed gaiety; and he acted his part so well, that I was doubtful whether I had not been altogether deceived.

"Then perhaps you are only out of health," said I, "instead of out of spirits? for I am sure that your hands are feverish."

"Now you have discovered it," said Ponsonby, laughing—"I am going to die!—Would you regret me?" said he: and then, in a tone of much feeling, added, as he put back my thick hair with his two hands, to kiss my forehead, and examine the expression of my countenance, intensely, as though he were taking a last farewell of it—"I will not ask you; for I am sure you would."

He now took up some paper and began to write, holding his hand before the paper, to prevent my seeing a single line.

"What are you writing?" I asked.—"Private business," was Ponsonby's answer.

On this I sat down to my pianoforte, that I might not interrupt him. Yet it struck me, that it must be something for me, or he would not have written it at my house.

Lord Ponsonby had often hinted that he wished to make a provision for me, during my life, of two hundred pounds a year. I imagined that this might be something of a promise to that effect: but as I knew Ponsonby, at that time, to be very poor, and much in debt, my resolution was taken at once. He will divide his purse with me, thought I, while he lives and loves me—and I will never look forward, nor provide for one hour after Ponsonby shall be lost to me.

As soon as he had sealed up a letter, which he put into his pocket, he looked at his watch, and starting upon his feet, said in a voice of real distress, "I must go!—Who would have imagined that it could be so late!"

"Must you go home already?" I asked.

"Not home; but to the House of Lords," Ponsonby replied. "But, my dear Harriette, I cannot lose you at this moment! Perhaps you were right, and my spirits may have been rather lower than usual tonight! Will you come down with me in a hackney-coach, as far as the House?"

I acquiesced willingly; and when we arrived there I begged to be allowed to wait for him. "I don't care if it should be all night," said I, "for you'll come at last, and we can drive towards your house together."

Ponsonby answered that I was very good; but in the greatest despondency.

In half an hour, he came to the coach-door, to say that the House would sit late, and he could not bear the idea of my waiting.

"All these things, my dearest Ponsonby," said I, "are mere matters of taste. I am very happy in waiting for you—very!" He did not again return to me for more than three hours. It was daylight. He seemed to be dreadfully unwell and fatigued. I had never seen him thus since the death of his father. He gave me, I think, almost a hundred kisses, without uttering a single word.

"You are much fatigued, dear Ponsonby," said I; "I only wish to heaven I might stay with you, and take care of you for ever."

"I have a letter for you," said Ponsonby, drawing the one which he had written at my house from his pocket, as we drove towards his own home.

"You must excuse my taking it," said I; "because, I will tell you frankly, I rather guess that it is to secure to me the provision which you have so often talked about."

He was peremptory.

"I am no liar, Ponsonby," said I; "and when I most solemnly declare to you that I will never accept of any annuity from you, unless you were to become so rich as to make one without the slightest inconvenience to yourself or your family—I hope you will believe me." I then tore the letter into many pieces, and threw it out of the coach window.

Ponsonby seemed almost ashamed of having had so little as two hundred pounds a year to offer; but even that was not without difficulty; for he was most magnificent in his ideas of gentlemanly expenditure.

Poor fellow! He had so little of it to spend; and from delicacy, he was afraid to say more on the subject of what he considered a trifle wholly unworthy of me.

As we drew near his door, Ponsonby pressed me close to his heart. "My dear Harriette," said he, "it is indeed, as you say, very hard upon us that we may not pass the whole of our lives together; but then he assured of this truth; and I hope that it may afford you consolation, happen what will; my affection for you, to whom I certainly owe some of the happiest hours I have ever known, will last while I exist."

The kiss which followed this declaration was as long and as ardent as our first! Yet, alas! how different the parting kiss of unfathomable anguish, given in the fervour of gaunt despair, to the first soul-thrilling embrace of wild, ardent ecstasy, which comprehends no limits, and which, like the last, could never be forgotten by me.

Ponsonby had affected me with his more than usual melancholy, and when I was about to take my leave, I felt that I could not speak; but I kissed his hand eagerly and fervently, as he was hurrying out of the coach. . . .

I have never seen him from that hour.

On the following evening, while I was expecting Ponsonby, I received a letter from him, the purport of which was to inform me that we had parted for ever. . . .

I remember little of the style or nature of the letter. Something I read about a discovery made by Lady Ponsonby, and a solemn engagement or promise, extorted from him to see me only once more; in which interview, he had intended to have explained and arranged everything; but could not. The perusal of this letter occasioned a mist to come over my eyes, my heart seemed to swell in my bosom so as almost to produce suffocation: and yet I did not believe it to be possible that we could have parted for the last time, or surely my anguish had burst forth in one wild cry, and then all had been still for ever!!

But hope was not yet extinct. I felt stunned, more by the sudden shock of such an idea being presented to my imagination as possible, than from any conviction of its probability. Dreadful! thought I, and shuddered, while I felt a cold dew, as from the charnel-house, overspread my whole frame; shall Ponsonby refuse to speak to me, and even look upon me as a stranger, after all our communion of feeling, after all that deep interest which he evinced towards me, so late as this very morning! Nonsense! palpable, gross absurdity! How I have been frightening myself! As if it were in human nature to be so cruel even to one's greatest enemy! And

Ponsonby's nature is so kind! and then a violent hysterical affection steeped my senses in forgetfulness, and relieved, for an instant, the bitter anguish of my heart. Then I suddenly recollected his parting kiss. Gracious God! could he have left me? My brain seemed absolutely on fire. I flew to the window, where for years I had been in the habit of watching his approach. It is not high enough, thought I, and would but half destroy me. I will go to him first, and my trembling hands essayed, in vain, to fasten the ribbons of my bonnet under my chin; but no, no, I will not risk her happiness. I am not really wicked, not so very wicked as to deserve this dreadful calamity. We are sent into the world to endure the evils of it patiently, and not thus to fly into the face of our God. If He is our Father, and I kneel down to Him with patience, this anguish will be calmed.

I locked my door, and then prostrated myself, with my face on the floor, and prayed fervently for near an hour, that, if I was to see Ponsonby no more, God would take me, in mercy, out of a world of such bitter suffering, before the morning. I arose somewhat comforted; but stiff, and so cold that my whole frame trembled violently. I swallowed some lavender-drops, and tried to write; blotted twenty sheets of paper, with unintelligible nonsense, and wetted them with my tears.

The book Ponsonby last read to me now caught my eye. No sense of religion could calm or save me from the actions of despair, while these objects were before me, and, hastily wrapping my cloak about me, I hurried into the streets. I walked on with incredible swiftness, till my strength failed me, all at once, and, panting for breath, I sat down on the step of a door in Half-Moon Street. The night was dark and rainy. I have a strong mind, thought I, and I will exert it to consider where I shall look for help and consolation, if Ponsonby has left me. As this thought struck me, the slow tear fell, unregarded, down my cheek. Death, was the answer my despair made me, only death can relieve me! But then what is death? How soon the vital spark of life is destroyed in insects. The poor moth, when writhing in torture of its own seeking, how often, and how easily I have put at rest! Ponsonby's neglect, Ponsonby's late passion, his smile, and his last, long kiss, cannot torture me after this little palpitation has ceased; and I held my fingers to my throat, to ascertain the strength of what seemed all of life about me. Yet I will suffer first, and suffer long, that I may pray for God's forgiveness, only be it my consolation that this will terminate all.

Alas! vain was my reasoning. There was no consolation for me. I was bent on writing to Ponsonby. I will return home, thought I, and shut myself up in the small room he has never entered. My trembling knees could no longer support me. I tried to rise, but could not. My lips were parched, my cheeks burned, and I was very sick. God is about to grant the prayer I have made to Him, thought I—ever sanguine in what I—wished I shall die by His own will.

I grew worse, and very faint. Sickness was new to me at that time, and now a slight touch of fear came over me. Alas! methought, I am going out of the world very young, and very miserably, and before I have written to Ponsonby. He would have returned to me. He loved me, and while there was life, there was hope. I might have been so exquisitely happy as to have been pressed to his heart again! though but once more, it would have compensated an age of misery. It is but in losing him I can appreciate my late wonderful happiness. I would have been his servant, or his slave, and lived on one of his smiles for a week, as a reward for the hardest labour. What am I? what was I, that Ponsonby should devote his precious life to me? No matter what I was! As I grew still fainter, I prayed for Ponsonby's eternal happiness, as though I had felt he required my prayers.

"Vy do you set there?" inquired a man who was passing, in the accent of a Jew, and receiving no answer, after examining me attentively, he added: "Poor ting! poor girl, you are ill! don't be afraid of a poor old Jew. Tell me vat I sal do for you." My heart was so deeply oppressed, that my strongest effort to subdue my feelings proved unsuccessful; and, at the sound of these few words, uttered in a tone of unaffected benevolence, I sobbed aloud.

"Poor ting! poor young ting! Got bless my soul (taking my hand) you are very ill, you have much fever, vat shall pe done?"

"I am really ill," said I, struggling to speak calmly, "and you will oblige me greatly, if you will have the kindness to see me to a hackney-coach."

The Jew hastened to comply with my request, and with real delicacy, assisted me into the carriage he procured for me, without making a single inquiry.

Arrived at home, my housekeeper was so alarmed and struck at my altered appearance, that she, after putting me to bed, sent for Dr. Bain, who assured me that I was in a high fever, and that my recovery depended entirely on my keeping myself very quiet.

I confessed to my physician, that there was something on my mind, which agitated me so violently, that I could find no rest, till I was allowed to write a long letter. He seemed to take a strong interest in my fate; and, after vainly imploring me not to attempt it, suffered my maid to place my writing-desk before me; but alas! I could not write.

My memory began to fail me, and my head was dreadfully confused; I remarked this to Dr. Bain, as I laid down my pen.

"My dear child," said the doctor, taking my burning hand with much kindness, "your pulse is so high at this moment, that nothing but the most perfect stillness can ever restore you. Only obey my instructions for three days, and I firmly hope that your fever will have left you, and you will be able to write without difficulty, on any subject you please."

The idea of dying without having addressed Ponsonby, caused me such extreme anguish, that I submitted, like an infant, to follow the advice I received.

"Only assure me, Sir," said I, "that I shall be able to write, to a particular friend, a very long, collected letter before I die—and my mind will become comparatively calm."

The doctor gave me all the comfort in his power, and promised to see me early in the morning.

I passed a very agitated night; I could not refrain from puzzling my poor confused brain, as to what I should write to Ponsonby. My letter was to decide my fate on earth, therefore must not be hurried, nor begun, till I had collected all the energies of my mind. I prayed that such eloquence might be granted me, as might persuade and lead Ponsonby, at least, to show some symptoms of humanity towards me.

It was six o'clock in the morning before the strong opiate, which Dr. Bain had prescribed for me, produced any effect. At that hour, quite exhausted in mind and body, I fell into a heavy sleep, which lasted more than eight hours.

On opening my eyes I saw, at my bedside, my dear sister Fanny and Dr. Bain: the latter was feeling my pulse. I felt very much agitated at seeing Fanny there.

Dr. Bain told her that my disorder proceeded, alone, from the agitation of my mind; but it, nevertheless, had produced such violent effects, as to make it advisable for me immediately to lose some blood.

I submitted to whatever was required of me; but I begged Fanny not to tease or question me, as to what had caused all this, assuring her that I could not talk on the subject without disturbing my senses, and I was earnestly desirous of obtaining a little calm reason, if only for one hour more, that I might compose a letter before I died.

Dr. Bain, as well as my sister, said and did everything the most tender friendship could dictate. To be brief, their kind attention and my own excellent constitution triumphed over the fever, which had been very severe, during five days. In a little more than a fortnight, I left my bed; and, though reduced to the mere shadow of what I had been, I found myself sufficiently collected to address the following letter to Lord Ponsonby.

Scarcely a month has elapsed since I possessed, or believed I possessed, with health, reputed beauty, and such natural spirits, "as were wont to set the table in a roar," all my highest flights of imagination had ever conceived or dreamed of perfect happiness on earth—I had almost said, in heaven! Alas! I had not considered how unreal and fleeting must ever be the glories of this life, and I was, as a child, unprepared for the heavy affliction which has fallen on my heart like a thunder-bolt, withering all healthful verdure, and crushing its hopes for ever.

In encouraging so deep an attachment for a married man, I have indeed been very hardened; but, till now, I call my God to witness, I have never, in my life, reflected seriously on any subject. Maturity of thought, it should seem, is required earlier, by certain characters than others; for I could affirm, on my death-bed, that, hitherto, I dreamed not of injuring any one of my fellow creatures. In short, while I loved all the world, and would fain have done them all good, I most respected Lady Ponsonby. This assertion may seem scarcely credible to young females, differently educated, or of less wild and childish dispositions; but, just arisen from a sick bed, I write not to deceive.

Three weeks of bitter anguish of mind and body have changed, or rather matured my nature so completely, that even the expression of my features bears another character.

My eyes are now open, and I feel that as the mistress of a married man, possessing an innocent, amiable, young wife, I could no longer be esteemed or respected by the only being whose respect was dear to me. As lovers then, Ponsonby, we have met for the last time on earth! . . .

Here I laid down my pen; because this idea affected me.

I have delayed writing to you, till I could address you with reasonable firmness, not with the mere ravings of passion. Think you so meanly of me, dear Ponsonby, as to fancy that I could be gratified at becoming a mere instrument of pleasure to you, after my cool judgment has told me that I should thus forfeit all right to your respect or esteem? You are a man of the world, and, as such, may confound what is termed a love-fit, with the deep affection you have, for three years, taken pains to inspire in my heart.

Love never kills, says the unfeeling world: yet, unfeeling as it may be, such a sudden desertion of your wife would have called forth, towards her, its deepest commiseration. Alas! the ceremony of marriage, read over to me by a thousand priests, could not have added one jot to my despair, while I, in vain, cast my cheerless eyes around the wide world, for a single ray of pity, which is ever denied me. But come what may, I have been blessed.

Had it pleased heaven to have bestowed on me the husband of my choice, there is nothing great, or good, or virtuous, that I had not aspired to: as it is, I am a poor fallen wretch, who ask of your compassion one line, or one word of consolation, to save me from despair.

Oh! I have known such moments of deep anguish, as I could never describe to you. Ponsonby, my dear Ponsonby! I throw myself on my knees before you; I raise the eyes you have so often professed to love and admire, now disfigured and half closed by constant weeping, towards heaven, and I ask of God to soften your heart, that you may not torture me beyond my strength. Recall, then, those dreadful words—we must part now, Harriette, and for ever! I too am a woman, and Lady Ponsonby desires not my death.

When you come and speak to me of what is right and virtuous, shall I not love virtue for your sake? Have I ever wished to disobey you? I do not ask you to visit me alone. Call on me with Lord Jersey. Come soon, and give but the assurance that still and for ever you will be all to me that honour and virtue permits; that once in every year, while I act virtuously, you will visit me, and encourage me with your friendship and approbation.

I am overpowered with faintness and fatigue, else I had many, many more arguments to urge. Hope, almost life, hangs on your answer; therefore, dear Ponsonby, be merciful, and so may God bless you!

HARRIETTE.

My mind was very much relieved after I had dispatched my letter; for I considered that I should certainly hear from Lord Ponsonby, if he possessed one spark of feeling toward me; and if he did not, of course my respect and affection must naturally abate.

I watched for the appearance of the postman, who usually brought my letters, from morning till night, with indescribable emotion; nor did I cease to hope, for a whole week. At last, however, I was convinced that the epistle, which had cost me so much labour of thought, was indeed entirely disregarded by the person on whom, I expected, it would have made a deep impression.

Somewhat of an indignant feeling began to take the place of affection. All my woman's pride was roused, and yet, methought this man, so cruelly unfeeling to me now, has watched my slumbers in breathless silence, and still he smiles, with the same brilliant expression, on others, and all about him are impressed with that dignified air of true nobility, that high reserve so delightfully and condescendingly thrown aside, in favour of the few who please him.

A slow, intermitting fever began to prey on my constitution. I felt a violent oppression of the chest, which increased so rapidly, in spite of all my kind friend, Dr. Bain, could do for me, that, in less than a month after I had addressed my last letter to Ponsonby, I could never find breath sufficient to enable me to ascend the stairs to my bed-chamber, without sitting down to rest more than once. I began to hate society; above all, I avoided anything like gaiety.

It was now that I believed in all I had heard, as to the wretchedness of this life, and I wanted to reconcile myself to my God. I will pass my heavy hours in doing the little good to my fellow-creatures, in my power, said I, one day, as I recollected my former slight acquaintance with a woman whom I knew to have been lately taken to Newgate for rather a heavy debt. She was Lord Craven's housekeeper, during the time I had lived with him at Brighton.

I ordered my carriage to the Debtors' door of Newgate. My mind was so deeply absorbed with one object, that the misery I saw there did not much affect me. The poor woman, Mrs. Butler, was surprised and delighted to see me.

"I wish I could pay your debt," said I, panting for breath, as usual, and speaking with pain and difficulty.

"My dear, dear young lady," said Mrs. Butler, looking at me with much compassion, "what has happened to that sweet, merry, blooming face of yours?"

It only required a single word, uttered in a tone of sympathy, to bring the ready tears into my eyes. Mine now fell, disregarded by me, down my pale cheek. "You," returned I, "are not the only person in affliction; but never mind, talk to me, my good woman, of anything except my unhappiness. I cannot pay your debt, with common justice to my own creditors; but this trifle I can spare, and you are very welcome to it." I then placed in her hand all I, at that moment, possessed in the world, except a single one-pound note.

Mrs. Butler really was, what she appeared, very grateful. I sat an hour with her, and promised constantly to visit her, and provide for all her little wants, as long as she continued in prison. When I was taking my leave, just as the last bell was about to ring, which was to exclude all strangers for the night, I observed an interesting young girl, of about fourteen years of age, in one corner of the room, weeping bitterly; near her sat an elderly lady, apparently in much affliction. A working man was in the act of making up a large bundle, out of I knew not what.

"Those poor people are in great affliction," said Mrs. Butler, observing what had fixed my attention. "The mother has seen better days; they have hitherto contrived to pay 3s. 6d. a week for the hire of their bed, which that man is now taking away, because their means are exhausted." I was instantly about to desire the man to put down the bed, when prudence whispered in my ear, that I had just given all I possessed but a single pound note. No matter, thought I, taking out my purse, poverty cannot add to such affliction of the mind as mine is. Again I paused. This lady has seen better days, and must be treated with more delicacy. I hastened towards her, and taking hold of her hand, to place my bank note in it, I whispered in her ear, my request that she would do me the favour to make use of that trifle, and, without waiting her answer, I hurried on after the man, who was now disappearing with the poor woman's mattress and bedclothes, and desired him to return with them.

The next morning I was surprised by a visit from the Duke of Wellington, who had, unexpectedly, arrived from the Continent the night before.

"How do you do? what have you been about?" asked His Grace: then, fixing his eyes on my pale, then, careworn face, he absolutely started, as though he had seen the ghost of some man he had killed, honestly of course!

"What the devil is the matter?" inquired Wellington.

"Something has affected me deeply," answered I, my eyes again filling with tears, "and I have been ill for more than two months."

"Poor girl!" said Wellington, as though he really would have pitied me, had he but known how, and then added, "I always dreaded your getting into some scrape. Do you recollect I told you so? How much money do you want?" said this man of sentiment, drawing near the table, and taking up my pen to write a draft.

"I have no money," I replied, "not a single shilling; but this is not the cause of my sufferings."

"Nonsense, nonsense," rejoined Wellington, writing me a check. "Where the devil is Argyle? Why do not you make him pay your debts? I will give you what I can afford now, and you must write to me, as usual, at Thomas's Hotel, if this is not sufficient.

"Good God! how thin you are grown! Were you sorry I left you? I remember you shed tears when I told you I was off for Spain. I am a cold sort of fellow. I dare say you think so, and yet, I have not forgotten that either: because there is no humbug about you; and, when you cry, you are sorry, I believe. I have thought of you, very often, in Spain; particularly one night, I remember, I dreamed you came out on my staff."

Wellington consoled me as well as he could, and sat with me nearly three hours. His visit made no impression on me, except that I was grateful for his kindness in leaving me the money I wanted.

The oppression on my chest increased daily, and I became so reduced as to excite the commiseration of a kind, opposite neighbour, who sent over her footman to know if the poor young creature she saw from her window, and who appeared so very ill, had proper advice, and friends in town to take care of her.

My grief seemed now to settle in deep despondency. I considered my late intimacy with Ponsonby as unreal mockery, a bright vision of the fancy. I believe that, were he suddenly to appear again before me, I should instantly expire. Dr. Bain, I know, believed that my symptoms bordered on a decline, and he wished me to try Italy.

In about a week, I paid a second visit to Mrs. Butler, although my trembling limbs could scarcely support me up the stairs of the prison; and, when I entered, I was absolutely speechless with the effort for nearly a quarter of an hour. Mrs. Butler was all gratitude, while expressing the concern I believe she felt, lest I should injure myself by venturing out in such a miserable state of health.

Observing in the room several women, who appeared to examine me with much impertinent curiosity, I asked Mrs. Butler if she knew what it meant.

"Why," said Mrs. Butler, "that woman, whose bed they were taking away from her, when you noticed her last week, knows you, and has been malicious enough to tell all the room, that you are a mere kept mistress, with whom she should be ashamed to converse."

I threw on the stranger, to whom I had given my very last pound, a hasty and indignant glance; but, neither the expression, nor the colour of anger, would dwell on a cheek bloodless as mine, and I might apply to myself, what Sterne said of his poor old monk, that nature had done with its resentments.

I lingered thus, for about two months, without any visible change in my health or spirits, except that I grew weaker and thinner every day.

All the kindness which could be administered to a mind diseased, I received from my mother and sister Fanny.

About this time, the Duke of Argyle arrived from Scotland. He was, no doubt, greatly shocked to see me so ill, although the cause of my melancholy state of mind being known to him, did not either flatter or interest him; more particularly as he had often himself remarked to me, that he wondered any woman alive could resist Lord Ponsonby.

I had always liked Argyle, and was glad to see him, and should have indeed found much consolation in his society, but that he loved to trifle with my distress, as it regarded Lord Ponsonby.

"I have just dined with Ponsonby," said Argyle to me one night, "and I never saw him look better. He showed me a letter containing an invitation from that nasty sister of yours, Amy, who wanted to have me last year."

That way madness lies: I could not listen to another word. I was rushing past Argyle, when he detained me, frightened at the wildness of my looks.

"It is all a joke, you credulous little fool," said he, running after me.

"I cannot run," said I, turning round, and panting for breath. "Pray, pray, leave me now. You torture me by staying. Come this evening, and I shall thank you for your visit." It was long before I could induce him to leave me.

The moment I was alone, I dispatched the following note to Lord Ponsonby:

I thank you that you renounced my prayers; for thus you cured me of half my esteem. It was my fixed determination never to intrude myself again on your attention; but the Duke of Argyle has mentioned to me this morning, my sister Amy having written to you. Once more then, Ponsonby, I implore you, as you would save me from self-destruction, satisfy my wretched mind, in what cannot injure Lady Ponsonby. Declare to me—nobody has or shall. . . . Ponsonby, I am addressing you for the last time. Have mercy on the dreadful agitation of my mind, and answer me directly. You are quite happy, Argyle says; and I, in the very flower of my age, am dying. One line can relieve me, perhaps, from madness! Your watch, chain and ring, are sealed up. I could not look on them. I never shall again; my poor eyes have looked their last on them, and you; and I shall never write to you again; therefore, God bless you! When age shall overtake you, in some moment of affliction, perhaps you will remember me, and what I could have been to you. Adieu.

I dispatched my letter, almost without hope. If he could resist the other, thought I, this is more stupid, and less likely to affect him.

The agitation Argyle's stay had occasioned, produced an increase of fever. I now began to think seriously of dying, and not without reason, being reduced to a mere skeleton, and having been afflicted with cough and extreme difficulty of respiration for almost five months.

Some days later my servant brought me a letter, by the twopenny post; the handwriting was Lord Ponsonby's. Gracious heavens, how my heart beat! I could not open it. I kissed it a thousand times, placed it next my heart—thought I should never have found courage to read it, and when I did, at last, in fear and trembling, for I had begun to doubt the probability of any good happening to me on earth, it was as follows—very short and not particularly sweet:

Why, dearest, will you consider these things so seriously? Upon my honour, upon my soul, I can say no, in reply to your question; and you may tell the Duke of Argyle that he is mistaken, if he thinks me happy. Do you remember what I said to you at our last meeting? and will you do me the justice to believe I did not deceive you? pray do. Adieu.

PONSONBY.

Does this man love me? thought I, half wild with the delightful idea, and shall we not meet again? Impossible! As friends, at least, we must, shall meet, or I will die in the attempt.

The letter gave me new life, I imagined myself cured. Gay visions of departed happiness filled my imagination. I placed myself before the glass, to contemplate the havoc which sickness and anxiety had made on my features, and sighed heavily. No matter! vanity whispered, I am more interesting; though not half so brilliant; and then I hoped he would not love me less for the suffering his neglect had occasioned me. This world, said I, is a blank without him. I have endeavoured and prayed for tranquillity of mind in vain, during many long months, which yet have brought me no consolation. Too well I know I must renounce him as a lover; but for ever out of his sight, I cannot exist, and longer, I will not. I will take him by surprise. I will wait for hours, days, years at his door; but I will hear his voice once more. Shall I continue to suffer thus for what his footmen, tradesmen and valet, enjoy freely every day?

I, who would sign my own death-warrant, but once again to kiss the dear hand which inscribed this beautiful little note! What have I done, so very wicked, that I may not ever again behold him? I will wait at his door, every night that I can ascertain he is from home, and, the first time he happens to return on foot, I cannot fail to see him; and one word he must say to me, if it is but to order me home. Something like the man who boasted of having been addressed by the Emperor Bonaparte: What did he say to you? somebody asked. *Va t'en, coquin*, answered this true Christian.

Well then, to conclude, since I am sure my readers are growing as tired of this dismal love-story as I am, I wandered, nightly, round Lord Ponsonby's house, which I believe I have said was now at the corner of Upper Brook Street, in Park Lane, for nearly a fortnight, to no purpose. He returned not before daylight, when I dared not show myself, or he either came in his carriage, or had not left his house. The night air so increased my cough, that, God knows where I found strength for these wild nocturnal promenades; but love does wonders! I passed the whole day, coughing, in bed, to obtain strength, at least to die at his door: for I had taken an oath to behold Ponsonby again, or die in the attempt.

One night, dread of observation from the watchman, or insult from the passing strangers, made me parade slowly on the opposite side of the street, before his house. The moon was shining beautifully, at near one in the morning. A magnificent, tall, elegant man, habited in black, turned hastily round the corner, from Park Lane, and knocked loudly at Ponsonby's door. Could I be mistaken? I felt, in every drop of my thrilling blood, and at the bottom of my heart, that it was Ponsonby, almost before I had caught a glimpse of him; and, darting across the street, with the light swiftness of former times, alas! *ils étaient passés, ces jours de fêtes là.* A bar of iron, across my chest, seemed to arrest my flight, and I was compelled to stand quite still for an instant. That instant decided my fate. I obtained Ponsonby's dwelling, as the porter shut him out from my sight. The anguish of that moment I will not attempt to describe.

My mouth immediately filled with blood. Whether this was the effect of mental suffering, or whether I had done myself an internal injury by over-exertion, I know not; nor do I scarcely recollect how I happened to find myself in a hackney-coach. All I know, for certain, as to the adventures of that miserable night, is, that I opened my eyes, at five in the morning, to behold Dr. Bain and a surgeon, who was binding up my arm to bleed me, my sister Fanny, in tears, and the Duke of Argyle, who stood at the foot of my bed, consulting with Dr. Bain. I know not why the kind scarlet fever attacked me in the midst of all my troubles; but that was the disorder under which I suffered.

I will not dwell on what I endured, during a fortnight; indeed, as I was so frequently delirious, I knew little about it.

At the end of that time, however, my life was despaired of; but, in a few days, the disorder took a favourable turn, and after lingering six weeks, during which I had full time to reflect on all the follies I had indulged in, and having, for more than a week, been desired by Dr. Bain to prepare my mind for death, my late passion assumed the character of madness. I considered Ponsonby's conduct, towards myself and his wife, as equally heartless, and undeserved by all I had suffered for him. I earnestly prayed that he might, hereafter, make his lady amends for the former neglect I had occasioned her. I no longer desired to see him. I have suffered too much, I often thought to myself, and will not dwell on the occasion of it, lest I lose sight of that charitable spirit towards all mankind, in which I hope to die.

During this severe illness, the Duke of Argyle was very attentive to me. He was now the only man living for whom I felt the least interest. My sister Amy knew this, as well as all my late suffering; yet I was scarcely considered convalescent when she made a desperate attack on Argyle's heart, and which he complained of, to me, in terms of strong disgust. One night, in particular, before I had left my room, he came to me after the opera.

"I have had a narrow escape," said Argyle.

"From what?" I asked.

"A rape!" was his reply.

"Who then, in this land of plenty," said I, "is so very hard up?"

"Your sister Amy," returned Argyle. "She asked me to see her to a coach; then insisted on setting me down—drove me, *bongré malgré*, to her house; and would make me walk upstairs and sup with her. I was as obstinate as a stoic. 'Why, where are you going?' inquired your sister Amy. 'To a sick relation of yours,' was my answer; at which Amy looked like a fury, as she wished me a good night."

"How you abuse her," said I. "Really, you seem to have entirely forgotten our relationship."

"Why," added Argyle, "she sets me the example."

I fought Amy's battles as long and as earnestly as though she had really loved me, assuring Argyle that she was not bold, and had been kind but to very few lovers.

Argyle, no doubt, from all I said, began to think he had made a valuable conquest, and, rather than the poor thing should die, and appear at his bedside afterwards, like unfortunate Miss Bailey, I suppose he determined to look at her again, the next time he met her.

At that period, I believe he could have attached himself to me very sincerely, more so than formerly. His old friend, Lady W—— was in a very bad state of health, and was not expected to live. Argyle lamented the prospect of her loss, with real friendship, and would have found consolation in my society, but for my late desperate passion for another; which, however, I should soon have overcome, now that all was still, and calm, and quiet about the region of my heart. This calm was heaven to a poor wretch who had undergone so much mental suffering. I could not account for it; or rather, I could still less account for all my former misery.

As soon as I was able to converse, I inquired after my poor protégée at St. George's Hospital. My housekeeper informed me that she still lingered, in a very hopeless state. The idea of dying without seeing me again appeared to affect her much. I desired my housekeeper to carry her everything she wanted, and to assure her that my very first visit should be to her, the moment Dr. Bain would permit me to leave the house. That very kind friend had so reasoned with me, about the sin and folly of trifling, as I had done hitherto, with the blessings of health, that I had passed my word to obey him in everything, on pain of incurring his lasting displeasure.

On the very first day I received permission to go out, while my carriage was waiting at the door, I was shocked by a most melancholy scene. The poor young creature, from St. George's Hospital, having resisted the persuasions and threats of the matrons, declaring that she would see me before she died, drove up to my door in a hackney-coach, literally in the agonies of death! My landlord, who had just called for his rent, hearing, from my servants, that a dying woman was come to me from the hospital, declared that she should not enter his house. What was to be done? We were all women, and could not contend. My footman would have had her brought in by force; but force was the very thing in which the most particlerst man as js, was most deficient. The poor creature held out her hands, entreating me, for the love of God, not to send her away from me, in her last moments. The scene was indeed disgraceful to humanity, and I was very much affected by it; but how could I help it; the landlord insisted she should not come in. There was no time to be lost, she must go to the workhouse.

"We will lose no time in contention with this unfeeling wretch," said I, "but I will go with you to the workhouse, and nurse you."

"God bless you! God bless you!" exclaimed the poor dying creature, faintly. "I am not afraid of dying while you are with me."

I will not dwell on a scene which, even at this distant period, I cannot remember without shuddering. In less than an hour after my poor protégée was placed on a miserable couch, in Marylebone workhouse, she expired in my arms, earnestly and piously recommending her soul to God.

CHAPTER 7

My HEALTH SUFFERED much from this shock, and it was more than a week after the poor girl's death, before I could again venture to leave the house. My sister Fanny at last prevailed on me to go and pass the day with her. There I met Julia, who had forgotten her constant swain, Colonel Cotton, though he still appeared to adore her. She had fallen madly in love with Sir Harry Mildmay, who, for a short time, seemed to return her passion, and was really attentive to her, till somebody at Melton Mowbray asked him, one day, what the deuce he was doing with an old woman who might be his mother? All the love Mildmay ever felt, for any daughter of Eve, originated in vanity, and was fed and nourished by vanity; therefore, I need not add that he cut Julia from that hour, and, from that hour Julia's passion for him regularly increased; although it was unmixed or unpurified by the least atom of affection.

I inquired after Sophia, who had not been permitted to visit me; because the scarlet fever was considered infectious. She was still living in the shabby, confined lodging Deerhurst had provided for her, and Deerhurst also continued to provide her with currant wine and raisin wine! He saw but little of her, and the less the better for the taste of Sophia, who declared that water was by no means an indispensable requisite at that nobleman's toilette. In short, he was as much afraid of it as though he had been bitten by a mad dog.

I desired to know who consoled her for Deerhurst's dirtiness, and Deerhurst's neglect, and was told, by Fanny, that Colonel Berkeley tried hard to make himself agreeable; to which Julia added: "He is there from morning till night."

"And how does Sophia like him?"

"She dislikes him particularly. Henry De Ross is less disagreeable to her, I believe; but Sophia does not trouble her head, for an instant, about any man; only she really does wish that Deerhurst would wash himself a little more, and in particular his head."

Fanny went on to say, that somebody told him what Sophia said, on this subject, and Deerhurst, having accused her of circulating these stories out of school, asked her if he was not remarkably nice in his person.

"I think so," Sophia answered, "very nice indeed, I always said so."

Being still very weak, I left them early in the evening, and, passing by Amy's door on my road home, I observed a carriage waiting, very like the Duke of Argyle's. I could not possibly be in love with Argyle, that was very certain. I had of late given too many absurd proofs of love for another; and yet I had never ceased to admire and like him. He had lately been my sole friend, and his attention had promoted my recovery. In short, my nerves had undergone a shock which, to this day, I have not recovered from, nor ever have I enjoyed, nor shall I, most probably, enjoy another hour's health.

At that time a mere nothing affected me. I hastily pulled the check-string, and requested my servant to inquire of the coachman, if that was really the equipage of His Grace. He was answered in the affirmative. I am ashamed to confess how much, and how long, this circumstance affected me. It was painful to my heart to acknowledge a sister so un-natural, and it caused another relapse. Amy heard the occasion of it, and, sporting fine feelings, one fine morning, after having, by my kind recom-mendation, lived with Argyle more than a month, and become pregnant by him, she came suddenly into my room, and observing my deathlike aspect, began to blubber downright!

Hypocrisy was ever disgusting to me. I had in full, warm, sisterly con-fidence, introduced her to the Duke, and praised her to him, till I changed his disgust into something like partiality; dressed her up in my own elegant clothes, because hers were always as shabby as they were showy, in the style of her black-pudding dinners and champagne suppers; and she intruded herself into my house, warm from the embraces of my lover, to show off tenderness! I experienced a sudden fit of rage, almost amounting to madness.

"You disgusting, deceitful creature!" I exclaimed, locking her in my room, and taking out the key; "since you have forced your company on me, you shall repent it." I then looked round for some instrument to execute vengeance! ! !

Readers, can you conceive anything half so monstrous, half so ruinous to black-pudding men, so destructive to the rising generation?

I was just thinking about killing her!

Amy opened the window, and called out to a boy in the street, that a wicked woman, who was no better than she should be, had locked her in.

"I shouldn't wonder," answered the boy, laughing and running away, "a pair of you, no doubt!"

I by this time was heartily ashamed of having been thus surprised into temporary madness, owing to the extreme irritability of my nerves.

"Go out of the house," said I, "for God's sake; there is something too indelicate and disgusting in your pity. You are very welcome to live with Argyle, if you can endure the idea. I certainly felt the loss of a friend, in my present low nervous state; but His Grace knows well that I have been in love with another for the last three years, one on whom your soft circular effusions made not the slightest impression, unless of disgust."

I hastened out of the room, and locked myself into my bedchamber. Amy's visit, I afterwards found, was in consequence of the anxiety Argyle had expressed concerning my health, and Amy guessed that she must show off sisterly affection, or Argyle would dislike her!

The next day Argyle visited me. He was very melancholy, and had scarcely shaved since Lady W——'s death, which had lately taken place. He reminded me that, when he dearly loved me, I never *gênée'd* myself or him; that he was now unhappy and could have devoted himself to me; but that he saw no hopes of a steady return.

"Yes! but then a sister!" said I, "the idea, to me, is so disgusting—but do not let us dwell on it, I forgive anything in your conduct which has caused me pain, and destroyed the possibility of our ever being more than friends, for the rest of our lives—and yet, I trust, we shall never be less. A very trifle affects me now; so do not be too vain, nor attribute to sentiment what is due to the scarlet fever. You believed me incapable of steady regard; because I did not fix my undivided affections on you after I had learned, from your own letter, now in my possession, that you could not be wholly mine. Is that fair, or rather are not you a terrible coxcomb, master Argyle?

"*Apropos*, for here must end all sentiment between us, so, to talk of something else, Mr. Colman accuses you of having cut him dead in the park yesterday, when he bowed to you."

"What a vulgar fellow!" Argyle remarked.

"Why vulgar?"

"It is a vulgar idea, and one which certainly never occurred to me; not because I happen to be Duke of Argyle; for a private gentleman's rank, in society, is the same as mine; therefore, what right have I to cut him? or what right would any duke have to cut a private gentleman? If a man does not return my bow, I take it for granted he is absent or not in the humour, or thinking of something else. Tell Mr. Colman he is an ass, my dear pretty."

"Argyle!" interrupted I, "no more dear prettys, if you please. I have left off being pretty; but, thank God, I am heartwhole, and propose remaining so to the end of my natural life. Nevertheless, whatever the cause may be, I am truly sorry to see you so changed, and so melancholy."

"Thank you," returned Argyle, sighing. "Then oblige me and don't tell anybody in the world that I am unhappy."

His Grace seemed to leave me with regret. I did not invite him to repeat his visit.

My health, soon after this, began to improve rapidly. My late fever seemed to have carried away all the oppression on my chest, except what was the mere effect of debility.

I took an early opportunity of paying Sophia a visit, and I had scarcely time to inquire after that young lady's *petite société*, before Colonel Berkeley was announced. It was in the evening, at about eight o'clock. He was very lively and agreeable, which I think was generally the case with him. The man bears an indifferent character, and perhaps with some reason; but I have always seen him pleasant, and I never knew or heard of his breaking his word. His fancy for Sophia did not prevent his being polite and attentive to me, as often happens with ill-bred young men of the present day.

In less than half an hour after Colonel Berkeley's arrival, in bounced Lord Deerhurst, in an agony of tears! !

"Oh Sophy! Sophy!" exclaimed His Lordship, blubbering and wiping his eyes with a very dirty, little, old red pocket-handkerchief—"Oh, Sophy, I never thought you would have used me in this way! !"

Sophy declared herself innocent, which was indeed the fact, as far as regarded Colonel Berkeley.

"I cannot bear it," continued Deerhurst, rushing out of the room, like the strolling representative of a tragic king in a barn, and, seating himself on the stairs near the street door, to sob and blubber more at his ease.

Colonel Berkeley looked at His Lordship, in utter astonishment, exclaiming, "My good fellow, what the devil is the matter?"

"Why! did you not——" he paused.

"Did he not what?" I asked.

"Oh, Lord! oh, dear!" roared out Deerhurst.

"Don't take on so, my Lord," interposed Sophia's fat landlady, offering His Lordship a glass of water.

Deerhurst accepted it with apparent gratitude, as though quite subdued.

"Could you have believed it, Madam?" said he. "Did you believe that young creature was so depraved?"

"What do you mean by depraved?" I asked. "Why, I can answer for it, Sophia has never given Colonel Berkeley the slightest encouragement, and beyond a mere yes or no, she never opens her lips to him."

"Oh! don't tell me! don't tell me!" still blubbered His Lordship, the big tears rolling down his cheeks.

"This is incredibly astonishing!" ejaculated Colonel Berkeley, in a very natural tone of surprise.

"What is incredibly astonishing?" I asked. "I am determined to understand this. In fact, I think I have guessed already. Lord Deerhurst, by the restoration of his annuity, will put two hundred pounds a year into his pocket on Sophia's first act of infidelity. You are his friend, and have done nothing but express your astonishment at His Lordship's tears and apparent jealousy, ever since he came blubbering into the room; therefore, since his arrival so quickly succeeded yours, I will lay my life, you two desperate *mauvais sujets* came here together."

"Nonsense!" replied Colonel Berkeley, laughing.

"I am now sure of it," added I.

Colonel Berkeley slyly nodded assent to my remark.

Deerhurst was smelling a bottle of hartshorn, which Sophia's landlady held fast, to the end of his nose. Berkeley addressed Sophia, in a whisper. Deerhurst jumped up, like a madman, and was leaving the room.

"My good fellow," said the Colonel, taking Lord Deerhurst by the arm, for this excellent acting had really deceived even Berkeley himself, whom His Lordship had brought to Sophia's door in his own carriage, for the express purpose of taking her off his hands, "if you really are annoyed at my visit, if you have changed your mind—only say so, and I give you my word I will not call on Sophia again. Be a man! don't make this noise and bellowing; but tell me, frankly, what you wish. You and I are old friends."

Deerhurst said that his feelings were wounded and his heart-strings cracked; therefore he must go home and get them mended: and he darted out of the house.

"What the deuce can all this mean?" said Berkeley. "The man really is unhappy. I must go after him."

"Take me with you," I said, "just to gratify my curiosity."

"With all my heart," replied Berkeley, "if my carriage is at the door."

"Did not you drive here in it?"

"No," whispered he, "Deerhurst brought me with him, and I desired my coachman to follow, with my *vis-à-vis*."

We found it at the door, and were set down at Lord Deerhurst's house in Half-Moon Street.

We were shown into the drawing-room, where, after waiting about five minutes, His Lordship half opened the door of his bedroom, which was the one adjoining, and showed us such a merry-looking face, *qu'il n'était plus réconnaissable.*

"Glad to see you both," said His Lordship, wiping his hands with a very dirty towel. "Will you come in? But you must excuse the disorder. You know it is a mere bachelor's room," continued he, lighting a long tallow-candle, by a short piece, which was burning in a broken candle-stick.

"Why don't you ride and tie, regularly, with your two muttons," said I, "when you want to be economical? and then no one would know they had not been allowed to burn on together with an equal flame, like you and Sophia."

"Oh Lord!" said Deerhurst, laughing, "I can't cry any more at this moment, for I have just washed my face."

"But seriously," Colonel Berkeley observed, "I have followed you, because, upon my soul, I do not understand you. I want to know whether my attentions to Sophia are really disagreeable; for I don't see how a man could command so many tears to flow at pleasure."

"Oh! there was a boy at Westminster could cry a great deal better than I can," said Deerhurst.

"I won't believe you," retorted Berkeley, laughing, "unless you'll sit down on that chair and favour me with another cry; and first ring for some proper candles, will you? How came these stinking butcher's candles in your room?"

"Bachelor, you know, bachelor!" said Deerhurst, grinning.

"What the devil has that to do with it?" exclaimed Berkeley.

Deerhurst excused himself, declaring that tears, even sham ones, must be spontaneous; "and yet," said he, sinking into an arm-chair, and again taking out the self-same dirty little red calico pocket-handkerchief, "and yet, though I appear a wild, profligate, hardened young man, I never think of that sweet girl, Sophia, without its bringing tears into my eyes"; and he blubbered aloud, and again the big tears rolled down his cheeks.

"This would melt a heart of stone," I observed, putting on my cloak, "so I am off."

"What! won't you have any more?" said Deerhurst, jumping up and laughing.

"Capital!" exclaimed Berkeley, taking up his hat.

"Why, you are not going to trust yourself in that rake's carriage alone?" said Deerhurst to me.

"I am afraid there is no danger," answered I.

"Some of the most virtuous ladies in England have been attacked by the gay Colonel, until they have called out murder; and two of them lost their diamond brooches, coming from the opera, before they could get hold of the check-string——"

"Or cry out, stop thief!" added I. "For my part I have more reasons than one for believing the Colonel to be very harmless in a carriage, or I should not have ventured. I, too, have heard of his gallant feats of prowess, in chariots and *vis-à-vis*! but I will tell you a story: There was a pretty, elegant French woman joined my party, one night, after the opera, and explained to me the mere accident which threw her on my charity for a safe conveyance home. I had already Fanny, Julia, and little Fanny, as we called my young niece, to carry home, and only a chariot. What was to be done? The rain fell in torrents. It was on a Tuesday night, and there was nobody in the round room that anybody knew, as that fool of a Brummell used to say, except Colonel Berkeley, who joined us immediately.

"In spite of the most prolific account I had heard of the gay Colonel, I considered my friend old enough to take care of herself; and, as to sending her three miles, in such a costume, at such an hour, and in such weather, the thing was out of the question: so I told Berkeley that I must intrude on his politeness to set my friend down. 'To oblige you, with great pleasure,' was his prompt reply, before he had even looked in the face of the young French woman, to whom I presented him, when he assured her his coachman waited for her commands.

"The next morning, I made it a point to call and inquire after madame's health. She thanked me for having procured her so polite an acquaintance. 'I hope he was polite,' said I, 'for to tell you the truth, I very unwillingly placed you under his protection.' 'Why?' asked my friend. 'To be frank with you,' I replied, 'Colonel Berkeley is said to be such a terrible fellow! that no woman can safely remain a single instant *tête-à-tête* with him, particularly in a carriage. I understand he attacks both old and young, virtuous and wicked, handsome and ugly, maid, wife and widow.'

"'And sal I be de only exception?' asked the French woman, in real dismay.

"'What then,' I inquired in astonishment, 'are you sorry he was not impudent to you?' 'I do not conceive what you have told me, impudence,' continued the French woman, '*nous prenons cela autrement, en France*. Di only impudence vat I sal never forgive, is dat Colonel Berkeley have presumed to make me de exception, and if I ever meet him in de street, *je lui cracherai au nez.*'

"'*Non pas! non pas!*' rejoined I, 'you are too pretty to have been an exception. It is a mere false character they have given the Colonel, or maybe he set it about himself. For my part, I will take the first opportunity of getting into his carriage, in order to convince you of another exception, that you may hold up your head with the best of us.' This night has already proved I was right."

"Oh, Lord, what a falling off is here!" said Deerhurst to Berkeley.

"I want you and Sophia to favour me with your company to dine at Richmond on Monday, and, if you will trust yourself to my care, I will drive my barouche," said Berkeley.

"Willingly," answered I.

We then took our leave, and Colonel Berkeley set me down at my own door, in perfect safety.

The next day, I dined with Julia; Fanny was of the party. Julia was raving about Sir Henry Mildmay, by whom she professed to be pregnant. The shy Julia glorified in this *faux pas*.

"What mortal could have resisted such an angel!" exclaimed Julia.

"And Cotton?" added I.

"By your advice," replied Julia, "I have refused to receive him but as a friend."

"Certainly," said I; "I do think it wicked to put ourselves in the way of increasing a large family of children, only to starve them. You are the mother of six already, which is five more than your slender fortune can support."

"I shall have seven thousand a year at the death of my brother, who is in a decline," said Julia, whose eyes were very red, as though she had been weeping.

To my inquiry, what was the matter? Fanny answered, that the foolish creature had done nothing but shed tears from morning till night.

"If I could only once more have Mildmay in my arms," said Julia, "I should have lived long enough."

"And who is to protect Mildmay's child?" I asked.

"I would rather die than apply to him for money," answered Julia; "but my poor child will never see the light," and she burst into tears, "unless I see its beautiful father once more."

"Will once do?" I asked.

"I would be patient and resigned if I could kiss his heavenly eyes once more."

"*Et puis?*" said Fanny.

"*Sans doute! ça va sans dire,*" added Julia.

"*Pas toujours,*" I remarked, "however," giving my hand to Julia, "there is my hand on it, it shall be done, Ma'am, and before this week is out, we pledge to you our royal word!"

Strange to say, this promise satisfied Julia, who immediately dried up her tears.

After dinner a young member of Parliament, of immense fortune, brought his carriage for Fanny. He was a Hampshire gentleman, of the name of Napier, who had been lately very attentive to her; but Fanny did not like him. He was a long-backed youth with very fine eyes, and that was all; a sort of home-bred young man, not ungentlemanlike, but wanting tact and spirit.

Soon after his arrival, Fanny took me out of the room, and asked me how I liked him.

"Oh! not in the least," I answered.

"I wish," said Fanny, "he would attach himself to poor Julia: her children, and her debts, and her natural turn for extravagance, will send her to a prison, unless a rich man like this would take her under his protection. Now, as I am determined not to have him myself, I have left them together, that he may draw her into conversation, and find out the truth of her being one of the most elegant women in England."

"You are very good," said I, laughing.

"What else can be done?" Fanny asked. "If Julia goes to prison, she will immediately destroy herself; and how easily this Napier, who has more than twenty thousand a year, could assist her, and pay off all her debts, seeing that he lives on three thousand, and possesses, in hard cash and at his banker's, more than a hundred thousand pounds."

When we returned to the drawing-room, Napier did seem to have fallen in love with her conversation. However, he soon placed himself by Fanny's side, to make as much love as usual. "This is very poor sort of amusement for me, ladies," said I, "so I shall wish you all a very good night."

Fanny declared that she would accompany me.

Napier called her a coquette, and a false deceiver, reminding her of her promise to allow him to see her home.

"Cannot help it," answered Fanny, kissing her hand to him, and hurrying downstairs.

Napier offered me his arm to follow, and Julia held up her finger, significantly, to me, saying, "Remember."

"*Oui, oui,*" was my reply, and after Napier had handed us into my carriage, we requested him to return and chat with Julia. "A niece of Lord Carysfort," added I, "daughter to a maid of honour, the Honourable Mrs. Storer, and the most graceful creature breathing."

"Why," said Fanny, bursting out into a loud laugh, "Harriette, that madman with his placard and his challenge to all the world, about Bayley's blacking, in Piccadilly, is a fool to you."

"Never mind," I answered, "so that we can but get her off, and save her from a prison."

Before the carriage drove from the door, we had the satisfaction of seeing Napier return to Julia—*et puis—et puis*—but I will tell what happened some other time.

On our way home, Fanny told me how irregularly her allowance from the late Mr. Woodcock was paid, and that her boy George's schoolmaster had been dunning her for money due to him, which she could not pay.

"How good you are, then," said I, "to make over your rich conquest to Julia."

"There is no goodness in that," answered Fanny, whose heart was so very warm that she was always afraid of incurring ridicule from the extreme of a good thing.

"Since life is now dull and grey for me without affection," I replied, "and all my bright illusions are destroyed for ever; I have most pleasure now, when I can make myself a little useful; so you must let me take George off your hands. I am richer than you are; I will, therefore, pay his schoolmaster, and you must send him to me tomorrow. When his holidays are expired, I will, myself, take him back to school." Fanny said I was very good, and I answered, fiddlestick! as I set her down at her own house.

My mind was now a complete blank. My imagination was exhausted, my castle had fallen to the ground, and I never expected to rebuild it, for even my cool judgment told me that Ponsonbys were not often to be met with.

I had no fancy for going downhill, so I bought a great many books, and determined to make them my object. I lived very retired, and when I did go out, or admit company, it was more because I was teased into it, than from any pleasure I found in society.

Little George Woodcock came to me the next morning, and, before the week was out, he had broke open my jewel-box, stolen my money, kissed my housemaid, and half killed my footman. I looked forward, with much anxiety, to the period for taking him back to school. His schoolmaster was an old Frenchman, who lived at Layton-stone. Julia's three sons, and my nephew, had boarded with him four years.

Luttrell called on me the following day, and was greatly amused with the engagement, which I told him I had entered into with Julia. He informed me that Fred Lamb was arrived from the court of somewhere, I think Sicily, and had expressed a very strong desire to be allowed to visit me.

"Tell him," said I, "that I am worn out and tired of the world, and good for nothing."

Luttrell being our father-confessor general, to whom we all related everything, I asked him if he knew how Napier's *tête-à-tête* with Julia went off.

"Oh, I have just left the enemy," answered Luttrell, alluding to Amy, "who told me that Napier had made a violent attack on the virtue of Lord Carysfort's niece, in consequence of my flourishing panegyric, which had only served to prove her adamant to all but Sir Henry Mildmay."

"*Apropos* of that gay baronet," said I, opening my writing-desk, "such virtue as you describe, in this fair daughter of a maid of honour, must not go unrewarded"; and I wrote a polite note to Mildmay, desiring him to call upon me in the evening.

Soon after Luttrell had taken his leave, old Smith, the haberdasher, was announced, with more returned bills.

Angels defend us! said I, what am I to say to him this time? I looked in the glass, settled my head-dress as becomingly as possible, and trusted to my charms and soft speeches for subduing his anger, as usual.

As I entered, I caught a full view of my friend Smith, in the glass; he was pacing the room with sturdy firmness, as though preparing himself for a desperate attack. His brow was knit, and, in his hand, he held the fatal black pocket-book, which I had no doubt contained my bills, six or seven times returned on his hands. *Avec tout mon savoir faire, je craignais de ratter le procureur,* as Laura says in *Gil Blas*; I therefore returned to my bedroom, unseen, and desired my faithful housekeeper, Mrs. Kennedy, to declare that her mistress had been seized with a fit, on her way downstairs, and that, during the last attack of this sort, with which she had been afflicted, she had actually bitten her nurse's thumb clean off.

"Will you like to step up, and see her?" added Kennedy.

"No, no, I thank you," answered Smith, putting on a pair of his thickest beaver gloves, as though to defend his thumbs. "Some other time, if you please. My compliments"; and he was hurrying away.

"You will oblige me by stepping upstairs," said Kennedy, "as I really am frightened out of my wits; and Miss Wilson requires at least three persons to hold her when in these fits, and our William is just gone out with a letter to Sir Henry Mildmay's."

"Very sorry to hear it," replied Smith, running downstairs. "I regret that I have such a particular engagement that I cannot stay another instant," and he immediately gained the street door, which he took care to fasten safely, as soon as he was on what he now conceived the right side of it.

In the evening, Mildmay arrived at the hour I appointed, believing, no doubt, that the poor tender soul, Harriette Wilson, would not survive his neglect. He was proceeding, in a very summary way, to practical love-making.

"*Attendez un instant, mon ange!*" said I. "I am Julia's friend; besides, I have no opinion of you."

"In what way?"

"In the way you wish to shine! I believe you to be cold, and I hate cold men."

"Try me," answered Mildmay.

"*Je ne demande pas mieux.* Give me the proof I am going to ask, of your real genuine ardour, and I shall hereafter look up to you as something superior to the rest of mankind."

"Explain!" said Sir Henry.

"Well, then, there is Julia, of whom I know, you are completely tired. Only enable her to praise you to me tomorrow evening, and I think I shall not be able to resist you."

"Will you promise?" Mildmay asked.

"What is the use of a promise, to such a beautiful creature as you, who know yourself to be irresistible?"

Mildmay looked pleased. I made him sing to me, and I must really have been very deficient in good taste, if I had not expressed my admiration of the sweetness of his voice and expression. When I had completely flattered and praised him into excellent temper, I made him promise to visit Julia, by two the next day.

"Shall I find you there?" Mildmay inquired, "and will you give me a kiss? otherwise, upon my honour, with the best possible intention to distinguish myself, I am afraid."

"Perhaps," said I, "you may find me with her; but, at all events, recollect that you did like poor Julia, and that I never, to the day of my death, will forgive you or speak to you, if you do not fulfil your promise tomorrow morning."

"You treat me very ill," said Mildmay, "and yet, I suppose, you must be obliged. Only mind, you must promise me there shall not be a scene between Julia and me. I cannot stand scenes, remember!"

"I was in hopes there would be act the fourth," retorted I; "but seriously, what do you understand by a scene?"

"Reproaches and hysterics, and all that sort of thing," answered Mildmay. "Do tell Julia it will be of no use but to spoil the moment, there is a dear creature."

"Poor Julia!" I retorted. "Only recollect her situation, and pray, if you ever wish me to admire or like you, do not be so very unfeeling."

"Yes, I have heard all, and a pretty piece of business it is altogether," said Mildmay, evidently much annoyed by it.

I refused to part with him till he had most faithfully promised, punctually at two the next morning. As soon as he was gone I dispatched the following note:

DEAR JULIA,

Sir H. Mildmay has this morning, given me his word and honour, on pain of my everlasting displeasure, that he will attend your moderate commands, tomorrow, exactly at two o'clock, on condition that you do not give him a scene. Make my excuses to him for not joining you both. I dislike to be second fiddle, of all things.

God bless you.

The next day, the one fixed on by Colonel Berkeley for our trip to Richmond, Sophia and the Colonel called for me at twelve o'clock, accompanied by that young savage, Augustus Berkeley, who appeared to be perfectly well-behaved in the presence of his brother, quite mild and humbled.

Sophia said it was a charming day.

"The atmosphere," I observed, "is heavy I think, and unhealthy."

"Oh, quite shocking," Sophia immediately replied, "I am absolutely ill with it already."

We drove down to Richmond as fast as four highbred horses could carry us, and Colonel Berkeley having ordered a dinner, as much too ostentatiously extravagant as Deerhurst's rural fête had been too scanty, proposed our rowing down the river for half an hour, while it was getting ready.

Augustus, at the word of command, took off his coat and waistcoat, and began rowing, while Berkeley was all attention to us.

"How delicious this is," said the Colonel.

"I never saw anything so beautiful," echoed Sophia.

I remarked that I was a little giddy.

"So am I," said Sophia, "very giddy indeed."

In less than an hour, I mentioned that the air of the river had given me an appetite, and Sophia, of course, had never been so hungry in all her life!

Colonel Berkeley, on landing, astonished the two boatmen by throwing them a five-pound note! The innkeeper entertained us in his best and most magnificent style. We conversed a great deal, for Colonel Berkeley can talk, which is not always the case, nor considered at all a necessary accomplishment in gentlemen of the present day. There are, in fact, various kinds of gentlemen. A man is a gentleman, according to Berkeley Craven's definition of the word, who has no visible means of gaining his livelihood; others have called Lord Deerhurst and Lord Barrymore, and Lord Stair, gentlemen; because they are Lords: and the system, at White's Club, the members of which are all choice gentlemen, of course, is, and ever has been, never to blackball any man, who ties a good knot to his handkerchief, keeps his hands out of his breeches-pockets, and says nothing. For my part, I confess I like a man who can talk, and contribute to the amusement of whatever society he may be placed in; and that is the reason I am always glad to find myself in the company of Lord Hertford, notwithstanding he is so often blackballed at White's.

Colonel Berkeley and I conversed on many subjects; but there was one which was a favourite with us both—plays. Berkeley was mad for acting Shakespeare's plays, I for reading them. We were both lost in wonder as to how the poet, or any one man breathing, could have acquired such a perfect knowledge of human nature, in every class of society, in every gradation, from kings downwards.

I, by this time, conceived I had talked quite enough, and I therefore endeavoured, with all my might, to call Sophia out, and draw her into some kind of conversation.

Berkeley was beginning to think himself trifled with, and, being naturally a little abrupt in such cases, he told her flatly that, if she meant to refuse him after all, she ought not to have admitted him so often.

Sophia continued to hint, with proper delicacy and due modest blushes, that her living with him or not, must depend on what his intentions were: in other words, she gently intimated that, as yet, she was ignorant what settlement he meant to make on her. The gay handsome Colonel Berkeley's vanity being now so deeply wounded, he in his sudden rage, entirely lost sight of what was due to the soft sex, at least to that part of it which had been so hard upon him.

"Do you fancy me then so humble and so void of taste, as to buy with my money the reluctant embraces of any woman breathing? Do you think I cannot find friends who have proved their affection, by the sacrifices they have made for me, that I should give my money to buy the cold-blooded being who calculates, at fifteen years of age, what the prostitution of her person ought to sell for?"

Sophia was frightened, and shed tears.

"Colonel Berkeley," said I, "we are your visitors, and wish to retire immediately from such unmanly insult as you have offered to us. Will you procure us some safe conveyance? no matter what."

Colonel Berkeley immediately begged pardon, with much apparent humility, saying, "I am a passionate, ill-tempered, spoiled fellow, and must throw myself on your charity; or, if you prefer it, my carriage is at the service of you both, and neither I nor my brother shall intrude, without your permission."

I shook hands with him, as did Sophia, and little more was said. We all returned home together, but in silence, and Colonel Berkeley never afterwards sought Sophia's society.

I got home about five o'clock, and found Fred Lamb in my little library, looking over my books. I felt annoyed by this intrusion; but Frederick appeared to take so strong an interest in all I had been reading, and doing, since we last met, that my heart failed me, after I tried to quarrel with him.

"I never saw a girl, except yourself," said Frederick, "possessing unbounded liberty from the age of fourteen, without a single friend, or anything better to guide her than her own romantic imagination, who yet contrives to grow wiser every year, to reflect, to read, and to improve her mind, in the midst of such flattery as you are surrounded by."

Fred Lamb did actually say all this; but I do not tell my reader that I was vain enough to believe above half of it; for, though I had bought my books to be ready, in case a fit of reading should happen to come over me, yet I must confess that, hitherto, I have not had a call, as Lord Headfort said.

Apropos, to what?

I'll tell you—

At Brighton, I used to make a general postman of the good Marquis of Headfort, who had long been our family's friend, equally at hand to congratulate us on our marriages, our simple fornications, our birthdays, or our expected deaths. Send all your letters to me at Brighton, under cover to Headfort, I used to say to everybody who could not frank, or were so cut off from the blessings of this life as not to have a member belonging to them. Headfort, having a packet of letters to bring up to me, every morning, from the Pavilion, to Prospect House! which was the dignified appellation my landlord bestowed on my humble cottage at Brighton, I requested he would rap twice only; according to the etiquette observed by other postmen.

"How much?" one day asked my stupid new servant, for which I discharged her on the spot, for how could one live with an animal so little alive to the sublime and beautiful! as to have mistaken the Marquis of Headfort, wrapped up in an old greatcoat, on a rainy day, for a common general postman! ! I was really very much shocked indeed.

"Come upstairs, my dear Marquis," said I, "and see me discharge this fool directly.

"Take off your greatcoat.

"Ah! *vous voilà, Marquis, de haut en bas. Dites donc, mon cher, en parlant du bas,* who do you make love to now? for it cannot be supposed a gay deceiver like yourself can be satisfied with old Mrs. Massey all your life, although that crim. con. affair of yours did cost you so much money."

"Oh, my dear child," answered poor Headfort, "it is more than ten years since Mrs. Massey has cut me dead, as her lover."

"Why?" I asked.

"Don't you know, my dear, that she has turned Methodist, and thinks it wicked."

"But then," said I, "it is still lucky for you that her conscience permits her to make use of your house, purse, equipage and private boxes!"

"Yes," said Headfort, "she still does me that honour; for which I pay very dear, particularly on a Sunday, when she reads me Letters from the Dead to the Living, till I am almost tempted to wish her own name at the bottom of them."

"With whom, pray, do you console yourself?"

"I have not had a call, my dear, for the last five years!"

"It will come on you when you shall be born again, by the assistance of Mrs. Massey's prayers," I remarked.

I am, however, wandering from my subject.

No matter, it was a very bad one!

It was Fred Lamb, who dined with me, read to me, talked of love to me, and looked all passion, just like the satyr of my vision.

What vision, pray? the reader asks; that is to say, if ever I should be honoured with a reader, which is not at all certain. I am ready prepared and armed for abuse of every sort and kind: but not to be read!! No matter! if this happens, it will be entirely Stockdale's fault, for not enlivening the work with pretty pictures, as I have suggested to him, and certainly cannot, by the most remote possibility, be owing to any demerit of mine!

Above all, I wanted Wellington to be exhibited, dripping with wet, standing opposite my street door at midnight, bawling up to Argyle, who should be representing my old Abigail, from my bedroom window. Good gracious! I quite forgot to tell this adventure!! How could I be so ridiculous and negligent? Never mind, you shall have it now—but there is poor Fred Lamb waiting all this time, in my select library! I can't help it—there's no getting on with Fred Lamb. I never could use him, to any purpose, in all my life; and yet there's matter enough in him too! What matters that? Let it stand over, or let it pass. Fred Lamb can read Zimmerman, which he will find among my books. It will teach him to love solitude and to profit by it, while my readers amuse themselves with the interesting adventure, which happened on the very night of Wellington's arrival from Spain, and which I beg a thousand pardons for not having made them acquainted with, in due order and proper time.

Good news!! Glorious news! Who calls? said Master Puff, the newsman. Not that anybody called the least in the world; but Wellington was really said to have won a mighty battle, and was hourly expected. Cannons were fired, and much tallow consumed in illumination. His Grace of Argyle came to me earlier than usual on that memorable evening; but, being unwell and love-sick, he found me in my bed-chamber, when, catching me in his arms, he swore, by his brown whiskers, that this night, at least, he would be a match for mighty Wellington.

"*Quelle bizarre idée vous passe par la tête?*" said I. "Surely you have forgotten the amiable Duchess, his bride, and all the fatigue His Grace has encountered, enough to damp the ardour of any mighty hero or plenipotentiary, for one evening, at any rate; therefore, trust me, Wellington will not disturb us tonight."

At this very moment, a thundering rap at the door was heard.

"*Vive l'amour! Vive le guerre,*" said Argyle: "*Le voilà!*" And hastily throwing my dressing-gown over his shoulders, and putting on one of my old nightcaps, having previously desired "the most particlerst man as is," not to let anybody in, hastily put his head out of my bedroom window, which was on the second floor, and soon recognized the noble chieftain, Wellington! Endeavouring to imitate the voice of an old duenna, Argyle begged to know who was at the door?

"Come down, I say," roared this modern Blue Beard, "and don't keep me here in the rain, you old blockhead."

"Sir," answered Argyle, in a shrill voice, "you must please to call out your name, or I don't dare to come down, robberies are so frequent in London just at this season, and all the sojers, you see, coming home from Spain, that it's quite alarming to poor lone women."

Wellington took off his hat, and held up, towards the lamp, a visage which late fatigue and present vexation, had rendered no bad representation of that of the knight of the woeful figure. While the rain was trickling down his nose, his voice, trembling with rage and impatience, cried out, "You old idiot, do you know me now?"

"Lord, sir," answered Argyle, anxious to prolong this ridiculous scene, "I can't give no guess; and, do you know, sir, the thieves have stolen a new water-butt out of our airy, not a week since, and my missis is more timbersome than ever!"

"The devil!" vociferated Wellington, who could endure no more, and, muttering bitter imprecations between his closed teeth, against all the duennas and old women that had ever existed, returned home to his neglected wife and family duties.

That's all!!

CHAPTER 8

AND NOW WE really must attend to the Right Honourable Frederick Lamb, plenipotentiary at the court of ———, with all its appendages and powers to have and to hold by, etc. etc. etc.

He was, then, very handsome, and clever, and as his passions were most ardent, he would grind his teeth in bitterness of wounded pride, if you did not happen to be affected with the same ardour. Now I hate a man of this complexion. I take these sort of things, when they happen to me, very differently. My love or passion for a man is at once destroyed, turned to burlesque ridicule, *le moment qu'on ne me rend pas la pareille.*

But, again, I am digressing from Fred Lamb! ! What is to be done? unless he turn freemason, and tie me to his apron strings! I wish I had let him alone, instead of handing him into my library; he is quite a weight on my mind! Perhaps the reader will allow me to cut the subject where it stands? But I should like to tell them about The Cock at Sutton, too.

Of course, you all know The Cock at Sutton? or, lest any lady or gentleman should be so deficient in tact, so behind-hand in topographical knowledge, so unacquainted with public characters, suppose I just mention that the celebrated athletic Jackson, the gentleman-bruiser and prize-fighter, once shouldered and insinuated himself into the good graces of the fair widow who kept The Cock at Sutton, which afterwards became his, for several years, by right of marriage and rights of a landlord: hence its celebrity.

However, the story I have to relate has nothing to do with Jackson, else I could about it straight; but there is a fatality attending on Fred Lamb, and, though I am bored to death with him, I don't like to miss telling you the story of The Cock at Sutton! and so here goes—to use mad Dr. Roberton's elegant expression.

I could only get Fred Lamb out of my library, by promising him that we certainly should meet once more, if only to sign and seal my forgiveness of his former violence.

"Well, then," said Frederick at last, "I shall come up from Brocket Hall the day after tomorrow, and I will call on you on my way to town, and if you do not desire and wish to see me, order your servant not to let me in;

for I should be very sorry to be accused of forcing your inclinations a second time."

The next day, being, of course, deeply affected with Fred Lamb's absence, I went to call on Julia, *pour me distraire.*

But where is your story of The Cock at Sutton? the reader inquires.

I am coming to that, by and by.

Julia's spirits appeared much improved since my last visit to her. "I see very well, by your altered look," said I, "that Sir H. Mildmay has been paying you a visit, and has fulfilled England's expectation, by having done his duty."

"True," answered Julia, with a deep sigh, which almost resembled a groan; "but I see very plainly that he is tired of me, though I would resign all the rest of my life, without a sigh, to be loved for one single week more by that angel Mildmay."

"My poor forlorn woman," I replied, "for God's sake recollect you are a mother! Whoever forgets that, is less than human. Think of your poor, dear, beautiful children. It is wrong, perhaps, to intrigue, under any circumstances, yet somebody who was wise, or who passed for wise, has said that there are exceptions to every rule. Mr. Napier is rich and free. I think that it depends on you to provide for your children. Consider, my dear Julia," I continued, taking her hand, and I saw a tear glisten in her eye.

"When do you expect Mr. Napier?" I asked.

"The long-backed, odious creature, will call here tomorrow," answered Julia.

"I wish something else could be done," said I, hastily, sympathizing in her disgust.

"Shall I write to your uncle, Lord Carysfort?"

"Do not mention that unfeeling wretch!" exclaimed Julia. "A legacy has been left me, which I cannot help thinking has been unfairly appropriated."

"Have you applied to His Lordship on that subject?" I inquired.

"I have written to him twice," answered Julia, "and my second letter was answered by His Lordship, in these words:

The person from whom you expected a legacy, showed a becoming horror and disgust at your vile profligate conduct, by withdrawing your name from his will."

"Rely on it," said I, "that honourable uncle of yours has taken due care of your property. But what can be expected from one thus destitute of every manly feeling of compassion, towards a poor, fallen, defenceless relative?"

Julia absolutely sobbed aloud. I never saw her thus affected; for she was not given to the melting mood. To change the conversation, I asked her what had become of another noble relative.

"He has paid nearly a thousand pounds for me, and declares he can do no more," replied Julia.

"No matter," said I, "Napier is your man. Since you could be unchaste to gratify your own passions, I am sure it cannot be wrong to secure the comfort and protection of six beautiful children."

"But Napier's vanity makes me sick," retorted Julia, impatiently. "The possession of my person would not satisfy him. He wants me to declare and prove that I love him; and the thing is physically impossible."

I thought of Fred Lamb, and was silent.

"What has become of Amy and Argyle?" I asked, after a pause.

"Amy," said Julia, "is very proud of Argyle, and also of her pregnancy, and lives in hopes that her unborn babe, by the Scottish laws, may yet be Duke of Argyle."

"She has bespoken a boy, then?"

"Of that too she lives in hopes," repeated Julia.

"And the Duke," inquired I, with something like a sickness of the heart, "is he as tender and as loving as ever?"

"I have heard nothing to the contrary," answered Julia.

I was not jealous, but disgusted. I had always wished to love my sisters dearly. It was very hard on me that they would not let me!

"If," said Julia, "I were to consent to Napier's wishes, and he did not provide for my children, I should go into the Serpentine river the very next instant."

"Here is a fuss about trifles," said I. "Why cannot we take these things as the French women do? *Ça lui fait tant de plaisir! pendant que ça me coûte si peu!*

"That is the way they argue, and very philosophically too. Your sin has been bringing all these children into the world; and now, *coûte qu'il coûte*, you must provide for them to the extent of your power." I concluded here my very moral advice, and took my leave, promising to join her in our opera box on the morrow evening.

The next morning Mildmay called on me. He reproached me with having deceived and made a fool of him; but all he could say or do could not effect any change of my sentiments in his favour.

He had also professed to love Julia once, and how had he requited her? Heaven defend me from the like humiliation, thought I, and which I should richly deserve, were I to encourage this cold-hearted, profligate, beautiful Sir Henry.

As soon as I contrived to get rid of him, and had dined, I went to join Julia at the opera house. The first man who came into my box was Fred Lamb; he appeared delighted to see me.

"When did you come to town?" I asked.

"This morning," Fred answered, "and I called on you; but you were either out, or denied to me."

"I passed the morning in my little library," answered I.

"You have made me very wretched," whispered Fred Lamb, pressing my hand with much passionate agitation. He looked remarkably well.

"Indeed, Fred," said I, "I did not mean it."

"Remember your promise then," added Fred Lamb, "and do, pray, dearest Harry, tell me, when you will throw away two whole days on me, in the country?"

"What shall we do there?"

"Get married," interposed Julia.

"Go to The Cock, at Sutton," said Berkeley Craven. "It is a delightful, pretty, rural place for a man to read rhymes and be romantic in; just fit for you, Fred."

"Are you ever taken with either a fit of reading, or a fit of romance, Berkeley?"

"Ask my young nephew here, who can tell you how I used to sit, and sigh, and drink brandy and water, with Mrs. Patten, after the play," answered Berkeley Craven.

"So much for your romance!" said I.

"And as to reading," continued Berkeley, "I will be bound to say that, among men who have received no regular education, not one has read more plays and farces than I have; and I always read the newspaper from beginning to end, except the debates."

The Duc de Berri next came in; and we all stood up till he was seated, as bound by etiquette; and then followed my young, new acquaintance, the Duke of Leinster, who stood up by himself, like a noun substantive, for want of a chair.

Now the said Duke of Leinster being a very stingy, stupid blockhead, whom nobody knows, I will describe him. His person was pretty good; straight, stout, and middle-sized, with a good, fair, Irish allowance of leg. It was a good leg, however, *mais en gros*; and I never saw anything more decided in the shape of curls, than those which adorned and distinguished Leinster's crop from all such heads of hair as are in the habit of resisting the curling tongs, when they do not happen to be red hot: *c'était, enfin, une belle tête.*

I do not see how a man could be well handsomer, without a mind. His Grace was, at that time, in the constant habit of assenting to whatever anybody said, good or bad. He was all smiles and sweet good humour. He would in fact have made an excellent husband for Sophia; yet, strange to say, he felt not the slightest inclination towards her; but Leinster is not the first fool I have met with, who required wit and talent in a mistress.

"How did your Grace's party on the river go off this morning?" I asked.

"Oh, it was charming," answered the Duke; with more of the brogue than was at all necessary for a lad who had been bred at Eton. "But, upon my honour," added Leinster, "the English are too stiff and abominable, for, just as I had stripped and began to row, they hallooed out 'Wait for His Grace! where's His Grace? where's the Duke of Leinster?'—as if His Grace, who happens to be a mere wild Irish boy, of nineteen, was not allowed to amuse himself in the same way that other lads do. I question if they did not expect to see me in a big wig," added Leinster.

"I knew I should find my noble cousin, the big Duke, here," said the young handsome Harry De Roos, peeping his Narcissus-like head into my box.

"Come in, you pretty Harry," said I.

"Oh! I am very melancholy," observed De Roos, blushing, as he took his seat.

"Upon my honour," said Leinster, "Henry is fretting for nothing at all. Wait now, while I tell you all about it."

"Indeed, and we are waiting," I answered.

"Why," Leinster went on, "his mother, my Lady De Roos, is going to send him down to a private tutor, tomorrow, and I have frightened him with my description of the Smiths, that's all."

"Who are the Smiths?" I asked.

"Mr. Smith is the name of the big Duke's tutor, whom he has just left," answered De Roos, "after enduring such wretchedness, for more than two years, as would have about finished me, I am sure."

"Nothing at all like wretchedness, upon my honour," retorted Leinster. "It is all Harry's spoiled way."

"Tell us, you big Duke, how you used to pass your valuable time, at this said bug-bear of a tutor, Mr. Smith's," said I.

"Listen while I tell you then," replied Leinster. "Myself and two other lads were under his care. We rose at six, and cleaned our own boots and shoes."

De Roos looked on his peculiarly delicate white hand and fingers, and sighed heavily!!

"And then," proceeded Leinster, "we took our breakfast, which consisted of thick slices of bread, with a little salt butter. After that we had three large books placed before us, and in which we were desired to read for five hours, taking down notes of whatever struck us most forcibly. At dinner, which consisted one day of a roast joint, the next of the same hashed, the third, ditto, minced, our society was enlivened by the three Miss Smiths!"

"What sort of animals were they?" inquired Julia, laughing.

"Gorgons, all three of them, and the youngest turned of thirty," said De Roos, with a heavy groan.

"Thank God, I have done with private tutors!" said Leinster.

"How do you like Oxford?" asked Julia.

"Delighted with it," replied the Duke. "*Apropos* of Christchurch. Do you know that Brummell is cut amongst us, and who do you think sets the fashions there now?"

"Yourself, perhaps."

"No, nothing is asked, but whether Harriette Wilson approves of this or that? Harriette likes white waistcoats—Harriette commends silk stockings, etc. I asked my friend, the young Marquis of Worcester, why he did not curl his straight locks? Harriette considers straight hair most gentlemanlike. On my asking him if he knew Harriette, the Marquis owned that he had never seen her, adding, 'I ran up three times to the opera, on purpose; but she did not make her appearance. Will you present me to her? I shall be much indebted to you.' 'Not I, indeed, upon my honour,' was my answer, 'and I am the only young man at Oxford, acquainted with you.'"

The Duc de Berri, who had been all attention to Julia, arose to depart, and we all stood up to bow him out, with the self-same ceremony with which we bowed him in.

To proceed, I refused to permit the Duke of Leinster to accompany me home, although he declared himself ready to mount the box, or to stand behind, with my dapper little footman! I was out of sorts, and out of spirits at the idea of having promised to meet Frederick Lamb at The Cock at Sutton on the following morning. Oh, this tiresome Fred Lamb! I wonder if any woman alive was ever in love with him, with the exception of the once celebrated Charlotte Windham; who would have taken him into keeping, at least so I have heard, and found him in washing, tea, sugar, and raw eggs, to the end of his natural life, had he not cut her dead, *pour mes propres beaux yeux.* Handsome! clever! young! a great plenipo, and the recorded son of the Earl of Melbourne! What would ladies be at? *On ne connait pas toujours son père, c'est un malheur; on est sûr, cependant, d'en avoir eu un, cela console!* as says Pigault Le Brun.

Fred Lamb certainly had a father, and, in my conscience, I believe him to have been a man of high rank, no matter whether he was a lord, a duke, or a prince, and what is more, his mother was a married woman; and yet, notwithstanding these multifarious advantages of both, I looked forward with disgust to the idea of meeting him, at The Cock at Sutton. How could I be so deficient in good taste?

On the following morning, I did not awake till twelve o'clock, when I rang my bell.

"*Madame, la voiture est à la porte,*" said my French maid, as she entered my bedroom.

"I cannot help it; so bring me a cup of chocolate, *pour me donner du courage,*" I replied.

Before I had finished it, the Duke of Leinster was announced, and I went down to him in my dressing-gown and slippers.

"Upon my honour," said His Grace, "I am very glad you do not keep your appointment with Fred Lamb. I have brought little George some strings to mend his fiddle with, and if you will give it me, I will string it for him."

I rang for the fiddle, and Leinster set to work in great glee.

"How did you get home last night?" I asked.

"Oh," said Leinster, "my brother, Fitzgerald, has found out such a woman!! Upon my honour, I never laughed so much in all my life. He told me she was Venus herself, just emerged from the froth of the sea! I wanted to go home and think of you; but Fitzgerald dragged me by force to No. 2, Upper Norton Street. We were shown into a parlour by an old dirty duenna, who assured us her mistress was engaged, and she regretted it of all things.

"'Good gracious!' said I, 'Fitz, you are not going to wait?'

"'Yes,' said my brother, mysteriously; 'she is in keeping, and has been these five years. I shall ruin her if I am found here, so pray be quiet. The gentleman who keeps her is a captain of horse-marines.'

"'For God's sake, let me be off,' said I, making the best of my way to the door. I can stand a lick or two, as well as most lads of my age and country; but, being in love elsewhere, and not quite come to my strength, I do not feel much inclined to encounter this horse-marine tonight.' However, Fitzgerald over-ruled all my objections, and kept me there, in perfect misery, for more than half an hour. At last, we heard the creaking of heavy boots descending the stairs. I scarcely ventured to breathe, expecting, every minute, to be called to account by the horse-marine, for being found concealed on his premises at past two o'clock in the morning.

"Upon my honour, I did not half like it! and only just fancy my horror when, instead of going out at the street door, as we both expected, this much-dreaded horse-marine strutted into the parlour, in search of his hat! He did not look much like a horse-marine, but reminded me more of a city hosier. Nevertheless, I made myself as small as possible, and strove to hide behind the scanty, red window-curtain. As to Fitzgerald, believing that all was lost, he became bold from desperation, and, folding his arms across his breast, he fixed his eyes steadily on his rival. The horse-marine, who had entered with the sort of strut which became a commander-in-chief of No. 2, Upper Norton Street, started back, instead of encountering my brother's fixed regard, and began to stammer out an apology. He had just taken the liberty of seeing the lady home safe, from the opera; he begged pardon if it had been wrong, he was sure no harm, nor disrespect was meant, etc.

"By this time, my brother, who, I assure you, is by no means such a fool as I am, saw exactly how the case stood, and that the horse-marine was but the creature of his fair mistress's imagination, a sort of circular bugbear, by which she contrived to frighten all her lovers, while she flattered their vanity with the idea that her acquaintance was an unusual *bonne fortune*, which their peculiar merits alone had obtained for them. This conviction being impressed on my brother's mind, he interrupted his rival, in the midst of his humble apologies, by playing himself for that night only, the character of the terrific horse-marine!! And, waving his hand, with much pomp, towards the door, as he fixed his back against the fireplace, said, 'No offence, my good fellow, no offence! only there is the door, you know, and, unless you prefer making your exit by the window, never let me see your rascally ugly face in this house again!'

"Upon my honour," continued Leinster, "I could not stand it any longer, and before the poor trembling wretch got to the street door, we both broke out into a roar of laughter, which was interrupted by the entrance of the frail fair one, herself, whom my brother immediately accosted thus:

"'Fair lady, since I have been allowed to make so very valuable an acquaintance as that of your horse-marine, my conscience will not permit me to interfere with his happiness'; and we hastened out of the house, before the lady could recover from her confusion and surprise."

"Now, Duke," said I, "there's the door," placing myself before the fire and pointing to it, in humble imitation of Fitzgerald.

Leinster took this gentle, delicate hint, with much good nature, and left me at about two o'clock. I felt really ashamed of myself, and, hurrying on my travelling dress, was soon with my maid, on our road to The Cock at Sutton. Fred Lamb was waiting at the door, and his joy, on perceiving my carriage, overcame all his late vexation.

"I shall be nicely quizzed and laughed at," said Fred Lamb. "Harry Windham and Lord Egremont alighted here this morning, on their road to His Lordship's house at Brighton. They asked me so many questions as to where I was going, that I was obliged to confess I was waiting for somebody to meet me. They remained with me an hour. 'Why, you will not wait any longer, surely,' said Harry. 'Who can the cruel fair one be?' It was too bad of you."

"Well, do not scold," I answered, "for I could not help it."

Fred Lamb had a book in his pocket, and he read to me, in the garden, while our dinner was preparing. His remarks on the fine poem he read were very sensible; but his manner of reading, like that of his brother William, I dislike: it might rather be called singing; and yet some say it is proper, and all admit it to be the fashion to read so.

We had an excellent dinner, and, as long as I saw daylight, I kept in pretty good spirits; but when the waiter brought us candles, and we seemed as though settled for the night at The Cock at Sutton, my heart completely failed me. I tried hard to reason myself out of this repugnance. I argued with myself that, since I had already been under Frederick's protection, one night more or less could not make much difference —but to leave him now, were to treat him really ill, and make, perhaps, a bitter enemy of a man well disposed towards me: but all would not do. I cannot help it, said I to myself, in a sort of frenzy; I would rather die than pass another whole night with Fred Lamb, now the thing is gone by, and I have been so attached to another. My case was desperate; for I almost equally dreaded telling Lamb I would not stay with him.

"Fred Lamb," said I, at last, absolutely pale with terror, "I really must return to town tonight. Do not ask me why, for you may be sure, if I wished to stay, I should not go; and, if I do not, my society cannot be worth having, to a man of taste, who can easily make himself beloved and desired by more likeable objects than I am. You will, I know, have a right to reproach me with caprice, because my good heart made me wish to avoid the appearance of unkindness towards an old friend, *mais vous savez bien que les passions ne se commandent pas.*"

Fred Lamb, on this occasion, behaved very well, and very gentleman-like, much as his pride and feelings were hurt. He ordered out my carriage, and accompanied me home with friendly politeness, nor did he make a single unpleasant observation on my refusal to remain there.

The favourite topic, on my arrival in town, was the Marquis of Anglesea's elopement with the wife of Sir Henry Wellesley. His Grace of Argyle was soon expected to console Lady Anglesea by the offer of his hand and heart, in case that good lady could contrive, by hook or by crook, by English law, or by Scotch law, to obtain her liberty.

Amy Madden, alias Sydenham, alias Argyle, had long been led to believe, according to her own account, that she was to become the legitimate wife of the Duke of Argyle. At last, when Amy was very near her confinement, Argyle, fearful lest the sad truth might fall heavier on her tender heart from a third person than from his own lips, one fine morning, after breakfast, having, no doubt, previously fortified himself with a bumper of brandy, for Amy was a practical Tartar, opened to her, with the utmost delicacy he was master of, the appalling fact that he was about to marry Lady Anglesea.

Amy had an hysterical fit, or was afflicted with sore eyes, I forget which; but I know that she was very bad, and vented her rage in all the refined expressions usual on these most celebrated occasions. It will scarcely be expected that I should feel much commiseration for her. When I state these facts, it must be understood that Amy said so; but then, will methodistical Luttrell add, with his eyes turned up towards the sky, or the ceiling, as the chance may be—if all the lies that have been uttered since the flood, were put into a scale with Amy's, they would weigh as a hair in the balance; so that, perhaps, the less I say on this matter the better.

At last, when a whole month had elapsed beyond the period Amy had named for the expected event, Argyle could keep on the mask no longer; and, having asked her, one evening, how she felt, and received for answer, that she was perfectly well and free from pain, he said, in a passion, "Why, Amy, you are surely a Johanna Southcott, and never mean to be confined at all." This was certainly very cruel, though, no less certainly, circumstances did rather appear to justify such a suspicion!

At last, oh, blessed news for Argyle! Amy declared she felt a slight pain;

but whether it proceeded from the sweet pledge of love she carried in her bosom, from wind, or from what else, Time was to determine: and my kind readers will probably recollect that, in a like protracted case, old Time determined against the late Marchioness of Buckingham, without the least respect to all the splendid paraphernalia which had been profusely got up for the anticipated joyful occasion. Amy, however, not being quite so stricken in years, Argyle bustled about, in the joyful hopes of a speedy deliverance, and said, "No harm in sending to Dr. Merriman, and getting the knocker tied up, and a little straw laid before the door!" As to the nurse, she had been in the house for the last month!

By the time the knocker was tied up, the straw laid down, and Dr. Merriman shown upstairs into her room, Amy declared herself quite well again, and so she continued for another week.

"Good Lord deliver us!" exclaimed Argyle.

"Amen!" responded the old nurse: for who would differ from a duke; however pleasant it might be to enjoy present pay and good quarters for doing nothing!

I cannot help pitying anything in labour, even a mountain! At length Amy herself really experienced the so often anticipated pains. She now declared that she could not stand it; and would not, what was more!

"Give me a pair of scissors!" said she, in a fury, to the doctor, "and I will cut my own throat directly."

Dr. Merriman answered, with perfect *sang froid*:

Apropos! I do remember this said Dr. Merriman, of Curzon Street, an apothecary, and often has he stood behind his uncle's counter to serve me, when I was a child, and fond of sweets, with a pennyworth of Spanish liquorice. His father was a respectable *accoucheur*, and had the honour to bring all my respectable family into this respectable world, one by one, except my youngest sister Julia; and he would have done as much by her, but that he happened to die one day, and the present Dr. Merriman, his nephew, formerly designated Sam Merriman, officiated, *faute de mieux*, my dear mother being too shy to endure the idea of a stranger.

As soon as he got possession of his dead uncle's carriage, he took the small liberty of cutting the shop, Spanish liquorice and all, and ventured to change the name of Sam, for the more dignified one of Doctor, but it would not pass current everywhere. Many refused to pay a fee, and voted him ignorantus, ignoranta, ignorantum! and so Sam, *à force de battre le fer*, contrived to take out a degree, and became Dr. Merriman, indeed, at any lady's service.

"My dear lady," said the Doctor to Amy, in answer to her request for a pair of scissors to cut her own throat, "my dear lady, I should be happy to oblige you, if you could first insure my own neck"; and then, turning to the nurse, as he warmed his hands by the fire, "I always let them halloo, and make just as much noise as they like; but, for myself, as it will be necessary for me to pass the night here, I shall thank you to give me some warm blankets, on that sofa: with a cup of tea, and a bottle of wine."

In due season, the gentle Amy was delivered of a fine boy by my old friend Sam Merriman, and was duly announced to be as well as could be expected. For another fortnight, Amy contrived to keep Argyle in London, as might be supposed, to his no small annoyance, just on the eve of his approaching nuptials with Lady Anglesea. The time, however, did at length arrive, when His Grace took his departure northward, to the destruction of all the airy visions which had long flitted before the anxious eyes of Amy, who had adorned them with ducal coronets, and almost every other attribute of a resolutely ambitious and selfish mind. She declared that her death must be perfectly an event of course; yet she got up in a month, as blooming and well as she had ever been in her life. It is true she worked herself up into a dreadful frenzy of passion, when anybody told her that the Duchess of Argyle was, or would soon be, in the way which all ladies who love their lords wish to be in; but she was easily consoled by adding a few years to Her Grace's age, or detracting from the Duchess's charms, personal or mental.

Enough of Amy. I hate to dwell long on any subject, unless, indeed, it were the merits of these, my most interesting and valuable memoirs! which I assure you might have been better still—but that Mr. Stockdale won't let me, or anyone else, study and correct them. "The merit of such a light work as this," stupidly says he, "is, that it is written without study, and naturally, and just as you converse. There are learned books enough, and more than people are aware of, all written with such correct precision as to defy the Edinburgh Reviewers themselves! and yet half of them do not take, although months have been spent in poring over heavy volumes, to secure the accuracy of a single date. This research is highly creditable in its way; but since the world, in their rage of variety, require a little of everything, write you in your own natural language, and of life, manners, and men, as they strike you, and, take my word for it, your own genuine spirit will please, and the book will sell." So here am I, seated in an easy chair, at No. 111, in the *Rue du Faubourg St. Honoré, à Paris,* writing, not for the benefit of my readers, but for my own amusement and profit to boot, and in the full expectation that my work is to pass the twentieth edition!!

CHAPTER 9

THE DUKE OF LEINSTER, Harry De Roos and Sophia were dining with me one night when, just as we were about to sit down to dinner, Lord Deerhurst was announced.

"Dear me, how tiresome," said Sophia.

"Do not send him here, pray," said Leinster and De Roos in the same breath. I went down to ask him what he wanted, and informed him of my dinner-party, with whom I knew he was unacquainted.

"Oh, I wish much to know the Duke of Leinster, so pray do introduce me," said Deerhurst.

"No," I answered, "I shall do no such thing. That's frank and flat. If you don't like Sophia to dine here, you may, with her consent, take her away with you, but I will never present you to any friend of mine. Sophia told you, this morning, that she was to meet the Duke of Leinster and his cousin."

"Certainly," answered Deerhurst, "I have not the slightest objection; but do, there's a dear, good creature, present me to the Duke of Leinster."

"You are, in all and everything, the meanest man on earth," was my civil remark.

"You refuse then?" said Deerhurst.

"I do," repeated I, impatiently, "and you must now allow me to wish you a good morning, as we are going to dinner immediately."

"Then," said Deerhurst, "I must introduce myself, that's all"; and, disregarding all I could say or do to prevent him, he ran into the drawing-room, took off his hat with a low bow, and said:

"Duke, allow me to introduce, and earnestly recommend to your notice, Viscount Deerhurst."

The Duke had no pride, and was very mean and stingy, nobody more so; but he paid his bills, and was what the world calls an honourable man. To do him common justice, I do not think he would like to break his word, however much it might be to his interest, and well as he loved money. He disliked Deerhurst's character, and was too natural, and not half polite enough, to conceal his displeasure at being so unceremoniously intruded upon. He bowed very slightly, without speaking, and the smile with which he greeted His Lordship was scarcely perceptible.

Harry De Roos was as proud as he was shy, and took no sort of notice of Deerhurst, beyond rising from his chair, when His Lordship turned from His Grace to his cousin.

Deerhurst's stock of assurance was not to be diminished by two mere boys. He seated himself near Sophia, ever certain of her unqualified approbation, at all events.

"Well, Soph, my love, are you glad to see me?"

"Yes, I am very glad indeed," replied Sophia.

"I'll tell you something, Lord Deerhurst," said I. "I do not like quarrelling with people, and especially in my own house; but, seriously, I must tell you that these gentlemen expected to meet Sophia and me only, and your intrusion is really a little cool."

Sophia said I was quite right, it really was very cool indeed, and she had heard His Grace request that we would fix on a day when nobody else was coming.

"If His Grace will say he wishes to get rid of me, I am off," remarked His Lordship.

What could the easy-tempered Leinster do less than declare his happiness to see him?

Deerhurst possesses talents, and can be very agreeable. He was growing tired of being cut by so many respectable people; therefore he set about winning the friendship of the Duke of Leinster. He talked of sailing, and boats, big fiddles, and Irish watchmen; praised to the skies such of the Irish nobility as lived on their estates, and imitated the Irish brogue as though he had been practising it all the days of his life. Leinster was delighted with him.

After dinner, Luttrell called to say that Amy gave her first party, since her confinement, on this evening, and had permitted him to say that, as it was a mutual convenience that we should meet, civilly, at parties, and neither friendship nor intimacy was necessary for that purpose, she was ready to ratify the engagement made between us, a few years back, to offer me no insult, and desired I would go to her, in the course of the evening, and bring as many of my male friends as I pleased.

I asked Leinster and De Roos if they would like to take me to Amy's with them?

"Most willingly," was their answer.

"Make no apologies for not asking me," said Deerhurst, "for, with all my impudence, I do not think I could face that Tartar of a sister of yours, without a special invitation."

"Are you fond of looking at jewellery?" I asked Luttrell.

"Very," answered Luttrell, "and I believe I am rather a good judge too."

"Then," said I, "Sophia, my dear, if you have brought your jewels with you, pray ask Mr. Luttrell's opinion of their value."

Sophia drew from her reticule two smart jewel-boxes, of Love, the jeweller's. "These are the jewels which were presented to my sister by Viscount Deerhurst," said I, as I handed them to Mr. Luttrell.

The box contained a necklace of large green glass beads, set in yellow metal. There was a leaden ring, with a blue bead in it, a small Tunbridge-ware tooth-pick case with

"When this you see, remember me"

superscribed on it, and two brass seals, one with the name of Sophia on it, the other with a little winged figure, evidently meant for a cupid, or a parrot; but it was very difficult to decide which it most resembled. Everybody laughed heartily, but the loudest laugh of our party was Viscount Deerhurst.

"And then," said Deerhurst, trying to recover himself, "and then, having won the young lady by dint of these valuable jewels, Robinson, the attorney of Bolton Street, first draws up an agreement to secure to her an annuity of three hundred a year, and the next day tells you his agreement is not worth sixpence!!"

There was only one of our society who carried politeness so far as to seem amused at such disgusting profligacy.

Luttrell looked with unqualified contempt on His Lordship. Leinster and De Roos, considering themselves too young to set an example, or reform the age, fixed their eyes steadily on the carpet, while De Roos's fair cheek was tinged with a deep blush. Sophia alone joined Lord Deerhurst in his laugh; declaring that it was very funny to be sure.

"Lord Deerhurst," said I, "Sophia is my sister, and, if she chooses to submit to insult and ill usage from you, it shall not be in my house, where you were not invited."

Sophia immediately worked herself up into a passion of tears, declaring that she did not want to be insulted, and would much rather not return to Lord Deerhurst, who, she was sure, was a very nasty man indeed, and hardly ever washed his head.

Deerhurst, carelessly, declared himself quite ready to support the dire calamity, and wished, of all things, Sophia would live with her sister Harriette.

"The man is not worth a thought, much less a tear," said I to Sophia. "You are welcome to my house, as long as I have got one to share with you; in the meantime let us drive to Amy's." Sophia did not accompany us; but retired with Lord Deerhurst, who had remarked in her ear, that I was jealous, and wanted him myself.

"I think Harriette is a little jealous really, so I'll go home with you, to make her mad," said Sophia.

And off they went.

Amy's drawing-room was quite full. She looked very well, and fairer, as well as less fierce, than before her confinement. Fanny appeared unusually lovely, dressed in a pale, pink, crape dress, which set off her rosy, white, delicate skin, to the greatest advantage; and with her unadorned bright auburn curls, waving carelessly around her laughing dark blue eyes and beautiful throat, she seemed the most desirable object in the room. Julia was very fair too; perhaps her skin was whiter than Fanny's, and of quite as delicate a texture; but it had not the vermilion tinge, and the blue veins were less defined. Both were of the highest order of fine forms. They were also of the same height, which was that best adapted to perfect symmetry; their feet and ankles were alike models for the statuary's art, and Fanny's shoes fitted Julia, as well as her own; but Fanny's hair was dark, and more glossy than Julia's. Fanny's teeth were beautiful, while Julia's, though strong, were uneven; and Fanny's smile was infinitely more attractive than Julia's, whose countenance was, in fact, as I think I have before mentioned, rather harsh than pleasing. Yet there was such a decided resemblance in their *tout ensemble* that everybody mistook Julia for Fanny's eldest sister.

This evening Julia, I suppose with a view to outshine us all, wore a dress of white silvered *lamé*, on gauze, and a Turkish turban of bright blue, fringed with gold. There was a voluptuous and purely effeminate languor about Julia's character, which was well adapted to the eastern style of dress. The large, straight, gauze sleeve did not at all conceal the symmetry of her beautiful arm. Fanny's dimpled arms were quite uncovered, and encircled with elegant but simple bracelets, composed of plaited hair, clasped with a magnificently brilliant ruby. They were both infinitely graceful. Fanny would lay her laughing face on her folded arms, reclining on a table, while she made some odd reflections; or she would fasten her pocket-handkerchief, or her shawl, across her head and ears, when she felt the air affect her head without inquiring of her glass whether she had thus added to or diminished her attractions; yet everything became her; or rather all were determined to think faultless her in whose beautiful eyes shone the warmest philanthropy, whose every word and action proved the desire she ever felt to make others appear to advantage.

Julia's attitudes, though graceful, were studied and luxurious, but always modest and effeminate.

Amy wore a yellow satin dress, fastened round the waist, with a gold band. Her profuse raven-locks were entirely unadorned, and her neck, arms, and fingers, were covered with glittering jewels of every colour. My own evening dresses were invariably composed of rich figured white French gauze, over white satin; and I never wore any ornaments in my hair, of which I was not a little proud; but my earrings were of unusual length, and consisted of diamonds, rubies and turquoise stones. A Mrs. Armstrong, whom Amy had lately patronized, was of the party. She was the *chère amie* of Colonel Armstrong, an aide-de-camp of the Duke of York. It was said of the Duchess, that she carried her charity so far as to send yearly presents to the mistress of her royal husband's aide-de-camp; but if this were really true, I have always heard that, in all but the ceremony of marriage, the mother of Colonel Armstrong's children, from her steady adherence to her protector, during seven years, and her resistance of temptation, which assailed her in every shape, deserved the encouragement of the great and the good.

In spite of the strict economy which she invariably practised, the Colonel had lately decided that his circumstances would not, in common prudence, admit of his running the slightest risk of increasing his family.

"We will be excellent friends, my love," said he to his better half, "but friends only." This may be very easy at the age of fifty; but his Lucy was still in the prime of youth, possessing very warm passions, and old as he was, she loved her Tommy dearly, and was very melancholy at his determination.

"We cannot have separate beds, you know, my dear," said Lucy; "because there is not a spare bed in the house."

"That is true, my love," answered her Tommy, "but it really must be all the same."

Lucy sighed heavily.

"Go and visit your friend Amy, my dear," said the kind Colonel; "it will enliven you; and since our family is not to be increased, I can afford to put my last dozen shirts out to be made. Now that our boy William can run alone, there is no necessity for my poor Lucy making such a slave of herself."

Alas! thought poor Lucy, I am terribly afraid of being tempted, in Amy's gay society; but she did not say so.

Lucy was a very neat, lady-like little creature, who used to wear very fine muslin gowns ornamented with her own beautiful embroidery. Her teeth were extremely white and regular, and her lips of bright vermilion; but I could not discern any other beauty in her. Nevertheless she was a great favourite with the men, and would make fifty conquests while Julia was bungling with one. Lucy had a way of disarming the most impudent, when they attempted to take the slightest liberty with her: not by her dignified deportment, nor by her wit; but by the mere simplicity of her truly modest carriage, which was so far removed from prudery that nobody knew how to offend her.

This evening was set apart for dancing, and Fanny and Julia, being the very best dancers in the room, were in their glory.

All the world were, or wished they were there, but many could not get farther than the passage, the whole house being so crammed. Among others was the man they call the dancing Montgomery, although, perhaps, I do him too much honour by putting him in print; he was such a slovenly unlicked cub, of what particular family I am ignorant; but it was clear this man had originally been designed by nature for a lout, only he went to Paris, and came home a dancer, every inch of him, below the girdle. As for his shoulders and arms, they continued as before; Frenchmen cannot work miracles, like German princes! but they converted into a fop this ready-made clown, to the utter discomfiture of our gauzes, and India muslins, which were sure to suffer, as often as we ventured to employ him to hand us tea, negus, or orgeat.

"Would you like to dance?" said George Brummell to Mrs. Armstrong, *en passant*.

"I have only just left off," answered she, rising and curtsying with much politeness; "but I am never tired of dancing."

"You have a dancing face," Brummell quietly observed, fixing his eyes steadily on her countenance for a second or two, and then passing on.

Poor Lucy, she afterwards declared to us, was never so ashamed and humbled since she had been born.

All this time, Montgomery's thick straight locks were steadily beating time, on his watery forehead, as he trod the mazy dance with all his might, footing it away most scholastically. He did indeed dance famously; but then he was always out at the elbows, which appeared to have no connection whatever with his feet, particularly on this eventful night, when one of his elbows came in such neighbourly contact with the eye of the poor Duc de Berri, who was just entering the room, while Montgomery was swinging short corners near the door, as sent His Royal Highness reeling backwards.

"*Rein, rien du tout,*" said the good-natured Duc de Berri, holding his handkerchief to his eye.

"*Il y a tant de monde ici, ce soir, et la salle n'est pas grande, comme vous voyez, monsieur,*" said Fanny to His Highness; as usual endeavouring to excuse and conciliate all parties.

"*Ma fois! je n'y vois goutte!*" said the Duke, laughing, with his handkerchief still before his eyes.

Montgomery came forward to express his regrets; but it was plain, from his manner, that he did not at all attribute the accident to anything like awkwardness on the part of himself or his elbows, of which he seemed not a part.

I think it was on this evening I saw Colonel Parker for the first time. He appeared to have seriously attached himself to my sister Fanny. He was an officer in the Artillery, and a near relation to Lady Hyde Parker, I believe. I was anxious to see poor Fanny comfortably settled; and her tastes being all so quiet, and her temper so amiable, I knew that riches were by no means necessary to her felicity. Colonel Parker possessed a comfortable independence, and was very anxious to have Fanny entirely under his protection. "She shall bear my name, and I will show her all the respect a wife can require, and she shall always find me a gentleman," said he. I could not, however, help thinking that Fanny, with her strictly honest principles, her modest, amiable character, and her beauty, ought to have been Parker's wife, instead of his mistress, and therefore I did not advise her to live with him. His person was elegant; fine teeth and fine hair, was, however, all he had to boast of, in the way of beauty; but Fanny did not like handsome men, and appeared very much to admire and esteem Colonel Parker. I do not exactly know what aged man he was; but I should think him under thirty.

The next day, I was remarking to my young admirer, the Duke of Leinster, that life was nothing without a little love; and then begged him to say who was best worth having.

"I think the Duchess of Beaufort's brother, Lord George Leveson Gower, the most desirable man I ever saw," said Leinster.

"How is one to obtain a sight of your beauty?"

"I cannot assist you; and if I could I would not," His Grace replied.

I do not care, said I to myself, after Leinster had left me; I am not going to sit down all my life to love this fool. I must have something for the mind to feed on.

I was interrupted, while making these wise reflections, by a visit from Wellington!

Here is a thing in the shape of an intellectual companion, thought I!

After Wellington had left me, I entirely forgot him: nay before; for I now recollect that he said something about my bad taste in talking on subjects irrelevant to what was going on; such as a remark I might have made about my rose-tree, or my dinner, when I ought to have been all soul!! No matter! The soul's fire is partly kept alive by dinner; or, whether it is or not, still dinner, or even a rose-tree, is infinitely more interesting than Wellington!

I now felt *le besoin d'aimer*, with almost the same ardour as when I used to follow the handsome stranger and his large dog, which induces me to believe that never did a fair lady die of love for one man, whilst others, equally amiable, were dying for her smiles.

In a fit of folly, I wrote a letter to Lord G. L. Gower, requesting him to come and meet me in the Regent's Park, at eleven o'clock on a Sunday morning; at the same time assuring him that desirous as I was, from all I had heard of his perfections, to make his acquaintance, yet, if he expected to please me, he must show me just as much respect, and humble deference, as though I had not ordered him up to Marylebone Fields to be looked at.

Lord G. L. Gower's reply was:

I do not usually answer such letters; but there is something so eccentric and uncommon in yours, that I cannot resist complying with your request; therefore you will find me at the appointed time and place.

G. L. GOWER.

As the hour drew near for fulfilling my engagement in the Regent's Park, I recollected that I did not, in the least, know the person of Lord G. L. Gower, and felt much puzzled how I should contrive to distinguish him from any handsome man who might happen to be enjoying the fresh air towards Primrose Hill. However, trusting to chance, or sympathy, or that instinct by which, according to Falstaff, the lion knows the true prince, I dressed myself with unusual care, and contrived to be punctual. I observed a tall, rather handsome, and gentlemanly man, looking about him; but as I felt at once that he was not, in any respect, cut out for the honour of filling up the void in my heart, I prayed the God of Love to send me a better subject.

However, there was nothing to be seen, at that early hour on Sunday morning, which in the least resembled a gentleman, or even, in their Sunday new coats and brand-new yellow-leather gloves, could be mistaken for one, that came within a mile of me.

This must be Leinster's Apollo, said I. How could I address myself to such a booby? True, this man may, perhaps, have a certain indescribable charm about him, a *je ne sais quoi*, which may not be discoverable at the first glance! I ventured to raise my eyes to his face, and, if I did not laugh, I looked as though I was thinking about it; and, on this, he spoke, and smiled, and blushed, and bowed.

I conceived that, having brought a man up to Marylebone Fields on such a terribly hot morning, it would not have been fair, or lady-like, to have dismissed him, until I had given his talents and powers of pleasing a fair trial. I walked him up to the tip-top of Primrose Hill, and then towards Hampstead, and then back again to Great Portland Street.

At last His Lordship made a full stop, while he took off his hat to wipe his face, declaring he could go no farther, as he was quite unaccustomed to walking, and the sun was so very oppressive. He, therefore, entreated that I would permit him to accompany me, immediately, to my house, if only to sit down and rest, or otherwise he apprehended—fever or sudden death!

I assured him that I was sorry, very sorry, and hoped such fatal consequences would not follow our little rural bit of pleasure; at the same time I could only express my regrets, while I frankly declared to him that he was not, in the least, the sort of person I wanted.

Lord George L. Gower was too proud, too well-looking, to be deeply wounded at my determination, so he smiled, and bowed, and wished me good morning, declaring himself much amused with the eccentricity and frankness of my character.

It will not do, I see, to lay one's self out for love, thought I, after His Lordship had left me. It comes, like money, when one is not thinking about it. Reading is a much more independent amusement than loving. Books one may cut, when one is tired of them; so I began immediately on arriving at home, with *Lady Mary Wortley Montagu's Letter*. The style was very unequal, I thought; I read as far as this passage: "Our vulgar notions that Mahomet did not own women to have any souls, is a mistake. It is true, he says they are not of so elevated a kind, and, therefore, must not hope to be admitted into the paradise appointed for the men, who are to be entertained by celestial beauties. But there is a place of happiness destined for souls of the inferior order, where all good women are to be, in eternal bliss. Any woman that dies unmarried is looked upon to die in a state of reprobation. To confirm this, I believe they reason that the end of the creation of woman is to increase and multiply, and that she is only properly employed in the works of her calling, when she is bringing forth children, or taking care of them, which is all the virtue God expects from her."

I threw the book down at this passage, beginning to feel very much ashamed of myself: I rang my bell, and sent to my bookseller for the *History of Mahomet*, hoping that most prolific prophet would put me in the way of obeying his commands, in case, after duly studying his laws, I were disposed to turn Turk.

CHAPTER 10

"It is all settled," said Fanny to me on the night before Mr. Dick's dinner-party, "and I am to be Mrs. Parker."

"I hope you will be happy," said I; "but I wish you were married."

"Why should poor Parker marry a woman with a ready-made family?" asked Fanny.

I declined offering an opinion, fearing to do harm.

Fanny was four years my senior, and possessed, perhaps, a larger portion of what is called common sense than myself. *Au reste*, the thing was settled between her and Parker, who were to proceed together to Portsmouth, where Colonel Parker's regiment was stationed, after they had passed a fortnight at Brighton.

"Suppose we make a party, and hire a house for you and Julia and me?"

"The very thing I wish," said Fanny; "for London is growing very stupid. We meet no one but the Honourable Colonel Collyer and Lord Petersham about the streets."

"Oh, yes!" said I; "we also see Lady Heathcote and Lady Windham."

"And that makes it worse still," added Fanny; "for I really believe, neither of those good ladies have missed Hyde Park or the opera one single night for the last twenty years, or changed the colour of their chariot blinds; Heathcote, rosy-red! and the gentle Ann's interesting yellow! How very tired I am of seeing these women!"

Julia called on me before Fanny had left, and our little excursion to Brighton was fixed for the following week.

When we had settled this important affair, my servant informed me that a lady requested to offer herself in the place of Miss Hawkes, my late *dame de compagnie*, who had just left me to be married to her cousin. I desired him to show her upstairs. She came tripping into the room with the step of a child. She wore short petticoats, and a small French bonnet stuck at the top of her head. I should imagine her age to have been about forty: indeed she owned to six and twenty.

"Who will recommend you, pray, Madam?"

"The Countess Palmella, wife of the Portuguese Ambassador, in South Audley Street; I have been educating her children."

I asked if the Countess's had been her first situation?

She replied in the affirmative.

"What were you doing before that, pray, Ma'am?"

"Why," said the lady, with much affectation, "you see I was daily, nay hourly, expecting to get settled in life. I had a small property, and I went to Bath. Several of my friends had found charming husbands at Bath. However, time slipped away, Madam, and, by some strange fatality or other, I exhausted my little resources, and did not manage to get settled in life: that is the truth of it."

It struck me that this curious woman, with the odd bonnet, would amuse me as well as any other lion, *pour le moment*, and, being acquainted with Amy's poor beau, the Count Palmella, I told her she might come to me the following day.

She seemed absolutely enraptured, as though mine had been an atmosphere which would rain men upon her, and our bargain was concluded. She was a straight, tall, long-backed lath of a woman, with a remarkably long face, small twinkling eyes, fine hair, and a bad skin, in spite of the white paint she used to beautify it. So much for Miss Eliza Higgins!!

The next evening found us all dining with Mr. Dick, who handed me down to dinner, Lord Hertford took care of Amy, Alvanley was ever Fanny's most obedient, humble servant, and Ward held out his finger to Mrs. Armstrong. Luttrell was as usual the life and spirit of the whole party.

"No; champagne, if you please. I can get Madeira at home," said Alvanley.

I do not recollect that any of us were very agreeable that night, though we talked a great deal. Hertford's subject was death, *pour encourager les autres*.

"Oh! it must be a dreadful tussle, at the last!" observed Alvanley, with such comical gravity of expression, as no pen could describe.

"Oh, Amy!" said Mrs. Armstrong as soon as we women entered the drawing-room, to which Mr. Dick conducted us himself. "Oh! Amy, my Tommy was so good and kind last night!"

"How do you mean?" cried Amy, abruptly.

"Guess," said Lucy.

"Very well, I do; but I cannot calculate the brave Colonel's forces."

"Oh! only once," Lucy answered.

"How absurd!" Amy remarked, turning towards the glass, and arranging her black locks.

Poor Julia scarcely spoke a single word the whole evening; indeed we had the greatest difficulty in persuading her to be of our party. She declared she could not endure to meet Amy, who had been making love to Mildmay, merely because Julia adored him. Mildmay had paid due attentions to Amy's ogling, had basked in the sunshine of her smiles for nearly a fortnight, and then, just as she was growing tender, had cut her dead.

A few days later I found the Duke of Leinster in my box at the opera.

"I am glad you have no men with you," said His Grace, with something like agitation of manner, "for I want to speak to you. Do you know, my friend, of whom I spoke to you, is come up from Oxford on purpose to try to get introduced! I know he must return to college tonight, and I am, I confess, rather anxious that he should be disappointed."

"Nonsense," said Julia. "Who is it, pray?"

"The Marquis of Worcester," replied His Grace.

"Is he handsome?" I inquired.

"Not a bit of it," said the Duke.

"What is he like?" Fanny asked.

"I do not know anybody he is like, upon my honour, unless it be his father. He is a long, thin, pale fellow, with straight hair."

"You need not be alarmed," said I; "I shall not be presented to your friend, if I can help it. I always tell everybody I know not to bring men here, without first coming up to ask my permission."

"I know you do," said Leinster; "since this is the answer Lord Worcester has received from several of your friends, to whom he has applied."

"There he is!" continued Leinster, leaning towards the pit. "Do not you observe a very tall young fellow, in silk stockings, looking steadfastly up at this box. Upon my honour, he won't wear trousers or curl his hair, because he heard that you dislike it."

"It is very flattering," said I, eagerly looking out for him with my opera glass, an example which was followed by Julia and Fanny.

The young Marquis was, at that time, too bashful to stand the artillery of three pair of fine eyes at once, and turned away from our eager gaze! but not till I had satisfied myself that he would not do for me one bit better than his uncle, Lord G. L. Gower, and, in the next five minutes, I had forgotten his existence.

Lord Frederick Bentinck now came and asked me when I meant to keep my promise of accompanying him to Vauxhall?

"Oh, we shall never get to Brighton," said Fanny, who doted on donkey-riding. "Harriette will keep us in town all the summer, as she did last year."

"Summer!" interposed George Brummell, entering in a furred great-coat. "You do not mistake this for summer, do you? A little more of your summer will just finish me," pulling up his fur collar.

"Upon my honour, I think it very hot," said Leinster. "It must be hot, you know, because it is August."

"I never know the difference, for my part," Fred Bentinck observed. "The only thing that ever makes me cold, is putting on a greatcoat; but then I have always a great deal to do, and that keeps me warm. Once for all, Madam, will you go to Vauxhall on Monday night? If you will, I will put off my sister, and accompany you."

I assented, in spite of everything Fanny and Julia could say to prevent me; for Fred Bentinck always made me merry.

King Allen put his long nose into the box, and his nose only. "Is Amy at home tonight?"

Fanny answered in the affirmative; adding, "But she is in her own box. Why do not you go to her to inquire?"

"Lord Lowther and some nasty Russians are with her," answered Allen.

"*À ce soir*, then," I said, kissing my hand to him, which was as much as to say, "Do not come in." He was kind enough to understand my hint.

"Remember Monday," said Fred Bentinck, as he left the box to make room for Mr. Napier and Colonel Parker, followed by the young Lord William Russell.

Just as Parker and Napier had left the box, Lord Deerhurst entered it, accompanied by a tall young man, and Lord William then took his leave, from the mere dread of intruding. "I do not often introduce gentlemen to ladies," said His Lordship, "and perhaps I am taking a liberty now; yet I hope you can have no objection to my making you known to the Marquis of Worcester."

I bowed rather formally; because I had before desired Deerhurst not to bring people to me without my permission. However, the young Marquis blushed so deeply, and looked so humble, that it was impossible to treat him without civility; but, having taken one good look at my conquest, and thus convinced myself that I should never love him, I conversed in-differently, on common subjects, as people do who happen to meet in a stage-coach, where time present is all they have to care about. Deerhurst was lively and pleasant; the Marquis scarcely spoke; but the little he did find courage to utter was certainly said with good taste, and in a gentle-manly manner.

Leinster was infinitely bored and annoyed, though he tried to conceal it.

"What do you think of him?" asked Leinster, whispering in my ear.

"I will tell you tomorrow," I replied; and, the better to enable myself to do this, I examined the person of the young Marquis for the second time. It promised to be very good, and his air and manners were distinguished; but he was extremely pale, and rather thin; nevertheless, there was something fine and good about his countenance, though he was certainly not handsome.

"There is a pretty, race-horse little head for you!" said Deerhurst, touching my hair.

"I never saw such beautiful hair," Worcester remarked timidly.

"Put your finger into it," said Deerhurst. "Harriette does not mind how you tumble her hair about."

"I should richly deserve to be turned out of the box, were I to do anything so very impertinent," interrupted His Lordship.

"Oh, no," said I, leaning the back of my little head towards Worcester, "anybody may pull my hair about. I like it, and I am no prude."

Worcester ventured to touch my hair, in fear and trembling, and the touch seemed to affect him like electricity. Without vanity, and in very truth, let him deny it if he can, I never saw a boy, or a man, more madly, wildly, and romantically in love with any daughter of Eve, in my whole life.

"May I," said Lord Worcester eagerly, as though he dreaded an interruption, "may I, on my return to town, venture to pay my respects?"

"Certainly," answered I, "if I am in town; but we are going to Brighton."

True love is ever thus respectful, and fearful to offend. Worcester, with much modesty, conversed on subjects unconnected with himself or his desires, apparently taking deep interest in my health, which, I assured him, had long been very delicate.

"You return to Oxford tonight, I believe?" said His Grace of Leinster to Worcester, who replied that he must start at six in the morning.

I advised him to take a few hours rest first.

"That will be quite impossible," Worcester answered, in a low voice.

The young Marquis's pale face certainly did grow paler, as he looked wistfully after Leinster, whose arm I had taken.

First love is all powerful, in the head and heart of such an ardent character as Worcester's; and there really was an air of truth about him which not a little affected me, for the moment; therefore, turning back to address him, after I had drawn my arm away from Leinster: "Perhaps," said I, in a low, laughing voice, "perhaps, Lord Worcester, it may be vain and silly in me to believe that you are disposed to like me; but, as I do almost fancy so, I come to wish you a good night, and to assure you that I shall remember with gratitude those who are charitable enough to think favourably of me."

Worcester began to look too happy.

"But do not mistake me," I continued, "for I am not one bit in love with you."

Worcester looked humble again.

"In fact," said I, laughing, "my love-days are over. I have loved nothing lately."

"Not the Duke of Leinster?" inquired His Lordship, whose anxiety to ascertain this had overcome his fears of seeming impertinent.

"No, indeed," I rejoined, and Worcester's countenance brightened till he became almost handsome.

Leinster approached us, with a look of extreme impatience.

"Good night, my Lord," said I, waving my hand, as I joined His Grace. Worcester bowed low, and hastened out of sight.

"If Leinster were not my friend," said Worcester to a gentleman, who afterwards repeated it to me, pointing to Leinster and myself as we stood in the round room, waiting for His Grace's carriage—"if that young man were not my friend, I would make him walk over my dead body, before he should take Harriette out of this house."

Oh, this love! ! this love! !

Amy's rooms were not full. It was her last party for that season. There was nobody in town, so *faute de mieux*, since Mildmay had cut her, she was making up to a Mr. Boultby, a black little ugly dragoon, whom she declared was exactly to her taste.

"Come to Brighton," said Amy to her hero.

He assured her that if his regiment had not been stationed there, he would have joined her, since he felt that he could not live out of her smiles.

"How can you strive to make fools of people?" said I.

"What do you mean?" inquired Amy, fiercely.

"Why, seriously, Mr. Boultby," continued I, "take my word, she has no fancy for you."

Mr. Boultby's vanity would not permit him to take my word, so I left him to the enjoyment of it.

Parker and Fanny appeared to be very happy together, and sincerely attached to each other. No husband could show more respect towards any wife.

Leinster was very dull, though too proud to complain.

"Confess," said I to His Grace, as soon as I could get him into one corner of the room, "confess that you are annoyed and unhappy, about Lord Worcester."

"I do think," said Leinster, "though I do not pretend to have any claim on you whatever, that Worcester, as my friend, had no right to intrude himself into your society tonight."

The evening finished heavily for me. I was bored with Leinster, who never had anything on earth to recommend him to my notice, save that excellent temper, which I now saw ruffled for the first time since I had known him: and Amy, who, it must be acknowledged, was in the habit of saying droll things, was this night wholly taken up and amused with that stupid, ugly Boultby! I therefore returned early, and Leinster put me down at my own door.

The next day I proposed to my new *dame de compagnie*, Miss Eliza Higgins, to dress herself quickly in order to accompany me into the park.

"How do you do? how do you do?" said Lord Fife, as he joined us near Cumberland Gate. "Who is your friend?" he continued, appearing to eye Miss Higgins with looks of admiration, much to my astonishment. "Am I not to be introduced to your friend?"

"*Et pourquoi pas?*" said I, naming Miss Higgins, with whom he conversed as though her acquaintance had been the thing on earth most devoutly to be wished.

After Lord Fife had left us, Miss Eliza Higgins could speak of nothing else.

"Charming man, Ma'am, the Earl of Fife! I have heard much of him; but never had the honour to be presented to him before. That is a man, now, a poor weak female would find it very difficult to resist. His Lordship is so condescending! so polite!"

When we were tired of walking in the park, I drove to the house of a married sister of mine, whose name we will call Paragon, since she was the very paragon of mothers, having drawn up a new patent system of education for her children, better than Jean Jacques Rousseau's, and unlike everybody else's.

Her family consists of two boys and two girls. The eldest daughter was then nearly seven years of age: her son and heir had scarcely attained his fifth year. "They shall never go to school," said my sister Paragon, "nor will I suffer them to be left, one instant, to the care of nurses or servants, to learn bad grammar and worse morals. Neither shall they be told of such things as thieves or murderers; much less shall they hear anything about falsehood and deceit. They shall never obtain what they want by tears, nor rudeness, after the age of two; and it shall depend on the politeness and humility of their deportment, whether they have any dinner or not; and nothing shall be called indecent, which is natural, either in words or deeds. So much for the minds of my children; and, with regard to their bodily health, I shall make them swallow one of Anderson's Scots Aperient Pills every night of their blessed lives! *et il n'y aura rien à craindre!*"

Sister Paragon was very pretty. She had the sweetest, most lovely eyes I ever beheld.

C'est bien dommage!

Paragon's husband was not in London when I called on her. She was sitting, with four of the most lovely children I ever beheld at one time.

Little Mary was in high spirits. She talked of love! and said she knew, very well, that everybody fell in love, and that she was in love, too, herself.

"With whom, pray?" asked Paragon.

"With my brother John," answered little Mary; and next she asked her mother when she might marry him, declaring that she could not wait much longer.

"To bed! to bed!" said mamma. "You must all go to bed directly."

"Already?" I asked. "Why, it is not six o'clock yet."

"No matter. I am tired to death of them, and they are always asleep before seven."

In less than five minutes, the children were all running about stark naked, as they were born, laughing, romping, and playing with each other. Little Sophia, who was not yet two years of age, did nothing but run after her beautiful brother Henry, a dear little laughing boy, who was about to celebrate his fourth birthday. Little Sophia, bred in the school of nature, handled her brother rather oddly, I thought.

"Surely it is Nature's own sweet work!" said Paragon.

"Mamma! mamma!" called out little Henry.

"What is the matter, my love?" said Paragon.

"Is Sophy to have my did—dle to keep?"

"No, my love," answered mamma with calm dignity, "not to keep, only to play with!"

When I got home, I had only ten minutes left *pour faire ma toilette.* As

Harriette Wilson

A letter from Harriette Wilson to Lord Byron, probably written
about 1812

Amy

Sophia

Julia

The Marquis of Worcester (one of the Dighton sketches: *Characters at the West End of Town*)

The Duke of Argyll: another of the Dighton series

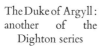

Lord Ponsonby. Sketch by Henry Bone of a portrait by Lawrence.
The inscription is torn. Perhaps it once read "Lord Ponsonby for
Miss Harriette Wilson"

High stakes at Crockford's

A domestic interlude. Lord Worcester laces Harriette's stays and toasts her breakfast muffins.

"First Come First Served." Wellington batters on Harriette's door while the Duke of Argyll (in her nightcap) sends him packing.

"The Cyprians' Ball." From *The English Spy*'s caricature of this celebrated annual event, showing the most famous demi-reps and their protectors. Harriette is seen at the right wearing a plumed turban. Amy is seated below the cellist.

The *ton* disport themselves at Almack's.

Lord Alvanley

Lord Nugent, "Fat Nugent,"
down from Oxford to pursue
the Cyprians

Cutting a dash in Hyde Park. The "starers" quiz carriages,
charmers and cavaliers. (From an engraving by George Cruikshank)

to Miss Eliza Higgins, Lord Fife's compliments had so subdued her, that she could not afford me the least assistance.

"A charming man the Earl of Fife!" she was repeating for at least the fiftieth time, when a note was put into my hand, bearing the noble earl's arms, and my footman, at that moment, informed me that my carriage was at the door.

"Any answer for Lord Fife, Ma'am?" asked my servant.

I hastily read the note, which contained His Lordship's request to pass the evening with me and my lovely companion. I did not show this to Miss Higgins on that occasion, because it seemed so very *outré* and un-hoped for, that I feared it might, from the mere surprise, have caused sudden death.

"My compliments only," said I, "tell His Lordship I am very sorry, but I cannot write, because I am this instant getting into my carriage to dine with Lord Hertford"; and so saying, I followed my servant down-stairs.

Lord Hertford had not invited one person to meet Julia, Fanny and me; but his excellent dinner, good wine, and very intelligent conversation, kept us alive, till a very late hour. I mean no compliment to Lord Hertford; for he has acted very rudely to me, of late; but he is a man possessing more general knowledge than anyone I know. His Lordship appears to be *au fait* on every subject one can possibly imagine. Talk to him of drawing, or horse-riding; painting or cock-fighting; rhyming, cooking, or fencing; profligacy or morals; religions of whatever creed; languages living or dead; claret, or burgundy; champagne or black strap; furnishing houses, or riding hobbies; the flavour of venison, or breeding poll-parrots; and you might swear that he had served his apprenticeship to every one of them.

After dinner, he showed us miniatures, by the most celebrated artists, of at least half a hundred lovely women, black, brown, fair, and even carroty, for the amateur's sympathetic *bonne bouche*. These were all beautifuly executed; and no one, with any knowledge of painting, could hear him expatiate on their various merits, without feeling that he was qualified to preside at the Royal Academy itself! The light, the shade, the harmony of colours, the vice of English painters, the striking characters of Dutch artists—*Ma foi!* No such things as foisting sham Vandykes, or copies from Rubens, on Lord Hertford.

But to proceed.

Lord Hertford showed us a vast collection of gold and silver coins, por-traits, drawings, curious snuff boxes and watches. He had long been desirous that Amy, Fanny, and myself, should sit to Lawrence, for a large family picture, to be placed in his collection.

Though the tea and coffee, like our dinner, were exquisite, Hertford made a good-natured complaint to his French commander-in-chief, about the cream.

"Really," said His Lordship, addressing us in English, "for a man who keeps a cow, it is a shame to be served with such bad cream!"

"I knew not," said I, "that you were the man who kept a cow. Pray where is she?"

"In Hyde Park," he replied, "just opposite my windows."

Lord Hertford then proposed to show us a small detached building, which he had taken pains to fit up, in a very luxurious style of elegance. A small, low gate, of which he always kept the key, opened into Park Lane, and a little narrow flight of stairs, covered with crimson cloth, conducted to this retirement. It consisted of a dressing-room, a small sitting-room, and a bedchamber. Over the elegant French bed was a fine picture of a sleeping Venus. There were a great many other pictures, and their subjects, though certainly warm and voluptuous, were yet too classical and graceful to merit the appellation of indecent. He directed our attention to the convenience of opening the door, himself, to any fair lady who would honour him with a visit incognita, after his servants should have prepared a most delicious supper and retired to rest. He told us many curious anecdotes of the advantage he derived from his character for discretion.

"I never tell of any woman. No power on earth should induce me to name a single female, worthy to be called woman, by whom I have been favoured. In the first place, because I am not tired of variety, and wish to succeed again: in the second, I think it dishonourable."

He told us a story of a lady of family, well known in the fashionable world, whose intrigue with a young dragoon he had discovered by the merest and most unlooked-for accident. "I accused her of the fact," continued His Lordship, "and refused to promise secrecy till she had made me as happy as she had made the young dragoon."

"Was that honourable?" I asked.

"Perhaps not," said Hertford; "but I could not help it."

We did not leave Lord Hertford till near two o'clock, when he kindly set us all down, himself, in his own carriage.

CHAPTER 11

THE NEXT MORNING, before I had finished my breakfast, a great big stupid Irishman was announced, by name Dominick Brown, with whom I had a slight acquaintance. He brought with him, for the purpose of being presented to me, the Marquis of Sligo. They sat, talking on indifferent subjects, for about an hour, and then drove off in His Lordship's curricle. Next came a note from Lord Fife, requesting permission to drink tea with me and my charming friend. Who would have thought it? said I to myself, laughing. Here am I playing second fiddle to Miss Eliza Higgins! for the amusement of her most charming man, the Earl of Fife. I wrote, on the back of his note,

Going to Vauxhall; but you may come tomorrow evening at nine.

I thought that Miss Eliza Higgins would have fainted when I told her that Lord Fife was coming to us.

"Oh dear, Ma'am, what would you advise me to wear? If you would not think it a liberty, and would lend me the pattern of your sweet blue cap, I would sit up all night to complete one like it."

"All this energy about drinking tea with a rake of a Scotchman—who you know would not marry an angel—and pretend to tell me that you are *une grande vertu*?" said I.

"Certainly," answered Miss Eliza Higgins, reddening.

"Fiddlestick!" was my sublime ejaculation.

Miss Eliza Higgins burst into tears.

"Nay," I continued, "this fit of heroics to me is ridiculous. I ask nothing of you but plain dealing. The fact is this, I am not curious but frank. Lord Fife wants to make your acquaintance, and it is not my wish to spoil any woman's preferment in whatever line of life, whether good or bad: so, guessing from all the raptures you have expressed at the idea of this rake's attachment, that the governess of the young Countess Palmella is no better than she should be, I have agreed to receive His Lordship; but, since these tears of virtuous indignation have convinced me of the injustice I did you, heavens forbid that I should be the means of bringing Lord Fife and a vestal together, for fear of consequences!" I then quietly opened my writing-desk, and began framing an excuse to His Lordship.

"Surely you are not putting off the Earl of Fife?" said Miss Eliza Higgins, in breathless agitation.

"I think it wrong to introduce such a gay man to an innocent woman," was my answer.

Miss Higgins entreated and begged in vain.

"Well, then," said Miss Higgins, "I confess that once——"

"Once what?" I asked.

"I had a slip—a—yes—a slip!" and she held her handkerchief to her eyes.

"What do you call a slip? do you mean a petticoat, or an intrigue?"

"Oh, fie! fie!" said Miss Eliza Higgins. "Intrigue is such a shocking word, and conveys a more determined idea of loose morals, than a mere accidental slip."

I still persisted in sending the excuse, declaring that, since hers had been only an accidental slip, she might recover it.

"Oh, dear! Oh, dear!" said Miss Higgins, as my hand was extended to the bell, "what poor weak creatures we are! I quite forgot the General!"

"General who?"

"Why, General—but you will be secret?"

"As the grave, of course."

"Did you ever hear of General Mackenzie?" said Miss Eliza Higgins, spreading her hand across her forehead.

"He was Fred Lamb's general in Yorkshire," I answered.

"The same, Madam, a fascinating man! and this is my excuse."

"True," said I, "and I remember all the servant maids, and Yorkshire milkwomen confessed his power."

"Most true!" said Miss Eliza Higgins, with a deep sigh.

"What, then, you have forgotten the Earl of Fife already?"

"Oh, His Lordship is quite another thing," said Miss Higgins, brightening.

"And another thing is what you wish for?"

"Oh, fie, Ma'am! indeed you are too severe. These little accidents do, and must happen, from mere inexperience, and the weakness of our nature. I entreat, I implore, Ma'am, do not refuse my first request. Who knows what may turn up?" In short, never was Brougham himself more eloquent! She, ultimately, prevailed; and all-conquering Fife was expected with rapture.

Before dinner, I went to call on Julia, by whom I had been sent for. Extreme anxiety had brought on a *fausse couche*; but Julia, being as well as could be expected, hoped still to be able to join us at Brighton, if not to accompany us there. My sister Sophia was sitting by her bedside, looking very pretty, and much happier than when she was with Lord Deerhurst.

Fanny called on Julia, whose house she had changed for one in Hertford Street, Mayfair, on her acquaintance with Colonel Parker, whose name, at his particular request, she had now taken.

The next evening, behold myself and Miss Higgins seated on the sofa, before our tea-table, in expectation of Lord Fife. Miss Higgin's new cap would have improved her beauty, had she not diminished its lustre by sitting up all night to finish it; but her fine hair, which was her solitary charm, was suffered to flow over her neck and shoulders in graceful, childish negligence. As for me, the part of second fiddle being altogether new to me, I took the liberty of appearing in my morning dress. Nine was the hour named by Lord Fife, and Miss Higgins had taken out her old-fashioned French watch, at least twenty times, since she entered the drawing-room, when the house-clock struck that wished-for and lagging hour.

"Is His Lordship punctual, generally speaking, pray, Ma'am?"

"Quite the reverse, I believe," said I, half asleep.

"You have a good heart, I know, Ma'am, and we females ought, naturally, to assist each other, in all our little peccadillos," remarked my companion.

"Well?"

"Why, Ma'am, I am going to ask your advice, who are better acquainted with His Lordship's tastes than I am. I was thinking now, that this little netting-box is pretty and lady-like! Shall I be netting a purse? or will it have a better effect to put on my gloves, and be doing nothing?"

Before I could answer this deep question, my footman entered the room, with a letter, sealed with a large coronet, and told me that a servant waited below for an answer.

"I will ring when it is ready, James," said I, opening the letter.

"It is an excuse from the Earl of Fife!" said Miss Eliza Higgins, growing whiter than her pearl powder.

Indignation kept me silent, after reading the following impertinent letter, from the Marquis of Sligo, to whom I had only been presented the day before.

My Dear Miss Wilson,

Will you be so condescending as to allow me to pass this evening, alone, with you, after Lady Lansdowne's party?

SLIGO.

I had not been so enraged for several years! I rang my bell with such violence that I frightened Miss Eliza Higgins out of the very little wit she possessed.

"Who waits?" said I, to James.

"A servant, in livery," was the answer.

"Send him up to me."

A well-bred servant, in a cocked hat and dashing livery, entered my room with many bows.

"Here is some mistake," said I, presenting him the unsealed and unfolded letter of Lord Sligo's. "This letter could not be meant for me, to whom His Lordship was only presented yesterday. Take it back, young man, and say, from me, that I request he will be careful how he misdirects his letters in future; an accident which is, no doubt, caused by his writing them after dinner."

The man bowed low, and took away the open communication with him.

"The Earl may yet arrive then?" observed Miss Eliza Higgins, recovering herself.

A loud knock at the door now put the matter almost beyond a doubt, and, in another minute, in walked the redoubtable Earl of Fife! in a curious black and tan broad-striped satin waistcoat, which was ornamented with a large gold chain. His watch was very gay, as were his numerous seals, at least twenty in number. Surely, thought I, as I threw a hasty glance at Miss Eliza Higgin's long, narrow, ill-shaped forehead, brilliant with agitation and pearl-powder, surely the man must be purblind, or, it may be, his eyes were filled with dust on Sunday, when we met him in the park. However, to my astonishment, His Lordship was all rapture, and did nothing but ogle my fair *dame de compagnie*, as though she had been really fair.

As to Miss Eliza Higgins, it had been previously settled and agreed on between us, that modesty was to be the order of the day.

"I am not so vain as to fancy myself altogether handsomer than you are, Madam," said the humble Miss Eliza to me, "and yet it is clear that the Earl of Fife prefers me; I therefore conceive that I may have appeared to him more timid and modest; therefore it will be better to keep up that character. Do not you agree with me, Ma'am?"

"Certainly," said I.

Miss Eliza Higgins kept up the farce to excess; scarcely venturing to raise her eyes from the ground, or utter a single syllable, beyond—"Yes," or "No, my Lord"—and that in a low whisper. She did, indeed, once venture to speak, pathetically, about her grandmamma, and her dear grandpapa. Lord Fife declared to me that she was an amiable creature, and he presumed to place a ring of some value on her finger, on which occasion Miss Eliza Higgins appeared to be growing rather nervous. He did not take his leave, until he had obtained her permission to write to her.

"Miss Eliza Higgins," said I, as soon as we were left alone again, which was not till after midnight, "my good Miss Eliza Higgins, this atmosphere, as you expected, has proved favourable to your wishes. It has done more than your six seasons at Bath. It has, in short, brought a noble earl to your feet. *Je vous en fais mes compliments.* We will now, if you please, say adieu. Make any use you please of your conquest, and accept my thanks for having been so truly ridiculous."

Miss Eliza bridled, muttered something about our sex's envy, and declared that she had proposed leaving me, herself.

"Agreed, then," said I, extending my hand, to shake hands. "I promise never to say anything but good of you to Lord Fife; at least not till he is quite tired of you."

Miss Eliza Higgins appeared satisfied, and wished me a good night.

"You will forward any letters that may arrive from the Earl of Fife?" said she, returning.

"Certainly."

"Why then I propose going to my grandmamma's tomorrow."

"*De tout mon cœur,*" I replied, and we parted.

In about a fortnight after the opera had closed, we all arrived at Brighton.

We had hired a good house, on the Marine Parade. Amy's admirer, Boultby, was one of our first visitors, and then Lords Hertford and Lowther, who were both on a visit at the Pavilion. For three whole days, Amy sickened us by the tenderness of her flirtation with Boultby, who sat lounging on her sofa, as though he had been a first-rate man. At last Amy grew tired of him all at once.

"Get up," she said, rudely pushing her inamorato off the sofa.

Boultby refused, like a spoiled child, and insisted on another kiss.

"Good heavens, get up then," said Amy, "and don't tumble my ruff. I came down to Brighton for the fresh air, and, for three days, I have inhaled none of it; but only your breath, as a substitute; and I am not sure that I shall like you. Here, put your head on this pillow," added Amy, putting down his head, and rolling a thick table-napkin about it. "So let me fancy you my husband, and in your nightcap. There," said Amy, holding her head first on one side, then on the other, in order to take a full view of his little, black, ugly face, which examination was not favourable to her lover.

"Get up this instant!" said she, with such fierceness as immediately set him on his legs.

"I told you so," said I, "but you would not believe me."

Boultby hoped his sweet Amy was joking; and he did well to make the most and best he could of the evening; for he was never admitted afterwards.

Lord Robert Manners, whose regiment was stationed in that neighbourhood, was very attentive to me. His Lordship is one of the most amiable young men I ever met with. His finely turned head might be copied for that of the Apollo Belvedere, and yet he has no vanity. In short, a more manly, honourable, unaffected being, does not exist; and much I regret the ill-health under which he has always suffered. His Lordship was kind enough to give me my first lesson in riding; often accompanied by the French Duc de Guiche, who was in the Prince Regent's regiment, and Colonel Palmer. The latter invited me to accompany Lord Robert to the mess-dinner at Lewes. It must more resemble a small select private party than a mess-room, as they seldom mustered more than seven or eight persons together at table.

Bob Manners, as Lord Robert is universally called, was remarkably absent, and spoke but little, yet he possessed a certain degree of quaint, odd humour!

"Those leathers are not bad; who made them?" asked George Brummell one day of His Lordship.

"Why, the breeches maker," said Bob Manners, speaking very low.

CHAPTER 12

LORDS HERTFORD AND LOWTHER were our constant visitors at Brighton.

One evening, when His Majesty had a party of ladies and gentlemen at the pavilion, we concluded that Lord Hertford would not be able to leave it. However, at nine, His Lordship arrived, accompanied by a hamper of claret.

"Much as I respect His Majesty," said Lord Hertford, "I cannot stand the old women at Brighton."

We received letters from Julia and Sophia, declaring they had changed their minds, and would not join us.

I saw a great deal of the Duc de Guiche, who used to be called, while in the 10th Hussars, the Count de Gramont, during my short stay in Brighton. He was very handsome, possessed a quick sense of honour, and ever avoided even the shadow of an obligation: I need not add that he, through strict economy, kept himself, at all times, out of debt. As an officer he was severe and ill-tempered; but well versed in military business: as a Frenchman, he was fonder of flirting than loving; and, with regard to his being a fop, what could a handsome young Frenchman do less?

I refused to see Dr. Bankhead, who had left his card, by Lord Frederick Bentinck's desire; because the world said he was a terrible fellow! However, being afterwards afflicted with an attack of inflammation in my chest, I ventured to send for this Herculean Beauty!

He cannot, thought I, be so very impudent as he has been represented to me by many, and particularly by Mr. Hoare the banker, who declared that maids, wives, and widows were often obliged to pull their bells for protection.

Dr. Bankhead came into my bedroom, with the air and freedom of a very old acquaintance.

"What is the matter, my sweet young lady?" said he, "and what can I do for you?"

"I see! I hear!" said he, interrupting me, observing that I spoke with difficulty. "Fever? Yes," feeling my pulse. "Oppression? ah! Cough? hey? Do not speak, my sweet creature. Do not speak! You have been exposing that sweet bosom!" endeavouring to lay his hand upon it, and which I resisted with all my strength of hand.

"Nay! nay! nay! stop! stop! stop! hush! hush! You'll increase your fever, my charming young lady; and then what will our friend Fred Bentinck say? quiet! quiet! There, don't speak; can you swallow a saline draught? and I'm thinking, too, of James's powders; but it is absolutely necessary for me to press my hand on that part of your chest, or side, which is most painful to you."

"Dr. Bankhead, excuse me. This is by no means my first attack of the kind, and I pretty well know how to treat it."

"There! there! then! be quiet, my dear young lady. I give you my honour, you have already increased your fever. Hush! you will take your draught tonight?"

"Dr. Bankhead, I must——"

"Nay! nay! there! keep yourself quiet, I entreat. Quietness is everything, in these inflammatory fevers, you know, my sweet."

"Dr. Bankhead, I must ring the bell."

"Hush! there! there then! I would not frighten you for the world: and I am apt to frighten ladies, I am, indeed! hush! be quiet! there then! hush! I am, indeed, as you may have heard, a most terrible fellow! Be quiet, my sweet lady! Swallow this glass of lemonade! There! now lie very still. In short, so terrible am I, that I frighten every woman on earth, except Mrs. Bankhead, and my Lady Heathcote!! hush!"

"Dr. Bankhead! this is an unmanly advantage of——"

"Oh, you naughty creature, to flurry yourself! I would not frighten you for the world! And, since I am so terrifying, take me altogether——"

"Dr. Bankhead, I'll ring the bell": and I tried to reach it.

"You shall have just as much, or as little of me as you please. Be still! pray! pray! and this is an offer I never before made to any woman: not even to my dear friend, Lady Heathcote."

Dr. Bankhead laid his giant-hand on my bosom, to demonstrate one of his former feats. My passions were now roused in a peculiar manner, and, catching hold of my bell, I never ceased ringing it till my maid appeared.

I desired her to show Dr. Bankhead out of my house, "and, above all things, do not leave my room without him."

"Good morning, to you, my sweet, comical lady," said Bankhead, and left the house.

In about two months we all grew tired of Brighton, except Fanny, who had never been happier than while galloping over the Downs with the first man she had really loved; perhaps the first who had treated her with the respect and kindness her very excellent and benevolent qualities so well deserved.

I often heard from Fred Bentinck, as well as from His Grace of Leinster. The latter joined me in London, towards the end of November. I had only been settled there a few days, when I was surprised by a visit from the young Marquis of Worcester, whose very existence I had almost forgotten.

He expressed his gratitude for being admitted; and sat with me for two hours, when our *tête-à-tête* was interrupted by Leinster. He then took his leave, having conversed only on indifferent subjects, without once touching on the passion Lord Deerhurst and several others had assured me that he entertained for me.

Leinster appeared much annoyed at the reappearance of Worcester, and talked of going to Spain.

"I am a great fool," said His Grace, "and travelling may make me wiser."

I shook my head.

"At all events," continued His Grace, "I shall be out of the way of seeing Worcester make love to you. I am no match for him, being of a colder and less romantic turn. Worcester would go to the devil for you; and will make you love him, sooner or later. I cannot contend with him, and, therefore, I have almost decided to go with my brother, Lord Henry, and young Fitzgibbon, to the Continent."

I went to call on Fanny, after His Grace left me. Lord Alvanley and Amy were with her, and her eternal admirer, Baron Tuille, who told us that Lord Worcester did nothing but inquire of every man he met, whether they had heard anything relative to the departure of Leinster for Spain.

"I've some news for you," said Fanny. "Sophia has made a new conquest of an elderly gentleman, in a curricle, with a coronet on it. He does nothing on earth, from morning till night, but drive up and down before Julia's door. Julia is quite in a passion about it, and says it looks so very odd."

"Talk of the devil," said Alvanley, as Julia and Sophia entered the room.

"Well, Miss Sophia, so you've made a new conquest?" said Fanny.

"Yes," answered Sophia; "but it is of a very dowdy dry-looking man."

"But then his curricle!" I interrupted.

"Yes, to be sure, I should like to drive out in his curricle, of all things."

"It is very odious of the fright, to beset my door as he does," Julia said.

"So it is, quite abominable; and, for my part, I hate him, and his curricle too," good-natured Sophia replied.

Worcester was riding near my door as I drove up to it. I stopped to ask him if he liked to join me at Astley's, where I proposed going, with the Duke of Leinster. He hesitated, and seemed really annoyed at the idea of Leinster being of the party.

"If you really wish it," said His Lordship, reddening.

"Oh, I shall not break my heart," I answered, "only it has struck me, and has struck others, that you liked me, therefore I conceived the proposal might be agreeable."

"I am afraid," said Lord Worcester, "that I shall be thought very intrusive and impertinent; but I am most anxious and desirous to be allowed to say one word to you, before you go to Astley's tonight."

"Leinster comes for me at half past seven," I replied, "so call at seven."

Worcester rode off, all gratitude.

I was surprised to find Leinster sitting at my pianoforte, in my drawing-room, when I got upstairs. "What, again at your hundred and fourth psalm?" said I, "after all the promises you have made to become less righteous?"

"I have a favour to ask," said Leinster, and the boy's usual open smile was fled, and he looked infinitely more interesting; because he was paler, and there was an air of sensibility about him, which was seldom the case.

"My dear little Harry," said he, passing his hand across his curly locks, "I am annoyed, and bothered to death, with Worcester's perseverance. I am going to Spain. I shall stay, perhaps, several years, and you and I may never meet again. I know you are going to remind me that you never professed any particular love for me, and that you never deceived me as to your love of liberty; but I am not asking anything of you as a right; I am only making an appeal to your good nature, when I entreat you not to receive Worcester's visits till I am gone, which will be, I hope, in less than six weeks. It should be sooner, but that I have many things to arrange, relative to my coming of age."

The simplicity, and feeling manner, in which Leinster delivered his little speech, affected me a good deal.

"Do not go, Leinster," said I, kissing the eye, where a tear was glistening; "and, as long as you will stay, I will tell Worcester I must decline receiving his visits."

"When," said Leinster, while a bright smile played on his full red lip, which was very pretty, and always looked as though a bee had stung it newly, "when will you tell him this?"

"His Lordship is coming here, at seven, and I will then give him his *congé, tout de bon*," said I.

Leinster hurried off, in high spirits, that he might get back in time to take me to Astley's.

Lord Worcester came to me before I had finished my dinner. He assured me that he now proposed to accompany me, if I still would permit him, to Astley's; "but," said Lord Worcester, after some hesitation, "you are, I am sure you must be, aware that my being present, to see the Duke of Leinster, or indeed any man on earth, conduct you home, is very hard upon me."

"I hope not," said I, "and certainly I am not aware of any such thing. You are neither my husband nor my lover, and you never made any professions of love to me; I hope you felt none; because—' and I hesitated in my turn.

"Because what?" said Lord Worcester, in almost breathless anxiety.

"Because my old friend, the Duke of Leinster, feels much annoyed at your visits, and——"

"And you assured me he was indifferent to you," interrupted Worcester.

"I said, I was not in love with him, neither am I; but I cannot bear teasing him; so, to be frank with you, and one must be frank when one is in such a hurry," continued I, laughing, "I have promised to beg of you, as a favour, not to come here any more."

Lord Worcester's face was scarlet first, and then pale as death: he took up his hat, half in indignation, and then put it down, in despair! Had I been more humble than I really am, I could not, with common sense, have doubted the deep impression I had made on Worcester.

"*Ecoutez, mon ami*," said I, holding out my hand to him. "I cannot account for the prejudice which runs high in my favour, among you young men of rank. I am inclined, rather to attribute it to fashion, or some odd accident, than to any peculiar merit on my part: still, flattered as I ought to be, and deeply grateful as I always am, it will yet be paying very dear for the impression which is excited in my favour, if, while my own heart happens to be free as air, and my fancy ever laughter-loving, I am to condole, all the morning, with one fool, and sympathise, the blessed long evening, with another; neither can I be tender and true to a dozen of you at a time."

"I did not," said Worcester, half indignantly, "I did not know that I was quite a fool; and, at all events, I shall not intrude my folly on you, if I am."

In vain he tried to pull his hat completely over his eyes. The tears did not glisten there, as they did in Leinster's; but they fell in torrents, as he attempted to take leave of me.

Oh dear me! said I, as I sighed an inward good-bye to the self-same harlequin-farces at which I had laughed so heartily many years before, when I accompanied poor Tom Sheridan to Astley's.

"What am I to do, Lord Worcester?" I asked. "Upon my word I would rather suffer anything myself, than cause unhappiness to those who love me, but I really must go to Astley's, I have not a moment to lose. My word is pledged to Leinster; but I believe that you love me better than he is capable of loving anything, and, since you are good enough to value my friendship, I will not cut you, indeed I will not," and I gave him my hand, which he covered with warm kisses and warmer tears.

"You must go now," I added; "I never break my word, and Leinster will be here directly; but, when he goes to Spain——"

"Does he go?" interrupted Worcester, eagerly.

"Everything is settled," answered I, "and, in less than six weeks, Leinster can torment you no more."

Worcester appeared to be overjoyed.

"And when he is gone, there will be no man you care about, left in England?"

"None: except indeed a sort of tenderness, not amounting to anything like passion, for Lord Robert Manners: and then I have a great respect for Lord Frederick's morals, and that is all! So now, my Lord, you must set off, and do be merry. You shall hear from me often, and, as soon as Leinster is gone, you are welcome to try to make me in love with you. If you fail, so much the worse for us both; since I hold everything which is not love to be mere dull intervals in life."

"I may not call on you then?" asked Worcester.

"I will write, and tell you all about it."

There was now a loud rap at the door.

"I am off," said Worcester. "I cannot bear to sit here a single instant, with Leinster. *En grace je te prie, mon ange, ayez pitié de moi, et ne m'oubliez pas.*" He dropped on one knee to kiss my hand, like a knight of old, and the next instant he was out of sight.

"Was that the Marquis of Worcester, who ran out of your house in such a hurry, as I was getting out of my carriage?" asked Leinster, as he entered the room, full dressed, his handsome leg, *en gros*, set off to the best advantage by a fine silk stocking.

"Yes," said I, "but I have desired him not to come again; so pray don't be sentimental. I have had enough of that, this day, to last me my life."

"You are very cold and heartless, which is what, from the expression of your eyes, I had never suspected," remarked Leinster.

"I was in love enough once," I rejoined, "God knows, and what good did it do me?"

After all, I arrived at Astley's just in time for my favourite harlequinade. The house was well attended. I thought that I observed the Marquis of Worcester, slyly glancing at us through the trelliswork of a stage-box: but I was not quite certain. After the piece was finished, I wanted to set Leinster down at his own door; but he declared himself so hungry, that he could not get farther than Westminster Bridge without a slice of bread and butter, quite as thick as those his tutor Mr. Smith used to provide him with. This luxury his footman procured, together with a tankard of ale, from a pot-house in the immediate vicinity of the theatre.

The next morning Fanny came to take leave of me. Colonel Parker could no longer be absent from his regiment, which was stationed at Portsmouth, therefore they proposed leaving London for that place on the following day.

"Remember me, kindly, to Lord Worcester, when you see him," said Fanny. "There is something in that young man's countenance I like so much, and his manners are so excessively high bred and gentleman-like, that I cannot think how you can resist him, and treat him so very coldly as you do. As to Amy, she is going stark mad to be introduced to him."

"With all my heart," said I.

Fanny told me, calling another subject, that Julia had not only surmounted her reluctance to Napier, but had become almost as fond of him as she had been of Sir Harry Mildmay; and that was the reason why she refused to join us at Brighton.

I inquired whether he seemed disposed to behave well to Julia, and her family.

"Oh, he is horridly stingy," answered Fanny, "and Julia is obliged to affect coldness and refuse him the slightest favour till he brings her money; otherwise she would get nothing out of him. Yet he seems to be passionately fond of her, and writes sonnets on her beauty, styling her, at forty, although the mother of nine children, 'his beautiful maid.'"

Fanny having her carriage at the door, I proposed our calling on Julia.

"I am going to take my leave of her," Fanny replied, and we drove immediately to her residence.

Julia, whose health had been very delicate since her last premature confinement, was gracefully reclining on her chaise-longue, in a most elegant morning-dress. She expected Napier to dine with her. Sophia was hammering at a little country dance on the pianoforte.

To our inquiry how her curricle-beau went on she answered: "Oh! he is always driving about this neighbourhood, and I think I have discovered who he is. I believe it to be Lord Berwick; but I am not quite certain. However, we are to be introduced to him, tomorrow, by Lord William Somerset, who has been here this morning to ask Julia's permission to present a friend. He did not name him, but assured us he was a nobleman of fortune, and of great respectability."

We wished her joy, and kissed her, and took our leave of Julia, as I afterwards did of Fanny, whose departure made me very melancholy. She was the only sister who cared about me, and we had very seldom, in the course of our lives, been separated from each other. We promised to correspond regularly, and I assured her that, when she should be settled at Portsmouth, if she acquainted me that she had a spare bed for me, I would certainly pay her a visit.

"Tell me all about Lord Worcester," said Fanny, "and you may say to him that it is lucky for Colonel Parker His Lordship never turned an eye of love on me."

I came home very dull indeed, and was informed that Leinster, who had been waiting for me more than an hour, had just left the house; but a genteel young Frenchwoman was still in my dressing-room. She came to offer herself, in the place of my late *dame de compagnie*, Miss Eliza Higgins.

"*Je vous salue, mademoiselle*," said I, as I entered my little boudoir. "*D'où venez-vous?*"

She informed me that she had been living with Lady Caroline Lamb.

I liked her appearance very much: it was modest, quiet, and unaffected. What a contrast to that Miss Eliza Higgins! She did not look as if she was twenty; but she assured me, *sur son honneur*, she was in her twenty-sixth year. I engaged her at once, declined to inquire her character of Lady Caroline, and requested her to come to me the next day.

I never talk much to servants or companions when they come to be hired. If I dislike their faces, I tell them I am engaged: if the contrary is the case, I desire them to come to me on trial. Wherefore should one ask them, you can dress hair? Are you quick, good-tempered, honest, handy, etc. etc., when one can as well answer all these questions, in their name, oneself, with a single yes?

I passed a restless night. No woman ever felt *le besoin d'aimer* with greater ardour than I. What could I not have been? what could I not have undertaken for the friend, the companion, the husband of my choice? *En attendant*, methought, Lord Worcester knew how to love: that was something; but then, where was the power of thought, the magic of the mind which alone could insure my respect and veneration?

"How did you like Lady Caroline Lamb?" I asked my new maid, and, when she had answered all my questions, I sat down to scribble the following letter to my sister Fanny at Portsmouth.

MY DEAREST FANNY,

The frank Lord William has left for you, must not be lost, although I really have, as yet, nothing new or lively to communicate. Your favourite, Lord Worcester, has not been admitted since you were in town, notwithstanding he writes me such letters! but I will enclose one of them, to save trouble, for one grows tired of all this nonsense. Poor Leinster is infinitely more attentive and amiable, since this powerful rival has put him upon his mettle. For my part, since the hope of mutual mind is over, I try, and make the best of this life, by laughing at it and all its cares.

My new French maid has just been telling me a great deal about her late mistress, Lady Caroline Lamb. Her Ladyship's only son is, I understand, in a very bad state of health. Lady Caroline has therefore hired a stout young doctor to attend on him; and the servants, at Melbourne House, have the impudence to call him Bergami! He does not dine or breakfast with Lady Caroline or her husband, who, you know, is Fred Lamb's brother, the Honourable William Lamb; but he is served in his own room, and Her Ladyship pays great attention to the nature and quality of his repasts. The poor child being subject to violent attacks in the night, Lady Caroline is often to be found, after midnight, in the doctor's bedchamber, consulting him about her son. I do not mean you to understand this ironically, as the young Frenchwoman says herself, there, very likely, is nothing in it, although the servants tell a story about a little silk stocking, very like Her Ladyship's, having been found, one morning, quite at the bottom of the doctor's bed. This doctor, as Thérèse tells me, is a coarse, stupid-looking, ugly fellow; but then Lady Caroline declares to her, que monsieur le docteur a du fond!

She is always trying to persuade her servants that sleep is unnecessary, being une affaire d'habitude seulement. She often called up Thérèse in the middle of the night, and made her listen while she touched the organ in a very masterly style.

R

Her Ladyship's poetry, says Thérèse, is equally good in French, in English, or in Italian; and I have seen some excellent specimens of her talents for caricatures. She sometimes hires a servant, and sends him off the next day for the most absurd reasons: such as " Thomas! you look as if you required a dose of salts; and, altogether, you do not suit me, etc." She is the meanest woman on earth, and the greatest tyrant, generally speaking, quoi qu'elle a ses moments de bonté; *but as to her husband, he is at all times proud, severe, and altogether disagreeable.*

Lady Caroline ate and drank enough for a porter, and, when the doctor forbade wine, she was in the habit of running into her dressing-room, to dédommager *herself with a glass or two of* eau de vie vieille de cognac! *One day, Thérèse, whose bedchamber adjoined that of William Lamb, overheard the following conversation between them.*

Lady C. I must and will come into your bed. I am your lawful wife. Why am I to sleep alone?

William: I'll be hanged if you come into my bed, Caroline; so you may as well go quietly into your own.

Lady Caroline persevered.

"Get along, you little drunken——" said William Lamb.

The gentle Caroline wept at this outrage.

"Mais où est, donc, ce petit coquin de docteur?" said William, in a conciliatory tone.

"Ah! il a du fond, ce docteur-là," answered Caroline, with a sigh!

Mind, I don't give you all this nonsense for truth; I merely repeat the stories of my young Frenchwoman.

Take Her Ladyship altogether, this comical woman must be excellent company. I only wish I had the honour of being of her acquaintance. Not that I think much of her first novel, "Glenarvon"; and she is, really, not quite mad enough to excuse her writing, in her husband's lifetime, while under his roof, the history of her love and intrigue with Lord Byron!! The letters are really His Lordship's, for he told me so himself. I once asked Luttrell, who was a particular acquaintance of William Lamb, why that gentleman permitted his wife to publish such a work?

"I have already put the very same question to William, myself," answered Luttrell, "and this was his reply: 'I give you my word and honour, Luttrell, that I never heard one single word about "Glenarvon," until Caroline put her book into my own hands, herself, on the day it was published.'"

Lady Caroline, I am told, always speaks of her husband with much respect, and describes her anxiety about his maiden speech in the House of Commons, to witness which she had, in the disguise of a boy, contrived to pass into the gallery:

But enough of Her Ladyship, of whose nonsense the world is tired. I admire her talents, and wish she would make a better use of them.

Poor Alvanley's carriage-horses, have, I fancy, been taken in execution. However, he said, last night at Amy's, that he had a carriage at the ladies' service, only he had got no horses; so we set him down.

"I cannot find any knocker, my Lord," said the footman, at our carriage door, after fumbling about for some time.

"Knock with your stick," said Alvanley, and then continued his conversation to us, "my d——d duns made such a noise every morning, I could not get a moment's rest, till I ordered the knocker to be taken off my street door."

Julia, most prolific Julia, is again in the way fair ladies sometimes wish to be, et vous? Your boy George is in high health; not quite as impudent and lazy as usual. Our dear mother has not looked so well, or more beautiful for the last ten years. She is very anxious about your health.

Brummell they say is entirely ruined. In short, everybody is astonished, and puzzled to guess how he has gone on so long! God bless you, my dearest Fanny. I meant only to write three lines, and here is a volume for you. Remember me kindly to Colonel Parker, and believe me ever,

Your affectionate sister,

HARRIETTE.

CHAPTER 13

VISCOUNT BERWICK WAS a nervous, selfish, odd man, and afraid to drive his own horses. Lord William Somerset was an excellent whip; but he had no horses to whip. Lord Berwick, like Lord Barrymore, wanted a tiger; while Somerset required a man whose curricle he could drive, and whose money he could borrow. The bargain was struck; and Tiger Somerset had driven Lord Berwick some years, when His Lordship, after having for more than a fortnight been looking at my sister Sophia, at her window, one day addressed the tiger as follows:

"I have, at last, found a woman I should like to marry, Somerset, and you know I have been more than twenty years upon the look-out."

"Who is she?" said Somerset, in some alarm.

Berwick told him all he knew, and all he had seen of Sophia.

"I think I know who you mean," said Tiger, "since you mention the house; because it belongs to Miss Storer, Lord Carysfort's niece, who has, I know, a fine young girl staying with her, whom Lord Deerhurst seduced."

"Seduced, already! you do not say so?"

"Most true, my Lord," said Tiger Somerset; "besides, I've often seen her, when Deerhurst used to take her out last year. She has no eyebrows, and——"

"I don't care for that, I love the girl, and will have her," was His Lordship's knock-down argument; and Lord William Somerset, having obtained permission from Julia, presented Lord Berwick to Sophia on the following morning.

Sophia would not hear of such a very nasty, poking, old, dry man, on his first visit; but the second day, she was induced to drive out in his barouche. On the third, she declared His Lordship's equipage the easiest she ever rode in; but then he wore such a large hat! In short, she could not endure him, even to shake hands with her. I never knew Sophia evince so much decided character, since she was born, as in her dislike of Lord Berwick; though she condescended to enter his barouche, and dine with him, accompanied by Julia or myself, yet no persuasion of Lord Berwick, no prayers that His Lordship had wit to make, could prevail on her to trust herself, for an instant, in his society. Things went on this way for several weeks. Berwick made very pleasant parties to Richmond, and did everything with princely magnificence. Worcester's good uncle, Lord Berwick's tiger, wanted Worcester to join their parties, and Worcester would not go anywhere without me.

My time being so gaily taken up, I had to reproach myself with neglect towards my sister Fanny. "Give me my writing-desk," said I to my maid, Thérèse, at past four in the morning, "for I have made a vow not to sleep till I have fully answered Fanny's last two letters," and which I did, as follows:

My Dearest Sister,

It is past four o'clock in the morning, and yet my conscience still keeps me awake till I have answered your two letters. Believe me, my neglect does not, in the least, proceed from want of affection. One is sometimes teased into going out, till one acquires a sort of habit of society, which it becomes difficult to throw off. Sophia's new lover, Lord Berwick, did not let me enjoy a single day in quiet; and not at all out of regard or respect for my superior merit; but merely because Sophia refuses to stir without me.

We were all at the play last night: that is to say, Julia, Sophia, Lord W. Somerset, Lord Berwick, and Lord Worcester, with your humble servant, in two private boxes adjoining each other. Lord Berwick teases Julia and me from morning till night. He wants us to persuade Sophia to receive a settlement from him, of five hundred a year, and to place herself under his protection. We do not like to advise at all on such subjects; and whenever he ventures to touch on them to Sophia herself, she begins to sob and cry, as if she was threatened with sudden death! I asked her, last night, why she accepted so many magnificent presents from His Lordship, and suffered him to put himself to such an immense expense, if she disliked him so violently?

"Oh, I never said I disliked his carriages, or his jewels, or his nice dinners," answered Sophia.

Lord Worcester is quite as indefatigable as Lord Berwick, in his endeavours to persuade me to accompany him to Brighton, His Lordship having just entered the tenth Hussars. Lord Berwick proposes taking a fine house at Brighton for Sophia and Julia, and sending down his plate, man-cook, etc., but Sophia says he may hire his fine house if he likes, but for her part she will live with Julia in a smaller one, though, at the same time, she shall have no sort of objection to become one at his dinner-parties, if Worcester and myself are present. Thus Sophia has set Lord Berwick to work, to plead Worcester's cause for him. I got into a passion one day last week, and declared I would not be teased out of my liberty, which I valued more than my life.

In the evening, Lord Worcester found me seriously ill, with an oppression on my chest, to which I am become rather subject. I could not have imagined that any young man, in any class of life, could have made such a good nurse! He ran up and down, from the kitchen to the drawing-room, twenty times, and poured out my water-gruel, and my tea, as though this had been his natural vocation. Seriously, I was very grateful. Nothing attaches a woman, in my weak, nervous, state of health, like these kind of attentions; and I must do justice to the excellent taste of Worcester, in never intruding his passion on me.

I am glad to hear that Parker looks forward with so much delight to the idea of becoming a father. It is a strong proof of a good heart, generally speaking. With regard to the repugnance you say you feel, in availing yourself of the invitations from ladies who believe you to be Parker's wife, I certainly, in your place, would never seek them; neither are you bound to say anything of yourself, which can prejudice society against you. You tell me that some of the ladies in your neighbourhood will take no excuses. Well, then, visit them, whenever you are in the humour, and, if they have good taste, they will be delighted with your society.

Amy has, at this present writing, a great deal of work on her hands, owing to our general change or projected change of administration. Worcester, Berwick, Parker, and Napier; all to win, and seduce away, at once!!!

Parker she has already made an attempt on: this you, with all your good-natured charity, have confessed: and the other night, at the play, we observed her sitting in a private box, on the opposite side of the house, with Baron Tuille. Her glass was pointedly turned towards Worcester, all the evening. After the play, while we were waiting for our carriage, Amy, with an affectation of childish wildness, made loud remarks on the elegance of Worcester's person, as we passed her. Our party stood on the opposite side of the room from that where the Baron and Amy were waiting. Worcester was, however, obliged to pass close to them, to inquire for Lord Berwick's servants, and Tuille, at the express desire of Amy, probably, tapped him on the arm, as he was hurrying along, and requested to have the pleasure of introducing Mrs. Sydenham to him. Worcester, in much confusion, bowed low, very low; but passed on, immediately afterwards, without uttering a single syllable.

What a bore for Amy! and yet it serves her right!

"I could not possibly avoid being presented to your sister," said Lord Worcester, on his return; and he spoke with such agitation and confusion, that it was impossible to help laughing at him.

256

"*You were not very attentive to her, as, I think, I could observe,*" *Julia remarked.*

"*I would not have spoken a single word to her, for the world, and I only wish, as a gentleman, it had been possible to have avoided bowing. Mrs. Sydenham has, by her perseverance, made herself so very odious to me,*" *was Worcester's reply.*

Lord Berwick laughed heartily at his extreme delicacy; so did Lord William; but Worcester is steady as a rock to me, and my interests. Not even ridicule, the sharpest weapon which malice can turn against the feelings and prejudices of youth, ever changes him one jot, even when it wounds him most severely.

"*Any unimpassioned, unprejudiced observer of Harriette's mind and character,*" *says Worcester,* "*must agree with me that it is much under-valued by that part of the world, to whom her eccentricities and careless observance of many established forms, only are known; but Harriette's goodness and singleness of heart approximate her nearer to my idea of perfection, than any human being I have yet met with, and her face and person, to me, convey all I can imagine most desirable.*"

I repeat this to you, my dear Fanny, merely to show the force and power of ardent passion in youth. Dieu! comme cela nous embellit!

You shall hear what becomes of me, next Tuesday, after Leinster will have left London. In the meantime, I need not say how truly I am yours, etc.

HARRIETTE.

When Lord Worcester had ascertained that Leinster was really safe on his journey to the continent, half wild with joy, he went and consulted Julia as to what she really believed was his chance of inducing me to go to Brighton. I had obtained his promise not to call on me, nor write to me, for at least three days after Leinster's departure.

"We shall only quarrel," said I to His Lordship, "if you come to me, rejoicing, as I know you will, at a circumstance which, no doubt, will affect me *pour le moment.*"

I passed a melancholy evening, after Leinster had taken leave of me. He was to sail from Portsmouth. Should he be detained by foul winds, even for a single hour, he promised to write to me. The first day, I refused to admit any visitor, and on the second, after his departure, I received a letter from him, to acquaint me that the unfavourable state of the weather might possibly detain him a week or more at Portsmouth. My resolution was taken in an instant: which wise resolution may be learned from the following letter, addressed to my sister.

My Dearest Fanny,

Leinster is at Portsmouth, waiting for a fair wind to convey him to Spain. I am too melancholy to keep my promise of receiving Worcester's visits; and besides, being desirous of shaking hands once more with the poor Duke, you will believe me really, and in truth, very anxious to see you. Therefore expect me almost as soon as my letter; and do pray be glad to see me, too.

I propose leaving London at eight o'clock tomorrow morning, till then, believe me,

Most truly yours,

Harriette.

After dispatching this, and a letter full of excuses to Lord Worcester, I began to assist my maid Thérèse to prepare for my journey to Portsmouth on the following morning. We arrived in time for dinner. Fanny was looking better than usual. Colonel Parker was absent, and she was kind enough to invite the Duke of Leinster to dine with us. His Grace was very glad to see me, in his dry way; but it was impossible to avoid making such comparisons between my two young lovers as were most favourable to Worcester.

Fanny did not like Leinster, and I felt rather cooled and disgusted, when she forced on my attention his extreme selfishness in leaving England without inquiring at all about the state of my finances. Leinster, much as he professed to esteem, respect, and love me, went out in a sailing boat every morning, instead of walking about with me. My pride took the alarm, and one fine morning, having previously arranged everything for my return to town, and taken leave of my sister, I coolly wished him *un bon voyage*, and, to his utter astonishment, jumped into the carriage which was to convey me to London.

I found a great many cards and letters on my table in town: and, what was better still, another blank cover, directed to me, containing two banknotes for one hundred pounds each!

Julia called on me the morning after my arrival.

"Do go to Brighton," said she. "You will never find anybody to like you as, I am sure, Lord Worcester does. I really would not advise you, but that I think he deserves you."

"I will consider about it," said I, "in the meantime pray tell some news."

Julia declared she had heard nothing lately. "Amy," she continued, "has found out a lady who once had a slip with your favourite, Ward."

"What does she say of him?" I inquired.

"Oh, that he was all fire and ice. He declared, on going to bed, that he should require at least three additional blankets, which comfort he had scarcely enjoyed a quarter of an hour, before he swore he was in a fever, threw off all the bedclothes, and opened the windows; and then came on his ague fit again."

"Oh, the amiable creature!" said I. "And how does Lord Berwick go on?"

Julia told me that he was quite as much in love with Sophia as ever.

"And Sophia?"

"Oh, Sophia hates His Lordship, if possible, more than ever, and declares she will not go to Brighton unless you decide to accompany Worcester there."

We were now interrupted by a visit from Lord Worcester. I will not attempt to describe his rapture, or how violently he was agitated at meeting with me. My readers, besides accusing me of vanity, would not believe such exaggerated feeling as he evinced to be in human nature. In short, I was pressed by Julia, entreated by Worcester, and inclined by gratitude, being, moreover, in a state of health which required nursing; therefore, without being in love, I agreed to place myself under his protection.

There certainly was much aggravation of sin, in my projected criminal intercourse with the Marquis of Worcester. Many women, very hard pressed *par la belle nature*, intrigue because they see no prospect nor hopes of getting husbands; but I, who might, as everybody told me, and were incessantly reminding me, have, at this period, smuggled myself into the Beaufort family, by merely declaring to Lord Worcester, with my finger pointed towards the North—that way leads to Harriette Wilson's bedchamber; yet so perverse was my conscience, so hardened by what Fred Bentinck calls, my perseverance in loose morality, that I scorned the idea of taking such an advantage of the passion I had inspired, in what I believed to be a generous breast, as might, hereafter, cause unhappiness to himself, while it would embitter the peace of his parents.

Seriously, I have but a very confused idea of what virtue really is, or what it would be at. For my part, all the virtue I ever practised, or desired to learn, was such as my heart and conscience dictated.

Now the English Protestant ladies' virtue is chastity! There are but two classes of women among them. She is a bad woman the moment she has committed fornication; be she generous, charitable, just, clever, domestic, affectionate, and ever ready to sacrifice her own good to serve and benefit those she loves, still her rank in society is with the lowest hired prostitute. Each is indiscriminately avoided, and each is denominated the same—bad woman, while all are virtuous who are chaste.

In Turkey, female virtue consists, as Lady Mary Wortley Montagu tells us, in losing no time, and being ever zealously employed in the pious work of increasing and multiplying.

The soldier's virtue lies in murdering as many fellow-creatures as possible, at the command of any man, virtuous or vicious, who may happen to be his chief, no matter why or wherefore.

The French ladies' virtue is, generally speaking, all comprised and summed up in one single word and article—*bienséance!*

Suppose we call it, *ça-et-là bienséance!*

It is a most prolific monosyllable, that same *ça*; only some people call it differently. However, to proceed with my story, for this same virtue and its attributes are puzzling me to death:

Viscount Berwick, in a magnificent equipage, drawn by four milk-white horses, or four of raven black, I forget which, led the way towards Brighton, followed by the more humble vehicles containing his cook, his plate, his frying-pans and other utensils. Soon afterwards, Julia and Sophia started in a neat little chariot, drawn by two scraggy black horses, *parceque Mademoiselle Sophie vouloit faire paraitre les beaux restes de sa vertu chancelante.* Lord Worcester I sent down alone, that he might hire a house, and have everything in readiness.

"But if I once join my regiment, I shall not be allowed to return," Worcester observed.

"No matter," said I, "my maid and myself can find our way to Brighton with perfect safety."

"I can ride ten or fifteen miles to meet you," Worcester said, and having made me promise again and again, that he might expect me, at a certain hour, on a certain day, he took his leave, and also set off for Brighton.

Two days later, just as I was growing tired of my journey and of the society of my maid, who, probably, was as much bored with mine, since she had fallen fast asleep, I observed the figure of an officer, or private, wearing some uniform which looked, at a distance, like that of the 10th Hussars, galloping towards us. As it approached, it grew a little more like the young Marquis, and yet, somehow or other, I could not reconcile it to my mind that he should wear regimentals. I had forgotten that circumstance, and felt disappointed. A gentleman always looks so much better in plain clothes. I was soon put out of suspense, by his kissing his hand to me.

Love is sharpsighted. In another minute or two the Marquis of Worcester was blushing and bowing by the side of my carriage. He told me that he had got a house for me in Rock Gardens, where he had left his footman, Mr. Will Haught, to get all square, that being the man's favourite expression. The said Mr. Will Haught was a stiff, grave, steady person of about forty. He always wore the Beaufort livery, which was as stiff as himself, and used to take his hat off, and sit in the hall, on a Sunday, with a clean pocket-handkerchief tied about his head, reading the Bible, offering thus, to the reflecting mind, these two excellent maxims: Respect God, but do not catch cold.

This Mr. Will was commander-in-chief of Worcester's servants. He had, indeed, been bred in the family, and was, I believe, the Duchess of Beaufort's footman before His Lordship was born, and though he wore a livery, he had since been raised to the rank of under-butler by the Duke of Beaufort. Why he was dismissed from that most honourable post, to follow the fortunes of his noble young master, I cannot tell; unless indeed Her Grace, touched and deeply impressed by the pious and respectful manner in which Will Haught was in the habit of binding up his temples, on a Sunday, with his clean pocket-handkerchief, while reading the Bible, had employed him as a spy, to watch over the morals of her hopeful firstborn. Be that as it may, we found Will quite as busy in settling everything for my comfort, as though I had been the Duchess's chosen daughter-in-law, for which he was making all square, upon the square, which means, I believe, in the way of honesty.

The coachman, Mr. Boniface, had also had the honour of driving the Duchess, in auld lang syne. We found him by no means so officiously polite and attentive as Mr. Will Haught: on the contrary, he was fast asleep, with his nice little *viellie cour* cotton wig all awry. We found a groom, in the Beaufort livery, at the door, waiting for His Lordship's horse, which he handed over, by the bridle, to the undergroom, and the undergroom sent a soldier with it to the stable.

What a bore it will be, to have all these lazy porter-drinking men in one's house, thought I, with very unmarchionesslike humility; but then I never set up for anything at all like a woman of rank.

Will Haught introduced my maid to a female servant, whom he had himself hired, and whom he desired to show her mistress's apartments to my woman. As to Lord Worcester, he was so excessively overjoyed at finding all his fears and dread of losing me at an end, that the moment he could contrive to get rid of Will Haught, he pressed my hand first to his trembling lips, and next to his heart, and then he burst into tears! which he, however, from the very shame, dried up as soon as he possibly could, and with the genuine feelings of affection and hospitality he asked me if, after the fatigue of my little journey, I should prefer passing the night alone.

"And where are you to sleep?" said I.

His Lordship informed me that he had a good bed in his dressing-room.

I then told him that, if he would permit me to pass this night alone, he would see me in excellent temper and spirits tomorrow. "At present everything is strange here, therefore, if I am a little melancholy, you must not, my dear Worcester, fancy it proceeds from want of regard for you."

It was impossible not to be reconciled to Worcester, while he thus acceded to all my wishes, reasonable or unreasonable. A good lesson, this, for many a fool who thinks to win a woman's heart by crossing all her desires.

An excellent dinner was well served, and while we partook of it, His Lordship informed me that Lord Berwick, whom he always called Tweed, wished to have dined with us, accompanied by Sophia and Julia; but he had not ventured to invite them, without first ascertaining whether it would be agreeable to me.

Lord Worcester's fine person looked remarkably well in the elegant evening uniform of the 10th, and I was so touched and won, by being allowed to have my own way, with such perfect liberty, in the house of another person, that when he handed me to the door of my bedchamber, and there took a most tender and affectionate leave of me for the night, I was almost tempted to regret that I had expressed a desire to pass it in solitude.

"It is a nice room," said I, "and the fire burns cheerfully. Do you think there are any ghosts in this part of the world?"

Worcester, however, was too modest in his idolatry, and had too great a dread of giving offence to me, to take my hint.

He merely reminded me that he was close at hand; and I had but to touch my bell to bring him in an instant to my side.

The next morning I was awakened by Lord Berwick's odd voice, calling to Worcester: "I have brought you some prime apples, which came from my country house this morning, and Sophia wants you both to dine with me today: in short, she will not come unless you do."

I hurried on my dressing-gown, and assured Lord Berwick that I should meet her with pleasure.

Lord Worcester said that he ought to be at parade; but declared, no matter what might be the consequence, that he could not and never would leave me again.

After breakfast, his two grooms rode up to the door with three horses: one of them was a delightfully quiet-looking lady's horse.

"Who is to ride that one which is without the saddle?" I inquired.

Worcester made Will Haught bring down from his dressing-room one of the most beautiful, easy side-saddles I ever beheld, richly embroidered with blue silk.

"Will you ride, Harriette?" asked Worcester. "If so, I hope you will approve of this saddle of my choosing, which shall always be kept in my dressing-room, that no one may use it, for an instant, except yourself."

We took a very long ride, and were joined by my former acquaintance Colonel Palmer, who pressed me, very politely, to accompany Lord Worcester to dine at the mess-rooms.

"Not today," said I; "certainly next week, with Worcester's permission."

Colonel Palmer fixed on an early day in the week, and kindly assured us he would get the mess-dinner kept back for an hour, knowing how fond Worcester was of late hours. He then ventured gently to hint something about Colonel Quinton's displeasure, at his having failed to attend parade that morning.

"I shall scold you," continued the Colonel, addressing me, "if this happens again."

Worcester and I rode about the country together, till it was nearly time to dress: the undergroom, who was waiting at my door for my horse, held out his hand for my foot, to assist me in dismounting, while his master was taking leave of Colonel Palmer; and I was just going to accept his assistance, when Worcester, in much agitation, desired him to desist, and never attempt such presumption again.

I assured His Lordship that I should not like him a bit the better, for dirtying his hands, or his gloves, with my muddy shoes; but he was peremptory.

Lord Berwick treated us most magnificently; but Sophia, the gentle, dovelike Sophia, was become so very cross and irritable to His Lordship, that it was disagreeable to everybody present.

After dinner we played at cards; and when we had concluded one of the most stupid evenings possible, Worcester and I took our leave.

The next morning, Lord Berwick called on me, to entreat that I would consider my sister's welfare, and persuade her to place herself under his protection.

"The annuity I propose giving her," continued His Lordship, "of £500, shall be derived from money in the funds."

"And so you really are, at last, caught, my Lord," said I, "fairly caught in love's trap? Now I am rather curious to learn what particular happiness you expect to enjoy, with a girl who, though she is my sister, I may say, as you and everybody know it as well as myself, never showed any character but once, in her whole life; and that was in her unequivocal dislike of you?"

"I do not mind that," answered His Lordship, "and by giving her whatever she wants, she may perhaps get over her dislike."

"Is it her beauty, then, which has won your heart?"

"In part," answered Berwick; "but chiefly the opinion I have formed of her truth. I could never live with a woman whom I must watch and suspect. Now, I am disposed to believe implicitly every word Sophia utters."

"And with good reason," I interrupted him, "for I am convinced that Sophia seldom, if ever, tells an untruth; and certainly there is something very candid and fair in her unqualified acknowledgment of dislike towards you, since she is evidently fond of all the good things your money can buy, and I think she particularly likes a good dinner."

"And therefore," Lord Berwick resumed, "as her friend, you ought to advise her to come to me."

I told His Lordship that I really could not overcome my reluctance to interfere in such matters.

"I want her to decide," said His persevering Lordship, "that I may give orders about buying the lease of a house for her in town, and furnishing it."

In the evening we all went into Lord Berwick's private box at the theatre, and were very merry, with the exception of His Lordship, who sat down, quietly, at the very back of the box, where he could neither see nor hear. Sophia did not once take the slightest notice of him. For my part, I asked him, several times, if he would not exchange places with Lord Worcester; but he assured me that he disliked seeing a play more than sitting in the dark.

"Sophia ought to chat with you, then, since she chooses to favour you with her company."

"Oh, I do not like to be talked to," said Lord Berwick.

On the morning of the day fixed on for our dining at the mess-room,

Lord Worcester received a severe reprimand from Colonel Quintin, for neglecting the drill.

We sat down at least thirty at table, and I was the only lady in company.

Colonel Palmer scolded me very much indeed about Worcester's missing parade of a morning. I assured him that I had done and would do all I possibly could to make him more attentive. The Colonel declared that, if he again missed the drill, he feared Colonel Quintin would act in a way to disgust Lord Worcester with the army altogether, and he should regret, much, his going out of the regiment.

As soon as we had left the mess-room, I told Worcester that he really must be at parade, by eight o'clock tomorrow.

Worcester again promised, and again broke his word, for which he was immediately put under arrest, and desired not to wear his sword.

When Colonel Palmer came to condole with Worcester, His Lordship was a good deal agitated and confused. I passed my word to the Colonel that, if he would get Worcester's sword restored to him, I would accompany him to drill, rather than he should miss it. The next morning, I actually accomplished being up, dressed, and on my road to the barracks, by half past eight o'clock, accompanied by Worcester.

Will Haught, who was in a terrible bustle on this occasion, asked, "Where is Miss Wilson to wait during parade, my Lord?"

"In my barrack-room," said the Marquis.

"Why, my Lord, there is nothing at all in it but a large trunk, and, you see, the room has never been put square like, and I should have wished to have got Miss Wilson a neat comfortable breakfast."

"Well, do your best," said Worcester, as we drove off.

I found Lord Worcester's barrack-room in a dismal state. However, though it was quite impossible for Mr. Will Haught to make all square, yet he procured absolute necessaries for my breakfasting every morning at the barracks. It was quite as much as we could possibly do, to get dressed in time for parade; and breakfast at home was wholly out of the question.

Behold me, now, regularly attending parade, like a young recruit, dressed in a blue riding habit, and an embroidered jacket or spencer worn over it, trimmed and finished after the fashion of our uniform, and a little grey fur stable-cap, with a gold band.

From the window of Worcester's barrack-room, I used to amuse myself reviewing our troops, but not after the fashion of Catherine of Russia. Sergeant Whitaker, teaching the sword exercise, used to amuse me the most. It began thus:

"Tik nuttiss ! ! the wurd dror is oney a carshun. At t'wurd suards, ye drors um hout, tekin a farm un possitif grip o'th' hilt ! sem time, throwing th' shith smartly backords thus ! Dror ! !" Here the men, forgetful of the caution which had just been given them, began to draw. "Steady there ! ! Never a finger or a high to move i'th' hed. Dror ! ! suards ! !"

We continued punctual at parade for more than a fortnight. Some of Worcester's friends generally joined us on our way from the barracks, to which place I frequently rode on horseback, when the weather would permit.

Young Edward Fitzgerald, who is a cousin of the Duke of Leinster, on one occasion galloped after us, and addressed Worcester: "What do you think ? there is a d——d old gallipot-fellow, has been gossiping about you, and tells everybody he meets the story of your being put under arrest, and having your sword taken away from you, for making such a fool of yourself about Harriette."

Worcester, reddening with indignation, said, "I must take the liberty of acquainting you, Fitzgerald, that the lady you call Harriette, I consider as my wife; and when I assure you that you will wound and offend me, if ever you treat her with less respect than you would show to the Marchioness of Worcester, I am sure you will desist from the familiarity of calling her by her Christian name."

Fitzgerald, goodnaturedly, assured him he had spoken with his usual thoughtlessness.

Some time after this, I received a long letter from my sister Fanny, to acquaint me with the absence of Colonel Palmer from Portsmouth, on particular business, and of her intention of passing a month with me at Brighton: it being nearly five weeks since she had become the mother of a lovely little girl, and her physician having recommended the bracing air of Brighton for the recovery of her strength.

Fanny's arrival was a holiday for us all. Lord Berwick hoped much from her extreme good nature and obliging disposition. Sophia, between Julia, Fanny and myself, was the more certain of not being left *tête-à-tête* with her nightmare, Lord Berwick, and Julia, whose very friendship partook of passion, shed tears of joy when she pressed her friend to her heart. My affection was calm, for it was fixed, and shall be eternal, if eternity is to be mine, with memory of the past.

Fanny declared we should all become good horsewomen before she left Brighton. She was, herself, a most beautiful rider. Accordingly, the morning after her arrival beheld a cavalcade about to start from my door in Rock Gardens: it consisted of Lords Berwick and Worcester, Mr. Fitzgerald, two young dragoons, whose names I have forgotten, Julia, Fanny, Sophia, and me. Lord Berwick was too nervous to trust himself on horseback, except on very great and particular occasions. I found much amusement in tickling up my mare a little, as I rode it close to his horse, in order to put a little mettle into them both. It was rather wicked; His Lordship declared he was not frightened for himself, but only for Sophia.

Lord Worcester took the opportunity to give Sophia a few instructions about holding her whip and bridle. Suddenly, when we were at least five miles from Brighton, Sophia quietly walked her horse towards home, leaving us to proceed without her.

"What can be the matter with Sophia?" we all inquired at once.

Fitzgerald feared he had said something to offend her.

Lord Worcester and Fanny galloped after her, to ascertain what was the matter, and how she expected to find her way home alone.

"Oh, nothing is the matter," said Sophia, very innocently, "nothing whatever is the matter, only he will go this way," alluding to her horse.

The whole party dined at my house, and Lord Worcester did the honours of the table with infinite grace.

When the ladies withdrew from the room, they had a thousand questions to ask each other. Fanny took upon her to say to Sophia that she conceived she was treating Lord Berwick very ill, in accepting so much from him, unless she meant to live with him.

Sophia began to cry, and I to laugh. Julia showed us some very romantic love-letters from Napier, whom she shortly proposed joining in Leicestershire.

Sophia, at Fanny's persuasion, now began to waver.

"Come," said Fanny, "what does it signify to you whether your lover is old or young, handsome or ugly, provided he gives you plenty of fine things; since you know you are the coldest girl in all England, and never felt a sensation in your life?"

"What do you call a sensation?" Sophia asked.

"Why," said Fanny, "I know you feel exactly the same in the society of men, as in that of women."

"How do you know?" continued Sophia.

"Well then I do not know," said Fanny; "so I beg you will tell us, and describe to us accurately, any symptoms you may have felt, bordering on passion or love: the latter sounds most amiable."

"Why, once," said Sophia, laughing.

S

"Once what?" Julia interposed.

"Come," said I, drawing my chair towards the fire, "let us hear all about your once."

"Well, then," resumed Sophia, "well, then; but you will promise not to tell?"

"Nonsense; who should we tell?"

"Well, then, you all recollect the handsome young cobbler, who lived in Chapel Street——"

"The cobbler! !" we both exclaimed, laughing.

"Yes, you may recollect, I used to get my shoes made by him."

"Well?"

"Well. I used to think the cobbler very handsome. Ah, you may laugh, all of you; but there is no answering for one's taste, you know. In short, I was incessantly calling on him with some excuse or another, such as asking how my shoes went on? or when they would be finished? and, when they were sent home, I used to carry my old ones to him, to ask if they were worth mending. One evening, when it was nearly dark, he ventured to press my hand, as he handed me my shoes. This I believe was done in trepidation; but I felt it very pleasant. Finding that I did not resent this first liberty, he began to kiss me, and I was so ashamed, I knew not what to say or how to push him away."

"What next?" cried we all three, eagerly drawing all our chairs nearer to her, and laughing.

"Why," said Sophia, blushing and hesitating, "why, oh, but the next thing was very nasty indeed!"

"What thing do you mean?"

"Why, a very shocking one."

"How do you mean, shocking?"

"Come, out with it," said Julia.

"Out with it, indeed," Sophia repeated, with a deep blush.

"Good heavens! surely he did not, you do not mean to say that the obbler actually did . . .?"

"Upon my word he did. . . ." answered Sophia.

"And was it on this memorable occasion, and this only, that you boast of having felt a sensation?" I inquired.

"Why, I never felt so oddly before."

"Mercy on me, and what did you do?" asked Julia.

"Oh, I was running out of the shop with my face and neck as red as scarlet; for you know I was scarcely thirteen years of age."

"And what prevented you?"

"Why, the cobbler; who took hold of my hand, and told me I had no call to be afraid of touching him, for he was quite clean."

We could scarcely ask her what happened next, being absolutely convulsed with laughter.

"Oh, nothing else," answered Sophia; "for I got away as fast as I could; but then it was more than a week before I could get the cobbler out of my head: however, it really will be a great shame if you mention this to Lord Berwick."

Fanny declared she would not miss hinting it, delicately, to His Lordship, for a hundred *louis d'ors*.

The gentlemen soon after came upstairs. However, all Fanny could relate publicly was, that Sophia, in her earliest youth, had had *une affaire du cœur* with a cobbler, and Lord Berwick declared he would never rest till he had heard all about it. Before the evening was over, His Lordship was led to hope, from what Sophia said, that, if he were to furnish an elegant house, she might, probably, be induced to inhabit it, with His Lordship, sooner or later.

In about a month or six weeks, Lord Berwick had fitted up a very nice comfortable house for Sophia, in Montague Square, and Sophia, after obtaining His Lordship's promise that she should sleep alone, at least for the first week or two, accompanied His Lordship to London.

CHAPTER 14

It is impossible to do justice to all the delicate attentions I received from Lord Worcester, during nearly three years. They never relaxed; but continued to the hour of our parting, exactly as they had begun. One day, when I was obliged to have a back double-tooth drawn, he turned as pale as death, being absolutely sick with fright: and long afterwards, he always wore the tooth round his neck. If, for only ten minutes, he lost sight of me, by my walking or riding on a little faster than himself, he was in such agonies that, as I returned, I was addressed, continually, by private soldiers of the 10th, who assured me, my Lord was running after me all over the country, in much alarm; and when, at last, he overtook me, his heart was beating in such evident alarm as was, even to me, who had been tolerably romantic in my time, almost incredible! He flatly refused every invitation he received, either to dinner-parties, balls or routs, and, for more than six months, he had not once dined away from me. His uncle, Lord Charles Somerset, who, I believe, then commanded the district, was growing very angry, and threatened to inform his brother, the Duke of Beaufort, as he feared we were really married. It was, as Lord Charles said, ridiculous, in a man of Worcester's high rank, to seclude himself quite like a hermit. "At all events," continued the worthy uncle, "I hope you will not fail to be here on my birthday, next week." Lord Worcester promised to make an effort for the birthday, while he frankly told Lord Charles that he should be always miserable, in any society, without me.

When Worcester returned home, and related the conversation to me, I begged and entreated him to comply with his uncle's desires, as to his birthday, at least.

"My dearest Harriette," said Worcester, "having bound myself to you for my life, for better or worse, and with my eyes open, I feel that we two make but one, in our faults, and I hate to go to any place, where you may not accompany me." I assured him that I had no desire to be invited, because I had no longer health to enjoy society; and, in short, I would not rest till I had obtained his promise that he would attend his uncle's engagement.

When the day arrived, Worcester said he could not endure my dining alone with that stiff Will Haught, who could not know how to serve me with what I liked, standing behind my chair.

"Well, then, you shall give me my dinner first," I replied.

For this purpose, I dined earlier than usual. As soon as I had finished my dinner, I gave him a gentle hint.

"You have no time to lose. Your pretty new yellow boots, with the rest of your magnificent, full-dress regimentals, Will Haught has spread out, to great advantage, in your dressing-room, *et vous serez tout rayonnant!!*"

"And why am I to be dressed up, there, while the person for whom alone I exist, or wish to live an hour, is left in solitude? Why am I to be a slave to Charles Somerset? I will not go, let the consequence be what it may," said Worcester.

Worcester's carriage now drove up to the door.

"My Lord, you have not a minute to lose," eagerly spoke Will Haught.

"Put up the carriage, and bring me some cold beef," answered His Lordship.

"What will you say to your uncle?" I asked.

"He be hanged!" was the reply.

At past ten o'clock, Lord Charles sent down a groom, on horseback, to inquire for Worcester, and state that the ladies waited for him to take his part in the quadrilles, which he had studied, for that night.

Worcester ran up into his bedroom, and called out, from the window, after putting on his nightcap, that he was ill, and in bed, and desired he might not again be disturbed at so late an hour.

It would be tedious to attempt relating all, or even one twentieth part, of the tender proofs of love and affection which Worcester was in the daily, I may say hourly, habit of evincing towards me. His Lordship has often watched my sleep, in the cold, for half, nay sometimes during the whole of the night, sitting by my bedside, rather than risking to disturb me by coming into it. On an occasion when I was induced to consult a medical man about a trifling indisposition, which was not in the least alarming, Lord Worcester wrote the doctor a most romantic letter, inclosing a fifty-pound note, and declaring that his obligation to him would be eternal, if he could contrive to be of the slightest use to me. He would send fur shoes and fur cloaks after me, in hot dry weather; because one could never be certain that it would not rain before my return. He took upon him all the care of the house, ordering dinner, etc., from having once happened to hear me say that I did not like to know, beforehand, what I was to eat; and always used to lace my stays himself, and get out of bed to make my toast for breakfast, with his own hands, believing I should fancy it nicer and cleaner, if the footman had not touched it.

When the Prince Regent, who then commanded the regiment, came down to the Pavilion, Worcester was in despair; for he saw no possible means to avoid visiting His Royal Highness. The dinner, which was given expressly for the officers of the 10th Hussars, he was obliged to attend. On that occasion, which was the first of his passing an evening from home, after giving me my dinner, he sighed over me, when he took leave, as though it had been to go to the Antipodes.

Lord Worcester's rapture, on his return, knew no bounds. "My dear Harriette," said His Lordship, "the Prince's band, at the Pavilion, was so very beautiful, that it would have been impossible for me, who love music to excess, not to have enjoyed it; therefore, as I abhor the idea of enjoying anything on earth of which you cannot partake with me, I went into a corner, where I was not observed, to stop my ears and think only of you. I must now tell you that the Prince has given me a general invitation, to go to him every evening, and I have settled my plan to avoid it. I intend to sham lame, and practise it at home, till I can limp, very decently and naturally, and then I will wait upon His Royal Highness and tell him that I have a sprain, which keeps me in constant pain, and confines me to the house."

Worcester began to practise on the spot, and being, in all things, a most excellent mimic by the following day limped famously.

He declared that he was melancholy to think that I might grow tired of our *tête-à-têtes*, while, for his part, he never desired nor conceived any more perfect happiness than passing every hour in the day alone with me.

In spite of my gratitude, which he yet believes in, because I proved it, not only in words but by all my actions, yet I did want a little varied society, that I might not fall into a lethargy; so, when Fanny went to join Colonel Parker in town, I begged hard for, and at last obtained, a week's permission of absence, from one who could refuse me nothing.

"You shall go, at all events, and I know I can confide in your honour," said Lord Worcester; "but I will not despair of obtaining leave from the Colonel to accompany you."

The better to effect his purpose, he went to Quintin with a box of cigars under his arm. Quintin accepted the cigars with perfect good will; but in answer to His Lordship's next request, for leave to pass a week in town, the answer was:

"No! no! my Lord, you must drill."

Worcester had a great mind to have asked him to return the cigars. Nevertheless, he kept his promise of permitting me to accompany my sister Fanny to London.

We found Sophia established in a nice house in Montague Square, which Lord Berwick, or rather his upholsterer, had furnished with much taste.

Nous lui demandâmes si elle faisait, encore, lit à part?

Elle répondait que non.

"And what sort of a man is Lord Berwick?"

"Oh, he is a very violent man, indeed."

Sophia insisted on Fanny remaining her visitor for a week, which invitation, as Parker had no fixed residence in town, she gladly accepted. Sophia had at her command a very handsome equipage, in which we all three drove out on the day after my arrival.

We called on sister Paragon, whom we found greatly agitated.

"What is the matter?" we both asked at once.

"Oh," said Paragon, "do you hear the screams of that infant?"

"Yes, how shocking! It is not one of yours, however," said I, as I counted her pretty little family, who, as usual, were all seated close to her side.

"They proceed from my landlady's child, whose mother insists I have half killed it, and that it never was in such pain before. In short, she declares she apprehends a convulsion fit."

"Why, what can you have done to the poor child?" Fanny inquired.

"I merely administered one of Inglish's excellent aperient Scott's Pills to the dear infant," Paragon replied, calmly.

"This perfectly accounts for all these cries," Fanny observed, and further declared that she had herself been put in perfect torture by the only one she had ever swallowed.

"Do you presume to judge of Inglish's Aperient, who have swallowed but one?" said Paragon, with dignified contempt; "why, it requires at least fifty boxes of it to pass downwards, before you can properly decide on the merits of this invaluable medicine! In the meantime, the bowels must be severely pinched into obedience. Everything depends on the force of habit. Now there is my little Mary, for instance, the dear little child has become so accustomed to a pain in her bowels, that if, by any accident, I put her to bed without a Scotchman, she always awakes in low spirits."

"Nevertheless, you must excuse my ever swallowing another, to the end of my natural life," said Fanny.

From Paragon's we drove to Julia's. She told us that she had made Lord Berwick pay her down several hundred pounds in ready money, for having interceded with Sophia and persuaded her to live with him.

"Well," said I, sighing, "you have a large family, and I suppose it is what we must all come to. However, I conceive myself, as yet, rather too young to take up this new profession of yours, Julia."

Julia defended her conduct, by assuring me she had not taken it up but for my sister's real interest: as a proof of which, she declared that she had strong reason to believe it was Lord Berwick's intention to marry Sophia.

Sophia said she would not have him.

"And why, pray?" we asked.

"Because," said Sophia, "because—I think it will be very shocking to swear never to have but one man."

I observed to Sophia that, perhaps, she would swear faith to her cobbler, by that sole in which consists a cobbler's sole hope, much more willingly.

"Oh," said Sophia, "I am very sorry I told you of my affair with the cobbler."

"Of his affair, you mean," I remarked.

"Nonsense," continued Sophia; "I shall never hear the last of it, as long as I live: for Julia has not only acquainted Lord Berwick, but she has made it out worse."

"I do not know how she could manage that," said Fanny.

We all dined in Montague Square. Lord Berwick appeared to be perfectly happy, although he scarcely ever opened his lips; but the little he did say was chiefly on the subject of cuckolds and cuckolding. His Lordship was horn-mad. He wondered how many men had been cuckolded that season, in London, without knowing it? He wondered, if a girl like Sophia was to be forced into the sin of adultery, some day, by some naughty man, whether she would bury the sad story in her own breast.

I assured him I neither knew nor cared.

After having been dumb for at least a quarter of an hour, Lord Berwick, *à propos* to nothing, burst into a loud laugh.

"What on earth are you laughing at, Lord Berwick?" Sophia asked, very crossly.

"My own thoughts," answered His Lordship.

"And what were they, pray?" I inquired.

"Only something that happened to come across me," said His Lordship.

We all insisted on knowing what had come across him.

"Why," said Lord Berwick, "I was just considering, to myself, what a remarkably serious face Joseph always has, in the pictures; a sort of unhappy physiognomy, as if he were saying to himself, it is all very well! Have you ever remarked this, Miss Wilson?" said His Lordship.

"Heavens forbid! why do you address yourself to me?" I asked.

"Joseph looks," continued Lord Berwick, without attending to my pious answer, "Joseph looks as if he thought it all mighty fine."

"How wicked!" said Fanny, trying to give a serious expression to her arch laughing blue eye.

"Horrible!" said Julia, drawing up her long, thin throat.

For my own part, I laughed loudly.

After dinner, His Lordship's discourse turned on marriage: the pith, meaning, and spirit of which, was to show cause why Sophia ought to become Lady Berwick. He could never rest, till he had made the excellent deserving Sophia, his lawful wife.

Sophia again declared she would not have him; but before I left the house, she was graciously pleased to say that she would give the subject due consideration.

The next morning I received a very long letter from Lord Worcester. He acquainted me, after three pages, full of deep regret at my absence, that his virtue had been in the most imminent danger, from the very active attempts of the paymaster's wife, of the 10th.

The story was this: the paymaster was a man of very savage temper. On the day I left Brighton, Lord Worcester happened to join him, on horseback, when he was riding with his young, frisky wife. Worcester, with his usual good breeding, had addressed himself, several times, to the lady, who, in return, it appears, had ogled Lord Worcester, unperceived by anybody in the world, except her good man, who had the impertinence to grow angry: when, being at a loss how to vent his fury on the spot, he tickled his wife's mare behind, in a way which, he knew well, would cause her to rear and plunge. The animal, so far from disappointing his hopes, we will, out of charity, suppose, rather exceeded them; since, but for the immediate protection and active support of Lord Worcester, at some risk to himself, the paymaster's wife would have been thrown over the cliff.

Lord Worcester, as a mere man, putting gallantry out of the question, could not have done less than afford every assistance to a young woman, under circumstances of such imminent danger. This fair lady, however, made up her mind that she had achieved a desperate conquest over the heart of the young Marquis.

The better to secure the prize, she, on her return home, composed a very pretty little pathetic effusion, beginning somewhat thus:

Could I, dear Lord Worcester, receive your tender kind attentions, without emotion? The soldier, who is to put this note into your hand, you will find trustworthy. At dusk, we may contrive to meet, just behind the barracks, any day when my husband is dining at the mess, etc.

Lord Worcester was so very inattentive as to take no notice of this broad hint from the paymaster's wife, who repeated it, in still broader terms, the following day; declaring that she would throw herself on his honour and humanity, to allow her to meet him, on his way home from the barracks, just behind a certain hill, as soon as it was dark, merely to advise her how to escape the much-dreaded violence of her husband.

Lord Worcester must inevitably pass the appointed spot, on his way home from the barracks; he therefore determined to take that opportunity of informing her, once for all, that he was steadily attached to me, and me only, for the rest of his life: but he was ill prepared for the desperate attack which was, on that evening, to be made on his passions and his virtue. His Lordship, after having fully explained his feelings and situation to the paymaster's wife, naturally relied on her pride for obtaining his immediate *congé*, but he knew not what he had to deal with. The mother of this said most amorously-disposed paymaster's wife, had seduced the *accoucheur*, while in the very act of bringing this fair young lady into the world. For this wicked act the poor *accoucheur* had, it is said, paid damages, and further, the injured husband had confined his frail *moitié* in a madhouse ever since.

"Oh, dear Worcester, do not say we are to part thus, never to meet again! I have never loved till now! Do kiss me! Pray do!"

"Since you really do love me," said Worcester, "I am bound, by gratitude, to prove my esteem for you, by insisting on your return home to your husband."

The heroine became still more demonstrative of her love! It occurred to Worcester, by this time, that there was a plot in all this, to obtain heavy damages from him; and that idea, added to the strong affection he certainly then entertained for me, made him ice itself, and he left the young lady near her door, to sing willow! willow! willow!

It was a great bore, but there were finer young men in her husband's regiment than Worcester, and so, rather than die of grief, the lady tried them all!

After relating this story, Lord Worcester went on to abuse his uncle, Lord Charles Somerset, for his malice in having written to His Grace of Beaufort on the subject of our connection, in a way to alarm him excessively. Worcester, in consequence, received very severe letters, both from his father and mother, insisting on his immediately leaving me, unprovided for, and without the smallest ceremony. These harsh, unfeeling letters excited in Worcester a spirit of defiance, such as mild remonstrance never could have produced. He repeated his solemn assurances to me, that no power on earth, not even my inconstancy, could destroy his everlasting attachment, or induce him, however it must destroy his repose, to leave me. He deeply regretted his not being of age, that he might immediately make me his wife, and then nought could separate us save death. He reminded me that the period of his becoming of age was not very far distant, and, in the meantime, if they pressed him, our marriage was not impossible. He begged his most affectionate regards to his sisters, Fanny and Sophia, and implored me, unless I would for ever destroy his happiness on earth, to promise to become his wife, and remain with him for ever, etc.

I immediately answered Lord Worcester, begging him not to irritate his parents unnecessarily. I did not touch on the subject of our marriage; but desired him to rest satisfied with my faith, and that I would never, willingly, cause him a moment's pain, while I had reason to believe in his affection.

In conclusion, I informed him that he might expect me at Brighton, without fail, in three days from the date of my letter.

A few days after my return to Brighton, Worcester put into my hand another romantic effusion from the paymaster's little impudent wife, whose want of pride disgusted me infinitely more than her want of chastity. For four more successive days, Worcester received the most ridiculous professions of the fiercest passion, written in a beautiful hand, on the best vellum, and sealed with cupids, hearts, darts and heaven knows what besides. These soft communications were slyly put in his hand by a little drummer, during parade.

Being really bored by her perseverance, I addressed the following cooler to her.

MADAM,

It is not my fault that you are treated so cruelly by Lord Worcester; for I gave you a fair chance of working on his affections, when I went to London. You must therefore, by this time, be convinced that, pour le moment au *moins, the case is hopeless. If, in your extreme distress, I can afford you any consolation, you have only to speak. Shall I forward you a lock of his hair? or get his portrait copied for you? Further I cannot do, myself, you know; and with regard to all your effusions, though they serve me excellently well for papillotes—à propos, where do you contrive to get such delightful soft paper?— still, I cannot be so unfeeling as to recommend your giving yourself the trouble of composing any more nonsense, since it merely serves for my use and amusement.*

I have the honour to remain, etc.,

H.W.

To my great astonishment, I received a very polite answer from the amorous paymaster's wife. Heaven forbid that she should cause any jealous pangs in my breast! She had never thought of injuring me, having been led to believe that I had left Lord Worcester, etc.

I answered this letter thus:

MADAM,

There is not the least danger in the world of your having the power to injure me. Lord Worcester, even if he had forsaken me, would, I know, like to choose his wife or mistress himself, instead of having one thus forced on him. I merely thought it fair to acquaint you, before you had wasted all your beautiful soft paper, that Lord Worcester was in the habit of bringing every one of your effusions to me, without reading them, or even breaking the seals. If, after this information, you chose to continue, croyez-moi, cela m'est parfaitement indifférent.

Yours obediently, etc.,

H.W.

In less than a month afterwards, the paymaster's wife had divided the love which had been all Worcester's, equally and fairly between the brave officers of the 10th Hussars! !

Vive l'amour et le sentiment!

In spite of all I could say or do to prevent it, Lord Worcester got horribly in debt. He was naturally extravagant, and everybody cheated him. As for myself, I might have been welcome to have brought away, in His Lordship's name, at any time, as many diamonds as either Wirgman or any other jeweller would have given him credit for; and yet I can say with truth that I never accepted a single trinket from him, in my life, except a small chain, and a pair of pink topaz earrings, the price of which was, altogether, under thirty guineas. I even did my best to prevent his buying these, which were brought to me, as the man said, by the desire of Lord Worcester, merely to inquire if I liked them. His Lordship being from home, the man said he would call for them when he returned.

When I saw Worcester, believing it was not too late to return the trinkets, and knowing him to be very poor, I told him that I never wore such things, and should esteem it a favour if he would not buy them. His Lordship assured me that it was now too late to return these; but I never suffered him to buy any more.

With regard to our house expenses, I could have regulated them for, at least, half the cost; but Worcester absolutely refused to allow me to trouble my head about them. Once I did venture to remark, when he was about to borrow a thousand or two, at enormous interest, that since the pious Will Haught always carried out of our house daily provision not only for himself, but his wife, and put down, in his pious accounts, more porter than any man could drink in his sober senses, I did not exactly perceive the fun or amusement of paying him very high weekly board-wages; but Worcester having slightly hinted this circumstance to the holy man, he cried and blubbered till he was almost in hysterics, and I declared myself quite unable to contend with a footman of such fine nerves. Still it provoked me to see the man, to whom I was bound, by gratitude, for his apparent devotion to me, teased and dunned to death, when I knew everything might have been made all square by proper economy; but it is really incredible how young, careless noblemen are used, between their tradespeople and their servants.

When the Duke of Beaufort discovered at what interest Lord Worcester was borrowing money, he threatened the money-lender with prosecution for fraud on a minor, if he did not sign a receipt in full for the bare sum lent; and these terms were accepted.

All this might be very pretty, and very fair; still my own opinion is that a bargain is a bargain. A man tells Worcester that he may have a thousand or two, on certain terms, or he may apply elsewhere, or go without it, whichever he pleases. Lord Worcester, who was nearly of age, and of very mature manners, obtained the sum, to take up a bill on which, as he declared to me, his father's credit depended. We cannot take upon ourselves to say that the lender did not put himself both to trouble and inconvenience, in order, at a very short notice, to put the desired amount into Lord

Worcester's hand; then, when His Grace of Beaufort's credit had been preserved by his son's punctuality, His Most Honourable Grace takes advantage of the mere accident of his son wanting a few months to be of age, to make him break his solemn word of honour, pledged to one who had relied on that honour. Yet the Duke of Beaufort passes for a very honourable man ! !

The opera season had begun, six weeks before, and I had engaged a very desirable opera box; but nobody cares for the opera the first six weeks of the season; and we who are very fine generally lend our boxes to our creditors, or our *femmes de chambre*, till about March or April. We were, however, tired to death of Brighton and old Quintin, and Worcester was waiting and watching for a good opportunity to address Quintin on the subject of leave of absence, having predetermined to cut the army altogether, in case he was a second time refused.

"I never meant to make the army my profession," said Worcester to me one day, "neither did my father desire it; but he conceives that every young man is the better for having seen a year or two of service. My object in teasing and hurrying my father, as I did, to purchase a commission, I frankly tell you was because, since my figure is better than my face, I hoped the becoming uniform of the 10th would render me a little, though a very little, more to your taste !"

"There !" said Worcester one morning to me, as we were riding past the barracks, "look at that young soldier : if you pleaded for him, and shed tears at the idea of his being flogged, jealous and mad as I should have been, I must have applauded your taste."

I assured Lord Worcester that his sarcasms could not wound me, on a subject where my heart so entirely and decidedly acquitted me; and I set about my examination of the man, whose beauty was to wash away all the sins any of our frail sex might be inclined to commit with him. He wore the dress of a private of the 10th Hussars; his age might be three or four and twenty; his height full six feet; and he was just as slight as it was possible to be without injury to his strength, or the perfect manliness of his whole appearance.

Nature had determined, for once in her life, to show the world what a man ought to be. He could neither read nor write, yet, either this man was naturally a gentleman, or his perfect beauty made one fancy so; for it was impossible to think him vulgar. There was much about the face of this young man which reminded one of Lord Byron; and yet, beautiful as he was, like His Lordship, supposing him to have been of the same rank in life, he would never have inspired me with passion. This, however, was very far from being the case, generally speaking. Many stories of his prowess, and of his conquests, were in circulation.

The Duc de Guiche mentioned to us one day at dinner, having met the handsome hussar, unusually smart and much perfumed, just as he was stepping into a post-chaise. His Dukeship insisted on knowing where he was going. The man hesitated, and appeared in much confusion; but the Duke was peremptory.

"My Lord—a lady——" said the soldier at last, deeply blushing.

"If that is the case," said De Guiche, "remember to bring back some positive proof of the lady's approbation; the honour of the regiment is concerned, mind."

The man, on his return, produced a twenty-pound note!

One morning, about a week after our meeting with the handsome soldier, I was a good deal affected by witnessing, from my window, the simple procession which was passing.

"There goes a poor soldier to his last home," said my maid, who happened to be sitting in the room with me.

The atmosphere was dense and heavy, while the rain fell in torrents on the heads of the mourners, and the wind whistled mournfully among the trees.

"He hears it not, poor fellow!" said I, "nor wind nor weather can disturb him more!"

As they passed on slowly, by my window, I observed that the funeral was attended by one of the officers of the 10th Hussars, to which regiment the dead soldier had been attached. I looked again. It was the Marquis of Worcester, and then I recollected his having mentioned something to me, in the morning, about having a soldier's funeral to attend. His Lordship looked unusually melancholy, and for my part, though I always considered this a mournful sight, I had never been so affected by a soldier's funeral until now.

"It is the dull weather which disorders our nerves," said I, brushing away a tear. "What is all this to me? Men must die, and worms will eat them."

I was going from the window, when my attention was arrested by the sight of a wild, beautiful young female, who rushed on towards the coffin. Her hair was dishevelled, and her eyes so swollen with tears that one could but guess at what might, perhaps, be their natural lustre.

Will Haught, at this moment, brought in my breakfast.

"Do you know anything about this funeral, or that poor young female who has just followed it?" said I to him.

"It is the beautiful young soldier, who died two days ago, of a brain-fever, Madam. That girl's name is Mary Keats. She was his sweetheart, and he loved her better than any of them great ladies as used to make so much of him."

CHAPTER 15

In a few days after this event, we were on our road to London, where I soon learned all the most minute particulars of my sister Sophia's marriage with Lord Berwick, from Fanny, who, with Colonel Parker, was still in town. Sophia, I am sure, never had it really in her contemplation to refuse so excellent a match; yet she had, for several weeks, delayed the ceremony, merely, as I imagine, for the honour and glory of having it said of her, afterwards, that Lord Berwick had obtained her fair hand, not without difficulty. The thing had struck Fanny in the same light; and therefore, in the view of hastening what certainly was a desirable event, she, one day, remarked to Sophia, that she had observed a degree of coolness in His Lordship's manners for several days past, and that she really fancied he was considering how he should get off the marriage honourably.

Sophia reddened in evident alarm.

Fanny affected not to have remarked her sister's anxiety. "It is lucky, my dear Sophia," she went on, "that you do not wish to be Lady Berwick, otherwise this change in my Lord's sentiments might have caused you the greatest misery."

"Oh, no; not at all; not in the least, I assure you," hastily answered Sophia.

"My dear," continued Fanny, "why do you take such pains to convince me of what you know I have never had cause to doubt? On the contrary, since I have now such good reason to believe that the match has become equally disagreeable to both parties, I propose, in order to spare your pride the slightest wound, you commission me to declare off for you, in the most decidedly unequivocal terms, declaring in your name that you will leave him for ever, on the very first moment that he renews the disagreeable subject."

"Why no—I think—you had better—better say nothing about it," said Sophia, with ill-disguised anxiety and evident confusion.

The next day, Lord Berwick received Sophia's permission to write to her father, stating his wish to become his son-in-law, and further begging my father to be present at the ceremony, which, with his permission, was to take place on the following day, for the purpose of giving his daughter away, that fair lady being under age.

My father was a proud Swiss, rather unpopular, and a deep mathematician. We were never, in our youth, either allowed to address him, or speak in his presence, except in low whispers, for fear of driving a problem out of his head. He valued his sons according to the progress they made in the science. For the girls he felt all the contempt due to those who voted x plus minus g a dead bore.

He was remarkably handsome, with white teeth, expressive eyes, and eyebrows which used to frighten us half out of our senses.

Lord Berwick, as well as many more, has often declared himself to have been much struck with that noble air for which my father was particularly distinguished.

The good gentleman was, of course, flattered, on his own account, and probably thought, with the man in *Bluebeard*, that

> 'Tis a very fine thing to be father-in-law
> To a rich and magnificent three-tailed Bashaw.

But I do not mean to say he did not rejoice in his daughter's welfare for his daughter's sake too, as that would be to decide harshly of any father, much less of my own. We will, therefore, take it for granted that, on this day, at least, *monsieur mon papa trouvait d'une forte belle humeur*; nay, my little sisters have since informed me that, when one of them, having had the misfortune to upset a box full of playthings, which made a violent noise in the room where he was, as usual, puzzling over a problem, just as they expected little short of broken heads, and were all running into the most remote corners of the room, until of the opposite wall they seemed a part, he surprised them, to the greatest possible degree, by saying, "*N'importe, petits imbéciles, venez m'embrasser!*"

Sophia was to be married at St. George's Church.

My father had a neighbour, who once insulted him with remarks about the profligacy of his daughters, and though the man had made very humble apologies, and my father had shaken hands with him, yet he never forgot it. This neighbour was a tradesman in a large way of business, and who lived in a very respectable style of comfort. He had several daughters, the ugliest, perhaps, that could possibly come of one father. There was no such thing as getting these off, anyhow, by hook or by crook, by the straight paths of virtue or the intricate road of vice. Not that I mean to say the latter had been attempted; but of this I am certain, if it had been, it must have been ineffectual.

On the eve of Sophia's marriage, as soon as my father had received Lord Berwick's polite invitation, he went to pay his good neighbour a visit.

"How do you find yourself this evening, my very excellent neighbour?"

"Purely, purely, thank you."

"And your amiable daughters? Any of them married yet? Any of them thinking of it, hey?"

G—— shook his head. "Husbands, as you well know, are not so easily procured for girls of no fortune."

"Indeed, Sir, I am not aware of any particular difficulty. You know my daughter Paragon has long been respectably married to a gentleman of family; and, as for my daughter, Sophia, I shall, please God I live, witness her wedding tomorrow morning, before my dinner."

"Who is she to marry, pray?" asked G—— with eager curiosity; and which my father answered by putting Lord Berwick's letter into his hands, to his utmost astonishment; and, before he had at all recovered from his fit of envy and surprise, my father took his leave, saying that he had many preparations to make for the approaching marriage.

The next morning, as my father was stepping into the carriage which was to convey him to Lord Berwick's house, in Grosvenor Square, well dressed and in high spirits, he was gratified by the sight of his neighbour, who happened to pass his door at that very moment.

This man, naturally envious, and having hitherto looked down with pity on my father's misfortunes in having such handsome daughters, or, at least, he affected to do so, although in his heart, perhaps, he had not despised his children the more, supposing it had been the will of heaven to have bestowed on them countenances less forbiddingly ugly, this man, I say, could not, under the pressure of existing circumstances, help giving some vent to his spleen, exclaimed—"Don't hurry! don't break your neck!" and then passed on, ashamed, as well he might be, at the littleness of his envy.

Just before Sophia's marriage, Lord Berwick spoke to her, to this effect: "My beloved Sophia, you are about to become an innocent, virtuous woman, and therefore you must pass your word to cut your sisters dead, for ever, and at once. I allude, particularly, to Fanny and Harriette."

"Yes—certainly—very well," was Sophia's warm-hearted answer.

"And you will oblige me by neither writing to them, nor receiving any letters from them."

"Very well; then I will give them up altogether," said Sophia, with much placidity; and yet we had never been, in the slightest degree, deficient in sisterly affection towards her; and Lord Berwick expected to inspire, with affection, this heartless thing who, for a mere title, conferred on her by a stranger she disliked, could at once forget the ties of nature, and forsake for ever, without an effort or a tear, her earliest friends and nearest relations; and not because she was more virtuous than they were, since, on the contrary, she had begun her career before other girls even dream of such things. She had intruded herself on the cobbler at thirteen, thrown herself into the arms of the most disgusting profligate in England at fourteen, with her eyes open, knowing what he was; then offered herself for sale, at a price, to Colonel Berkeley, and when her terms were refused with scorn and contempt by the handsome and young, she throws herself into the arms of age and ugliness for a yearly stipend, and at length, by good luck, without one atom of virtue, became a wife.

Sophia, having the command of more guineas than ever she had expected to have had pence, did nothing, from morning till night, but throw them away. She would go into a shop, and ask for two or three Brussels veils—send a beggar's family to an expensive tailor, to be clothed —build a little island on a pond—buy a dressing-box of fifteen hundred pounds price, and all within a week. Lord Berwick was often reminded that this silly girl would ruin him, without comfort or benefit to herself; but his answer was, that he could not endure to scold the innocent creature, but must trust to her common sense for shortly finding out that all this extravagance could not last, even if he possessed four times as large an estate.

Lord Berwick, in less than twelve months after his marriage, was so involved, as to be under the necessity of making over the whole of his property to his creditors for I do not know how many years.

Our young sister, Charlotte, then about seven years of age, was a sweet, lovely little creature, and promised to be one of the finest dancers of the age. She had been some time a pupil of Monsieur Boigera, of the opera house.

It was not the profession my mother would have preferred, but Charlotte promised to do wonders in it, and with her striking beauty, there could have been little doubt of her marrying well from the stage; and a mother who has fifteen children to provide for, cannot do as she pleases.

Charlotte had already made her *début* as Cupid, and delighted everybody who saw her, when Lord and Lady Berwick, seized with a fit of pride, which they nicknamed virtue, begged leave to snatch the child from such a shocking profession, and they undertook to bring her up and provide for her under their own eyes. My poor mother joyfully closed with this apparently kind offer, and immediately made Charlotte forsake the profession which, with her talents, must have made her fortune, with or without marriage, to go and live with Sophia.

The child, when at her country seat, became a great favourite with the wife of Lord Berwick's brother, Mrs. Hill, and all went on charmingly till Charlotte began to look like a woman, and one of such uncommon loveliness as to attract the attention of all the elegant young men in the neighbourhood. Sophia could not endure this. Even at the opera, many a man has preferred offering his arm to Charlotte; nay, it was said, a country gentleman of very large property was expected to make Charlotte an honourable proposal. This was too much. Poor Charlotte, after having forsaken the profession in which she must have succeeded, to be bred up in luxury, among nobility, who looked on her as half an angel, was bundled off to a country school, there to earn her daily bread by birching young vulgar misses, and teaching them their French and English grammar; and there has poor Charlotte been forced to bloom unseen, wasting her sweetness on the desert air, ever since.

Patronage is a fine thing!!!

I should like to know what Charlotte says about it, as she sits darning her cotton stockings on a Saturday night.

My time, in London, passed on pleasantly enough at this period, as I went wherever I pleased. The only drawback to my comfort was, that the Duke of Beaufort did nothing but write and torment Lord Worcester to leave me, while Worcester's love seemed to increase on the receipt of every scolding letter. He daily swore to make me his wife, and professed to be wretched whenever I desired him not to think of marriage.

Her Grace of Beaufort's letters to her son, which I always had the honour of perusing, were extremely eloquent on my subject. The Duchess, unlike Lord Frederick Bentinck, was fond of hard words. *This absurd attachment of yours, for this vile profligate woman, does but prove,* wrote this noble personage, *the total subjugation of your understanding.*

In answer to this nervous paragraph in one of Her Grace's epistles, I beg leave to correct the word subjugation. Not that there is any harm in it, on the contrary, it is a very learned kind of a full sounding expression, and looks handsome in a letter; but then it is too learned to be so ignorantly misapplied. Her Grace, in her zeal to be fine, must have mistaken it for something else, since I can offer an unanswerable reason why her hopeful son, Worcester, could not have his understanding subjugated, even by the wonderful charms of Harriette Wilson, and that in four simple words: He never possessed any.

Her Grace, in her infinite condescension, then goes on to state that the said Harriette Wilson is the lowest, and most profligate creature alive. In short, so very bad, that she once sent for her own immaculate brother ! ! ! alluding to my having ordered up that worthy man to Marylebone fields, one morning before breakfast. After continuing this most ladylike style of abuse, in detail, enlarging on my former little sins and peccadilloes, she writes, in a postscript—*Of course, Worcester, your own sense* (she forgot that it was subjugated) *will teach you to conceal this letter from the person of whom I have spoken so freely.*

"It is very hard upon me!" said I one day to Lord Worcester, after reading one of Her Grace's flattering letters. "I was well disposed towards you, and towards your family, for your sake. I have constantly refused to accept expensive presents from you, and I have saved you from gambling, and various other vices and misfortunes, to which you would otherwise have been, shall I say, in humble imitation of Her Grace, subjugated? I have refused to become Marchioness of Worcester, over and over again, believing that such a marriage would distress your family, and in return, your Duchess-mother, with the usual charity of all ladies who either are, or pass for being, chaste, insists on my being at once turned adrift into the streets, and entirely unprovided for."

At last there came another, very severe letter, from the Duke of Beaufort, insisting on Lord Worcester immediately joining him at his seat near Oxford.

Worcester declared that he would not go, while I insisted that he should not disobey his father.

"Do not irritate His Grace," said I; "but on the contrary, strive to set his mind at rest, by assuring him that I wish you too well to marry you. True, the Duchess is very abusive, rather vulgarly so, perhaps, all things considered; but I have no wish to deserve harsh language from your mother, in order that I may think of it with calm indifference."

Worcester spoke very handsomely on this subject. "I love my father and mother," said he, "and it would go to my heart to disobey them, if I saw them inclined to act with justice and humanity towards you. As it is, I could not resign them for ever, without the deepest regret: at the same time, I solemnly declare to you, upon my honour and soul, if it were necessary to make a choice, and I must lose, for ever, either you, to whom I conceive myself bound quite as sacredly as though we were really married, or my whole family, I would not hesitate one instant, not even if they could cut me off with a shilling. I should prefer, ten thousand times over, driving a mail-coach for our daily support, and living with you in a garret, to any magnificence that could be offered me without you."

His Lordship was miserably agitated, when he found that I seriously insisted on his leaving me to join his father; and perhaps he had, for this once, ventured to disobey me, had not his uncle, Lord William Somerset, at the Duke of Beaufort's request, called on us, and insisted on not leaving the house till he had seen Worcester safe off in the Oxford mail.

Now what am I next to amuse my readers with? no! that's a vanity, I meant to ask, what I should try to amuse them with? Worcester is gone to his papa's at Badminton; and I, being sworn to constancy, have no other beaux to write about.

Let us inquire what my sister Fanny is doing. She looked very serious when I called upon her, as she sat nursing Parker's pretty little daughter and kissing it.

"Colonel Parker is going to Spain," said Fanny to me, the moment I entered her room, and I saw a tear trembling in her bright eye.

"So must half the fine young men in England," was my reply.

"Parker is the only man on earth who has ever treated me with true respect and kindness," continued Fanny, "and my attachment to him is very strong; more so, perhaps, than you think for."

I told her that I could not doubt her love for the father of her infant.

"I am not romantic," Fanny went on to say, while sitting in a musing sort of attitude, and seeming quite inattentive to my last wise speech. "It is not in my nature to be in the least romantic or sentimental, yet, when Parker forsakes me, I shall die of it!"

"Fiddlestick," I answered, "you are always talking about dying, merely because your nerves are weak, and, in the meantime, I never saw you look better in my life: when does Colonel Parker set off?"

"Tomorrow night," she replied.

"He will write, of course?"

"He has promised to do so by every post."

I had seldom seen Fanny so serious. I begged her to come to me as soon as Parker had left her, and promised to do everything in my power to enliven her.

She told me that Julia wished her, of all things, to board with her again, as soon as Parker went to Spain, "and," continued Fanny, "I feel so melancholy that I think I shall avail myself of her invitation, provided she will permit me to furnish a spare empty room she has in her house, and keep it entirely to myself. Do you know," continued Fanny, "I, who used to abhor solitude, even for a single morning, am now become very fond of it? I love to think, and to read; and the more serious the work, the better it suits the present tone of my mind. I have lately been copying the passages which have most struck me, and, when you look them over, you will be astonished at my change of sentiments and taste."

Worcester sent me about six sheets of foolscap, scribbled all over in every corner, once a day, and on Sunday he rode nine miles to overtake the coach, with a volume! ! He had, he said, been accused by the Duke, his father, of wishing to make me his wife, and he had found it impossible to deny that such was, in fact, his first hope. His father used very harsh words, and Worcester's courage and firmness had consequently increased. Suddenly, the Duke had changed this high tone, and taking his son by the hand, addressed him with much apparent feeling. This, as I afterwards learned from His Grace's brother, was a mere coldblooded plan, settled between these two hopeful gentlemen, who had agreed that their best chance was to touch up the young Marquis with a little bit of sentiment.

"My dear, dear boy," said Beaufort, "you must forgive me, if the extreme anxiety you have for such a long time occasioned myself and your poor mother, has, for a season, made me lose my temper. I see that your feeling for Harriette is real, and beyond your power to overcome, at present. Indeed, if she is good to you, I desire that every care and attention should be paid her, and you shall return to her, and be teased no more on the subject: only pass your word and honour to me, as a son, and as a gentleman, that you will never marry her, and you shall hear no more from either of us on the subject."

Worcester, in his letter to me, where he described this scene, professed to have been deeply affected by it, and to have passed the following night and day in tears, yet he firmly refused to comply with his father's request. *Et tout fut consternation, dans le plus beau et le plus agréable château qu'on puisse imaginer! !*

All those letters from Lord Worcester having been since returned to the Duke of Beaufort, that honourable nobleman, with his son, may be pleased to deny that such letters were written. However, after referring my readers to the celebrated Henry Brougham, M.P. of Lincoln's Inn, and another highly respectable counsellor of the same place, named Treslove, who have both read the whole of Lord Worcester's correspondence (why they did so, shall be told hereafter), I will leave them to form their own conclusions as to the truth or falsehood of what I have written, or shall write, on the subject of those worthy wiseacres, the Beauforts! !

Worcester concluded this letter by declaring he could not and would not remain any longer absent from me, and that I was all the consolation which was left him on earth, since his father was about to turn his back on him for ever.

I answered this letter immediately, to this effect:

If, my dear Worcester, you do not immediately write, to give me your honour that you have set your father's mind at rest, by having complied with his late reasonable request, you lose me now at once and for ever. For I shall go where you will never find me. What happiness, think you, could we enjoy, at the expense of making your parents miserable? They have good reason for what they request, and to save the time it would take you to contradict this last assertion of mine, I declare to you that I never will be your wife.

I have said enough, I am sure, to convince any man worthy the name, and therefore you will have made friends with your father, and be on your road to join me, very shortly after the receipt of this letter. So till then, God bless you; but, remember, I can be firm and keep my word.

In three days after I had dispatched the above letter, Worcester returned to me, having made the Duke of Beaufort the promise he had required. We now enjoyed something like quietness during the remainder of our stay in London.

Worcester appeared to have suffered much during his visit to his father's, for he was so much paler and thinner, I really thought him consumptive. It was ever His Lordship's pride and delight to drive me about the streets or the Park, and to accompany me wherever I went. He but seldom went into society, and when he did, he always refused to dance, much as he used to like it. In short, his passion for me, which, from the very first, seemed so ardent that I knew not it was in human nature that it could be susceptible of increase, became stronger with the difficulty of indulging it.

"My brother is a fool," said Lord William Somerset one day to us. "I would have cured you both in less than a month, and made Worcester hate you most cordially."

"How, pray?" I inquired.

"Why," continued Lord William, "merely by shutting you up in one of my country houses together, making it my request that you never left each other an instant, to the end of your lives."

Some short time after my sister Sophia's marriage, she received, from

Lord Deerhurst, half a year of the annuity he had made her. My eldest brother was requested to call upon His Lordship, for the purpose of restoring the amount into his own hand, and which commission my brother executed, without, I believe, exchanging a single syllable with that most disgusting nobleman, who ever has been a disgrace to the peerage.

Fanny, in due time, received very kind letters from Colonel Parker, although they were certainly less warm than some of those he had formerly addressed to her. Napier's love for Julia seemed to grow with what it fed on, and this fair lady had been twelve times with child, and was actually turned forty, or as the French say, *elle avait quarante ans, bien sommés.*

In short, she was fat, fair, and forty, though her name did not begin with F; so I beg my fair readers who may be under fifty years of age, never to think of despairing.

Little Kitty, the Lady of Colonel Armstrong, went on very modestly and quietly still, with her dear Tommy, although he now steadfastly adhered to his former resolution not to risk any increase of his family.

Amy continued very steady, and constant in her love for———variety!

We were all regular at the opera house, both on Saturdays and Tuesdays.

Sophia looked very splendid in her opera box since her marriage, particularly when she wore all the late Lady Berwick's diamonds, and her own to boot. Lord Deerhurst, I observed, for several successive nights made it a point to sit in a box by himself, next to Sophia, and fix his eyes on her the whole of the evening. Not that he regretted or cared for her, but merely because, in his infinite vulgarity and littleness of soul, he gloried in insulting Lord Berwick's feelings, and conceived it high fun to ogle at Sophia's box, and then wink at his companions in the pit: but Lord Berwick was wise for once in his life, for he ever treated Deerhurst's low impertinence with the profound contempt it merited, nor condescended once to make a remark on it, even to his wife, although neither of them could have been blind to what was so very pointed.

To revert to the Beaufort story, *mais, c'est perdrix, perdrix, toujours perdrix!*

The Beaufort story may be *fort beau!* and yet, my readers may happen to require a little variety: at all events, if they do not, I do, for there is nothing on earth I think more adominable than to be hammering always at the same thing.

Therefore, the little anecdote which I proposed relating, merely to vary the story of the Beauforts, was about a prude, or rather a lady who went by that name. For my own part, I am miserably deficient in grammar, and a thousand more things, and among many others, I am ignorant of the true, genuine, and real meaning of the word prude.

A French *coquette* will call any woman a cold passionless prude who, being attached to her husband and family, shows symptoms of impatience or disgust whenever a chattering fool presumes to pour his regular cut-and-dried, stupid flattery into her ear.

Some call a prude, a woman who steadfastly resists being kissed by a man for whom she has no regard, at a time when her heart is devoted to another.

Pooh! nonsense! says the impatient reader, a prude is a woman who sticks up for ridiculous punctilios in such trifles as are of no real consequence.

True! but then I never yet happened to meet with this sort of thing. I have only seen base copies of it, in women without any real modesty, who affected excessive niceness; but I cannot fancy a woman the worse, or the greater prude, for showing, naturally, any degree of modesty which she may really possess.

The lady I alluded to just now, was nearly forty years of age, but she was still handsome, although she had entirely ceased to think about the adornment of her person. She was naturally sensible, and misfortunes had made her serious. The most delicate flattery which could have been offered from the lips of youth and beauty, would not have been extremely irksome to one, who, having loved a good husband dearly, and lost him, had for ever devoted her mind to other pursuits, as often as she could turn it from melancholy reflections.

I remember hearing this very excellent creature abused for being a nasty, stiff, tiresome prude, because she seriously assured a stupid, ugly fop, who was teasing her with the most insipid impertinence, that the style of his conversation was extremely disagreeable to her.

However, prude or no prude, this good lady was kind enough to receive my visits at all times, with an appearance of real satisfaction.

We wanted to go to the play, for we were both in love with Elliston; but we had no party, and what was worse, no private box. I have never in my life frequented the public boxes, and we scarcely knew our way in, or our way out, from that side of the house; yet, when two women take a thing into their heads, it is not a trifle can induce them to balk their fancies; so, after we had finished our dinner, my friend the prude declared that she was quite old enough to act as *chaperonne* to me, and, going in our morning, quiet costumes, without rouge or ornaments, she was sure no man would dare to insult us.

"In short," continued Prude, for so we will call her, since I do not think it fair to make her real name public, "in short, I never believe in such stories as women often relate to me, about being insulted by the other sex. For my part, I have ever been in the habit of using my liberty, and going where I please, and alone too, when it suited my humour, taking it for granted that, if I am decently and modestly dressed, and conduct myself with perfect propriety, it is impossible the men can mistake me for anything but what I really am; and if they did, the frown of indignation, which a virtuous woman can put into her countenance, cannot fail to awe the most determined libertine."

"*Nous verrons*," said I, as I placed myself before the glass to practice a frown of virtuous indignation, for that night only! but frowning was not my forte, and I made such ridiculous, ugly faces, without looking in the least awful, that Mrs. Prude burst into a loud laugh, requesting me, in God's name, to leave the frowning part of our evening's entertainment entirely to herself.

I did not half like going to the play, without the protection of a gentleman, or a private box, "It is all very well for you," I said, "but I happen to have no character to spare!"

However, Prude soon overruled my objections, and sent for a hackney-coach to convey us to the theatre.

We were quite delighted with Elliston in the "Honeymoon." We could not, of course, obtain seats in the dress-boxes, in our morning attire, but we had good seats upstairs; and though the men did cast many a sly look at me, yet no one ventured to address us. Even if they had so presumed, I knew that my friend's awe-inspiring frown would set all to rights, *parceque c'était Madame, elle-même, qui me l'avait assuré.*

I was at that time, very striking; for I never could pass anywhere unnoticed. I do not say this by way of paying myself a compliment, but merely to relate a fact, in which everybody who was then acquainted with me will bear me out. I always hated to be stared at by the mob, and I did my best to prevent it by the simplicity of my evening dresses, which were invariably composed of white gauze or muslin; and my head was always dressed after the fashion of the Irish people's potatoes, *au naturel;* but it would not do. I often wished to be more interesting, and less remarkable; *mais quoi faire?*

"I cannot conceive why these men stare at you in this manner," said Prude.

"Thank you, Ma'am, for the compliment," answered I, laughing.

"I do not mean to say that you are not handsome," continued my very liberal friend; "on the contrary, I think your countenance remarkably fine; but still I wonder why the people look so much more at you than at any other fine, handsome woman who may be in the house!"

"God knows! I do not thank them for their preference," said I, waxing half angry, as I observed the fixed, intense gaze of a young man who, for the last quarter of an hour, had been eagerly watching every turn of my head.

He was a very fashionable-looking man; but not at all handsome. I felt convinced, from that certain *air de famille*, that he must be a Stanhope, although I had never seen him before. It was neither Lincoln Stanhope, nor Fitzroy, nor that great unlicked cub who was turned out of his regiment for blacklegging, or leaguing with blacklegs. These three I had often met. It must be Leicester then, thought I, having heard that Lord Harrington had a son of that name, who was less handsome than his brothers.

"It will not do to attempt frowning at that young man," said I to Mrs. Prude, "as it may have the effect of making him laugh, as it did you at dinner time; but I will fix my eyes on him with an expression of dignity, which is more in their natural character, and try if they will do."

The young man was not vulgarly bold, nor impudent, and his eyes fell under my fixed gaze. He was not immediately behind us; but occupied the second bench to my left. I had no objection to his looking at me modestly. In fact, I rather liked it, being neither more nor less than a mere woman; but I hate vulgarity or assurance in men.

I wanted to have another look at Leicester Stanhope, and which I at last contrived to accomplish slyly. He is ugly, methinks, and yet I prefer him to any of the handsome Stanhopes, for there is something of better feeling, and more expression in his eyes. I dare say this is not, in fact, the case, and that I merely preferred his ugliness to his brother's beauty, because he was the only one of the family who ever seemed to admire me, even for an instant.

No, now I recollect myself, this is a libel on my own attractions: I remember Lord Petersham, after having, for several years, been in the habit of talking to me, and shaking my hand, with the same *sang-froid* one would have expected at fourscore, one Sunday morning, when we crossed each other's path, at Hyde Park corner, paid me the following most flattering compliment.

"You are decidely a very fine creature, but all that I have known for the last three years, and also that you are the wittiest, cleverest creature in London."

Now Lord Petersham know no more of my wit than that of the man in the moon, only it was the fashion to call me clever and witty, and who-ever had said otherwise would have, himself, passed for a fool.

When the play was over, we were a little at a loss how to find our way out; but after wandering up one passage, and down another, we came to a large room, lighted well up, and seeing so many people enter it, we con-cluded that we had only to follow them. However, we had no sooner made our appearance in it, than we were led to imagine that every man we met must have suddenly lost the use of his senses. In vain did poor Prude practise her infallible awe-inspiring frowns! ! They did but excite merriment.

"What! are you the bawd?" said one of them, rudely lifting up her bonnet.

"What do you ask for this pretty black-eyed girl?" inquired a drunken man in a dashing light green coat and a red waistcoat, and large tally-ho pin in his shirt, touching me in the most indecent manner; and when I resisted these disgusting liberties with all the strength of my little hands, they only fell into roars of laughter.

"Are there no constables here?" asked Prude, in a loud voice.

"Bravo," exclaimed a flashly-looking youth in top-boots, bearing in his hand a cane, with which he tapped an old constable who was near the door, "I say, my boy, that woman insists on having you to go home and sleep with her; but she is perfectly welcome, so that she leaves me her daughter"; and he tried to pull my arm under his.

"Good heavens! what shall we do?" said I, while the tears of anger trembled in my eyes, as I threw a hasty glance round the room to look for protection: and saw Leicester Stanhope, for it was really him, follow-ing us at some little distance, and shrinking back, that I might not ob-serve him, evidently half ashamed of the admiration he had evinced towards a woman who walked the lobby! ! For it was indeed that most respectable saloon, in which Prude and I were making an exhibition of our pretty persons, owing to the merest ignorance.

All the world seemed to be in this room, which was something like the round room at the opera. How could we help fancying it was the right way out? in short, we had tried and could find no other. It was immensely crowded, and, as we moved on slowly, every step we took exposed us to fresh insult of the grossest and most disgusting nature. Stanhope seemed determined to see the end of it all, *à la distanee.*

"How can that young man stand by, and see two women so shockingly insulted, and not come forward to offer his protection?" said Mrs. Prude, observing Stanhope.

At this moment we came in close contact with some females, whose language made our blood run cold. I hesitated, while I was almost tempted to interest Mr. Stanhope to protect us to a carriage: a horrible-looking, fat, bloated man, in a state of brutal intoxication, being actually about to thrust his hand into my bosom, Stanhope took a hasty glance at my countenance, and, observing it crimson up to my very eyes, he did, as by some ungovernable impulse, *qu'était plus fort que lui*, hastily place his person before me, as a protection, nay almost in defiance of the fat man.

"I believe I am addressing a Mr. Stanhope?" said I to him, in much agitation.

Leicester bowed with an appearance of great reserve.

"Being acquainted with several of your brothers," I continued, "I must take the liberty to entreat you will either protect us to a hackney-coach, or employ some honest man to do us a kindness you see we stand so deplorably in need of."

"Is it possible that you seriously wish to avoid all this impertinence?" asked Leicester, in evident but gratified surprise.

Both Mrs. Prude and myself actually fell back a pace or two, as we fixed our eyes on him in speechless astonishment at his manner of asking this question.

"Do not you really know what place this is? Do not you know that you are in the lobby?" asked Stanhope, whispering in my ear.

"Oh, dear me! good gracious, Mrs. Prude, we are in the lobby, with all the very worst women!" said I, and I thought Prude would have fallen back in a fainting fit.

Leicester Stanhope politely offered me his arm, and hastened to convey us out of the house. He afterwards set us down in safety, at my own door, requesting permission to inquire after my health the next morning.

For some weeks after this, Leicester was, or affected to be, in love with me, and was constantly making up little parties to the minor theatres, for my amusement. One night Amy caught a glimpse of us at some public place, I forget which.

"Kitty," said Amy to Mrs. Armstrong, "there is Harriette with a new man. I must go and call on her, without fail, tomorrow." I was consequently honoured with her early visit the next day.

"How do you do, Harriette?" said kind Amy. "I called to inquire after your health; because you looked rather pale last night, at the—*Apropos!* who was that elegant-looking man with you?"

Having answered her first question, she begged to know when I was likely to see him again.

"Leicester Stanhope wants me to go to Drury Lane tonight, and has taken a private box for me."

"Oh! pray do admit me of your party," said Amy, "for I am so very dull, and ill."

I understood her perfectly, and was well aware of two things—first, that she would try hard to make Leicester fall in love with her, and secondly, she would, by various little spiteful hints, uttered in a tone of innocent *naïveté*, do her best to inspire him with contempt for me: but what did I care for Leicester Stanhope, or any one of his stupid race, beyond the mere pastime these attentions might afford me *pour le moment*? therefore I invited Amy to join us.

In less than a fortnight from that evening, Amy and Leicester were to be found ruralizing together at a retired pot-house at Putney, or Clapham, or some such place, for their honeymoon!

I forget which of them got tired first; but I know one of them was tired in less than a week, and Amy returned to town, and her dear variety!!

CHAPTER 16

I, TOO MUST return to my dear Worcester! whose noble father had allowed him six or eight months more to grow tired of me, during which time nothing very remarkable occurred, except that Worcester's love and passion absolutely did increase daily, although that was what I had imagined to be morally and physically impossible.

His Grace now became furious again, and so did his gentle Duchess. Their Graces were both in town, and tormented Worcester hourly. The Duchess often declared, in the presence of a female servant, who afterwards repeated it to me, that she should prefer seeing her son dead under his horse's feet to his becoming my husband? His Grace thought that we had been privately married.

Worcester was desirous that I should disguise myself, and go with him to Gretna Green.

"Have you forgotten the promise you made to your father?" I asked.

"It was a conditional promise," answered His Lordship, "and my father has broken the conditions. You see that he refuses to let me live on with you in peace, and again and again I most solemnly swear to make you my wife, whenever I can obtain your consent! !"

Worcester was over head and ears in debt, and on this subject the Duke was eternally lecturing, as in duty bound; declaring, for his own part, he had never, when he was Marquis of Worcester, exceeded his allowance, or incurred a single debt.

I do not mean to dwell on the subject of Worcester's love, and Worcesters' devoted attentions to me, as I conceive nothing more uninteresting. His love never varied the least in the world, nor did we ever quarrel!

We returned once more to Brighton, and after continuing there for about two months, Worcester's troop was ordered to be stationed in a small village near Portsmouth, to guard the prisoners.

Quintin offered him the choice of changing his troop; but Worcester said, if I did not mind passing a short time at a wretched little village, he would much rather not leave it.

I was perfectly willing to accompany him; and on the day appointed for our leaving Brighton, four post-horses were put to Worcester's travelling chariot, which was to carry me to our destination. The distance was about forty miles, and the troop, with the Duc de Guiche, Worcester, and Lord Arthur Hill, were to rest one night on the road.

I never once entered the carriage; but rode in a line with the officers, dressed in my regimental cap and habit, like a little recruit. We all lodged together in the same deplorable pot-house. Our bedroom served us for parlour, kitchen, and hall, and we dined together in the only spare room there was, in this apology for an inn, furnished exactly in the usual style of such places; to wit, twelve immense, high-backed, black leather chairs, too heavy for anybody, except Bankhead, to move; and the wainscot adorned with such pictures as—a fox chase, and then the Virgin Mary, and cheek-by-jowl with that holy woman, Bellingham, the murderer of Perceval; next a print of King George the Third, in his parliamentary robes—a country map—the holy apostles sitting at the last supper, and a poll parrot, done in what is, I believe, usually called clothwork; plenty of sand on the floor, and plenty of wine glasses, tooth-picks, and cruets on the sideboard.

It poured of rain every day and all day long, during the first fortnight of our residence in this earthly paradise; and we further enjoyed the exquisite odours which had been accumulating, time out of mind, from beer and tobacco ! ! The weather also being windy, as well as rainy, the signboard, on which was depicted a flaming red bear, danced more merrily than musically at our window.

Here Worcester, once upon a time, laid his lordly head upon a large mahogany table, after wiping away the sour beer which fantastically varied its surface, and, with infinite enthusiasm, delivered himself to me in such soft words as, "Oh Harriette, my adored, delicious, lovely, divine Harriette, what perfect happiness is this ! passing, thus, every minute of the day and night, in your society ! ! God only knows how long I shall be permitted to enjoy all this felicity; but it is too great, I feel, to last. Nobody was ever thus happy long. They will make my going abroad a point of honour; but even then, my beloved angel-wife will accompany me ! yet alas ! how dreadful it will be to see you exposed to the dangers and inconveniences of war !"

I had a real tenderness and sisterly affection for Worcester, at that time. I should otherwise have been the most ungrateful, callous, and inhuman creature breathing; and I really was about to make a very tender, warm, and suitable reply; but, at that critical moment, the woman brought in a large platter of ill-dressed veal cutlets and bacon, followed by the Duc de Guiche, and the fat Lord Arthur Hill.

After our sumptuous dinner, Lord Arthur proposed our driving over to Portsmouth, to see the play.

We went accordingly, and having hired a large stage-box, and seated ourselves in due form, all the sailors in the gallery began hissing and pelting us with oranges, and made such an astounding noise that, out of compassion for ourselves, as well as the rest of the audience, we were obliged to leave the theatre before the first act was over, and we were followed by a whole gang of tars, on our way to the inn. They called us Mounseers—German moustache rascals, and bl——dy Frenchmen.

I know not whether the sailors objected to the dress of dragoons in general, as being a German costume, or whether it was our French Duc de Guiche who had caused all the mischief. However that may be, His Grace of Beaufort having got hold of the story from the neswpapers probably, declared, with his usual liberality towards me, that the English tars at Portsmouth could not endure the idea of my not being legally married to Worcester; want of chastity being held in utter abhorrence among the crews of our Royal Navy, as a sin they have no idea of, and one which is never, by any chance, practised by them.

His Grace of Beaufort at last obtained leave for Worcester to join him at Badminton; and being, as he said, rendered perfectly miserable, every hour that his son continued within the magic circle of my spells!! he wrote to insist on Worcester joining him in a few days.

Worcester, when he read these commands from his father, looked as if he had received his death-warrant.

I cannot, however, say that I was sorry to exchange this miserable, muddy village for my comfortable house in town. Not but Lord Arthur Hill had something comical about his manner, which I thought amusing enough, yet there was no real fun nor humour in the Duc de Guiche, although he often laughed in much the same stiff and unnatural style as his shirt collars.

Lady Charles Somerset was very fond of this young foreigner, and almost considered him as her son. Perhaps she rather expected he might become her relation one day or other, since he was always romping with her two bold daughters, who, as Worcester informed me, were to be found continually, in a morning, sitting on His Grace's knee, and allowing him to kiss them, and, as Worcester fancied, to do much more.

One day, when Worcester refused to pass before De Guiche, as a matter of etiquette, while the young Frenchman, who was then called the Count de Gramont, refused to move forward, in spite of all Worcester could say, I became quite impatient, and tired of waiting.

"How is this?" said I to De Guiche, when at last we were seated at table. "Why do you hesitate to go first, if your rank is highest; and if it is not, how happens it that Worcester, who is generally so *au fait* on all these subjects, is mistaken?"

"I am, in fact and truth, the Duc de Guiche," said His Grace; "but since, for some serious reasons, I do not take that title in England, and as I never expect to enjoy it in my own country, I consider it all nonsense; and, being called Count in the regiment, it would look strange that I should take the precedency of Worcester."

Now I am on the subject of Brighton, I must relate another little anecdote, which ought to have been mentioned earlier. Young Berkeley, as my readers may remember, during the last visit he paid me, which happened on the very morning of my departure from town to join Lord Worcester for the first time, declared, upon his life and soul, that, since he knew himself to be a much handsomer man than His Lordship, he would contrive to be even with me, if I so far presumed to differ in opinion from him, as to prefer the latter. What he said made so little impression on me, that it did not even once occur to my recollection after I had left London, until I was reminded of it by a report of a very disgusting nature, which Augustus had taken care to circulate about town, till it came to Worcester's ears: namely, that the girl whom Worcester wanted to marry was an old flame of his and his brother's, and that both had often passed the night in my house.

Worcester appeared greatly annoyed at this wicked falsehood, and anxiously inquired of me what grounds there were for it.

I assured him, most solemnly, of what I now repeat, with the same candour and anxiety, that I never gave the least encouragement to either of the young Berkeleys, Henry and Augustus, to pursue me.

"But, my dear Worcester," said I, "it will really not be worth while to give all this nonsense a second thought. You will have rather too much upon your hands, should you resolve to vindicate and defend my virtue, after the manner of Don Quixote; and, provided nothing is said against me or my conduct, since I have known you, I think common sense points out that you had better leave the rest to find its own level, *parceque je ne m'en suis jamais donnée pour une grande vertu; mais tout au contraire, comme vous savez bien!*"

I am not like those ugly women and cross old maids, who abuse the world or the world's judgment of my actions. Generally speaking, I have found the world acts fairly, justly, and often very liberally, towards me.

It is certainly, perhaps, a misfortune in many respects, for a woman to become the fashion, which was my case; for what second-rate man does not like to be in the fashion? Nay, there are few, very few, who would not affect pride in the possession of what their betters have coveted in vain!

"I beg you fifty thousand pardons," bawled Lord Petersham to me, one morning, from his or some other person's gay barouche, as I stood at my drawing-room balcony; "but, to save time, will you answer me one single question, from your window? I only want a yes or a no, as I am sure I can take your word."

My house being half in the country, I begged His Lordship to make as free as he pleased.

"Did you," asked His Lordship, forcing a little, mean-looking man, who was seated next to him, to stand up upon his two feet, while I surveyed him, "did you ever see this man, in your born days?"

"Never, to my knowledge," was my reply.

"Then you can declare, at all events, that you never made his acquaintance?" asked Petersham.

"Certainly I can; and your friend will unhesitatingly confirm the truth of what I assert."

"*Tout au contraire*," said Petersham, "he has been amusing us with an account of a former *petite affaire du cœur* he had with you."

"He does me honour," I rejoined, "although he knows I was never so completely blessed as to have been in his society."

"That's quite enough," said Petersham, giving me a significant little wink with his left eye, kissing his hand, and driving off, all at the same moment.

I must now return to Lord Worcester, or rather to my house in town, he having left Portsmouth to join his incensed papa and mamma at Badminton.

The Duchess was a very moral character, and when her first-born was a little boy, he frequented naughty women, and was, in consequence, afflicted with a naughty disease. During his confinement under this attack, the Duchess read him affecting lectures on the enormity of the sin of incontinence, which leads to a complaint with the name of which I shall not soil my pages; but the Duchess designated it by a new name, and declared that the Almighty had sent it to him as a judgment.

Worcester thought the vehicle unlikely to be made an instrument of God's wrath, and laughed not a little at the sublime idea his mother entertained of Things!

When I got to town, everybody was talking of an amorous adventure of Charlton and Horace Seymour. The latter was a gay, dashing son of Lord somebody Seymour, of the 10th Hussars, whom everybody knows and few care much about.

Charlton was a stupid young fellow, of no particular family, with very red hair; so red, that Sir Harry Mildmay had like to have lost the possession of a beautiful young woman from it.

She was a lovely creature, according to his account; and her name was Kate North, and her protector was Lord Reay, and Kate North was nothing loth:

"But then," said Sir Harry, "who could——after carroty Charlton?"

However, meeting Kate one day in Hyde Park, in Lord Reay's barouche, she struck the gay baronet as being so very unusually handsome, that he resolved to put Charlton's red hair out of his head; and in two days more, Kate North and Sir Henry were on their road to his country house in Hampshire, and poor Lord Reay was left at home to cry willow! willow!

Mildmay's love for Kate increased, during the first four-and-twenty hours of their sweet honeymoon; the second was not quite so sweet.

"Don't go into that room, my Henry. You must not, indeed you must not enter that room, darling," cried bonny Kate in a loud voice, observing, with dismay, that her lover had slipped out of his bed, and was making his way towards a little dressing-closet, in which she had, during his last long nap, found it necessary to enter.

"Why not, pray?" asked the delicate, violet-breathing Mildmay (for so Julia used to call this gay baronet), who began to suspect that a man might chance to be in the case.

"Oh—upon my word and honour, you must not—shall not go into the closet!" screamed out dainty Kate, as she leaped from her bed.

"The devil I must not!" said Mildmay, as he entered the forbidden chamber, and saw—no, he did not examine it—his nose—that won't do, it is so vulgar—his olfactory nerves elicited the first evidence, which convinced the baronet that there was something more than customary in that closet, *qui sentait autrefois de musc et de la rose.*

"I am quite satisfied now," said Mildmay.

The seduction of two little milliner-girls by Charlton and Seymour made more noise in the world than all four were worth; or rather caused more, since the story, with Charlton's love letters, were printed and cried all over London, price only one penny.

"As to our having to pay," said carroty Charlton to me, one night at the opera, when I questioned him respecting it, "that I fully anticipated and was quite ready to do : but what reduces me to absolute despair, by having for ever destroyed my future chances of preferment, is this publication of my circulars, which have served me as love letters from a boy, up to this very period, with the mere alteration of names and dates!''

I condoled with Mr. Charlton, and then went home to condole with Worcester, who was daily sending me the most dismal accounts of the persecution he had to encounter at home.

I have lost my parents, wrote His Lordship in one of his letters. *They refuse to acknowledge me as their son, and yet they attempt to shut me up here by force. This I should have resisted, and have returned to you last week, but that my mother declares herself ill, and my father asserts that she is not likely to recover her late accouchement, while her mind is so dreadfully agitated. For my part I can neither eat nor sleep, and both my father and uncle admit that they have tormented me, till I am seriously ill. I implore you then, my adored, beloved, darling Harriette, to come to me. I never close my eyes in sleep, without awaking in the great fright and agony, having dreamed that you were taken away from me for ever.*

He then went on to beg and entreat of me, if I had the least pity for him, to disguise myself as a country woman, or a common servant, in a coloured gown and checked apron, and go in the coach to a certain inn at Oxford, where he would contrive, unknown to his father, who should believe him in his bed, to await my arrival at past twelve o'clock at night, which he said was the hour at which the afternoon coach got into Oxford. He then made me at least a thousand humble apologies for having wanted me to disguise myself, and take all this trouble, assuring me that, if I went to Oxford in my usual style and character, someone or other would probably meet me on the road, and he could not describe what would be his parents' indignation and anger, in case my visit to Oxford came to their knowledge.

Were I to give my readers these letters, in Worcester's own expressions, there would be no end to them, since every other word was angel! or adored wife, or beautiful sweet Harriette, or darling sweetest! sweetest darling! dearest dear, dear dearest, etc., so perhaps they will prefer taking all these sweets at once, that I may proceed quietly with these most amusing and very interesting memoirs.

At about three o'clock on the day after I had received this letter from Lord Worcester, as my sister Fanny was standing at her window, pleasing herself with her pretty little daughter Louisa, a hackney-coach stopped at her door, and out of it sprung a lightfooted spruce damsel, clad in a neat coloured gown, thick shoes, blue stockings, blue check apron, coloured neck-handkerchief, cloth cap, and bright cherry-coloured ribbons. In the next minute, this bold young woman had given both Fanny and her daughter Louisa a hearty kiss!

"Good gracious! my good woman," exclaimed Fanny, pushing me gently aside, and, in the next instant hearing a loud laugh in the room, for I had not observed Julia and Sir John Boyd sitting at the other window, till they joined in our merriment.

"Lord help the woman," said Julia, "what can have put it into her head to appear, this beautiful weather, in such a costume?"

"It is a new style of travelling dress," said I, "and I am going to introduce the fashion. What do you think of my cap? It cost eighteen pence, and my blue stockings? but I can't stay gossiping with you fine ladies, or I shall lose my place in the stage. However, do just look at my nice little brand-new red cloak."

"You don't seriously and really mean to say you are going to travel that figure, and in the broad face of day too?" said Fanny.

"I must! I must! Worcester says, if I don't want to be beaten to a mummy by papa Beaufort, I must go to Oxford in disguise."

"Disguise, indeed!" said Julia.

"You will be found out by your taper-waist, and large bosom," said Sir John.

"Why, what is the matter with it, Sir John? is it not very decently covered by this smart coloured handkerchief?"

"Yes; but it's all too pretty, and your stays are too well made."

Julia's maidservant, who had not recognized me as I flew past her up the stairs, now entered the room, with a message from my hackney-coachman, who was waiting at the door.

"The coachman, Ma'am, desires me to tell the young woman, that he shall expect another sixpence if she does not come down directly."

"Oh laws a mighty! and here I hasn't a got a sixpence in the world more than what's tied up here, in this here bag, on purpose for to pay my fare to Oxford," said I, holding up a small red bag.

Julia's maidservant looked in my face, and seeing everybody ready to laugh, found it impossible to resist joining them.

"Why, the Lord defend me! Miss Harriette, is it really you?" she asked, opening her eyes as wide as possible.

"You see, Sir John, the delicacy of my shape has not stood the least in my way with the coachman, who did not discover the *air noble* under this costume! but I must be off directly."

"Good-bye! God bless you, mind you write to me directly, and tell me everything that happens to you," said Fanny.

"That all gave me a kiss, round, for the form is kissing a woman in blue stockings and a check apron, and I was soon seated in the stage-coach, which was being loaded at the door of the Green Man and Still, or as the Frenchman dated his letter, *chez l'homme vert et tranquil.*

"You're not apt to be sick, are you my dear?" inquired a fat-faced merry-looking man, with a red handkerchief tied over his chin, who had already, with a lady whom I fancied might be his wife, taken possession of the two best seats.

I assured them that I was a very good traveller.

"Because, my dear, you see, many people can't ride backwards; and there's Mrs. Hodson, my wife, as is one of them."

"Oh, the young woman is not particler, I dare say," said Mrs. Hodson, with becoming reserve.

In short, not altogether liking the words my dear, as they had been applied to me by her husband, she thought it monstrous vulgar.

A lady in a green habit, who was standing near the coach door, now vowed and declared her travelling basket should be taken out of the boot, where it had been thrown by mistake, before she would take her seat.

The coachman in vain assured her it was perfectly safe.

"Don't tell me about its safety," cried the angry lady, "I know what your care of parcels is before today."

"Come, come, my good lady," said Mr. Hodson, whom I recognized as a London shoemaker of some celebrity, "come, come, Ma'am, your thingumbobs will be quite safe. Don't keep three inside passengers waiting, at a nonplus, for these here trifles!"

"Trifles!" burst forth the exasperated lady, "are females always to be imposed upon in this manner?"

" *Monsieur Le Clerc!*" continued the lady, calling to a tall thin Frenchman, in a light grey coat, holding under his arm an umbrella, a book of drawings, an English dictionary, and a microscope, "*Monsieur Le Clerc,* why don't you insist on the coachman's finding my travelling basket?"

"Yes, to be sure, certainly," said the Frenchman, looking about for the coachman.

"*Allons, cocher, madame demande son panier. Madame* ask for one litel someting, out of your boots, directly."

"Did I not desire you to mention, *Monsieur Le Clerc,* when you took my place, that the basket was to go inside?" demanded the lady.

"Yes, *oui*," answered the Frenchman eagerly. "I tell you, Mr. *Cocher,* dis morning, six, seven, ninety-five times, madame must have her litel—vat you call—over her knee."

"I'm sorry for the mistake, sir; but it would take a couple of hours to unload that there boot, and I must be off this here instant."

"Come now, aisey there, aisey," bawled out a queer poor Irishman, with a small bundle in his hand, running towards the coach, in breathless haste. "Aisey! aisey! there, sure and I'm a match for you, this time, anyhow in life," continued he, as he stepped into the coach, and then took out his handkerchief to wipe the perspiration from his face. He was so wretchedly clothed, that Mrs. Hodson eyed him with looks of dismay, while drawing her lavender-coloured silk dress close about her person, that it might not be contaminated. I was, indeed, surprised that this poor fellow could afford an inside place.

The lady and her French beau, seeing no remedy, ascended the steps of the carriage in very ill humour, and they were immediately followed by a man with much comic expression in his countenance. He wore a would-be dashing threadbare green coat, with a velvet collar; and his shirt collar was so fine, and so embroidered, and so fringed with rags, that I think he must have purchased it out of the Marquis of Lorne's cast wardrobe. His little Petersham-hat seemed to have been *remit de nouveau,* for the third time at least.

"Lord! Mr. Shuffle, how do you do? who would a thort of our meeting you in the coach?" inquired Mr. and Mrs. Hodson, addressing him in a breath.

"Delighted to see you both," said Shuffle, shaking hands with them.

"And now pray, Mr. Shuffle, if I may be so bold, what might have brought you up to London? what antics might you be up to, hey? Are you stagestruck, as usual, or struck mad by mere accident?"

"Thereby hangs a tale," said Shuffle.

"What! a pigtail? I suppose you're thinking of the shop."

"Not I, indeed," Shuffle observed, "I've done with wig-making these two years; for really it is not in the nature of a man of parts, to stick to the same plodding trade all his life, as you have done, Hodson."

Hodson replied that he knew his friend Shuffle had always been reckoned a bit of a genus, and, for his part, he "always knode a genus," half a mile off, by his threadbare coat, and his shoes, worn down at the heels.

"*Apropos!*" said Mrs. Hodson, "by the by Mr. Shuffle, you forgot to settle for that there pair of boots, before you left Cheltenham, six months ago."

"Very true, my dear lady," answered Shuffle, "all very true: everything shall be settled. I have two irons in the fire at this time, and very great prospects, I assure you; only do pray cut the shop, just now, and indulge me with a little genteel conversation."

"A genteel way of doing a man out of a pair of boots," muttered Hodson; "but I'll tell you what, Mr. Shuffle, you must show me a more lasting trade, or one with more sole in it, before you succeed in making me ashamed of being a shoemaker."

"And pray," continued Hodson, "where's the perpetual motion you were wriggling after so long? and then your rage for the stage, what's become of that? Have you made any money by it?"

"How is it possible," answered Shuffle, "for a man to make money by talents he is not permitted to exert? 'Sir,' said I to the manager of the Liverpool theatre, 'I have cut my trade of wig-making dead, and beg to propose myself to you, as a first-rate performer.' 'Have you any recommendations?' inquired the manager, eyeing me from head to foot. 'Yes, sir,' I replied, 'plenty of recommendations. In the first place, I have an excellent head.'"

"For a wig! a good block, I reckon," interrupted Hodson.

"'In the second place,'" Shuffle continued, "'I have the strongest lungs of any man in England.'"

"That is, unfortunately, the case of my good woman here," again interrupted Hodson.

"'And as for dying, sir,'" still continued Shuffle, "'I have been practising it for these two years past.'"

"Upon red and grey hair, I presume?" said the incorrigible Hodson.

"'Sir,' said the Liverpool prig," so Shuffle went on, "'Sir, our company happens to be, at this moment, complete.'"

Shuffle declared that he had now resigned all thoughts of a profession, the success of which must, often, depend on a set of ignorant blockheads, and turned his thoughts to love and experimental philosophy.

"I say," was Hodson's wise remark, looking very significantly at his friend.

"Well, sir, what have you to say?" Shuffle inquired.

"Blow me, Shuffle, if you aren't a little——" Hodson paused, and touched his forehead.

"Don't meddle with the head, friend, that's not your trade. Oh, by the by," Shuffle continued, "talking of heels, I want to consult you about a new sort of elastic sole and heel, after my own invention: one that shall enable a man to swim along the river, like a goose, at the rate of fifteen miles an hour! ! I have just discovered that the goose owes its swiftness to the shape of its feet. Now, my water-shoe must be made to spread itself open, when the foot is extended, and close as it advances."

"Well done, gentlemen," interposed the poor Irish traveller, "this bates the cork jackets, anyhow in life!"

"Who the devil are you, sir?" asked Shuffle, "and what business have you to crack your jokes?"

"The only little objection that I see to your contrivance," continued Pat, "is that the patent shoe will be just after turning into a clog, as soon as it gits under water, good luck to it."

"The devil take me if that warn't a capital joke! so well done, master Pat," said Hodson.

"Is that an Irish wig you have got on your head, Pat?" Shuffle asked, by way of being even with him.

"For God's sake, sink the shop, Shuffle, and let's have a little genteel conversation," said Hodson, imitating Shuffle's late affectation of voice and manner.

"Pray what do you Irish know about wig-making?" asked Shuffle, disregarding Hodson.

"And may be you would not approve, nather, of their nate compact little fashion of breaking a head, perhaps?" inquired Pat, very quietly.

"Come, come, my comical fellow," said Hodson, "don't be so hot. Mr. Shuffle only meant to remark that it was a pity to wear a red wig over your fine head of hair."

"Arrah, by my sowl! and is it under it you'd have me wear it?" asked the Irishman.

Nothing of very great interest occurred during the remainder of our journey, except that Shuffle seemed disposed to hire Pat as his servant. The Frenchman found fault with everything at table, drank *eau sucré* and studied in his dictionary. The lady in the green habit scorned to address even a single syllable to a person in the humble garb I wore, and I never once opened my lips till we arrived at Oxford, and I was set down at the Crown Inn. There at the door, stood Worcester, as large as life, looking eagerly down the road after the carriages. I hastily placed my arm under that of Worcester, who so little dreamed of seeing me arrive in such attire that he pushed me rather roughly on one side.

"My dear Mr. Dobbins," said I, for that was the name we were to go by at the Crown, where he believed he was not personally known; "Mr. Dobbins! don't you recognize your dear Mrs. Dobbins?"

"Good God, my love! how came you alone, this miserable night?" and Worcester handed me upstairs, all joy, and rapture, and trembling anxiety lest I should catch cold. In less than a quarter of an hour, thanks to his good care, I was in a warm bed, and an excellent supper was served by the side of it, with good claret, fruit, coffee, and everything we could possibly require.

We talked all night long; for we had much to say to each other.

Worcester declared that he looked forward to no hope nor rest, until we should be really married.

I entreated him to consider all the inconveniences of such a match. "Your father never will forgive you, remember!"

"That I shall deeply regret," answered His Lordship; "but I must and will choose my own partner for life. You and I have passed weeks, months, years, together, without having had a single quarrel. This is proof positive, at least, that our tempers harmonize perfectly together, and I conceive that harmony of temper between man and wife is the first and greatest blessing of the wedded state."

I was too frank to deny that I perfectly agreed with him, in this particular.

"I was never happy till I knew you," continued Worcester, "and I am sure, as I am of my existence, that you are the only woman on earth to whom I could ever be constant to the end of my life, and not break my oath. When all is over, my father must submit to necessity."

"It may not be," said I, mildly. "Nay, it shall not be. Your parents, harsh as they are towards me and my faults, shall not have cause to curse me, neither shall you."

Worcester was greatly agitated; and, when all else failed, tried to laugh me out of my resolution. "We will go to Scotland together, in the mail." said His Lordship.

"And who shall be the father to give me away, and be a witness to prove my marriage?" I asked, merely to make a joke of a subject I was tired of treating seriously.

"You shall wear this pretty dress," said Worcester, "and my coachman, Boniface, shall come down to the North with us, to give you away. I dare not trust Will Haught; he shall know nothing of our departure till he has missed us."

"Boniface, of course, must be gaily dressed," said I, "and wear a large nosegay."

"True," proceeded Worcester, "and a white waistcoat."

"Shall the waistcoat be made with pockets and flaps, pray?"

"Why, perhaps that might look handsomer."

"Very well," said I, "perhaps pockets and flaps, perhaps not. Let the matter rest for the moment, and now, with regard to this long journey to Gretna Green, to look for a dirty blacksmith, I think that really will be unnecessary."

"How can it be avoided, till I am of age?" Worcester eagerly inquired.

"Why, I have spoken to that most reverend, pious, and learned divine, Lord Frederick Beauclerc, on this important subject, and he declares himself willing to officiate on this occasion, and marry us, privately, by special license, provided you agree to grant him *les droits du seigneur*."

Worcester inquired what that meant.

"Simply, *les droits du mari* for the first night."

Worcester, having by this time discovered that I was only laughing at him, appeared deeply wounded and offended with me.

"My love, what is to be done?" I asked, "I, as your friend, your real friend, wish you to be comfortably reconciled to your parents, and, by making me your wife, you lose them for ever, without doing me any material good; for I have no ambition, nor hankering after rank, and, I confess, my conscience does not reproach me with any particular crime, attached to my present quiet mode of life, since I have no children; else I should, for their sake, judge differently. Let us hope the best, enjoy the present, and be merry, pray, or I might as well have remained in town."

By degrees Worcester recovered his spirits, and, perhaps there never was an hour, during our whole acquaintance, in which he was so devoted to me, so madly, passionately fond of me, as during my visit to the Crown Inn, which proves how the passion of love is ever increased by difficulties, till it, at last, acquires such a degree of enthusiastic ardour, as persons in the full, easy possession of what they desire can form not the least conception of.

Alas! how fleeting are our moments of happiness! Poor Worcester was obliged to leave me by nine in the morning, after handing me into a hack-chaise; because he could not bear the idea of my being again addressed by any low man who might happen to be my fellow traveller, when my dress would induce them to mistake me for a servant.

Just as I had got about a mile from Oxford, one of Worcester's uncles passed my chaise: if I recollect right, it was Lord Edward. He stared at me, in my odd costume, as though I had been the ninth wonder of the world. However, I hoped, since I had never in my life spoken to His

Lordship, and merely guessed him to be a Somerset, that he would have remained at least in some little doubt as to my identity.

The next morning's post convinced me of my mistake. Worcester, in a very long dismal letter, acquainted me that I had been seen in a very odd unladylike kind of dress, close to Oxford. Worcester assured his father that it was quite impossible, as I certainly should not have gone to Oxford without acquainting him of the circumstance. The Duke and Duchess condescended to laugh at him as a weak, silly dupe to a vile and profligate woman; asked him what good he fancied I could be doing, by travelling about in disguise? and why, if it had been good, I looked so confused, and appeared so anxious to hide my face from his uncle, as to have actually covered it with both my hands? His uncle further declared that I was both deformed and ugly, which rendered his infatuation the more absurd.

Worcester, in reply, declared his aunt so very ugly, that the man who had chosen her for his wife, must for ever give up all pretensions to taste; and then he asked them why they imagined two of the handsomest men of this, and perhaps of any age, Lord Ponsonby and the Duke of Argyle (my readers must excuse my placing Lord Ponsonby first) should have been so much in love with deformity? and, if they were, it was, of course, a proof that my mind must have been of that superior cast, as made ample amends for the defects of my person.

There were two young men, at that time, on a visit with Her Grace of Beaufort, who is known to have always encouraged a very motherly kindness of feeling towards young men, particularly when they were well looking. Perhaps she wanted them for her daughters; and yet, that beauty soon fades, is the cry of most moral mammas. However that may be, and I have not in the least presumed to entertain a doubt of Her Grace's virtue, according to the English acceptation of that word; the two young men I have just now mentioned, and who so vehemently joined the hue and cry against me, were, Montagu, the eldest son of a lady in Portman Square, who used to give charitable dinners to the poor chimney-sweepers once a year, and Mr. Meyler, a young Hampshire gentleman, in the possession of very large West India property, of at least five and twenty thousand a year.

This youth had lately become of age, and, as everybody informed me, was very handsome. Worcester assured me that this young sugar-baker, as Lord Alvanley was pleased to call him, expressed himself in such strong terms of disgust, in reference to me, that His Lordship had been obliged to desire him never to use my name in his presence again.

Meyler, however, *dédommagé'd* himself with his favourite, the Duchess of Beaufort, to whom Worcester had presented him when they were both at Christchurch together. He always agreed with that lady, as to the subjugation of her noble son's superior parts; "for," said Meyler, "it would be impossible for any man, in his right senses, to be in love with that woman called Harriette Wilson; she may have been better once; but she is now in ill health, spoiled by flattery, and altogether the most disgusting style of woman I know."

"Are you acquainted with her, then?" asked the Duchess.

Meyler confessed he had never spoken to me; but added that he saw me every night in my opera box, and in the round room afterwards; and, in short, from having often conversed with my acquaintances, he knew just as much about me, as if he had been so unfortunate as to have been personally acquainted with me.

This inveterate abuse from a stranger, whom I did not even know by sight, somewhat excited my curiosity, nay, more, my emulation perhaps: *car j'avais quelque fois le diable au corps, comme aucune autre.*

"If," said I one day to Fanny, "if all this abuse of me could be reconciled to good taste in a gentleman, and this Meyler is really so handsome, t would be worth while changing his dislike into love, *seulement pour lui apprendre à vivre.* At all events, there is novelty in being an object of disgust to any man, just when Worcester has so cloyed me with sweets! Where can one get a sight of Meyler?"

"Sir John Boyd is a relation or particular friend of his," said Fanny, and, on the first opportunity, Sir John was consulted.

"No woman can do anything with Meyler, in the way of love," said Sir John; "for Meyler really don't know what sentiment means, and that is why I cannot conceive what he is always doing with that fine strapping woman, the Duchess of Beaufort, who appears never so happy nor so comfortable, as when he is perched upon a high stool by her side. Meyler is a mere animal, a very handsome one, it is true, and there is much natural shrewdness about him, besides that he is one of the most gentlemanlike young men I know; but you may read his character in his countenance."

"What is that like?" I asked.

"It is beautiful," said Sir John Boyd, "and so peculiarly voluptuous that, when he looks at women, after dinner, although his manner is perfectly respectful, they are often observed to blush deeply, and hang down their heads, they really cannot tell why or wherefore."

"And who does he love?" I inquired.

"His affections are, I believe, at this moment, divided between a Mrs.

Bang, a Mrs. Patten, and a Mrs. Pancrass, all ladies of Covent Garden notoriety. Meyler is a hard drinker, and a very hard rider, and a good tennis and cricket player, prides himself on his Leicestershire stud, and his old English hospitality, and he is no fool, though he hates reading ; and that is all I know about him, except that I don't believe he would like to be constant for a single fortnight to the most lovely or accomplished woman on earth. In short, he holds all women very cheap, and considers them as mere instruments of pleasure, with the exception of the Duchess of Beaufort, whom he calls a paragon."

"*En voilà assez*," said I, "*de votre bel sauvage*. Perhaps you will show him to me some day, not on Ludgate Hill, but at the opera ?"

CHAPTER 17

THINGS WENT ON worse and worse at Badminton, and I was now delighted that they did so, being altogether most miserably tired of the Beaufort story.

The Duke of Beaufort, at last, sent a notorious swindler of his acquaintance, who has since been confined in chains for forgery, one Mr. Robinson, who, as I have heard, had long been in the habit of doing dirty jobs for noblemen. Robinson declared that I had it in my power considerably to relieve the anxiety and distress of mind to which I had reduced the Beaufort family, by returning all letters in my possession, containing promises of marriage made by the Marquis of Worcester to myself.

"In short," said Robinson, "if you will take an oath, at Westminster Hall, that you have delivered into mine, or His Grace of Beaufort's hands, every letter, or copy of a letter, from Worcester, now in your possession, you may make your own terms with his Grace."

Though I never cared for myself, and I am afraid I never shall, yet, when one is dealing with a notorious rogue, it seems silly to become his dupe: I therefore requested to have a week allowed me to decide. This time being granted me, because I would have it so, I consulted a most respectable counsellor, Thomas Treslove, Esq. of Old Square, Lincoln's Inn, who had been acquainted with my family when I was quite a child and living with my parents.

Mr. Treslove, after reading Lord Worcester's letters, containing his repeated and solemn promises of marriage, at my particular request, declared, what I have no doubt he is ready, this day, to repeat, merely that he conceived the letters, if brought into a court of law, to be worth twenty thousand pounds to me, and, when I afterwards consulted Henry Brougham, Esq., M.P., of the same place, he entirely agreed, in opinion, with Mr. Treslove.

I inquired whether my situation, previous to my having been under the protection of Lord Worcester, made any difference.

"The court would not discuss that point, nor take it into the smallest consideration for or against you," said Mr. Treslove. "You have, for any-

316

thing which can be proved to the contrary, in all probability been prevented from establishing yourself eligibly or comfortably in life, by having received the most solemn promises of marriage from the Marquis of Worcester. If, from the extreme generosity of your disposition, you, instead of hurrying the thing forward, wished His Lordship to take time for consideration, you have the stronger claim on that family, supposing them to be people of honour. The Duke has no witness of your having ever refused the Marquis; on the contrary, you tell me, His Grace will not believe a single syllable of the matter. Lord Worcester has, by the dates of these letters, been pledging his faith to you for the space of two years; and, I conceive, the damages, if he should now declare off, would be rated, at least, at twenty thousand pounds!"

The next day I had second interview with Mr. Robinson, to whom I repeated the opinion of Counsellor Treslove, and assured him that gentleman was ready to put it in writing, if necessary.

Robinson said that it would not be required; for the Duke expected all this, and indeed he thought I might make better terms, without exposing the secrets of a noble family in a public Court of Justice.

I promised Mr. Robinson that His Grace should receive my decided answer by the next day's post.

Robinson said this would not be regular, and it had better pass through his hands.

I begged to be excused, declaring that I must and would manage matters in my own way; and Mr. Robinson was at length compelled to leave me, although in a very ill humour.

The following morning Worcester arrived in town, with the Duke and Duchess of Beaufort. Those worthy parents had again adopted the pathetics, finding it impossible to manage Worcester in any other way.

"My poor father is very wretched," said Worcester, "and my mother, when I left the house this morning, was almost in hysterics, because I will not consent to go abroad without you; and I never can or will attempt it."

"Do you think they would feel happier if they were in possession of your promises of marriage?" I inquired.

"Certainly," answered Worcester. "His Grace would, in fact, make any sacrifice to obtain them, though in the end, they could not serve his wishes, since I will never give up the hope and full expectation of becoming your husband."

Poor Duke! said I, musing to myself, after Worcester had left me, on the pomps and vanities of this wicked world. I perhaps, though very innocently, been the cause of much uneasiness to him. Not that this matter is quite certain either; for Worcester might have, by this time, completely involved his father's estate. It had, indeed, been his wish to do this, but that I laboured to prevent him, and he is not only a few thousands in debt, owing to the very small allowance his father makes him. I have never done the Duke or his family any real injury, and I never will; nay, I should like to prove myself anxious for their happiness, only their all being so severe upon me, and so very abusive, is such a damper. I will make the Duke of Beaufort like me, and regret his former severity, continued I, opening my writing-desk, and after five minutes more deliberation, I addressed a letter to His Grace of Beaufort, as nearly as I can recollect, in these words:

Your Grace has been very severe on me and my errors; but, if you imagine they are of a nature to destroy domestic comfort, I can easily forgive all the very harsh expressions which yourself, as well as Her Grace, in letters I have seen of her own writing, made use of on my subject. I will venture to remind your Grace that I was very far from seeking the acquaintance of your son. In short, but for such perseverance as I have seldom witnessed, I had never placed myself under his protection. I knew not that in doing so I was likely to destroy the peace of any human being. In short, if I had not respected yours, I had long since become your daughter-in-law. Having now inspired Lord Worcester with a very strong affection, something is surely due to him, from gratitude, neither would my conscience acquit me if, out of respect for the parent I never saw, I were to act with inhumanity towards the son who would sacrifice all for me. I have pledged myself solemnly not to desert him at present; but, what I can do, in perfect good faith to Worcester, I am very anxious to perform, for the relief of his noble father's mind. I will not sell the proofs of respect and affection which have been generously tendered to me; but, as I conceive they cannot be put to better account than that of relieving the anxiety of a father's mind, I have the greatest pleasure in forwarding them to your Grace, and am ready to take any oath that you may require, as to my having now enclosed you the whole of Lord Worcester's correspondence in my possession or power. All I ask in return, is to be considered by your Grace with somewhat less of ill-will, and that for your own sake, as well as that of the Duchess, you will feel some confidence in the goodness of my heart, in the sincere wish I do, in truth, feel, that your son may turn out all and everything you can desire.

Only point out what I can do more, for the tranquillity of Lord Worcester's parents, which shall not become a breach of faith and humanity towards himself, and I declare to your Grace that you shall never see me hesitate, from anything like a selfish motive. I have the honour to remain, with sincere wishes for the happiness of Lord Worcester's parents,

> *Your Grace's most obedient,*
> *and very humble servant.*

> HARRIETTE WILSON.

His Grace of Beaufort never, in any way, condescended to acknowledge the receipt of this letter, which I carried myself, and left with his porter in Grosvenor Square; yet the Beauforts were ever a high-bred race! but I conclude high-bred and well-bred must be two things, for it never could be well-bred of His Grace to refuse to acknowledge the above, to say nothing of the extreme selfishness and want of feeling of the noble Duke, who, having obtained what he wished for the present, returned to Badminton, to which place he insisted on Worcester again accompanying him.

During another month, Worcester declared to me that his parents, relatives, and his father's friends, tormented him beyond his patience; and that young Meyler had begged him to leave me, as though he had been begging for his life, humbly entreating him to forgive the liberty he took with him, which alone arose out of his brotherly affection and respect for the Duchess, etc.

Worcester generally contrived to get over to London every two or three days, though but for a few hours; and, when that was impossible, I met him at a village ten miles on this side of Brighton.

One morning I received a letter from Worcester, so blotted over, from one end to the other, that it was scarcely legible, and some parts appeared actually to have been defaced by tears. Such an incoherent scrawl I never had known him, nor anybody else, write before! It was all over wives and angels, and eternal constancy, and eternal despair!! with miseries and tortures without end. In short, it was out of all compass miserable, and out of all rules, or direct right angles, or parallel lines. All I could make out of this scrawl, as certain, was that Lord Wellington, at the request of Worcester's father, who had made it without his son's knowledge, had appointed him his aide-de-camp, and that go he must; for there was no remedy, or it would be called cowardice, if he hesitated. Nevertheless, he had sworn not to leave London, unless he had been allowed to pass a whole fortnight, entirely, with me. This had been granted, and I was to expect him in two days after the receipt of his letter, which ended with earnest entreaties that I would promise to accompany him to the Continent; and, lastly, His Lordship informed me that his father would arrive in London, on the same morning with his letter, for the express purpose of attending a levee, and demanding a private audience of his present Majesty, to beg permission for Worcester to leave his regiment, and join the Duke of Wellington in Spain.

I knew not, nor had ever suspected, how much Worcester's loss would affect me, until there was no remedy, and my case desperate, for well I knew that I should never be permitted to follow up the army in Spain, even had I been disposed to make the attempt. I burst into a violent flood of tears.

It now struck me very forcibly, that Worcester had deserved all my devoted attachment, and that I had not been half grateful enough to him. That he would lose his life in Spain, I felt convinced, and that since his regiment remained in England, I should have his blood on my head. What was to be done? My crimson velvet pelisse, trimmed with white fur, and also my white beaver hat, with the charming plume of feathers, were spread out in my dressing-room, ready for Hyde Park, and conquests!! and poor Worcester, perhaps, might soon be numbered with the dead! food for worms!!

After a second flood of tears!! on went the red pelisse and charming white hat, and, in less than half an hour, behold me standing at the Duke of Beaufort's street door, awaiting the answer to my humble, single rap, with a little note in my hand, containing these few words, addressed to the Duke.

I earnestly entreat your Grace to permit me to speak a few words to you before you attend the levee this morning.

Your most obedient, humble servant,

HARRIETTE WILSON.

When His Grace's huge, fat porter opened the door, I made a desperate effort to conceal my tears, which had been flowing in abundance ever since I had read poor Worcester's letter, just as if I had received his dying speech; and I delivered my little note, requesting to be allowed to wait for the Duke's answer. The porter looked on me suspiciously: he seemed to be considering His Grace of Beaufort's moral character, as his eye glanced from my face downward, as though it had struck him as just possible that I might have come, thus unattended, for the purpose of swearing a child against his noble master.

"Are you quite certain that it is the Duke himself you want to see, and not the young Marquis?"

I assured him that I wished much either to see the Duke, or to receive an answer to my note.

As the man again looked under my large beaver bonnet, I felt the tears gush into my eyes.

"His Grace shall have the note directly," said the porter, in a tone of compassion, observing how I was trembling, as I really half expected the Duke of Beaufort would order one or two of his tall footmen to put me on the other side of the door. I saw the porter give my note to a servant in livery, desiring him to take it to His Grace's valet.

"The Duke," said the porter, turning to me, "is dressing for the levee; so you had better take a seat."

I did so, and while I was almost choked with the efforts my pride caused me to make, in order to conceal my tears from a parcel of curious, impudent servants, who, for near twenty minutes that I was suffered to remain in the hall, were eyeing me with very impertinent curiosity, the kind porter again addressed me, almost in a whisper, with, "Ma'am, your note has been put into His Grace's own hands, and he is reading on it; so I dare say he will ring his bell, and we shall hear if there is any answer for you."

I waited another quarter of an hour, in a very miserable state of suspense, and in real bodily fear of being kicked out of the house.

At last, as I sat with my handkerchief to my eyes, and my face turned towards the ground, I heard someone, in a mild, gentleman-like voice, call from the bottom of the stairs, to inquire if the person was waiting, who had brought the last note. I raised my head, and, seeing a handsome-looking man, in a court dress, who appeared to be a very little older than Worcester, I grew brave, as I always do from desperation, conceiving everything was now lost, and that the Duke had descended from his usual dignity, for the purpose of seeing justice done to the orders he was about to issue for my being kicked into the street.

"Did you bring this note, pray?" asked the Duke, addressing me, since his first question had not, it seemed, reached the dull ear of the fat porter.

"I did, your Grace," answered I, firmly.

"Then do me the favour to walk this way," continued the Duke, opening the parlour door, and closing it after him.

"What can he be going to do to me?" thought I, trembling from head to foot.

"My bell was broken," said His Grace, "and, for the last ten minutes, before I came down, I could not make anyone hear; but I assure you that

I had no idea that you yourself were waiting in my hall. I conceived it was your messenger."

The least sound of kindness, to one already so very low and nervous, is enough to affect one. The tears I had made such efforts to conceal from the servants would be restrained no longer, and I was not, like the Duchess on a former occasion, almost hysterical, but quite so; and the more I laboured and prayed for calm, the more impossible it was to obtain it; so, as I stood sobbing aloud, in the middle of the Duke's large dining-room, with my handkerchief held to my eyes, the Duke of Beaufort and myself really cut two very pretty figures!! and I much wish Stockdale would get a print of it!

"I am not aware of your motive, Miss Wilson, for favouring me with this visit," said the Duke.

And, as I attempted to apologize, my tears fell still faster and faster, till they quite choked my voice.

The Duke, seeing that mine was real agitation, and not affectation, condescended to unbend a little.

"Sit down," said His Grace, drawing an easy chair towards me. "I beg you will sit down and compose yourself, and don't think it necessary to speak till you are more calm. I hope you believe that I felt very much shocked that you should have waited in my hall? upon my honour, I had not a conception of finding you there, when I went downstairs, because I could not make anybody hear."

At length I succeeded in recovering myself, so far as to state to His Grace that, on the receipt of Lord Worcester's letter, I had felt so very much shocked at the idea of being the sole cause of His Lordship being sent into danger, while his regiment remained quietly in England, that, really, I found it impossible to resist making an effort to prevent it, by proposing to His Grace to do all in my power to induce Lord Worcester to consent to our separation; and even if I failed, rather to agree to go abroad myself, and keep my residence a secret from his son, than that he should, for my sake, be exposed to danger.

The Duke declared that even had he been inclined to comply with my request, and he honestly confessed he was not, it was now too late; "and really, Miss Wilson," continued His Grace, "it was, from the first, folly and madness in you ever to have fancied Worcester could or would have made you his wife."

"Your Grace still believes me desirous of the honour I might obtain, by forcing myself on you as your despised relative?" said I, indignation drying up my tears at the idea of being so misunderstood, "and further, you imagine that if I wished, and would consent to marry your son, I should fail to accomplish my designs?"

"Certainly," answered His Grace, proudly.

"Duke!" said I, fixing my eyes mildly, but firmly, on his face, "you neither deceive me nor yourself by that assertion, for you know the contrary. I am——" and I felt my heart swell with something between grief and indignation, "I am," I continued, "naturally good, but you will, among you, harden my heart till it becomes cold and vicious. Since nothing generous, and no sacrifice, on my part, is understood or felt, even when I would serve others, and while I only think of them, you will not, or you cannot understand me. Allow me, then, to tell you the fault is in your own character; I will not say in your heart, but in your want of heart."

The Duke, being of gentlemanly manners, to give everybody their due, sought to appease matters a little.

"I did not mean to hurt your feelings, I assure you," said His Grace, "perhaps I expressed myself improperly. I only wanted to observe to you that such unequal marriages are seldom, if ever, attended with happiness to either party, as witness Lord Egremont, and several more I could name."

"Do not trouble yourself, Duke, since I am, and I always was, determined not to marry your son; upon my word, I am; and, if you again give me the lie, or speak to me as though you entirely disbelieved this positive assurance, which has been repeated to your son so often, while on his knees he has implored me to become his wife, I shall say you do so because I am a woman, and cannot call you to account for it. Your Grace would use more ceremony with a man; but my object for the great presumption of thus intruding on you, was the hope of being able to suggest some plan which would render it unnecessary for Lord Worcester to join the Duke of Wellington's staff. You have answered me on that subject, and I have now the honour to take my leave of your Grace."

"Not yet," said the Duke. "Pray stay till you are more tranquil. Shall I get you a glass of water?"

I declared it was unnecessary; but he insisted on my waiting, while he himself went into his dressing-room to procure one.

"Now I hope you are quite convinced that your being left in my hall was contrary to my knowledge, and gives me real concern?" said the Duke, after I had swallowed the glass of water he presented to me.

I bowed in acknowledgment of this apology. "I have spoken to Lord Worcester's father for the first and, in all human probability, for the last time in my life," said I, feelingly; because I really, for Worcester's sake, felt a regard and respect towards his father, at that time.

"And if it should happen so?" inquired the Duke of Beaufort.

"Will your Grace shake hands with me?" said I, timidly, and without presuming to offer my hand.

"With great pleasure," answered the Duke, and, after shaking hands, rather cordially, he himself conducted me into the hall, and called loudly to the porter to attend and open the door for me.

Worcester came to town on the following morning, and for all the Duchess could say or do, Worcester insisted on passing the whole of every day with me.

"My Lord," Will Haught would say through the key-hole of our bedroom, "my Lord, the Duchess desired me to tell you that she has a great deal of business to settle with you today, about, in short, about all manner of things, my Lord."

"Very well, that is enough, Will," His Lordship would answer.

In another hour this torment would knock again.

"My Lord, Her Grace looked rather displeased this morning. The Duchess was almost in a passion."

"You be d——d! go along!" was the elegant reply.

"My Lord" (in another hour), "you see I'm tired of standing in this here room, and the Duchess this morning—I assure you, my Lord—your Lordship knows what I mean, Her Grace had got a very particular look in her face; you know, my Lord, how she looks when she's vexed like, and takes on, you know, my Lord."

"Go to hell!" vociferated Worcester, from the emergency of the case, although he had by no means the habit of swearing.

"I'm going, my Lord," answered Will Haught.

Everything was arranged, in a week, for my accompanying Worcester to Spain. My female attendant was hired, and my trunks really ready; but, as new objections continually offered themselves to this plan, Worcester was reduced almost to despair, and looked so miserably ill that everybody he met made the observation.

The army was not expected to be stationary. If I remained at Lisbon, I should see no more of him than by remaining in London. The misery, expense, and privations, perhaps insults, I must endure in my attempt to follow the army, could scarcely be surmounted; and Worcester could not deny that I should make a coward of him; that fight he could not, supposing I might be suffering under sickness or difficulty. At last it was finally decided between us as a thing impossible. We must then be separated for one year, since there is no remedy: "but," said Worcester, "I shall declare to my father that, at the end of that time, we will part no more. He has implored me to make a trial of a year's absence, and I have consented; but in twelve months from the day I leave you, supposing I am not on my road to join you in England, remember you are to come to me."

This I promised, should the thing be practicable.

At all events, no power on earth, he solemnly vowed and declared a thousand times over, and as solemnly wrote it down, that neither man nor devil should separate us longer than twelve months, during which time my last kiss was to be virgined on his true lip.

"If ever you prove false to me, or I to you, let all inconstant men be called Panders, and all false women, Cressids," said Worcester, or he ought to have said so. In short, he spoke to this effect, only he spoke more strongly; for, in his zeal, I believe he hoped we might both go where he had sent Will Haught, if ever we were inconstant; and yet he was leaving his beloved, surrounded with flatterers and spies of the Duke, in the gay city of London.

"Never mind, my love," said I, "for, if my residing in the metropolis makes you miserable, I'll go and bury my wonderful charms in a village, and so immortalize it for ever!"

But Worcester declared that all the comfort he was capable of feeling, at that moment, was in my honour.

"*Mais, ne sais-tu pas que je l'ai perdu?*" I inquired.

"*N'importe. Si je place ma confiance, mon ange! c'est en toi,*" said Worcester.

All this joking, on serious and affecting matters, is really in monstrously bad taste! I cannot conceive how I can be guilty of such heartless unfeeling behaviour! But, after all, being now in the daily habit of meeting this profligate Marquis of Worcester about Paris, with the sister of his late wife, and seeing him look as if he did not even know me by sight, while I often forget, until he has passed, where or when I have seen that man before, the face being familiar, and perhaps the name even forgotten—Oh, by the by! I say to myself, if I meet him a second time in the same morning, now I think of it, that long-nosed, tall man is Worcester. And just in this way does his own treacherous memory, no doubt, treat his own dearest dear! own beloved! ever adored, and ever to be adored! delicious! sweet! darling! wife! Harriette.

Worcester declared that he would not leave me, until his father would make me an allowance, at least, during his absence from England. For

325

this purpose, about three days previous to his departure, he brought Mr. Robinson, as he said, from the Duke of Beaufort.

Robinson declared that anything Worcester could sign, by way of annuity or allowance, would be good for nothing; "but," he continued, "I am come to pass my word, in the Duke's name, that the allowance Worcester requires for you, shall be paid to you, in regular quarterly payments, after all your house debts, etc., have been discharged."

"Of course, Worcester, I may trust to this assurance made in your presence?" I inquired.

Worcester was sure his father would act up to his engagements, and I, being in grief, and naturally careless in money matters, believing, too, that I was in the power of gentlemen, and gentlemen of strict honour, assured them I was under no alarm, and never expected to be left to starve, while I endeavoured to do my duty, and then the subject dropped.

On the last day we passed together, we certainly shed a super-abundance of tears. Poor Worcester was half blinded with his: and, seriously, a man going to be hanged could not well have appeared more discouraged or dismayed.

"I will write at least a quire of foolscap to you every day," said Worcester, "and may God bless my adored wife, and bless me only just as I am found ready to sacrifice my life for her happiness." In short, but for Lord William Somerset, who absolutely dragged him out of the house a few minutes before the Falmouth mail started, I almost believe he would have preferred love to glory, and given old Wellington the slip.

I passed the night entirely without rest, in spite of all the efforts I made to recover my spirits. He is gone. Nothing can bring him back. Well, should he not be killed, it is a good thing for a young man to see a little service. It won't do for me to lose all my life in fretting: and fifty more such wise remarks did I repeat to myself, and yet I could not forget poor Worcester's extreme kindness and attachment.

In two days more I was visited by Robinson, who used every argument in his power, to convince me of the folly of ever expecting to live with Worcester again.

"Why not act with common sense?" said Robinson. "There is His Grace of Beaufort ready to provide for you, in the most comfortable manner possible, for your whole life, in short, as I told you before, you may make your own terms, conditionally, that you never speak or write to His Lordship again."

I begged Mr. Robinson not to lose his time in teasing me when I was out of spirits. "Pray acquaint the Duke that Worcester refused to leave

England until I had solemnly pledged myself to write to him constantly, and wait for him a year, from the day of his departure, and then tell me if the Duke commands me to break my written oath, and ill-use his son?"

"If he does, will you do it?" Robinson asked but considering this an impertinent question, I refused to answer it, and again the worthy man went away, in a very ill-humour, declaring that, for his part, he could not treat with me.

CHAPTER 18

FANNY WAS MY constant visitor after Worcester had left England, and did all in her power to amuse and enliven me. Worcester had promised to make the acquaintance of Colonel Parker, in Spain, and send her word how he went on, who he made love to, and, in short, all the news about him he could possibly scrape together. Fanny was very grateful to His Lordship, for having, himself, suggested this plan to her. She was still living with Julia, and Julia was yet beloved and adored by Mr. Napier, who might have been her son in point of age and appearance.

My opera box had been engaged for that season, and paid for, before Lord Worcester thought of being ordered off to the Continent, and Fanny and Julia had each of them purchased a ticket from me; yet I did not like the idea of going there without His Lordship. I knew I should feel dull, and that the Duke and Duchess, whose box was opposite mine, would make their observations on whatever I did, and might report mere nothings in a way to disturb poor Worcester's feelings.

"I will not go tonight," said I, in answer to Julia's pressing entreaties, and I kept my word.

The following Saturday's opera was expected to be unusually brilliant. All the fashionable world was in town: there was a new ballet, too, and a new French dancer; and Fanny declared it to be the height of folly to have paid two hundred guineas for an opera box without making use of it.

"Well," said I, "since Worcester cannot well be shot by the enemy previous to his reaching headquarters, I may as well take the opportunity of seeing two or three more ballets; for, as to indulging in gaieties while a parcel of shots are flying about his head or across his brain, is not in my nature." This last was, by the by, a very foolish idea, but a nervous woman will often fancy impossibilities, and that was my case. However, I determined to cut all public amusements as soon as I knew Worcester to be in contact with the enemies of old England.

We were all three unusually well dressed on that evening; for our finery was new, and we humbly hoped in very good taste. On this night, too, I may say, without flattering myself, that there was no lack of humble servants, and devoted pretenders, among the gentlemen in waiting, who crowded about me, believing, of course, that, in the absence of my jealous Lord, it would be no difficult matter to obtain favour in my sight, and, whether I was the style of woman they liked, or just the reverse, still it was always worth while cutting out a man who had been so proverbially in love as Worcester. No doubt, argued such tasteless beings, who, for their own part, saw nothing at all remarkable about me, no doubt, she must improve, wonderfully, on acquaintance: at all events, it is worth trying what she is like. In short, if it had been to have turned my head by flattery, *il y avait vraiment de quoi*; and it has been remarked by several persons in high life, who knew the world well, that it would have been easy for me to have secured, at that period, not less than a dozen annuities.

Amy was rather gay too that season, in her box next to mine, and the Honourable Berkeley Paget had cut his wife and all his family to accompany her, by her particular desire, about the streets and in all public places. In short, he lived in the same house with her, and seldom quitted her for an instant. Everybody cried out shame, and some few, such very moral men as the Duke of York, actually cut him dead, and refused to receive him at Oatlands, even on public nights: for, beyond all doubt, a man ought to be of royal blood before he presumes to commit adultery, except in private, like Lords Cowper and Marlborough.

Fanny and Julia were both looking remarkably well, and many a beau turned his head wishfully towards our box, anxiously waiting to observe a vacancy for one.

Brummell, Lord William Russell, Frederick Bentinck, Lord Molyneux, Captain Fitzclarence, Lord Fife, Duc de Berri, Montagu, Berkeley Craven, and a great many more were visitors.

A young man whose name I have forgotten came to request the favour of being allowed to present Mr. Meyler to me.

This Meyler was the young, rich, Hampshire gentleman who, Worcester assured me, had professed to entertain such a violent dislike toward me. Both Fanny and I at once concluded that he wanted to come to me as a spy, either at his favourite the Duchess of Beaufort's suggestion, or his own.

"Don't see him," said Fanny, "I am sure he will make mischief."

For my part, as I have before informed my readers, *j'avais, de temps en temps, le diable au corps*, and I liked the description that Sir John Boyd had given me of that young gentleman's style of beauty and expression; and I was, besides, rather curious to see how such a man would set about disliking me! and I wished the Duchess to be aware that I was not to be had. No doubt, thought I, since Meyler is such a mere profligate, he proposes succeeding with me at once, merely to laugh at me afterwards, and acquaint Worcester what a loose woman I am. He may not be aware that I know him to be the friend of Worcester's family.

Having made all these wise reflections to myself, while the young man chatted with Julia, I addressed him to inquire what sort of a person he intended introducing to me.

"Oh, a charming, beautiful youth, whom all the ladies are in love with," was the reply; and I desired him to bring Mr. Meyler to me immediately.

He took me at my word, and soon returned, to present to our notice a man, certainly of very interesting appearance, and with a most expressive countenance. His manner too was particularly unaffected and gentleman-like, and the tones of his voice were very sweet: nevertheless, it was easy to discover, in spite of his naturally good breeding, that he held me rather cheap.

In short, to put the idea of respect to me out of the question, he attempted to give me a kiss as we descended the stairs together; but though I refused decidedly, it was done rather coquettishly, on purpose that he might be induced to renew the attack at some future day, with a little more ceremony.

At about three o'clock the next day, my servant announced a gentleman, who refused to send up his name, merely saying that he lived in Grosvenor Square, and wanted to speak to me.

I was about to insist on knowing who my visitor was before I admitted him, when the idea struck me as just possible, and I requested he might be shown upstairs.

It was the Duke of Beaufort!

I was surprised at receiving a visit from His Grace, and still more so, when I found that he really had nothing particular to say to me. He hesitated a good deal, looked rather foolish, and wished, for my own sake, as well as his son's, that I would abandon all hopes, and leave off corresponding with his son.

"Duke," said I, interrupting him, "was it not your first and most anxious wish that Worcester should go abroad?"

"It was."

"Well, then, Lord Worcester positively and absolutely refused to leave London, until I had pledged myself, in the most solemn manner, to continue faithfully his, and not place myself under the protection of any other man, for one twelvemonth from the day he should leave England. Do you still ask me to break my oath ? "

The Duke, from very shame, perhaps, was silent, and stood against my door, fidgeting and hesitating, as though he would have proposed something or other, but that he wanted courage.

After a long pause, he suddenly, and with abruptness, said, "Who makes your shoes ? "

I fixed my eyes upon His Grace in unaffected astonishment at this irrelevant question.

"We will say nothing of the feet and the ankles," continued His Grace.

This compliment was so very unlooked for from such a quarter, and struck me so very odd, that I felt myself actually blushing up to the very eyes, and I immediately changed the conversation from my feet and ankles, to the young Marquis and the peninsula war.

His Grace, when he took his leave of me, had made no single proposal, nor said one single word, which could in any way assist my guess, as to why he did me the honour to call on me.

I received two more very long letters from Falmouth: the last was written in despair, agony of mind! etc. to use Worcester's own words, and put into the post on the very eve of His Lordship's sailing for Lisbon.

On the following Saturday, just as I was seated in my opera box, Meyler occurred to me again, for the first time, and I was rather curious, at least, to know whether he meant to visit me any more. Perhaps I was half desirous that he should. It is true he could be nothing to me, and besides he was so abominably cool and impertinent, and then he had declared that he thought me anything but desirable. Still, I told Fanny, I should like to have one more look at him, before I died or retired into the country, merely to ascertain if the expression of his countenance was really as beautiful as it had struck me to be at first sight.

Fanny declared that it was very wicked of me to wish anything whatever about the matter; but Julia said Meyler had, if possible, a more delicious face than ever her own adored Harry Mildmay; and, for her part, she candidly owned he had but once to put the question to her, and alas, poor Napier! !

However, Fanny might have spared her sermon, since neither Julia's virtue, nor mine, were put in any sort of danger; for all the notice Meyler took of either of us, was through his opera glass, as he sat in the Duchess of Beaufort's box.

Considering that, by this time, Meyler really disliked me, I began to sympathize with him in his feelings; and having determined to cut him,

W

wherever we might hereafter meet, I amused myself with talking to half the gay world, careless of everything but time present.

Julia having paid Amy a visit in her box, and mentioned to her that I thought Meyler very beautiful, Amy immediately dispatched the first man she could find, of his acquaintance, to invite him to her supper after the opera.

I declared to Julia, if that was the case, I would not go to Amy's, as I had taken a disgust at the idea of meeting Mr. Meyler; and I returned to bed immediately on leaving the theatre.

I passed much of my time in scribbling every little event which occurred, to Worcester, and the rest mostly with Fanny and Julia, having changed my residence to one which was within a few doors of Julia's.

Meyler, as Amy afterwards informed us, did not attend to her invitation.

One Tuesday night, as Julia was not ready, nor had even begun to dress when I called for her, I went to the opera alone. Judge my surprise, on entering my box, to find the front fully occupied by two immensely fat city-sort of ladies, and an elderly stupid-looking man in powder.

"There must be some mistake, I fancy," said I, civilly.

"How do you mean, Madam?" asked the powdered man.

"This is my private box, and you may see my name on the outside of it."

The party, in great haste, produced three bone-tickets, which they had purchased for eight shillings each at Mr. Ebers's.

"They are the three tickets I am in the habit of disposing of every night. Lady Castlereagh does the same thing; but nobody ever thinks of intruding their society on me here. The tickets are sold for the pit."

"For the pit, indeed!" said one of the ladies, with indignation, "the pit!! who ever heard tell of such a thing? You're much more fitter, Ma'am, for aught I know, to go into the pit yourself than we are. Is our dress a pit-dress, or a gallery-dress, Ma'am?"

"I fancy, Madam, you are thinking of the play or Astley's. You are not accustomed to the opera, I see, or you would not fancy anything too fine for the pit. I assure you, you will all three cut a brilliant figure there," said I.

A little Captain Churchill, of the Guards, came into my box at this moment, and opened his little eyes as wide as his astonishment could stretch them, at seeing my party.

"Mr. Churchill, these two ladies have bought my tickets of Ebers, and they insist on taking up the front of my box."

332

"Oh, Madam," said Churchill, addressing the eldest, "you really must not expect to make such a very magnificent appearance, for only eight shillings."

"Silence!" said the fat, powdered gentleman, with dignity, and Churchill stared impudently in his face, and burst out into a laugh.

"This is unwarrantable conduct, sir," said the stranger, "and I must call the box-keeper, if you hinder my whole party from witnessing the performance."

"Excellent! upon my word, capital! We are really very much obliged to you all, for being such monstrous good fun," said Churchill, holding his sides.

"Box-keeper!" roared out the powdered man, and one of them immediately attended his summons. "These people are a great nuisance, box-keeper, and they want to make us believe that we have no right to sit in our own box!"

"Excuse me, sir," said the man, "this box belongs to this lady. It is Miss Wilson's own private property."

"And pray are not these the tickets of this box?" the stranger inquired.

"They certainly are," replied the man, "and I have no right to refuse you admittance; but it is a regular understood thing, when ladies dispose of their tickets, they are for the pit."

"Don't tell me about your regular understood thing," said the enraged gentleman. "We have come up to town on purpose to witness an Italian opera, and we have procured tickets for this box. Now I'll tell you what, young man, if you don't make these people silent, I shall apply to a constable, and have them turned out."

"Oh! how very good!" said Churchill, again laughing, and looking at the party through his glass. "Did you all three come up by steam, or how?"

The box-keeper vainly endeavoured to look serious, while informing them that he really could not take upon himself to request me or my friend to be silent, when we were inclined to converse or laugh in my own box, as it was what everybody did; and many went there for no other purpose but to chat with their friends.

I requested the box-keeper to send Ebers to me, while the fat ladies were turning up their eyes, and throwing out contemptuous remarks on the man for having attempted to impose on them with such an improbable story as that of people putting themselves to the expense of going to the King's Theatre, when they only wanted to converse, and had no wish to see the performance.

"Let us make ourselves so disagreeable to them that they will be glad to go," said I in French, which language, from their stupid faces, I concluded they had not studied.

"I have been trying that plan for the last ten minutes," answered Churchill; "but how can *la belle Harriette* ever expect to succeed in disgusting others?"

"You shall see," said I, "although I am going to be very vulgar; but the case is desperate, for it is death to be stuck behind these fat people, and I shall be quizzed and laughed at for a month, for changing my two sister-graces, whom I expect every minute, for these two furies." I then fixed my eyes steadily on the ladies' finery, particularly their head-dresses. Then Churchill would take a peep at their feet, and laugh again, louder than ever.

"Insufferably impertinent!" said the youngest lady, fanning herself violently; but still they kept their seats.

Mr. Ebers came into the box to express his regrets; and he did all in his power to convince the ladies that it really was never meant that those who purchased tickets for the night should enter the private boxes of ladies who disposed of their tickets.

"And pray, sir," said the eldest lady, bridling, "do we look like people who would bemean ourselves by going into the pit?"

"Don't let's have no more to do," said the powdered gentleman, pompously. "Mr. Ebers! we request you to prevent this bold young man and woman from making a noise, as we comed here for to see the opera, not to listen to all the absurd things you choose to tell us. When we want you, we will call on you in your own shop!"

"Do sit down, Mr. Ebers," said I, pointing to a chair, which he accepted for a few moments, merely to repeat his regrets that we had been so intruded upon.

I was now determined to have these people out, *coûte qu'il coûte*.

"Madam," said I to the ugliest lady, "I take it for granted, from your appearance, that you are a lady of strict virtue."

The woman stared at me!

"Consequently," I continued, "it must be painful for you to continue with a woman so notoriously wicked as I am, and in my private box, too! just as if you were a particular friend of mine."

"Now, Hopkins! what's to be done?" said the two ladies, at once.

"I am not joking," continued I, "as you will soon ascertain beyond a doubt, since I expect the pork merchant with whom I have promised to pass the night, every instant."

"All quite true, Madam," said Churchill, quietly, "and further, I was her companion last night. It was her respect for you, which has made her so very anxious to have you out before she sends for the bottle of brandy she usually takes here; because she is the most violent creature in the world, after she has got a little here," pointing to his forehead.

"Mr. Hopkins!! come out!" said the ladies, and out they all bundled.

Churchill followed them some paces down the passage, and returned handing in Julia and Fanny.

Fanny could not, for the life of her, help laughing, and yet she was so good, and loved me so dearly, she could not but feel hurt that I had given myself so bad a character.

"Why make yourself out worse than you are?" she asked.

"Never mind, dear Fan, plenty of people are left to make the best of themselves. One wants a little variety in life."

I passed a merry night, and, as Mr. Nugent was bringing me to a hackney-coach, as a carriage was out of the question on the Duke of Beaufort's princely allowance, I observed Mr. Meyler waiting, as if on purpose to speak to me slyly, as I passed just by the Haymarket entrance to the theatre.

And Harriette Wilson had refused to become Marchioness of Worcester, to be waited for, in a corner, by a vile sugar-baker! Oh! ye gods! I wonder I did not drop down dead on the spot! but, as Lord Byron says,

> There is no spirit now a days!

so I merely flew into a passion.

Meyler's beautiful dimple, as he smiled on me, did not disarm me in the least.

"Mr. Meyler," said I, *en passant*, "it is not necessary for you to conceal yourself in by corners, in order to acknowledge me, and for this very simple reason, I wish to be allowed to decline your acquaintance."

"But why?" asked Meyler, following us up.

"Merely that I consider you a dead bore!" I added, as I stepped into the hackney-coach, and was followed by Julia. Fanny had retired early with Colonel Parker.

Nugent directed our coachman to Camden Town, and then wished us a good night; but we had scarcely got clear of the throng of carriages, when we observed a man in silk stockings running after us, bawling to the coachman to stop!

It was Mr. Meyler, who came up to the coach window, quite out of breath, to beg, very earnestly and humbly, that we would permit him to enter the carriage, just for a few moments, while he made his apologies, and explained things.

"It is so perfectly unnecessary, Mr. Meyler, that I hope you will not detain us any longer."

"Mrs. Johnstone," said Meyler, addressing Julia, beseechingly, "pray intercede for me. Do pray allow me to speak to you five minutes. You may put me down again at White's, in St. James's Street, if you are tired of me."

"Oh! there can be no harm, since we are two," said Julia.

And in spite of all I could say or do to prevent her, she pulled the check-string, and Meyler seated himself by my side, declaring he was willing to prove at the very next opera, how desirous and how proud he should feel to acknowledge and protect me there, or anywhere else.

I told him I had merely spoken in haste, as the thing struck me at the moment; that it was forgotten the next, and, if I had been rude, I was ready to apologize, rather than be teased any longer on a subject which must be so uninteresting to all parties. Situated as I was, with his friend Lord Worcester, and being about to retire into Devonshire till His Lordship's return, what was the use of making acquaintances?

"Oh dear," said Julia, "what shall I do?"

"What has happened to you, pray?" I inquired.

"Oh, I am ruined—I shall be ruined! The man will arrest me, for his bill. I had all the trouble in the world to get two twenty-pound notes out of Napier, at the opera tonight, for the purpose of settling his bill with them early in the morning, and they are gone!"

Poor Julia, as she turned over her reticule for the last time, appeared the image of despair. We had only just entered Pall Mall. Meyler, glad to be employed, rather than be turned out altogether, entreated us to wait in the coach, while he ran back to search my box for Julia's banknotes.

Julia, being more in debt than she dared to acquaint her stingy lover, Napier, with; and really dreading the bailiffs every hour of her life, was miserably agitated at this accident; and, being pregnant, as usual, she was seized with violent sickness just as Meyler had left us.

"What will become of me?" said she. "I must drive off directly. I would rather go to prison than disgust that charming young man with my sickness."

I thought it cruel to keep her waiting, since she was so very ill, and therefore, seeing the watchman standing in his box, I offered to let her set me down and drive off without me.

"How can you wait, in this dress, in the middle of the streets?" Julia asked.

I told her I would put my shawl over my head, and present the watchman with a shilling, desiring his protection for a few seconds, that I might not miss Mr. Meyler with the banknotes.

Julia grew worse, and I made the coachman drive her home without me.

In about ten minutes, Meyler came running towards the spot where I stood, and appeared to be looking eagerly about for our hackney-coach.

"Here, Mr. Meyler," said I, tapping him on the arm.

"No, no, not tonight," said Meyler, pushing me from him without looking at me.

"It is Harriette," said I, and he turned round in much astonishment.

"You here alone?" said Meyler, "good heavens! I beg you ten thousand pardons."

"Julia was seized with such a violent headache and sickness, that it was misery for her to remain an instant; therefore I made her drive home without me."

Meyler was evidently delighted to find me alone, in the streets; but having discovered that nothing was to be done with me, without a little more ceremony than he at first considered would be necessary, he began by expressing his regrets that no money was to be found, and, still more, he lamented having just lent his carriage to Lady Castlereagh.

"How could I be so stupid?" said he; "but you will allow me to set you down, in a hackney-coach?"

"Certainly not," was my reply; and, lest he should again run after me, I declared that, since the evening was so warm and moonlight, I proposed walking home, if he insisted on accompanying me; and we actually walked, full dressed, from Pall Mall to Camden Town! during which said long walk, Meyler endeavoured to make himself as amiable as possible, and took his leave at my door, without teasing me for anything except permission to call on me, some morning.

He was so very pressing that I was, at last, foolish enough to say he might pay me a visit, at Julia's, on the following Thursday; and he left me quite satisfied and delighted, with having obtained so much more than he had expected from my manner of receiving his advances at the beginning of the evening.

I omitted to acquaint my readers that, just before the departure of Lord Worcester, Her Grace of Beaufort took it into her head to break the seals of my letters. It was very odd that so immaculate a lady could venture to cast her chaste eyes on the private letters of Harriette Wilson—the vile, profligate Harriette Wilson—addressed to her lover! Moreover, it was surely dishonourable and dishonest: at least, it would have been called so if I had done it; and then the Duchess declared to her son that my last letter was such an indecent one, she could not read it, and she proceeded to reason on the immorality of a paragraph at the very bottom of my paper; which proves true the old saying—liars must have good memories.

N'importe!

I called on Julia, the next morning, to acquaint her that I had taken the liberty of inviting Meyler to her house, because I knew it would make Lord Worcester miserable if I were to receive him in my own.

"I like your making apologies," said Julie, "when you know how very much I admire the lovely creature Meyler. *Apropos,*" continued Julia, "my two banknotes were in my bosom all the while, and I want, very much, to apologize to that dear little blooming, arch-looking man, for all the trouble I have given him."

I could not but fancy Julia was not so much my friend as she ought to have been, considering how anxious I had always shown myself for her welfare, in thus encouraging Meyler; and I went home more than usually interested about Lord Worcester; because Julia tried to make me neglect him.

In this humour, I sent off a few lines to Mr. Meyler, begging to be excused from my promise of meeting him at Mrs. Johnstone's. All this is infinitely amiable of me, I reflected, with much self-complacency, for I was very dull by myself, and Meyler, as to externals, was much to my taste.

Julia informed me, in the evening, that Meyler had sat with her, for more than two hours, hoping to see me, and had gone away much disappointed.

The next day, I received a letter from him, begging permission to call on me; and, as I sent no answer, he took the liberty of coming to my house without permission, and I had some difficulty, and so had my servant, in getting him out of it, and which was not till he had made every possible effort to see me, for he went upstairs, and tried to open the door of my sitting-room, which I had locked.

The moment he was very fairly out of my house, I addressed the following note to him.

Miss Wilson presents her compliments to Mr. Meyler, is under the necessity of informing him that she requires a little more respect than he seems disposed to show towards her. Mr. Meyler might have taken it for granted that, if she had been at home this morning, and disposed to receive his visits, she should not have been denied to him.

Camden Town.

On Saturday, I could not well turn Meyler out of a box in which Julia had a share without her consent, and I was teased and talked into allowing him to set us down; but nothing could induce me to admit him into my house, nor to remian alone with him an instant, anywhere.

I had promised to send Worcester a journal of everything I did; and it really is so little in my nature, that it is scarcely in my power, to be artful; and so, as I would not walk about Camden Town, to enjoy a *tête-à-tête* by moonlight, Julia was pressed into the service, and we all three wandered about the fields, and Meyler sighed, and talked downright sentimentally about leading a chaste life for my sake, and sending away all his women! At this, of course, we both laughed; but Meyler continued in the same humour for two months longer. I never received a single visit from him at my own house, and insisted, over and over again, that he should not be admitted into my opera box; but Meyler had so many little winning ways, really they were overpowering to a poor weak woman! He would tap at the door of my box, and Julia would open it, and assure him that I should quarrel with them both if she admitted him: and Meyler, instead of looking cross, would sigh! and point to a rose in his bosom, and desire Julia to tell me that it was the rose I gave him a week before, and he had preserved it with the greatest care. Then he would go downstairs, and then his legs were so beautiful, and his skin so clear and transparent, and Meyler was sentimental for the first time in his life!

Really all these things, and thirty thousand a year besides, were enough to melt a heart of stone: and, as we were going out of the opera, we were sure to see Meyler's bright smile, as he stood watching for us. Then, if there was the least difficulty about coaches, etc., he would come up and say mildly that his carriage was at the door, and, if we would use it, he would not enter it, but go home in a friend's. In short, Meyler was so very humble, persevering, and indefatigable, that he contrived to see and converse with me every day of my life, in spite of all I could do to prevent him, although I never once admitted him to my house, or to a *tête-à-tête*, and I wrote Worcester a full and most exact account of all my proceedings. I even went so far as to tell him, I really was afraid Meyler's attentions might create a very strong fancy, notwithstanding I certainly had no esteem for him. To prevent the possibility of this, I proposed retiring into some quiet village in Devonshire.

This my readers, I mean my young and handsome readers, will admit was a sort of thing easier said than done. London was so very gay! Meyler so very attentive! *Tout le monde* seemed so very much to admire my person, and delight in my conversation! and I was about to leave all this for a dull village, where I was to pass one of the most brilliant years of my life in perfect solitude.

"I will make any settlement on you you may please to ask of me," said Meyler, "if you will but leave Worcester, and live with me."

"You have told me this at least fifty times already," I replied, "and you really may spare yourself any further useless trouble. I must follow the dictates of my heart, whatever may become of me. There will be a consolation in a clear conscience, and, in leaving Worcester, I should feel that I deserved the worst that could happen to me, and both your lives might be lost in a duel; or, if Worcester was killed abroad, having first cursed me for my conduct, I should never get over it: else, you know I am full half in love with you, and Worcester knows well I was never, one bit, in love with him."

"Then, if you do love me," said Meyler, "I will hold myself disengaged, and wait for my chance of you, during the whole of that year you have promised to wait for Worcester's return."

I laughed at Meyler's promises, assuring him I had not the least faith in them.

Worcester was eternally writing to me, and nothing could be more romantically tender than his letters. No power on earth could tempt him, or should ever induce him, while he breathed, to even bestow a single kiss on any woman's lips but mine, etc. Then followed very excellent descriptions of battles, with a long account of Parker for Fanny.

These very kind letters at length determined me to leave London.

The last evening I passed in town was truly a dull one, to me. No doubt, thought I, this gay, young, volatile creature, surrounded as he is by temptation, will forget me in less than a month! I am unprovided for, and am leaving every friend on earth, to wander about for a lone lodging, in a dismal village. It cannot be helped! Worcester's mind must be set at rest; because there was nothing he was not ready to do for me.

"Where is there a village?" said I to Luttrell, who informed me that there was a village called Charmouth, within thirty miles of Exeter, which, as he once passed through it, had struck him as particularly picturesque.

"That will do," said I, sick of the dry, dull subject; and I took a place for myself and my *femme de chambre* in the Exeter mail without further delay.

Meyler was half cooled, as soon as I was quite determined to leave London; but still he was very melancholy.

Might he write to me? he inquired.

"Yes," said I, "but your letters will be shown to Worcester, mind; so you must confine yourself to mere friendship. If, however, circumstances force me to leave His Lordship, and you are good enough to remember me with kindness, I will gladly come to you."

"In a year, then," said Meyler, "if Worcester does not return?"

"All that must depend on circumstances," I replied.

Meyler shed one tear at parting—*c'était beaucoup pour lui*, and he gave me a gold toothpick-case, with some of his hair in it; so, having taken leave of Fanny and Julia, fancy me, and my maid, in the Exeter mail, on our road to Charmouth.

In about two weeks after my arrival in this village, my reader may imagine me sitting at a little rural thatched window, in that beautiful country, addressing the following long letter to my sister Fanny.

CHARMOUTH, DEVONSHIRE.

My DEAREST SISTER,

I really am afraid you will accuse me of want of affection towards you, in having suffered a whole fortnight to elapse, without acquainting you of my arrival in this part of the world. The fact is, my constitution is really good for nothing, and I have only just recovered the fatigues of two successive nights passed in the mail-coach.

To begin, then, we got here at about six in the evening, without anything in the least romantic having occurred to us; for we were neither ravished, upset, nor thrown into a pond just as a lovely youth happened to be passing by.

One of these incidents ought really to have occurred; mais enfin que voulez-vous? It was a beautiful May evening, when the mail-coach set us down at a little country-looking sort of pot-house, in this village. I was wretchedly oppressed by melancholy and fatigue! I inquired for beds, and was informed, by very good luck, that my landlady's only bedroom, containing two small, neat, white beds, was at our disposal. The staircase was a ladder, or rather a ladder was the staircase. We will not be particular. I was soon in bed, and my maid contrived to procure me a cup of tea, which is all I remember happening to me till about eight the next morning, when the broad sun, shining in my face, for want of window-curtains, induced me to rise. As for my maid, she was already dressed, and busy with my trunks, searching out my clean linen. I am sorry, really, for the most noble the Marquis of Worcester! but the fact is, my very first thoughts on awakening, and my most sincere regrets, were for the miles which now separated me from poor little beautiful Meyler. In short, having done everything right towards Worcester, I loved him much less for that very reason.

After our breakfast, we inquired for a guide, to show us some of the beauties of that part of the country.

"My little boy will take you over to Lyme Regis. He is particularly cute, and can tell you more than I can," said the good landlady.

Behold us, then, on our road to Lyme Regis, with a little cute Devonshire lad for our guide. I cannot describe the scenery, like Mrs. Radcliffe; I wish I could; but, alas! I have not an idea of the kind, and yet I can feel and enjoy it. Lyme Regis is a sort of Brighton in miniature, all bustle and confusion, assembly-rooms, donkey-riding, raffling, etc. etc. It was sixpence per night to attend the assemblies, and much cheaper if paid by the season. We went to a little inn and dined. From the window, I was much amused to see the number of smart old maids that were tripping down the streets, in turbans or artificial flowers twined around their wigs, on the light fantastic toe, to the sixpenny assembly-rooms, at five in the evening!! They were very pleasantly situated, near the sea, and as we walked past their windows, we saw them all drinking tea and playing at cards. There were, amongst them, persons of the highest rank; but the society was chiefly composed of people of very small independent fortunes, who, for economy, had settled at Lyme Regis; or of such as required sea-bathing; natives either of Exeter or any neighbouring town. There were plenty of furnished lodgings to be let at Lyme Regis; but I determined, if possible, to establish myself at Charmouth, that place being so much more to my taste.

"It will be impossible, Madam," said the landlady where we dined, "since Charmouth is a very genteel village, inhabited by persons of small fortunes, who would not condescend to let lodgings, or take in boarders. There are not, perhaps, three dozen houses, in the whole village, and certainly not one lodging-house. All are independent and proud, except the owners of a few huts, round about that neighbourhood, to whom the gentry of Charmouth are very kind and charitable."

"Well then, I must return, much against my will, to establish myself here," said I. This idea increased my melancholy! for I hate, and always did hate, anything like London in miniature! give me town or country en grand! Solitude, or the best society; but I abhor little sixpenny assembly-places.

At eight o'clock in the evening, we arrived at our humble inn at Charmouth, in a donkey-cart, and immediately retired to rest. Next morning at a little after seven the gay and fashionable Harriette Wilson was to be seen strolling about the little village of Charmouth, as though it had been her native place, and she had never heard tell of the pomps and vanities of this very wicked world, or the sinful lusts of the flesh, etc.

We carefully examined every house we passed, for a bill indicative of lodgings to let: but in vain. They all appeared to be inhabited by some respectable individual, neither rich nor poor. We had walked twice through the village, and round about it, and were bending our steps towards our little pot-house, in mute despair, when my attention was arrested by the striking loveliness of a young lady who was watering some flowers at one of the windows of a house I had before admired for its peculiar neatness. She smiled so very graciously that I was encouraged in my wish to address her. The moment she saw me make towards the little street door, she ran and opened it herself. After many apologies, I entreated to be informed if I was likely to succeed in obtaining board and lodging with any private family at Charmouth. The young lady entreated me to walk into the parlour and sit down. We chatted together for about a quarter of an hour, like people who had taken a liking to each other, and then she left me to speak to her mother on the subject of procuring me a comfortable residence. In a short time she returned, and presented me to two very respectable-looking women, in deep mourning, as her mother and aunt. After a little more conversation, Mrs. Edmond, which was the name of the young lady's mother, spoke to me, to this effect: "I am the widow of an officer in the navy, whose death, when abroad, I learned ten years ago from a brother-officer, who had been present, and came here to convey his last requests to his family; since that moment, having for ever renounced the world, I live only in my child, and have nothing to do, on earth, but attend to and promote her happiness. She feels greatly disposed to benefit by your pleasant society, and has made it her anxious request that I will offer you an asylum in my house; therefore, if you like to inhabit a snug room, which faces the country, it is at your service, and you may keep it entirely for your own use. I have also a servant's room for your maid, and, if you can accustom yourself to our family dinner, the thing is arranged at once."

I could scarcely conceal my surprise, at finding such good, innocent, confiding people, ready thus to take a stranger in without making a single inquiry. However, as I determined to act with the strictest propriety, and conform to the established rules of the family, to be regular at church, too, for the sake of example, I conceived that it was certainly not incumbent on me to turn king's evidence against myself, as to my former irregularities, or, as my friend Miss Higgins would say, little peccadilloes. I pressed them to name terms, for me and my maid, at once, and the price they asked for being troubled with us both was so ridiculously moderate, that I insisted on doubling it, and refused to hear another word on the subject.

Everything, which the warmest affection or the oldest friendship could have *dictated, was put in practice for our comfort and accommodation. I had a nice bed-room, adjoining the snug little sitting-room, where I am now writing; but I have swelled my letter to such an enormous length, that I must defer saying any more about these good people, till my next. I am very anxious to hear from you, and I confess I should like to know if Meyler has entirely forgotten me.*

Pray write soon, to a poor melancholy recluse, and believe me ever,

Your most affectionate sister,

H.W.

P.S. How do Amy and her schoolmaster of Athens go on?

CHAPTER 19

TWO DAYS AFTER I had dispatched this letter, the little postwoman (for we had no postman), a good old soul, trotted *à l'Esterhazy* down the hill with a lanthorn; the mail used to come into Charmouth at ten o'clock at night, and Eliza Edmond and I had watched this poor creature, every night, during almost a fortnight, from my little window, as the light of her lamp appeared for an instant, and was lost again, while she stopped to deliver her letters. At last she stopped at our door, and presented two heavy packages for Mrs. Wilson.

The kind, warm-hearted Miss Edmond came flying upstairs, and was breathless when she delivered them.

"One of these is a foreign letter, and, no doubt, from your husband," said Eliza, kissing my cheek, while her eyes sparkled with such unaffected benevolent joy as made her beauty appear more than human.

I hastily examined the address of the first which was presented to me: it was from Lord Worcester, and the real anxiety I felt to learn his safety overcoming all curiosity about Meyler, I broke the seal of this, while the other, unexamined, had fallen to the ground.

"It is from your husband, then?" asked Eliza, and, having answered her in the affirmative, she had the delicacy to glide out of the room, like a spirit, before I was aware of it.

Worcester had already been in one action. He had prayed to me, as to his tutelar saint, kissed my chain, which he wore about his neck, and his party had been successful. He wrote in high spirits, and gave me what, by excellent judges of those matters, was afterwards considered one of the most accurate descriptions of a battle ever written by any officer. The letter ended, like all the rest of his letters, with vows of eternal love and fidelity; and he assured me that he had already learned to speak Spanish. What a clever man this might have been, had he but the habit of reflection, methought: for Lord Worcester's memory often astonished me.

Having finished reading Lord Worcester's letter, I hastened to examine the second epistle, which had fallen to the ground. It was, as I suspected, or rather as I hoped, from Meyler. He had at first, he said, determined to forget me, since there was so very little chance of our ever meeting again.

However that, as he was pleased to add, was out of the question. He was in fact unwell, and required Devonshire air. I must not be surprised, therefore, to see him in my neighbourhood. He had only once called on Julia, since I left town; because, seeing my friends only added to his melancholy, now I was gone. There was nothing like Worcester's sort of rapture in his letter, yet something melancholy and interesting about his style of writing, which appeared perfectly unaffected.

Meyler was anything rather than romantic: his manner and voice were particularly pleasing at all times; but the former had, generally, something of melancholy, till he had drank a few bottles of claret, though not at all noisy or ungentlemanlike, he appeared all animation and happiness.

I was a good deal affected by his letter, and the idea that I had no chance of seeing him again; nevertheless I immediately answered his letter as follows.

CHARMOUTH.

MY DEAR MR. MEYLER,

I must candidly confess that I am glad that you have not forgotten me; and I wish you happy, with all my heart and soul; but, believe me, I cannot prove myself more desirous of being liked and esteemed by you, than I have done and shall continue to do.

As I keep my faith to Worcester, so hereafter will you be inclined to trust me, if any unexpected circumstance should oblige me to separate from him. In the meantime, I must throw myself on your honour and kindness. As to your idea of intruding your society on me in Devonshire, I assure you that, on the very day of your arrival, I shall hold myself in readiness to leave these very hospitable, new friends, who have been so very kind to me; but you are, of course, only joking! How, in fact, can I be so ridiculous as to fancy, for an instant, the rich, handsome, gay Meyler, would so far astonish the natives of this little village as to come and establish himself among us? How you would laugh to see me, in my quiet straw-bonnet, trotting down the hill to church, and lending my arm to the curate's father, aged ninety-five! After church, I appear in the character of my Lady Bountiful paying visits to the sick, followed by my maid, bearing my good host's medicine, with my own wine and broth. Charity is stimulated where, here the number of poor is so limited that, by each of us contributing our mite, we may hope to meet only smiling, happy faces in our walks.

Last week I found a poor woman, and six fine, beautiful children, without a roof to her house: for a trifle, I made it a comparative paradise, and now Miss Edmond and her mother are employed in making up the stuff-frocks I purchased for the children. But enough of Harriette Wilson as Lady Bountiful.

I suppose you will soon get into Parliament, à présent que vous avez vingt et un ans bien sommés. Do you see much of your favourite the Duchess of Beaufort now? Pray tell me all the news you can scrape together. Of course, the Beauforts have received news from Lord Worcester long ago? My last letter from His Lordship, which I received with yours, had been delayed by being directed to London. My old beau, Wellington, is going on famously, thanks to the fineness of his nerves, and his want of feeling, and his excellent luck. I do not mean to say he has not a good notion of commanding an army; for, though I do not understand things, I am willing to take it for granted that this is the case.

I will now take my leave, with sincerest wishes for your welfare and happiness; therefore, whether we meet again or not,

God bless you,

H.W.

Though I remained a year at Charmouth, I really can remember no one incident that occurred to me, during the whole of my *séjour* there, worthy the attention of my readers.

Mrs. Edmond was invariably obliging, gentle and melancholy; her sister, my Aunt Martha, as Eliza Edmond used to call her, was a very merry, comical old maid. Eliza was, without any one exception but that of my beloved mother, the most truly virtuous being, according to my acceptation of the word virtuous, which does not mean chastity only, I ever met with in my whole life.

Eliza was too religious, too devoted to the observance of every form of the Christian faith, to have cast an eye of love on anything but a parson; and her heart would therefore have been safe, but that, unluckily, a certain black-eyed, most libidinous divine, having been thrown into her society, just before I became acquainted with her, his hypocrisy had proved more than a match for poor Eliza's simplicity; and she had loved him, from the belief that he was most pure and holy. My readers may conceive what her feelings must have been, when this first object of her warmest, devoted love, finally declared to her that their marriage must be kept secret, since his family would never receive her as their daughter.

From that hour, Eliza had never seen her lover, and no power on earth could have induced her to consent to a single interview.

"You are, then, very proud, Eliza," said I to her, after her mother had related this story to me in her presence.

"Do you call my love of God pride?" asked Eliza. "If ever I had married, my husband, after my God, would have been nearest my heart.

Could I respect the husband who would deceive his parents? or would you have had me force myself into a family which despised me?"

I never saw Eliza so agitated, and, observing the crimson blush on her cheek, I said, "You are very proud, Eliza, after all, that is the truth."

Eliza's quivering lip was now pale as death, as she raised her eyes to heaven, and, in the next instant, she rushed out of the room.

Eliza's mother placed her hand gently on my shoulder, seeing that I was about to follow her daughter.

"Eliza is gone to pray," said Mrs. Edmond, mildly. "You have frightened her; but, it was not, I am sure, intentionally. You know not how very delicate is her conscience; how pure, yet how ardent are her feelings! Pray go to her in about a quarter of an hour. I would not have her dwell longer on what you have said; for Eliza is consumptive. She will be taken from me soon enough, by God's will; we must not cause her unnecessary agitation."

Eliza, generally speaking, was more cheerful than persons usually are when they are dying; and nobody expected that poor Eliza would live beyond five and twenty.

We were often invited to little family tea-parties, where we passed our time comfortably enough, though most gay London ladies would have been bored to death; but I thank Nature for bestowing on me a contented disposition.

Meyler wrote to me constantly: sometimes he was melancholy; then he determined to join me, whether I would or not; he next declared that I was cold and selfish, and that he would forget me: at last, he almost teased me out of a promise, or rather a half-promise that if, at the end of the year, there were new obstacles thrown in the way of my joining Worcester, or His Lordship's returning to me, I would put myself at once under Meyler's protection.

In the meantime Lord Worcester corresponded with me as regularly and lovingly as I could possibly desire, and so did Fanny. In answer to one of my letters to her, written nearly three months after my arrival in Devonshire, I received the following:

MY DEAR HARRIETTE,

Many thanks for your last kind letter, in which you inclose my Lord Worcester's, containing so much news of Colonel Parker. I was, indeed, in want of consolation; for I am very melancholy, and my cough is still rather troublesome, although not bad enough to have prevented my attendance at the opera, which closed but last night for the season.

All the gay world are constantly asking me about you. As to Mr. Meyler, we have seen but little of him. Last night, however, we observed him in the pit; and so did Amy, who was of our party: she immediately sent somebody down to request him to join us, and her messenger returned, bringing Meyler with him. He looks very well, and, as usual, particularly interesting. He asked Julia and me at least a thousand questions about you. Amy, to change the disagreeable subject, invited him to sup with her; but he begged to be excused, provokingly adding that her house would make him melancholy, by reminding him of you. Amy could scarcely conceal her ill humour at this answer. Julia asked him if he really meant to say he had not forgotten you, all this time? and he seriously declared that he had never loved you better, nor any being else half so well: and then the poor little man sighed quite naturally, as though he could not help it; but though I do not mean to hurt your vanity, I fancy there was something of ill health in that sigh of his. However, perhaps this is a mere fancy of mine, for Mr. Meyler himself, who ought to be the best judge, professes to be in remarkably good health, and he is known to ride very hard in Leicestershire. But there is something so remarkably transparent about Meyler's skin, it is, in fact, a church-yard-skin, like my own, I think, I hope I am mistaken, too: for it would be hard to die, in the bloom of youth and beauty, beloved by everybody, and with thirty thousand a year.

My children, thank heaven, are all well, although I really feared my dear Louisa would have died last week, owing to my extreme folly in having suffered myself to be persuaded into administering one of Inglish's Scott's pills to the poor baby, out of sister Paragon's box. All Pandora's box of evils could scarcely have done more mischief. The child was absoluetly convulsed with pain, while provoking sister Paragon looked on, calmly declaring that it was the first duty of an aperient to gripe the patient as much as possible.

Pray write a very long letter soon, and believe me, at all times, your most affectionate sister,

FANNY PARKER.

His Grace of Beaufort had passed his word as to the regular, quarterly payment of an allowance, which Worcester stipulated should be paid me if he left England; yet four months had now elapsed, without my having been able to obtain a single shilling from the Duke, or even an answer to my letters, in which I assured him that all my ready money was gone, and that I was entirely destitute of the means of existence.

The Duke, perhaps, hoped to starve me into putting up with the first, man I could find; at all events, it was clear I might have starved, or begged, or thrown myself into the streets, before he would have offered me the least assistance while he could possibly have avoided it; and, in this amiable conduct, I take it for granted he was upheld and encouraged by his most interesting Duchess.

I was now in debt, a whole quarter, for board and lodging. Never having once doubted the Duke's word of honour, conveyed to me by his man of business, in the presence of his son; and, being so far from London, I sat down to consider who I could possibly consult, in that part of the world, as to what was to become of me.

The only person in my neighbourhood whose face I had ever seen before, was an old, cracked sort of a general, his name I have forgotten. I never had but a mere bowing acquaintance with him, from the circumstance of his being my next door neighbour in London, where he bore the character of a terrible deceiver of maids and maidservants! In short, I do not believe there was a single girl of that description, within two miles of us, with whom he had not scraped a kind of acquaintance.

When I saw him first, at Charmouth, I cut him dead; but being now really anxious to consult someone who knew a little about me, I took the liberty of nodding to him the next time I met him.

"Oh, oh, my fair neighbour! I really feared I had been so unfortunate as to have offended you. How do you do, pray?"

We then entered into conversation, and as I discovered that he, like half the rest of the world, had heard all about Worcester and me, I consulted him as to what was to be done.

"Don't you know Fisher, the lady-killer of these parts?" he inquired.

"Heaven forbid!" said I.

"Why so?" asked the General. "He is a most particularly sharp fellow, and being a lawyer, who knows who you are, and all about you, he is the very man to consult."

"But then, I am so afraid of the persons with whom I am living," said I.

"Be assured," answered the General, "that Fisher will be secret as to your business. I will tell him you mean to apply to him, and you may depend upon his honour. I am sure he will put you up to a plan of making that shabby Duke of Beaufort treat you better."

"But why is he called a lady-killer?"

"He is the beauty of Devonshire. Such black eyes! and six foot high!" answered the General.

"The very things I hate in a man, so I am safe, and may consult your Mr. Fisher, and yet hope to die a natural death after all."

I took my leave of this comical old man, and on the very same evening addressed the following note to the gay Mr. Fisher, of Lyme Regis.

Sir,

A friend of yours has, I trust, acquainted you with my motive for wishing to see you. As the family with which I am staying is unacquainted with my real situation, I should wish to consult you without their knowledge, if you will be kind enough to say how that can be managed. If you will tell me the proper hour, in the morning, I will go to Lyme Regis.

> *I remain, Sir,*
> *Your most obedient humble servant,*
>
> H. Wilson.

"What sort of a man is Mr. Fisher, the attorney, of Lyme Regis?" said I to Eliza, after I had carried my letter to the post office.

"Oh, he is a very gay man indeed; a very shocking man, they say; indeed, I have heard that he makes love to several women at the same time, although he is a married man; but it would be uncharitable of us to suppose anything so wicked as that."

I could not help laughing at poor Eliza, who must have been meant for the golden age.

The next evening, the little old postwoman, for whom Eliza and I had been watching till we were nearly worn out, condescended to bend her steps, little lanthorn and all, towards our door. Down flew Eliza and, this time, presented me with three letters; the postmark on one of them was Lyme Regis; so, guessing this to be from Eliza's terrible man, Mr. Fisher, I put it into my reticule unopened. The other two were from Meyler and Worcester. I beg His Lordship's pardon, for putting him last; it was not, certainly, done with any intention to offend, but quite naturally. Meyler, having tried every other argument to induce me to leave Charmouth and Lord Worcester, now ventured on a threat!

"You have a husband, with whom you are, it seems, quite satisfied; or rather a lover, for whom, too, you cheerfully resign me, and the income I have offered you, to assist those methodistical Edmonds, in feeding their pigs and chickens! *Grand bien vous fasse!* I, too, shall take unto myself a wife, as the Quaker says, and verily the spirit has moved me towards a certain fair one, and in sundry places."

The letter continued with some Melton news, and an account of his having hurt his right arm, which would prevent his playing at tennis for the rest of his life. He would rather have lost half his estate, upon his honour. He was, at last, chosen for Winchester, after a severe contested election, which had cost him twenty thousand pounds; but then it was well worth that sum to be independent. Not that he should be very active either way. In fact, Lord Bath had been kind enough to point out to him the best seat in the lower house for taking a nap.

Meyler's letter ended with many tender professions and entreaties that I would go to him.

Worcester's letter, of three sheets, crossed and recrossed, only contained matter for four pages, leaving out the dearest darlings! angel-wives! loveliest, sweetest, adorable, own own, everlastingly to be worshipped, etc.

We are, says Worcester's letter, only my readers must hold in mind that I am leaving out His Lordship's ohs and ahs! *we are within a stone's throw of the enemy. God only knows whether I shall be permitted to see you again or not. Your chain is round my neck, and as for your picture, I could not press my lips near enough to your sweet delicious eyes, without taking off the glass; and now, alas! I have kissed the left eye out, altogether, with your under lip. I am dreadfully melancholy! but, being so close to the enemy, pray don't tell anybody. If ever your heart beats against my own, and I leave you again, may I——*

But oaths are all nonsense, particularly those of noble lords, marquises, and dukes; besides, if I were to go on with the most noble the Marquis of Worcester's letter, I might tumble upon something indecent. Who knows; we are but mortal! even marquises and dukes are but mortal! and the weather is so hot in Spain and Portugal!

Poor Worcey! You ought to have seen me provided for, and yet I can never quite forget how dearly you loved me, when you gave up all society, endured almost a parent's curse! nay, more, gave up hunting! and offered to support me by driving a mail-coach!!

No, young man: never mind what I sometimes write and say. Upon my honour; upon my soul, to give you the expressions out of Lord Ponsonby's last letter, I do not, and never shall quite forget you!

The third letter was, as I supposed, from the provincial Adonis, Mr. Fisher; as follows:

MADAM,

Since secrecy is an object with you, I request you will come to my chambers just after it is dark, on Thursday next, that being the only hour I can command, as free from the interruption of clients; it being my constant habit to refuse admittance to strangers after daylight, although I do not leave my chambers till my papers are all arranged for my clerks, who attend here before eight in the morning.

> *Obediently yours,*
>
> CHARLES FREDERICK FISHER.

What a wretch! said I, to myself, as soon as I had read Mr. Fisher's eloquent epistle. I meet this dirty Devonshire lawyer after dark, indeed!! I wish Worcester was here. If he had really loved me, as he affects to do, he would have died rather than have left me to be thus insulted by this black, dirty, nasty, six-foot-high country attorney!! Meet him at dark!! What could one do with such a wretch, either by day or night, or any kind of light? The monster!! To flatter himself for an instant.

I hastily opened my writing-desk, and addressed the following letter to Beau Fisher.

SIR,

Whether I am, or am not, Lord Worcester's wife, be assured that he has too much respect for me, to permit a country attorney to insult me by his invitations to meet him in the dark. You may, of course, do as you please, with regard to the secrecy I mentioned; but it is my, and Lord Worcester's pleasure, that you never presume to insult me again with your odious and very humiliating proposals.

> *I remain your most obedient,*
>
> HARRIETTE.

After I had put this letter in the post office, the next morning, I strolled down to the sea coast, and again met the old general. He came skipping towards me, in great glee.

"You are the very person I wanted to see," said he. "I saw Fisher last night, and he told me he had just answered your note, to assure you that he should feel happy in being able to render you the slightest service."

"Pray don't mention Mr. Fisher to me," answered I, with much dignity.

"Why not?" inquired the General, in surprise.

"Why, he has written me the most insulting letter possible. He desires me to go to his chambers at dark."

"Impossible!" said the General.

"How do you mean, impossible?" I asked.

"Do you really mean to say that Fisher ever hinted anything like a wish to be favoured by you?"

"How do you mean, favoured?"

"May I speak plainly?"

"I beg you will, General," answered I, impatiently.

"Do you really believe Fisher wanted to intrigue with you?"

"You may well be surprised at the wretch's presumption," said I.

"No," interrupted the General, "Fisher would never surprise me by his presumption. I know him too well for that; but, since you permit me to be frank, I will tell you what Fisher said of you the other day."

"Go on."

"You promise not to be offended?"

"I never was offended in the whole course of my life with persons for whom I have no regard, although one sometimes might seem indignant when vulgar people presume to be too impertinent."

The General commenced: "Says Fisher to me, the other day, says Fisher, just as you were passing by, 'What in the name of the devil can Lord Worcester see to admire in that ugly piece of goods? why, I vow to God, I would not have her if she were to fall on her knees to me. She has not a good point about her.'"

"How very funny it will be if I have mistaken his intentions," said I, and I burst into a loud laugh: the idea struck me as so perfectly absurd and comical!

At ten in the morning, I opened my eyes, and saw Eliza's pretty smiling face at my bedside, with a letter in her hand.

"A manservant has just brought this letter, from Lyme Regis, and waits to know if you have any answer to send back?" said Eliza.

I was seized with such a violent fit of laughter, after the perusal of Mr. Fisher's letter, that poor Eliza really thought I was mad. It was as follows:

MADAM,

Your misinterpretation of my last note, is, indeed, truly astonishing! I can only assure you, madam, upon my honour, that I have not, and I never had, the slightest wish or intention to meet you, but as a man of business.

Your very obedient, humble servant,

C. F. FISHER.

"What can you be laughing at so violently?" Eliza inquired.

"Oh, you must excuse me," answered I, still laughing.

"Any answer for the servant?"

"Oh, yes. Pray ask him to wait a few minutes," said I, addressing myself to my maid: and I then hastily wrote the following answer to Mr. Fisher's tender effusion:

SIR,

By your letter, I have to apprehend that there was no real cause of alarm! I cannot express my dismay, but must console myself with the hope, and in the belief, that you are all a century behind hand, as to good taste, in this part of the world.

I beg to remain, Sir,
Your most obliged, and very devoted, humble servant,

HARRIETTE.

I waited another month, in the vain expectation of receiving the promised allowance from the Duke of Beaufort, and then I wrote to him as follows:

Lord Worcester agreed to go abroad, on condition that I was taken care of, and I promised to remain in England for one year, during which time you pledged yourself to send me a quarterly allowance, or rather your man of business pledged himself, in your name, in the presence of your son.

I conceive a conditional engagement to be null and void, when the conditions are not fulfilled. I therefore propose immediately joining Lord Worcester in Spain, in case I do not receive a due remittance from your Grace by return of post. I cannot help adding, that I should be very sorry to act with such want of feeling, towards my greatest enemy, as you have invariably shown towards me, who have, from first to last, made every sacrifice in my power for your peace and happiness.

I remain,
Your Grace's most obedient,
humble servant,

H. WILSON.

By return of post, I received a very polite answer from the Duke of Beaufort, inclosing me a quarter's allowance, with some very plausible excuse: I really forget what it was; but I think he said the delay was not his fault, but Mr. Robinson's. Mere nonsense, of course; since my frequent applications could not have miscarried, and His Grace never once condescended to write till I threatened to join Worcester, after which he was afraid to lose a single post.

I am now growing tired of Devonshire, and so, I hope and trust, are my readers. I propose giving them very little more news from that quarter. I remained there exactly twelve months, during which time the only two persons I beheld who had been before known to me, were Lord Burghersh, whose estates are, I believe, in that part of the world, who opened his eyes wide with astonishment, at meeting me and the old general there.

My dear mother and sister Fanny regularly corresponded with me, and Meyler was more sanguine than usual, as the year got to a close. He declared that he had no sort of fancy for anybody on earth but me, nor ever had since the very beginning of our acquaintance. Worcester also wrote, in high spirits, stating that nothing should detain him in Spain an hour after the expiration of twelve months.

At last, oh killing news! just as I was in the expectation of Worcester, to fly away with me from Charmouth, which was all in his road from Spain, came a letter, it ought to have been sealed with black wax, to say that the Prince Regent, rather than Worcester should return to love and me, was about to oblige the Duke of Beaufort, while he gave the brave and dandy warriors of the 10th an opportunity of distinguishing themselves. To be brief, Worcester's regiment was ordered abroad. Could he possibly, he wrote, come home at such a moment? But then, his own darling angel, sweet Harriette, would come to him! Of this he felt sure, etc.

"My dear Eliza, I must go to Spain," said I, as soon as I had finished this letter.

The whole house was in tears.

Eliza's aunt, Martha, declared that she would accompany me to Falmouth, and see me sail. "I am old enough, and thank God I am no beauty," said Aunt Martha, "and I may do what I please with my own little fortune. I have never yet been ten miles from my native place, and I want to see the world."

Fresh floods of tears were now forced out for my Aunt Martha; however, go she would.

"The worst of it is," continued Aunt Martha, "that my habit is five and twenty years old, and as to travelling without a habit, that is quite impossible."

"I think, between us all three, we can alter it into something smart and fashionable," said Eliza, and the next hour saw them occupied in unpicking, cutting, and basting, at my Aunt Martha's most ample calico habit.

At last we were seated in the Falmouth mail, on a fine clear summer morning. We travelled all day and all night, and poor Aunt Martha was half dead with fatigue, on the following evening, when we were set down at the first-rate inn at Falmouth.

We begged the chambermaid to conduct us immediately to a good two-bedded room.

"Oh, ladies," announced the woman, pertly, "you must take what you can get; for we are so full that I don't know where on earth to put half of you, owing to the wind having been so directly contrary for more than three weeks. Thus ships are, every day, coming in, while all the passengers for Spain have been waiting at Falmouth these three weeks, and we have got a consul, or ambassador, or something great, of that kind, who has occupied all our best rooms for the last fortnight, with his secretaries and black footmen, and all the rest of it."

"Had we not better try another inn?" said I to my Aunt Martha.

But she declared herself so very ill and fatigued, having never travelled before, that she could not move.

"And if you could," said the chambermaid, "you would only fare the worse for your pains, since there is scarcely a bed to be found in all Falmouth."

"Well, what can you do for us?" I inquired despairingly, for I was both tired and spiritless.

"Why, as luck would have it, a gentleman as was going to Spain, is just gone off by the London mail, because he had no more patience to wait here for change of weather, and his room has got two little beds in it; but it is up in the garrett."

"Never mind," said poor Aunt Martha; and we were soon settled for the night, in a very comfortless-looking room, far away from either chambermaids or waiters, and nothing like a bell was to be discovered.

For the three first days of our inhabiting this garret, we really ran the risk of being starved, as it was impossible to procure any attendance. True, in scampering about the house to search for bread, tea, or butter, our noses were regaled by the excellent ragouts, as the Consul's black servants were carrying them to their master's table.

We were very anxious to look about us a little; but Aunt Martha had been told that Falmouth was such a wicked town that, for four days, we had kept our room.

The fifth, finding it impossible to procure any single thing to eat, good or bad, owing to the arrival of another vessel from the Peninsula, we were absolutely forced out of our delicate alarms, and resolved to go out and purchase a cold tongue and some biscuits.

As we entered the inn, after filling our reticules with eatables, we stepped back, while the Consul or Ambassador, I forget which, who ate up all our dinner, and was the chief cause of such a terrible famine in the inn, stepped into his gay carriage. I thought I had seen his face; but I really could not recollect where. He appeared to recognize me too, by the manner he looked at me. We mounted up into our dismal room, very much out of spirits, having ascertained that the wind was exactly in the same unlucky quarter.

The next day, the chambermaid brought me a polite note from the Consul, to request the favour of our company to dinner, as often as we could make it convenient, *sans cérémonie*. He had often had the pleasure of seeing me in London, or he should not have taken the liberty, which he had the less scruple in doing, having been led to understand we were so very badly attended on.

"Well! this is something like!" said my Aunt Martha, bridling; for I forgot to inform my readers, that my Aunt Martha was still on the right side of fifty, and though her countenance had never, even in her youngest days, possessed any other attraction than an expression of extreme good nature and animation, still that was something; and then, her habit, which was composed of curiously fine cloth, had not been altered into as becoming a form as possible. On the whole, my Aunt Martha, while she admitted I must have been the principal attraction, really did hope she had stood for something in this invitation.

"How I regret not having seen something of life a little sooner," said Aunt Martha, as she stood before the glass, settling her ruff.

Aunt Martha was so long settling the form of her lace-cap, that the Consul and his two secretaries were waiting dinner for us when we entered the room. He politely introduced the young gentlemen to us. The name of the handsomest was Brown; I have forgotten the other. I whispered to the Consul, at the very first opportunity, that my friend was unacquainted with my situation, or the name of Lord Worcester, believing me to be an officer's wife, of the name of Wilson; and he promised to be discreet. He was a very pleasing man, of about forty-five or fifty, and, being really under such obligation to him, for his great politeness, I am particularly sorry that I cannot recollect his name. I hope, if ever he condescends to read my memoirs, that he will, through this medium, accept my thanks.

The dinner was served up in the very best style of elegance. What a contrast to our scanty fare in our garret! After dinner, the young men proposed going to the play, since Mathews was engaged there for a few nights. The Consul, however, declared we must excuse him, but good-naturedly requested the secretaries to chaperon us there, promising to have a good supper for us on our return.

"Oh, if I had but slipped my new purple silk dress into my portmanteau," whispered Aunt Martha.

On our return from the play we found an excellent supper ready, and the good Consul was himself making us some punch, in case we should happen to be tired of champagne and claret. After supper we had a waltz. Mr. Brown kindly undertook to give my Aunt Martha her first lesson, which created much merriment. It was nearly three o'clock before we got to bed, and, in this manner we kept it up for almost three weeks, dining regularly, when not otherwise engaged, at the Consul's table.

I had been an unusual length of time without letters from Lord Worcester, and as I could not doubt their being immediately forwarded to me by Mrs. Edmond, if any had arrived at Charmouth, I grew uneasy; and having learned, by accident, that a young officer who had just arrived from headquarters was in the house I requested, in a note, that he would allow me to ask him a few questions. He came to me instantly, and in answer to my various inquiries about Worcester, with whom, he said, he was not personally acquainted, he hinted something of a story, that Mrs. Archdeacon, the sister of the paymaster's second wife, who formerly made such an attack on Worcester's virtue at Brighton, and who was living with her husband at Lisbon, had been ran away with by the Marquis of Worcester.

"Are you certain of this?" I inquired, without, I confess, much agitation.

He was not, he said; but it was a fact that Mrs. Archdeacon had left her husband, and gone up to the army with somebody. He knew that the Marquis, when he last came down to Lisbon, had been in the habit of dining with Mr. Archdeacon and his wife.

This fool! thought I, after tormenting his parents, and keeping me here, lest he should die!—after refusing the prayers of his father, whose very life seemed to depend on leaving me, suddenly takes another woman away, notwithstanding his last letter was as full of solemn vows of ever-lasting constancy as any he ever wrote. What steadiness could I expect from such an ass as Worcester? I'll go to London: that's settled! Life is short, and I have been quite patient enough. I don't care one straw about money; but I must have something like enjoyment of some sort, before I die. Another story decided me. I heard two days after my interview with the officer, it was whispered about Lisbon, that, supposing Harriette Wilson made an attempt to join Lord Worcester, the English Ambassador had the power to get her put on board an American ship, and sent to America!

"I have received letters which require my instant presence in London," said I to my Aunt Martha, at which, though she expressed the greatest surprise, still she was delighted, as I did not mean to leave England. Next day I took my place in the mail.

It was a tremendously long journey; but I was tired of the country, tired of suspense, disgusted with the whole set of Beauforts, and dying to be refreshed once more by the sight of Meyler's bright, expressive countenance.

The mail stopped a short time at Charmouth, where I left my Aunt Martha, took a most affectionate leave of the whole family, and, late the next night, I arrived at my sister Fanny's house in London.

CHAPTER 20

MEYLER WAS IN the country, unacquainted with my arrival. Fanny declared it would be absolute madness not to make the Duke do something for me, before I wrote to Meyler, and, in short, absolutely teased me, day and night, till I wrote to His Grace, to say that I was now ready to put myself under the protection of Mr. Meyler, as soon as he should have provided for me, according to his first proposal of giving me £500 a year. The Duke wrote declaring that he had never offered so much. I had the proposal of that sum from His Grace's man of business. I now offer you £300, continued the Duke, in his letter; more than that I must decline.

It was not in my nature to stick out for money, so I agreed to the £300, and the Duke set his attorney to work to draw up the papers.

In the meantime, when I least expected it, came two large parcels from Worcester. He had not seduced Mrs. Archdeacon, for Mrs. Archdeacon had followed him up to the army, whether he would or not, and he had sent her back immediately, and wished her dead for her disgusting assurance: and he adored me, etc. etc., as usual.

I then wrote to the Duke of Beaufort, to say that I could not immediately put myself under the protection of Mr. Meyler, owing to circumstances having changed; therefore he must not get the annuity made out under that idea. Soon after this, the Duke heard of Mrs. Archdeacon, and, believing his son had forgotten me, kindly wrote me word, he would now do nothing for me, and I might starve if I did not like to live with another man.

I could no longer endure the Duke's excessive selfishness calmly, and therefore assured him that I had still many letters, with promises of marriage, from Lord Worcester, written since those I had delivered up to him, trusting to the frail reeds, his generosity and honour, all which were, at that time, in my possession.

The Duke now wrote me a most insulting and impertinent letter, declaring that, if I were humble and civil, he had no objection to giving me a small sum for my letters; but recommended me to be moderate in my demands, otherwise he should not think them worth attending to, or taking any notice of. This time the Duke had the honour of putting me in a passion, and I consequently wrote to this effect.

Your Grace must excuse my flattering, with civility, you whose conduct has been so invariably selfish, mean, and artful towards me, as to have, at last, inspired me with perfect contempt. Having your promise of £300 provided I fulfil certain conditions, without one bit of the civil humility you recommend, I beg to acquaint you that, if the annuity is not made out directly, I will publish the promise of marriage, and put an execution into your house for the annuity.

This letter had the desired effect, and the annuity was made out immediately, although I forget what excuse the Duke offered to me for reducing it to two hundred a year, or why I consented to the reduction. This last annuity was drawn out, with a condition that I should never once write to Lord Worcester, nor hold any kind of communication with him. Mr. Treslove, of Lincoln's Inn, advised me not to accept a restricted annuity; but I declared I could not but fancy myself safe, since Worcester, of course, in case he should be the cause of my losing this, possessed too good a heart to suffer me to be unprovided for : so the thing was witnessed and signed, and I gave up all the letters once more to His Grace of Beaufort, who having written to acquaint his son of what he had done for me, and on what conditions, Lord Worcester wrote a parcel of very pathetic letters to my sister Fanny: he wished me happy: he knew well that he should never be allowed to see me again: he did not think I could have agreed never to write or speak to him again: he had heard that I was with Mr. Meyler; but, even in that case, he could not fancy my having cut him.

Three or four letters came to Fanny, in the same style. At last, he wrote to me : it was impossible to resist addressing me, cruelly as I had left him, etc. etc.

"So it is, very mercenary, cruel, and unnatural," said I to Fanny, after having finished His Lordship's letter to me: "in short, were he to be killed abroad, I should never enjoy another hour's rest"; and, in spite of all they could say or do to prevent me, I wrote to tell Worcester, that I trusted to God, and to his good heart, for seeing that I was somehow provided for; but that nothing should again induce me to cut him, while I believed him still fond of me, and unhappy for my sake.

Soon after I had dispatched this letter, the first half year of the allowance becoming due, I received £100 from the Duke of Beaufort's attorney, and in less than a month afterwards, the same attorney applied to me for the £100 back again——

"What do you mean, pray?" I asked.

"Why," answered the attorney, "Lord Worcester has acquainted his father that you have written to him, and therefore, since you are not entitled to that £100, the Duke insists on its being returned."

"Upon your honour, does the Duke really wish to take from me the means of existence, even if I effectually, and for ever, separate myself from his son?"

"Of course," answered the attorney.

"And the Duke of Beaufort wishes to see the woman who, but for her generosity and feeling towards his family, had long since been his daughter, thrown on the wide world without a shilling?"

"He certainly is very angry with me for having paid you the £100, which I must lose out of my own pocket if you do not return it, since His Grace, being no longer obliged to do anything, will never give you twenty pounds as long as he lives."

"Not if I continue separated from Worcester?"

"Certainly not, even then. The fact is, His Grace believes that his son has left you altogether."

"What, then, is to become of me?"

"That is a matter of perfect indifference to His Grace, and also to me. I only want to know if you mean to oblige me to obtain the hundred pounds back again by law." I rang the bell. "Show this man downstairs," said I, and I retired to my dressing-room.

Strange as it may appear, I was not, in any respect, put out of spirits at the idea of having lost £200 a year, and I do not believe I should, at that time, have eaten less dinner than usual, if I had lost £200 again: so little did I care for money, or anything money could buy, beyond clean linen, and bread and milk; but I was deeply hurt to think that, do what I would to deserve it, no one would like me; and there was nothing on earth, half so desirable, half so consoling, to me, as the esteem and steady friendship of others. For this I had left the gay world, and buried myself in a village. It was to ensure the esteem of the Beauforts, that I refused to become one of them. In a very desponding temper, I sat down and wrote to Meyler, as follows:

It is long, very long, since I heard from you, and, like the rest of the world, I take it for granted you have forgotten me, else I had been yours, and yours only, as long as you were disposed to protect me. I always liked you; but twice the love I ever felt towards you would not have made me act unfeelingly towards anybody breathing, while I knew or fancied they deserved my gratitude. The reward for this steadiness in what I believed was right, is, that all have forsaken me: even Lord Worcester has turned against me, and written me romantic professions latterly, in cold blood, on purpose, as it seems, to betray me, by the goodness of my heart, with sending him an answer, which, by law, would deprive me of the small annuity which had been granted for my future existence.

The money is nothing!—I never cared about money; but all this harsh treatment wounds me more than I can describe to you. And you, too, have forgotten me, n'est-ce pas ? *If you have not, I hope you will tell me so, by return of post. In the meantime, God bless you, dear Meyler.*

HARRIETTE WILSON.

By the earliest post, Meyler wrote me a letter, the style of which was unusually romantic. He should be in town on the same day I received his answer. He had believed me in Spain, and had relinquished all hopes of me for ever. He had won a considerable wager by my dear, kind letter; but was too happy to enrich himself at any man's expense, therefore refused to accept a guinea of it. *I don't think,* Meyler went on, *I don't believe you would again say I am cold, if you could read my heart at this moment, and understand how deeply impressed I feel, with gratitude towards my beloved Harriette. Never mind Worcester's annuity, for you and I will never part.*

I would not marry any woman on earth, and I am sure I shall never entertain so high an opinion of another, as I have had good reason to encourage towards you: so yours, beloved Harriette, for ever and ever: full of happiness and haste to follow this letter, yours most devotedly affectionate,

RICHARD WILLIAM MEYLER.

It is not my intention to dwell on Meyler's love, or Meyler's raptures, since such subjects, in prose, are very prosy. Meyler struck me as having grown much more handsome than when we last parted; but this might be only my own fancy, having seen nothing like a beauty, except Beau Fisher, during the last twelve months.

We hired a very excellent house in the New Road, close to Gloucester Place, and, for the first fortnight we were both in love, and did not quarrel: but, alas! in rather less than three weeks, I discovered that Meyler, the lively Meyler, was one of the worst tempered men in all England! This was very hard upon one who, like myself, had been spoiled and indulged by a man who was ever a slave to my slightest caprices! I cannot describe Meyler's temper, for I never met with anything, in the way of temper, at all to be compared to his. It was a sort of periodical temper;

and when he had passed a whole day in sweet soft conversation, I was perfectly sure that a storm was at hand for the next day, and vice versa.

At first I would not stand it, the least in the world; and used to kick him out of bed the moment he began to run restive, and then he would turn out, in the middle of the night, to return to his house in Grosvenor Square, and I, to show my indifference, would make a point of joining any gay evening parties.

The next day, Meyler never failed to make his appearance, looking most penitent, arch, and beautiful.

"Why don't you cut her dead for two or three days," said Amy to Meyler, "and rely upon it, she would sneak after you, and that would be much better than your sneaking after her in this manner."

"So I would, Mrs. Sydenham," Meyler used to answer; "so I would, only some man would——in the meantime, perhaps."

I must confess I was sometimes a very tyrant towards Meyler; and yet I know my temper is naturally good; but my feelings towards Meyler were all made up of passion. I neither esteemed nor trusted him; and yet I was never so jealous of any other man. There was, in fact, an expression in Meyler's countenance, of such voluptuous beauty, that it was impossible for any woman to converse with him, after he had dined, in cold blood. One night, as he sat in the Duchess of Beaufort's box, I left my own, and sent in the box-keeper, on the Duchess's side of the house, to request he would come out and speak to a person in the passage. He immediately obeyed my summons. "Meyler," said I, in a hurried tone of voice, "if you return, even for an instant, to the Duchess of Beaufort's box, we part this night, and for ever. I cannot endure it." "Then I will stay with you, all the evening," said Meyler, flattered rather than angry with me, for such jealousy, as he knew I had never felt towards Lord Worcester.

"Why will you agitate yourself for nothing?" said Meyler, when we got home, this being his good-tempered night.

"You know you did once love the Duchess of Beaufort," I replied.

"Never," said Meyler. "Worcester and I, you know, were at Christchurch together," he continued, "and one day, when I was too young to have ever compassed an intrigue in any higher line than what boys usually find in the streets of Oxford, he presented me to his mother, who, you know, is a very fine woman of her age: this you will the more readily admit, because there is certainly a very striking resemblance, in your picture. No woman, in fine clothes, would have come amiss to me at that time; and I certainly felt a very strong desire for the Duchess; but without entertaining the shadow of a hope, notwithstanding she always distinguished me with unusual attention, as you must have heard from others as well as from myself; till, one night when I was staying at Badminton, in the absence of the Duke, I happened to say that the cold had affected my lips, and made them sore. It was as late as twelve o'clock. Her Grace desired me to accompany her to her dressing-room, that she might give me some cold cream. When I entered, her night-clothes were hanging to air, near the fire. We were alone. I hesitated. In another instant, I might have ventured to take this midnight invitation as a hint; but unluckily, my Lady Harrowby, who probably suspected something improper, entered the room like our evil genius."

This story Meyler was in the habit of repeating to his friends, and I particularly remember his inquiring of Mr. Napier, who is also a friend of Her Grace of Beaufort's, whether he imagined the Duchess might have been had on that evening; and Napier said, in answer, that whoever, in the absence of her husband, was to invite him to her dressing-room at midnight, he should feel bound, in common gallantry towards her, to attempt———whether he had felt disposed or not.

Meyler has repeated this story to so many people besides myself, Napier, and Sir Harry Mildmay, that it will be folly to affect a denial of it. Meyler's greatest enemy never accused him, yet, of uttering an untruth.

Meyler led me but an unhappy life, during the first year of our living together. His jealousy was downright selfishness; for he would be jealous of my pianoforte, if that instrument amused me. He was, in fact, always jealous, unless I was counting the minutes of his absence. If I procured a private box, to witness a play, *tête-à-tête* with my sister Fanny, he would send a note, by his coachman, to this effect: *Dearest Harriette, I send a carriage to convey you to the play, to prove my wish to put no restraint on your wishes; but if, for my sake, you would stay at home, I should feel both grateful and happy, and will return to you as soon as possible.*

He often left me, to pass a week with the Beauforts at Badminton, and this never failed to render me completely wretched. "My God," said Meyler one day, striking his head violently with his hand, "what am I to do? I would rather blow my brains out, than be thus the slave of any woman. Mine is not the passion of a day, or a year. I shall never cease to love you; but I must enjoy a little liberty."

I was much struck with what Meyler said. This sort of affection may be more lasting than Worcester's late unnatural rapture, which went off all at once, thought I to myself; and Meyler is so rich! so very, very beautiful, and it would be so shocking to lose him altogether. I will therefore put up with him, in his own way, as long as I have reason to believe him constant to me. I ought to be grateful, since I know that half the women in London would fain tempt him to forget me.

The next day, Meyler agreed to dine with me, and set off, after dinner, to Badminton. He came, I know, in fear and trembling, for he expected me to fret, and shed tears, as usual, at the idea of his going to Badminton. So far from it, I played him all his favourite airs on the pianoforte, gave him an excellent dinner, and drank my proper allowance of champagne, with spirit; hoped he might pass a pleasant week at Badminton, and, feeling full confidence in his affection, should make myself happy, with my books and music, till he returned.

"What is the matter?" I asked, suddenly observing that he could neither eat nor drink. He only sighed!

"Do, my pretty, little Meyler, tell me what you would be at?"

"It would be impossible for you to keep up such delightful spirits, knowing I am about to visit a fine woman, if you loved me," said Meyler, despondingly!

"Oh, nonsense!" I exclaimed, "you have assured me you never mean to leave me, and I believe you, because you never yet told me a lie; and a jealous woman is the most disgusting animal imaginable, you know; so let us enjoy time present, since you are so soon to leave me."

"I see you are delighted to get rid of me," said Meyler, "and I could never love, nor believe in the love of any woman who was not madly jealous of me. I see your affection, and therefore I hate you, Harriette: so, in order to punish you, I will not go to Badminton at all."

"Bravo! You'll stay then with me?" said I, kissing him. "Indeed, indeed, I but acted with indifference from dread of disgusting you; but now, since you will stay, I am so very, very happy."

Meyler, being satisfied that it would make me miserable, set off for Badminton early the next morning. In the evening, I went to my sister Amy's, where, among many others, I met Lord Hertford. "Is it possible, think you," I inquired of His Lordship, "is it possible to pass one's life with a man of bad temper?"

"Better live on a bone," answered His Lordship, with his mouth full of cold partridge.

"What do you know about living on a bone?" I asked, laughing at him.

"Oh, pray make up your mind, at once, to leave that vile, ill-tempered Meyler," said Fanny; "for his jealousy is really mere selfishness, and though he goes to balls and parties every night of his life, and does not return till five or six in the morning, he never fails to call here for Harriette, in ten minutes after she is set down, declaring he is miserable till he knows her to be safe in bed, and there he leaves her."

"Cut him, cut him, by all means," said everybody at once.

Lord Hertford wanted to set me down; but I positively refused. "Well, then," whispered His Lordship, "you really must pay me a visit at my little private door in Park Lane. You say you are going to the play tomorrow night, and you know you can rely on my discretion. The King dines with me; but His Majesty will leave me before the play is over, and I will open the door for you myself, after my people are gone to bed, and you shall find everything ready and comfortable." "You may then depend on seeing me," said I, and I took my leave.

The next evening, Fanny, Julia, and I were all seated in a private box, at Covent Garden, by seven o'clock, accompanied by two friends of theirs, whose names I have forgotten; and we were, I think, afterwards visited at the theatre by Lord Rivers.

"Are you hungry?" said I to Julia, just as the curtain dropped.

"Very," they both answered in a breath; and Fanny declared that nothing made her so hungry as sitting out a long play, after hurrying to it before she had half-finished her dinner. I said that we now lived in the age of fairies, and that a good-natured one would, this night, tap some door with her wand, and it should fly open and disclose a magnificent repast, served out on gold and silver, and composed of every delicacy which could possibly be imagined.

"What is the use of putting one in mind of all these good things," said Fanny, "when, for my part, I shall think myself happy if my maid has saved us a bone of mutton, or even half a pint of porter, these hard times?"

"No, what would you say if I had discovered a fairy, witch, or magician, who would, this very night, do all I have named for us?"

They were a long while before they would listen to me; but from my earnestness they at last really began to think I had hit upon some odd plan of giving them a fine supper, and promised to be led by me. Both of them had, once, been shown Lord Hertford's private apartments, some years back, from Seymour Place; but they had never seen the little private entrance out of Park Lane, and had nearly forgotten the whole together. We were set down, by my desire, at some short distance from Lord Hertford's little private door, and it was such a dark night, I was obliged to feel my way to it.

"Where on earth are you taking us to?" said Julia, in alarm. "Here are no houses, and this place is really dangerous. For God's sake let us return to the carriage directly."

"Pray don't be alarmed, and, in half a minute, you shall see what the good fairy has provided for us."

Having arrived at the little low door, which resembles that of a cellar, I tapped gently, three times, and the door was immediately opened by Lord Hertford, who was, absolutely, struck almost dumb at observing that he had three fair ladies to entertain instead of one. He just looked.

> How happy could I be with either,
> Were t'other dear charmers away.

However, though of course he was disappointed, he was too well-bred to complain; and therefore turned the whole affair into a joke, saying he cut a comical figure, coming downstairs thus shyly, with his miniature key, to let in a whole party!

The little winding staircase, covered with red cloth, conducted us to his beautiful apartments, where a magnificent supper was laid, just in the fairy style I had described. Everybody was agreeably surprised except His Lordship, who fully expected to have passed the evening *tête-à-tête* with me. Nevertheless, I must say, he contrived to support this terrible disappointment with infinite good humour, and we returned, at three in the morning, delighted with our English night's entertainment, in which we partook the feast of conviviality as well as of reason, and the flow of wine as well as of soul.

Meyler returned to town in less time than he had named, because some man had laughed at the idea of my being constant. He soon began to quarrel again, as usual. At the opera he was offended if I stood in the room with my sisters. "I will retire before the curtain drops, if you accompany me," I used to say; but Meyler had fifty people to chat with in the round room. He was a particular friend of Sir Harry Mildmay. Both were Hampshire men, and members of the same county; and the gay Sir Harry had ever a mind for all his friends' wives or mistresses, ugly or handsome: he was, therefore, continually setting us by the ears; merely because I was among the few who had refused him.

"Meyler," he would say, after having seen him standing near me in the room at the opera, "Meyler, why the deuce do you stand there with Harriette Wilson every night, like a frightful shepherd, to be laughed at? Why don't you take to intriguing with women of fashion? Do you know, man, that you are by no means an ugly fellow?"

"I never thought I was anything like an ugly fellow, Sir Harry," answered Meyler, speaking slowly.

On another opera night, as I was waiting at the top of the stairs, with my sister Fanny, for Meyler to take me home, Sir Harry came flying up to me, in affected surprise. "You here!" he exclaimed—"Why I thought it was your ghost?"

"How so?"

"I really imagined that it was you who went out just now with Meyler!"

"Is Meyler really gone without me, then?"

"I have this instant seen him hand a lady into his carriage, and step in after her," answered the Baronet.

I felt myself reddening with indignation. It rained fast. Fanny and Julia were going, in Mr. Napier's chariot, quite a different road, and there was no place to spare for me, and not a soul left in the room, except Lady Heathcote and her party, and Amy, who was watching me, at a distance, with a host of beaux. "My carriage is much at your service," said Sir Harry Mildmay, "and I shall be very happy to set you down at your own door."

"What, has Meyler gone off, and left you here by yourself?" said Amy, joining us, and speaking loud enough for Lady Heathcote to hear. Her Ladyship looked as if she was much amused with the whole occurrence. I have a terrible proud spirit of my own, and, greatly as I disliked the idea of seeming to encourage Sir Harry Mildmay, the temptation was now irresistible; so, putting my arm under his, and skipping gaily past Dr. Bankhead's dear friend, Lady Heathcote, I said I would forgive Meyler for cutting me, as often as he was disposed to send me such a very amiable substitute. It was a dark night, and Mildmay's coachman drove like mad. Judge my surprise, on finding myself set down at Sir Harry's house in Brook Street, when I thought I was in the New Road. Sir Harry took hold of my hand, as I stood on his steps, and laughingly tried to pull me into his house.

"Really, Sir Harry, this is too absurd! Eloping with me as though I were an innocent fool, who could be led to do any one thing which clashes with my humour!"

Sir Harry, at last, finding it impossible, either by jokes or earnestness, to induce me to enter his house, begged I would get into his carriage to be carried to my own house.

"No," said I. "No power on earth shall induce me to enter your carriage again."

My anger towards Meyler, for his supposed neglect, having now cooled, I was beginning to be very unhappy about him, and very much out of humour with Sir Harry.

"I will walk home," I said, "or at least walk till I can find a coach, and I insist on your leaving me this instant."

"That, my sweet Harriette, is quite impossible: and since you are so obstinate as to insist on risking to catch your death of cold, by walking home without a bonnet, I must accompany you."

"It is quite fine again now," answered I, and off I set, accompanied by Sir Harry, having first fastened my shawl over my head.

My house in the New Road had a garden before it. I felt dreadfully afraid of finding Meyler there; and I almost wished Mildmay to remain at hand to protect me; in case he should grow violent before I could convince him of my innocence.

"If Meyler is not there, I will come in," said Sir Harry. I was really astonished at his assurance.

"What do you think Meyler would say, if he found you in his house?" I inquired.

"Oh! hang Meyler! we would lock him out."

I could not refrain from laughing at Mildmay's excessive impudence.

"Is Mr. Meyler in the house?" I tremulously asked of the servant, who was coming down the garden to open the gate for us. The maid told me that Mr. Meyler had been there half an hour ago, and appeared much agitated when they informed him I was not returned from the opera house.

"Where did he direct his coachman to drive to?"

"I think to Mrs. Sydenham's, Ma'am," was the reply.

I said that Mildmay was determined to enter the house with me; and, dreading the consequences of such a very mad action, I desired the servant to shut us out, since I should go and look for Mr. Meyler.

"Don't, don't," said Mildmay; but I insisted, and the street door was closed upon us. We stood in the garden; and then, for near a quarter of an hour, I begged, entreated, and implored Mildmay to leave me, but in vain. Every instant I expected the return of Meyler: yet, frightened and agitated as I was, under the impression that I had thoughtlessly committed an imprudence, for which I was likely to pay very dear, Sir Harry would have no mercy on me.

At last, as good luck would have it, two drunken men observed us among the trees, as they passed the house. It being rather moonlight, and, not dreaming that the owner of it would be standing there, at two o'clock in the morning, with a gay man in silk stockings, they naturally concluded me to be some poor creature he had met with in the streets; so, knocking with their sticks between the iron railings of the gate, they bawled out, "I'll trouble you, sir, for ground-rent, if you please."

"Ground-rent! ground-rent! D——n your impudence," said Sir Harry, running after them; and I immediately knocked till my servant opened the door, when I rushed into the passage, and safely barred out the gay Baronet, in spite of his irresistible beauty.

In about another half-hour, Meyler's carriage drove up to my door. I was in a dreadful fright; for the provoking Mildmay had confessed to me, at last, that he had not seen Meyler go out; but, on the contrary, he had left him in the upper room, talking to Lord Palmerston. It was past three o'clock in the morning. I knew him to be very passionate. He will kill me, of course, said I to myself, as he entered the room. Judge what was my surprise, when Meyler, pale and trembling, took hold of my hands, kissed them, and then fixed his very expressive inquiring eyes on my face.

"You will not deceive me," said he: "of this I am quite certain."

I immediately declared, upon my word, I had nothing to conceal, having done nothing wrong.

Meyler was in raptures.

"When I came into the room to look for you, with the intention of bringing you home," said Meyler, "the first person I saw was Lady Heathcote; and I could not help thinking she looked very oddly at me, and as if she had been inclined to laugh at something; and then I missed you from amongst your sisters. Having, upon inquiry, been told by Amy that Mildmay had taken you away in his own carriage, I asked for Julia and Fanny; but they were gone with Napier; and to Julia's house I drove immediately. They knew nothing of you; and Napier laughed so, at my evident agitation, and would have made such fun of me, all over the town, that my fear of the world, for which you always scold me so much, made me put the most violent restraint upon myself, to endeavour to conceal my anxiety, by remaining quietly where I was for a quarter of an hour. However, they saw through it all; and I left them, to call at your sister Amy's house. Amy said everything she possibly could, to make me believe you were with Mildmay. I left her in disgust; and determined to come here, once more, before I called on Sir Harry."

I then told Meyler by what falsehoods Mildmay had induced me to accept his protection.

"I shall never be the least angry with Sir Harry, as long as you steadily refuse him," said Meyler; "because I have, for some time, wanted such a story to laugh at him about; he having so many against me, with which he takes upon himself to amuse the females of my acquaintance."

This incident roused the little indolent Meyler to pay me unusual attention, for the next several weeks. *Ainsi va le monde!*

One morning, when I called on him at his house in Grosvenor Square, I found him reclined on his chaise-longue, in a very pensive attitude. On a table, before him, was a most unbecoming military cap, which appeared to belong to the militia, or might have been worn, for aught I knew, by the hero of some corps of volunteers.

"What is the matter, Meyler? and why is that frightful cap stuck up before you?"

"Ah!" said Meyler, with his usual slight, but sentimental sigh, "frightful indeed! Fancy a little, quiet, country-gentleman, like myself, sticking such a thing as that on his head!"

"What necessity can there possibly be, for disfiguring yourself so?"

"Why, you see, I am obliged to be Captain of the Hampshire militia, of which Lord Palmerston is Colonel and Commander," continued Meyler, heaving another sigh, and looking most interestingly pensive, while his eyes were steadily fixed on the cap.

I could not help laughing; for there was, in fact, an originality about Meyler's manner of saying mere trifles, which it would be impossible to describe. And then he spoke so very slow, and his mouth was such a model of beauty, that even nonsense came gracefully out of it.

"Meyler has brought his large dog over with him, from Hampshire," said Mildmay to me one evening at the opera; "and he is at least half an hour saying his name."

"What is his name?"

"Why Ch-a-n-c-e," answered Sir Harry, mimicking him.

"Meyler is not stupid," said I.

"Why, no," replied Mildmay. "Meyler possesses a good understanding, when one can give him a fortnight to consider things; but whenever impulse is required, he is of no use on earth."

"I don't k-n-o-w t-h-a-t," I rejoined, imitating Meyler. "Some of his impulses are particularly good, I assure you."

"Do you know that Lord Worcester is expected to bring home the next dispatches?" said Fanny to me one night, when we met in our opera box.

"It is all the same to me," I replied, "since he could be so selfish and vilely shabby as to acquaint his father I had written to him. I shall never respect or like him again." "Yet," said Fanny, "I have this morning received a letter from His Lordship, who writes of you in a very tender style. *A friend of mine*, says His Lordship's letter, *saw my sweet, darling Harriette in Hyde Park, looking lovely. God bless her! What would I give, but to see her pass, at this moment, even though she refused to acknowledge me.*"

"Oh, that's enough," said I, interrupting Fanny, "I am quite in a fidget, and cannot guess what Meyler is about, that he does not visit us tonight, as usual. I understand he is going to the Duke of Devonshire's dress party, and the idea torments me wretchedly."

I turned many an anxious glance towards the Duchess of Beaufort's box, in vain, as well as towards the door of my own. The curtain dropped without our having seen anything of Meyler.

As I was descending the grand staircase, in a very ill-humour, a well-known voice, from the little dark passage, called me by my name. Conceive my astonishment at seeing Meyler, screwed up into a close corner, quite alone, in full regimentals. Fanny and I began to laugh heartily at him.

"Good gracious, Mr. Meyler, is it you? Why not show yourself to the admiring world, after the trouble of making yourself so very fine?" said Julia.

"I am going to the Duke of Devonshire's dress-ball, where there will be plenty more fools in the same ridiculous sort of costume; and where, I hope, I shall not feel so much ashamed of myself; but here, I cannot for the life of me summon courage to face my acquaintance; and so, here have I been stuck up, in the dark, for the last two hours, trying to get to your box: yet ashamed even to venture to my own carriage, till everybody shall have left the house." How we, all three, did laugh at the poor little interesting hero! and yet he looked so handsome, and his red coat reflected such a fine glowing tint on his transparent, pale cheeks, that I was selfish and wicked enough to determine against his exhibiting himself at His Grace of Devonshire's. Lord Hertford joined us in our little dark corner.

"Do not go, Meyler," said I, "pray do not go to the Duke's tonight."

"And why not?" Lord Hertford asked.

"Because it will make me wretched," I answered.

"However," said Meyler, "this is the first time of my being invited; and as all the world will be there, I really must go. You may take my carriage, and I will get home to you as soon as possible."

"Do you return to Grosvenor Square first?" I inquired.

"Yes," said Meyler, as he handed me into his carriage; and then directed the coachman to take me home; but I had scarcely got into Piccadilly, when the fit of jealousy seized me with such overpowering violence, that

I suddenly pulled the check-string, and requested to be conducted to Meyler's house. When there, I, unannounced, walked up into his dressing-room.

"Meyler," said I, "I have given way, at all times, to your caprice and jealousy. This once, humour mine, and I shall feel most grateful. My health and spirits are low tonight. Pray cut the Duke, and return with me. It is the first time I ever interfered with your amusements, therefore do not refuse me." Meyler was obstinate.

"Well, then," said I, "I shall not return home alone. I propose going to Lord Ebrington's, and making love to him." This speech would have disgusted most men; but I knew Meyler.

"I am sure you would not leave me for Ebrington, handsome as he is," said Meyler.

"Upon my word I will, and this very night, if he is to be found, and you refuse to return with me." "Well, then, I must return with you," said poor Meyler, throwing off his unfortunate regimentals, and preparing to accompany me home.

The next time I met Lord Hertford, he told me I was very wrong, and ought to have had more sense than to have attempted bringing Meyler home by force.

"You, on the contrary, are very right, my Lord," answered I; "but then I really could not help it."

Soon after this, Meyler went to hunt in Leicestershire, where, according to the rules of their society, I was told I could not accompany him. However, though Meyler and I were eternally at variance when together, yet we were very miserable and jealous whilst separate. One day I lost all patience: and, ordering post-horses, went to join him at Melton by surprise. He appeared delighted to see me; and I was invited to dine, every day I should remain in Leicestershire, at their club. The house was very comfortable, and their dinners most excellent; so much so that I remember Meyler afterwards enticed away their man-cook, who died in his house in Grosvenor Square. And further, I remember that, while the said dead cook's body was in Meyler's house, his religious feelings would not permit him to peruse some books which were lent him, I believe, by Lord Alvanley. These books, to say the least and best of them, were what Lord F. Bentinck would have called very loose.

The members of the Melton Club led what I considered a very stupid sort of life. They were off at six in the morning, dressed up in old single-breasted coats which once had been red, and came back to dinner at six. While they sat at table, it was the constant habit of a few wretched, squalid prostitutes to come and tap at their windows, when those who were not too sleepy were seen to sneak out of the room. The rest snored and drank till ten, and went to bed till hunting-time again.

The evening hunt dress is red, lined with white, and the buttons, and whole style of it, are very becoming. I could not help remarking that these gentlemen never looked half so handsome, anywhere in the world, as when, glowing with health, they took their seats at dinner in the dress and costume of the Melton hunt; and, when the signal of those horrible, dirty prostitutes was slyly attended to, by either Mildmay, Lord Herbert, or Berkeley Craven, I could not help saying, *Mon Dieu! Quel dommage!* Once, Meyler got into a desperate rage, and declared me to be such a loose, profligate, wicked woman, that he was really afraid to leave the room, even for an instant, lest I should offer myself to some of those very handsome and most amorously disposed young gentlemen, as an indoor substitute for the dirty, shivering, frail ones without; but this my readers are aware was vile, infamous scandal! since there exists not the man or woman who can prove I was ever unfaithful in my life, while I professed truth, and while I believed others true to me. But we are told, now I come to reflect, that whosoever has even thought about it, hath committed adultery in her heart. And so, with regard to Melton, and thinking about it, I really do not know what excuse to make for the thought, which, I am afraid, did strike me, very forcibly indeed. However, of course, every rule has an exception; and, if women will tap at windows, for the sole purpose, and beautiful young men will retire for the sole purpose, why the idea is forced upon one; and, whether one likes it or not, is all a chance, you know.

CHAPTER 21

I FORGET WHETHER Meyler got tired of me, or I of Melton, or of him; but, certain it is, I very soon returned to town. Meyler had no mind, no romance about him. His person was charming; but that won't do, even with gentleman-like manners, for one's everyday companion. Meyler was not up to me, either in hand or heart.

I could have been more constant, I often used to say to myself, by way of excuse, when I felt anything like a new fancy coming across my imagination; but then he who suited me was married, and how can such an active mind, such a warm imagination, live on air?

These reflections used to occur to me latterly, as often as I happened to meet Lord Ebrington, with whom I had now only a mere bowing acquaintance. Formerly, when I was very young, we had, mutually, sought each other. I always thought him very handsome and sensible-looking, and what, to me, is better than all the rest, he appeared as shy, proud, and as reserved, as Lord Ponsonby; but, on acquaintance, we had discovered that we were too much alike in temper to agree. Afraid of each other, we could do nothing together, so we cut in a week; except as to the mere bow, which could not, in common civility, be avoided, when we passed each other.

Lately, since I had found Meyler's temper become so provoking, it had struck me, more than once, that, if Ebrington were to try again, we might agree better. However, there were three reasons why I did not make the first advances to His Lordship. In the first place, though Meyler was a torment to me, my jealousy prevented me from throwing him upon the world: in the second, I could not deceive any man: in the third, I said to myself, why should Lord Ebrington like me now, when my health and freshness are gone, though he did not care for me in the days of my earliest youth and beauty! The case is hopeless, thought I, after casting one wishful look, behind me, on Lord Ebrington, who, meeting me, on my entrance into town from Leicestershire, smiled sweetly, as he made me a very graceful bow.

When I returned from Leicestershire, Colonel Parker was arrived from Spain, and Worcester hourly expected with dispatches. My father proposed separating himself from my mother, and retiring to his native country, the Canton de Berne, should the expected peace be proclaimed; and he, as well as Lord Berwick, wished my mother to reside with the younger part of her family, in France.

Lord Worcester, when he brought over the dispatches shortly afterwards, appeared, from what my sister Fanny, whom he often visited, told me, to have taken rather a dislike to me, or he was trying to do so, and he strove hard to muster up another passion, for another woman. The only flattering part of this melancholy fact was, that every woman he made up to, had been reckoned like me in features or expression. He made a dead set at a French woman who was a sort of caricature of me, and the poor lady fell in love with the gay Marquis in earnest. She was very thin and bony, as Worcester told Fanny, and all the first night of their honeymoon, she caressed, and caressed, and caressed, saying, *ah que je t'aime! que je t'aime!* and yet nothing would do; he could not manage to prove his gratitude in the way the lady wished and naturally expected.

"It is, no doubt, owing to the great fatigue I have experienced, in bringing over dispatches," said Worcester; "but tomorrow night, I shall make a satisfactory return for your kind and affectionate devotedness."

However, the second night came, and passed away, without the lady having been gratified by, even, one of the promised proofs. The third morning sun shone on no more brilliant scenes of marital prowess; and, on the fourth night, madame felt such irrepressible disgust, that she kicked the triumphant dispatch-bearer of the bungling Wellington out of bed:

> And made the fair,
> In wrath declare,
> The Aide-de-Camp a fumbler.

While Lord Worcester was in town, Fanny had permitted him to visit her, for the sole purpose of endeavouring to make him do something for me; but Lord Worcester seemed to have lost every atom of feeling in the wars, and from a shy, sensitive, blushing, ardent boy, had returned a cold-blooded and most shameless profligate, like the great, the glorious wonder of his age, Wellington!

France being now open to us, Meyler expressed his intention of taking a trip to Paris. We had some very serious quarrels, just at that time.

"Meyler," said I to him, a short time before we went abroad, "you and I cannot live together. You are honest enough to acknowledge that your temper is abominable; for my part, I do not believe that there exists a woman who could endure it. I hold myself no longer, therefore, under your protection, mind. I don't mean to say that I will be unfaithful to you: but from this hour I am my own mistress, and you, when we meet any visitors, are to be turned out, the first moment you treat me with a want of politeness." Meyler could not bear this plan for any length of time, and we had, in one month, mutually agreed to part at least twenty times over, and then made matters up again. The deuce was in us both. We really hated each other, and yet sheer jealousy kept us together. At last Meyler assured me that, though he had often talked of parting, he had never been so determined till now.

This resolution made me, I do confess, very unhappy. To conceal my real feelings, I dressed gaily, I went blazing to the opera, and to every other place of resort where I might expect to meet Meyler's friends, one of whom told me that Meyler was actually staying at Melton, quite alone, the hunting season being at an end. In about three weeks, he came to town. I dreaded encountering him at the opera, since we were to cut each other dead, and yet the effort must be made. He shall see me merry, and surrounded with handsome admirers, if I am to die the next hour. The little, provokingly handsome sugar-baker must not know that I still remember him, and am dying for his kiss.

For several opera nights I saw Meyler, in the Duchess of Beaufort's box and in the round room, and we mutually cut each other. At last he cáme slyly up to our party, and addressed my sister Fanny. His beautiful, white *petit* hand was held towards mine, and I pressed it, *malgré moi*, for an instant, without speaking to him, and, the next moment, found myself seated in his carriage, on our way home.

"Don't tell my friends," said Meyler. "I have so sworn never to speak to you again that I shall not be able to support their incessant quizzing."

"We shall never again attempt to live with each other," said I. "Our tempers never can assimilate, and I will be as free as the air we breathe; but you may, indeed you must, come and visit me."

"Swear then, upon your honour and soul, that you will acquaint me, if you should prove unfaithful to me."

I did swear not to deceive him: and then we hoped to go on more comfortably under our new arrangement.

"I shall go to Paris in my own carriage, and establish myself in my own lodgings," said I; and to this proposition Meyler was obliged to agree. He promised to follow me, and be there a week after my arrival.

My dear mother had disposed of her house at Brompton, very unwillingly, in compliance with the wishes of Lord Berwick and her husband.

Her departure, as well as mine, was delayed by a circumstance which I will now relate.

Colonel Parker, being one of those sort of animals whose constitution requires variety, had been, of late, cooling towards Fanny, his most amiable, and I will swear, most faithful companion, the mother of his child, too, and merely because he had been in possession of her person too many months for his habit of vanity.

The Colonel, having left Fanny one morning, to pay a visit to a relation of his, where he was to meet his cousin, Fanny asked him, in joke, if he was certain he should not make love to her.

"Love to her!" exclaimed Parker, "she is the greatest fright imaginable. I wish you could once see her. It would set your mind at rest for the remainder of your life, on that head at least." The lady's name was Popham, if I recollect right.

As Parker promised to return to Fanny in a week, she grew uneasy when almost a fortnight had elapsed without seeing or even hearing from him. At last somebody told her that he was in town, and residing at an hotel in Vere Street. Fanny set off that very instant, by herself, and on foot, to the hotel, declaring her conviction of its utter impossibility. She was, however, dreadfully agitated, *quand même*. She met Parker on the steps of the hotel, and placed her hand upon his arm, absolutely breathless and speechless.

"Fanny," said Parker, "you are, no doubt, surprised that I did not either go to you, or inform you of my arrival in town." Fanny looked earnestly in his face—"but"— continued Parker—and he hesitated.

"Pray, speak," said Fanny, and she pressed both her hands on her left side. She had, of late, often complained that she felt pain there, but at that moment it was agonizing, and seemed almost to produce suffocation, which might have been seen by the purple tint of her quivering lips.

"I have bad news for you," said Parker, rather confused than agitated. "I am going to be married," he continued, observing that Fanny could not speak.

At these words, Fanny's whole countenance underwent such a violent change that Parker was terrified; and, calling a hackney-coach, they stepped into it, and came home together, while I was sitting with Julia, at whose house Fanny still resided.

The little sitting-room, which Fanny had furnished and fitted up for herself, was a back parlour, looking into a garden. Her veil was down, when she descended from the coach, and, though we expected they would have come upstairs, Julia and I determined not to interrupt them. I was to pass the day with Julia: and, when the dinner was on the table, the servant was desired to knock at Fanny's door, and inform Colonel and Mrs. Parker, that we were waiting. The servant brought us word that they must beg to be excused. I became uneasy, and, without knocking, or any further ceremony, entered the room. Fanny was sitting on the sofa, with her head reclined on the pillow. She was not in tears, and did not appear to have been shedding any; but her face, ears, and throat were visibly swollen, and her whole appearance so changed that I was frightened.

"My dear Fanny, what is the matter?"

Fanny did not even lift her eyes from the fixed gaze on the ground.

"Colonel Parker," said I, "for God's sake, tell me what has happened."

"She heard some unpleasant news, too abruptly," said Colonel Parker.

"I implore you not to inquire," said Fanny, speaking with evident difficulty. "I would not be left alone, this night, and I have been on my knees, to intreat Parker to remain with me. He refuses."

"Surely you do not mean to leave her, in this state!" said I, addressing Parker.

"I can do her no good. It is all too late: since my word is passed, and, in ten days, I shall be the husband of another. My presence only irritates her, and does her harm."

"Fanny, my dear Fanny," said I, "can you make yourself so completely wretched, for a man who acts without common humanity towards you?"

"Pray, pray, never expect to console me, in this way," said Fanny impatiently. "I derive no consolation from thinking ill of the father of my dear child."

"Come to bed, dear Fanny," said I, taking hold of her burning hand.

"Yes, I shall be better in bed."

We assisted her upstairs. She seemed stupefied, and could neither speak nor shed tears. At about one, Parker left her.

Fanny kept her bed for two days, and on the third she thought herself much better.

"All I entreat of you, is to keep secret from me the day of their marriage, and everything connected with it," said Fanny.

We promised to do our best to prevent her hearing a word more on the hateful subject.

Fanny changed the conversation immediately, and forced herself to go into society as usual; but her lips now assumed a blueish tint, whenever she made the slightest exertion, or hurried upstairs, or walked fast, and she would put her hand on her left side, and say, "there is something very wrong, and odd, about my heart: of that I am certain; and so, as it may be of use to others, perhaps to some of my sisters, I hope that, when I am dead, you will have my body examined."

There was a man, a brute, I should rather say, whose passion she had good-naturedly laughed at, who actually brought her a piece of Parker's wedding cake, and informed her of the day, and hour, on which they were married. Fanny almost went on her knees, to implore us not to enter her bedroom, for the whole of the next day. After that, she appeared nearly the same as usual, except that she coughed rather more, and began to discover that a single glass of wine always produced fever; but she looked as fresh and lovely as ever. Her character, however, was completely changed, from gay to serious, and she was always occupied in writing or reading.

When I went to France, Fanny's mind had been much relieved by some kind letters from Parker, assuring her that he would, on his return to town, always visit her and his child. He even led her to believe that his marriage had been merely a convenient one, in order to obtain promotion in the army, and that his heart had never changed.

Fanny talked soon of joining me in Paris. Meyler, with whom I had not once quarrelled since I had received him only as a visitor, promised to follow me in a week. As to Julia, she could not leave her dear, long-backed Mr. Napier for a single day. Ladies on the wrong side of forty become so very tender!

Lord Frederick Bentinck drove me, in his tilbury, the two first stages on my road to Dover, and then, after a world of good advice, and many questions as to where I expected to go after I was dead, he took his leave, and I continued my journey towards Paris, accompanied by my *femme de chambre* and my young provoking nephew, George Woodcock.

We were, all three, so weary when we reached Paris, that, having hired some handsome rooms in the Rue de la Paix, we kept our beds for about two days and a half. On the third day, we went out to look about us, and were much struck and pleased with the Place Vendôme, and many more places which have been sufficiently described by others.

"We are free as air, you know, my dear," said Meyler, on the very first night of his arrival in Paris. "I have been most true to you for more than two years, nor am I tired of you now, in the least; but never having had an intrigue with a Frenchwoman, and being here, for the first time, of course I must try them, merely for fun, and to have something to talk about. You know, a young man with thirty thousand a year must try everything, once in his life; but I shall love you the better afterwards."

"A delightful plan," said I, striving, with all the power of my mind, to conceal my rage and jealousy, "provided it be mutually followed up, and I can conceive nothing more agreeable than our meeting about once a week or so, and passing a day together, for the sole purpose of hearing each other's adventures."

"Oh, nonsense! mere threats," said Meyler. "I don't believe you will ever be inconstant. You are, in fact, too constant for Paris. One has enough of all that hum-drum stuff, in England. I am sure I have had enough of it, for the last two years, and begin to wish there was no such thing as constancy in this dirty world."

I could have almost murdered Meyler for this insulting speech; but that pride made me force myself to seem of his way of thinking.

"Where are you staying?" I inquired, with affected carelessness.

"At the Hotel de Hollande, exactly opposite your own door," he replied.

"Never mind," said I, "I shall not have time to watch you."

"What are you going to do this evening?" Meyler inquired, growing uneasy, and more in love, as he began to believe in my indifference.

"Oh, I have made a charming new acquaintance already. An Italian lady, who resides in this hotel, has invited me to dine with her," said I.

"Will you present me?" Meyler inquired.

"Why no, that would be too cool a thing to do, till I know her better."

"Tomorrow morning then, I suppose, you are to be found, in case I should not be otherwise engaged, at about two."

"Why no, not so, for my carriage is ordered at ten in the morning, and I shall be out the whole of the day, with a French party, seeing sights."

"Where shall I see you, then?" said Meyler, vexed, fidgety, and almost forgetting his project of making up to French women, since the chief enjoyment and zest of such a pursuit was expected to arise out of my jealousy.

"Why, really, Meyler, this plan of as free as air, which you know you proposed, is so decidedly to my taste that I cannot sufficiently express to you my obligation. I began to wish, with you, that there was no such thing as constancy in the world, particularly when I recollect how very Darby and Joan-like we lived together in London; but I dare say we shall meet at the opera, towards midnight, and if we don't, never mind, love," said I, kissing my hand to him, as I went towards the door.

"Where are you going, then?" asked Meyler.

"To a party, in the hotel, to whom my Italian friend presented me yesterday. *Au revoir, mon voisin,*" said I, and then called Monsieur François, my new *lacquais de place.* to conduct me where I was to pass the evening.

I had acted my part well, and satisfied my pride, but not my heart. No matter. It won't do to play the game of hearts in Paris, and, wherever we may be, we must take the world as we find it.

At this French party, I expected that the men would be tumbling over each other in their too great zeal to show me their national politeness. Quite the contrary, the young Frenchmen were as indifferent as even Brummell himself, to every woman turned of twenty; but the old high-bred, high-born Frenchmen were all remarkably intelligent, polite and agreeable.

I did not see Meyler again till the following evening at the opera, when, being both tired of shamming more indifference than we really felt, we went home together. Meyler was looking remarkably handsome and well. He told me that Lord Ebrington was in Paris, and had promised to present him at court the next day.

"What do you think of His Lordship?" I inquired.

"He is one of the handsomest, most sensible, and distinguished looking young noblemen in Europe," Meyler replied.

"Very well, I am glad you like him, and I am glad he is here; because, if you treat me too ill, or again mortify me by saying you are sick of my constancy, and wish nobody was constant in the world, *alors, vois-tu, on peut se consoler*,"

"*Point de tout*," answered Meyler, "for, of course, if Lord Ebrington had any fancy for you he would prove it. I am not such a vain fool as to believe any woman breathing would have me, or remain an hour with me, if she could be even tolerated by Lord Ebrington."

"Now Meyler, pray don't go out of your way to provoke me. You cannot, nobody can, or ever did imagine I would stay with a man whom I disliked, merely for his money: and further, what pleasure do you find in striving to wound and humble my vanity thus, as if I was and had been constant to you from necessity alone?"

"I did not say you could not get others. I know to the contrary. I only said what I firmly believe, which is that, were you, this very night, to send a note to Lord Ebrington, inviting him to your bed even, he would not come."

Thus did this provoking creature delight in teasing me, and the next half-hour he would seem passionately devoted to me.

For the first month, Meyler went everywhere, and I led a very gay life: that is, with regard to going every night to parties, masquerades, balls, and other amusements. One day, a friend of Meyler's, Bradshaw, told me that Meyler led a most dissipated life, and made up to at least half a dozen Frenchwomen in a week. The idea had not struck me with such force of truth before, and I was suddenly oppressed with very low spirits; so writing an excuse to the party where I was expected to sup, I sat down at my window to watch the door of Meyler's hotel, which was opposite to mine, for the arrival of his well-known little elegant chariot. The moment it caught my eye, I dispatched my servant with a note begging him to come over to me immediately. He obeyed my summons in very ill humour, declaring that I made him feel as though he had a net thrown over him, and that it was impossible to be happy without perfect liberty. This harshness to one like me, who had been hitherto so spoiled and indulged, affected me with the deepest melancholy. I felt it the more too from being in a foreign country.

"Meyler," said I, almost in tears, "I wish all the world to enjoy perfect liberty, and you must admit that, generally speaking, it has been my request that you only remain with me while my society is pleasant to you; but this night I am unwell, and my spirits are greatly depressed by what Mr. Bradshaw has told me. You know I am not a likely person to wear the willow, or be long unhappy, if you have ceased to prefer me to all other women; but, this night I would entreat and consider it as a favour, if you would remain with me for an hour."

"Can't you enter into the secret of my temper?" said this most provoking little man in his usual impressive, slow way. "Can't you understand that, were you to make it your particular request that I should sit down on that chair at the very moment when I was about to do so, it would be the very reason why I should determine against it?"

"Common delicacy, such as is due to yourself as a gentleman," I continued, "might induce you not to wound my pride, or insult me by leaving me, at the moment when I have every reason to believe it is for the purpose of visiting another woman; one, too, of that class which is even unsought by any Englishman who may fall in their way. This has been told me by your friend; but if you will give me your honour that such is not the case I will believe you."

"You are not my father confessor," answered Meyler roughly, and then ran downstairs, got into his carriage, and drove off without further ceremony.

If I had bowed in meek submission to Meyler's will, and endured all this unfeeling, insulting treatment in humble silence, wetting my solitary pillow with my tears, perhaps some might have voted me a saint, from which opinion I take the liberty to differ. We must, as I think, treat those capricious men as we find them. Meyler's affections were not to be so preserved, even if it had not been contrary to my nature and my spirit to submit to undeserved insult without offering *la pareille*. Had I been a wife or a mother, I might have thought differently; as it was, anger now took the place of tenderness. I should have preferred being pointed at by the whole world, as one of the most profligate women breathing, rather than that anyone should imagine me capable of wearing the willow for a mere sugar-baker, who could forsake me and openly seek the society of the lowest women in preference to mine.

At this moment, choosing whom I might prefer myself as an instrument to execute my proposed vengeance, was quite secondary consideration. I thought only on the person who might be most likely to inspire Meyler with jealous rage and envy.

I very soon decided upon Lord Ebrington, as being the man Meyler professed to think most desirable, and, at the same time, whose attention he conceived it would be most difficult for me to obtain, and I wrote as follows:

MY DEAR LORD EBRINGTON,

You and I made each other's acquaintance when I was very young, and soon parted. By mutual consent we cut each other's acquaintance. Yesterday I saw you looking remarkably well. You were in Meyler's barouche. You have sense enough to love candour, and, when women mean the same thing, you have the same respect for them, whether they go a roundabout way to work, or straightforward. In a word then, I am willing to renew our acquaintance, believing it just possible that, if you were tired of me long ago, when I was quite a different sort of person, you may like me now; while, at the same time, I may be less afraid of you than I was formerly. Qu'en pensez-vous?

H.W.

Answer:

Will ten o'clock this evening suit you? If so, I shall have much pleasure in visiting you.

E.

Revenge is sometimes sweet, even to the most forgiving lady, when the manner of it is not too desperate. Ebrington came. He was then particularly handsome and sensible, and his manners were as gentle, shy, and graceful almost as those of Lord Ponsonby himself. Few women could have disliked a *tête-à-tête* with Lord Ebrington. The thing was scarcely possible, supposing he had been in the humour to make them like it. The fact is I gloried in being a match for Meyler's vile impertinence. Naturally frank, I did not conceal the real state of things from Ebrington. I paid his vanity a wretched compliment, he said: but still he should have been proud to have accepted my invitation under any circumstances.

Ebrington was not a new lover. I had known him long before I ever saw Meyler; but he was proud, and reserved, and shy, and he had not taken the trouble to draw me out, or discover that I professed any more quickness than girls in general. I always thought the expression of his countenance remarkably fine, and now that we conversed more freely, and I had an opportunity of judging of his very agreeable qualities from his lively pleasant conversation, it was impossible to avoid drawing comparisons by no means favourable to Meyler, who, though perfectly graceful and gentleman-like, was far from well read, and, as for conversation, he seldom spoke at all. Moreover, at this instant, I had good reason to believe the provoking little reptile was actually in the arms of some frail, very frail, Frenchwoman.

I asked Ebrington, while we were taking our chocolate the next morning, in my very gay, luxurious dressing-room, how he came to be so cold a lover at a time when I was certainly handsomer and in the very first bloom of my youth.

"I cannot account for it," answered Ebrington; "but, since you love candour, I will tell you that you did not then inspire me with any warmer sentiment than such general admiration as one cannot help feeling towards any fine girl. We met by accident, and soon parted, I believe without much regret on either side.

"Since that," continued Ebrington, "I have heard of nothing but Harriette Wilson wherever I went. I could not help wondering what Ponsonby or Worcester had discovered in you that was so very charming, and yet could so entirely have escaped my observation."

"You vile, impertinent monster!" interrupted I.

"Never mind, dear Harry," continued Ebrington, "for I love you dearly now."

"And I like you twice as well as I did six or seven years ago," I retorted.

"Very complimentary to us both," said Ebrington. "In fact, you are now exactly what I always liked. Formerly, you were too shy for my taste. I would have given anything that you had sent for me merely because you fancied me. Nothing can be so gratifying and delightful to my feelings, as the idea of having inspired a fine woman with a strong, irresistible desire to make me her lover, whenever the desire is not a general one."

Ebrington did not leave me till past two o'clock in the day, having obtained my permission to return to me early on the same evening. About half an hour after his departure Meyler entered my room, and, as was invariably the case after he had used me harshly, was all smiles and tenderness. "My dearest Harriette," said he, "I confess Bradshaw told you the truth. I have been intriguing, since I came to Paris, with almost every Frenchwoman I could find. *Que voulez-vous?* It is the nature of the animal. I am not naturally sentimental. Frenchwomen, being a great novelty to me, inspired me for the moment; but I could never visit any one of them a second time. So much the contrary, that I ran away from anyone I had once visited, when I met them in the streets, with feelings of the strongest disgust. Last night has cured me of intriguing with Frenchwomen. I returned home more in love with you, dearest Harriette, than ever. In short, I was dying to see you, to kiss you, and ask your forgiveness on my knees: but it was too late, your house was shut up, and I dared not disturb you."

"You will never disturb me again," answered I, very quietly.

"What do you mean?"

"I have seen Lord Ebrington."

"What! When we passed your house in my barouche."

"I am not so platonic as to have been satisfied with that. No, I sent for him: but you know, you affirmed that I might do this with safety, since you were sure he would not obey my summons. *Qu'en pensez-vous actuel-lement?*"

"Pray," said Meyler, trembling from head to foot, "put me out of suspense."

"*Je ne demande pas mieux, je t'en réponds,*" answered I, "only," and I looked at him as I advanced towards the door for safety, "only promise not to beat me nor break my head."

"Nonsense! Pray, pray don't torment me."

"Why not? You felt no remorse in vexing me, last night."

"Yes, indeed I did, after I had left you."

"And of what service was that to me, think you? However, I never wished to deceive you nor any man. Briefly then, I beg to inform you that I sympathize with you in your love of variety, and you will, I am sure, give me credit for excellent taste, when I inform you that I have made a transfer of my affections from you to Lord Ebrington, who passed the night here, *et qui doit faire autant ce soir.*"

I expected abuse; but, at all events, something like coldness of manner from Meyler. *Oh! que les hommes sont bizarres.* Quite the contrary. Meyler's spirits sunk into despondency: he actually shed tears, which, with him, was a very unusual event. He was now at my feet, the humble, sighing, adoring, suppliant lover again.

"You have a good heart, Harriette," said he, "and, whatever my faults may have been, I am now sufficiently punished. My health, as you know, has been seriously affected lately. I therefore implore you to send away Lord Ebrington and give me one more trial. I will be as constant and as attentive to you as you can possibly wish."

The little interesting sugar-baker looked very pale; but always very handsome. I say little, from the mere habit I had acquired, with more of his friends, of calling him little Meyler; for his person was very well proportioned, and altogether of the full middle size; but then the expression of his features possessed that soft style of beauty which would have been suitable to a woman.

To proceed, Meyler remained with me without his dinner till past eight o'clock. He would not eat, and could not leave me. At nine, I expected Lord Ebrington, who believed me watching for him with tender anxiety. By this time, fasting and fretting had made poor Meyler seriously unwell. I was not destitute of humanity towards even the worst of my fellow creatures; but it is not, was not, and never will be in my nature to forget insult, nor to love any man after he had practised open infidelity towards me.

"Meyler," said I to him at last, just as the clock was about to strike the hour of nine, and I was in momentary expectation of seeing Lord Ebrington enter the room, "since you have stayed here so long, and appear really annoyed, I will not turn you out of the room to admit another man."

I then hastily scribbled a few lines of apology to Lord Ebrington and handed it to my woman, requesting her to carry the letter down to the porter's lodge to be delivered to His Lordship as soon as he should enter. Meyler was all joy and wild rapture: more in love, perhaps, even, than on the day I first went to him, after he had been pining for one whole year and a quarter. For my part, the idea that so many of the lowest women had lately been favoured with his smiles entirely prevented my sympathizing in his feeling. Ebrington seemed at least to respect and love me. He was handsome, accomplished, of high birth, and not quite turned of thirty.

I was already beginning to prefer His Lordship, and was it to be wondered at, all the circumstances considered? Meyler wanted me to promise never to see nor speak to Ebrington again; but, as it was contrary to my taste and principles to leave any man I had once favoured, as long as he gave me no cause to complain of him, I told Meyler he had better waive the subject, for I would positively make no promise, one way or the other. With this answer he was obliged to be content.

CHAPTER 22

I HAD CHANCED to make the acquaintance of a very pleasing female. She was an Italian widow, of exactly my own age, with the true, soft, Italian expression of countenance. A native of Naples, she had accompanied her son to Paris for the purpose of placing him in a celebrated college. He was a delicate, bilious-looking, interesting child of eleven years of age, with large, pensive, black eyes, and thick black fringes to them. He wore, in common with all the youths of that institution, a large cocked hat, with a tight, military blue coat, faced with a lighter shade of the same colour. His appearance formed an odd contrast to that of my young nephew, George Woodcock, whom I had brought to Paris with me. George was a fair, fresh-coloured, remarkably strong, active boy, with white, thick, curly hair, dressed in a light blue jacket and trousers, with a small ruff round his throat. He did not know one single word of French: nay, more, was such a complete John Bull as to declare upon his word and honour that he would take all the care he possibly could not to learn it. All he feared and dreaded was that the vile jargon should come to him by itself, in spite of all he could do to prevent it.

My Italian friend, whose Christian name was Rosabella, inhabited the same hotel with me. Her constant visitor was a most sanguine Bonapartist, who had formerly been employed by that Emperor as Ambassador to the Court of Naples. I forget this man's name; but I remember he treated Rosabella with the affectionate kindness of a father.

Rosabella was naturally as frank as myself. In our second or third interview, she informed me that she had married at the age of thirteen, by her parents' commands, an old Frenchman whom she hated, and who might, in point of years, have been her grandfather; that her disgust and dislike towards her better half was at its height when she was accidentally thrown into the society of Monsieur l'Ambassadeur, who, in the course of due time—in one, two or three years, I forget which—had completely won her heart, and the result and pledge of their love was her only son, the young Carlo, who was a prodigy of learning for his age. No expense, which could be imagined by fond parents as likely to forward or facilitate his studies, was spared or ever neglected. He had a private tutor kept for him at the college, and whom Rosabella would constantly invite to her table. All her hopes on earth were centred in her child, who slept on a bed of down and drank only of the most delicate wines. He was already a good poet, and rhymed in four different languages; but the poor child appeared to me to be actually dying a victim to severe study, combined with want of exercise. His mother indeed took him home every Saturday night, and he remained with her till the following Monday; but she made him draw plans by way of recreation, with his tutor, almost the whole of the day.

At the time we became acquainted, poor Carlo was afflicted with an oppression on the chest, attended with a cough, and Rosabella, having remarked the bright bloom on George's cheeks, snatched her poor little, interesting skeleton of a child to her heart, and half smothered him with the ardour of her kisses, and then burst into tears. I endeavoured to console her with the assurance I felt, that Carlo only required air and relaxation in order to recover his health.

"He shall have a week's holiday," said poor Rosabella, "and play with your nephew all day long, merely to try its effect."

I interpreted what she said to my nephew, who immediately seized hold of the delicate Carlo, saying, "Come along with me, little Boney. There's a castor for you," taking up the child's large cocked hat, which was full half as big as himself, and, pressing it down on his head by main force, "one may see you're a Boney in a minute. Never mind. I won't be such a coward as to leather you till you get stronger, for fear I should kill you; so come with me, my little fellow, and I will teach you to swim and play at cricket."

"*Plaît-t'il?*" said Carlo, raising his large languid eyes to George's face from the pencil he was cutting.

"*Veux-tu jouer avec le petit Anglais, mon enfant?*" inquired Rosabella.

"*Volontiers,*" answered Carlo, throwing aside his pencil and gracefully bowing to George, as he took off the huge military cocked hat, which George had fastened tight on his head by dint of hard thumps on the top of it with his fist.

"Come along," said George, dragging Carlo forward to the spacious courtyard below.

The contrast which these two children of exactly the same age exhibited, both in their characters and persons, was too striking to have been overlooked, even by the most careless observer: for my part, it furnished me with no inconsiderable source of amusement.

. . . . . .

The next morning I received the following letter from my sister Fanny:

MY DEAR HARRIETTE,

My journey to Paris is put off for the present, and our dear mother will arrive without me, accompanied by our brothers, George and Charles, with Jane, Charlotte and Rose. My spirits are not at present equal to any sort of exertion. Parker has inquired often, and kindly, after his child, and has twice been to visit me; but I will not dwell on this melancholy subject. I am writing in Parker's old bedroom. Methinks the bed looks like a tomb. However, reflection is all nonsense. I would fain tell you something in the shape of news, but really, I scarcely ever leave the house. Brummell's sun, they say, is setting, which, you'll answer, was the story long ago; but, since that, I am told Brummell won twenty thousand pounds, that is too now gone, and he is greatly embarrassed. Poor Lord Alvanley they say is just in the same plight. Napier's passion for Julia continues to increase. I will not call it love or affection, else why does he u ith his twenty thousand a year suffer her to be so shockingly distressed? On the very day you left England, Julia had an execution in her house and the whole of her furniture was seized. I really thought she would have destroyed herself. I insisted on her going down to Mr. Napier at Melton by that very night's mail, to whom I wrote, earnestly entreating him to receive her with tenderness, such as the wretched state of her mind required. A man of Mr. Napier's sanguine temperament was sure to receive any fine woman with rapture, who came to him at Melton Mowbray, where petticoats are so scarce and so dirty; but, if he had really loved her, he surely would have immediately paid all her debts, which do not amount to a thousand pounds, as well as ordered her upholsterer to new-furnish her house.

Would you believe it? Julia has returned with merely cash or credit enough to procure little elegant necessaries for Napier's dressing-room, and, for the rest, her drawing-room is covered with a piece of green baize, and, in lieu of all her beautiful knick-nacks and elegant furniture, she has two chairs, an old second-hand sofa, and a scanty, yellow cotton curtain. Her own bed was not seized. It is now the only creditable piece of furniture in the house of Napier's adored mistress, one of the richest commoners in England, who is the father of her infant.

Ward has been making love to me lately. The other day, he said something to me which I fancied so truly harsh, coarse, and indelicate, that it produced a violent hysterical affection, which I found it impossible to subdue.

Ward wanted me to submit to something I conceived improper. When I refused, he said, with much fierceness of manner, such as my present weak state of nerves made me ill able to bear, "D——d affectation."

392

Sophia and Lord Berwick appear to go on in the old humdrum way. Nobody visits them in their opera box, except our brother John. In fact, I believe Lord Berwick will not permit them. Harry De Roos declares Sophia to be most ridiculously jealous of her sister Charlotte's beauty.

God bless you. I enclose a few lines for my poor boy, George, and beg you to believe in the lasting affection of

Your sister,

FANNY.

I had scarcely finished reading my letter when Lord Ebrington called on me.

"You have behaved very ill to me," said His Lordship.

I assured him it was not my fault; that I had frankly assured Meyler that it would no longer suit me to continue on the same terms with him in which we had formerly lived.

"But still you admit him, just as usual," retorted Ebrington.

"Because Meyler is so violent in his temper, and just now, so uneasy in his mind, which, added to his indifferent state of health, is more than I can resist. Meyler will not remain long in France; but while he is here, my heart fails me when I attempt to turn him out of my house, and he must be permitted to visit me; neither will I shock nor disgust him, while he is in this constant and penitent humour, by allowing him to find you so often here."

Ebrington, being very proud, did not show half the disappointment he really felt. I refused to tell His Lordship to which theatre I was going in the evening, lest his visit to our private box should annoy poor Meyler; for I still felt something like affection for him, although I could never speak to him, or think of him, without getting into a passion.

About this time Amy, if I recollect right, came to Paris with Nugent and Luttrell: at all events if she was not actually the companion of those famous inseparables, she must have followed them immediately. I remember all three paying me a visit together, and inviting me to visit them in the Rue Mont Blanc.

"What then, do you all live together?" I inquired.

"We have each separate apartments, in the same hotel," they replied, and I agreed to call on them.

As for Meyler, he continued to be all a woman could possibly wish him, as long as there was rivalry with Lord Ebrington; but, as soon as ever His Lordship had, or seemed to have, relinquished the pursuit, Meyler left off being amiable by slow degrees, till he became just what he had been before Ebrington had made an infraction in the complete harmony of our *ménage*. At that time Lord Hertford's remark occurred to me: "Better live on a bone, than with a man of uneven or bad temper."

In one of Meyler's fits of dogged humour, he asked me if I imagined he was vain enough or dupe enough to believe that I had given up such a man as Lord Ebrington for him. "You know, as well as I do," continued Meyler, "that you are only making a merit of necessity. Ebrington got tired of you!"

I bit my lips with indignation, as ladies are wont to do on these occasions; but I remained silent, considering that most dignified.

"As you will," I replied; "be it as you will, only pray, pray, a little peace if you please, and a little respite from these eternal quarrels, or part we must and part we will!"

I began to grow thin and to lose my appetite owing to the wretched life I led with Meyler, and I often asked myself why I endured it. I must have been naturally steadfast in my attachments, or possessed a very good heart. One of these, I hope, cannot admit of a doubt. At length, Meyler began to despair of putting me in a passion by anything he could say on the subject of Lord Ebrington having cut me dead, and of my having made a merit of returning to him, *faute de mieux*. This was what his jealous, suspicious temper made him really believe, and he never gave a woman the credit of any single good motive for what she did or said. "Perhaps," observed Meyler, in his zeal to tease and provoke, "perhaps Ebrington likes you still and wishes to visit you, while you are so excessively cold-blooded as to leave the man you like to stay with me, because I am so much richer."

"Which of us two must leave the room?" said I, taking up my bonnet and ringing my bell in a violent passion.

Meyler had never seen me so violently disturbed, and half afraid he might have gone too far, he affected to turn the whole into a mere joke, when he took leave of me, as he said, to dress for dinner.

The very instant he had turned his back I wrote a note to Lord Ebrington, declaring, whether he ever wished to see me again or not, Meyler and I were now really separated: but that it would certainly make me happy, if he were disposed to convince me he was not offended by what I said to him at our last meeting, by coming to me directly.

Lord Ebrington, who lived in my neighbourhood, was at home, and immediately answered my letter in person. Though his pride had not permitted him to show any symptoms of regret when he was dismissed, yet he very willingly expressed his delight and satisfaction at being reinstated.

"Meyler has accused me of leaving you, to endure his vile temper, merely for his fortune, and that accusation has decided the business. I will therefore receive your visits just as publicly as you please and when you please, for as long as ever we shall both agree together."

Ebrington stayed so long with me, that I was obliged to offer him some of my dinner. In short, difficulties never fail to increase passion even in the coldest breast. Ebrington however, as a lover, was far from cold at any time; but a man may possess very warm passions with a cold heart. Ebrington acknowledged that his heart was cold; at the same time it was on this day rather unusually warmed.

"I love heart in women," said Ebrington, "and am grateful when feeling of any kind is evinced towards me."

His Lordship's extreme gentleness of disposition appeared very attractive when set in contrast with Meyler's tormenting, dogged humour. In short, ours bid fair to grow into a strong, mutual fancy, if not to real, true love, *selon les règles*.

I could not get Ebrington out of the house. He remained with me from five in the evening until past three on the following day, when, after obtaining my promise to receive him again on the same evening, he took his departure in full dress, having called on me the day before, merely with the intention to make me a flying visit on his way to a large dinner-party. Ward, who, as I have before said, had accompanied him to Paris and lodged with him at the same hotel, entered his room just as he had sat down to a second breakfast, without changing his white silk stockings, etc.

"*Déjeuner restoratif, apparemment?*" said Ward, bowing to him, and mawkish as this may seem in print, it was certainly the most amusing attempt at wit I ever heard from that quarter: although Nugent accuses him of having uttered many more good things.

Ebrington's pretty cabriolet, which he had sent for, was scarcely driven from the door when—enter little Mr. Dick Meyler, M.P., and sugar-baker, as pale as a ghost! I was really shocked, having seldom seen him look so ill, and I took hold of his hand, which was as cold as death.

"Why, Meyler, will you force me from you, if you really have the smallest attachment for me?"

"I saw Ebrington's cabriolet, and had no stomach for going out to dinner yesterday; so down I sat at my window to watch for His Lordship's departure. In about an hour, I saw Ebrington's head put out of your window to order his servant home. I sat at my window till past two o'clock in the morning, watching for Lord Ebrington."

"And did not you then begin to hate me?" I inquired.

Meyler shook his head, and the tears were actually gathering in his eyes.

"What an unaccountable creature is man!" exclaimed I.

"Ultimately," continued Meyler, "I threw myself on my bed, and fell into a feverish sleep, during which I dreamed that both you and Lord Ebrington were trying to destroy me."

I now felt so tormented between pity for Meyler's unhappiness and disgust at the idea of being longer the slave of such a temper, which no kindness or attention could mend, because it was ever misinterpreted, that I heartily wished Ebrington in Italy, that Meyler might leave me without fear to join the Leicestershire hunt, since August was fast approaching.

"Anything on earth will do, for a quiet life," said I to Meyler. "I have suffered too much already. My nerves and health are nearly destroyed, and, if this is the perpetual tax upon a little wit or a little beauty, I would I were a homely idiot and the mistress of some clean little hut, where people would let me alone. I can do very well without love, for I can always find plenty of things to laugh at and amuse myself with, only do for heaven's sake let me alone; for nothing you can now say or do shall induce me to be tormented with your society."

"Then I will very soon take my departure for London," answered Meyler, despondingly, "for I see you are really in earnest. Only promise me that for the short time I feel under the necessity of remaining in Paris, in order to give a fair trial to my medical adviser here, of whom I think highly, not to let me see Ebrington visit you."

"I want rest," said I, "and I cannot be teased just now. *Allez, mon ami. Amuse-toi bien,* and be sure to tell me when you go to England, that we may take leave of each other."

Meyler was no doubt affected, and felt deeply at particular moments; but he was a hard liver, and his heart was a cold one. He loved riding and good claret better than the finest woman in the world, so that, the first burst over, I have no doubt, with Bradshaw's help, with whom I knew I was no favourite, he soon learned to support the dire calamity of my loss, assisted by some gay, pretty Frenchwoman, of rather more refined manners than those of his lost Dulcineas. However that might be, he never attempted to visit me during another fortnight or more.

Being tired of the idea of a mere animal, whom I had loved for his beauty, I began to grow in love with mind. Ebrington passed the whole of his time with me; but he never brought his cabriolet to my door, and I strictly enjoined him to watch in every direction for Meyler before he ventured to approach my house, in order to spare that little gentleman, if possible, the disgust of seeing him enter. Much as I abhorred deception, I considered this a matter of common delicacy towards a man with whom I had once lived as a wife; but to have denied myself the society of a person so very pleasing, merely to gratify Meyler, who had so coarsely insulted my feelings, I conceived to be quite unnecessary, particularly as I often observed him go out in his barouche with a party of male friends, evidently in improved health and tolerable spirits. Meyler's spirits had never been high since I had known him, owing, probably, to a decayed constitution, for even when I first saw him, strong and blooming as he seemed to the careless observer, he had symptoms of decline about him; and one of them was that lovely transparency of skin and the occasional blue tint of his lips.

Ebrington and I were excellent companions. We both knew the world well, and well we both knew how to laugh at it. We often strolled in the Tuileries, or down the Champs Elysées.

Ebrington, in point of every exterior quality, perhaps too in many of his general habits, was a model for English noblemen. Nevertheless, though he never scolded, nor found fault with anybody, he often put me in a passion. If one kept him waiting, or refused even his most trifling request, he would not condescend to complain, and yet there was something about the freezing reserve he assumed on such occasions, which my pride and feeling could ill brook. There was no affectation in this; but much genuine, innate pride. His Lordship was a connoisseur in pictures and statues, and a most enthusiastic admirer of Napoleon, to whom he said he had some idea of paying a visit at St. Helena. In short, the only time I ever heard Ebrington speak like a man of warm feelings, was one evening as we stood in the Place Vendôme, canvassing the merits and the faults of Bonaparte.

It was long since I had been fairly and truly in love. I might very likely have begun again with Lord Ebrington, but that there was a certain hauteur about his character, added to a disposition to be severe and satirical, which rendered him at some moments quite odious. *Au reste*, few men could, when he happened to be in the humour, render themselves more pleasing to a woman than Lord Ebrington.

Since Lord Ebrington had accompanied to the Continent a party who were impatient to be on their road to Italy, after passing a few more weeks with me he began to talk of taking his departure.

"If we like each other again, we will renew our acquaintance on your return," said I, "but pray let us make no promises. I am so delighted to have obtained my liberty, that I am resolved to permit no man on earth to infringe it."

Ebrington, with his cold heart and his proud disposition, naturally loved to feel himself unshackled as well as I did, however he might regret the idea of leaving me. I think Lady Heathcote was one of the party he was to accompany to Italy. Ebrington at last took his leave of me, promising to make Paris on his way back. Our parting was affectionate: it might have been enthusiastic on my part, but that I could not help thinking Ebrington naturally selfish. Yet, since I found him an intelligent, delightful companion, I regretted him for a whole day and night.

The next morning Meyler entered my room before I was out of bed.

"Thank God, Ebrington is off for Italy," said he; "and, knowing you were alone, how could I resist paying you a visit?"

"I am glad to see you, poor little Meyler; but how very pale you are!"

"I have had a severe attack of liver," answered Meyler, "which confined me six days to my bed."

"Indeed, if I had known that, I would have gone to see you. I thought you were gone to Brussels or Versailles, when I did not see you pass in your carriage."

"I am going to England," said Meyler. "Paris does not agree with me, neither will I ever again attempt to live with any woman breathing. You are the first, and shall be the last. I now know myself and my temper, and feel that my only chance of enjoying health or quiet is in living alone; my nerves are so terribly irritable.

"I shall go to England in three days," continued Meyler. "May I see you constantly till I go?"

It was not in my power to refuse this request from one whom I fancied to be dying in the very bloom of youth; and we passed two whole days together, without once quarrelling. Meyler's late indisposition had, in fact, left him too weak to contend, while I humoured him as though he had been a child.

We slept in separate beds, in the same room; and, on the night previous to Meyler's departure for England, just as we were composing ourselves to rest, Lord Ebrington walked up to my bedside! I screamed aloud. Perhaps I mistook him for a ghost, or, it might be, I dreaded the effect this *mal apropos* visit might have on poor Meyler's shattered and irritable nerves.

"Dear little Harry, have I frightened you?" said Lord Ebrington, in speechless dismay.

I pointed with my finger towards the small French bed, where poor Meyler was still calmly sleeping, and Lord Ebrington hastily bolted from the room. I then got out of bed, and, after steadfastly examining Meyler's features to ascertain that he really slept, seized my lamp, and hastened to awaken my English maid, who slept in a closet adjoining my bedroom, which was situated next to the entrance-room.

I asked her how she came to be so forgetful as to leave the key on the outside of the ante-room.

Martha was frightened to death and begged my pardon; hoped nothing had been stolen.

"A man has entered our bedroom," answered I, and Martha was thinking about fainting!

"Don't faint," said I, "but secure the door instead." I then crept quietly back to my bed, resolved not to tease poor Meyler by acquainting him with Lord Ebrington's unexpected return. I however wrote to His Lordship early the following morning, desiring him not to make his appearance until Meyler should have left Paris.

For more than a month after Meyler's departure for Melton Mowbray, I continued in very low spirits about him. Lord Ebrington, after travelling two whole days along a flat, ugly country, was seized with a fit of love for me, or disgust of flat countries, I am not sure which.

"Suppose we turn our horses' heads towards Paris again?" said Lord Ebrington to Lady Heathcote, on the third morning after they had quitted that gay, delightful city. Now it happened to have been long shrewdly suspected, that my Lady Heathcote could refuse Lord Ebrington nothing. However that may be, certain it is, she did not refuse to return to Paris with the rest of the party, which consisted of—I forget who.

Ebrington, on the wings of love, flew to his faithful Harriette, whom he expected no doubt to find like fair Lucretia, surrounded by her virgins, at their spinning wheels; instead of which—but I told all this before.

I fancy his vanity was irreparably wounded with what he saw on his arrival. He had left me in tears, and returned almost under the impression that he should save me from despair. He was half in love with me for my tenderness of heart. We might have travelled to Italy altogether, and I would have rather made the tour of Italy with Ebrington, than almost anybody I knew, now that he had quarrelled with Ward, or rather cut and parted company with him. No wonder! who could travel with Ward? However, Meyler spoiled my preferment with Ebrington by hurting His Lordship's vanity and thus damping all his ardour.

We passed about a week together, during which time I was continually talking of poor Meyler and lamenting his precarious state of health. Ebrington took his leave of me and of Paris. Could I wonder at it?

CHAPTER 23

THE NEXT DAY, Henry Brougham, M.P., engaged me to dine with him at Verié's in the Palais Royal. He had invited Nugent and Luttrell to join us, but not Amy.

After dinner, we went to witness Talma's performace in one of Racine's tragedies, Brougham being a very great admirer of French dramatic poetry. Before we parted, I took the liberty of consulting him on the subject of my annuity from the Duke of Beaufort, which His Grace refused to pay me, owing to my having been induced to write a few lines to Lord Worcester, contrary to the letter of the bond.

Brougham said boldly, and at a public dinner-table, that it was a mean, paltry transaction, the object of the Duke being fully obtained by my final separation from his son, to seize hold of such a pretext for depriving me of a bare existence. He advised me to bring the case to trial by all means; had no doubt of its success; afterwards wrote to me from England to the same effect, and I showed his letter to young Montague, who was a friend of the Duchess of Beaufort, and often on a visit to her at Badminton. This gay young man was, however, now passing a few weeks at Paris.

Before Brougham went to England he very kindly promised to give me every assistance in his power, provided I would take the advice he so strongly recommended, of proceeding against His Grace of Beaufort.

"In the first place," said Brougham, "Lord Worcester could not in common decency, even supposing it were possible that he wished it—and I will not for an instant imagine that possible, or in human nature—but even if he wished to bring your letter, written under such circumstances, in evidence against you, shame must hold him back."

Everybody agreed with Brougham. Even his friend Montague said that, of course, Lord Worcester would not think of turning witness against me in a court of justice.

I asked Montague how he could excuse his friend the Duke of Beaufort for acting so very selfish and mean a part towards me, who had trusted so entirely to his honour.

"Why, as for the Duke," said Montague, "he was wholly guided in this business by Lord Worcester. For my part, I do not want to enter on the subject of what you may or may not deserve from Lord Worcester; but this I will say, that be your merits or demerits what they may, I think Worcester ought not to leave you unprovided for. It was due to himself and to his high rank after what had passed, that you should not be thrown upon the wide world, and so I will tell Worcester as I tell you, were he here at this moment. In Worcester's place I would most unquestionably have seen you provided for."

I disliked the idea of proceeding against the Duke of Beaufort: however, I promised to take the matter into serious consideration, and Brougham took his leave of me and of Paris nearly at the same moment.

During my stay in Paris Lord Herbert was introduced to me by Mr. Bradshaw. It was at a large party. I remember that I was very much struck with Lord Herbert's beauty, for it was generally believed that he was married to the Duke Spinelli's sister, whose name I have forgotten. As we had much conversation together, I asked him if this was really the case.

"No, to be sure not," answered His Lordship, to whom the subject appeared to be very annoying. "She answered my purpose very well while I was there. We, in fact, never met, during her husband's existence, but at the risk of both our lives in the event of a discovery, which was not at all impossible. Our only place of rendezvous was the garden. The very night her husband died I made a bet that I would accomplish my wishes as usual; and I won it."

Had Lord Herbert's profligacy not been so extravagant, I should probably have fallen in love with him; but profligacy, and such profligacy, in a man, was ever disgusting to me. Not that I love a saint: but rather something which is most luxuriously sly and quiet.

As I was one day taking a solitary drive up the Champs Elysées on my road to the Bois de Boulogne, the Duke of Wellington galloped past my carriage. He did look at me; but passing so rapidly I was uncertain whether he recognized me or not. In another instant he had returned and was at the side of my carriage.

"I thought it was you," said Wellington, "and am glad to see you are looking so beautiful. I'll come and see you. How long have you been in Paris? When may I come? Where do you live? How far are you going?"

"Which of these questions do you desire to have answered first, Wellington?" I inquired.

"I want to know where you live?"

"At thirty-five Rue de la Paix."

"And may I pay you a visit?"

"When you like."

"I'll come tonight at eight o'clock. Will that suit you?" I assented, and shook hands with him. His Lordship was punctual and came to me in a very gay equipage. He was all over orders and ribbons of different colours, bows, and stars, and he looked pretty well.

"The ladies here tell me you make a bad hand at Ambassadorship," said I to him.

"How so?"

"Why, the other day you wrote to ask a lady of rank if you might visit her, *à cheval?* What does that mean pray?"

"In boots, you foolish creature! What else could it mean?"

"Why the lady thought it just possible that the great Villainton, being an extraordinary man, might propose entering her drawing-room on the outside of his charger, as being the most warrior-like mode of attacking her heart."

"You are a little fool," said Wellington, kissing me by main force.

Wellington was no inducement for me to prolong my stay in Paris, and as Bonaparte was now on his way from Elba, I began to prepare for my departure. The English were all hurrying away in a state of great alarm.

My mother, having settled herself in a small house just out of Paris, expressed her determination to remain where she was; so did Amy. They were neither of them in the least alarmed. For my part, besides being very anxious to see my sister Fanny, my finances required that I should return to London.

One fine day, as I walked along the New Road, on the outskirts of London, I met Prince Esterhazy. He pulled up his horse, to inquire about my health and learn where I was to be found. I gave him a very incorrect address, and his groom had on the following day failed to find me out. The Prince then set off in his curricle, to search for me himself, and having found a house in the neighbourhood where I had formerly lived, he wanted the owners to take charge of a letter for me, which was rudely refused. On the third day the Prince's servant was again dispatched on the same errand, and he was at last successful.

"I have been two whole days vainly endeavouring to find you out, Madam," said the servant, while delivering into my hands the Prince's note, which contained an earnest request for me to appoint an hour to receive his visit.

I named Sunday at two o'clock.

A few days later the Prince entered and, throwing off his large German cloak, shook hands with me.

"Prince," said I, "I know you don't come here to make love to me, which knowledge renders me the more curious to learn what you do come here for."

"Why," said the Prince, "I have a high opinion of you, and always had."

I bowed.

"In short, I have great confidence in you, and I am going to point out to you how we may serve each other very effectually. I want a friend like you. It is what I was always accustomed to have in Paris. In short, I want to make the acquaintance of some interesting young ladies. I hate those which are common or vulgar; now you could make a party here in this delightful, pretty cottage, and invite me to pay my court to any young lady of your acquaintance, perhaps your sister!"

"Do you allude to an innocent girl, Prince?" said I; "and do you really imagine that, for all your fortune, paid to me twice over, I would be instrumental in the seduction of a young lady of education? And, if I would, would you not yourself scruple, as a married man, to be the cause of misery to a poor young creature?"

"There are many girls who determine on their own fall," said Esterhazy. "All I want is that, when you see them going down, you will give them a gentle push, thus," said he.

"Prince," I replied, "I will never injure a woman while I breathe, and I will assist and serve those of my own sex whenever I can, as I always have done. No innocent girl, however inclined she may be to fall, shall receive the push you suggest from me. On the contrary, I will always lend my hand, as I did to my sister Sophia, to try to prevent her from falling, or to lift her up again. If I knew a poor young creature, deserted by her friends and her seducer, and you would make a provision for her during her life, I would for her sake, not for yours, perhaps present her to you."

"Perhaps I would make a settlement on her," said Esterhazy; "but mind, she must be very young, very fair, and almost innocent."

"Why, Prince, you are like the ogre in *Tom Thumb*. And all the while you have the enjoyment of the most beautiful wife in Europe!" said I.

"Oh Harriette! a wife is altogether so very different from what is desirable, no sort of comparison can be made with them," replied His Excellency, taking up his cloak.

In two days he came to me again, in a dirty greatcoat, all over wet and mud, just at my dinner-time. He placed himself before my fire so that I could not see a bit of it, with his hat on, and declared he was much disappointed at not having heard from me.

"Take your hat off, Prince," said I.

"I never take it off, nor behave differently to the first duchess in the land! It is my way. I cannot alter it. I am too old to mend. I saw two of the most lovely sisters, walking with their mothers today. They would not measure round the waist more than so much"—describing to me the circumference with his hands. "I watched them home, to No.———in ——Street. Do pray contrive to get acquainted with them."

"You had better leave my house," said I, beginning to be truly disgusted at the very honourable employment which this princely representative of Imperial dignity, morality, disinterestedness, and humanity wished to force upon me.

"At all events, take off your hat, Prince, and let me see the fire!"

"I tell you I will do no such thing," asseverated the Prince, with the dignified positiveness of his own Imperial master.

"*Où ôtes ton chapeau, monsieur le prince, où va-t-en au diable! comme je t'ai dis auparavant,*" said I, in a passion.

"*Je prendrai le Parti,*" said the Prince, leaving the room.

"*Et tant mieux,*" I observed to him, as he went downstairs. I am indeed most inexcusably forgetful, I should otherwise have described, in its proper time and place, that famous masquerade which was given by the members of Wattier's club to all the nobility in England, in honour of peace between Great Britain and France, which occurred prior to my leaving England. It was the most brilliant assemblage I had ever witnessed. Amy, Fanny and I were promised tickets from the very beginning; but poor Julia was not popular. After making vain applications to half the town, and to all the members of the club who were stewards of the feast, she at last addressed herself to Lord Hertford.

"I am not a member of Wattier's; therefore I cannot obtain a lady's ticket for you," said His Lordship; "but, if you like to go in boy's clothes, I have one at your disposal; but not transferable, mind."

Julia was very shy and did not like boy's clothes; but Julia's legs were perhaps the handsomest in Europe, and then Julia knew there was no remedy: so, after accepting Lord Hertford's polite offer with many thanks, I accompanied her to Mr. Stultze, the German regimental tailor and money-lender in Clifford Street.

It was just before I left England for Paris. I cannot think why I am so very careless as not to put more order into my memoirs. However, when a person gives a bad dinner, and apologizes for not giving you a better the apology is always more insufferable than the dinner.

We asked Stultze's advice about a modest disguise for Julia, and he referred us to a book full of drawings therein exhibited, the dress of an Italian or Austrian peasant-boy and girl, I forget which; but I remember that Julia wore black satin small-clothes, plaited very full round the waist, *à la Cossaque,* fastened tight at the knee, with a smart bow, fine, black, transparent silk stockings, black satin shoes, cut very short in the quarters, and tied with a large red rosette, a French cambric shirt, with beautifully small plaited sleeves, a bright blue, rich silk jacket without sleeves, trimmed, very thick, with curiously wrought silver bell-buttons, and a plain round black hat with a red silk band and bow.

I, as Julia's fair companion, was to wear a bright red, thick silk petticoat, with a black satin jacket, the form of which was very peculiar and most advantageous to the shape. The sleeves were tight, and it came rather high upon the breast. It was very full-trimmed, with a double row of the same buttons Julia wore. My shoes were black satin, turned over with red morocco; my stockings were of fine blue silk, with small red clocks; my hat was small, round, and almost flat, the crown being merely the height of a full puffing of rich pea-green satin ribbon. The hat was covered with satin of the same colour, and placed on one side at the back of the head. The hair was to fall over the neck and face in a profusion of careless ringlets, and, inside my vest, an Indian amber-coloured handkerchief.

Stultze brought home our dresses himself in his tilbury, on the morning of the masquerade, being anxious that we should do him credit. Everything fitted us to a hair. The crowd was expected to be immense, and we were advised to get into our carriage at five in the afternoon, as, by so doing, we should stand a chance of arriving between nine and ten o'clock, at which hour the rooms were expected to be quite full.

Fanny chose the character of a country house-maid. She wore short sleeves to show her pretty arms, an Indian, glazed, open, coloured gown, neatly tucked up behind, a white muslin apron, coloured handkerchief, pink glazed petticoat, and smart, little, high, muslin cap.

What character in the name of wonder did Amy choose? That of a nun, forsooth!

We were actually on our road, seated in the carriage, from the hour of five till nine. At last we arrived and were received at the first entrance-room by the Dukes of Devonshire and Leinster, dressed in light blue dominos. They were unmasked, this being the costume fixed on for all the members of Wattier's club. No one else was to be admitted but in character. The newspapers described this most brilliant fête in glowing colours long ago, and much better than I can do; I will therefore merely state that it exceeded all my highest flights of imagination, even when, as a child, I used to picture to my fancy the luxurious palaces of the fairies described in my story-books.

One of the immense suite of rooms formed a delicious, refreshing contrast to the dazzling brilliancy of all the others. This room contained, in a profusion almost incredible, every rare exotic root and flower. It was lighted by large ground glass, French globe-lamps, suspended from the ceiling at equal distances. The rich draperies were of pale green satin and white silver muslin. The ottomans, which were uniformly placed, were covered with satin to correspond with the drapery, and fringed with silver. Mixing carelessly in the motley throng, I did not discover this charming spot till I had been there some time.

On our entrance, the Duke of Devonshire presented us with tickets for a raffle. "These," said His Grace bowing low, without in the least guessing who we were, "these tickets will entitle you to one chance each in the lottery, which will commence drawing at twelve o'clock."

The two best characters in my opinion, were the Honourable Douglas Kinnaird as a Yorkshireman in search of a place, and Colonel Armstrong as an old, stiff, maiden-lady of high rank in the reign of Queen Anne. He wore no mask; but his face, though curiously patched and painted, was easily known. He sat on a bench, with his hoops and ruffles and high powdered head, his point laced lappets, etc., fanning himself, and talking to his young maids of honour, who sat one on each side of him. Everybody who passed stopped to examine him with much doubtful curiosity, which was constantly followed by a loud laugh, and exclamations of, "It is Colonel Armstrong!" "Ha! ha! ha!" "Capital!" Those who could command their countenances among the ambassadors, and men who bore high characters, for that night at least, addressed him in the most obsequious manner, with "I hope Your Ladyship caught no cold at Lady Betty's last night. Immense crowd! Charming evening!"

Armstrong answered all these orations, sticking close to the character and with the most dignified politeness, while the loud, vociferous roars of laughter which were bestowed on his successful efforts to make himself so very ridiculous, never once tempted him to move a single visible muscle of his odd countenance.

Douglas Kinnaird was unfeelingly severe on almost everybody in their turn. To one gay fashionable mother, whose name I have forgotten, he said, "Why, Missis, you've been hawking them girls all over the world for these last six years, and sin they be made to hong upon hond like, maybe they'd go off better all of a lump, if you was to tie um up in bunches you see, as they do cherries, look ye. I manes no offence."

Meyler looked very interesting and handsome, in his blue domino of rich *Gros de Naples*. I had given him leave to find me out if he could, and I guessed that he was busily but vainly employed in the pursuit. I waltzed and danced quadrilles with half the young ladies and gentlemen in the room.

"Is that a boy, or a girl, think you?" was the question from every mouth, as Julia and I passed them. "The leg is a boy's, the finest I ever saw," said one; "but then that foot, where shall we find a boy with such delicate feet and hands?" Still it remained a puzzle, and everybody seemed undecided as to the sex of Julia.

At last, Meyler discovered my sister Fanny by her voice.

"Pray point out Harriette to me," said Meyler, "for I am tired and worn out with my fruitless search."

"That is Harriette," answered Fanny, directing his attention to a young flower-girl who, with her disguised mincing voice, kept him a quarter of an hour in suspense, before he could ascertain the joke Fanny had practised against him; and it took him a second quarter of an hour to find Fanny again.

"Oh you little, wicked, provoking creature!" exclaimed Meyler, at length, catching hold of her hand. "I now vow and declare not to relinquish this fair hand until you conduct me to your sister."

"Upon my word and honour that nun is my sister," answered Fanny, leading him towards Amy, who was standing near her in conversation with Colonel Armstrong.

"Thank you," said Meyler, releasing Fanny's hand in his zeal to join the nun.

Fanny was out of sight in one instant, and, in the next, Meyler had discovered his mistake and resumed his pursuit of her.

William Lamb, who is very handsome, wore a magnificent Italian dress, supported no character, and looked so stupid, I could not help fancying that Lady Caroline had insisted on his showing himself thus beautiful, to gratify her vanity: for, to do William Lamb justice, his character is in truth a manly one, and I will venture to say this said tawdry dress was never one of his own choosing.

I know not how I came to lose my party, just as the grand supper-rooms were thrown open to accommodate, as I should guess, at the least five thousand people. I was in a great fright lest I should lose my supper. The rooms were suddenly deserted. I found myself alone; but it was only for an instant. A gentleman in a rich white satin Spanish dress, and a very magnificent plume of white ostrich-feathers in his hat, suddenly seized me in his arms, and forcing over my chin my mask, which was fastened loosely to admit of air, pressed his lips with such ardour to mine that I was almost suffocated; and all this without unmasking, but merely by raising for an instant, the thick black crape, which fully concealed the lower part of his face. I would have screamed, but from a dread of what might follow.

"This is most unmanly conduct," said I, as soon as I could recover my breath.

"My dear, dear, sweet, lovely Harriette," said the mask, "I implore your forgiveness of a poor married wretch, who hates and abhors the wife whom circumstances oblige him to fear. I have been mad for you these five years. I knew you were here, and how could I fail to discover you? I shall never on earth have such another opportunity, and I had taken an oath to press my lips to yours as I have now done, before I died."

"I believe this to be all nonsense," answered I, "so pray tell me who you are."

"So far from it," answered the mask, with mysterious earnestness, "that, after what has passed, were you to discover me I would blow my brains out."

"Not surely, if I were secret as the grave itself?"

"I would not trust you! But come, I am keeping you from your supper. I accompanied my wife in the disguise of an Italian monk, and having only this instant changed it for the gay one I now wear, I will venture to hand you down to supper, and place you at the greatest distance from my own family; but I entreat one more kiss, dear Harriette, and if ever the fates make me free, then you shall not doubt my affection. The feelings you have inspired in me are unaccountable, even to myself. I am in love with your character."

"Are you old?"

"Guess my age," answered the mysterious mask.

"To judge of you by the nonsense you talk, I should say twenty; but by your voice, your hands, and your person, I should say five and thirty."

"No matter which," said the mask, sighing, or making a feint to sigh. I do not pretend to say it was a true, genuine sigh! "No matter; for I shall, I fear, never enjoy your society more."

I liked his voice, and there was something romantic throughout this little adventure which pleased me. I was in high spirits, and the mask's beautiful dress was set off by a very fine person : and so, when he again insisted on more kisses, I candidly confess I never once dreamed of calling out murder.

"Come," said the mask at last, dragging me hastily towards the supper rooms, "you shall not lose your supper for such an insignificant wretch as I am : and yet, had I known you before my marriage, my dearest and most generous of all human beings, you should never have been exposed to the cold-blooded, unfeeling wretches who have always taken such an unfair advantage of you."

"Why be a slave to any unamiable woman ?" I inquired.

"Political necessity," replied the mask, in a low whisper.

"Do you think I believe all this incredible, romantic nonsense ? Why, you are some strolling player perhaps !"

"No matter : for we are not likely to meet again," the mask said coldly.

"I am glad," added he, "that the little you have heard and seen of me is disagreeable to you; for, neither wife nor children nor politics should have kept me from Harriette Wilson, if it had been possible for her to have loved me only half as much as she once loved——" he paused.

"Who ?"

"Ponsonby."

"Do you know Lord Ponsonby ?" I inquired, with surprise.

"It is of no consequence. You are losing your supper. I will conduct you to your own party."

The mask now hurried me along so fast, that I arrived at the table panting for breath.

"Make room for your sister," whispered the mask in Fanny's ear, as soon as he approached her, and the next moment we were both seated.

"Is there nothing in the tone of my voice or in my manner which seems familiar to you ?" questioned the mask, in a low voice.

"Nothing, positively."

"And my kisses ? Think you that you felt them tonight for the very first time in your life ?"

I started, and threw a hasty earnest glance on the person of the stranger ; for there had indeed seemed magic in his kiss; and, while his lips were pressed to mine, I did think on Ponsonby, yet it was quite impossible that this should have been His Lordship, who was, I knew, on the Continent. Neither was it his voice nor his person.

"Tell me; did you several times receive money sent to you in a blank envelope by the post?"

"And was it you who——?"

"No, not I," interrupted the mask. "A mere accident made me acquainted with the circumstance, and yet I am always near you, I watch over you like a poor wretch, as I am," said he, seizing my hand, and, pressing his lips most ardently on every part of it, he arose from the supper-table and was out of sight in an instant.

Before I could recover my astonishment, a man habited as a friar came towards me, and bending his head close to my ear said, in a tremulous voice, affected by real agitation, or, if otherwise, it was excellent acting, "Farewell, daughter! Every night I shall fervently pray that you and I may love each other in a better world!" It was the stranger-mask, who again vanished from my sight never to return.

Supper consisted of every rare delicacy, in and out of season. The wines were delicious, and the members of Wattier's club were as attentive to us as though they had all been valets, and bred up to their situations like George Brummell, who, by the by, was the only exception. Instead of parading behind our chairs to inquire what we wanted, he sat teasing a lady with a wax mask, declaring that he would not leave her till he had seen her face.

I love a masquerade; because a female can never enjoy the same liberty anywhere else. It is delightful to me to be able to wander about in a crowd, making my observations, and conversing with whomsoever I please without being liable to be stared at or remarked upon, and to speak to whom I please, and run away from them the moment I have discovered their stupidity.

At last I found myself in the still quiet room I have before described. It was entirely deserted, save by one solitary individual. He was habited in a dark brown flowing robe, which was confined round the waist by a leathern belt, and fell in ample folds to the ground. His head was uncovered, and presented a fine model for the painter's art. He was unmasked, and his bright penetrating eyes seemed earnestly fixed, I could not discover on what. "Surely he sees beyond this gay scene into some other world, which is hidden from the rest of mankind," thought I, being impressed, for the first time in my life, with an idea that I was in the presence of a supernatural being. His attitude was graceful in the extreme. His whole countenance so bright, severe, and beautiful, that I should have been afraid to have loved him.

After watching his unchanged attitude for nearly ten minutes, I

BB

ventured to examine that side of the room towards which his fine head was directed; but there was nothing visible at all likely to fix the attention of anyone after the first *coup d'œil*. "Can this be a mere masquerade-attitude for effect, practised in an empty room?" thought I, being almost convinced that I had not been observed. His age might be eight and twenty, or less; his complexion clear olive; his forehead high; his mouth, as I afterwards discovered, was beautifully formed, for at this moment the brightness of the eyes and their deep expression fixed the whole of my attention. "Surely that man's thoughts are occupied with intense interest, on something he sees, which is beyond our common sight or conception," said I, encouraging the mysterious turn of ideas which had obtained the mastery over my imagination; "and I will speak to him." I approached slowly, and on the points of my feet. The stranger seemed not to have observed me; for he did not change his position, nor did his eyes move from their fixed and penetrating gaze on what seemed but space and air, until I came up, close to him, and addressed him thus:

"I entreat you to gratify my curiosity. Who and what are you, who appear to me a being too bright and too severe to dwell among us?"

He started violently, and reddened, while he answered rather peevishly, "You had better bestow your attention on someone more worthy of you, fair lady. I am a very stupid masquerade-companion"; and he was going away.

"Listen to me," said I, seizing one of his beautiful little hands, urged on by irresistible curiosity, "whoever you are, it is clear to me that my intrusion bores you. I promise to leave you at liberty in one quarter of an hour; nor will I insisit on your disclosing your name, and I promise you shall not know mine."

The stranger hesitated.

I had addressed him in French; because I wore a foreign costume, and had promised Meyler, when he presented me with a ticket, that I would remain the whole evening incognita.

The stranger hesitated.

"Don't you understand French?" I inquired.

"Perfectly."

"Well then, take out your watch. In one quarter of an hour you shall be free from all my persecution; but, give me that time, pray do!"

"Agreed," said the stranger smiling, as he gracefully offered me his arm.

"This," said I, pressing the arm I had taken, "this seems, I am sorry to say, to be mere solid flesh and blood. I had fancied——"

"What?"

"Why," continued I, half ashamed of myself, "upon my word and honour, I do confess I thought you something supernatural!"

The stranger's countenance brightened, and he asked me eagerly if I had ever seen him before.

"Never, nor am I naturally superstitious or weak."

"I am not much like the world, I believe," said the stranger; "but I am merely one of ye."

"Does not that satisfy you?" I inquired.

"No; I would be more or less: anything rather than myself; but what is all this to you? Are you a Frenchwoman?"

"No; English."

"Nonsense!"

"Fact, upon my word."

"*Allons!* I like even an Englishwoman better than a Frenchwoman. Not, I assure you, from any national prejudice in their favour; but Frenchwomen are my aversion, generally speaking."

"No matter, I do not require you to like me, for you are too handsome to love in vain."

"What! Then you really could not return my passion?"

"No, upon my word."

"So much the better," answered he; "for I am sick to death of woman's love, particularly tonight."

I looked at the stranger with earnest curiosity.

"Who can you be?" said the stranger, in evident surprise, "and why, if you dislike me, were you so very desirous to speak to me?"

"Who on earth could dislike you? Now would I forswear love, which has hitherto been my all, to follow you to banishment or to death, so that I could be considered your equal, worthy to be consulted by you as a friend; for, though I do not know you, yet I guess that you are on earth and that there's nothing like you. I could pity you, for your fifty thousand weaknesses and errors, adore your talents, and——"

"Here is a high flight," interrupted the stranger, "I can now guess who you are; but dare not name the person I take you to be, lest I offend. Yet," and he paused to examine my person and my feet, "yet, it is impossible it can be anybody else. Why did you affect not to know me?"

"Indeed I do not know you: and it has only this instant struck me, for the first time, that you must be Lord Byron, whom I have never seen."

"And you are Harriette Wilson."

We shook hands cordially.

"I know you hate me, Lord Byron," said I.

"On the contrary, upon my word, you inspired me with a very friendly disposition towards you at once. I was in the humour to quarrel with everybody, and yet I could not resist offering you my arm."

"You did not, I fear, believe in women's friendship and affection, towards men they could not love."

"Why could not you love me? Mind, I only ask from curiosity."

"It is a foolish question."

"I agree with you. Love comes on, we know not why nor wherefore, for certain objects, and for others never will come."

"And yet, I think, I can describe why I could never entertain anything like passion for you. Your beauty is all intellectual. There is nothing voluptuous in the character of it. Added to this, I know that such a man as you are, ought not, or if he ought, he will not, make women his first pursuit; and, to love at all, he must feel pride in the object of his affections. I might excite your passions; but then, such contempt as you have lavished on poor Lady Caroline Lamb would kill me."

"Is there any sort of comparison to be made between you and that mad woman?" Lord Byron asked.

"No matter! I would never put myself in the power of a man who could speak thus of any lady whom he had once professed to love."

"How do you know I ever did?"

"Those letters, in Her Ladyship's novel, *Glenarvon*, are much in your own style, and rather better than she could write. Have you any objection to tell me candidly whether they are really your originals?"

"Yes! they are. But what of that? Is it not absurd to suppose that a woman, who was not quite a fool, could believe in such ridiculous, heartless nonsense? Would not you have laughed at such poetical stuff?"

"Certainly. Those letters would have done more to convince me of your perfect indifference, than even your silence and neglect. Nobody ever did or can impose upon me by a heartless love-letter. *Quand le cœur parle, adieu l'esprit.*

"You must be ill or unhappy, to be so violent and gloomy," I continued, "and, while your genius is delighting all the world, it is hard, and deeply I lament, that you do not enjoy such calm tranquil thoughts as I shall pray may yet be yours."

"Who shall console us for acute bodily anguish?" said Lord Byron, in a tone of wild and thrilling despondency.

414

"We are all more or less subject to bodily sufferings. Thank God, they will have an end," I said.

"And what then?" inquired His Lordship.

"We will hope, at least, that bodily pain and anxiety shall cease with our lives. This, surely, is a reasonable hope. In the meantime, yours cannot be all made up of bitterness. You have enjoyed exquisite moments of triumphs, and you have written the *Corsair!*"

"True! I cannot deny that my sensations are sometimes enviable. You have already done me good, and you and I are now, I hope, sworn friends. Something has this day ruffled me beyond my stock of patience. I must leave you; but we shall meet again, and you will let me hear from you I hope. Or do you mean to forget me? I may not long continue in the same country with you; but wherever I am, it will console me to know that I am remembered kindly by you."

"Do you wish to leave me now, then?" I asked.

"Yes."

"Thank you for being candid, and God bless you, dear Lord Byron," said I, this time raising up my mask, that I might press his hands to my lips.

"*Amuse-toi bien, mon enfant,*" said Lord Byron, drawing away his hand from my mouth, to give me an affectionate kiss.

I saw no more of him for that evening; and rejoined the noisy merry throng. Fanny passed me, followed by Meyler, who was still tormenting her to tell him under what disguise he must look for me.

"There," said Fanny, "Harriette is among those ladies. There are not more than eight or ten of them, and I declare to you that I will not point out Harriette from the rest, say or do what you will." Meyler, in his anxiety to make us all speak to him, suffered Fanny to depart in peace. He did not once address me, but stood puzzling between a gipsy-girl and a flower-girl, till I was induced so far to take compassion on him, as to place my hand in that of the gipsy, making signs for her to tell my fortune, as though I had been representing a dumb woman.

Meyler examined my hand and nails attentively, and then called me by my name.

"I could swear to this hand anywhere; but how you have tormented me tonight," said Meyler.

The novelty of my dress seemed to make the impression on Meyler which a new woman might be expected to make on a man who, like him, was so fond of variety. He was quite in raptures, and refused to leave my side an instant during the remainder of the evening, lest any famous knight-errant should carry me off in a balloon.

At eight o'clock in the morning an excellent breakfast was served. It consisted of coffee, tea and chocolate; and, when I returned home at half past nine o'clock, I heartily wished that the whole *fête* would begin again.

Very soon after this I left London for Paris, as I have already described, and I must now carry my readers back a few pages, to that part of my memoirs where I have stated that my finances required my return to London.

Somewhere about this time John Mills of the Guards insisted on falling in love with me, merely to prove himself a fashionable man. Being a friend of Meyler's, I could not easily avoid making his acquaintance. He was rather well informed: but a stiff, bad imitator of Meyler's gentlemanly carriage and manner: a sort of man who would rather have died than not been a member of White's club, at the door of which he always wished his tilbury and neat groom to be found, between the hours of four and five. From that he went into Hyde Park, for such was the fashion, and he had a chance of meeting Brummell and Meyler there. The former was just now getting into disgrace. The story was this:

Brummell, Alvanley, and Worcester agreed to raise thirty thousand pounds on their joint securities. Brummell having made Worcester believe that he was at least competent to pay the interest of the debt, the money was raised, and the weight of the debt was expected to fall on the Duke of Beaufort, who, after strict inquiry, ascertained that Brummell was deeply involved and without even the most remote prospect of ever possessing a single guinea. When Meyler heard this he became furious, both on his friend Worcester's account and his own, declaring that Brummell had borrowed seven thousand pounds from him, which he had lent in the fullest conviction that Brummell was a man of honour.

I asked Meyler how he could be so very stupid as to have been deceived, even for an instant, about Brummell.

"Why, did not everybody think so?"

"Certainly not. Brummell was pretty generally known for a man destitute of feeling or principle; but he looked well at an assembly, and was the fashion."

"I would forgive him the seven thousand pounds he has robbed me of; but, on Worcester's account, I shall expose him tomorrow at White's."

"Why not let Worcester fight his own battles?"

"That is just what, for the Duchess of Beaufort's sake, I wish to prevent."

416

"I think you may trust Worcester, who has no sort of inclination to fight Brummell nor anybody else."

"No matter. Brummell I will certainly expose; because he has basely obtained a sum of money from my friend."

"So has Lord Alvanley."

"But then, Lord Alvanley may at least contrive to pay the interest; therefore it was not so complete a fraud. Nevertheless, I hold it my duty, as an independent gentleman, never to give my countenance nor society to a man who has done a dishonourable action. I shall therefore cut Lord Alvanley wherever I meet him, notwithstanding no man delights more in his amusing qualities than I do; but, believing that society would be much improved by general firmness of this kind, no power on earth should prevail on me to swerve from this my fixed determination."

Meyler strictly adhered to this resolution to the day of his death. Even when he met Lord Alvanley in the Duchess of Beaufort's box, or no matter where, he never spoke to him again. Alvanley used to rail at Meyler for this, as might naturally be expected, calling him a d——d methodistical grocer, etc.

The little sugar-baker kept his promise of exposing Mr. Brummell at White's club, where he placed himself the following morning for the sole purpose of saying to every man who entered that Mr. Brummell's late conduct both towards the Marquis of Worcester and himself, had been such as rendered him a disgrace to society, and most unfit to remain a member of that club. Tom Raikes, I believe it was, who acquainted Brummell the next day of this glowing panegyric on his character.

Brummell addressed a few lines to Meyler, begging to be informed if such had really and truly been the expressions made use of.

Meyler answered that not only he had used expressions, but that he further proposed returning to the club on the following day, for the sole purpose of repeating them between the hours of two and four, to anybody who might happen to be present, and, if Mr. Brummell had anything to say to him in return, he would be sure to find him at White's during that particular time.

Brummell never made his appearance in London after the receipt of this letter, which gained Meyler the nickname of the dandy-killer. Since then, dandies have gone out of fashion.

Brummell, finding himself on his last legs, made the best of his way to about a dozen of his former acquaintances, from most of whom he had already contrived to obtain large sums of money.

"Play has been the ruin of me," said he to each of them in turn. "I

417

now throw myself on your compassion, being in a wretched plight; for I have been led into such scrapes, as oblige me to leave London at a minute's notice, and I have not a guinea to pay post-horses."

Many of them gave him a fifty-pound note; so did John White I believe; but first, he expostulated with the beau, and asked him what excuse he could offer for having already obtained such large sums from one who knew so little of him.

"Why," said Brummell to several of these half-and-half sort of gentry, "have not I called you Dick, Tom, and John, you rogues? And was not that worth all the money to you? But for this, do you fancy or flatter yourselves that you would ever have been seen picking your teeth in Lady Foley's box, or the Duchess of Rutland's? John Mills above all!"

Brummell was soon after this established in Calais, and half the world went to see him, as though he had been a lion.

CHAPTER 24

Lord Byron paid me frequent visits; but I really cannot recollect whether it was just at this period or later in that year or the next. No matter; Voltaire says somewhere that provided there was a battle, it does not signify when it took place. His Lordship's manner was always natural, sometimes very pleasant; but generally egotistical. He would listen to one's conversation just as long as he was entertained by it and no longer. However, he very good-naturedly permitted one to grow tired of him in the like manner, which was more than many great men could pardon. Once he talked with me on religion till I grew weary and absent. He then fixed his expressive eyes keenly on my face for an instant, as if to read my thoughts before he ventured to proceed, and complacently changed the subject, observing, "I have tired you to death on religion. Let us talk of the gay world, men and women! Perhaps you may find me less tiresome."

"You are never tiresome on any subject; but I was vexed, and tired of the vain attempts I have been making to change such opinions as seem to engender black melancholy, in the mind of a man superior and amiable, as you would be with a happier temper. It was indeed the very height of vanity and folly in me, to have hoped for an instant that anything I could say would influence you."

"The strong proof that you have affected me by much which you have been saying, is the energy and nerve with which I have been striving to refute your arguments during the last half-hour. Do you believe I should have taken all this trouble, if you had said nothing to strike me or throw new lights on a subject which is often tormenting me?"

Lord Byron gradually recovered his serenity, and, before we separated, we had mutually indulged in many a laugh at the expense of false prudes: ladies who put their heads into their pillows, while affecting to cry nay, and, at the same time, *elles se prêtent à la circonstance*. But never mind what we laughed at, or how absurd our conversation, so that poor dear Lord Byron got rid of his sombre melancholy.

We met on various occasions previously to his separation from his wife;

and His Lordship made me very happy one day, by assuring me that there was a soothing kind of softness in my temper and disposition, which, joined to much playful humour, had more than once saved him from feelings nearly allied to madness.

Speaking one day of the severe critique published by the Edinburgh reviewers on his first work, entitled *Hours of Idleness*, I mentioned my surprise at His Lordship having been so irritated and annoyed by it.

"I can easily conceive a stupid, prosing poet, who felt his own inferiority and despaired of writing anything better, becoming furious at such absurd scurrility; but I should have expected you to have read it without feeling your temper ruffled; though, in fact, your poetry was perhaps a little lame: but the satire directed against it became pointless, from its unnatural severity."

"And where did you ever see a stupid, prosing poet, who did feel his own inferiority?" asked Lord Byron. "As a boy, I certainly had a strong suspicion that I possessed unusual abilities; but I was by no means convinced of it: and I often felt myself very deficient in things which it was incumbent on any man to know. I offered my work to the public in fear and trembling; for I knew but very little of the world, and was foolishly sensitive."

Speaking of vanity some time afterwards, Lord Byron remarked, laughingly, that he was tired of praise as Lord Byron, because it now became a thing of course; but still he felt at all times proud and grateful, when any stranger took him for a very fine fellow.

"I, one day," he continued, "determined to try what effect I could produce on an untaught servant-maid. She was very pretty and not, I think, deficient in natural abilities, though it is really very good of me to say so; for she could not endure me! I made myself very smart too at our second meeting, and she became a little more reconciled to me before I left England. However, she certainly was much more in love with a young shopkeeper in the neighbourhood."

Although for my part I never affected friendship for Mr. Brummell, either in his day of triumph or since his disgrace, yet curiosity induced me to inquire about him as I passed through Calais, *en route* for Paris.

"*C'était un homme charmant,*" his French language-master informed me. "*Qu'il avait un ton parfait; que, c'était aussi étonnant qu'heureux qu'il n'eut jamais appris à parler Français, en Angleterre.*"

I made the beau a hasty visit, just as the horses were being put to my carriage. My inquiry, "*Si Monsieur Brummell était visible?*" was answered by his valet, just such a valet as one could gave given the beau in the acme of his glory, *bien poudré, bien cérémonieux, et bien mis, "que Monsieur faisait sa barbe."*

"*Pardon,*" added the valet, seeing me about to leave my card, "*mais Monsieur reçoit, en faisant la barbe, toujours Monsieur est à sa seconde toilette, actuellement.*"

I found the beau *en robe de chambre de Florence*, and, if one might judge from his increased *embonpoint* and freshness, his disgrace had not seriously affected him. He touched lightly on this subject in the course of our conversation, *faisant toujours la barbe, avec une grace toute particulière, et le moindre petit rasoir que je n'eus jamais vu.*

"Play," he said, "had been the ruin of them all."

"Whom do you include in your all?"

He told me there had been a rot in White's club.

"I have heard all about your late tricks in London," said I.

Brummell laughed, and told me that in Calais he sought only French society; because it was his decided opinion that nothing could be more ridiculous than the idea of a man going to the Continent, whether from necessity or choice, merely to associate with Englishmen.

I asked him if he did not find Calais a very melancholy residence.

"No," answered Brummell, "not at all. I draw, read, study French, and——"

"Play with that dirty French dog," interrupted I.

"*Finissez donc, Louis,*" said he laughing, and encouraging the animal to play tricks, leap on his *robe de chambre de Florence*, and make a noise. Then, turning to me, "There are some pretty French actresses at Paris. I had such a sweet green shoe here just now. In short," added Brummell, "I have never been in any place in my life, where I could not amuse myself."

Brummell's table was covered with seals, chains, snuff-boxes and watches: presents, as he said, from Lady Jersey and various other ladies of high rank.

The only talent I could ever discover in this beau was that of having well-fashioned the character of a gentleman, and proved himself a tolerably good actor; yet, to a nice observer, a certain impenetrable, unnatural stiffness of manner proved him but nature's journeyman after all; but then his wig—his new French wig was nature itself.

At Paris, I found most of my friends just as I had left them a few months earlier. Rosabella was delighted to see me. Nugent's old blue remise was still kept in constant motion, rattling about the dirty streets of Paris after his favourite women, and Amy's eyes still rolled and ogled her ugly Swiss banker, Monsieur Grefule, who being still cruel, my pen was employed to melt his Swiss heart; but one might as well have attempted to thaw a Swiss mountain-cape of ice.

I think it was during this visit of mine to Paris, that I happened to be in want of money, an exigency by no means unusual with me; and, having considered who was most likely to give it me, after vainly applying to Argyle I fixed on Lord Byron, who was at that time in Italy: and I addressed him as follows:

PARIS, 15TH MARCH.

MY DEAR LORD BYRON,

I hate to ask you for money, because you ought not to pay anybody: not even turnpike men, postmen nor tax-gathering men: for we are all paid tenfold by your delicious verses, even if we had claims on you, and I have none. However, I only require a little present aid, and that I am sure you will not refuse me, as you once refused to make my acquaintance because you held me too cheap. At the same time, pray write me word that you are tolerably happy. I hope you believe in the very strong interest I take, and always shall take, in your welfare: so I need not prose about it. God bless you, my dear Lord Byron.

H.W.

By return of post, I received the following answer:

RAVENNA, MARCH 30th.

I have just received your letter, dated 15th instant, and will send you fifty pounds, if you will inform me how I can remit that sum; for I have no correspondence with Paris of any kind; my letters of credit being for Italy; but perhaps you can get someone to cash you a bill for fifty pounds on me, which I would honour, or you can give me a safe direction for the remission of a bill to that amount. Address to me at Ravenna, not Venice.

With regard to my refusal, some years ago, to comply with a very different request of yours, you mistook, or chose to mistake the motive: it was not that "I held you much too cheap" as you say, but that my compliance with your request to visit you, would just then have been a great wrong to another person: and, whatever you may have heard, or may believe, I have ever acted with good faith in things even where it is rarely observed, as long as good faith is kept with me. I told you afterwards that I had no wish to hurt your self-love, and I tell you so again, when you will be more disposed to believe me.

In answer to your wish that I shall tell you if I was "happy," perhaps it would be a folly in any human being to say so of themselves, particularly a man who has had to pass through the sort of things which I have encountered; but I can at least say that I am not miserable, and am perhaps more tranquil than ever I was in England.

You can answer as soon as you please: and believe me

Yours, etc.,

BYRON.

P.S.—Send me a banker's or merchant's address, or any person's in your confidence, and I will get Langle, my banker at Bologna, to remit you the sum I have mentioned.

It is not a very magnificent one; but it is all I can spare just now.

Answer:

PARIS, 30 RUE DE LA PAIX.

Ten thousand thanks, dear Lord Byron, for your prompt compliance with my request. You had better send the money to me here and I shall get it safe. I am very glad to learn that you are more tranquil. For my part, I never aspired to being your companion, and should be quite enough puffed up with pride, were I permitted to be your housekeeper, attend to your morning cup of chocolate, darn your nightcap, comb your dog, and see that your linen and beds are well aired, and, supposing all these things were duly and properly attended to, perhaps you might, one day or other in the course of a season, desire me to put on my clean bib and apron and seat myself by your side, while you condescended to read me in your beautiful voice your last new poem! . . .

It would serve me right, were you to refuse to send me what you promised after my presumption in writing you this sermon. However, I must be frank and take my chance, and, if you really wish to convince me you bear no malice nor hatred in your heart, tell me something about yourself; and do pray try and write a little better, for I never saw such a vile hand as yours has become. Was it never a little more decent? True, a great man is permitted to write worse than ordinary people; mais votre écriture passe la permission. Anyone, casting a hasty glance at one of your effusions, would mistake it for a washer-woman's laboured scrawl, or a long dirty ditty from some poor soul just married, who humbly begs the favour of a little mangling from the neighbouring nobility, gentry and others! Look to it, man! Are there no writing-masters at Ravenna? Cannot you write straight at least? Dean Swift would have taken you "for a lady of England!"

God bless you, you beautiful little ill-tempered, delightful creature, and make you as happy as I wish you to be.

HARRIETTE.

Can I forward you a bundle of pens, or anything?

Answer:

RAVENNA, MAY 15TH.

I enclose a bill for a thousand francs, a good deal short of fifty pounds; but I will remit the rest by the very first opportunity. Owing to the little correspondence between Langle, the Bologna banker, I have had more difficulty in arranging the remittance of this paltry sum, than if it had been as many hundreds to be paid on the spot. Excuse all this, also the badness of my handwriting, which you find fault with and which was once better; but, like everything else, it has suffered from the late hours and irregular habits.

The Italian pens, ink and paper are also two centuries behind the like articles in other countries.

Yours very truly and affectionately,

BYRON.

I should have written more at length, in reply to some parts of your letter; but I am at "this present writing" in a scrape (not a pecuniary one, but personal, about one of your ambrosial sex), which may probably end this very evening seriously. Don't be frightened. The Italians don't fight: they stab a little now and then; but it is not that, it is a divorce and separation; and, as the aggrieved person is a rich noble and old, and has had a fit of discovery against his moiety, who is only twenty years old, matters look menacing.

I must also get on horseback this minute, as I keep a friend waiting.

Address to me at Ravenna as usual.

Lord Byron wrote me many letters at different times; but I have lost or mislaid them all, except those which I have herein given, and can show to anyone who may be pleased to question their being really originals.

Here's a disaster—a multiplicity of disasters in short, as Lady Berwick said one day, when the compound evils fell upon her. First, Peacock did not send her shoes home. Secondly, Lord Berwick threw a large, hot leg of mutton at his well-powdered footman's head. I will tell you why: the stupid cook insisted on serving it up, unadorned by the smart piece of writing-paper which is usually wrapped round the shank-bone. His Lordship had expostulated so often that, this time, he hoped to imprint the fact more strongly on the memory by dousing the untouched, greasy joint against his lacquey's brain. Now Sophia, it so chanced, was fond of a slice of mutton. Thirdly, that little man in St. James's Street, who sells box-combs, I forget his name, cut her hair at least an inch too short on the forehead. Fourthly, Sophia could not match the silk she wanted to finish a purse she happened to be netting for her handsome harp-master, Boscha of——notoriety.

"One thing coming upon another," said Sophia, turning up her eyes as she sat with her feet on the fender; "one thing coming upon another, I feel I shall go mad." But, heavy as were Her Ladyship's afflictions, they cannot reasonably be named in the same day with the tragic misadventures which have been lately heaped on my poor little devoted shoulders.

I had proceeded nearly thus far with these my most valuable memoirs, and nearly thus much had been kindly forwarded by the late, good-natured, obliging ambassador, Sir Charles Stuart.

Hélas! les voilà passés, ces jours de fêtes! Sir Charles is sent to India, and his place supplied by that selfsame beau whom I one Sunday trotted up to Marylebone Field in the dog-days, and did not order him home again till he was expiring with fatigue and perspiration. It just now occurs to me that I styled him Lord George, instead of Lord Granville Leveson-Gower, an error which I hasten to correct and in all humility atone for: but it really is difficult to bear in mind the names of those who do not excite in us the least interest. Now that the case is altered, my readers perceive how readily I correct myself, having addressed His Lordship to this effect:

My acquaintance with your Lordship is very slight, since we have met but once in our lives, and that was a long while ago. Nevertheless, I hope you will prevent my feeling the loss of my late kind friend, whom everybody likes, as far as permitting me to forward my letters in the bag.

You will thus, my Lord, serve me just now most positively and effectually, for which condescending kindness I shall ever remain your Lordship's obliged and most obedient servant,

H. WILSON.

Lord Granville sent me a stiff formal note, which I have neither time nor inclination to look for, stating his regrets that, owing to certain regulations at the Foreign Office, he was compelled to refuse my request.

To which I replied:

MY LORD,

I was looking about for a fool to fill up my book, and you are just arrived in Paris in time to take the place, for which I am indebted to you.

Yours obliged and obediently,

H.W.

In the following week, this most upright plenipo's conscience growing slack, he slackened the strings of the bag so far as to admit the private correspondence of an acquaintance of mine, whose name he may learn whenever he thinks it worth his while to apply for it to me, who am his near neighbour.

To proceed with my disasters: the next was a pressing letter from Stockdale, handed to me by bag, declaring that he must have the rest of my memoirs, because folks began to think it was all a hoax, as Liston or some other funny fellow says. *Que faire?* Having, by some wonderful chance or providence, contrived to scrape together two hundred francs, I determined to cross the Channel once more; for I hate to break my word.

Arrived at Mr. Stockdale's house, "willa" I would call it were it at all Cockneyish, I handed him over, as a plenipo-pacificator, the chief part of my delectable memoirs. I conceived that my disasters were now completely at an end, and I looked forward to a rich harvest, with unbounded applause.

Unfortunately, Stockdale, in a courteous fit, acquainted the immortal Wellington that I was about to publish part of his private life, under the impression, of course, that every act which relates to so great a hero must be interesting.

Will it ever be believed? His Grace, in the meek humility of his heart, has written to menace a prosecution if such trash be published. What trash, my dear Wellington? Now, I will admit, for an instant, and it is really very good of me, that you are an excellent judge of literature, and could decide on the merits or demerits of a work with better taste and judgment than the first of Edinburgh reviewers. Still, in order to pronounce it trash, we should fancy that even Wellington himself must throw a hasty glance on one of its pages at least. Quite the contrary. Wellington knows himself to be the subject, and therefore wisely prejudges the book trash one fortnight before it sees the light! So far so good! But when my own Wellington, who has sighed over me and groaned over me by the hour, talked of my wonderful beauty, ran after me, bribed Mrs. Porter over and over again, after I refused to listen to her overtures, only for a single smile from his beautiful Harriette! Did he not kneel? And was I not the object of his first, his most ardent wishes, on his arrival from Spain? Only it was such a pity that Argyle got to my house first. No matter! Though Argyle was not his rose, he had dwelled with it; therefore, what could my tender swain Wellington do better than stand in the gutter at two in the morning, pouring forth his amorous wishes in the pouring rain, in strains replete with the most heartrending grief, to the favoured and fortunate lover who had supplanted him, as Stockdale has indulged me by getting so inimitably delineated. When, I say, this faithful lover, whose love survived six winters, six frosts, six chilling, nay, killing frosts, when Wellington sends the ungentle hint to my publisher, of hanging me, beautiful, adored and adorable me, on whom he had so often hung! *Alors je pends la tete!* Is it thus he would immortalize me?

I'll e'en make my will, and so good-bye to ye, old Bombastes Furioso.

Yet I scarcely know how to take leave of the subject, it affects me so deeply! I should not have been half so much afraid of hanging, only I was subpœnaed on a trial at the Old Bailey a short time ago, as witness against a poor girl who stole a watch out of my house. She acknowledged the fact, and was honourably acquitted!

"Och! the divel fly away wid all the world!" shrieked out my Irish cook, a widow who had just lost her husband. "Sure my darlink's watch has been stolen out of the kitchen."

She came flying into my room when I was ill in bed, and frightened me half out of my wits.

"Nonsense!" said I. "Who could steal your watch, think you?"

"Och! Don't bother me now. Sure it was the last thing my own darlink husband clapped his two good-looking eyes upon, before he died, and I'll murder every mother's son of you, but I'll have my watch!"

"Why, not a soul has been here during your absence, except a very interesting young woman, who did not appear to be more than seventeen years of age. She has left her direction, as she wanted to be my house-maid. I desired her to let herself out, and to be sure to shut the street door after her. On her head she wore a straw bonnet with green ribbons; but my room was rather dark, and that was all I noticed of her. I scarcely think I should know her again."

My Irish cook raved, roared, stormed, and bellowed along the streets, on her way to a magistrate, from whom having obtained a warrant, she passed three whole days in wandering about London to look for young women with ribbons on their bonnets. Of these she contrived to coax three or four to walk with her to my house; but, alas! they did not include the person she wanted. At last she chanced to meet with a young female about seventeen years of age, who blushed deeply when she mentioned to her having been cruelly robbed of a watch. Without hesitation she seized her by the arm, and observing how the young woman trembled, under a promise of pardon prevailed on her to confess the theft, and immediately had her taken into custody. Next day two officers made me accompany them to Marlborough Street public office. The girl was fully committed for trial and sent to Newgate, where I visited her, and expressed my astonishment that so young a girl could commit so daring a robbery. Her plea was, that a soldier had seduced her, she was pregnant by him, and he loved her no longer. In short, her only chance of being admitted to visit him rested in her having money to give him. Love had made her so deperate, that she stole my Irish woman's watch on her way downstairs, merely to ensure one more interview with her faithless lover.

Oh this love! this love!

For more than a week I was shut up all day long in the witness-box at the Old Bailey. The first evening, only petty offences were tried. Two men for pig-stealing, a gentleman for stealing a piece of pickled pork, and concealing it about the lower parts of his person. This, notwithstanding it was a fundamental error, was pardoned, and excited an expression of loud applause from the gallery auditors. The judge reprimanded the noisy throng with proper dignity, assuring them that, if this indecent conduct was repeated, they should be severely punished.

The next morning I saw three men condemned to be hanged. The same judge sat upon the bench. These dreadful scenes were new to me, and I was overpowered with a violent hysterical affection, for which I expected seven years transportation at least; but the judge, it should seem, preferred the sound of sobs and tears to applause, from mere habit, for he took no sort of notice of me. I forget his name. He was a very old man, and spoke as if he took much snuff. I know not whether he or Denman is most respected: but this I know, that, for my own part, next to not being hanged at all, *plaît a M. Wellington*, I should like Denman to pronounce sentence upon me: so pleasing a voice and so persuasive manner I never witnessed, and the most placid, benevolent countenance! No one could see him on the bench, and not feel the comfortable conviction of his earnest wish to save the unfortunates, if it were consistent with his duty. Now I could not help fancying that the learned and snuffy judge was a little more convinced of the wholesomeness and convenience of hanging, than either Denman or our good King George.

Young Law, Lord Ellenborough's son, was a very smart, fine, young gentleman; and his impatience of temper passed, I dare say occasionally, for quickness. His wig was never straight on his head. I rather fancy he liked to show his own good head of hair under it. He was constantly explaining to the witnesses what the snuffy judge said to them, from very impatience, and then again he would explain to my lud on the bench the blunders and mistakes of witnesses.

Young Law cross-questioned an old woman in an antique costume.

"When you first beheld the deceased did you, for your own observation, conceive him to be in a dying state?"

"He said he was very bad, sir."

"I do not ask you what he said, my good woman. I want to know what your own opinion of his health was."

"Why, Lord, sir, everybody said he was in a bad way: upon my word they did."

"Come, come! This won't do, upon my word! What's upon your word to do with it? Don't you know you are on your oath? What—was—your—own—opinion, as to the man's state of health?"

"Oh law!" said the witness, and then paused. I thought, really, that she was calling him by his name. "Oh law! I think he must have been but poorly! very so so, indeed."

"My Lud," said young Law, tossing up his little head with such uncontrollable impatience towards the bench, as to shake out a cloud of powder from his wig, "my Lud, I am no match for this woman. She had better be examined by someone more competent."

The good woman was desired to leave the witness-box.

Good-bye, judge snuffy. Heaven knows how soon you and I may meet again, thanks to the great Wellington. It is a nervous subject to me, yet I cannot help reverting to it. However, let us change it and proceed with my memoirs.

There is surely something harsh and unmanly in threatening a woman with any kind of law or prosecution, unless she were to do something much worse than telling the truth: and there is a double want of gallantry in threatening a fair lady, whose favours have been earnestly courted! *N'est-ce pas?*

Yet, if all the lords and law-givers are like Wellington, in the habit of threatening poor devils of authors and booksellers with prosecution, hanging, and destruction, as often as they are about to publish any facts which do not altogether redound to their honour and glory, while they modestly swallow all the *outré* applause which may be bestowed on their luck or their talents for killing men and winning battles, I can no longer be surprised that even Beaufort has maintained his good character up to this present writing, since publishers will quake when heroes bully.

There's no spirit nowadays.

CHAPTER 25

ANOTHER HERO IN a passion! Another lover threatens prosecution! No less a personage than that most prolific plenipo, the Hon. Frederick Lamb, who yesterday called on Stockdale to threaten him, or us, with prosecution, death and destruction, if his conduct towards me in times auld lang syne was printed and published in any part of my *Memoirs*, after Part I, which he acknowledged that his counsel had informed him he could not lay hold of. No wonder that he is sore. I have certainly told, as the Hon. Frederick Lamb was well aware must be the case, harsh truths of him, I confess: but then it will disgust one to think that a man would feel such violent passion for a girl, without the heart to save her from absolute want afterwards. Yet I never deceived him, and I endeavoured to live on nothing, at my nurse's in Somerstown, *pour ses beaux yeux*, as long as I possibly could. When I say nothing I mean nothing, in the literal sense of the word. Frederick had never given me a single shilling up to the time when hard necessity obliged me to accept the Duke of Argyle for my lover.

As to Frederick Lamb's rage at my publishing these facts, he was fully acquainted with my intention; and had he, now that he is in better circumstances, only opened his heart, or even purse, to have given me but a few hundreds, there would have been no book, to the infinite loss of all persons of good taste and genuine morality, and who are judges of real merit. But I hate harping on people's unkindness, and vice versa, I cannot omit to acknowledge the generous condescension of Earl Spencer, who, though I have not the honour to be in the least acquainted with him, has very repeatedly assisted me. In short, His Lordship has promptly complied with every request for money I ever made to him, merely as a matter of benevolence.

Lord Rivers, with whom I have but a bowing acquaintance, has not only often permitted me to apply to him for money; but once, when I named a certain sum to him, he liberally doubled it; because, as he kindly stated in his letter, he was so truly sorry to think that one who possessed such a generous heart as mine should not be in affluent circumstances.

Lord Palmerston also, one fine day, did me a pecuniary service without my having applied to him for it. Neither can I express half the gratitude I feel, and shall entertain to the end of my life, for the steady, active friendship Mr. Brougham has invariably evinced towards me, actuated, as he is, solely by a spirit of philanthropy. When I see a man of such brilliant talents pleading the cause of almost all those persons whose characters I have sketched in these pages, with such honest warmth and benevolence of feeling, as Brougham did yesterday, to say I look up to him and love him, is but a cold description of the sentiments he inspires in my heart.

"A pretty list indeed," said Brougham, alluding to my characters, as advertised in the newspapers by Stockdale. "Almost every one of my particular friends is among them! The poor Duke of Argyle! What has he done? I am very angry with you. I don't really think I can shake hands with you."

"I have strictly adhered to the truth."

"Yes; but then, who wants to have their secrets exposed! Secrets, some of them, sixteen years old."

"Who do you think would have entrusted me with their secrets fifteen years ago? Besides, why don't my old friends keep me among them? They are all rich. I have applied to them and they refuse me the bare means of existence. Must I not strive to live by my wits? You say you have not read even the first part of my book. How do you know that it is severe?"

"Well! perhaps not! The Duke of Leinster tells me that it is not severe, nor does it, he says, contain any libel."

"To be sure not! Why, as His Grace goes on, he will find that I give him credit for a little more intellect than even a Newfoundland dog! *Que voulez-vous?* But I wish to explain the Duke of Beaufort's conduct, certainly."

"Aye! true! The Duke of Beaufort treated you shamefully. You are very welcome to tell the world that I am your counsel in that business; that I said then, and repeat now, that he took a shameful advantage of your generosity. There, you behaved only too well."

"Thus then, though many of you are angry with me, you all agree in being disgusted with the heartless selfishness of the Duke of Beaufort. The Duke of Portland says he cannot conceive or understand it. So say Montague, Fred Bentinck, Headfort, yourself: in short, if Beaufort means to fight all those who call his treatment of me infamous, he may gain the high-sounding epitaph of fighting Bob before he knows where he is: so farewell Beaufort. I would not change hearts with you. May you meet with all the respect you merit here, and forgiveness hereafter. I have certainly deserved better from you."

"Well! never mind Beaufort," said Brougham, "tell all the truth of him; but, as to the others, pray don't be severe. Write something from your fancy, I cannot endure the idea of all this. You perhaps do not address your letters correctly when you want money. You are so careless. I was once desired to send you some in a great hurry, and there was no date to your letter! I am sure these old friends of yours would provide for you, if applied to civilly."

"I tell you, you judge of them by your own excellent heart: you, who have never refused me any assistance I asked you for, nor any act of friendship in your power, while I have not nor never had any claim upon you. There is the Duke of Argyle, who used to write thus:

"*If at any future time you are in trouble and will condescend to apply to me, you shall be as welcome as my sister; for indeed, I am afraid, I love you.*

"Well, I have, at His Grace's request, condescended to apply civilly, stating my distress, and humbly entreating for anything he could conveniently afford, at least fifty times: and I have never received one single shilling, nor any proof of friendship since it pleased him to become *le beau papa*. Everybody who knows me will admit that I have all my life been disposed to like Argyle, to pardon all his sins against me, and inspire others with a favourable opinion of his heart and character; but the invariable excessive selfishness and want of feeling which His Grace evinces towards me has, at length, I confess, disgusted me."

I have a few more high characters in reserve to sketch for the benefit of my readers; but they are too noble and brilliant to come in at the fag-end of a work. I mean therefore to conclude these *Memoirs*, and take my rest for a month or so, in order to collect my ideas for a new work in two volumes, which ought to be printed on the most expensive hot-pressed vellum, wholly and solely for the express purpose of immortalizing His Grace of Richmond, the Marquis of Londonderry, Lord Maryborough, Grand Master of the Mint, and of the Art of Love, and Mr. Arthur Chicester, contrary to their particular wishes; and at his own earnest, urgent and especial desire expressed in a letter now in my possession, the Earl of Clanricarde.

Oh muse, etc. etc. etc., grant me eloquence to do justice to my subjects on that great and mighty occasion! In the meantime let me conclude, or rather let us proceed to draw these anecdotes into something like the form of a conclusion, because I their writer am tired of them, if you the reader of them are not.

One day, while I was dressing to drive out in my carriage, my servant informed me that Fanny had just called on me, and was in the drawing-room. I was surprised that she did not come up to my bedroom, that being her constant habit whenever I happened to be at my toilette. I hurried on my pelisse, and went down to join her. She was sitting near the window, with her head reclined on her hand, and appeared more than usually pensive.

"My dear Fanny," said I, "what is the matter? Why did not you come upstairs?"

"I feel a weight here," said she, laying her hand on her heart. "It is not a weight of spirits only; but there is something not right here. I am sick and faint."

"A drive in Hyde Park will do you good," said I, and we were soon seated in the carriage. Turning down Baker Street we saw Colonel Parker. Fanny was greatly agitated. He did not seem to have observed us.

"I dare say he is only just come to town, and means to call and see his child," said I, hoping to enliven her. We then drove twice up the park, and Fanny made an effort to answer the beaux who flocked around the carriage, with cheerfulness. Suddenly she complained to me again of sickness, occasioned by some pressure or tightness about the heart.

"I am sorry to take you from this gay scene," said poor Fanny, "but I am too unwell to remain." I immediately pulled the check-string, and desired my coachman to drive to Hertford Street, Mayfair, where Fanny was then residing. After remaining with her half an hour she begged me to leave her, while she endeavoured to obtain a little sleep. She made light of the sickness, and told me to call and take her into the park on the following day. I did so, and just as I was stepping out of my carriage in Hertford Street for that purpose, Lord Hertford came running downstairs to join me, from Fanny's apartment.

"Don't get out, Harriette," said he, "as you will only lose time; but go directly for a surgeon. I was going myself. Fanny is very ill, and her physician has prescribed bleeding, without loss of time."

In the most extreme agitation I hurried after the surgeon and brought him with me in my carriage. Fanny was now affected with such a violent palpitation of the heart that its pulsations might be distinctly seen at the opposite side of the room through her handkerchief.

"I am very ill, Harriette," said the dear sufferer, with encouraging firmness, holding out her hand to me; "but don't frighten yourself. I shall soon get better: indeed I shall. Bleeding will do me good directly," continued she, observing, with affectionate anxiety, the fast gathering tears in my eyes.

I called Lord Hertford aside, and addressed him: "Tell me, I earnestly implore you, most candidly and truly, do you think Fanny will recover?"

"I do not think she ever will," answered Hertford.

"Nonsense!" said I, forcing my mind by an effort to disagree with him. "Fanny was so perfectly well the day before yesterday, so fresh, and her lips so red and beautiful; and then many people are afflicted with these palpitations of the heart, and recover perfectly."

"If her pulse beat with her heart, I should have hopes; but her pulse is calm, and I have none. Disorders of the heart are incurable."

Instead of wishing to display feeling, Lord Hertford seemed ashamed, and afraid of feeling too much.

For another fortnight, Fanny's sufferings were dreadfully severe, and, being quite aware of her danger, she requested that her body might be examined after her death for the benefit of others. My readers will, I hope, do me the justice to acquit me of affectation, when I say that this subject still affects me so deeply, I cannot dwell upon it. All the world were anxiously, and almost hourly, inquiring if there were hope: Sir William Knighton and Sir John Millman, her medical attendants, gave us none, or very slight hopes, even from the first hour.

Fanny never slept, nor enjoyed a single interval of repose. Her courage and patient firmness exceeded all I had imagined possible, even in a man. Once, and once only, she spoke of Colonel Parker; for it was the study of every moment of her life to avoid giving us pain. Fanny called me to her bedside: it was midnight.

"Harriette, remember, for my sake, not to be very angry with poor Parker. It is true, you have written to say I am ill, and he refuses to come and shake hands with me; but then, believe me, he does not think me so ill as I really am, or he would come. Oblige me by forgiving him! Now talk to me of something else: no more of this, pray!"

I pressed her hand and immediately changed the subject. She begged, when we told her of Lord Hertford having had straw put down by her door, and of all his constant, steady attentions, that, when he came next, she might see him and thank him. In consequence of this request, he was admitted on the following morning. Fanny was not able to talk much; but she seemed gratified and happy to see him. When His Lordship was about to depart, she held out her hand to him. Hertford said, in a tone of much real feeling, "God bless you, poor thing," and then left the room.

A monster, in the shape of a nurse to Colonel Parker's child, Louisa, took this opportunity to remain out with the infant the whole of the night! I will no longer dwell on this subject; for, indeed, I cannot.

Fanny was my only friend on earth. I had no sister but her. She was my hope, and my consoler in affliction, ever eloquent in my defence, and would not have forsaken me to have become the wife of an emperor, but God willed Fanny's death.

> I saw her laid low in her kindred vaults,
> And her immortal part with angels lives.

Only three weeks had elapsed since Fanny's lovely laughing countenance, as she drove round the ring in Hyde Park, excited the admiration of all who beheld her. Her life was ebbing fast, when her friends acceded to her earnest desire to be removed to a more airy situation.

Reclined at length on a couch, in her new apartment, Fanny's spirits appeared so much improved as to encourage hopes which had become extinct.

"Do you not breathe with rather less pain?" I asked, while I pressed her cold damp hand between my own.

"At all events," answered poor Fanny, "I would rather die here, than in the close apartment I have just quitted. How sweet and refreshing the flowers smelt, as I was carried along the garden! I did not see them, for I could not endure the light. I wish I could," continued Fanny, fixing her clear, still lovely blue eyes on my face beseechingly. "The prospect, I understand, is most beautiful from the room above us; but I shall never see it."

"Do, dearest Fanny," said I, making a violent effort to conceal my tears, lest they should agitate my suffering sister, "let me open one of the shutters a very little. The air is mild and delicious, and the heat no longer oppressive, as it was when you passed through the garden."

The last ray of the setting sun fell on poor Fanny's pale, beautiful features, as I drew back the curtains. It was one of those lovely evenings in the month of June, which often succeed a thunderstorm, and the honeysuckles, which clustered round the windows, emitted a rich and fragrant perfume.

I asked her if the fresh air did not enliven her a little.

She requested to have her head raised, and I rested it on my bosom.

"Alas!" said poor Fanny, "gloriously as the sun is setting, I may now behold it for the last time!"

Cold drops hung on her fair, lovely forehead. I feared that the slightest agitation would destroy at once the fragile being I held in my arms, and yet, mastered by the strong impulse of irresistible tenderness, I suddenly imprinted a kiss on my sister's dying lips.

The last tear poor Fanny ever shed trembled in her eyes. Forcing a smile, I now endeavoured to address her with cheerfulness, and administered her last draught of goat's milk, which she held firmly in her hand without requiring my assistance.

"I did not believe I should shed another tear," said Fanny, brushing away the drops which were stealing slowly down her fair, wan cheeks. "Pray for me, Harriette! Pray that my sufferings may soon cease."

"I do pray for you, my poor sister, and God knows how earnestly. Be assured, dearest, that your sufferings will very soon cease. You will recover, or you will be at rest for ever. Remember my love, that we have all committed many faults, and you may be called upon to suffer yet a few more hours, as your only punishment, before you are permitted to rest eternally with your God. Yet a little fortitude, my dearest Fanny. It is all that will be required of you."

Fanny seemed deeply impressed with what I had said. Her agony was at that moment dreadfully severe. She crossed her hands on her breast, and there was something sublime in the stern expression her features assumed, while she suppressed the cries which nature would almost have wrung from her. She compressed her lips, and her brow was contracted. In this attitude, with her eyes raised to heaven, she appeared a martyr, severe in virtue and almost masculine fortitude.

"I am better," said Fanny, half an hour after having made this strong effort.

"Thank God!" I ejaculated, taking hold of her hand.

"What o'clock is it?" she inquired.

"Near seven."

"I am very sleepy. I could sleep, if you would promise to continue holding my hand, and would not leave me."

I placed myself close to my sister, with her cold damp hand clasped between both of mine.

"I am near you, always, dearest," said I. "Sleeping or waking, I shall never leave you more." Fanny threw her arms once more round my neck, and with a convulsive last effort pressed me to her heart.

436

"May the Almighty for ever bless you!" said she, and, sinking back on her pillow, a gentle sleep stole on her senses. I watched her lovely countenance with breathless anxiety.

In less than an hour poor Fanny opened her eyes and fixed them on me with a bright smile, expressive of the purest happiness.

"I am quite well," said Fanny, in a tone of great animation.

Again her eyes closed and her breathing became shorter.

Suddenly, a slight convulsion of the upper lip induced me to place my trembling hand on my sister's heart.

I felt it beat!

Joy flushed my face with a momentary hectic—

And then, hope fled for ever!

Fanny's cheek, still warm and lovely, rested on her arm. The expression of pain and agony was exchanged for the calm, still, innocent smile of a sleeping infant.

I had felt the last faint vibration of poor Fanny's heart.

It was some time previous to the death of my sister, that I was induced by the advice of Mr. Brougham and Mr. Treslove to commence proceedings against the Duke of Beaufort for the recovery of the small annuity he had thought fit to deprive me of.

I have already related the circumstances of my having refused to marry Lord Worcester over and over again, solely to relieve the minds of his parents, and further went down to Oxford to implore Worcester, by all his future hopes of happiness, to pass his solemn word to the Duke and Duchess never to marry me; and it was only at my request he could be induced to promise to go abroad for one year, on condition that his father made me an allowance. This the Duke gladly agreed to, and sent Worcester to me, accompanied by his attorney, to ask me what I required.

"Enough to pay for my board only," was my reply. "Nor do I require bonds or signatures. The Duke is a gentleman, and will take care that the person who has complied with all his wishes shall not come to want. Of that I am well satisfied."

Robinson told me to fear nothing, and down I went into Devonshire, where I might have wanted bread, without obtaining a shilling or an answer to any one of my letters addressed to His Grace, had I not, after waiting four or five months, been obliged to threaten that I would join Worcester in Spain. This, and this only, brought a polite letter, enclosing two quarters of the promised allowance, from His Grace.

I should like to know if His Grace or his noble son will take upon them to deny any of these facts, or that he did not desire me to make my own terms if I would not marry Worcester? and for which, all the world are crying "Off! Off! Off!" to the Duke of Beaufort, just as if he were Kean the actor. At all events, the facts I am now proceeding to relate were public.

Neither Brougham nor Treslove could be induced to believe that, since the Duke of Beaufort had bestowed a small annuity on me for the purpose of separating me from Lord Worcester, it could ever be His Grace's wish to rob me of that annuity, while the intent and purpose of it was fulfilled. I had indeed written a few lines to Lord Worcester, trusting to their humanity to forgive me for the exercise of mine; but, since my letter did not interrupt the object of the bond, which was to separate us, nobody would believe that the Duke wished to throw on the world me, who might have been his daughter, without the means of existence.

"The Duke will prefer giving you fifty thousand pounds," said the Duke's attorney to me.

My answer was, "Were I selfish, I would marry Worcester."

To satisfy these incredulous gentlemen, I renewed my applications to His Grace; but they were unattended to, as before.

As the day of trial drew near, I expressed my astonishment to my legal advisers that they wished me to bring forward a case like this, which I must inevitably lose if Lord Worcester produced the letter I wrote to him, which was directly in the teeth of the conditions of the bond.

"Fear nothing," was Brougham's answer. "Lord Worcester cannot appear in it without irremediable disgrace and loss of character."

"How can you imagine it possible," asked Brougham, "that Lord Worcester, the man who for years together has sworn to make you his wife, can appear in evidence against you, for the purpose of leaving you destitute, and effectually robbing you of the trifling independence which you were gracious enough to be satisfied with, when you might have been Duchess of Beaufort?"

I was at last almost convinced that Lord Worcester could not act thus.

"If he does he ought to be ashamed of himself," said Fred Bentinck, "and so I shall tell him. I always tell everybody exactly what I think of them for my part."

The day of trial arrived. The very hour approached, and Worcester had not obeyed his father's peremptory summons to come up to town and attend as evidence against me. The Duke, knowing there could be no other witness, was in a terrible fever of agitation, as my attorney told me.

Just at the last, when the furious Duke had given up all hopes of his son, he, in a great fright, proposed to my attorney to pay him twelve hundred pounds, rather than stand the event of the trial alone, and Brougham had scarcely given his written consent to this compromise, which was immediately signed, when the most liberal, generous, high-minded, and noble Marquis of Worcester stepped out of his travelling carriage, and came driving towards the scene of action, with my poor, ill-fated letter in his hand. Such at least is my attorney's account of the business. He may be referred to by the incredulous. I was not present.

Thus was I indebted to the Duke's fears of wanting a witness, or being hissed out of court, for the sum of twelve hundred pounds, which was handed to me as soon as I had accompanied the attorney to Westminster Hall and taken the following oath:

"THE KING'S BENCH,
"Between Harriette Wilson, Plt.
and
"His Grace the Duke of Beaufort, Deft.

"Harriette Wilson of———the above named plaintiff, maketh oath, and saith that she hath, in the schedule hereunder written, set forth a full and true list of all the letters, papers, and writings in her possession, or power, written by the Marquis of Worcester to this deponent, and that she hath not retained or delivered to any person, any copies, or extracts of them, or any or either of them, save and except any extract that this deponent may have sent or delivered to the above defendant."

And now good-bye Beaufort.

My readers will believe that my poor sister's death affected me deeply, and my health suffered seriously from my anxiety and want of rest. About two days after I had seen my dear sister buried, Amy appeared to feel something like compassion for the weak state in which she found me. She suddenly took me in her arms, and told me she feared I should die, and then burst into a flood of tears, as she added that she knew well she had never been kind to me!

Everything was forgiven from my heart and soul at that moment; but Amy soon ran up a fresh score of offences, just in her usual way.

I cannot in justice help relating Sophia's kind attention to her sister

Fanny in her last moments. Not that there was merit in one sister loving another, who was too amiable ever to have made a single enemy in her life: one whom the most cold-blooded and unfeeling could not but love: yet still I am glad I can, with truth, affirm that Sophia did her duty in this instance, and Amy also, in the daytime. The night-watching devolved entirely on me; but whoever else might have watched poor Fanny I would never have quitted her.

From the hour of my sister's death, my dearest mother's health visibly declined, and exactly three months after Fanny had breathed her last, I followed my parent to her grave. From that period I was for more than two months confined to my room, and, generally, to my bed, with a violent liver complaint, or I know not what.

"It is liver," said Dr. Bree, "and she must swallow plenty of mercury."

"No such thing," said Dr. Nevinson. "It is neither more nor less than over-excitement of the nerves, with too much anxiety, fatigue, and distress of mind."

"All this has disordered her liver," reiterated Dr. Bree, who has written a book on people's livers.

"I won't stand it," said Dr. Nevinson; "and, before Harriette begins upon your mercury, I will call in Dr. Pemberton."

"Never mind that cough, Ma'am," said Pemberton; "you may keep it till you are eighty, and it will be an amusement to you. It is only a nervous cough."

However I continued very ill in spite of all these gentlemen could do for me.

When my spirits and health were at their very worst, I was informed that poor Julia was dying and wanted to see me. I could not refuse her request. Her features bore the fixed rigidity of death when I entered her room. Her complaint, like her late poor friend's, was a disease of the heart, and there was no remedy.

She talked much of her dear Fanny, and said she had been certain from the first that she should soon follow her to the grave.

I insisted on writing to Napier, who was at Melton Mowbray.

"No! no!" said poor Julia. "If you will lend me your carriage, I am sure I shall be able to join him in a few days. I shall soon be better."

I wrote notwithstanding, and Napier came to her, kneeled by her bed-side, read the service of the dead, and then—and then he again read prayers to her. All this he afterwards told me himself.

"You must have killed her," said I, "in so dreadfully weak a state as she was in."

This conversation took place some weeks after her death.

"Nonsense," replied Napier. "Why say such cruel unfeeling things to me? Upon my honour, there was no chance for poor, sweet, dear Julia, who was the image of death when I—Oh, Julia! Angel Julia! I cannot bear it!" he added, pulling his hair, and throwing the handsome pillows of my new sofa all about the room.

"*Doucement! doucement! s'il vous plaît*," I observed. "Julia was my friend, I regret her certainly; but my feelings are so deeply affected by the death of my adored mother, whom God knows how I have loved, that there is scarcely room in my heart for any other grief, and, at all events, I don't quite see the use of your knocking my new sofa about."

"Very true," said Napier, suddenly jumping up; and, having wiped his eyes with the back of his hand, he began briskly to make fierce love to me.

"But Julia?" said I.

"Oh, Julia!" retorted he, banging another pillow on the ground, "I had her laid out in state, and wax candles were kept burning round her coffin for a fortnight: and I paid half of all her debts!"

"Suppose you had paid the whole?"

"Nonsense! They were very thankful for half."

"And what is to become of her poor children?"

"A noble relative has taken one, and Lord Folkestone another, and Mrs. Armstrong is consulting me about the rest."

I am now about to return to Paris, from where I propose sending Stockdale this volume or continuation of my *Memoirs*, provided you are all grateful and civil for the trouble I have already given myself; but I will pause now, at this period of my endeared parent's death; for my habits and character became more serious and melancholy from that hour. Meyler's sudden death too, which happened soon afterwards, certainly added much to those cold, desponding sensations, with which I was now often affected.

There was nothing on earth, not even Fanny nor Lord Ponsonby, I ever loved, as I loved my mother. I do not dwell on the subject, nor in the manner of her death; because it is to me a very sacred one. No one, not even Amy, will call my affection for that beloved, that sainted parent, in question.

One night I dreamed that I saw my dearest mother standing at the top of a high hill or mountain: so high that her head seemed almost to touch the clouds, and her drapery was of such indefinite texture, that I doubted whether I saw a shadow or a real substance. She looked very pale and beautifully placid, as she pointed towards the heavens, fixing her eyes on my face.

I would have given half my existence when I awoke for such another dream! With which I will for the present conclude, after wishing to all, a good night and pleasant dreams, and slumbers light.

LETTERS

AND

BIOGRAPHICAL NOTES

LETTERS

The FOLLOWING TWO letters were probably written between 1812-20.

HARRIETTE WILSON TO LORD BYRON

MAY 31st.

I have received the 1000 francs and must repeat my very sincere thanks to you, dear Lord Byron; though it was too bad to cut me off with such a shabby short letter and such an excuse—just to choose the very moment when the Horse was waiting and the divorce going on. However, it is a very nice dear little letter, written more after my style than your own and, if you were not aware of it, so much the more flattering to me—I love the little cramped hand too now, and know every turn of it.

Pray, dear Lord Byron, think of me a little now and then (I don't mean as a woman, for I shall never be a woman to you) merely as a good little fellow who feels a warmer interest in all that happens to you and all that annoys you than anybody else in the world. Forget me when you are happy; but in gloomy moments, chilly miserable weather, bad razors and cold water, perhaps you'll recollect and write to me. You can easily judge by a woman's scribbling whether her heart is with it, and you know I love you honestly and dearly. Alas! I can never prove it by any sacrifice. . . .

I am truth *and nothing but the truth. I looked at you for half an hour together one night and while studying your very beautiful countenance I could fancy a new sensation produced by the pressure of your lips to mine, beyond what my nature could endure—wild and eager as your poetry—terrifying by its power to* wither *and destroy me.*

Jupiter was all powerful in a cloud and ladies have been known to admire a Horse, *but there is a quieter, better, more voluptuous feeling for a woman, and* you can't *give it her.*

Besides, I never loved any but blue eyes. Are you as dark as at the Masquerade, or were you painted? Nothing, I suppose, will ever bring you to Paris, not even your friend T. Moore; yet I will hope that we shall one day (some twenty years hence) take a pinch of snuff together before we die; and as you watch me, in my little pointed cap, spectacles, bony ankles and thread

stockings, stirring up and tasting my pot au feu, *you'll imagine Ponsonby's,
Worcester's and Argyle's* Angelick Harriette ! !

I have made a new conquest lately—Lord Francis Cunningham; but I hate
boys *so I have been setting him to hunt and pull out my* grey hairs *to destroy his*
Illusions. *He found ten and I did not know I had one.* "Better get a Monkey,"
you'll say, than *a fine young* blue-eyed *man of one and twenty. What a fool he
must be! When you and I meet, I shall set you to work at the* brown ones, *for
I mean to attack them as soon as the grey predominates. It is more dignified to
keep to one colour,* n'est-ce-pas ? . . .

I trust and hope "at this present writing" *you are out of your scrape, or I shall
be the more sorry because I know you did not love* her *enough to make the
scrape worth while. Pray, dearest, let* me *love you,* tell me to love you.

I am at a very harmless *distance, you know. . . .*

Votre Affectionée,

BEAU PAGE.

God bless you ; nobody knows anything about loving you but myself.

HARRIETTE WILSON TO LORD BYRON

"*This comes* hopping" *to say I have lost* lots *of my liking for you*—Il
vaudrait bien le peine de faire payer un port de lettre pour si peu de chose !
But now you have *paid it, you may as well learn all about it, you know.
Strange to tell, I never heard of* Don Juan *till I found it on Galignani's table
yesterday and took it to bed with me, where I contrived to keep my large* quiet
good-looking brown eyes open (*now, you* know, *they are very handsome) till I
had finished it.*

Dear adorable *Lord Byron, don't make a mere* coarse *old libertine of yourself.
When everybody advised you not to publish your* English Bards, *you would
mind nobody.* I am nobody : *therefore attend to me. What harm did the Commandments (no matter by whom composed, whether god or mortal) ever do you
or anybody else, and what catch-penny ballad writer could not make a parody on
them? When you don't feel quite up to a spirit of benevolence, the encouragement of which you are pretty sure contributes more to one's earthly happiness
than anything else, in* gratitude *for the talent which, after all, must have
caused you exquisite moments in your time, throw away your pen, my love, and
take a little* calomel. *I wish the Deuce had all the papers, pens and ink burning,
frizzling and drying up in the very hottest place in his dominions, rather than
you should use them to wilfully destroy the respect and admiration of those*

who deserve to love you and all the fine illusions with which my mind was filled. Ecoutez, mon Ange. *It is not in my power or my nature to forget any kindness shown me (supposing I had not half loved you before) but I would not, even* to you, *who in a wrong-headed moment wrote it, lie under the imputation of such bad taste as to admire what in your cool moments, I am sure, you must feel to be* vulgar *at least.* . . . *In the very act of writing you felt half ashamed of what you wrote; and so* don't, *dearest Lord Byron, keep "all on" to the end of time mistaking mere false pride and* temper *for a bad heart; for you* know *all you have done or written that was wrong has caused you to regret, that convinced yourself alone (or rather you and I, my* Angel) *of the natural goodness of your disposition. Only, you are* spoiled. *Lord, if you could only suffer for one single day the agony of mind I endured for more than two years after Ponsonby left me, because Mrs. Fanny would have it so, you would bless your stars and your good fortune, blind, deaf and lame at eighty-two, so that you could sleep an hour in forgetfulness or eat a little bit of* batter pudding. *Heavens! how I have prayed for* death, *nights, days, and months together, merely as* rest *from suffering and* you! *whom everybody loves or wishes to love.* . . . *Don't bore yourself to answer my nonsense. I* hate *people to bore themselves for me.* Reading *Don Juan made me think of you all day; and so I could not go to bed without presuming to write to you again. But I won't quarrel with you for not answering. Only, pray, don't say anything* harsh *to me.* . . . *I don't forget this most flattering expression in a former letter of yours:* "I now trust this most brilliant acquaintance may be permitted to end." *I was more* angry *than* hurt *then, knowing myself not deficient in natural or affecting brilliancy. I thought you a* coxcomb *and myself a much better subject; but* now *if you are unkind to me I shall die of it. In the meantime, I am dying for want of sleep; so God bless you, dear Lord Byron, and good night.*

HARRY.

HARRIETTE WILSON TO E. BULWER-LYTTON

PART OF A letter from Harriette Wilson to Edward Bulwer-Lytton, probably written in 1829. She was forty-three and living in Paris on her memories and the profits of her *Memoirs*, while he had become the newest, most fashionable English novelist:—

SIR,

Though I have disliked reading all my life unless it be Shakespeare's plays, yet I got to the end of Pelham. *It was not a book to my taste either, for I thought the writer was a cold hearted man, and his light chit-chat was pedantic, smelling of the Lamp—not so good as my own. But then it was a sensible book, the fancies brilliant, the thought deep, the language very expressive. In short I got to the end of it. The Disowned I liked better still, and felt very much obliged to you for writing one of the few books I can come to the end of, with all my desire for amusement. But that imbecile (Mordaunt) who allow'd his wife to be starved like a helpless block-head, his want of French philosophy made me sick. Do you consider that man virtuous or sensible whose little soul makes him ashamed of doing his duty in that state of life into which it may please God to call him? He had arms and legs, health and intelligence—why did not he clean his wife's room and white-wash the walls, earn her by his daily work a mutton chop, and then fry it for her à la Maintenon? There's no such thing as starving in England for an intelligent man who will turn his hand to anything rather than endure to see the beloved of his soul die of hunger. No, that man ought to have been sent to the treadmill.*

Now for Devereux, I have nearly finished the first vol. and am so charmed with it, that I have laid it aside to tell you how proud I should be if you felt disposed to honour me with your acquaintance. I merely suggest this to you because life is too short and too miserable for us to afford prudently to risk the loss of a possible pleasure for want of asking for it, and it is just possible that we might derive pleasure from being acquainted—not very probable, however, because I am not a bit agreeable except to those who are predisposed to like me, and who appear to feel and understand all that is original or eccentric or amusing or likeable in my character at once. I am very shy, and when people do not flatter and encourage me by making me feel sure of their predisposition to like me, I am not a bit amiable because I am genée. I am not, and never was, a general favourite; but nobody likes me a little or forgets me when they have once liked, understood and been liked by me. I am very ignorant and can't spell, but there is this advantage in not reading, you are all of you copies and I am the thing itself. You are sure if I say anything to strike or please you that it came out of my own little head.

What do you think about it? Perhaps you would like my society better than I should like yours. . . . I am not ugly, as they describe me in the papers; but on the contrary rather handsome, particularly by candlelight when I am amused—although I was born at ten minutes before eight o'clock, the 22 February 1786 and christened at St. George's Church—I love to be particular.

I am not my own mistress, but if en tout bien et tout honneur you were to write me a word that you would not object to favour me with a visit some day— or will you take a walk with me some evening? I am much pleasanter to begin with when I am walking, because if it is dark I thus get rid of the shyness or nervousness which is constitutional with me and renders me a bore to strangers until I am encouraged delightfully by a certain inward conviction that they like me enough to be indulgent.

> Yours truly, and with high
> respect for your superior talents,
>
> HENRIETTE ROCHFORT
> *Author of* The Memoirs of Harriette Wilson.

THE FOLLOWING ARE some extracts from another letter written by Harriette Wilson to Edward Bulwer-Lytton in 1829, where it is evident that the elegant and cautious young man refuses to respond to Harriette's advances. That is, he encourages the flattering correspondence but refuses to compromise himself by meeting her in person. But Harriette, hungry for amusement, and for echoes of that world of clever, high-bred men which she had once known, refuses the rebuff and tries to interest him in her novel *Clara Gazul*. But he will have neither the lady nor her book, and we feel he is the loser.

OCTOBER 1ST, *deux heures après minuit*

(1829)

Though my sister gave me your letter before dinner (in answer to mine of "the six weeks ago instant") I had no opportunity of reading it till this moment. I am sleepy and my fire is out, and yet, the matter having hold of my thoughts, I should not rest till I had expressed to you my regret that you like me, since you refuse to shake hands with me. On sait à peu près ce qu'on veut, I had therefore philosophically made up my mind to endure your silent contempt, but since you are benevolently inclined towards me, it is really rather hard upon me this— dead cut. From your style of writing I did not expect to find you a very agreeable companion for a post-chaise, etc., nor did I desire that we should meet under the impression that it was at all incumbent on us to be more agreeable than our neighbours. The very thought and fever of such a wish would only serve to redden our noses and dampen our spirits. I conceived, as a sensible man, you might be amused with the novelty of a woman who is always true to nature, no matter how bizarre may be her thoughts, creed or wishes. However, if you won't make friends with me you won't, and I must stick to my "Yours of the 15th came safe to hand on the, etc."

If, however, you believe I wished you to neglect others for so insignificant an individual as myself, you have done me injustice. Believing you married, I only desired the honour of your acquaintance under the impression that love or desire for me now was entirely out of the chapter of possibilities, and that no wife would pay me the compliment to object to my occasionally enjoying the benefit of a little chat with her husband. I should have been proud and obliged if hereafter you would have been at the trouble of looking over my unfinished new Work—the only thing I have ever written at all to my own satisfaction with regard to romance, the language and the spirit of it. But why should I have presumed to expect so much condescension from you? The work must take its chance; I'll publish it with all its blunders of ignorance, because I like it myself, and expect others may do so too, since everybody tells me I had never had any vanity. What I am now writing (a sort of female Gil Blas not quite so loose as Faublas) gives me much more trouble. It appears that we grow humble and difficult to be pleased as our eyes open on the glare of our own vast and melancholy deficiencies. No matter, you won't, and nobody else shall, meddle with my novel. I will tell you what would make a perfect novel—you write it all but the love scenes and send them for me to draw.

The papers forced me to allude to my person *and* voice, *since who would like the few they admire to be impressed with the false idea of their hideousness and their* coarse voice *?—knowing that my voice is* very good *and that no time can quite spoil a fine face, though it may not be a pretty one. I told you the exact truth, namely that I am forty-three, very* journalière, *often* joliment abattu, grace à Dieu, *particularly when I can't sleep, which happens four nights out of six, handsome (for those who like the Siddonian expression) occasionally when I have slept, never very ugly in the face, and as pretty as ever in person, which, by the by, does not appear under the disguise of my costume which is as loose as my morals—to use the newspaper's expression, while in fact I am a true, faithful wife leading about as innocent a life as a hermit can well do. . . .*

You say you are six foot broad. I should from my ear (not my grammar) say "six feet"; which word is right? I know from your writing that you are thin, bilious and severe, I should say dry, not graceful; but one wants variety, I should like your shrewd wisdom for a change; harsh it might sound to a lady's ear, after the gentle, voluptuous, graceful, luxurious Argyles or Ponsonbys, but the rude scenes of age and harshness must come and is to nous autres *who have been loved and doted on,* the tax upon beauty. *The contrast and neglect must be borne, and borne by me like a man, for Lord Ponsonby used to say of me that my advantage over other* sweet fair *ones was that besides my pretty bosom and effeminate qualities, softness of temper etc., I really was " an* excellent fellow*" (bon camarade). So to preserve the impression in my favour, now I am growing old I must be a* better fellow *than ever, in which character I forgive your* *cut and wish you every success, every possible happiness that can be obtained in a world* fait exprès pour nous enrager.

Adieu,

HARRY.

One more letter follows: it is a melancholy postscript, Harriette's last appearance, written from a seedy address when she is evidently in great straits. Probably the colonel has now left her, having run through most of the money derived from the *Memoirs*. Even so, that old irrepressible note of banter still sounds. She heads her letter thus:

69 *Vauxhall Bridge Road*
Pimlico. Nov. 1832.
Lively!
Pastoral!

I'm desperately ill, and mind wears out with body, but I fear you will be so very unhappy if you don't hear from me now and then, before I die . . .

She goes on to discuss Bulwer-Lytton's latest book with intelligence and spirit. She ends casually. The rest is silence.

BIOGRAPHICAL NOTES

ALVANLEY, WILLIAM ARDEN, 2ND BARON, 1789–1849. At one time an officer in the Coldstream Guards. A celebrated dandy and one of the greatest wits of his day, he was described by John O'Connell (with whose son he fought a duel) as 'a bloated buffoon,' and by Greville as 'to the last degree reckless and profligate about money; he cared not what debts he incurred.' On one occasion when his debts were being compiled by a methodical friend, Alvanley discovered next day that he had overlooked one debt of £55,000. In 1831 he married Arabella, daughter of the Duke of Cleveland, but had no issue. He has been called the perfect example of a Regency buck, in both appearance and spirit.

ARGYLL, DUKE OF. GEORGE WILLIAM CAMPBELL, 6TH DUKE, 1766–1839. Until his succession to the dukedom in 1806, he was the Marquis of Lorne. 'An amiable, thoughtless man, who whistled away the cares of life.' He possessed huge estates in Scotland, centred around Inveraray Castle. He was Vice-Admiral of the West Coast of Scotland, Keeper of the Great Seal, and later Steward of the Household to King William IV and Queen Victoria. In 1810 he married Caroline Elizabeth, the former wife of the 1st Marquis of Anglesey, whom she had divorced.

BEAUFORT, DUKE OF. HENRY CHARLES SOMERSET, 6TH DUKE, 1766–1835. Head of one of the noblest English families (a descendant of John of Gaunt), and father of the Marquis of Worcester, Harriette Wilson's lover. He was Lord Lieutenant of the Counties of Monmouth, Brecknock and Gloucester, Lord High Steward of Bristol, Warden of the Forest of Dean, etc. etc. He married Charlotte Sophia Leveson-Gower, daughter of the 1st Marquis of Stafford, and sister of Lord Granville Leveson-Gower.

BERRI, DUC DE. CHARLES FERDINAND DE BOURBON, 1778–1820. A Prince of the Blood, second son of the Comte d'Artois (later Charles X). Born at Versailles, he emigrated during the Revolution, and was with the army of Condé and arrived in England in 1801, where he rejoined his family. The Duc de Berri fought against Napoleon and entered Paris with the Allies in 1814 and 1815 where he became notorious for the license of his conduct. In 1816 he married the

Princess Caroline of Naples, a charming, gay, courageous girl through whom the degenerate French monarchy hoped to re-establish itself firmly. (It was said that of all of them the Duc de Berri was the only prince capable of begetting an heir.) However, his first two children died in infancy. In 1820, some months before the birth of the Duchesse de Berri's third child, the Duke was assassinated one night as he left the opera. His posthumous child, the Comte de Chambord (Henri V), lived, for the most part, banished from France.

BERWICK, LORD. THOMAS NOEL HILL, BARON BERWICK OF ATTINGHAM, 1770–1832. He married at St. Marylebone, on February 8, 1812, Sophia (a minor), daughter of John Dubochet. Lord Berwick died at Naples. His widow survived him by forty-three years, expiring at Leamington in 1875.

BROUGHAM, LORD. HENRY BROUGHAM, 1ST BARON BROUGHAM AND VAUX, 1778–1868. The great advocate, Lord Chancellor and the defender of Queen Caroline at her trial for adultery in 1820. Brougham first emerges as a feared and hated force in politics around 1812. An ornament of Whig society, his cynical nature earned him the nicknames of 'Wickedshifts' and 'Beelzebub' given him by the diarist Creevey. His enthusiasm for the South of France first launched the little town of Cannes as a fashionable centre.

Creevey, whose sharp eyes remarked most things, tells us that 'Brougham's hatred of her (his wife), *absolute hatred*, is too visible.' Brougham married a Mrs. Spalding, daughter of Thomas Eden. Creevey found her the ugliest of her sex, the most unaccountable person he had ever known. 'A Gentleman's Daughter who resembled the commonest Pot Girl.' He accused her of being 'forever on the languishing tack instead of the cursing and swearing she is so distinctly made for.'

BRUMMELL, GEORGE, 'THE BEAU,' 1778–1840. Although of comparatively humble origin his name has become the synonym for elegance. His father, the son of a valet, had risen in the world until he became Secretary to the Prime Minister, Lord North. He was later High Sheriff for Berkshire. George was sent to Eton where, handsome, clever and a good sportsman, he laid the foundations for his entry into the beau monde where he became the protégé of Georgiana, Duchess of Devonshire. He rapidly rose to a position of supremacy among the *ton*. He was their *arbiter elegantiarum*. Although he never appeared to be particularly interested in any one woman, all of them fought to secure his presence in their opera boxes or at their dinners. He was a cold fish, egocentric to the point of madness, a calculating *arriviste* who reckoned on his audacity to carry him along at a rate of living few could afford. The Prince of Wales made much of him until the

Beau's arrogance became insufferable. Byron said of the fit of Brummell's coat that 'it seemed as if the body thought.' His follies, extravagances and love of high play at last ruined him. Swamped in debts, he fled his creditors to France where the good offices of his remaining friends eventually obtained him the post of British Consul at Caen. Soon his creditors there, too, began pressing him. An awful spectre of his former self, he died insane, in conditions of abject misery, cared for at the last by the Sisters of Charity.

BYRON, GEORGE GORDON, 6TH BARON BYRON, 1788–1824. The celebrated poet whose verses inflamed the public from one end of Europe to the other. A sulky, spoiled Adonis, whose genius did not excuse his boorishness. A poseur who drank vinegar to keep his figure and whose 'Byronic curls' were maintained by curl-papers, according to one eye-witness. A most fascinating rebel, he was embroiled in scandals without number and at last fled England for the Near East. He dabbled in orientalism, swam the Hellespont and settled in Italy. The infatuated Lady Caroline Lamb summed him up as 'mad, bad, and dangerous to know,' which must have delighted the poet since he liked nothing better than to pose as daemonic. Mme. de Staël found his prevailing mood one of profound melancholy. He was irresistible to all kinds of women, who smothered him by their advances. He looked, said Stendhal, 'like Talma in the role of Nero. He suffered from his ostracism, though he took a sort of masochistic enjoyment in fostering it, and silly women would run out of the room as he entered. . . . His own caste revenged themselves on the *writer*, by persecuting the *man*, though they could not succeed in snubbing his birth, or breeding, or brilliance.' He contracted a disastrous marriage to Miss Milbanke, niece of Lady Melbourne, and died young, disillusioned and splenetic, fighting for Greek independence. Childe Harold's pilgrimage was done.

CARYSFORT, JOHN JOSHUA PROBY, 1ST EARL OF, 1751–1828. Joint Postmaster General and Keeper of the Rolls in Ireland. A cultivated, poetically inclined individual, always much grieved at the conduct of his niece, Julia Storer (or Johnstone).

CRAVEN, WILLIAM, 2ND EARL OF CRAVEN, 1770–1825 Son of Elizabeth, Lady Craven, the intrepid traveller, who married, *en secondes noces*, the Margrave of Ansbach and Brandenburg. Lord Craven was Colonel of the 84th Foot, Aide-de-Camp to the King, 1798–1805, Lord Lieutenant of Berkshire. In 1807 he married a provincial actress, Louisa Brunton, whose father, once a greengrocer in Drury Lane, had become manager of the Norwich Theatre, where Louisa appeared with considerable success.

DEERHURST, LORD. GEORGE WILLIAM, COVENTRY, 10TH EARL OF COVEN-
TRY, 1784–1843. An eccentric who always appeared to be in a great
hurry; known for his habit of rushing down Piccadilly after any
pretty passer-by. 'Unusually sparing of soap and water,' in 1811 he
married, *en secondes noces*, 'Mary with £100,000,' daughter of the
6th Duke of St. Albans. He grew more and more intractable until at
last he died insane.

DEVONSHIRE, DUKE OF. WILLIAM GEORGE SPENCER CAVENDISH, 6TH
DUKE OF DEVONSHIRE, 1790–1858. Son of the celebrated Georgiana,
Duchess of Devonshire, he succeeded to the title in 1811. Enormously wealthy, he was Lord Chamberlain of the Household and
Ambassador Extraordinary to St. Petersburg at the coronation of the
Czar Nicholas I, a special mission which was said to have cost him
£50,000 over and above the sum granted by his government. Perhaps owing to his deafness, he led a rather retired life, concentrating
his energies on Joseph Paxton's designs for laying out the gardens at
Chatsworth, and the erection of a conservatory which covered an
acre of ground. He was to some a benign, poetic figure, to others
very cold and aloof. He never married but appears to have been, in
his youth, something of a social force. Raikes speaks of him as having
launched the waltz on English society. 'No event ever produced so
great a sensation . . . as the introduction of the German waltz in
1813. Up to that time the English country dances, Scotch steps, and
an occasional Highland reel formed the evening recreation of the
first circles. But peace was drawing near, foreigners were arriving
and the taste for Continental customs and manners became the orde,
of the day. The young Duke of Devonshire, as the Magnus Apollr
of the London drawing-rooms, was at the head of these innovationo
. . . Old and young returned to school, and the mornings which has.
been dedicated to lounging in the park were now absorbed at homd
in practising the figures of the French quadrille, or whirling a chaie
round the room to learn the step and measure of a German waltz. . . r
What scenes have we witnessed in those days at Almack's, etc.! What.
fear and trembling in the debutantes at the commencement of a
waltz, and what giddiness and confusion at the end! It was perhaps
owing to the latter circumstance that so violent an opposition soon
arose to this new recreation on the score of morality. The anti-
waltzing party took the alarm, cried it down, mothers forbade it,
and every ball-room became a scene of feud and contention.'

EBRINGTON, HUGH FORTESCUE, 2ND EARL FORTESCUE OF CASTLE HILL,
1783–1861. Viscount Ebrington until 1841, he was M.P. for Barn-
staple, 1801–7, Lord Lieutenant of Ireland, 1839–41. Lord Steward
of the Household to Queen Victoria, 1841–50. Not much is known

about this gentleman. He appears to have been of a studious character, which is not, however, the impression Harriette gives. He obtained his M.A. at Oxford in 1810 and became a Fellow of the Royal Society in 1817. His widow survived him for thirty-five years, only dying, at the age of ninety-one, in 1896.

ELLICE, EDWARD ('BEAR'), OF INVERGARRY, 1781–1863. M.P. for Coventry and Secretary to the Treasury, an influential Whig politician whose fortunes derived from enormous properties in Canada. He married first Lady Hannah, sister of Earl Grey; and later, Lady Leicester, widow of the 1st Earl.

FIFE, JAMES DUFF, 4TH EARL OF FIFE, 1776–1857. Major General in the Spanish army and a great lady-killer. Protector of La Mercandotti, the celebrated Spanish ballerina who became the rage of London at the age of fifteen, Lord Fife was said by some to be her father. In any case he lost her to the wealthy dandy, 'Golden Ball' Hughes. A current couplet read:

> 'The fair damsel is gone, and no wonder at all
> That bred to the dance she has gone to the Ball.'

FITZCLARENCE, CAPTAIN GEORGE, 1794–1842. One of the ten children born to the Duke of Clarence (later King William IV) and Mrs. Jordan, the actress. In 1831 he was created Earl of Munster.

FREELING, MR., LATER SIR GEORGE HENRY FREELING, 1789–1841. Commissioner of Customs and the inaugurator of various reforms in the Postal Service. (The 'essential service' which he rendered Harriette may be an occasion mentioned by Julia Johnstone, who states he once stood bail for Harriette, when she had been apprehended for debt and languished in the debtors' prison in St. Martin's Lane.)

GUICHE, DUC DE. ANTOINE GENEVIÈVE HARACLIUS AGÉNOR, DUC DE GRAMONT, 1789–1855. Holder of one of the greatest titles in France, he was born at Versailles in the first year of the Revolution. His family emigrated to Russia, then to England. At the age of nine, the young Comte de Gramont (as he then was) was given the brevet rank of 2nd lieutenant in the Russian Regiment of Tauride. Arrived in England in 1802 at the age of thirteen, he was given a commission in the Prince of Wales' regiment, the 10th Hussars, which paid for his education. He fought against Napoleon under the English colours. He was a universal favourite, dazzlingly handsome and considered perfectly irresistible to women, according to Gronow, who also stated he was 'a grand seigneur in word and deed, quiet in manner, a chivalrous, high-minded man. The most perfect gentleman I ever met with in any country.' He married the beautiful sister of Comte d'Orsay, the dandy, succeeded his father as Duc de Gramont in 1836 and died in Paris where he had returned with the Bourbons.

It is of interest to recall that it was his son, the Comte de Gramont, born in 1819, who became the protector of Marie Duplessis, the original of the *Dame aux Camélias* and first launched her in the world of Parisian high gallantry. In 1848 he married the daughter of Lord Mackinnon and, entering the Diplomatic Service, was Ambassador to Rome during the formation of the Kingdom of Italy. In 1870 he was Minister of Foreign Affairs, a position he did not fill with distinction, for when war was declared against Prussia and the French saw that Germany was uniting against them contrary to what the Duc de Gramont had led them to believe, he was forced to resign. He lived retired, embittered, a finished man and one who is remembered less for having been Minister of Foreign Affairs than for having been the lover of *La Dame aux Camélias*.

HERTFORD, FRANCIS CHARLES SEYMOUR-CONWAY, 3RD MARQUIS OF, 1777–1842. Sometimes referred to in the *Memoirs* by his earlier title of Lord Yarmouth. A wealthy, dissolute man of appetites, who appeared to some of his contemporaries to have no single redeeming feature but who appears very favourably in the *Memoirs*. His mother, the second Marchioness, was for some while mistress of the Prince Regent and during this time Lord Yarmouth enjoyed every royal favour. In 1812 he was appointed Vice Chamberlain of the Household. In 1798 he married Maria Emily, putative daughter of the Duke of Queensbury ('Old Q') by the Marchesa Fagniani. Lord Hertford appears as the Marquis of Steyne in *Vanity Fair*, and as the Marquis of Monmouth in *Coningsby*. Greville harshly wrote of him, 'No such example of undisguised debauchery was ever exhibited in the world.' In his late sixties, when he was broken with various infirmities and suffering from a paralysis of the tongue, 'he was in the habit of travelling about with a company of prostitutes who formed his principal society. What a life, terminating in what a death! Without a serious thought or a kindly feeling . . . faculties far beyond mediocrity, wasted and degraded, immersed in pride without dignity, in avarice and sensuality . . . all his relatives estranged from him and surrounded to the last by a venal harem who pandered to his disgusting exigencies.' Thus Greville in a severe obituary. It is perhaps worth extending this note to speak of Lord Hertford's two sons, if they were such, which is open to doubt, though he accepted the eldest as his heir and the second, Lord Henry Seymour, as his son, though he cut him off without a penny. Both were celebrated characters in Parisian life. The 4th Marquis was a great collector and connoisseur of French art. He left his fabulous possessions to his secretary, Sir Richard Wallace. Sir Richard passed as his secretary, was said to be his son, but was in all probability yet another illegitimate son of La Fagniani. Eventually Sir Richard bequeathed his treasures to the British nation and they are known today as the Wallace Collection, housed in Hertford House, London.

La Fagniani's other son, Lord Henry Seymour, although never acknowledged by his father, inherited a vast fortune from his mother and lived in Paris, where he passed into history as the personification of the crazy, rich English milord. In fact, he never set foot in England. He was dubbed 'Milord l'Arsouille'—Milord the Oaf—and was an eccentric, cruel, caustic dandy, spendthrift and sportsman, who spent his life among jockeys and prostitutes. 'Please put my boots outside the door,' he is said to have commanded one of these charmers. 'They will return the compliment before long.' He founded the Jockey Club de France, was its first president and may be said to have established horse racing in France. Eugène Lami has left a picture, *Calèche de Lord Seymour*, during Carnival in 1835, in which we can see the wild, extravagant way of life this man personified.

LAMB, LADY CAROLINE 1785–1828. Only daughter of the Earl of Bessborough. 'The cleverest, most agreeable, absurd, amiable, perplexing, dangerous, fascinating little being that lives,' said Byron, before her frenzied pursuit exasperated him. She married William Lamb, later Lord Melbourne. Their only son died young, mentally defective. Her conduct was too startling even for the tolerant Whig aristocracy to which she belonged. Her infatuation for Byron led her to dress as a page and follow him from house to house, and culminated in a scene at a ball where she slashed her wrists with a broken glass, determined that all the world should be aware of her emotions. After her husband separated from her she lived at Brocket, their Hertfordshire home. By a strange chance, out driving one day, she encountered Byron's funeral cortège. The shock of this increased her eccentricity to the point of near madness. She died of dropsy, aged forty-two, still on affectionate terms with her forbearing husband, who had continued to visit her during all the years of their estrangement.

LAMB, FREDERICK JAMES. 3RD VISCOUNT MELBOURNE, 1782–1853. Third son of the 1st Lord Melbourne. A rather ponderous young man, and, although considered 'a sad dog with the ladies,' quite eclipsed by his brother William. He was gazetted to the Royal Horse Guards in 1803, and left the army to enter the diplomatic service in 1810, becoming Minister to Madrid in 1825. In 1841 he married Alexandrina, Countess von Maltzan, daughter of the Prussian Envoy to the Court of Vienna. In 1839 he was created Baron Beauvale of Beauvale, and succeeded his brother as Lord Melbourne in 1848. His widow survived until 1894.

LAMB, WILLIAM. 2ND VISCOUNT MELBOURNE, 1779–1848. A perfect example of the cynical Whig aristocrat, although, in fact, a very moderate Whig and opposed to all the more progressive measures. 'Why not leave it alone?' was a favourite phrase of his. He liked 'easy men' and an easy life, but married Lady Caroline Lamb whose eccentric behaviour and infatuation for Lord Byron caused convulsive scandals and brought about their separation. In 1828 Creevey wrote, 'Never man was so improved as Wm. Lamb, whether from gaining his title or losing his wife I know not.' He was a fine classical scholar, 'exceedingly handsome, good-natured, often paradoxical, coarse, terse, epigrammatic, acute, droll, with fits of silence and abstraction.' In his sixties he became the young Queen Victoria's adored Prime Minister and confidant, the supreme power behind the throne until, at last, his place was taken by the Prince Consort.

LEINSTER, DUKE OF. AUGUSTUS FREDERICK FITZGERALD, 1791–1874. This Irish duke was the godson of the Prince of Wales. Educated at Eton from 1806 to 1810, he appears to have been scarcely out of school before he was ensnared in Harriette Wilson's toils. It would seem he was handsome, parsimonious, prudent and not a very taking young man. In 1818 he married Charlotte Augusta, daughter of the Earl of Harrington, and did not figure greatly in any of the contemporary memoirs, living chiefly on his Irish estates.

LEVESON-GOWER, GEORGE, AS HE IS CALLED IN THE MEMOIRS. PROPERLY GRANVILLE, 1ST EARL GRANVILLE, 1773–1846. Son of the 1st Marquis of Stafford. A complacent Apollo, for many years the lover of Lady Bessborough, and a pampered favourite of Whig society. His mother wrote in 1794, warning him against '*artful women*. . . . You have a naturally pleasing manner, are well-looking, and have a good understanding.' Married in 1809 to Lady Bessborough's niece, Harriet, daughter of the 5th Duke of Devonshire, he was Ambassador to Paris, 1822–41.

LUTTRELL, COLONEL, 1757–1849. A natural son of the 2nd Earl of Carhampton. He was a brilliant wit, 'the last of the conversationalists,' and an inseparable friend of the poet, the funereal-looking Samuel Rogers. Luttrell was a most agreeable man whose fine intellect was concealed, like his kind heart, behind a frivolous and cynical façade.

MELBOURNE, PENISTON LAMB, 1ST VISCOUNT, 1744–1828. Father of Fred Lamb, Harriette's protector. The son of Sir Matthew Lamb, he was created Lord Melbourne of Kilmore in 1770. He was made Gentleman of the Bedchamber to the Prince of Wales in 1784, and became an English peer in 1815. Brocket Hall, Hertfordshire, was the family seat, and, in London, Melbourne House was an important centre of Whig politics. He married Elizabeth (1749–1816), daughter of Sir Ralph Milbanke of Halnaby, Yorkshire, a fascinating and astute woman whose charms considerably furthered her husband's career. Her friendship with the Prince of Wales accounted for many of Lord Melbourne's advancements. Her children were said to be by different fathers; it was commonly held that William Lamb, later 2nd Viscount Melbourne, was the son of Lord Egremont; but she and her husband always remained on the best of terms and no one disputed that she was a devoted mother. 'As long as she lived she kept me right,' wrote William after her death. She was Byron's adored confidante, '*ma tante*'; it was her niece, Miss Milbanke, 'the Princess of Parallelograms,' who became his wife.

MILDMAY, SIR HARRY, 4TH BARONET, 1787–1848. M.P. for the city of Winchester; in 1809 he married Charlotte Bouverie, who died in 1810.

PALMELLA, COUNT DE SOUZA HOLSTEIN (AFTERWARDS DUKE OF PALMELLA), 1786–1850. Regent of Portugal in 1830. Portuguese Ambassador to the Court of St. James's. Ugly, swarthy and wealthy, he was very much fêted. During the Peninsular campaign, when the Portuguese soldiers were subsidized by the English army, Portugal was a key nation, and Palmella ranked with such ambassadors as Esterhazy and Talleyrand. In 1813 Wellington told Lord Liverpool, 'the Portuguese are now the *fighting cocks* of the army. I believe we owe their merits more to the care we have taken of their pockets and their bellies than to the (military) instructions we have given them.'

PALMERSTON, LORD. HENRY JOHN TEMPLE, 3RD VISCOUNT PALMERSTON, 1784–1865. The great Foreign Secretary, Home Secretary, and Prime Minister, whose distinguished career continued far into Queen Victoria's reign. In his salad days he enjoyed what Gronow described as 'the mazy waltz,' and was constantly at Almack's, one of the first to essay this exotic measure; he was, says Gronow, 'to be seen describing an infinite number of circles with Princess de Lieven.'

PETERSHAM, LORD. *See* STANHOPE, CHARLES.

PONSONBY, LORD. JOHN ERIC PONSONBY, 2ND BARON AND LATER 1ST VISCOUNT PONSONBY OF IMOKILLY, 1770?–1855. 'The handsomest man of his time,' who on one occasion owed his life to his good looks. As a young man he was in Paris during the Revolution when feeling ran very high against England and every Englishman was held to be an agent of *ce sacré Pitt*. Several were hanged from the street lamp-posts before any arguments or protestations could begin. As the young Ponsonby was walking down the Rue St. Honoré he was seized by an infuriated mob, yelling their bloodcurdling cry, *à la lanterne!* as they set about stringing him up to the nearest lamp-post. The noose was round his neck and he had been jerked off the ground when some of the women rushed forward, cut the cord and freed him, crying that he was too handsome a boy to hang.

Besides the powerful effect of his good looks Ponsonby was said to possess 'a tact and perfection of manner which rendered him irresistible.' He succeeded his father in 1806. In 1803 he had married Lady Frances Villiers, daughter of the 4th Earl of Jersey. A portrait of her by Opie shows a grave, dark, classically beautiful young creature, the loveliest debutante of the season. Ponsonby fell in love on sight and they were married before she was sixteen. She lived rather apart from the world, being very shy and deaf—legacy of an attack of scarlet fever. Her husband was said to be always much in love with her, but always at great pains to conceal it from her too. In 1825 Lord Ponsonby was appointed Ambassador to Buenos Aires, to Constantinople in 1832 and to Vienna in 1846. He made a most admirable ambassador, although he abhorred making speeches. Sir John Drummond-Hay, one of his staff at the Porte, recounts that when the Ambassador was received by the Sultan for the first time, in great state, he struck an attitude and, with an impassive face, majestically counted up to fifty, pausing occasionally on a number, smiling on others, raising his voice in emphasis and ending 'forty-eight—forty-nine, *fifty!*' as if it were some particularly felicitous phrase. The Turks, who could not understand a word of English, appeared much gratified. The Ambassador's interpreter then stepped forward and read in Turkish the excellent speech which the Ambassador had prepared and the ceremony finished in style with the Sultan graciously replying and Lord Ponsonby, with further bows, continuing to count impressively from fifty up to eighty. On leaving he explained to his bewildered staff that he wasn't going to be bothered to memorize a speech that none of Sublime Porte could understand anyhow.

Another example of his highly unconventional but practical methods is recounted by Major General Sir John Ponsonby in his book on the Ponsonby family. On one occasion the Sultan, feeling that the Corps Diplomatique, headed by Lord Ponsonby, did not show sufficient humility and sufficient awe when entering the Royal presence, caused a very low door to be built, through which the diplomats had to pass to enter the Hall of Audience. This door was so low that it was necessary to crawl through on all fours. Lord Ponsonby, suddenly confronted with the new door, turned round without a moment's hesitation and crawled through backwards, presenting a splendid expanse of white satin breeches to the waiting Sultan and his viziers. This, said one of his attachés, was typical of

Lord Ponsonby, of his coolness, his sense of humour and his practical methods of dealing with unexpected situations.

PONSONBY, WILLIAM. 4TH EARL OF BESSBOROUGH, 1781–1847. Home Secretary under Lord Melbourne, 1834–5, Lord Lieutenant of Carlow and Kilkenny, in Ireland, 1846–7. In 1805 he married a daughter of the Earl of Westmoreland. His mother was the celebrated Lady Bessborough who, with her sister Georgiana, Duchess of Devonshire, queened it over Whig society and has left us such entrancing letters. His sister was the mercurial Lady Caroline Lamb.

REGENT, THE PRINCE, AFTERWARDS GEORGE IV, 1762–1830. The First Gentleman of Europe, a great patron of the arts, who continued the Royal Collections begun by Charles I, and the first monarch since Charles II to be fashionable. He was a sportsman, dandy and *débauché*, and possessed great personal charm, which, however, he did not always care to exercise. His behaviour towards both Mrs. Fitzherbert, his unacknowledged wife, and Queen Caroline, his consort, was odious. He was greatly under the sway of his successive mistresses, from whom he took his tone, often with deplorable results. His excesses finally destroyed his health and looks and he died, a dropsical wreck, no trace left of the dazzling figure once known as Prince Florizel.

SOMERSET, LORD CHARLES, 1767–1831. Brother of the 6th Duke of Beaufort, Governor of the Cape of Good Hope, a sermonizing sort of man who spent much time trying to prevent his nephew, Lord Worcester, from becoming involved with Harriette Wilson.

SOMERSET, THE REV. LORD WILLIAM, PREBENDARY OF BRISTOL, 1784–1851. Another of Lord Worcester's uncles also employed by the Beaufort family in their efforts to dissuade the Marquis from marrying Harriette. A celebrated whip, he loved to drive, but being too poor to afford his own curricle, he often acted as 'Tiger' to his friend Lord Berwick.

STANHOPE, CHARLES. 4TH EARL OF HARRINGTON, 1780–1851. Better known as Lord Petersham, which title he held until 1829. One of the most celebrated of the Regency bucks, a captain in the Prince of Wales Light Dragoons, Lord of the Bedchamber, 1812–20. The perfect example of a dandy. His dun-coloured liveries were inspired by those of the French *noblesse*. Lady Bessborough believed he wore stays, 'what Misses us'd to wear some years ago.' He collected rare kinds of snuff and exotic teas, and never ventured abroad before six o'clock in the evening when he was to be seen strolling down St. James's, or lolling and lisping among his fellow dandies at White's. His manner was as affected as his lisp, and he wore (a great rarity at that time) a little pointed beard expressly to emphasize his alleged likeness to Henri IV.

STANHOPE, LEICESTER, LATER 5TH EARL OF HARRINGTON, 1784–1862. The third son of the 3rd Earl, he succeeded his brother, Lord Petersham, in the earldom of Harrington.   Colonel of the 1st Life Guards, Deputy Quartermaster General, 1817–21.   Deputy Adjutant General in the East Indies, 1815–17, where he saw considerable service.   He travelled to Greece on questions of Greek independence, where he met Byron, and after the poet's death he brought home his remains.   In 1831 he married Elizabeth, daughter of William Green of Jamaica.

STOCKDALE, JOSEPH, 1770–1847.   Bookseller and publisher.   He specialized in literature of a dubious character and was at one time concerned with various Societies for the Suppression of Vice, or organizations which called attention to such diversions as illustrated editions of Rabelais, 'Generating Bedsteads' (no doubt the kind that Lady Hamilton, when still Emma Hart, had adorned and rendered so particularly lively), or those snuff-boxes which contained, hidden under the lid, drawings of a most inflammatory nature and which had, we are told, 'a ready Market in Boarding Schools for Young Ladies.'   Stockdale, who was once the young Shelley's publisher, edited Harriette's *Memoirs* and some people think he wrote a large part of them.   As Harriette's publisher he was sued for libel and damages by an insignificant person who, it is thought, was put up to taking action by a number of better known gentlemen happy to find a cat's-paw. Stockdale lost the case and had to pay heavily.   Next, Mr. Fisher, the attorney and lady-killer of Devonshire who claimed Harriette had libelled him, sued Stockdale for defamation of character.   Again Stockdale lost the case.   He was soon ruined, being next embroiled in a series of litigations which landed him in the Debtors' Prison.   During this confinement he profited by extracting from his fellow prisoners the most startling disclosures concerning a number of distinguished people.   These disclosures his wife was preparing in brochure form, with a view, we suppose, to their publication or—at a price—their suppression.   They do not seem to have been published, and Stockdale fades from sight—a most obnoxious character.

VORONZOV, COUNT.   As we do not know his first name it is impossible to say to which one of this numerous Russian family the *Memoirs* refers. Count Simon Romanovich Voronzov (1744–1832) was Russian Ambassador to England from 1785 to 1806, when ill health obliged him to resign.   However, he remained in England till his death twenty-six years later.   He was brother of the celebrated Princess Dashkov who took part in the *coup d'état* which placed Catherine the Great on the throne of Russia. His son Michael became Prince Voronzov, Field Marshal and Governor of Odessa, long remembered for his unsympathetic conduct towards the rebel tribes during the Caucasian wars. Count Simon's daughter married the 11th Earl of Pembroke. It is probable that the Count Voronzov mentioned in the *Memoirs* was either the young Michael or some visiting relative. It seems unlikely that it was the Ambassador himself, though it is possible.

WARD, JOHN WILLIAM. 1ST EARL AND 4TH VISCOUNT DUDLEY, 1781– 1833. Secretary for Foreign Affairs in Canning's administration, 1827–8. An excessively absent-minded man whose vagueness bordered on insanity and who, according to one observer, 'affected to be absent but, in fact, no one ever forgot himself so seldom.' He does not seem to have been an agreeable character. The Princess of Wales complained that he ate like a hog. Lady Charlotte Bury found him 'an unpleasant companion at table. Then his person looks so dirty; and he has such a sneer in his laugh, and is so impious as well as grossly indecent in his conversation that I cannot like this clever man.' After such opinions it is not surprising to learn that he never married.

WELLESLEY, MARQUIS. RICHARD COLLEY WELLESLEY, 1760–1842. Eldest son of Lord Mornington and brother of the Duke of Wellington. Governor-general of India, 1797–1805. He married Mlle. Hyacinthe Gabrielle, his mistress for nine years, by whom he had had several children prior to the marriage. He was a rigid moralist and insisted on a strict observance of the Sabbath in India among all the many different religious creeds over which he ruled so autocratically. On his return to England he appeared an embittered, 'sultanized' Englishman whose direction of the Foreign Office was much criticized. He held the mob in contempt, took refuge in classical studies and the friendship of Lord Brougham. He had none of his brother Arthur's large-hearted grandeur.

WELLINGTON, ARTHUR WELLESLEY, 1ST DUKE OF, 1769–1852. Field Marshal, Ambassador, the 'Iron Duke,' fourth son of Garrett Wellesley, 1st Earl of Mornington, was born in Ireland about three months before Napoleon. To his mother the 'Iron Duke' was just 'my ugly boy Arthur'—fit food for powder; to which end he was early sent into the army. But to contemporary society, and women in particular, he was 'the Beau.' Very young he decided that to achieve success he must be single-minded. He burned his violin, abandoned the study of music for that of military tactics, and rose rapidly to the rank of Colonel. In 1798 his brother, Richard Colley, Marquis of Wellesley, was appointed Governor-General of India; but it was the younger brother, Arthur, then fresh from the battlefields of Seringapatam, who really ruled. On his return to Europe his brilliant series of victories in both the Peninsular campaign and the Low Countries won him the nation's acclaim. Back in England, as Napoleon's conqueror he was fêted and loaded with honours. Yet, 'No woman ever loved me; never in my whole life,' he confided to a friend. Nevertheless, many women said they found him irresistible. He was a handsome, dashing figure, elegant and impressive, surrounded by an aura of victory. He had married an inconspicuous Irish girl, Kitty Pakenham, daughter of the Earl of Pakenham, largely, it would seem, because she had waited ten years for him. The marriage was a dismal failure. Two sons were born, but the Duke and Duchess spent little time together. The Duchess was shy, short-sighted, homely and lacking in the poise and social sense her great position demanded. The Duke remained outwardly loyal, however, and was with her when she died. His was an astute, generous, chivalrous nature, without meanness or rapacity. A great aristocrat by birth and bearing, his particular brand of common sense, tact and breadth of vision made him the confidant and arbiter of three successive sovereigns. His power was absolute over the Regent (later George IV), William IV and Queen Victoria. Indeed he was perhaps the only person to whom Queen Victoria ever deferred, once the Prince Consort had established his sway. To mark their gratitude for Wellington's final defeat of Napoleon the nation presented him with Apsley House which still stands at Hyde Park Corner, and which is unofficially known as No. 1, London.

WORCESTER, MARQUIS OF. HENRY SOMERSET, LATER DUKE OF BEAUFORT, 1792–1854. Dandy and sportsman; he joined the 10th Hussars in 1810 and was aide-de-camp to Wellington, 1812–14, in the Peninsular campaigns. Having sown his wild oats with Harriette Wilson, he settled into an unimpeachable tenor of life by marrying in 1814 the niece of the Duke of Wellington, Georgiana Frederica Fitzroy, who died in 1821. But in 1822 he married her half-sister, Emily Frances, and a contemporary letter states: 'I heard by the last post of Worcester's marriage with E.F. What a complication of folly and, I should fear, eventually of misery. He never was and never can be steady to any one thing or person.' He lived principally at Badminton, became M.P. for West Gloucestershire, was an admirable landlord, a great patron of field sports and Master of the Beaufort Hounds. His widow survived until 1889.

BIOGRAPHICAL NOTES
ON THE PRINCIPAL DIARISTS
OF THE REGENCY

CREEVEY, THOMAS, 1768–1838. Diarist and letter writer, son of a Liverpool merchant and onetime sea captain, but thought very possibly the illegitimate son of Charles, 1st Earl of Sefton. He was called to the bar in 1794 and practiced between London and Liverpool. In 1802 he married the charming widow, Mrs. Ord, who, by her influence with her many high-placed friends, greatly advanced her husband's career. Creevey entered Parliament as M.P. for Thetford, nominated by the Duke of Norfolk. A warm friendship sprang up between Mrs. Creevey and Mrs. Fitzherbert, the Prince Regent's mistress or wife, and further advanced the Creeveys in those fashionable and political circles, which Creevey negotiated so adroitly.

The years passed, punctuated by delightful letters exchanged between all the members of the Creevey–Ord family, Creevey's journals, and his voluminous correspondence with friends; all these are rich sources of information on the period. Creevey missed nothing. High politics, high life, gossip, intrigue, family affairs, and international politics. His pawky wit is particularly evident in the nicknames he bestowed on many of the characters of whom he writes. Lord Broughton found him not always agreeable and summed him up thus: 'One who would let no principle of any kind stand in the way of his joke.... He spared no one.... He had that lively perception of the ridiculous which goes to make an entertaining man. Raillery of the present and destruction of the absent were his weapon for general talk; but when serious he showed sound and honest views, both of public and private duties, and discovered qualities which might adorn a higher character than he had endeavoured to acquire.'

GREVILLE, CHARLES CAVENDISH FULKE, 1794–1865. Political diarist and grandson of the 5th Earl of Warwick. Left Eton in 1810 to become a page to George III and later private secretary to Lord Bathurst. He obtained the sinecure Reversion of the Clerkship to the Privy Council, to which he owes much of his authority in writing of the inner workings of both the political and social life of his times. His passion was horses. He was one of the oldest members of the Jockey Club and managed the racing stables of his close friend the Duke of York from 1821 to 1826. His *Memoirs* are a wonderfully evocative account of a whole age. He was an epicure, a good friend, 'a loving cynic,' and had that detachment and attention to detail which mark the best diarist.

GRONOW, REES-HOWELL, 1794–1865. Son of a Welsh landowner, whose estates, Court Herbert, were in Glamorganshire. At Eton he became the close friend of Shelley. In 1812 he was gazetted Ensign in the Guards and saw service in the Spanish campaigns. He was one of the finest dandies and men about town in the early years of the century, and one of the few officers admitted to Almack's Club, which set up to dictate to London society. The Duke of Wellington, it may be remembered, was once turned away, and went meekly, because he was not suitably dressed (said Almack's) to enter the sacred portals. Captain Gronow fought at Quatre Bras and Waterloo, and later became M.P. for Stafford. In 1831, declared bankrupt, he left London to live chiefly abroad. His *Recollections* are fascinating but often very inaccurate accounts of his life and times.

RAIKES, THOMAS, 1777–1848. Diarist. Son of the promoter of Sunday schools and, in violent contrast, close friend of the Regency dandies and often their butt—'though he did kick sometimes.' A solid, sober man whose curiosity led him to record great events and small in the society of both London and Paris, the French capital being his home during the latter part of his life. His father had been a governor of the Bank of England, and his family conducted its merchant's business in the city—to the east of fashionable Mayfair. Thus to the noble snobs of St. James's and the West End where he passed his evenings, playing high at White's or Crockford's (often with Beau Brummell, his friend since Eton), he was known as 'Apollo,' since he rose in the east and set in the west. His diaries range over a huge field of early nineteenth-century daily life. In 1829 he travelled to Russia, and his *Russian Journal* gives us, besides many things of interest, a sadly unenthusiastic picture of the poet Alexander Pushkin.

INDEX